The
FAMILY
Encyclopedia of
BABY, TODDLER
& CHILDCARE

Consultant: Dr R.M. Youngson

Robinson
LONDON

Robinson Publishing Ltd
7 Kensington Church Court
London W8 4SP

Previously published as *My Child* partworks by Marshall
Cavendish Partworks Ltd, 1990.

This revised paperback edition first published in the UK by
Robinson Publishing Ltd 1998.

A copy of the British Cataloguing in Publication Data for this
title is available from the British Library.
ISBN 1-85487-890-5

Important note
This book is not intended to be a substitute for medical
advice or treatment. Any person with a condition requiring
medical attention should consult a qualified medical
practitioner or suitable therapist.

For the sake of continuity, the baby or child is referred to as
'he' throughout; similarly there may in places be more
references to mothers than to fathers or parents. Certainly
no prejudice is intended and this is very much a book for
both parents.

Edited and designed by Grapevine Publishing Services
Cartoons by David Mostyn
Printed and bound in the E.C.

Foreword

Babies and children can be something of a mixed blessing. There is no more rewarding experience than to watch and guide them as they grow and mature and when everything is going well their vivacity and charm is an endless delight. But it is also true that parenting can be a fraught business and children a source of considerable worry and concern, particularly when for any reason they are ill or unhappy.

After 25 years in medicine and ten years as a parent myself, I have come to see children as a curious mixture of resilience and vulnerability. Their resilience can be seen in the effortless way in which they can take the changing world in their stride and their ability to be struck down by viral illness one day, and to be up and running about the next.

Their vulnerability takes two forms: the physical and emotional. Physical vulnerability arises from their relatively immature immune systems so if there is anything 'going round' they always seem to catch it, necessitating repeated visits to the doctor with episodes of bronchitis, ear infections, wheezy chests and so on. This also explains why they are so prone to allergic conditions like asthma and eczema. Their emotional vulnerability arises from the difficulties of both being dependent on others for their security and the struggle to assert their independence and individuality.

Within this perspective this book sets out in its first section to give a broad overview of how parents can expect their child to develop from the moment he or she is born right up to the immediate pre-school years. The early tests and check-ups are explained and the processes of normal growth and development and acquisition of skills are outlined.

Next there is an A–Z which covers the widest range of everyday issues with sensible advice on how to approach everything from bathing to bee stings, from measles to moodiness, from safety to sleeping. It covers sensitive issues such as favouritism, sibling rivalry and 'spoilt' children with practical suggestions on how best to avoid confrontations while meeting your child's needs effectively. Games and activities are suggested to stimulate your child while helping them to learn about the world around them.

The Family Encyclopedia of Baby, Toddler & Childcare is quick and easy to use, comprehensive and commonsensical. I commend it highly.

DR JAMES LE FANU

The First Four Years

New Babies: Getting to Know Your Newborn

Do not be too surprised if your new baby does not look exactly as you had expected. It takes time – usually about two weeks – for his body to become accustomed to life outside the womb. During this period, you may notice all sorts of changes: skin colour, blotches that come and go, hair in unexpected places and lumps and bumps. Because they are so routine and usually clear up of their own accord, doctors and midwives may neglect to warn new parents what to expect, often causing unnecessary worry.

If you had a vaginal delivery, your baby's head will appear long and pointed. This is because the bones are specially designed to overlap each other as the baby travels down the birth canal. This causes no damage to the brain and the bones soon move back.

Your baby may have a large firm swelling on one or both sides of his head, called a cephalhaematoma. This is caused by pressure from the uterine muscle during labour and it will soon go down. The swelling is outside the skull – rather like a large bruise – and puts no pressure on the brain. Again, it needs no treatment.

If you had a forceps delivery, you will notice bruising and shallow indentations on either side of your baby's head. They will disappear in a couple of days without treatment. Similarly, if your baby had a monitor attached to his head during labour, this may leave a bruise which will soon disappear.

A feature of all newborn babies is their fontanelles. These are the soft spots on your baby's head where the skull bones – which move during birth – have not yet fused together. This fusing is not completed until your baby is about two years old. The most noticeable fontanelle is on the top of the head and you may notice a pulse beating there. Many new parents feel inhibited by these soft spots when they first handle their newborn, but the fontanelles are covered and protected by a tough scalp. Nevertheless, you should make sure that these soft spots are never pressed hard.

If your baby's skin looks yellow, he may have physiological jaundice. This is not a disease, but happens because a baby's blood has a high content of red cells which are broken down after birth. This breaking down causes an increase of a yellow pigment called bilirubin, which causes jaundice. It usually clears up by the time your baby is a week old.

Another feature you may notice is that your baby's feet or hands are bluish in colour. This occurs because your baby's circulation is not yet working very well, so that blood does not always reach his extremities, especially if he has been asleep or still for a long time. Moving him gently will get the blood circulating again. This movement is also appropriate if your baby looks red on his lower half and pale on the upper half. This is caused by blood pooling in the lower half of his body when he has not been moved for some time. It soon goes when you turn him over.

Blue patches, or "Mongolian blue spots", are common in babies with dark skin – especially those of African, Mongolian or Mediterranean descent. They are temporary accumulations of pigment under the skin. They have nothing to do with Mongolism, nor are they bruises. Babies are often born with small red marks on their skin, especially on the eyelids, forehead or at the back of the neck, just under the hairline. Known as "storkbites", they are caused by the enlargement of the tiny blood vessels near the surface of the skin and usually disappear by 18 months at the latest. "Strawberry marks" appear after a couple of days and gradually fade over the years. Some types of birthmark, however, will not go away, so ask your doctor if you are worried.

Babies in the womb are protected by a white, greasy substance called vernix. While some are born with only a little of it, others are covered with it. It provides a natural barrier against minor skin infections and hospital policies vary as to whether they wash it off after birth or not. If left, it will soon be washed off as you clean your baby. Large amounts in the skin folds are usually wiped away to prevent irritation.

New babies are often spotty. Milia are small white spots over the bridge of the nose, while neonatal urticaria are red spots with yellowish centres. These spots are nothing to worry about and occur because of the immaturity of the baby's skin. Never squeeze them.

Many babies are born with dry peeling skin, especially on the palms of the hands or the soles of the feet. This dryness soon disappears and does not mean that your baby will suffer from eczema.

Your new baby may be bald or, especially if he is born late, he may have a large amount of rather coarse hair. Whatever type he has, most will fall out to be replaced with new hair. This may be of a completely different colour and texture from what he first had.

You may notice a condition called cradle cap, which can look like dandruff. It happens because the skin on your baby's head, as elsewhere, is peeling and the oil from his scalp is bonding the scales into a brown cap. It will clear up if left, although you can try massaging in a little olive oil, leaving it for two hours and then gently combing it out.

At birth the umbilical cord will be cut about 10 cm from your baby's tummy. It will then be clamped with a special plastic clip and the stump will be left to shrivel up and drop off. Your midwife will keep a close check on the stump and tell you how to clean it. Tell her, or your doctor, if you notice any redness or discharge from the stump.

A new baby's genitals are large in proportion to the rest of the body and the scrotum or vulva may also look red and angry. Both boys and girls may also have swollen breasts which contain a small quantity of milk. Girls may also bleed a little from the vagina or have a clear or white discharge. All of these are caused by some of your hormones that have crossed the placenta and entered your baby's bloodstream.

The solution in all cases is to leave well alone. Any swelling will soon go down and as he grows his genitals will seem more in proportion to the rest of his body. Never squeeze your baby's breasts.

A boy's testicles develop in the abdomen and drop down into the scrotum just before 40 weeks. In some babies, especially those born pre-term, the testicles are "retractile" – they can be moved into the scrotum but will return to the abdomen of their own accord. They generally move down permanently by the time the baby reaches his expected birth date, but if not, an operation may be necessary later.

Temporary puffiness of your baby's eyes is normal after birth because of the pressure on his head, and will soon go down.

If the eyes have a yellowish discharge which forms crusts on the lids and lashes, your doctor will prescribe drops or a special solution for bathing them.

Until their eye muscles have strengthened, babies often find it difficult to focus, and one eye may appear to wander out of focus. If your baby cannot align the eyes by three months, mention it to your doctor. A fixed deviation should be reported immediately.

Your baby's ears may seem disproportionately large, may stick out or be an odd, almost unfinished shape. They will change shape as he grows and he will also "grow" into them.

A new baby's tongue may appear to be attached to the bottom of his mouth along almost its full length. This is nothing to worry about as the tongue will grow mainly from the tip during his first year.

Another characteristic you may notice is that his tongue is white all over. This is a normal result of his all-milk diet, but patches of white on an otherwise pink tongue should be mentioned to your doctor as it may be a sign of illness. Another result of his milk diet may be blisters on his lips caused by sucking.

Many babies are born with very long nails as they have been growing in the womb. Cut them with special baby scissors. Newborn babies often keep their hands clenched at all times during the first few weeks.

Your baby may sneeze whenever he opens his eyes. This happens because light stimulates the nerves to the nose as well as the eyes. It does not necessarily mean that he has a cold, and is not cause for concern.

Many newborn babies also hiccup a lot because of sudden, irregular contractions of the diaphragm. Again, this is nothing to worry about and will soon pass.

A baby's breathing may vary in several ways. It can be so light and shallow that at times parents may fear that their baby has stopped breathing. At times it may be very fast and noisy, while at others it may be irregular.

He may also snuffle loudly as the bridge of his nose is low and the air has to travel through very small nasal passages. This snuffling will disappear as the bridge of his nose gets higher. If it stops him sucking when feeding, your doctor may prescribe nose drops.

All these variations are normal. However, if his breathing becomes laboured or his chest is sharply drawn in with each breath, consult a doctor immediately.

Your baby's first stools will be greenish-black and sticky. This "meconium" is the substance that filled your baby's intestines in the womb and has to be got rid of before ordinary digestion can start.

Babies vary enormously in the frequency with which they open their bowels – some, especially breastfed babies, do so as often as four times a day, others only every two or three days.

What comes out also varies. It may be thick or fairly liquid, greenish, yellowish or brown and may be different every time. Breastfed babies tend to pass fewer stools as more of the milk is digested, and their stools smell less than those of bottle-fed babies. These variations are nothing to worry about but if you notice any blood or mucus in the stools, contact your doctor as this can be the first signs of an intestinal infection. Always report diarrhoea.

Your new baby will pass urine frequently – up to 30 times a day. If he stays dry for periods of four to six hours, mention this to your midwife or doctor as it may indicate a urinary tract blockage.

Early check-ups

Shortly after the birth of your baby and before you are discharged from hospital, a paediatrician will come to check over him to ensure that everything is "present and correct". Immediately after the birth, the doctor will look at how well your baby is breathing, whether his extremities are still blue, and whether he responds well to stimuli. His reflexes will also be tested: if his cheek is brushed, he will turn his head and open his mouth to look for the breast (the rooting reflex); he will grasp a finger put in his palm so firmly and tightly that he can be lifted up; if startled by a sudden movement as if he is about to be dropped, he will throw up his hands to grasp the holder and tremble (the Miro reflex); and when he is held upright he will make walking movements with his feet (the stepping reflex).

Other tests done on your baby while still in hospital will include feeling the upper part of his mouth to make sure there is no cleft in the palate, bending and moving his legs around to check that his hips are not dislocated and, for a boy, the doctor will see if the testes have descended. The baby's tummy will be felt to see if the liver and spleen are normal or enlarged and his head will be felt to check the position of the skull bones.

Your baby's weight, length, and head circumference are measured too, to check that he is within the normal range; these measurements are useful for checking that the baby is growing well later on. Your baby's weight is usually checked every day while you are in hospital and then occasionally by the community midwife when you are at home. This is to check that the baby has regained his birthweight by the time you are discharged from midwifery care ten days after the baby's birth.

On about the eighth day after the birth a blood sample will be taken from your baby's heel and sent off for analysis. This is the Guthrie test, which detects the presence of a rare metabolic defect called phenylketonuria in which the body cannot metabolize a substance found in certain foods, particularly milk, breakfast cereals and potatoes. If it is undetected, toxic products build up, causing severe brain damage. If detected early, the baby can be fed a special diet which will enable him to grow healthily. The disorder is rare and you will only be contacted after the test in the unlikely event of the result being positive.

Premature babies

A premature or "pre-term" baby, is a child born before 37 complete weeks of pregnancy. If your baby is born between 34 and 37 weeks he is likely to be a bit smaller than a full-term baby and will need to be monitored more carefully, but he may not need to be cared for in a special unit and may stay with you in the ward. Even babies born as early as 22 weeks into the pregnancy can survive, but they will need to be kept in the special care baby unit (SCBU). The smaller (or less mature) your baby is, the more attention he will need, but with today's amazing scientific equipment the chances of survival for even the tiniest baby are good.

Most pre-term babies are quite normal apart from the fact that everything about them is small and generally immature. A pre-term baby looks tiny and fragile and probably not nearly as vigorous as a full-term baby. His head will look large in comparison with the rest of the body, with large fontanelles, and his abdomen will protrude well above his small chest. His skin will be papery thin and red, and he may be rather hairy.

The reason he looks red is because you are able to see his blood vessels through his transparent skin. His ears may look a bit odd as they are soft and very flexible and if the lobe is pushed forward it will stay there. The palms of his hands and soles of his feet are smoother than a full-term baby's, as they haven't had time to develop creases. His arms and legs will be very skinny and the skin may hang in folds off his frame as he has hardly any body fat. Pre-term babies tend to lie with their limbs splayed out, not in the curled position of full-term babies.

In girls, the genitalia may appear prominent because the outer folds have not yet developed, and boys may have undescended testes.

Premature babies are prone to a range of complications: any newborn baby is liable to lose heat, but a pre-term baby is more likely to do so as their temperature control system is not well developed, and because they lack insulating body fat. Breathing difficulties are also common: "respiratory distress syndrome" is a condition typical to pre-terms with their immature lungs. This can sometimes be compensated for by supplying air at a slightly increased pressure, although for most very small babies the doctor will decide to take over the breathing process by using a ventilator. This does not necessarily mean that the baby is unable to breathe, but it helps control the baby's oxygen intake more exactly. Many babies under 30 weeks will require ventilation from the minute they are born.

The sucking reflex may be poorly developed, so the baby will be fed through a tube placed through his nose and down into his stomach. Once in place, this will not be uncomfortable for him, and as he grows he will start sucking and feeding normally.

Jaundice is common in full-term babies, but even more so in the pre-term whose liver is particularly inefficient. It is usually treated with phototherapy (light therapy) in which the baby is undressed and put under ultra-violet light with his eyes covered. This is painless and helps break down the bilirubin which causes the condition. Very occasionally, a baby may need a blood transfusion.

Pre-term babies are prone to infections, so although gowns and masks are no longer routinely worn in special-care baby units, it is very important that you wash your hands before handling your baby.

Special care baby units are usually close to your room in the hospital, and though you will not be able to have your child beside your bed you will be able to spend all the time you want with him in the unit. In the early stages, your baby will probably be kept in an incubator – a transparent perspex box with two circular openings on each side to allow you access to your baby without taking him out. The temperature and oxygen levels in the incubator are carefully controlled, and your baby is monitored by fine wires stuck on his skin.

The special care baby unit, although technical and efficient, is a very friendly, welcoming place. You may be able to stay in hospital with your baby as long as you like, but you will probably prefer to go home as soon you feel strong enough. Although you will not have to do as much for your baby as you had expected, you will still be tired and will need time to rest. You can of course visit as often as you like, and bring in friends and family to introduce and show off your brand new baby.

Having a pre-term baby can be very worrying, but small babies are a lot more robust than they look, and once the first few critical hours are over and he is settled in the unit, he has survived the worst and will gain strength daily. You will also gain confidence fast. You should be able to hold your baby soon after birth even if only for a short time, as soon as his breathing has been established.

Even if your pre-term baby relies on non-human equipment to a large extent for his well-being, you are still just as essential to him for his survival. Your milk will nourish him, even though he cannot yet get at it himself. You will be helped to express your breast milk which is given to him by tube until he has grown enough to breastfeed normally. If he is very small or has breathing difficulties, a lot of handling is not good for him, but you should touch and stroke your baby and talk to him, and the nursing staff will be happy to share his care with you as much as possible.

A more mature pre-term baby will not need to be in hospital much longer than a full-term child would, but very small pre-term babies will usually need to stay in hospital until about the time they would have been expected to be born. (When measuring your baby's development, the doctor will count his age from the time he should have been born rather than his actual birthday. If your baby was only slightly pre-term he will catch up with his peers within a year, and even a very premature baby will have caught up with his friends before he's two years old.)

By the time you are discharged, you should be used to handling your baby, but be prepared to feel quite insecure and anxious. This is quite normal, and you will soon gain confidence and be able to enjoy your baby. You won't be completely on your own, as the baby unit's doctors will want to keep an eye on your baby for a while after you are discharged. They will check his progress when you take him to the outpatient clinic.

Remember:
● All babies should be put to sleep on their backs. Placing babies face down can increase the risk of cot death.

The First Six Months

For the first six months of his life your baby grows and develops in all sorts of exciting ways, changing visibly every day and acquiring basic physical skills at a phenomenal rate. He will change from a pink "parcel" of arms and legs to a responsive, inquisitive and self-willed little being as he starts to gain control over his body. This is a great time to watch your baby develop, as you start to notice all the unique and special parts of his character and get to know him as a person.

In the first few months of his life, your baby will like to lie on his tummy for short periods. This will strengthen his neck and back muscles and give him the chance to kick his legs. Put bricks, balls and soft toys near him, where he can see them, and soon he will reach out to touch them.

At first, if you lie him face down, your baby will be all scrunched up with his knees up under his tummy, but by six weeks he will be lying with his legs out behind him. In this position he will squirm around, kicking his legs and thrashing out with his arms, so don't be surprised if you find him in a different position from the one you left him in.

If you hold up your three- to five-month-old son as if he were about to swim, he should look like he is doing the breaststroke. This is an ideal starting point for rough-and-tumble play. He will love this type of game and, at the same time, he will learn about balance and speed.

Your baby needs to feel secure; he needs to feel confidence in himself at each stage of his learning. With confidence, he will feel good about doing new things like crawling to the other side of the room out of your sight. You are the one to instil this confidence, so start by offering him physical assurance – handling him gently, smoothly and firmly. For instance, when you put him down, don't remove your hands until the mattress takes his weight; don't pick him up suddenly without warning, let him feel your touch around him before lifting him up; and talk to him when you are out of his sight so he knows that he has not been abandoned. You can help him feel secure by wrapping him up tightly in your arms, and let him feel freedom by leaving him to wriggle around with no clothes on, between nappies, if he seems to enjoy the sensation.

Your tiny baby will copy you when you move your lips and tongue, in an early endeavour to communicate by imitation. You may even discover your child smiles in response to you much earlier than the usual six weeks. The first smile is a big reward for parents, as it is often the first sign of positive interaction.

Hand-to-eye co-ordination

A newborn baby's short-sightedness continues until he is about four months old, but over this period his vision will change from a staring sort of gaze to a lively, interested observation. For the first three months your baby will lie with his head to one side when he is on his back. Nine out of ten babies look to the right, while the other ten per cent look to the left. Interestingly, the direction in which your baby looks has nothing to do with right- or left-handedness; it is purely arbitrary and just means that if you don't position his toys accordingly, he won't be able to see any of them.

At two to two and a half months, he can track a moving object and can focus more quickly than before; and by six months he will have learnt to calculate the distance between himself and an object, enabling him to lift up his arm and grasp it in one smooth action.

Your baby not only has to learn how to achieve certain skills, he also has to get to know his own body. At first, he has no idea that this arm or leg is his own. To him, everything he sees or touches is new, and apparently random. Sooner or later he will accidentally knock the figures on his bouncing chair, mobile or the rattles strung across his pram or cot. He will like this and will want to make it happen again, so he will repeat the movement of his arm. He will do this over and over, moving his arms and legs excitedly, glorying in his own cleverness and new-found skill.

In this way he learns to control his own body – a major achievement for him. He has learnt to do something for himself without your help. By two or three months he will be able to reach out and knock the mobile on purpose and laugh as he makes the dolls swing round and round.

Communication

Although your baby cannot talk in the first six months, he can certainly communicate. The vocabulary of his cries and yells may not be rich or subtle, but it is effective enough for his basic needs.

By five to six weeks old, your baby will be starting to control the air passing over his vocal cords, changing the shape of his mouth and using his tongue and lips. The result of this technical mastery will be a responsive cooing to the sound of your talking. The sounds he makes are mainly vowel sounds such as "ooo" and "aaa".

By three to four months your baby has also added consonant sounds such as "mmm", "ppp" and "bbb". At about five months old he will start putting the two together, making babble sounds like "da", "ka" and "ba". At this stage in his language development he is merely practising making tuneful sounds; he has no concept of what these "words" mean, even if mummy and daddy may like to think so. You can encourage his verbal ability by talking to him, and by leaving spaces in your conversation for him to "talk" back to you.

At around six months, when lying down, he will stretch out his arms in anticipation when he sees that you are going to lift him up. Also at approximately six months, he will imitate your cough and may try to attract your attention by coughing. He will also laugh aloud when you play peep-bo games. These are all positive signs that intellectual development is progressing well.

Health checks

The first major check-up is your baby's postnatal or six-week check. This will normally involve taking him to your own doctor's surgery or to your local health centre. If there was any early concern about your baby's health you might be asked to return to the hospital for these tests. The check-up comprises a general physical examination of your baby and the same tests that were carried out after the birth, to check that nothing was missed. The doctor may be able to tell how your baby is doing by the disappearance of some of the early reflexes that were present after birth and can also check that a boy's testes are descending if they had not done so before.

The doctor will probably want to ask you how the baby is feeding, sleeping and whether you have any worries. This is a good time to bring up problems such as a lot of crying, difficulty in settling to sleep, and frequent night waking. It often takes many weeks to get into any kind of routine, though most babies do settle down by three months, sleeping for longer periods and having fewer episodes of colicky crying, much to the parents' relief.

A mother's most frequent worry in the early weeks is how her baby is feeding. Most first-time mothers want to check their baby's progress by fairly frequent weighing over the first few months. A rough guide for weight gain is that a baby should gain on average 170–225 g (6–8 oz) a week, but remember this is very variable. Some babies are fast growers, others slower, and both can be equally healthy. Breastfed babies tend to gain weight in spurts, perhaps not gaining much for two weeks then putting on a lot of weight; this is normal. Breastfed babies also sometimes gain weight more slowly than bottle-fed ones, not because they are less well nourished, but because it is much easier to overfeed a bottle-fed baby.

Six to Twelve Months

In the second half of his first year, your baby's manual skills will really take off as he starts using his hands to bring the world to him.

At six months he will be reaching out with two hands to grasp a teddy or rattle. Then he will try to bite teddy's nose off as he finds out about shapes, tastes and textures by putting everything into his mouth.

At seven months, the rattle he picks up with one hand will be transferred to his other hand while he chews on it; later he will move the rattle from one hand to the other without using his mouth. This is clever stuff, illustrating that he has learnt not only how to move his arms and hands the way he wants, but also to use them to do different things at the same time.

By the time he is 11 or 12 months, your baby will be using his fingers to prod, poke and point. Pointing is a crucial stage in his manipulative development and one that he will delight in – look at the way he enjoys ringing the bell and pushing knobs on his activity centre.

Sight – and out of sight

From six months onwards your baby will be very alert to his surroundings, straining to touch objects that are out of his reach but that have caught his eye. When he sees something he likes, he will want it.

Offer him a brick and he will grasp it in the palm of his hand; show him another and he will take that too, and if you show him a third he will want that one too and probably take it, even if it means dropping the other two in order to have the new "prize".

However, it will take him about 18 months to realize that objects and people continue to exist even though he can no longer see them, so he is bound to cry and become very distressed the moment he can't see you. He will want to follow you, not wishing to lose sight of you even for a minute or two, which can make your life quite difficult.

Help him learn that people and objects still exist even when they are not in view, by playing games. At six to seven months, you can try letting him find a spoon or ball placed inside a paper bag or a teddy bear hidden halfway under a blanket or a cushion. Of course the favourite game of a one-year-old is to throw toys out of the pushchair to see them disappear then reappear miraculously when mummy repeatedly picks them up!

Language
In the second half of your baby's first year he will begin to babble. He will make lots of sounds which join vowels and consonants to form "syllables" which, by nine months, he will join together to produce long streams of repeated sounds, like "dadadadadadad". What he is doing is practising all the sounds which make up the language he will use. Although the sounds do not mean anything yet, he needs to learn how to make them using his "vocal equipment" – breath, vocal cords, tongue and lips.

Movement and play
From not being able to sit up alone, your baby may now be crawling and possibly almost walking by the end of his first year. Achieving the balance to turn around and reach for a toy while sitting is one of the first signs of physical independence. Moving forward requires more co-ordination but enthusiasm will never be lacking! The first tentative steps will be equally exciting for both baby and parent.

When your child is about six months old, introduce him to the delights of a mirror. Sit him on your knee while you hold the mirror at the level of his face. Ask him who is in the mirror, and point both to him and to the reflection. It will take him about another six months to fully appreciate that it is him in the mirror, but he will still find his "little friend" an amusing and entertaining pastime.

Most of his development, in fact, will take place by him "mirroring" you. A great deal of play focuses on imitation and he will quickly learn to clap his hands, play "Pat-a-cake" and wave bye-bye, by following your example.

He will love playing with you. Games such as "Peek-a-boo", tickling and lifting him high in the air will make him laugh and squeal, and he will want them played over and over.

Your wilful one-year-old will leave you in no doubt when he is annoyed; he will throw his body back and stiffen and protest loudly. But for all the times he refuses to co-operate there will be the times when he shows you that he loves you by coming over to cuddle and kiss you. Your relationship is becoming more and more intense as he begins to realize who he is and who you are.

Developmental check

Between seven and nine months your baby will be ready for a further general development check. You will be asked if he is sitting unsupported, crawling, pulling himself upright, rolling over, playing with rattles and other toys? Does he respond to sounds, does he smile in greeting, and how does he respond to strangers? The answers to some of these questions may be self-evident, but not all babies "perform" on demand, so it's important for you to say how he behaves at home.

Your child's hearing and eyesight will be tested at this stage, too, although many variables can confuse the results, for example if a child is frightened or distracted by the strange surroundings, or if his hearing is temporarily affected by a recent cold.

These regular developmental tests are there to help. They can pick up any problems in the early days, so that prompt treatment can help prevent more serious problems later on. Remember that the doctor may rely on you for information about any potential problems which it may be easier for you to spot at home than for him in his surgery.

Twelve to Eighteen Months

Unless he is a bottom shuffler, your baby may be walking at fifteen months, though his gait will resemble that of a robot. He is likely to waddle along with his feet wide apart and his arms outstretched to help him balance.

He will now be so confident about standing up alone that he will be able to stand and play at a table or windowsill. If you watch him standing, playing with his toys, you will notice that when he wants to get down to pick up a toy he has dropped, he will probably just fall down with a bump.

Your baby will now be able to creep upstairs on his hands and knees quite safely, but when it comes to getting back down he will probably need to creep backwards very slowly. Make sure you are around when he is learning how to tackle the stairs. It is important that he learns to do this safely for it will allow him to become more independent.

Playing outdoors is great fun for a child of this age. In the garden he will be able to push his toy dog around on the grass, walking with it to examine the flower beds. As well as improving his balance, this will help him to develop imaginary play.

At fifteen months, your baby will also be starting to kneel without support. In this position he will be able to play with toy cars, pushing them, and learning to let them go. This is quite a skill and you can help him by providing a ramp he can run his cars down before letting go.

Your baby's manual skills will have greatly improved since his first birthday. He will be able to hold a brick in each hand and bang them together to make a noise, and then place one brick on top of the other to make a tower. This is the beginning of his ability to match and classify objects into categories such as colours and shapes.

He will also be starting to hold a crayon in the palm of his hand to make marks on a piece of paper. Over the next few months, his control will develop, allowing him to make backward, forward and round scribbles.

Understanding language

At this stage in your baby's life you will begin to notice how he starts to understand your words. He will hear you make the sound "sock" as you put on his sock and he will begin to associate the word with getting dressed, just as he once associated the sound of a spoon on a plate with dinner time. He will also start to understand "doing" words such as "dance" as you hold his hands and jiggle to his favourite record. Games such as "this is the way we touch our nose" will help him to expand his vocabulary and to understand the association between words, objects and actions.

It is often difficult to understand your baby's first few single words because they may be interspersed with babbled noises. It can also be difficult because the words often lack endings, so milk is "mil".

You will quickly catch on to his speech, however, and learn to understand what he is saying. Do not be misled though, those single words can carry quite a message. For example "mil" could mean "I want my milk" or "I don't want my milk" or "I've spilt my milk".

Although your baby may only be able to say a few single words, he will understand many more. You should be able to see him act on simple instructions that you give such as, "Come to mummy," "Say bye-bye," or "Clap hands," as well as respond when you call his name. He will also show you how much he understands by the way he uses objects familiar to him. For instance, if you give him a comb he will comb his own hair.

Vision

Your baby's senses are now becoming very sophisticated and he will want to test them out and practise putting them together. Everything is approached with an insatiable curiosity. He will want to empty out a handbag and examine each object carefully. He will drop a handkerchief to see how it falls, suck a perfume bottle to see how it tastes, unscrew a lipstick to see how it marks and shake a purse to see how it rattles. All the time he is learning. You will need to keep a close eye on him at this stage, otherwise you run the risk of finding lipstick smeared over the walls!

Social and emotional

Your baby will start to show you he is getting older by taking a more active part in household activities. He will hold his own beaker to drink, unless he wants you to hold it because he is tired and wants a cuddle. He will start to help you dress him by holding out his arm or leg and by eighteen months he will be able to take off his shoes and socks. Do not expect him to co-operate all the time though; sometimes he will simply want to play.

For a few months after his first birthday your baby will need to be near you and be reassured by your presence. He will play alone quite happily as long as he knows you are around and he can come over for a kiss or cuddle. He is likely to be very affectionate at this time and through his actions he will tell you he loves and needs you.

From between twelve and eighteen months, however, his conflicting emotions between the drive for independence and his unrivalled feelings of love for you will result in emotional turmoil and tantrums.

One of the biggest milestones for you during this period will be when your toddler gains control over his bladder, although it will take many months from the time that he first starts to realize that his bladder is full, to using the potty effectively! Do not expect him to be "dry" until after he is two, and do not put any pressure on him – he will do it in his own time.

Eighteen Months to Two and a Half Years

The time when your toddler is between 18 months and two and a half years can be difficult for a parent. He will be developing a strong sense of independence, frequently expressed as "No! Let me do it." He will seem to have a massive ego because he thinks the world revolves around him. But it is also a time of great rewards, as he shows you that he wants to become a person like you, often by imitating everything you do.

Physical feats

Your toddler needs to practise physical skills to gain strength in his muscles and develop balance and co-ordination. He will climb on to chairs, tables and stools to look out of windows or to open doors. He will have no sense of danger, only exploration.

You need to strike a balance between allowing him to explore in order to learn and protecting him from damaging himself.

Bricks and pencils will help him to improve his dexterity, and so will learning-to-thread toys. Give him items with different sized loops so he can experiment with threading them on to anything longer and thinner than the hole.

From about 18 months you will begin to see your toddler acting out pretend situations such as feeding his teddy. Make-believe is extremely important for your child's development.

When he is pretending, he is picturing things in his mind as he wants them to be. He will need to be able to manipulate pictures and games in his mind if he is to learn to manipulate thoughts like you do. He will also be able to act out his resentment by being cross with his teddy when you have said "no" to something he wants.

Emotional development

For your child these 12 months are likely to be fraught with powerful emotions, as he struggles to move from babyhood to the independence of childhood. These emotions often result in violent tantrums. He is plagued by feelings of jealousy and anxiety. He is often frustrated at having a body that constantly lets him down.

When he is not exerting his independence, he may well be clingy, demand you feed him like a baby and cry when you leave the room. These swings of behaviour and emotions leave you both feeling confused and possibly in conflict. You need to respond to him as a toddler – not as a baby, or you will hold him back, and not as a pre-school child, or you will put him under too much pressure. Accept his mood swings, give him independence, but supervise him and protect him from danger.

Sight, sound and language

Your toddler will now get great pleasure from picture books and will recognize fine detail in his favourite illustrations. At around 18 months he will particularly like looking at lift-the-flap books. He will also enjoy story-books with rhymes and actions and joining in the repetitions and sound effects. Make up your own stories, incorporating sounds to go with the pictures in the book.

Books about children's activities will also be popular. Your toddler will be able to identify with what is happening in the story, for instance with the little boy getting up and getting dressed.

Your hard work in the first 18 months, when you held long, one-sided conversations, will now start to pay off. Your child will continue talking in what sound like real sentences but with more and more understandable words appearing. He may be using about 6 to 20 words by the time he is 18 months old, adding new words almost every day until he is using about 200 when he is two and a half years old.

His understanding, though, is much greater than he is able to communicate by spoken words. Simple requests like "go and get mummy's slippers" will get a result, perhaps immediately, perhaps five minutes later. However, do not always expect the result to be what you asked for.

Some areas of his understanding are becoming quite sophisticated. He can remember things from day to day – and knows, for instance, that the tree stays in the garden, even when he is not there to see it. He can hold images in his mind, he is freed from the here and now, and he can work things out, try them this way and that, and remember what he has tried before.

Memory is still a variable quality at this age, however. It is very short, and your child will have little ability to think ahead. He will, therefore, have great difficulty waiting for anything he wants, even for a second. If he wants it, he wants it right now. Even as you take the wrapper off the chocolate bar, he will be clamouring for it.

Toddler to Pre-school

The realization that your sweet little baby has become an active, thinking toddler may suddenly hit you one day, but this will not have happened overnight; it has been a gradual change. He will have changed from someone you have tried hard to please, to a person who tries hard to please you and will have become a child with immense physical capability and dexterity.

Developing through play

Young children need to stretch their developing muscles as much as their minds and robust physical activities are important at this age.

Once he can jump from the bottom step of the stairs two feet together, he is ready to start practising his skills on a climbing frame, as long as the floor is cushioned and you are around to supervise.

He may now be able to balance momentarily on one foot as long as he concentrates, and he will become confident walking up the stairs, one foot to each step.

You can encourage his balancing skills and allow him to be physically active even in a small space. Make an obstacle course using furniture. Try making tunnels with chair legs; caves with cushions; mountain ledges with solid tables and narrow bridges using a plank resting on books. He will find all of this fun, and it will fire his explorer's imagination as he invents games.

The shape and size of toys are now more important than their colour. Introduce pillars and arches into his building bricks to extend the scope of his construction. This will help him to learn about volume, size and rudimentary multiplication. He will pile bricks up with a definite structure in mind, and build bridges with tunnels if you show him a model of one. Do not underestimate the complexity of these skills – they show that he understands that a new object can be created from a number of small objects.

Your three-and-a-half-year-old will find an increasing need to express himself through drawings. His little fingers will be able to control a pencil well while he copies circles, makes crosses and attempts to draw potato men. At this stage his figures will have stick legs emerging from a round head, but later he will start to put bodies into his people drawings. Let him progress at his own speed; do not rush him. He is drawing what he sees and feels is important.

Something all children enjoy at this stage is cutting shapes out with scissors. By three and a half they will be good at this. Your child will be able to use blunt ended scissors to cut out small shapes and glue them on to pictures, or sprinkle lots of cut up pieces of paper on to a sticky shape. As well as helping to develop his manipulative skills, this will also encourage his creativity.

Making music gives a feeling of pleasure and achievement, but children are not born with musical ability and the pre-school years are a very important time to start developing this. Encouragement now while it is easier for your child to learn to recognize variations in pitch and tone will pay off later.

The best first musical instrument is a xylophone, especially one from a music shop, which gives a better quality of pure tones. He will get to know sounds which get higher and lower, louder and softer. Home-made musical instruments are very useful as well – plastic tubes in water, paper on a comb, a cork, plastic or wood hammer on a milk bottle or tin lid will all help develop an "ear" for music.

An improved ability to use his mind develops a whole fantasy world of imaginary play for your child. The pretend play of the 18-month-old has developed into elaborate make-believe games. Dressing up for a tea party or setting the table for his imaginary friend are important to help his thoughts and understanding progress.

Talking and questioning

Your child will probably be a dreadful chatterbox between three and four. With about 500 words in his vocabulary, he will say about 20,000 a day, often talking incessantly to himself. By three years, most of what he says should be understandable to other people but as he learns to use grammatical sentences he will make some very funny mistakes.

Often at this age your child may become very conscious of physical differences in the sexes, especially when he notices a friend's little girl naked whilst they play in the paddling pool. As he asks, "What's that?" all he wants is its name and perhaps the matching name for what he has. Answer calmly, concentrating on giving the answer to a specific question he will understand, in a way that you feel comfortable with. There is no reason why the subject should cause embarrassment. It is likely to be quite a few years before he fully understands physical differences and why they occur.

Caring and sharing

You will certainly notice the difference between two and three years when your child starts to play with other children, instead of alongside them. He will begin to understand the concept of sharing and will share make-believe worlds with his playmates.

He can now see you as a person in your own right, he has become capable of genuine sympathy and concern, not only to you but to his playmates, and characters on the TV. So his hugs when you are upset are an attempt to make you feel better, not to get your attention. Now he can understand that you want to do something for the same reasons that he wants to, for example, being with friends. This will make bargaining very appealing; such ploys as saying, "If you play quietly for five minutes whilst I speak to Grandma, then I will let you help me bake Daddy's birthday cake," will allow you to resolve almost every potential conflict that may arise.

Your child will now start to learn about his world by watching and listening instead of the earlier trial and error "doing". He is really starting to use his mind to work out the solutions to problems. He will also start to use you as he now understands what you say to him, and will consequently bombard you with the questions "What?" "Why?" and "How?".

Abdominal Pain

The abdomen, or "tummy" as it is often called, contains a number of organs, including the stomach and intestines, liver, pancreas, spleen, kidneys, ureters, bladder, and nearly all the sex organs in girls. It also contains a huge network of blood vessels and the abdominal lining, or "peritoneum".

Tummy ache is one of the most common complaints in children and can be a symptom of both physical and emotional problems. Anxiety is a very common cause of tummy ache in both children and adults: in times of stress the body automatically increases the squeezing action of the intestine.

Some emotional causes will be easy to identify – for example, going to playgroup may bring on tummy ache for a shy child. Often, however, it is difficult to tell whether the tummy ache has a physical or emotional source and you may need to enlist the help of your childminder, health visitor or doctor.

A tummy ache will vary in timing, type and severity, from mild discomfort to severe colic, depending on what is wrong. Check for any other symptoms such as unusual bowel motions, problems with urination, vomiting, rashes or signs of infection. They often give a clue as to the cause of the tummy ache.

A number of illnesses can cause abdominal pain – measles and mumps for example – but it can also be caused by indigestion, a swallowed object, asthma, reaction to medication and rarely, food allergy among others. In children especially, seemingly unrelated infections and complaints such as tonsillitis or middle-ear infection, can also be the cause of pain in the abdomen.

If the pain is accompanied by vomiting or diarrhoea it may be caused by an infection of the bowel or, if severe, by appendicitis.

On its own, however, tummy ache is usually a very minor problem which lasts no more than an hour or so. It can be caused by "wind" and may come on when the child has eaten too much, eaten unusually rich food or eaten too quickly and swallowed too much air so that there is more gas than usual in the intestines.

Certain foods, such as beans, cabbage or sprouts and leeks often cause gas in the intestines and give a child wind. The intestines are also very sensitive and respond to excitement or worry, so after-party tummy aches are common.

When the tummy ache seems fairly mild, sipping hot water or being patted on the back like a baby usually relieves wind, and most cases of tummy ache in children can easily be soothed by a warm (not scalding) hot-water bottle and a cuddle. It should not be necessary to give your child medicine, but a little gripe water may help. Usually a tummy ache, with no other symptoms, will go within two or three hours if treated in this way.

If the tummy ache lasts longer than a few hours, or is bad enough to make the child lie down, or if it is accompanied by vomiting or diarrhoea, it may be a symptom of some illness, quite possibly gastroenteritis. In this case, the pain will seldom be continuous, but will be worse just before an attack of sickness or diarrhoea.

Although most forms of tummy ache are nothing to worry about, children do get tummy ache if they are ill with kidney problems, pneumonia, meningitis and diabetes, as well as rare but serious digestive disorders. If you are worried about a pain because it recurs or seems very severe or lasts a long time, or if your child has other symptoms which worry you, ask your doctor's advice.

Abscesses

An abscess is a gathering of pus around a local infection. It can range from a simple stye, pimple or boil, to a tooth abscess or a serious internal abscess.

The pus shows that the body has been fighting the infection, and there are bacteria in it as well as the infection-fighting white blood cells.

The earliest sign of a skin abscess is a red, hot, painful swelling which later becomes filled with pus. Nearby lymph nodes may become swollen and tender. Internal abscesses are often accompanied by fever and a feeling of being generally unwell.

Sometimes abscesses clear by themselves, without any discharge. A hard, painless lump remains which will disappear after a few months.

A small, superficial abscess may either discharge pus on its own accord, or may be surgically drained.

Abscesses need medical attention and may require a small incision made under local or general anaesthetic, while a gumboil needs to be treated by a dentist if the trouble persists. Antibiotics are often given to ensure there is no danger of the infection spreading.

Adoption and Fostering

For couples who cannot have children, adopting or fostering a child is their only hope of having a "child of their own". But these are also options which many people consider after they have started their own family.

The reasons range from wanting to have a companion for an only child, to seeing their children become independent and feeling they can cope with another one. And some parents simply feel that theirs is a happy family and that they want to share their happiness and love with one or two more youngsters.

Adoption

The first step in finding a child to adopt is to approach an adoption agency. Some of these agencies are run by independent charities, although most are part of the social services department of local authorities throughout the country.

When you contact an agency you will find out what restrictions they impose on would-be adopters. Many local authority organizations, for example, only consider applications from people living locally. Other agencies specialize in finding families with a particular religious faith.

Race can be a limiting factor: wherever possible agencies now try to match children with a family of the same racial and cultural background as that of the "birth parents".

These racial policies have developed in recent years to help increase the degree of understanding and sympathy between parents and their adopted children. While a very young child seldom has any direct experience of racism, by the time he has become a teenager he is aware of his racial identity and what it means in society. Black and Asian families will be better equipped, out of their own experience, to provide the child with the confidence and sense of identity that will help him cope with problems he will encounter.

If you are hoping to adopt a very young child you should be prepared for disappointment as there are many more suitable families available for these babies than there are children to be adopted.

Because of this, the agencies can set conditions which limit the number of adopters they consider for these children. You may have to prove that you are unable to have more children of your own. There is often an age limit of 35 for the woman and 35 or 40 for the man, and you will probably have to have been married for at least three years.

Older children and those with special needs – children who may be physically or mentally handicapped or emotionally immature because of an unhappy early childhood – may be placed with families which do not meet such strict requirements but you must be sure you will be able to cope.

Once you are considered suitable to adopt a child, you will then be invited to a series of interviews with social workers. These meetings allow the social workers to gauge how serious you are about adoption and help them decide what sort of child would most benefit from becoming part of your family. Adoption is a way of giving a family to a child and your family will be assessed according to the needs of a child, not the child according to the wishes of the family.

Couples are interviewed together and separately, and searching questions are asked so that the agency can discover as much as possible about the family. In the process, you will probably learn a lot about yourselves – how strong your marriage is, what are your strengths and weaknesses, as well as your views about children, education and discipline. The social worker will then visit you at home and will try and judge how your children would get on with a new member of the family.

The stringent procedures that are followed at this early stage mean that most adoptions are highly successful.

After the agency has a complete picture of you and your family you will begin to wait. It could be weeks, or even years, depending on the criteria that must be met.

The first meeting with a potential adoptee is usually a low-key affair in the company of someone from the agency. Perhaps you will meet for half an hour one afternoon. If, after the first meeting, and from what you have been told about the child, you want to take it any further you might take him out for a day, or a weekend perhaps.

Everybody feels nervous at first and the agency's social workers will still be available to explore any doubts you may have.

Once a child comes to live with you there is a period of three months before the adoption order is signed by the court and the child becomes your own. If there is any serious risk that the new family will not be successful it is obviously best to stop the process as soon as possible – preferably before a child moves in.

Children vary as to how easily or quickly they settle into a new family. In general, the older the child, the longer he will take to settle in. Often older children have been living in an institution for some time and they are not used to family life, or they may have lived with a variety of foster parents.

The older the child, the more you will have to explain how your family works, as well as accepting elements of his own personality – habits of speech, ways of doing things – that would not have developed in a younger child.

Your own children may resent the new child at first, just as they would if you had a baby. If your new child becomes the eldest in the family, the second older may resent his new position. Many eldest children, however, enjoy having someone to look up to, someone who is more capable than them. Some children resent being expected to be the most mature youngster in the family and welcome the opportunity of being less in the limelight.

There may be a "honeymoon period" at first, when everyone, yourself, your new child and your existing children included, will be on their best behaviour for a few days or weeks. Often this is followed by a difficult time when your new child tests you to find your limits of acceptable behaviour.

However difficult it may be to begin with, most children really want a stable, loving family and the vast majority of adoptions are considered successful by everyone involved, even if there are problems initially.

In the past, families sometimes tried to hide the fact that someone had been adopted, or put off telling a young child.

Now it is recognized that the earlier you tell a child the better he will come to terms with his place in the family. It is easier for a child to grow up with the idea of adoption than to discover later and have to suddenly view his entire childhood in a different light.

When adopted children reach the age of 18 they have the right to see their birth certificate. A few children may try to find their birth parents, although many will be satisfied with just an outline picture of their origins.

Fostering

Many children in care do not need a permanent new family as they are still in contact with their parents. Sometimes the parents are going through temporary difficulties, such as homelessness, imprisonment or illness. Sometimes adoption is being considered, but the parents are still hoping their situation will change to allow them to be able to look after their children in the future.

Looking after someone else's child used to be known as being a foster parent. Now that the importance of maintaining contact with the child's parents is accepted the term social workers use is "foster carer".

If you think your family has room for one more child on a temporary basis, offering your services as a foster carer could provide a valuable spell of love and security to a child in need.

To become a foster carer you apply to your local social services department. You need not necessarily be married or well-off financially for your application to be successful. You will go through a series of interviews similar to those undergone by would-be adopters.

The demands on a foster family, however, are different from those on a couple who adopt a child. Although you would be caring for a child 24 hours a day, there will be times when they visit, or are visited by their own parents. You will be working with someone from the social services department as well as the child's family in order to help a child through a sometimes stressful time.

Most foster carers have children of their own and if you are considering fostering, bear in mind that your children will have to welcome the idea as much as you. They may come to be close friends with someone who then moves back to his own family. They may also resent the extra energy you will have to spend on an "outsider".

Some children are in care because their behaviour is too difficult for their own parents to cope with. Lying, stealing and destructive behaviour will not necessarily stop overnight out of gratitude for your care.

A young child in foster care may take time to settle in. You can make the change easier to cope with by finding out as much as possible about routine medical problems, likes and dislikes and so on from the social worker; respecting the child's sleeping patterns; giving the child the kind of food he is used to; welcoming favourite toys, especially comforters or cuddly toys and dolls that provide a link with the past; making any changes in the child's routine gradually and only as much as is necessary to help your family run smoothly; welcoming contact with the child's parents and reassuring them that you are not taking over the child for good.

Being a foster carer is not easy but you will always have the help and support of a social worker to call on.

While adopting a child allows you to enter completely into the role of parent, the relationship between a child and foster carer will vary according to the age of the child and the length of time he stays in the family. Some older children may not want to become emotionally close to you. Some children only need foster carers for a few weeks during an isolated family crisis. Sometimes a family fosters a child for two or three years and everybody involved considers him one of the family, just as if he had been adopted. If a child does stay with a family for a year or more it is not uncommon for them to consider adoption.

Aggression

Aggression comes in many forms, not just fighting. A tantrum can be a form of aggression because it is an attempt to control someone else by using unreasonable behaviour.

Verbal violence is another form. Shouting and hurling insults can be as hurtful as kicking and hitting. Sometimes it does more permanent damage to the victim. What is said in rage cannot always be unsaid. Children can be very cruel in this way and constantly picking on the victim verbally is a potent form of bullying.

You may wonder whether people learn to be violent or whether they are born with this tendency. This is known amongst psychologists as the "nurture or nature" argument. Both seem to be true when it comes to aggression in children. Most toddlers explore violence and fighting for a while, but learn to control their tempers as they get older. When children of more than six years old are frequently violent, however, it suggests that they have been taught, probably unwittingly, that violence is acceptable.

Children learn by example and may think that whoever hits hardest and shouts loudest wins. It is unrealistic to smack your child and then expect him to do as you say and not as you do.

There is no real answer as to what extent physical aggression can be considered a passing "attempt at self-assertion". It largely depends what age the fighting goes on to. What is normal and natural in a two-year-old can be an alarming display of anti-social behaviour in an eight-year-old. It also depends on how often it happens. A two-year-old may have frequent outbursts of violent or aggressive behaviour – children commonly enter the fighting and tantrum stage around this age. By the time your child is three his outbursts may still be fairly violent, but will probably occur less frequently as his language skills improve. At four or five he will have a good degree of control over his behaviour, although there may still be the odd outbreak of violence.

When your child enters the "terrible twos" he begins to explore his power to control events and people. Up until then his world has been totally dominated by the adults around him. They have decided when he should eat, when he should go to bed and with whom he should play. Not unnaturally, he wants some say in what happens to him but does not have the words to discuss it. He explores other, more direct, ways of controlling things – tantrums and fights.

Even if fighting does not get him what he wants, it at least gives vent to his frustration and allows him to test the boundaries, finding out just how far he can go. He has learnt the word "mine" and many fights with friends are about possession of a toy. The attitude seems to be "What's yours is mine and what's mine is mine".

These tantrums and fights often seem to have a pay-off, a reward. Sometimes he will gain possession of a toy by giving his friend a hefty thump; at other times his friend will win the battle. Either way, they cannot help feeling that fighting works.

Everyone has feelings of aggression and rage but we learn to control them. It is the lack of control in children when they fight that is so distressing. How you feel about your child when he is kicking, hitting, screaming threats and spitting depends a lot on how you yourself were taught to deal with your own feelings of anger.

You may have been taught that it is bad or even wrong to have such feelings, let alone act on them. This leads to a sense of guilt and shame at experiencing strong emotions such as anger and aggression. When you are teaching your child to control his behaviour it is important that he has a clear understanding of the difference between feelings and actions.

The truth is that there are no bad feelings, only bad actions. To feel jealousy and rage is merely human. To act on these feelings with physical violence is what does the damage. Thinking "I could kill him" is very different from actually doing it. You must make clear to your child that you understand he was angry when he hit his friend but that it is his actions that you disapprove of, not his feelings.

If you catch your child in the act of bullying a playmate it is important that you make it clear to him that such action will not be tolerated. Smacking him so that he knows how it feels to be at the receiving end is not a good method however, as answering violence with violence merely gives him the idea that "might is right".

Attempting to reason with your child when he is still purple with rage is also pointless, because he is in no condition to listen to you. Your child needs time to "cool off" before he can listen to reason. Remove him from the situation by putting your arms around him firmly but gently so that his movements are restricted.

Soothing noises and strokes on the back can help to calm him. If, when you remove him, he throws a tantrum then ignore it. Tantrums are no good without an audience. When he has finally calmed down you can reassure him that you love him while explaining that you do not like his behaviour – and telling him why not.

You may find your child's violence very shocking, but it is important not to withdraw your love, however appalled you are.

Some children appear to be naturally dominant and others seem to be more passive or submissive. There seem to be several reasons for this.

Gender has something to do with it. Boys are expected to be more "go-getting" in our society, while girls are taught to be gentle, caring and unselfish. Aggressive behaviour in girls is often seen as unattractive.

If a child is taught that strong emotions such as rage, jealousy and resentment are bad, they are likely to bury these feelings. This repression sometimes produces a meekly submissive child whose emotions may break out in unpredictable violence.

Regardless of whether your child is the aggressor or the victim – and the chances are he will be both at different stages of his development – this violent age can be very upsetting for all concerned. The good news is that most children grow out of it in time and develop into peace-loving adults who rely on talking and "diplomacy" to get what they aim for, rather than their fists.

◆ See also, **Bullying**, **Temper Tantrums**

Allergies

If your child is allergic, his body will over-react to something that he eats, breathes or touches. The cause of the reaction is called an "allergen". Your child's body will produce antibodies as if this allergen were a threat or disease – which generally it isn't – and the allergic response may show itself as asthma, eczema, hay fever, migraine, urticaria or diarrhoea. An allergic reaction is rarely life-threatening, though symptoms can be dangerous and are at the very least very uncomfortable for the person who suffers them.

Allergens can be almost anything – common ones are house dust mite droppings, pollen, certain foods and animal fur. Susceptibility to more than one allergen is common. Numerous contact substances can cause allergies.

The "dose" is important. Your child may display few symptoms when the contact with an allergen is slight. For instance, there may be little response to exposure to a friend's cat, but if a cat is brought into the family home, your child may suddenly display a strong allergic response.

Other factors are significant, too. Allergies are not contagious, but they often run in families, though the type of allergy may differ. Where you have hay fever, your child may develop asthma. The nature of allergic symptoms also change with age. For example, a baby with eczema may grow out of it only to develop asthma, then grow out of this and develop hay fever instead as a teenager!

The tendency to allergy is called atopy. This is a genetic disorder causing a susceptibility that interacts with environmental factors to cause allergy.

The symptoms of an allergy will vary widely and are linked to many things, including the strength of the allergen and your child's individual susceptibility.

When an allergen meets its antibodies, certain cells are caused to release powerful substances, including histamine, that irritate the tissues.

Allergic Disorders

Name	Allergen	Symptoms	What you can do	Treatment
Asthma	Animal fur, pollen, house dust mite droppings, some foods, fumes. Infection, exercise or emotional upset may worsen the reaction	breathing difficulties, wheezing	Avoid obvious allergens where possible, keep dust down, calm and reassure your child	Inhaled drugs, close medical supervision
Anaphylactic shock	Wasp or bee sting, peanuts, serum injections	Faintness, possible collapse, severe breathing difficulty	Take your child to hospital at once	Once the emergency is over, carry adrenaline to treat future reactions
Contact dermatitis	Skin contact with allergen, e.g. soap powder on clothes, jewellery, bubble bath	Itchy, blistery inflammation	Avoid contact with allergen – rinse clothes well and avoid soap and bubble baths; keep child's fingernails short	Specialist dermatological care
Eczema	Foods such as cow's milk, wheat products, eggs or food additives	Severe red rash on face, neck, hands and limbs	Identify allergen with medical help, keep child's fingernails short, dress in smooth cottons not rough materials, avoid soap	Specialist dermatological care
Food allergy	Cow's milk, wheat, eggs, strawberries, peanuts, citrus fruit, shellfish and food additives, but many others	Various, e.g. tummy upset or pain, nausea, diarrhoea, "colic-like" symptoms, eczema, irritability, runny nose, wheezing; if acute, swollen tongue and lips	Breastfeed for as long as possible, don't give solids before four months, avoid wheat, citrus fruits and eggs in the early stages of weaning and watch for reactions. Get medical advice on diet if allergies are suspected or in family history and keep to the diet	Elimination and provocation test to identify allergen – under medical supervision

Name	Allergen	Symptoms	What you can do	Treatment
Hay fever (Allergic rhinitis)	Pollen, dust, animal fur, carpet underlay, feathers and other substances can trigger similar reactions	Blocked or runny nose, sneezing, sore and itchy eyes and nose	Identify allergen if you can, keep windows shut and avoid open air if pollen count high, keep dust down	Prick test for diagnosis, antihistamines and nose drops
Migraine	Sometimes caused by certain foods, e.g. wheat, chocolate, cheese	Severe headache; possible tummy ache (abdominal migraine)	Discuss with doctor, provide rest and comfort, avoid allergens if known	Varies – possible elimination diet test if due to food
Urticaria	Foods, drugs, handling certain plants, animal fleas	White weals, surrounded by red, irritating swelling, appear on skin	Avoid allergens if known, relieve itching with calamine lotion	Calamine lotion, homeopathic preparations, antihistamine pills, if severe

Usually symptoms will show up in the parts of the body which are exposed to the allergen, so an airborne allergen, such as pollen, mostly affects the eyes, nose and air passages, causing a runny nose, sneezing and breathing difficulties. An allergy to metal will usually affect the skin, and food allergies may cause tummy ache or diarrhoea. But allergens often get into the bloodstream, and can then cause symptoms almost anywhere.

If the cause can be clearly identified – for example, if your child develops a rash after eating strawberries – then the allergen can easily be avoided, but often the exact cause cannot be precisely pinpointed. Subjecting your child to a barrage of tests to find out may be time-consuming, distressing and expensive.

It is wise, however, to avoid obvious allergens if your child seems susceptible or if there's a history of allergy in your family. Therefore, keep down dust in his bedroom, dress him in natural fabrics, especially underclothes, restrict the use of chemicals in the home and take care with food – particularly when weaning.

Your doctor may suggest a combination of identifying allergens, some avoidance and medication to help symptoms. Anti-allergy medicines and applications in the form of inhalants, cream, drops, tablets or lotions often help.

◆ See also, **Asthma**, **Eczema**, **Food Allergy**, **Hay Fever**, **Rashes**

Artificial Respiration

If your child has stopped breathing, you must use artificial respiration to get air into his lungs as soon as possible.

The chances of saving your child's life will be greatly increased if you have been taught the proper technique by a qualified instructor.

Do not carry out the technique on anyone who is breathing normally.

Your child's breathing could be stopped for a number of reasons:

● The nose and mouth could be covered by a pillow, the airway between mouth and lungs could be blocked by food or a small object that has gone down the "wrong way", the child's own tongue, vomit or broken teeth.

● The airway can also be closed by swelling caused by swallowing a scalding or corrosive liquid or by an insect sting.

● Any tight constriction of the neck, as in strangulation, has the same result.

● Sometimes the airways close up naturally, because of noxious gases or medical conditions such as bronchitis or asthma.

● Breathing may also stop if the child has inhaled smoke, gas or dust.

● Electrocution, pesticides and damage to the spinal cord can all stop your child's respiration, as can an overdose of drugs such as sedatives or pain-killers, which is why lockable bathroom cabinets are essential.

Do not rush in and start artificial respiration without thinking first. What has stopped the breathing?

● If the room is filled with gas, open the windows.

● In the case of electrocution, switch off the current before you touch the child.

● If the child is choking, turn him upside down and slap him on the back.

● If the child is drowning, rescue him from the water, and start artificial respiration immediately.

Whatever the cause of the emergency, the outcome of asphyxia (suffocation) is the same. If obvious, remove the cause of the difficulty immediately as breathing may start. Breathing may become deeper and more rapid while the pulse speeds up as heart and lungs fight to get oxygen into the blood.

As the blood's oxygen content falls, the skin turns blue, particularly in the face, neck, hands and feet.

The child eventually loses consciousness and may go into convulsions. Finally, respiration fails and the heart stops.

The brain will suffer irreversible damage if it is totally starved of oxygen for more than about four minutes. Everyone should know how to give artificial respiration – when an accident happens, there will be no time to look it up in a book.

The "kiss of life"

1. Remove any obstructions from the mouth and throat. Tilt the head back to get maximum access to the airway.

2. Pinch nostrils, take a deep breath and after firmly sealing your lips over the child's mouth, blow steadily to inflate the lungs.

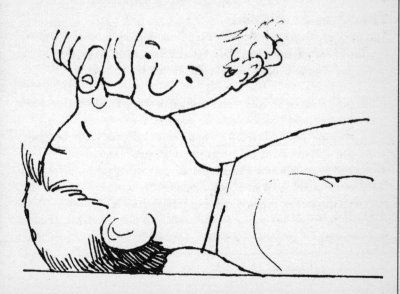

3. Take your mouth away and watch the chest sink. Give five more breaths quickly. Continue until his breathing starts again.

4. If you are giving the "kiss of life" to a small baby, place your mouth over his mouth and nose together when you gently breathe out.

Remember:

● Always think before you start – should you open windows, switch off electric current?

● Give the first five breaths as quickly as possible to get a surge of oxygen into the blood and prevent irreversible brain damage.

● Do not blow too hard – remember a child's lungs are smaller than your own.

● Keep a close watch on the heart. Check for a pulse with the fingertips at the sides of the Adam's apple.

● If there is no pulse, start cardiac massage.

● Keep going – the child's life may depend on it.

● When the child starts breathing, place him in the recovery position – lying on his front with lower arm behind his bottom, upper arm and leg bent at right-angles at elbow and knee, and with head to one side to prevent choking.

The Silvester method

This method should only be used when facial injuries prevent you giving the "kiss of life", if strong poison has been swallowed, or if copious vomiting means that mouth to mouth would push vomit into the lungs.

1. Place the child on his back with a cushion or blanket under his shoulders.

2. Bend the head well back to clear air passages.

3. Kneel facing the child's feet with your knees either side of his forehead.

4. Grasp the child's wrists and cross them over on his lower chest.

5. Rock your body forward and keeping your back straight, press down lightly and steadily, using your body weight for two seconds.

6. Lean back on your heels, bringing the child's arms up and out in a wide arc until his hands are on the ground with arms fully extended. Hold for three seconds.

◆ See also, **Cardiac Massage**, **First Aid**, **Strangulation**, **Suffocation**

Asthma

About one child in ten develops asthma at some stage in childhood. It is one of the commonest chest problems in children and can cause endless misery and some danger unless it is treated properly. Fortunately, many children outgrow it and those who don't can grow up perfectly well and lead a full life, with the proper treatment. The risks of asthma must never, however, be underestimated.

Asthma involves a severe narrowing of the bronchial tubes which lead from the windpipe into the lungs. They carry the oxygen we breathe in to all parts of the lungs and the carbon dioxide we breathe out back into the windpipe. The narrowing of the tubes results from the contraction of the muscle in their walls and swelling of the membrane lining them. The difficulty is most obvious when breathing out. For this reason, asthmatics tend to inhale in short gasps and breathe out with a long wheeze – a result of the effort required to breathe against the obstruction.

Asthma is brought on by a number of factors, ranging from breathing polluted air to emotional upset, which makes it rather a complex problem to treat. The cause of asthma is the body's own release of histamine in response to breathing substances as varied as house dust containing house mite droppings, animal fur, paint fumes, pollen and fungal spores among others.

Viral or bacterial infections of the throat can cause similar irritations which is why asthma tends to get worse with chest infections or colds. We also know that emotional upsets or anxiety may occasionally worsen an asthmatic condition, though how this happens is not clear. Cold air or vigorous exercise, especially running, can also trigger an attack. Certain drinks, foods and preservatives can also produce an asthmatic response.

The typical asthma attack is characterized by a sudden shortness of breath and wheezing, which is sometimes accompanied by coughing. The bringing up of phlegm is not a prominent part of the attack and would suggest that the child may also have bronchitis. Generally speaking, asthmatics are more prone to chest infections caused by a failure to clear the lungs fully. Many children develop a hunched look which is brought about by the constant effort of breathing.

In some cases, the onset of asthma follows a seasonal pattern as the pollen count rises. This pattern is often accompanied by irritations to the nose and sneezing, which we usually refer to as hay fever.

Of course, allergies to house pets and the house mite will occur all through the year as the allergen is constantly in the air. The house mite is particularly keen on living in warm places, like beds, and for this reason asthma attacks often seem to happen at night. In fact, coughing at night in children may well be a result of this allergy and is often an early sign of the onset of asthma.

The treatment for asthma depends on the severity of the attacks, but it is broadly divided into two: emergency treatment for severe attacks, requiring a visit from the doctor or admission to hospital, and everyday self-medication to prevent an attack occurring, which is known as prophylactic or preventive treatment and can be carried out at home. Monitoring of the severity with a home peak expiratory flow meter, and charting the results, are essential if severe attacks are liable to occur.

Emergency treatment is designed to bring relief as rapidly as possible by getting drugs quickly into the lungs to dilate the bronchial tubes and control the lining inflammation. These drugs can be given by injection or inhaler. Some cases may require a "nebulizer". This device is powered by electricity and produces a fine mist or spray of the drug dissolved in sterile water. This mist can be inhaled through a mouthpiece or a mask. The child should obtain relief within a few minutes. In the case of a very severe attack, the doctor will often give a steroid drug to be taken by mouth for a few days. This reduces inflammation in the lungs and prevents the attack from developing any further.

Regular treatment is designed to prevent severe attacks and to allow the sufferers to lead as normal a life as possible. Asthmatic children may be tested for allergies so that steps can be taken to avoid the allergen that upsets them, although in the many cases where the child is allergic to house dust mite droppings, this is obviously very difficult.

A number of prophylactic drugs are available which cut short the abnormal response that asthmatics suffer. These may be taken by mouth or by inhaler three or four times a day. These drugs all considerably reduce the risk of asthmatic attacks and must be taken regularly.

Steroid drugs can also be taken in very low dose by inhaler to prevent asthmatic attacks. Since they are inhaled directly into the lungs, there is practically no absorption of the drug into the system and negligible risk of any side-effects.

Most asthmatics will have their condition worsened or even triggered by everyday substances and once the cause is identified, the only course is to avoid it by, for instance, keeping the house as clear of dust as possible, avoiding petrol fumes and tobacco smoke, certain "reactive" foods and also sudden exertion and emotional stress. However, it is difficult to be specific, as what affects one asthmatic may not actually have any effect on another. But it is accepted that regular, controlled exercise rather than sudden exertion does have a beneficial effect and all asthmatics should be encouraged to take as much regular – but strictly controlled – exercise as they can manage.

Although there is no absolute cure, regular treatment with prophylactic drugs will do much to reduce the occurrence of attacks.

◆ See also, **Allergies**

Athlete's Foot

Athlete's foot is an annoying and unpleasant fungal infection. Fortunately, it usually responds well to treatment and can be prevented fairly easily. It is not very common in small children, but anyone in the family can get it and pass it on if precautions are not taken.

Athlete's foot is a form of Tinea (Epidermophytosis). It is caused by a fungus on the surface scales of skin, and can be brought on by poor personal hygiene and carelessness in drying the feet.

People who suffer from sweaty feet are particularly at risk and the infection can be aggravated by airless, plastic shoes which prevent the feet from breathing. Epidermophytosis can affect any part of the skin (*see also* Ringworm).

The fungus lives on dead skin shed from the moist, sweaty areas between the toes. However, it may also inflame and damage surrounding areas of live tissue which is when the discomfort starts.

The first signs of athlete's foot are irritation and itching between the toes followed by the skin beginning to peel. The feet may smell too.

In bad cases, painful red cracks, known as fissures, appear between the toes. In more severe cases the toe-nails can even be affected, becoming either soft or brittle as the fungus invades them.

Imidazole creams are very successful in the treatment of athlete's foot. These need to be applied daily until two or three weeks after the symptoms have disappeared.

Where the infection is severe and the nails have been affected, your doctor may prescribe a medicine to be taken orally which is effective within a few weeks. To prevent re-infection, however, it is necessary to use an antifungal powder daily.

Athlete's foot may be avoided by taking the following precautions:

● Wash your child's feet daily with soap. Clean any dirt from under the nails and between the toes.

● Dry between each toe thoroughly with your child's own towel. Do not let anyone else use this towel.

● Dust the feet with antifungal powder. (To prevent re-infection, put powder in the child's shoes and socks as well.)

● Make sure your child has clean cotton or wool socks daily. Avoid nylon socks and plastic shoes. Put your child in open shoes if his feet feel sweaty.

Baby Talk

Although we still don't know exactly how a child learns to speak, we do know that all children follow a similar learning pattern and that babies understand a lot about language long before they utter their first words. For instance, your baby will become familiar with the rise and fall in your speech which indicates a question or statement, and he'll also learn the art of conversation which dictates that first one person speaks, then another answers. Consequently, when he starts to make his own sounds, he knows to pause afterwards, looking to you to respond.

One of the wonderful attributes of childhood is the ease with which young children pick up languages, especially if they hear them at home. This is particularly noticeable where each parent has a different mother-tongue. Children of such a couple will invariably speak both languages without confusing the two. In some cases, however, children do become confused, so if you and your partner speak two languages and your baby seems to be making little progress in either, it may be best to talk in just one language until he is fairly fluent, and only then introduce the second.

Just as all children do not learn to walk at exactly the same age, so language development is different for each child. Therefore, don't be tempted to make close comparisons between your child and another child of the same age. Remember, too, that a child who is slow to speak is not mentally slow: there appears to be no connection between early language development and overall intelligence. In fact, for one reason or another, many very bright children are late to form their words. Evidence also suggests that children have spurts of development in one field, then another. So a child who is running around at a year may not speak until much later, whereas a talkative 14-month-old may still be crawling on hands and knees.

As soon as your baby is born, he utters his first cries – desperate pleas to be noticed. These first efforts to communicate may sound all the same to others, but you will soon identify and interpret different cries. You will know when your baby needs to be fed, changed, amused or just given a cuddle. You'll also be able to hear if your baby is distressed or unwell. As well as crying, your baby will also start to make little burbling noises when he's content and comfortable.

A baby is able to identify different sounds during this time and he will soon learn to recognize your voice and know that when he hears you, you are coming to give him attention. Research shows that at this stage, a baby only responds positively to the mother's voice when her face is also in view.

Talking above his head to another adult will not, therefore, comfort him; so, try to talk directly to your baby, and look at him when you speak.

You will probably also notice an affectionate reaction after a month or so – your baby may gurgle or hold out his arms when you come near. At around six weeks, he will probably be smiling at the sound of your voice too. He may also make a noise and wait for you to reply, as he begins to understand the various forms and patterns of adult communication.

In addition, you may notice that he repeats the same sounds over and over again, and will practise these conversations when on his own, as well as with you.

From about six weeks, the gurgling progresses into "cooing" noises such as "ahh" and "ooh". These vowel sounds are soon joined by consonants. P, b, t, d, and eventually nasal sounds like m and n will creep into his vocabulary, and he will soon be saying words like "ma" and "da". But, much as you would love to believe otherwise, these sounds are more likely to be made by accident as he experiments with his new ability.

The seventh and eighth months are usually the "babbling" months, when your baby will extend and improve his speech. He will also become increasingly responsive to your voice and the voices of others, and to all sorts of music.

He'll begin to introduce shouts or exclamations, such as "ai", and will try to imitate you when you sing or tell a nursery rhyme. He will watch you closely, looking at your lips and mouth when you talk, and turn to watch any reply that's made by you. This is a time of great learning and he'll soon be ready and eager to move on to the next stage of language development.

Over the next few months, your baby's speech will become noticeably more sophisticated. He'll start to introduce rises and falls in his speech pattern, and string small words together in a sentence-like format, such as "baba-ma-da-da". This is called "jargoning", which will soon develop into proper speech.

You will notice "sentences" that sound like questions, demands, and statements, and near to his 11th or 12th month, he will probably say his first "real" words.

Your baby's first words will be determined by his physical abilities to say certain sounds. He'll start by saying words which are familiar to him, such as "cat", "dog", "ball", "cup", and so on. Don't expect perfect elocution from the start; many of his words at this stage will be simplified and mispronounced.

It is often difficult, even frustrating, to keep up a conversation with a tiny baby who can only respond with "oohs" and "aahs". Use his toys and books as sources of stimulation. Play with his dolls and teddies, explaining what you are doing as you pretend to feed them, put them to bed and dress them. Do the same thing when bathing, dressing and feeding him. For instance, say "Mummy is putting on Daniel's socks", "Here's Daniel's bottle of milk", and "Look at Daniel's teddy". Whenever possible, call him by his name, rather than "you", so he can learn to distinguish himself from others.

Try to use the names of objects, people and animals, rather than saying "it", when talking to him. For instance, if you hide a ball behind your back, don't say "Where is it?" but "Where is the ball?". Substitute "Look at the dog" for "Look at it", and "What's Daddy doing?" in place of "What's he doing?". He will also be able to understand simple instructions, such as "no", "get your spoon", and "bye-bye". In fact, even though he won't be able to pronounce the words himself, he will understand a lot of what you say to him.

There are all sorts of games you can play which will help in language development:

● "Ring-a-ring-a-roses" – lift your baby up and bring him down at the appropriate time.

● "Round and round the garden like a teddy bear" – he'll love the actions and being tickled, of course.

● Play with toy animals and act out the noises they make, as well as repeating their names.

● Read books which have only one word to each colourful illustration. Talk about colours and shapes of things on the page, as well as the actions.

● Sing nursery rhymes with accompanying actions and props, such as toys and teddies.

● When giving him a bath, play with his ducks and boats, and include the sounds they make, their various colours and their shapes. Talk about the taps, water, soap and towels, and what they are used for.

● "This little piggy" – count his toes and fingers.

● Talk to him in front of a mirror so that he can see himself smile and form sounds – babies are fascinated by their own image.

● "Peek-a-boo" – encourage him to say "boo" to you too.

To improve his language development, it is important to encourage your baby from the word go. A baby will only learn speech if he hears it around him, so the more you talk to him, the more he will know. Babies who are not given this type of stimulation throughout their early years will still learn to speak, but they tend to be less fluent and articulate in later life than those who had more attentive and supportive parents.

When your baby can coo and gurgle, look at him and repeat his sounds back to him. Add new sounds like "boo" or "ma" for him to imitate. But don't be tempted to talk to him all the time in baby language. Use proper but simple sentences, and pronounce the names of objects clearly. Also, make sure that he can see your mouth as you talk and speak directly to him, so that he can learn how to use his mouth, lips and tongue to form words and make specific sounds.

To reinforce the connection between what your baby sees and what he hears, repeat the name of an object. When talking about his teddy, for example, say "Look at teddy. Teddy's got a hat on. Teddy's waving goodbye", and when looking at cows, say, "The cow says moo. The cow is brown. The cow eats grass." Always talk about things your baby can actually see; he won't yet understand concepts like "yesterday" or "tomorrow".

A good way of helping him to understand sensations, rather than objects, is to create situations which illustrate them. Act out your conversations with your baby. Hold him up in the air and say, "Up you go." Then bring him down, saying, "Daniel's going down," with the accent on "up" and "down".

Exaggerate your statements and questions, using bodily movements to emphasize your meaning. When asking a question like "Does Daniel like his milk?" make sure your voice rises and falls to suggest a question. And look at him, as if waiting for a response; he may not be able to answer yet, but he will understand and may smile or point.

When your baby does start to use "real" words, encourage him by using those words in your sentences. Introduce new words which sound similar for him to attempt, but remember that some sounds, like "s" and "z", are difficult to make out and he will probably not be able to pronounce these for another year or so.

Inevitably, you will understand your baby's speech before anyone else. Take time to translate his first words and encourage him when he says a word correctly. If he mispronounces a word, such as "rabbit" as "wabby", don't immediately jump to correct him, but simply restate it correctly, "It's a lovely rabbit". It's often frustrating when your baby either cannot say a word, but almost has it, or mispronounces words. Whatever you do, don't show impatience as this may silence him completely. Happy children are usually quite vocal, so if he suddenly stops making noises, you'll know something is wrong.

Don't worry if your child calls things by the wrong name at first. For instance, he may call a ball a "cat" – not because he thinks it's a cat, but because it may be the only "real" word he can say. Time and practice will help him match his words with the correct objects. However, in the early months, don't bombard him with too much sound. Take each stage at his pace and don't try to rush things – he will learn in his own time and over-eagerness on your part may not help his progress.

Younger siblings do tend to learn to speak sooner than others, as they are encouraged by their older brothers and sisters. However, occasionally an older child may understand and interpret for the younger one, leaving no reason for the little one to communicate with "real" language, thus delaying his development.

Twins are often slow to talk, although you may find that they chat quite happily together in their own exclusive language. This is quite normal and is not cause for concern – they will eventually use "real" words when they start to mix more with other people, especially other children.

If, however, your child obviously doesn't understand what you are saying by 12 months, or if he hasn't made any attempt to speak by the time he is one and a half, you should consult your doctor to ensure that all is well.

One reason may be deafness. If your baby is severely deaf, you will probably have noticed before this time. Slight deafness is often more difficult to detect in very young children. If you suspect that your child has hearing difficulties – if, for instance, he doesn't react much to loud noises – mention it to your doctor who may want to carry out further tests.

Temporary deafness is quite common during the first few years when children are prone to colds and ear infections. But all the same, take him to the doctor if anything seems to be impairing his hearing, as delaying a proper medical diagnosis may allow the condition to worsen.

Babysitters

For some parents the search for a good, reliable babysitter is often a difficult one. However, this need not be the case, and whatever you do, don't sit at home night after night without a break because you feel there is no one available to look after your child. As you know, it's not an easy task looking after children all day, and everyone, including you, needs a break away from the dirty nappies, and some time to be yourself and not just somebody's "mummy" or "daddy". On the other hand, unless you're confident that your child is in the hands of a capable, responsible person, you'll be worried all evening and it will spoil your enjoyment.

Simply following some general guidelines should make the task of finding the right person a good deal easier. Find a child carer with whom your little one is familiar. This is particularly important for older babies and toddlers who may become distressed and frightened if they wake up to find a stranger in the house – a situation which can be most upsetting for child and sitter alike. Always ensure that your child and babysitter are introduced before you go out. It may be worth asking the babysitter to come to the house a few hours before you leave. Perhaps you could even arrange for the sitter and your child to share a meal, and allow time for them to play or read a book together for a while before bedtime.

If you have a young baby, make sure that your babysitter knows how to change a nappy and is confident about feeding and so on. Also, ensure that they know where you keep the baby's changing and feeding equipment.

If your baby likes to be comforted in a particular way, remember to explain this to the babysitter before you go out, leaving her in charge for the evening. Ideally, you should try and settle your baby yourself before going out, and should not leave them if they are unwell.

Many parents find teenagers are very willing to babysit. This can prove quite satisfactory if the teenager is mature in her outlook and has some experience with children of the same age as your own. Remember too, that the suggested minimum age for a babysitter is 14 years, and if your sitter is relatively young, do not give her too much responsibility or leave her alone in the house for too long.

It may also be prudent to ask your babysitter not to bring along any friends, unless you've agreed with her in advance, or you may find your home is turned into an "open house" while you are away – not the safest situation for your baby or your home!

Ultimately, your choice of babysitter will be quite a personal one, and it is really up to you to decide who you feel is trustworthy and capable of looking after your young ones. After all, some 16-year-olds are very mature and may have experience of looking after younger brothers and sisters; others of 20 or more are not nearly as knowledgeable about childcare.

When you do find a suitable sitter, try to use her on a regular basis so that your child becomes used to the fact that when you go out the same person will look after him. Many children actually enjoy the company of babysitters and look forward to their arrival. Do make sure, however, that the sitter knows how you discipline your children, as many youngsters get very excited when someone different is in charge. Older children, in particular, may tend to "act up" or show off in these circumstances.

And always leave a number where you or a close friend or family member can be contacted if necessary.

Knowing that the search for a reliable babysitter can be difficult and that the cost can often be off-putting, some mother and baby groups have created their own self-help babysitting circles. Each tends to operate on a local basis and provide childcare (daytime and evening) for all members of the group.

Some circles work on a token basis, whereby each member has a photocopied list of the names and numbers of all the other parents involved. Each member has six tokens with which to "buy" and "sell" babysitting services from other parents in the circle. It costs one token for a sitter up to midnight and two tokens after midnight. The parent who offers the babysitting receives one or two tokens each time she looks after another's children. Parents who go out a lot will eventually use up all six tokens after which time they must return the favour to earn back tokens so that they can then go out again.

Other groups have different schemes, but all are based on the same idea of giving and receiving babysitting services free of charge to other members of the group.

If all else fails, there are always professional babysitting agencies to fall back on, many of which are advertised each week in magazines. Your local library could advise you where to look. Each operate different schemes, but most are fairly reliable.

The babysitters are often trained nannies or have some kind of childcare qualification. The agencies usually ask for at least two references which are then followed up, and all prospective babysitters are asked into the agency for an in-depth interview to ascertain their reliability, personality and so on, before they are put on the books.

You will probably be asked to pay the agency a predetermined fee in advance for the service; the individual babysitter will then expect to be paid an hourly rate on the night. Most agencies also insist that you arrange transport home for the sitter after 10.30 p.m.

Although these services can be useful on occasion, you can never rely on getting the same babysitter each time you require one, so there is little chance for your child to build up a relationship with the carer. Services can also become quite expensive if used on a regular basis.

If you do use an agency it is best to employ one that has been recommended to you. Although the majority are highly respectable, there are always odd exceptions to the rule and no one wants to take any chances with their child's welfare. Remember also to ask the agency how they screen candidates, and if you have any doubts, ask for references that you can check personally. Charges vary enormously, and you may simply have to shop around to find a service and a sitter that suits you best.

If you are planning to go out at weekends or over holiday periods (Christmas and the New Year are particularly difficult times), try to book your babysitter well in advance to avoid disappointment. Remember that babysitters have social lives, too! If you are really set on going out on certain dates around Christmas, and your babysitter seems rather unenthusiastic, try offering her a slightly higher rate of pay, or some kind of "bonus" like a pair of cinema tickets or a record voucher. This may serve as recompense for her missing a few evenings out at such a sociable time of year.

Once you have found a reliable babysitter, you will feel free to go out and enjoy yourself. Take the precautions outlined above and you should have no reason to worry.

◆ See also, **Nannies**, **Work (Going Back To)**

Bandages

Bandages are needed in first aid, and can be used for many different purposes: to hold a dressing in position and give added protection; to prevent movement of an injured part of the body; to stop bleeding or reduce a swelling by applying pressure; to give support; or to hold a splint in position.

Bandages are available in a variety of sizes and shapes and can be made from any cloth-like substance such as calico, linen, cotton, muslin, crepe, flannel or even paper.

● Triangular bandages can be used as a whole cloth to hold a dressing in place or as a sling.
● Roller bandages are rolls of open-weave cloth of different widths for varying parts of the body. Their advantage is that they cannot easily be applied too tightly, but they are more difficult to secure.
● Crepe bandages are the most popular type of bandage. Their elastic strength makes them easy to apply and ensures that they stay firmly in place. Care has to be taken not to cut off the blood supply by bandaging too tightly. Release the pressure immediately if you suspect this.
● Tubular bandages are used to bandage fingers or limbs with the aid of a special applicator.

As well as keeping the above in your first-aid kit, you should also have a stock of sterile dressings, and tape or safety pins.

It is generally easiest to secure a bandage using adhesive tape, but as children often pull and tug at them, you may find it better to use a small safety pin (through the outer two layers) or a reef knot when tying the ends of a bandage.

Bandaging a wrist

1. Fix the bandage round the wrist and take it diagonally across the back of the hand, round the palm and under the fingers.

2. Carry the bandage across the top of the fingers to the little finger, round the palm again and across the back to the wrist. Continue until the hand is covered, and secure.

Bandaging a knee

1. Start from the inside of the knee and make one straight turn, carrying the bandage over the knee cap and right around the leg.

2. Take the bandage round the thigh, then round the calf. Continue turns, covering a little more each time. Finish off with a spiral turn just above the knee.

Any bandage that is applied too tightly to a swelling part may cut off the blood supply to the injured area and may cause permanent damage. If the bandage isn't loosened or is left for too long, gangrene may develop.

To test for good circulation in a bandaged limb, press one of the nails. The skin beneath should go white immediately and, when released, the blood and the pink colour of the nail should return within two seconds.

Do not use bandages if the area requires regular observation, if a limb is broken or if the child is seriously injured and you have called an ambulance to take him to hospital.

Bathing Babies and Children

Most parents are shown how to bath their baby while still in hospital but this crash course can seem woefully inadequate once you are at home. It may help to know that even some of the experts own up to bathtime nerves once they have a baby of their own to care for, and that babies are remarkably resilient and will thrive in even the most inexpert hands.

It is sensible to take things slowly and try not to set yourself unmanageable standards. Young babies do not actually need to be bathed every day and a bath every two or three days will suffice, as long as you clean your baby's face, hands and bottom daily.

Try to set aside half an hour to bath your baby so that you are more relaxed. Indeed, the baby's "hygiene" is part of the daily routine and needs this time. Lay out everything you need, and perhaps organize bathtime in the evening when another adult is around to help.

Always make sure you have the following to hand before getting down to bathing a new baby:

- Bath or sink with towel to wrap around taps
- Big soft towel
- Bowl of boiled water
- Cotton wool
- Soft facecloth
- Baby shampoo
- Soft baby brush
- Oil
- Nappy changing equipment
- Clean nappy
- Clean clothes
- Waterproof apron

You can bath your baby anywhere in the house where it is warm and comfortable. Babies do not have to be bathed in the family bathroom. Some parents find it easier to use a baby bath made to fit on to the main bath but as babies only need a little water, it is easy to carry the baby bath to another room where there is more space. If you are going to use a specially designed baby bath with a stand, make sure it fits properly and that the stand is sturdy. Some baths are part of the changing unit, but if you use one of these, ensure that the mat or cover lifts off, or slides away completely, and cannot drop down on to the baby while he is in the bath.

Many mothers find bathing baby easier in a washing-up bowl or in the bathroom or kitchen sink, where the height is comfortable and worktop space is often available. If you do use a wash basin, wrap a towel around the taps to stop dripping and to prevent baby touching them. You don't want to risk banging his head or burning him on the warm metal of the hot tap. If the bath surface is slippery, you should line it with a hand towel or nappy, or use a non-slip bath liner.

When filling baby's bath, run cold water first so that the bottom of the bath is not too hot. If you are using a sink with a mixer tap, run cold at the end as well, to ensure that the tap is not hot. A few drops of oil added to the bath will help if your baby's skin is very dry. Almond oil is ideal, and the unbranded type can be bought very cheaply over the counter at the chemist. The water should be "blood heat" – about the same as your baby's blood temperature, which is 29.4°C (85°F).

Before putting your baby in the bath, test the water temperature with your elbow or the inside of your wrist to make sure it feels just right – neither too hot nor too cold. If you don't trust your elbows, you can always buy a special thermometer.

Tiny babies soon get cold, so limit the time your baby is completely undressed. Leave your baby's vest on while you clean his outer regions with baby lotion and, when you take it off, wrap him in a soft towel so that he doesn't feel naked and insecure.

With baby snugly wrapped in the towel, clean his eyes, ears and nose. For newborn babies you will need some warm boiled water in a small bowl and some cotton wool balls. Later unboiled warm water is fine.

Cleanse your baby's eyes first with moistened cotton wool, using a fresh piece for each eye. Wipe gently from the bridge of the nose outwards. Then clean the outside of your baby's ears and behind them with moist cotton wool. Never poke about with cotton wool buds. Wipe baby's face with damp cotton wool, cleaning around the nostrils and mouth to remove any remove any dried milk or dribble.

When it comes to actually "dunking" baby in the bathwater, if you establish a secure technique of holding your baby it helps. As you unwrap baby from the towel, put your left arm under his shoulders, and hold him with your thumb over his shoulder and fingers hooked under his armpit. Slip your right arm under baby's legs and hold on to his opposite thigh. Then gently lower him into the water. Soothe him, talk and smile to calm him and to make him feel less vulnerable.

Hold your baby's head and shoulders up, with his lower body in the water, resting on the bottom of the bath. Still holding him securely under his shoulders, use your free hand to wash him. Don't use soap for the first few weeks because babies need the natural oils in their skin. After about six weeks you can opt for either the traditional bar of baby soap, or a mild baby bath liquid which is added to the water. The liquid makes baby less slippery and means you don't have an extra item to cope with.

Don't leave your baby in the bath too long, because tiny babies can't regulate their body temperature very well, and never leave your baby unattended in the bath, not even for a second while you turn to retrieve something. It is extremely easy for a child to drown even in very shallow water, and statistics show that there is a significant number of accidental drownings in the home.

To take him out of the bath, slip your free hand under his bottom and gently lift him out on to the towel. Wrap him up snugly, give him a cuddle and make sure you dry all his nooks and crannies. Forget baby talc – it can chafe the skin and can make babies cough if applied too liberally.

The hospital will probably give you some surgical wipes to clean your newborn baby's navel while it is healing. (This does not mean that you cannot bath the baby, but ensure that you dry the navel properly after the bath.)

Many parents are fearful of cutting a new baby's tiny nails and it isn't really necessary to do this for a few weeks unless your newborn baby is scratching himself. When nails do need cutting, it is easiest done after the bath when they are soft. Use a small pair of round-ended baby scissors, gently cutting the nails along the line of the fingertips. You may feel more confident if you do this tricky task while baby is asleep. If your baby is a sound sleeper he won't fight you, and you won't feel so nervous and worried that you might cut his skin. Or you can get someone to divert his attention, say, with a song or toys.

On days when you are not going to be bathing your baby, "topping and tailing" is a perfectly good alternative method of cleaning your baby without risking a cold, or fearing that you drop his slippery little body. To "top and tail", undress your baby to his vest and nappy, and lay him on a flat, firm surface at a comfortable height. Have everything ready in advance. Cleanse his eyes, ears and face with cotton wool dipped in warm boiled water as you do before you give him a bath. Using a new piece of cotton wool clean your baby's hands and dry gently with a soft towel.

Next, take off his nappy and clean the nappy area with a damp soft facecloth if he is merely wet. (Natural sponges are ideal for washing baby, but they are dear.) If he is dirty, use baby lotion and cotton wool to clean him.

When cleaning the nappy area, don't try to clean inside your baby girl's vulva. It is not only unnecessary but medically unsafe. Only the outer part needs washing. But clean her from the front and wipe backwards to her bottom, so that you don't cause infection by carrying any bacteria from her bottom to her bladder. And again when cleaning your baby boy's nether regions, wash the outer skin only, and don't try to pull back an uncircumcised foreskin to wash him. Remember, the "hidden parts" of the body look after themselves better than we can, so just wash the outside of his genitals and dry gently in the folds.

Small babies may make you nervous when you are holding them in water, but at least you are in control. Many parents discover, however, that bathing a toddler can also be a tricky business. Small children often go through a phase when they scream at the idea of having a bath, and parents despair.

However, a routine of cleanliness and hygiene is essential and so parents have to find ways of making bathtime pleasurable. Bath toys, or empty shampoo bottles, and appealing sponges or flannels, are ideal for allaying bathtime fears. In establishing an early delight in bathing, your child will naturally grow into habits of cleanliness which should last a lifetime.

Bedwetting

At some point during their third year, most toddlers manage to stay dry through a whole night. This normally happens a few months after they have learnt to control their bladders during the day. No two children are the same, however, and some may take longer than others to achieve this milestone in life.

Staying dry through the night has more to do with bladder size and family traits than anything else. A toddler's bladder may simply not be large enough to hold the overnight build-up of urine. Or, whereas one child might wake up when his bladder is full, another one may sleep so heavily that he cannot. Boys are more prone to bedwetting than girls, although no one knows why this should be.

If by his fourth birthday your child is still bedwetting regularly, take him to the doctor who will check that there is nothing wrong physically. He can also advise you about different training methods to help overcome this frustrating difficulty.

Bedwetting sometimes afflicts a child who has already successfully reached the dry night stage. In this case, stress is very probably the cause. Common reasons for stress in toddlers are the arrival of a new brother or sister, starting a new school, or even illness.

If your child suddenly starts to wet his bed again, find out what is worrying him and try to minimize the problem. Indulge him, let him behave in a babyish way – some children revert to thumbsucking or demanding a bottle for example, when a new baby arrives. Don't let him know you are bothered about the bedwetting until he is used to the new situation, or you may end up in a vicious circle.

Bear in mind that stress may also affect a child who has not yet quite managed the dry night stage and may be what is preventing him from getting there.

If your child is slow about staying dry through the night, be patient and don't try to rush things along. Your anxiety could make your child nervous and the situation worse. Try the following tips:

● Don't deny him a drink before a daytime nap or at bedtime – it's not worth the anxiety this will cause.

● Rather than risk wet sheets, keep your child in nappies at night, even if he doesn't use them during the day.

● Do get him to empty his bladder before putting him to bed.

● Pot him just before you yourself go to bed, without waking him up completely – he will respond to the coldness of the pot.

● Pot him first thing in the morning, as soon as the household starts to make noises.

Bee Stings

Bee stings can cause severe pain and, for the very young, the old and those prone to allergies, are potentially the most dangerous of insect stings in this country. Most other insect stings cause only minor irritation that can be cooled with a cold compress or calamine lotion. A bee sting requires a little more care.

If there is a bees' nest in your attic or near your house have it removed by an expert as soon as you spot it. Don't allow your child to approach a swarm of bees, or play close to flower beds where there are bees.

A bee always leaves its sting behind. So, if your child is stung, always first suspect a bee if you have not actually seen the insect and look for the black sting which may still be embedded in his skin. The puncture area around a bee sting is surrounded by a blanched area and then a reddish area, usually swollen.

Either gently scrape the sting away with the edge of a credit card or ease it out with a pair of tweezers, without squeezing the attached poison sac.

The venom of bee stings is acid. Treat the puncture area and surrounding swelling with a counteracting alkaline solution from your pharmacist. Then make your child rest and watch for any signs of shock.

If your child has had a previous bee sting and has developed an allergy, he may suffer from breathing difficulties or signs of shock such as faintness, a shallow rapid pulse and sweating. This severe reaction is known as anaphylactic shock. Take him to a doctor immediately.

A sting in the mouth can be very serious as any swelling might impair breathing. Give the child a mouthwash of one teaspoon of bicarbonate of soda in a tumbler of water, then make him suck an ice cube. To reduce the swelling of the tongue or throat, put a cold soothing compress on your child's neck. Take him to a hospital emergency unit immediately, and take the dead insect with you, if you can find it.

Bites

Domestic pet bites

Families often live with a wide range of domestic animals any of which is capable, under provocation, of biting children. Bites may be superficial needing only minor first aid and a cuddle, or they may be serious enough to require stitches.

Where an animal bite has not broken the skin, gently wash the area and apply a soothing ointment. As long as there is no swelling or other symptom of infection, this, along with loving attention, will be sufficient.

Rabies is common in some countries, so if your child is bitten outside the UK you must take him immediately to a doctor to see if he needs protection against rabies. Most bites will heal over without any problems, although deep gashes could leave a scar.

As a preventive measure you should teach your child to respect all animals and to treat them with caution and kindness. Don't let him use pets as toys; a mauled kitten, puppy, or even hamster can bite if handled roughly. Your child should never approach other people's pets until he has permission to do so and is sure that the animal is friendly. Some dogs are not used to children and might react to sudden movement. On the other hand, don't make your child afraid of dogs. A nervous screaming child can make a normally calm dog aggressive.

Dog bites are the most serious danger to children. Make sure that you can control your own dog, under any circumstances; if necessary, take it to obedience classes. Never leave your child to play unsupervised with any animal even if you are told it is safe.

Snake bites

Different countries are home to different species of snakes. Some are harmless, others are poisonous and a bite from them requires urgent action.

The only poisonous snake in Europe is the adder, which is about 75 cm long when fully grown, with a broad head. It may be grey, yellow or reddish brown with a black zigzag along its back. Although the adder's bite is rarely fatal to an adult it will cause swelling and pain as well as possibly sweating and vomiting which can make a child seriously ill.

If your child is bitten by a snake:
● wash the wound, but do not suck out the venom. Comfort your child, treating him for shock if necessary.
● rush him to the nearest casualty department.
● don't let him walk as this will move the venom around the body and make it worse.

In an emergency:
● If the skin is broken, clean the wound, then take your child to the doctor, as an infection could occur and cause complications.

Other Common Bites and Stings

Source	Prevention	First Aid	Later Treatment
Jellyfish	Do not bathe in water known to be frequented by jellyfish. Get child to shore and pick off pieces of jelly fish with sandy hands.	Cleanse the area stung	Seek medical help, especially for the sting of Portuguese Man of War
Mosquitoes	Wrap up after dark. Avoid stagnant water. Burn a mosquito coil by the bed. Apply insect repellent	Apply surgical spirit; cologne or cold water will do if this is not available. Repeat as necessary	Avoid scratching. Take antihistamine tablets if swelling is severe
Ants	Do not sit on uncovered grass or disturb ants' nests. Wear an insect repellent.	Treat with bicarbonate of soda paste	None is usually necessary
Ticks	Do not sit on grass used normally by sheep or cattle. Keep dogs and cats free of ticks.	If the tick is embedded in the skin use petroleum jelly, oil, alcohol or petrol to loosen its grip and remove it with tweezers.	Soothe tick bites with calamine lotion.
Fleas	Keep dogs and cats free of fleas.	Treat bites with calamine. Badly affected children should see a doctor.	Use a suitable powder on animals, clothes, bedding and cushions.

● Check that your child's tetanus immunization is up-to-date – he could need a booster.

● If the bite is deep or you cannot stop the bleeding, take your child to the hospital immediately in case he needs to have stitches.

◆ See also, **Bee Stings**, **Wasp Stings**

Black Eye

In the rough and tumble of everyday life, energetic young children can suffer all kinds of bumps and bruises, including black eyes. Although alarming, they are rarely serious.

The first sign of a black eye is a yellowing of the tissues around the eye, which will gradually turn black. There may also be rapid swelling, even to the point where the eye is almost closed. The swelling should go down in a couple of days.

The cause of a black eye is a direct blow to the eye area. The skin here is thinner than on the rest of the face, so blood released under it is more obvious than elsewhere. This blood must be reabsorbed from the tissues before the colour returns to normal.

No treatment is usually necessary. If, however, you are not sure of the cause of a black eye or if the blow to the eye area was severe, take your child to your doctor or a hospital casualty department.

Rarely, what looks like an ordinary black eye is caused by a fracture at the base of the skull, but then the bruising usually shows beneath both eyes. In such cases, seek hospital treatment immediately.

◆ See also, **Bruises**

Bleeding

However badly your child is bleeding, your first priority is to make sure he or she is still breathing and the heartbeat is present. Then check for foreign bodies in the wound. Small pieces of gravel or dirt can be wiped off, but anything larger may be plugging the wound and stopping further bleeding. Do not attempt to remove it. Severe, pulsating (arterial) bleeding must be controlled by direct firm pressure using a pad, such as a folded handkerchief.

Foreign bodies – bandaging the wound

After controlling the bleeding with pressure on either side of the wound, cover very gently with sterile gauze. Build up a layer of pads or cotton wool around the foreign body until you reach at least its own height. Do not pull the gauze tight over the object. Secure dressing firmly by bandaging either side of the object. Bandage once over the object only if you have built up the dressing around it.

Bleeding from the ear

Make the child comfortable with his head tilted towards the injured side. Do not put anything inside the ear to stop it bleeding as this could cause further damage. Cover the whole ear with a sterile dressing and secure with tape or a bandage. Watch for any signs of shock which may develop. Take him to the doctor as quickly as you can. If your child is not too distressed, do your best to find out what caused the bleeding to save time at the doctors.

Scalp bleeding

The scalp bleeds very freely, so scalp wounds generally look much worse than they are. Control the bleeding by applying pressure through a pad and take the child to the doctor to check for concussion or possible fracture as soon as possible. Just because your child is still conscious does not mean that he is not concussed.

Nosebleeds

Nosebleeds are quite common. If your child has a nosebleed, sit him on your knee with his head forwards over a bowl. Loosen any tight clothing around the neck and pinch the soft part of the nose for about ten minutes. Your child will need to stop crying before he can breathe through his mouth, so comfort him as much as you can. If the bleeding has not stopped after ten minutes, apply pressure again for another ten minutes. If the nose continues to bleed after 30 minutes, take your child to a doctor. Do not let him run around or blow his nose for about four hours after the bleeding has stopped.

Bleeding from the eye

If your child's eye is bleeding, do not attempt to remove anything which may be embedded in it.

● Lay your child on his back, supporting his head. Keep him as still as possible. Place a sterile dressing or pad over the closed eye. Secure with tape or a bandage and take him to the nearest hospital.

Controlling bleeding from a limb

1. Raise the injured limb above the level of the heart. You may need to lay the child down.

2. Apply direct pressure to the wound with thumb or fingers, ideally through a clean dressing. Press the edges of the wound together if necessary.

3. If an object is sticking out of the wound, press around it, not on it. Maintain the pressure until you see a lessening in the flow of blood.

4. Cover with a sterile dressing large enough to overlap the wound.

5. If blood starts seeping through, place another dressing on top of the first one. Bandage in place. Do not try to use a tourniquet unless you have expert knowledge.

6. Treat for shock, if necessary (see Shock) and seek medical help at the nearest hospital.

Impalement

If your child falls on to railings or spikes and impales himself, do not attempt to lift him off. Support the weight of his body and limbs. Tell whoever phones the emergency services to give all the details so they can bring the necessary equipment to cut the child free. This will normally involve the Fire Brigade. While waiting for the emergency services to arrive, keep the child as calm and as still as possible to prevent him from injuring himself any further.

Amputations

If a child has lost the end of a finger or toe, for example, the doctors may be able to sew it back in place if hospital attention is received quickly enough. Control the bleeding as described earlier, but take extra care not to damage the stump as you press. Pressure immediately above the wound rather than directly on it will help, though it may be less effective. Put the severed part in a clean plastic bag. If possible, wrap the bag in some material, and put it in a container of ice. Make sure that the ice does not come into direct contact with the severed tissue. Get to hospital as quickly as possible.

Internal bleeding

If you suspect internal bleeding, you must get your child to hospital as quickly as you can. It is not easy to diagnose, so play it safe and go to the hospital if you note any of the following symptoms:

● Shock after a violent injury but no sign of blood.

● Pattern bruising – the imprint of clothes can be seen in the bruise.

● Blood coming out of the mouth (especially bright, frothy blood), or the anus or passed in the urine.

● Severe swelling around an injury.
● Sudden severe pains in the chest or abdomen.

Internal bleeding can result from a number of causes including broken bones, crush injuries or simply a hard blow to the body, though it can also occur with a penetration injury. Tell the doctor if you know or suspect what the cause could be.

Boils

Boils can occur anywhere on the body, but they appear most often on the face, eyelids, back of the neck, upper back and buttocks. They especially favour places where clothing rubs, such as the neck area along the collar line.

There are three main types of boil – those caused by a hair follicle becoming infected; carbuncles (now very rare), which are two or more boils occurring next to each other; and styes, a boil in one of the eyelash follicles.

Almost always boils will clear up by themselves. However, treatment may be necessary to eliminate any risk of their spreading.

Boils are caused by certain bacteria called staphylococci, some of which live harmlessly on the skin all the time. These bacteria usually only cause trouble when their numbers become excessive.

Diabetics can have a series of boils when their blood sugar concentration remains high. This is because the bacteria breed faster when there is sugar present in the tissues.

When the skin is broken, boils develop rather more easily.

A boil starts gradually with a tender area under the skin. It becomes hot and red and may be surrounded by swelling. A centre of pus develops where the fight against the infection is fiercest. On places like the ear or nose, where the skin is tight and the surrounding tissue cannot stretch, the condition is very painful indeed.

Although boils usually clear up by themselves, you can help them to form a head and ease the pain at the same time by bathing the area with hot water or by applying a hot flannel or poultice. A kaolin poultice can be made by heating kaolin paste in a pan of boiling water until it is moderately hot, then spreading it thickly on some lint. This is covered with gauze and applied to the boil. Test the heat of the poultice against the inside of your arm before putting it on your child.

Although small boils can be gently squeezed without much danger, it is wiser to leave them alone.

Large or painful boils must never be squeezed, nor should you squeeze any boils or carbuncles, large or small, between the eyes and the nose as you risk infection spreading to the brain.

Once a boil has burst and the pus begins to drain, a dry dressing should be applied daily.

As soon as the pus from a boil has been released and the central core of dead tissue is gone, the boil heals. This may take about a week. Occasionally the body's defences will get the best of a boil, and the inflammation will subside without bursting.

A small boil will heal without leaving a noticeable scar, but large boils and carbuncles do form scar tissue which may shrink over the months, but never disappear altogether. The best way to reduce the risk of scarring from a large boil is by early treatment. The sooner you take your child to the doctor, the sooner the boil will be brought under control and damage kept to a minimum.

The following may help to prevent the occurrence of boils:

● Keep the skin bacteria down by daily washing.

● Take extra care when washing areas where there is rubbing, such as the buttocks and neck.

● Powder neck and buttocks to reduce friction and sweat formation.

● Change flannels daily.

● Avoid tight collars and underwear made of nylon.

◆ See also, **Styes**

Bonding

Bonding is a topic you will read about in most childbirth and baby books. It conjures up romantic pictures of the mother falling instantly and overwhelmingly in love with her newly-delivered child.

All traumas of giving birth swept aside, this love-at-first-sight scenario is seen as standard. In fact, the reality can be very different, and very normal.

The time it takes to feel the first stirrings of love varies from person to person. For some, the immediate feeling is exhaustion and relief that the labour is over. For others, the feelings of responsibility can overwhelm all other emotions. Many women describe feeling trapped. For some women, learning to love their child can take a while.

When the experts started stressing bonding it was largely to re-educate the professionals. They wanted to change the delivery room practice of separating the babies from their mothers in the name of medical routine. This deprived mothers and fathers of early moments with their new baby – important moments that could contribute to the bonding process.

Allowing parents getting-to-know-you time was the ideal, but the expectations of its effects were possibly too high. While many mothers find bonding with their babies is helped by close physical contact after the birth, there is no evidence that being deprived of this does in reality prevent bonding in any way.

Early contact is just one contribution to the forming of maternal love. Mothers who have had difficult or Caesarean deliveries, or whose babies have needed to be in the special care unit, do not automatically get off to a disastrous start in their relationship with their children.

In the past, hospital routine didn't allow mothers time with their babies after birth and newborns were whisked away to be checked and then consigned to the nursery. Nevertheless, mothers still formed loving bonds with their babies.

Now that we are led to expect a natural, trouble-free birth followed by a thunderbolt of love, it is little wonder that many women who experience neither feel let down and guilty. But it is not unnatural not to feel instant motherly love for your newborn child; he can take time to grow on you.

When your baby arrives he may be very different from what you expected. You may have anticipated a miniature version of you or your partner only to be presented with a tiny, ugly, red infant who resembles neither of you. You may have spent your pregnancy carrying an imagined "darling" daughter, only to be handed a son.

Pregnant women can be persuaded that they are carrying a girl or a boy by old wives' talk of how the baby is lying or how much it kicks. They may think they will find it easier to mother either a daughter or a son. Grandparents may place advance orders.

When expectations don't match reality many a mum can feel confused, but there is a very simple answer – time. Love can arrive later than the baby, and discovering the bond can take days or weeks. Forget all the myths about one sex being less trouble than the other; both will be troublesome and both rewarding.

For some parents the realities after giving birth are far from the happiness they anticipated. They may have to face problems they thought would never happen.

Mothers may feel desolate and deprived if their babies are premature or have problems that mean they need time in incubators in special care units. Instead of having a baby in their arms, the parents are faced with a tiny, fragile infant, often dependent on frightening gadgets and tubes. It seems the baby belongs to the hospital, not them.

But the situation need not be totally black. If possible, the parents will be allowed to touch their baby through the incubator's special glove holes. When the time is right, they can gradually begin to help with his care. If the mother wants to breastfeed, she can try to express milk.

When these mothers eventually take their babies home, relief will be mixed with fear. They need all the help they can get from partners and relatives because looking after babies who need extra care is stressful. But as the anxiety subsides and the baby thrives, they will be able to catch up on the closeness they have missed.

There are other parents, however, who need special help because they have "special children", ones with long-term problems or handicaps. Faced with these realities, parents may be completely stunned and the level of grief felt can be very similar to that experienced when someone you love dies.

Trying to come to terms with this situation is full of pain and sometimes parents are only protected by disbelief or anger. Time and the help of friends, support groups and caring professionals can ease the stress, if not the hurt. Eventually, parents may be able to see past the sadness, find hope for themselves and their babies and begin to make positive plans for the future.

One reason for encouraging more early contact and mothering and less professional interference is that new mums can be made to feel inadequate if the experts take control. But no matter how much motherly involvement is encouraged in the early days, many mums feel fearful and inadequate when facing the total responsibility for a tiny infant.

It is not unusual in the isolation of motherhood to feel unequal to caring for a new and vulnerable baby. Confidence, like love, takes time to grow.

If a baby is continually fretful or colicky, mothers naturally worry. At times, feelings of resentment at being housebound by this dependent infant can blot out the expected glow of maternal love.

Being deprived of sleep and the ability to escape the 24-hour duty of motherhood often makes women feel exhausted, trapped and inadequate. It may seem impossible to admit that you feel miserable and put-upon, but support will work wonders.

Don't be afraid to discuss your feelings with others. You will be surprised to find that many a seemingly radiant mum has felt guilty, gloomy and confused. It helps to know that you are not bad mothers but beleaguered mothers whose feelings are both natural and normal.

Early "baby blues" are a well known feature on the maternity ward. "The weepies", which afflict many mums, are regarded as a normal occurrence by the medical staff.

The person to turn to is your partner. He, on his part, may be feeling totally bewildered by your tiredness and tears. Also, if he's a first-time dad, he's learning parenting, too. Together, you've got to get used to three major changes. Living with a third person, being a parent, and seeing your partner not just as a lover and friend but as your baby's mother or father. A new dad can feel extremely traumatized by the birth. Not many men are prepared for the way they feel during labour and delivery. It is an intense and upsetting time for a man, seeing his loved one in agony and not being able to help much. Once at home he might have a week off work to be with you and the baby, but after that he'll only be there for evenings and weekends. This realization is a big shock for both parents, and can be the beginning of a very difficult division of labour in the home.

Because you are with the baby all day and every day you will naturally build up a closer relationship more quickly than the father can. If you're not careful this can lead to the father feeling "dethroned" from his position as the most important person in your life, which can quickly make him jealous and resentful. The trick is to try to adapt to life as a threesome rather than hark back to the old baby-less days of yore. And the worst thing for a nervous new dad is to have you standing over him telling him he isn't doing it right – if you criticize he may very well stop offering to change nappies altogether.

The more contact a father has with his baby, the better – especially early on. It may be hard for him to switch from wheeling and dealing at the office to coming home and wiping the baby's bottom, but versatility is a skill that every parent soon grows adept at.

The early stages of getting to know your baby will probably also see the birth of your protective instinct. This need to protect your child at all costs can be very powerful stuff. Many women say that it surges over them like a kind of tidal wave at real or imagined threats. It can be a magnificent feeling and it can also be quite frightening in its intensity. Either way, it is quite normal.

Women who, before they became a mother, tended to be rather passive, can be really surprised at how aggressive they can become if they feel that their babies are threatened in any way.

When your child is about five months old, your hormone balance will probably have returned to more or less normal. This will help you a lot. Your level of anxiety will be greatly reduced. You will have begun to get used to the idea that your life is now completely different. You will be a bit more relaxed and so, as a result, will your baby.

Along with the stresses and strains of the first few months you will have had the reinforcement of some truly magical moments. These times will help you over the tough bits. You will feel immense pride at your child's achievements. You will have times when you feel unqualified love for your child. You will be filled with tenderness simply by watching your contentedly sleeping child.

Older siblings

Bonding with a new baby can be a complex business for older siblings too, who can react in many and varied ways to the new arrival. They may start to behave in a more babyish way, or possibly become destructive and difficult. Your child may also express feelings of resentment to you or your child.Among all the mixed emotions, however, there is likely to be a strong feeling of pride at having a new baby, coupled with a powerful protective instinct, which will endure as the bond between the children is forged.

◆ See also, **Fatherhood**, **Motherhood**, **Postnatal Depression**, **Sibling Status**

Bottle Feeding

Despite the rise in breastfeeding, bottle feeding is the most popular method of feeding newborn babies. This is so for a number of different reasons. Some women find breastfeeding physically difficult or don't have enough milk. Others find it uncomfortable or inconvenient. The big advantage of bottle feeding is that it allows the father to be involved in the process and helps him get close to and bond with his new baby.

All babies need milk as their only food for the first four to six months of their lives. Infant formula milks are made from cow's milk, which has been specially modified to make it suitable for young babies.

Cow's milk contains more mineral salts and protein than a baby's delicate digestive system can deal with, which is why it is modified before being used.

Infant formulas are either whey- or curd-based. Whey-based formula is usually recommended during the first few months as it is more easily digested. Curd-based formula, which usually takes longer to digest, is often given to older babies.

Some babies have an allergy to cow's milk. If your child does, a soya infant formula may be advised. Never give your baby soya formula unless recommended by your doctor, midwife or health visitor.

You'll need to sterilize your baby's bottles and equipment before use to help protect him against infection. You can do this with special sterilizing units or in a large plastic container. You'll also need sterilizing tablets or solution from the chemist. Microwave ovens are not suitable for sterilizing.

Most sterilizing units hold four to six bottles, so you'll need to sterilize and prepare bottles twice a day – morning and evening. This way you'll have enough feed ready whenever your baby wants it. As he grows, the number of feeds will decline and you'll be able to make up all the feeds he needs for the day in a single batch.

Formula manufacturers take great care to make a feed which will give your baby a balanced diet. This balance will be upset if you make the feed too strong or too weak, so follow the manufacturer's instructions to the letter. Never add other foods or sugar.

You'll gradually learn how much milk to make up. The instructions on the tin will guide you. As a rule of thumb, a baby needs about 150 ml of milk per 1 kg of body weight (2½ fl oz per 1 lb) every 24 hours.

Babies' appetites increase as they grow and some need more than others, so you might want to put 30 ml (1 oz) more feed in the bottle than is normally suggested.

Feed your baby whenever he's hungry and you'll soon recognize his feeding pattern. At first he'll probably need feeding every three or four hours. Many babies need more frequent feeds than suggested, so make sure you have extra bottles made up and ready in the fridge.

Experiment with different teats – latex and silicon, conventional- and nipple-shaped – to find the one that best suits your baby. Check the holes too – medium or large – to ensure that the milk will flow out adequately: hold a filled bottle upside down; milk should drip out at a rate of one or two drops per second. If it drips out more slowly, your baby may take a long time to feed and get tired before he has had enough. But if it's too fast, your baby may choke and get more wind. Always check for splits and discard any damaged teats as well as any old ones that have become flabby.

To warm a bottle from the fridge quickly you should stand it in a bowl of hot water for a few minutes. Always test the feed's temperature on the inside of your wrist before feeding – it should feel neither hot nor cold.

The things that are important in breastfeeding, such as cuddling, stroking and talking to your baby, are just as important if you bottle feed. Your baby can see your face, knows your voice and learns very fast about the world around him, so make feeding time an enjoyable and relaxing experience.

Find a comfortable chair that supports your back and hold your baby in the crook of your arm so his head is supported. Your baby should be slightly sitting up and cuddled against you. Make sure he's not lying horizontally.

Hold the bottle so that the teat is always full of milk, place it in his mouth above the tongue, being careful not to push it too far back. Pull on it slightly and let your baby suck until he needs a rest.

Babies often suck the teat flat, which causes a vacuum and no milk comes out. If this happens, take the bottle out of his mouth to let the air in and then just pop it back in again. After a few feeds he'll learn to let go of the teat every now and then.

Most babies take what they want in about 20 minutes. If your baby is much slower than this, discuss it with your midwife or health visitor.

Halfway through feeding, move your baby to the other arm. This will give your baby a new view to look at and your arm a rest. It's also a good time to wind your baby if you think he's swallowed any air.

To remove a bottle, just pull the teat away gently but firmly and your baby should release the bottle. If he doesn't, gently slide your little finger into the corner of his mouth to break the suction.

Winding brings up any air that's been swallowed during feeding or crying prior to feeding, and helps to prevent the wind from causing your baby any discomfort or pain.

To wind your baby, hold him upright on your shoulder with a bib or towel over your shoulder to catch any dribble. Gently rub or pat your baby's back between the shoulder blades. Alternatively, you can sit your baby propped up on your knee with his chin supported between your finger and thumb, then pat or rub his back. Or, lay the baby on your lap, face downwards, with his head turned to one side, and again, pat or rub his back. Don't pat or rub too hard as you may jerk him and he'll bring up some of the feed. A gentle upward stroking movement is usually the best.

Most babies do bring up a mouthful or two of milk when being winded. This "possetting" can be alarming at first, but it doesn't do any harm. Some mothers worry because the milk looks curdled, but this is simply due to the effect of the stomach acid on the milk during the first stage of digestion.

If your baby possets, check the hole in the teat. If it's too large he may be taking in too much feed too quickly, and if it's too small he may be sucking in a lot of air because he has to suck very hard. If more than a mouthful or two comes up, or if your baby possets regularly, report it to your doctor, midwife or health visitor.

Bottle feeding basics

● Always wash your hands before sterilizing, preparing and giving feeds.
● Sterilize every piece of equipment you use.
● Follow all instructions exactly.
● Keep opened packets of formula in the fridge.
● Cool made-up formula immediately by putting it in the fridge.
● Keep all bottles refrigerated until required.
● Give warmed-up milk to a baby immediately.
● Throw away any left-over feed.
● Don't use artificially softened water to make up feed – it usually has too much sodium.
● Never use "natural mineral water" as this can contain high concentrations of minerals unsuitable for infant feeds.
● If you're using bottled water, always boil it first.
● Don't feed your baby lying flat. It's difficult for him to swallow in this position and he may gag or be sick.
● Never leave your baby propped up on a pillow or cushion, with the bottle. He might inhale milk and choke, or swallow too much air.
● Don't force your baby to finish the bottle after he's stopped sucking. He knows when he's had enough.
● Don't try feeding your baby if his nose is blocked. He can't swallow and breathe at the same time, so ask your doctor for nose drops which can be used before each feed.

● Never change your milk formula without consulting your doctor, midwife or health visitor.

◆ See also, **First Foods**, **Hygiene**

Breastfeeding

Breast milk is the perfect and complete food and drink for a young baby for the first four to six months of life. As well as having exactly the right balance of "ingredients", instantly available and at the right temperature, breast milk contains anti-infective substances which protect your baby's health and help him avoid infection and illness.

You can continue breastfeeding your baby for as long as you want to – it helps provide nourishment and comfort even for older babies on solid food.

The other reason you may choose to breastfeed is that it's such an enjoyable thing to do ... watching your baby grow and knowing it's all because of you is a special pleasure. Breastfeeding is a lovely way of offering your baby security and closeness, and many mothers look back on this period as a very precious time.

Every woman produces breast milk, whether or not she intends to breastfeed her baby. In fact, your breasts start preparing for breastfeeding as soon as you're pregnant. You might notice your breasts feel fuller as the milk producing and storing tissue starts to develop.

During pregnancy, your breasts produce colostrum, a straw-coloured fluid which your baby will have in the first few days after birth. You may even leak a little colostrum before you give birth – this is quite normal, so don't be alarmed.

On the second, third or fourth day after delivery – sometimes later – your breasts will begin to produce milk. If you don't breastfeed your baby, this initial production of milk will cease, and your breasts will "dry up". However, if you do, your body gets the message that breast milk is needed, and will continue to produce it.

The message gets through because hormones (the chemical messengers that circulate in the blood) take instructions from one part of the body to another. The two vital hormones involved in breastfeeding are stimulated by the action of the baby sucking on your breast. When the baby sucks, he stimulates prolactin, which is the milk-making hormone, and oxytocin, which causes the milk to flow into the ducts and down towards the nipple.

It's this that gets the whole milk production and supply line going – and the more your baby sucks, the more milk you'll make. That's why a mother with twins makes twice as much milk as a mother of one single baby, and why there's no need to be worried if your baby seems extra hungry at any point – as long as you feed him as often as he wants, you'll make enough milk for him. It's also why introducing bottles of milk or water is rarely a good idea, especially in the early weeks when your breasts need plenty of stimulation to get feeding established. A bottle fills your baby up, satisfies his need to suck and takes away his desire to come to the breast. Your body responds to this by making less milk, because the stimulation to the supply is decreased.

If there are signs you're underproducing, you can increase your milk supply by feeding more often – waking your baby up to feed him if necessary, so you fit in extra feeds when you can. Aim to feed every two to three hours for a couple of days. Also, make sure your baby is well latched-on so he can milk your breast efficiently, getting the rich creamy hind milk as well as the thinner fore milk. And allow him to stay on one breast for as long as he wants, before moving him to the other side.

If your baby is gaining weight satisfactorily, he produces six or more wet nappies a day, his cry is good and strong, and your doctor is happy with his health and progress, then you're both doing fine.

The very first feed can take place soon after birth. Many babies are beautifully alert and responsive in the first hour after delivery, and if you and the baby are well, ask for help in putting him to your breast. Don't worry if you don't have the chance to feed as soon as this, though – just try later.

To feed efficiently, a baby needs to be well latched-on to the breast. It's sometimes called "being fixed". Hold your baby so his chest is facing yours, with his head supported. If he's ready to feed, he may well start to open his mouth; sometimes you may have to help him a bit by stroking his lips with your fingers or with your nipple.

His mouth needs to be wide open so he can draw the nipple far back into his mouth, and also to allow his jaws and tongue to work on the breast to stimulate the milk. When his mouth is wide, move his head against your breast, making sure he can take the underneath part of the areola into his mouth as well (this is where you may need to help as you can't see this bit).

Incidentally, there's no need to wash your breasts or nipples before you feed. Just wash them (without soap, which is too drying) as part of your normal showering or bathing routine.

Breastfeeding can be a slow process, especially at the beginning. It's as if nature has devised a special system to force you to rest and recuperate after giving birth – after all, you can't rush round doing other things when your baby needs feeding. You have to sit or lie down, and the surge of hormones as the feeding starts actually helps your body to relax.

Don't let your baby chew on the end of your nipple: he can make your nipples very sore very quickly if he does this, and he may not be able to stimulate enough milk. This sounds complicated, but it isn't! Sucking comes quite naturally to babies and as they soon master the technique, you'll soon stop having to think about whether he is sucking or chewing. Let your baby feed for as long as he wants to on the first side. Then, when he takes a natural break, and doesn't seem to want to return to the breast, sit him up and rub his back to "wind" him. You can change his nappy if you want to. Offer him the second side. He may or may not take it. At the next feed offer the unused side first.

In the early days and weeks, you might find yourself feeding very often in response to your baby's hunger. It's not unusual for a young baby to go to the breast a dozen times a day or night!

A new baby feeds often because his stomach is very small and empties very quickly, especially with breast milk which is so easily digested. It's also because breast milk production needs frequent stimulation at first in order to get it well-established. As time goes on, your baby is unlikely to need feeding as often as this, and you'll notice that he edges towards a pattern of feeding approximately every three or four hours.

At this early stage, each feed may last more than an hour by the time your baby has stopped and started, you've winded him and changed him, rubbed his back, offered him the breast again because he still seems unsettled ... and in the evenings, many babies like to be on and off the breast for hours, so you really lose all sense of separate feeds when your baby is very small and nuzzling at your breast.

This stage passes, and by the age of three to four months, most babies have settled into a feeding pattern and feeds have become a lot shorter. Both you and your baby will be feeling comfortable and easy together, and you will have the intense satisfaction of knowing that you have given your baby the best "natural" diet for his young and growing body.

Expressing

You may need to store your own milk so that someone else can feed the baby. The process of squeezing out the milk is called "expressing" and there are both electrical and hand pumps to help you do this. It is worth knowing how to express if your baby needs special care or your partner wishes to help you with the feeding routine.

Begin by washing your hands and sterilizing the pump and bottles. The best time to express milk is in the morning when you have most milk. Showering the breasts gently may help if you have difficulties.

There are three types of hand pump: the syringe type, the bulk type, and the battery-operated type. To use a syringe pump fit it over the nipple and pump it so that suction draws out the milk. Pour the milk into sterilized bottles labelled with the date.

Once you have expressed your breast milk, it can be fed to your baby by bottle or with a spoon. Some mothers express and store their milk on a regular basis so that they can go out to work. Milk can be stored in the fridge for 24 hours, but you can also keep it in the deep freeze, where it will last for three months.

Stored milk may separate into layers of different densities. It does not mean the milk has gone off but simply that the different elements in the milk are separating. To thaw the milk, run hot water over the bottle, then stand that in hot water to warm the milk. Once the milk has been defrosted it must be consumed in a few hours.

Breastfeeding problems
Sore nipples

Your nipples may become sore at first. If your baby is sucking on the nipple alone, it will be very painful and is also not an efficient way for him to get the milk out. He should take in the whole of the areola (the dark area around the nipple) as well. Try to hold your baby close to you and encourage him to open his mouth wide by placing your nipple near his mouth for a moment, then move him towards the breast, keeping his bottom lip towards the edge of the areola. When his mouth is properly positioned, his lower lip will turn out slightly – use a mirror or ask a midwife to check – and feeding should not cause soreness. If you have difficulties with positioning, ask for help and keep asking until you are sure you've got it right.

Don't wash your nipples between feeds as this can make them soggy; ordinary bathing or showering is quite sufficient. Between feeds wear absorbent breast pads, which should be changed regularly, and keep your nipples dry. If your nipple becomes cracked or inflamed you will feel a sudden sharp pain as your baby latches on to your breast. You can use an emollient cream or Vitamin E oil as a preventive measure, but sparingly. If the nipple is allowed to get too soft, it will take a long time to heal. Allowing a small drop of breast milk to dry on the nipple may also help, as will exposing it to the air.

If your baby has thrush in his mouth, this can be transferred to your nipple and vice versa. This irritating problem will not be resolved until you both get the correct treatment from your doctor. You can continue to feed while your nipple is sore, but use the side which is not sore first, and only use the sore nipple for a short time, or, if this is unbearable, hand express the milk from that side. A breast shield, a latex ring which fits over your nipple, sometimes helps. These can be obtained from pharmacists. Simple painkillers can be taken and will not affect your baby. Sore and cracked nipples usually heal remarkably quickly provided they are treated promptly.

When milk first "comes in" your breasts may become so full that the nipple becomes flattened, making it difficult for your baby to get a good hold. This is known as breast engorgement and can be very uncomfortable. The best way to relieve the pressure in your breasts is to feed your baby, but if your breasts are too full you may need to soften them by expressing a little milk before beginning to feed. Lean over a basin and let the milk drip and massage the sides of your breast towards the nipple. The midwife will help you to learn the technique. However, if your breasts are very engorged, expressing may be too painful. In this case, draping your breasts with warm flannels in a warm bath may be enough to encourage a little milk to flow out and allow your baby to get hold of your nipple. If you are in a lot of pain, ordinary painkilling tablets such as paracetamol may be taken.

This stage may last from just 24 hours up to a whole week, but be assured it will pass, whatever you do. However, the answer is not to feed your baby less. In order to get breastfeeding properly established, you need to offer your baby the breast very often, even if you feel very uncomfortable, as your baby's sucking is the key to starting the milk flowing freely. Keep the sucking time short, perhaps two minutes on each side, but don't reduce the frequency. Your baby may seem unsatisfied and restless, and even refuse the breast at times. This is quite common, and a little perseverance and support at this stage usually overcomes the problem.

Lumpy breasts

If you notice that one of your breasts is becoming lumpy and sore or if you notice an area of red skin on your breast which feels harder than normal, you may have a blocked duct. This often stems from engorgement or wearing too tight a bra. Get the milk flowing and start feeding from the affected side, leaning forwards and stroking over the lumpy area while your baby is sucking. Make sure the breast is completely empty – hand express after the baby has finished feeding. If the blockage is not cleared, it can lead to mastitis, which affects 9 per cent of breastfeeding mothers.

Mastitis

This happens when the milk flow is blocked and the milk leaks into the surrounding breast tissue. You may feel ill and feverish, and be running a temperature. Consult your doctor, who will probably prescribe antibiotics. In the early stages mastitis is often not an infection, but if it is not cleared up quickly it is likely to become one and the breast may even have to be drained surgically. It is also important to feed your baby frequently on the affected side, as the constant flow will help clear any blockage. Again, if your baby doesn't empty the breast, express the remainder of the milk. Bathing your breast in warm water can ease the discomfort, or try applying a warm or cold compress over the painful area. Again, it is quite safe to take a simple painkiller such as paracetamol.

Breast abscesses

These are very rare. They start with your feeling a soft, painless swelling or noticing a shiny red patch on your breast and you may see some pus in your milk. Stop feeding from the affected side at once and consult your doctor, who will give you antibiotics immediately. If that does not resolve the problem the abscess may require incision and draining. You can continue to feed your baby from the other breast, and in this instance a few complementary feeds may be needed.

Fast flow

It is possible for your let-down reflex to be too efficient, so your milk flows out too quickly and chokes your baby as soon as he sucks. You can slow the flow by expressing a little before you start to feed or by applying pressure with your fingertips above and below the areola as your baby feeds.

Breast milk jaundice

This rare type of jaundice occurs when a mother's breast milk contains an unusual chemical which makes the baby's liver less efficient at dealing with finished red blood cells than it should be. The chemical has no effect on the mother and once a doctor has ruled out all other possible causes for the jaundice, no treatment is required and nor should breastfeeding stop. The baby will remain yellow as his body adapts and his liver builds up to full efficiency, but once this has happened, the jaundice will disappear.

Drugs and breastfeeding

Avoid all drugs if possible but there may be times when you need to take them, particularly if you are experiencing breastfeeding problems and need to take painkillers. If your doctor gives you a prescription, always say that you are breastfeeding and check that any drugs you are taking are safe for the baby. Check with your pharmacist as well if you buy medicines over the counter. However, most drugs will have little effect on your baby, although antibiotics may make his motions loose and diuretics may reduce the amount of milk you produce. If you need to take tablets for epilepsy, it is usually absolutely safe to breastfeed.

◆ See also, **Weaning**

Bronchitis

There is often confusion about the word "bronchitis" because it is used to describe two totally different conditions. Acute bronchitis occurs in children; chronic bronchitis occurs in adults.

Acute bronchitis is an inflammation of the main bronchial tubes – the bronchi – caused by a bacterial or viral infection. It may develop suddenly, following a head cold or a sore throat.

Bronchitis usually occurs more frequently in winter, in damp cold climates and in heavily polluted environments. Chilling, overcrowding, fatigue and living with parents who smoke can all help cause bronchitis in young children.

The initial symptoms are often a head cold, running nose, fever and chills, aching muscles and possibly back pain. This is soon followed by the most obvious feature: a persistent cough. At first it is dry and racking, but later it becomes phlegmy. It is worse at night.

The best treatment is bed rest in a warm room. Paracetamol will reduce the fever and cough medicine may relieve the cough. If your child is very young, your doctor will tell you what is best to give him. Antibiotics are usually needed to eliminate bacterial infection.

Broodiness

Few women are totally immune from a sudden surge of desire or an enduring emptiness that is known as "broodiness". Whether you are already a mother, a dedicated career woman, 18 years of age or going on 40, the feeling that happiness is a tiny baby of your own can be irresistible.

Some experts explain this by saying that biological instincts are programmed into all living creatures to guarantee the survival of their species. Biology may well influence these desires but so does the society in which we live. In the world of today where many women have jobs and careers, a woman is still only believed to be totally fulfilled when she has a baby. So it is hardly surprising that women equate fulfilment with motherhood.

It is usual for girls, unlike boys, to be cared for principally by someone of their own sex – their role model. Little girls grow up identifying with the role of their mothers. They expect to have a baby of their own one day; it seems both natural and desirable and they learn mothering skills, which are simply waiting to be put to use.

Given the environment in which most of us grow up, it becomes almost impossible to separate biological from socially produced "maternal instincts". Freud had a theory that for women the early feeling of being incomplete (that is, not being endowed with a penis) can only be resolved by having a baby. But then, of course, Freud was a man!

Wanting a child is not the exclusive domain of women; men get broody too. Just as some women marry because they want children so, too, do some men. In some cultures a man will make sure that his lover can bear children before he even considers marrying her.

Men may feel broody because they want to produce an heir, to create a family or because they find parenthood rewarding and a tiny baby irresistible.

Sometimes a man desperately wants a first child or another child when his wife does not. She may not be ready to tie herself down or to take time out from her career, while her husband is longing for a family. She may still be recovering from a difficult birth or be finding it hard to cope with a young child, while her husband, enjoying his infant, longs for more babies.

Similarly a wife can long for a baby or want to give her child a brother or sister while her husband shuns the idea, afraid of the burdens of being the breadwinner. This refusal only makes the broody partner feel even more broody and desperate for another baby. Out of this situation resentment and conflict are likely to arise, especially when one partner in a relationship feels that the other does not understand or share their desires.

It is no use simply papering over the cracks; relationships break down when a couple cannot agree over such an important issue as whether and when to have a baby. If a husband and wife talk about their fears and feelings, understanding and agreement can often be reached.

To long for the gift of a child and then to experience the rewards of parenthood is the ideal. If you have enjoyed pregnancy with its status and cosseting, if you have found mothering a tiny baby a happy experience, you may want to recreate that time. But fortunately most women do not keep becoming pregnant simply because they feel the tug of love that makes them broody. Some women do, however, become victims of their maternal desires. They long for another baby and another and all too soon have to face the reality of a family short of space, money and precious time for each individual child.

You may want another baby because the one that is rapidly growing out of the baby stage gave you such joy or because you imagine that the next one will be different, easier, more the ideal you dreamed of. It is all too easy to become increasingly frustrated by the tantrums of your truculent two-year-old if you are fondly longing for the tranquillity of a new dream baby. It is as well to remind yourself that a new baby will become a difficult two-year-old in his turn.

If the time is not right to add to the family it helps to concentrate your love on the child you already have. A little more babying and cuddling will remind you that this toddler is still your baby, and stop you missing the closeness of the baby days.

As women get older there is an inescapable realization that time will eventually rob them of the choice with the end of their childbearing years. What experts describe as "the biological clock" ticks a message that often makes a woman decide to have a baby – or one last baby – before it is too late and she can no longer conceive.

Women who feel broody or caught up in the internal conflict of wanting and yet not wanting a baby can actually suffer increased menstrual pain or premenstrual tension as their bodies wonder whether they have conceived as they hoped, or whether they are relieved or unhappy when they have not.

Of course, nowadays, because there seems to be more freedom of choice, women imagine that when they choose to have a baby their wish will be granted. But for many couples fertility problems deny them a much longed-for child. Their unhappiness is made more difficult to bear when all their friends seem to have babies and thoughtless relatives enquire as to when they are going to "start a family".

Anyone who fails to become pregnant after a few months trying to conceive should see their doctor who will refer them.

Ulterior motives

Feeling broody may be a basic urge but the urge to conceive can result from wanting a baby to put things right or to upgrade our status. A baby may be desired to save a marriage, to stop a partner straying, to compete with a sister or brother's family or to produce the first grandchild for parents or in-laws. When you say you are "feeling broody" you should stop and think what your motives may be for wanting a baby.

You may find yourself focusing on friends as they feed and cuddle their new infants, and watching mothers pushing buggies in the park. But, in fact, you are seeing only what you want to see and shutting out the realities of sleepless nights, colic, dirty nappies, and frayed nerves.

Baby-snatching

Many women look into prams and feel a desire to have just such a baby to love and hold. This feeling is common and normal. The much publicized, rare cases of baby-snatching involve far more than mere broodiness.

The baby-snatcher is usually the sad victim of mental and emotional problems that are manifested in the act of snatching a baby. Once caught they are likely to be sent for medical treatment for their underlying illness.

Bruises

Bruises are formed by small blood vessels breaking and bleeding beneath the skin. As the blood collects, dries and is then reabsorbed by the body, a bruise runs through its familiar pattern of changing from purple to greeny-yellow and finally disappearing altogether.

All children will bump and bruise themselves regularly when they are growing up. In most cases no treatment beyond "a kiss to make it better" is necessary. If the skin is broken, it may need a little more attention.

If the bruise is under a finger- or toe-nail and is very painful, you should ask the doctor about it as he may feel the blood should be let out. If the blood underneath the nail is released, this will relieve pain, reduce the risk of infection and help prevent the nail turning black. However, it will not always be necessary. Bruises where the skin is very near the bone, as on the skull, ribs, arms and legs, may also need to be checked in case the bone underneath is fractured.

An icepack or a cloth soaked in cold water will limit the pain and swelling if applied quickly. Severe bruising should be checked by a doctor as it is likely to be accompanied by swelling which may make a broken bone difficult for an inexperienced person to diagnose. Bruising that occurs without injury requires immediate medical attention.

Bullying

Bullying in children is often a front for faked confidence. Many children attempt to compensate for any failings or weaknesses they feel they may have by asserting themselves over others through physical or verbal aggression. Needless to say this is a distressing situation for the parents of both bully and victim.

If you have reason to believe your child is bullying others, let him know that what he is doing is wrong, but reassure him that you love him. Tell him that he is too nice a person to pick on others. If he is helped to feel worthwhile, rather than worthless, he may cease to feel the need to bully. It may be good to arrange for him to play with older children for a while. They will be able to hold their own in any dispute and he will not be "rewarded" for his violence by getting his own way.

If, on the other hand, your child is very passive and tends to be on the receiving end of bullying, teaching him to be assertive will help. One very useful way to do this is to act out little scenes with him that include ways of standing up for himself without resorting to hitting or shouting. Arranging for him to play with younger children can help to give him the sense of "being boss" instead of being bossed.

◆ See also, **Aggression**

Burns and Scalds

Burns

Toddlers who do not understand the dangers of playing with fire are especially vulnerable to burns.

Burns are medically classified according to the depth of damage to the skin – first, second and third degree. A first-degree burn harms only the top layer of skin: sunburn and the slighter burns that happen in the kitchen are examples of this. A second-degree burn penetrates the outer layer and damages the underlying layer, while third-degree burns destroy all skin layers. Hospital treatment is needed for all serious burns, but prompt first aid can do a lot to limit pain and damage.

Scalds

A scald is a burn produced by steam or boiling fluid such as water or fat. The treatment is the same as for burns (see below).

Remove any clothing that has become hot from boiling fluid, fat or steam. If the clothing has already cooled, however, do not remove it.

A scalded mouth or throat can be caused by your child drinking a very hot fluid or inhaling steam. If the thin layer of skin that lines the mouth and throat gets damaged it will swell very quickly and, in severe cases, can block your child's breathing. Make him wash his mouth out to cool the tissues, then give him frequent sips of water to drink.

Electrical burns

These may look quite small on the surface but serious damage underneath can result. An electrical burn requires quick action. First of all, switch off the current. If this is impossible, break the contact by standing on something dry and pushing the victim away with a wooden chair. Get immediate advice.

Chemical burns

Battery acid, drain cleaners and lime used in building are some of the commoner causes of chemical burns. In the case of a chemical burn, quickly remove any soaked clothing without touching the chemical yourself.

Wash away the chemical by flooding with running water. Chemical splashes in the eye must be flushed out immediately under a running tap for a minimum of ten minutes. Take your child to hospital as soon as you can for follow-up treatment.

Treating burns

1. Always begin by cooling the burn. Major damage can be done by the heat from a burn penetrating deep into the body, and the application of cold water will help reduce this effect. A small part, like a fingertip or wrist, can be held under a running tap; a larger area should be plunged into a bucket or sink full of cold water.

2. Areas like the face or chest that cannot be kept under water should be covered by a thick cloth, soaked in cold water. If the cloth gets warm and dry, renew cold water and re-apply. Continue cooling the burn for at least ten minutes. This quickly relieves pain and reduces the formation of blisters. Repeat until pain is relieved.

3. A large burn or a burn on the face should be covered with a non-fluffy dry dressing after cooling. Do not apply a lotion or ointment, and avoid touching the burn itself. Use the inside of a sterile surgical dressing or a clean handkerchief, handling it as little as possible. Cover with more folded padding and loosely bandage.

In cases where a child's clothing is on fire:

● Get the child on the floor, flames uppermost so they rise away from the body.

● Use water if possible to extinguish flames. If not, smother the flames with a rug or heavy coat. Press it firmly round the body so as to extinguish all burning.

● Remove smouldering clothes but do not try to tear away any material sticking to the skin.

● Never roll the child around. This will only expose different areas to the flames.

● Remove anything such as a bracelet which could constrict the burnt area if it swells.

● Do not prick any blisters or apply anything but cold water.

Most burns are easily prevented. Look around your house and check for the following:

● Are there any open fires without guards?

● Have you left any matches or lighters lying around?

● Trailing electrical wires and sockets – are they within reach? Loop wires out of the way and fit sockets with safety plugs.

● Kettles and pans of boiling liquid – could your child pull them over himself?

● Are there any dangerous chemicals where a curious child could find them?

● Do you have a fire extinguisher or fire blanket?

Car Journeys

However exciting your destination, whether it's a holiday, seeing granny or visiting favourite friends, if you are travelling with small children, just getting there can be hell.

Sadly there's no simple formula for containing babies, toddlers and older children in relative quiet for long periods in a car but there are several ways you can make the best of a day on the road. Good timing and good planning both help enormously, as does being a dab hand at diversionary tactics when tempers start to fray. Whenever and wherever you choose to travel, for your child's safety he should always be restrained in a car seat appropriate to his age.

Just as some children are better travellers than others, so you will find your own children go through different stages depending on their age. Babies and toddlers may be relatively easy to take travelling. The motion of the car often lulls them to sleep for much of the time and when awake they are frequently entertained by what they can see through the window. On the other hand, once they suddenly decide they're hungry, need a clean nappy or simply want to be lifted out of their seat you have little option but to stop as soon as possible. It's difficult to placate a hungry or miserable baby, and driving while they're crying can be extremely distracting if not positively dangerous.

Small children who like to be constantly on the go are probably the worst travellers. Not surprisingly, they soon feel bored and restricted in a car, and so become restless and quarrelsome. Be prepared to stop regularly for refreshments and trips to the loo and, equally important, a chance to unwind a little. Playing games and joining in with rhymes and singalongs will keep toddlers and older children amused for variable lengths of time. Tapes of stories and songs can give you a break but may drive the adults all mad in the process.

Most parents find their children will sleep in a car for at least some part of a journey. Since it would be folly not to encourage this, make sure you bring one or two favourite bedtime toys and a blanket to cover them when they fall asleep. Baby seats, especially the reclining types, are designed for sleeping infants and will support their heads well. However, once your child is big enough for a booster seat, he may find it more difficult to find an easy sleeping position. It's a good idea to bring a few cushions for him to lean his head against and check occasionally to make sure he doesn't wriggle out of his seat belt in an effort to lie more comfortably.

If your children do sleep happily in the car, you will find it helps to start your journey at a time when they would normally be asleep – either very early in the morning or in the early evening. For a morning start, children can be bundled from bed to car wrapped simply in a dressing gown or duvet. With luck they will go back to sleep before they know what's happening and this should give you several hours of peaceful motoring.

Alternatively, start a journey just before bedtime. As the evening progresses and the novelty of the journey wears off, they will probably drift

off to sleep. Many children will sleep the entire night through in a car and, providing you don't mind night driving, it's an excellent way of covering the miles. The only drawback is that you can't make prolonged stops for your own refreshment. However, if you share the driving and take a flask of coffee with you to help you stay awake, this is a small price to pay.

If you do decide to travel by day, be prepared for the trip to take longer than you'd planned. Depending on the length of your journey, a stop of five minutes every hour can help relieve pent-up energy in a restless four- or five-year-old but try to get a good distance behind you before the first break. A stop for petrol just after you have left home can be very disconcerting for a small child who's all geared up for a long trip. Similarly, try not to leave just before a mealtime. A stop for lunch ten miles from your home town would only lead to all-round despondency and while packed lunches are a good idea, it is better to save the sandwiches for later when their appearance will make a welcome diversion.

If you're not restricted to motorway services, make the most of all the options available and vary your stops as much as possible. For example, if the weather is fine, a picnic lunch anywhere off the beaten track, such as by a river or in a meadow, will give everyone a chance to stretch out and will set you all up for the next part of the journey. Later in the day, supper in a roadside restaurant which has swings and slides for the children to play on will be a great treat and give them plenty of opportunity for letting off steam.

There is an advantage to stopping at a roadside restaurant or motorway service station – they do cater for children. Highchairs are usually available and child-size portions invariably appear on the menus. If you bring your own baby food into the restaurant the staff should be happy either to heat up a small amount in their microwave or to provide a jug of hot water.

Of course, the ideal is to plan exactly when and where you make your stops but if you have as tiny baby with you, you'll have no alternative but to stop whenever he needs attention.

It is important to remember that a baby should never be taken out of his restraints while the car is still moving, however urgent and desperate the cries. Travelling with a baby on your knee in any circumstances is extremely dangerous – tests have shown that if a car stops suddenly, a baby can easily be crushed between whoever is holding it and the front seat. So steel yourselves to the squawks until you find a safe place to pull up and deal with the problem.

If your baby is bottle-fed, make up as many feeds as you will need and put them in a cool bag before you set off. Alternatively, you could buy a supply of the ready-prepared cartons of formula milk and empty one into a sterile bottle just before a feed. It is a good idea to carry a flask of hot water with you so you can warm each bottle as you need it.

Breastfeeding mums are saved all this bother. A quiet feed in the car park before you enter a restaurant to eat is the best way to ensure a peaceful meal for the rest of the family. If they're available, take advantage of the mother and baby facilities at service stations for feeding and changing your baby in comfort.

Once your baby is eating at family mealtimes, stopping for frequent refreshment isn't so imperative. Sandwiches en route can be enjoyable and satisfying, not to mention cheaper than a sit-down meal. Small children need careful catering. Pack food that makes as little mess as possible and make sure it is in manageable, bite-size portions. The best rule of thumb is to take foods your children actually like and will eat enthusiastically. Ham, cheese, peanut butter or anything else fairly dry is relatively easy to eat in sandwiches, unlike, say, egg mayonnaise which can be extremely messy. Very diluted squash or fruit juice is thirst-quenching so keep a large bottle handy. Give children their drinks in spill-proof beakers or buy small individual cartons of juice with straws. It's a good tip to insert the straw and take a large sip yourself before handing these over to prevent juice squirting everywhere as soon as your child grabs the carton with a gleeful squeeze.

After several hours of travelling and intermittent nibbling you can hardly expect to arrive anywhere in the same clean and tidy state in which you all set off. Travel in comfortable everyday clothes which don't show dirt and are easy to clean. Pack a change of clothes for each child and perhaps a spare top for yourself, in case of minor "accidents".

Along with clothes and nappy changing gear you will need a bag with dampened flannels, or some baby wipes, and a copious supply of tissues or kitchen roll to be kept close at hand for use throughout the journey. A spare carrier bag is essential to serve as a rubbish bin – keep another as an emergency sick bag!

Remember, if you do have a child prone to car sickness, make sure he travels on the seat behind the front passenger so that if necessary, you can stop and he can get out quickly and safely. Make sure he wears thin, cool clothes for travelling and open the window periodically to keep fresh air circulating. Encourage him to sit up and look ahead, and don't let him look at books or read or write while travelling.

If you know that the trip ahead will be a long one, be prepared with a supply of activities and games. It's a good idea to keep a bag of toys at the ready. Choose these carefully, avoiding any with little bits or pieces which could drop off and get lost. Hand out toys one by one, taking back each one as it's finished with.

For babies, try pictures stuck to the back of the car seat, mobiles tied securely or other objects that will dance on a short string above the cot or car seat, a soft toy to cuddle, a cloth or plastic picture book. Toddlers and small children will enjoy song and story tapes, picture books, hand puppets, cars or trains. Avoid noisy toys such as whistles, balls, and anything that two children are likely to fight over.

Alternatively, you could make a holiday trip into a real treat by presenting each child with a special booty bag at the beginning of the journey. Fill the bag with any number of interesting items that they haven't seen or played with before – perhaps a new puzzle, a little purse, or a magic slate. Include a piece of fruit or a small pack of sweets, and, if you have time, wrap up a few items in advance – it all adds to the excitement of receiving new toys.

When toys become tiresome, older children may like to listen to a story tape or enjoy a tape of rhymes and songs. Some parents are all in favour of equipping children with personal stereos for the duration of a long journey in the hope that they, the parents, can miss out on having to hear that same story again and again and enjoy at least a few minutes peace and quiet.

But whatever the activity of the moment, you can be sure that interest will eventually wane and that the children will be clamouring for attention of some kind or other and assurances that the journey won't be lasting much longer. Be ready to strike back with a choice of engaging games which can involve as many family members as possible. One word of advice, though: if any of your children get travel sick, don't play games that require reading or writing, and don't forget most young children sitting in the back can't actually see much out of a car window, so "I-spy" games have their limitations. You will quickly discover that different games suit different age groups.

"Lion hunt" is one game which children 18 months and upwards will find great fun. Start a story "We're going on a Lion Hunt," adding sound effects and actions (if space allows!) at appropriate points in the story. For instance, "We opened the gate (groan of gate opening), we walked through the long grass (shusha, shusha), we swam across the river, we climbed the tree..." and so on. The story generally ends with discovering the lion in a cave and it chasing you home, back through all the same obstacles, of course, all of which need sound effects and actions filling in at great speed and in the reverse order.

The game "Beep beep" will keep alert two- to six-year-olds on their toes. Explain that you're going to tell a favourite fairy tale or story, but that you're going to play a trick occasionally by putting in the wrong words. Every time anyone notices, he's got to say "beep beep". For instance, "There were once three bears who lived in a ... bucket". Children who enjoy this game will like to play the storyteller sometimes.

"Who am I?" is a good guessing game that can be spun out over many miles. Think of an object and let everyone take turns to guess what you're thinking of by asking questions to which you only answer "yes" or "no". For instance, if you pick a car as your mystery object, and your questioners ask "Are you alive?", "Do you move?", "Do you have wheels?" and so on, they would be well on the way to making a correct guess. Younger children will probably need a little help at first in asking the right questions but they will quickly get the hang of it.

All this energetic input, keeping your children happy and occupied in the back seat, can be quite a drain on your own resources. Even if the aim of a trouble-free trip is attained you may well arrive feeling shattered yourself. If possible, give yourself a break from being chief cheer leader by swapping places with the driver now and then.

◆ See also, **Safety**, **Travel Sickness**

Cardiac Massage

Cardiac massage, or cardiac compression, is the name given to the First Aid technique which is used to start the heart beating again after failure by pressing on the chest.

Six to 12 seconds after his heart has stopped, a child will lose consciousness. No pulse can be felt. Within 15 to 30 seconds, breathing will stop. The skin turns grey and the pupils dilate (enlarge).

First aid is urgently required to re-start circulation and breathing. Within three or four minutes of circulation stopping, the heart will become damaged because of lack of oxygen. Although the heart may be re-started at this point, the brain will suffer irreversible damage.

If cardiac massage is successful, heartbeat may be restored within a few minutes. It is worth continuing for at least 10 minutes even if there is no sign of a returning pulse.

Cardiac massage should be given immediately, combined with artificial respiration, as breathing will also fail. If possible, one person should give artificial respiration – one breath after every five heart compressions – while another concentrates on the cardiac massage.

● Make sure the child is lying on his back on a hard surface.

● Check for a carotid pulse by extending the head backwards and feeling with all four fingertips (one or two in very small children) in the groove between the Adam's apple and the strap muscles of the neck. Allow at least ten seconds to be sure no pulse is present.

● With the closed fist, hit hard on the lower left side of the breast bone: this may start the heart beating.

● Give five breaths (*see* Artificial Respiration).

● Move your hand to the lower third of the breastbone. Place your palm at the point where the last ribs join it. Use two fingers only for a baby.

● Press down about 3 cm (1 in): the movement should be regular and rhythmical at a rate of about 100 beats per minute.

● Do this five times then give two full mouth-to-mouth ventilations.

● Continue alternating compression and ventilation.

● Check carotid pulse every two minutes.

● Stop cardiac compression once you feel the pulse again.

Generally, if the hands are placed in the right position and heart compression is done properly, no damage, such as broken ribs, should occur.

Note
If your child has a cardiac arrest when his mouth is full of food, turn his head sideways and use a finger to clear any obstruction. Then follow the steps above.

◆ See also, **Artificial Respiration**, **First Aid**

Catarrh

This common complaint may be no more than a temporary irritation which can be relieved by treatment at home. But if it lingers, see the doctor.

The membranes lining the nose and the windpipe help to warm and moisten the air flowing into the lungs, but they also help to trap dust and germs in the mucus. It is therefore quite normal for the nose to have some mucus present at all times, but an excess of mucus in the nose is usually called "catarrh". Since the mucous membranes extend to the windpipe, excessive mucus may also be produced in the chest.

The commonest causes of catarrh are an allergy, infection or other irritation of the mucous membrane lining the nose to which the membrane responds by producing more and more mucus.

Physical irritation of the lining of the nose can occur with dusts or cigarette smoke, so if your child is in a dusty or smoky atmosphere, he may be prone to catarrh.

The most obvious symptom of catarrh is a runny, irritated nose with some blockage. If it persists for more than a few days, a cough may follow because the catarrh tends to extend down the back of the nose into the windpipe. The cough is often worst at night and in the morning but clears during the day.

The treatment depends to a large extent on the cause. If your child's catarrh is caused by dust or smoke in the atmosphere, then try to remove the irritant from the air he breathes. For a cold, you can help to relieve catarrh by using a steam inhalation. This will liquify the thick mucus and allow you to blow the child's nose more effectively. A decongestant nose spray from the chemist may help for a few days.

Hay fever and other allergies do not respond well to these sprays but may be helped by antihistamine tablets which can be obtained on prescription.

If the catarrh is caused by allergy to fur or feathers, your child should avoid animals and feather-filled pillows in the house.

Steam treatment can also be helpful (but care must be taken with the boiling water). If catarrh persists for more than four or five days, take your child to the doctor.

Chickenpox

Being so easily caught, chickenpox is almost a natural hazard of childhood. It does not last long, it rarely has serious complications and effective home nursing is a simple matter.

It is a childhood illness because although babies are born with a natural ability to resist the infection (passed on by their mother), by the age of one or two this wears off.

The chickenpox virus is present in the child's spots, but it is transmitted by droplet infection. A child who already has chickenpox spreads clusters of the virus in the tiny droplets of water which are exhaled as a matter of course with every breath. When another child breathes in an infected droplet, the virus starts to multiply and another case of chickenpox begins.

Once the virus has entered the child's body, there is an "incubation period" of about a fortnight while the virus spreads. After this, the first a child will know of his illness may be a 24-hour period of vague headache, feeling unwell, occasional slight fever and sometimes a blotchy red rash which quickly fades.

The first spots will appear within 24 hours. They usually start on the trunk and face, only mildly affecting the arms and legs.

The spot starts as a pink bump which within five or six hours becomes raised to form a tiny blister containing clear fluid which is full of viruses. These "teardrop" spots gradually become milky in colour. Then they form a crust and finally a scab.

During this period, the child may be fretful and run a temperature of around 38°C (100.4°F). Some children may only have 30 to 50 spots while others may have several hundred.

Immediately the crust forms, the spots begin to itch and this may last until the scabs drop off, leaving your child with normal skin, after one or two weeks.

Chickenpox spots come out in crops, so that new ones will appear every day for three or four days.

When examining the skin, you will notice that the spots will be at different stages even in the same area. This is typical of chickenpox and quite normal.

Children with a high temperature who feel unwell may prefer to stay in bed or lie downstairs. Otherwise, there is no medical reason to enforce strict bed rest. The majority of children require no treatment at all.

Any pain from sore throat or headache is best relieved with paracetamol. As there is no medical cure for the virus, the condition is left to take its natural course. Severe itching can be helped with application of calamine lotion or an antihistamine drug. Should any of the spots become infected, they will take longer to heal. Try to persuade your child not to scratch the scabs as this will increase the risk of secondary infection and scarring.

The majority of children with mild chickenpox start losing their scabs after about ten days and will then be completely clear of spots within two weeks. Scabs which fall off on their own do not leave a scar.

Chickenpox infection produces life-long immunity but may lead to shingles later in life. Dangerous complications of chickenpox are extremely rare. Most children feel well enough to play around the house during the illness.

Children who are taking steroid drugs or those suffering from leukaemia are the likeliest to be seriously affected and in whom the condition may be fatal. In a very small number of cases, a severe form of pneumonia is caused by the virus.

In other rare cases, there may be bleeding into the spots so that the patient becomes ill from loss of blood. Brain inflammation may also occur – particularly if the child has mistakenly been given aspirin. (Do NOT give this to under-12s – especially with chickenpox.)

The most common complications arise from infection of the skin at the spot, causing boils, or one or two other skin conditions.

Childcare

◆ See **Babysitters**, **Nannies**, **Work (Going Back To)**

Choking

Choking is one of the most common accidents among babies and children. If the child can cough, there is less to worry about as obviously some air must be getting through. It is frightening for the child, however, so stay calm yourself. Food or drink which has gone down "the wrong way" may be coughed back up the nose. This can be painful but it is not dangerous.

If the child does not cough, but gasps, turns red and then greyish or blue while obviously panicking, his airway is blocked and you must act quickly.

Open his mouth and hook your finger around the object or piece of food to see if you can get it out of his throat. Don't worry if you make him retch – it could help dislodge the obstruction.

If you cannot clear his airway with your finger and the child is under a year old, lay his head down over your knees and on top of your forearm. Give him four smart pats between the shoulder blades with the heel of your other hand. If he continues to choke, turn him over and put two or three fingertips on the lower end of his breastbone. Press down quickly and smoothly four times. Repeat the sequence of pats on the back alternating with pressure on the front until the obstruction is dislodged. Be ready to give artificial respiration if breathing stops altogether.

Lay an older child on his back and put the heel of your hand just below his ribcage, above his tummy button. Press smartly upward and inward between six and ten times until the object is cleared. If he is still not breathing, give artificial respiration.

Choking accidents may be prevented by bearing in mind the following:
● Never leave your baby alone when he is eating or drinking – particularly if he is drinking from a bottle.
● Keep small objects such as beads, balloons and toy parts away from him.
● For older children, certain foods such as hard sweets or popcorn are easy to choke on.
● Peanuts should not be given to small children as they not only go down the wrong way easily but also contain an oil which can irritate and inflame the lungs even after the peanut has been removed.

◆ See also, **Artificial Respiration**

Colds

◆ See **Common Cold**

Comfort Habits

Some children are generally more anxious than others simply because of their different personalities and emotional make-up. One four-year-old will be delighted and full of excitement at the prospect of starting playgroup whereas another will become extremely upset and anxious long before his first day at nursery.

Children often express their anxiety in ways that puzzle adults. If they are upset they may rock themselves, hug their comforters, or go and sit quietly in a corner. At any of these signs you should consider whether there is anything which could be causing him distress such as the arrival of a new baby, starting or changing nursery school, or maybe some tension between you and your partner.

On the other hand, some behavioural patterns which you may think are caused by anxiety might really be part of any child's "normal" development – these may include not eating much over a period of time when your child is about 18 months, going through a clinging phase at around one year, having frightening nightmares or occasional periods of rocking.

Habits are quite common in children, they are rarely permanent and most children outgrow them by the time they start school. It is only if your child devotes long periods of the day to rocking, thumb-sucking, mastur-bation or other "bad" habits, and shows other signs of disturbance, that you should consider getting professional help.

Problems can start early. At about six to eight months your baby will want some independence but at the same time be anxious about losing his closeness to you. To deal with this conflict and to comfort himself he may begin rhythmical movements like thumb-sucking, rocking, stroking a cuddly toy or sucking a dummy or cloth.

These so-called "comfort habits" tend to occur at certain times such as when he settles down to sleep, and when he is upset, stressed or bored.

A comfort object can remain in use for years without signalling any particular emotional disturbance. Soft comforting objects like a blanket or toy will probably be most important to your child when he is about two years old. Gradually your child will start to give up the comfort object of his own accord and you may want to encourage this when you feel he doesn't depend on it in the way he used to.

If the object is very big – like a cot blanket – you could try surreptitiously to make it smaller when it is no longer needed as a blanket. For example, cut it in two so you have half in reserve when it needs washing.

When your child starts at playgroup, encourage him not to take his comforter with him. Suggest that it is for home use, especially at bedtime. Remind him occasionally that when he is a "big boy" he will no longer need this special comforter, not even to keep him company at night. But don't press too hard if your child is not ready to give up his comforter yet.

Thumb- or finger-sucking starts quite early on in life. Although it is often regarded as a sign of inadequate opportunity to suck, it is merely the comfort habit most likely to develop – and the object of desire is always there and available. Don't worry about it as long as your child is happy and active most of the time. If he spends long periods in a sleepy state, doing nothing but sucking his thumb, though, then he either needs other activities and more stimulation, or he may be worried about something and need more comforting from you.

On the other hand, if you personally find your child's thumb-sucking objectionable and excessive and if you are worried that it might damage his teeth (a possibility if the habit continues after the age of six years when the

second teeth begin to come in), there are a number of things you could try to put a stop to it.

The old home remedies of putting mustard or plasters on thumbs are usually not effective for any length of time. In the same way trying to talk him out of it before he is ready may only increase his determination to carry on, or may even upset him so much that he actually needs to do it more! Instead every time your child starts sucking his thumb you could make a game of asking him to clench his fists for three minutes.

Another method is to reward your child for not sucking his thumb. If you notice that your child sucks when he is tired, try putting him to bed earlier. If boredom seems to be the cause at other times, give him more attention and distract him by playing a game together or going for a walk.

Being rocked is comforting for a child and head-banging can for some obscure reason give similar pleasure and comfort. By the end of the first year there are very few children who do not sometimes rock or head-bang. Either habit only becomes a problem if it turns into the only way he knows of getting attention or if it becomes an all-important source of comfort. In some children head-hanging only occurs when they are worried or upset.

Being prepared for this type of behaviour may enable you to stop these habits from taking a firm hold by providing alternative satisfactions and amusements.

Frequent masturbation or playing with himself is a habit that disturbs a lot of parents, even more so when it happens in public. But try to remember that it is a natural stage of development for your toddler to explore his body, and to him it's not very different to sucking his thumb or trying out different tastes or textures.

However, a bored or unhappy child may find that masturbation is the best comfort he has. And there is little point in telling him to stop unless you are going to deal with the problem of boredom or unhappiness. A tense family atmosphere may cause a child to masturbate to soothe himself. He will continue the habit with even more persistence if he finds that this also brings him a lot of attention. Try therefore to pay as little attention to it as possible and distract him with an absorbing game.

Other habits seem to be more a result of tension or concentration than to give comfort. These include nail-biting, stuttering and stammering, licking lips, picking at scabs or sore places, nose-picking and hair-pulling, and although quite common things they may be just as disturbing or alarming to you.

These habits may occur if your child is concentrating on something – for example, watching TV or drawing a picture – and is not really aware of what he is doing. If tension or anxiety is behind it, you may be able to identify the cause and dealing with this may be sufficient to stop the habit. But more often than not there is no obvious cause – no one event or concern which has set it off. Nevertheless, once a particular habit gets going it becomes entrenched and hard to stop – as many an adult will be forced to admit.

Most children stammer or stutter at some time. It is a normal stage of language development and often happens when they get over-excited. Rather than getting impatient, help your child to calm down. Tell him to pause, take a breath and speak slowly if he is getting into a tangle. It is not wise to make a big fuss and draw attention to his stammer. If at the same time your child shows other signs of tension and anxiety, look for any underlying cause.

The chances are that your child will grow out of the stammer. If it seems to be persisting, say for longer than nine months, it could be helpful to discuss the problem with a speech therapist, who can be contacted through your child health clinic.

Other stress-related habits are fiddling with hair or even tugging it. If your child habitually yanks his hair it may be a symptom of some distress. Again, do try to find the cause of the problem and if you can't, seek your doctor's help.

If your child bites his nails occasionally there is no need for concern. If it continues for an extended period it may be because of a particular worry. To counteract this rather unsightly – and unhygienic – habit, encourage your child to try new activities that involve using his hands. Also show him how to take pride in caring for his hands, keeping them clean and nice to look at.

Generally, the best way of dealing with habits is to ignore them and not get emotionally worked up about them. If the habit has become well established, make a determined effort to ignore it and give your child a lot of attention when he is not showing the habit. You may find a reward system – like a star chart – helps to motivate your child to try harder not to bite his nails or pick scabs.

However, child experts have pinpointed times of special stress for a child – such as the death of a loved one, separation, starting at nursery, moving house, the arrival of a new baby or the creation of a new family after divorce – and claim that if your child is undergoing any of these this may well be the reason why he reverts back to behaviour or habits which he had previously left behind.

Emotional problems can also turn your child into a worrier. He may quickly lose confidence as a result and become anxious when difficulties arise. To help rebuild his confidence you could tell your friends, in front of your child, how pleased you are with any achievement, protect your child from failure, and avoid using negative statements like, "I knew you wouldn't be able to do that."

Children may never mention how upset they are even though they have plenty of opportunity to do so. They lack the ability to talk about their fears or think them through; so in times of stress it is wise to look out for any non-verbal signs of anxiety.

Ultimately, anxiety, and the habits your child acquires to release it, can be mastered and to some extent controlled by understanding the source of his emotional strain and by carefully planning how to free him from it. By teaching your child to relax you will give him the idea that worries and tension can be brought under control. Try relaxation techniques together, such as listening to some quiet music that your child is fond of, or reflecting on a happy day you had together in the past. You may also, however, have to be firm and confident in the way you respond to your child's habits, worries and fears. Sometimes the habit will survive the original anxiety and if the child is as keen as you to leave it behind, it is then that you can count on his co-operation to "kick the habit".

When a problem persists and is making your child worried and upset, then you and your child may need help to see the problem in a new way. It may also help you to cope with and handle stress-related habits. Try asking other parents what they know of the local services (one of the best-informed people is likely to be your doctor). Voluntary groups for parents can be very supportive and give you an idea of how other people have coped, and don't be put off by a referral to a family therapist or psychiatrist – these people are trained and experienced in helping with any emotional problems your child may have.

It is worth bearing in mind that in order to develop into a well-rounded person, your child needs to have met and overcome challenges. Surviving a stressful experience will make your child stronger and will prepare him for the inevitable stresses and disappointments he will face later.

Common Cold

Babies up to the age of about six months benefit from the natural immunities they get from their mothers, especially if they are breastfed. This means that in the early days they catch fewer colds. After that, you are in what could be termed "cold war territory", and it is not a war that you can win. Little children often get half a dozen colds a year. This is quite normal. Despite all the advances in medical science, no one has yet come up with a way to prevent or cure the common cold so unfortunately, you are highly unlikely to fare any better.

Colds are caused by viruses. Not a single virus but about 200 strains of them, which is why your child can get one infection soon after another. A virus cannot be killed off by antibiotics, so a cold simply has to cure itself, relying on the body's defence system. This usually takes from five to 14 days, whatever you do in the meantime.

Contrary to popular belief, children do not catch colds from getting wet or being out in a chill wind. They catch them from other people. Colds are transmitted by contact, so if you can stop well-meaning admirers with colds from touching your baby, so much the better. But even so, the chances are that playmates at nursery school or someone in the supermarket will bestow a cold upon your child.

A cold infects membranes in the nose and throat, producing the typical symptoms of a runny nose and sore throat and sometimes a slight cough. When your child's defences are weakened by a cold virus a secondary infection can sometimes set in. His nose may run with a nasty yellow discharge and his tonsils, adenoids and neck lymph nodes may become swollen. This is the time to see the doctor, who will check your child's throat and ears for infection and prescribe antibiotics if necessary.

As a straightforward cold can't be cured or treated, comfort is the only help you can usefully give a small child. He will be less distressed if you administer plenty of reassuring cuddles. Forget your normal daily routine in

Complications of Colds

Complication	Possible symptoms	Cause	Treatment
Otitis media (infection of middle ear)	Earache	Infection by bacteria in mucus from nose or throat; violent nose blowing can push mucus along Eustachian tubes, or swollen tonsils and adenoids can cause blockage and build-up of mucus	Antibiotics and probably nose drops (to aid drainage) from doctor. "Runny" ear may indicate a burst ear-drum and needs urgent treatment to prevent later deafness
Tonsillitis and infected adenoids	Sore throat; general aches and pains; headaches; vomiting; fever	Infection by germs entering through the mouth or nose; can lead to otitis media	Antibiotics from doctor; paracetamol for pain and fever; tonsils only removed after repeated tonsillitis, and adenoids if causing repeated otitis media
Sinusitis (infection of sinuses, the small cavities in the skull)	Pain above or below eyes; fever; thick discharge from nose; persistent catarrh	Infection from mucus which has filled sinuses	Antibiotics and nose drops to reduce swelling of membranes
Cold sores	Painful sores around the lips and nose	Infection by the Herpes Simplex virus which attacks when resistance to infection is lowered	Ointment or cream prescribed by doctor. Sores should disappear in a week or so

favour of extra attention and play, which will help your child forget that he is feeling under the weather. Ice cream is a treat that soothes a sore throat and a gentle baby cream or lotion applied to his nose will stop the skin getting too dry. A paracetamol syrup may ease discomfort, and a vapour rub on the chest, or a few drops squeezed from inhalant capsules onto pyjamas or pillows can help your child's blocked nose at night.

◆ See also, **Catarrh**, **Coughs**, **Herpes and Cold Sores**, **Sinusitis**

Concussion

Concussion is a bruising of the brain, usually when the head receives a blow. It may also occur if the head is shaken violently. Young children are especially susceptible to concussion as their skulls are still relatively soft and more susceptible to blows.

The child may lose consciousness, usually for just a few seconds, but sometimes minutes. In very severe cases, he may remain unconscious for several weeks.

When the child's head is knocked or shaken, the brain may suddenly be forced against the skull with sufficient pressure to cause bruising. Shaking may result in bruising to several areas of the brain. A single blow tends to cause bruising below the site of the impact, where the skull is forced against the brain, and sometimes on the opposite side of the head too, possibly because of the jarring effect.

In mild cases, the child may simply feel giddy for a little while and complain of a headache, which can persist for a day or two. If the injury was caused by a blow, a painful bump will usually be found on the head.

If the child seems confused about what happened, or cannot remember, this indicates that he has probably been unconscious. In more serious cases, the child may remain unconscious for some minutes and, on coming round, may have problems with muscular control – you may notice slurred speech, for instance.

The symptoms of concussion usually disappear as the damage to the brain gradually heals. However, a severe blow to the head could cause the child to remain unconscious in a coma for several weeks.

● If you find your child unconscious, check his breathing and heartbeat. If either is absent, start resuscitation immediately (*see* Artificial respiration) and have someone send for an ambulance.

● If any blood or other liquid is discharged through the ear, call an ambulance immediately.

● Clean and dress any wounds. In the case of deep cuts, stop the bleeding first (*see* Bleeding) and call a doctor or take the child to a hospital.

● Even if the child appears to recover quickly, take him to a doctor for a check-up. Watch out for signs of difficulties with muscular control.

The current recommendation is that anyone with concussion should remain under observation in hospital for at least 24 hours, in order to watch out for signs of a sub-dural haematoma (a blood clot that compresses the brain).

Confidence

A lack of confidence can be crippling for a child: and it can and does go on to blight people's lives. It may stop them from ever fulfilling their potential in all kinds of areas, including education, careers and relationships. In extreme cases it can lead to isolation and even mental illness.

Words commonly used in connection with confidence give some clues as to its nature. Confidence can be shaken, knocked, undermined and even lost. It is often a fragile thing, tough to get but so very easy to lose. It is one of those things that is only really noticed when it is not there.

Confidence is not something we are born with. It has to be encouraged to grow. In order for you to help your child develop genuine, rock-solid assurance it is important to realize that it is the product of a sense of self-esteem, and the knowledge that he is a worthwhile person.

The more fragile kind of confidence, the kind that can be lost, is not built on this solid foundation and therefore cannot withstand the knocks and setbacks that life dishes out. Confidence that is born of a good self-image can and does.

It is not always recognized that confidence can be faked. People can develop quite a "front" to disguise a basic lack of self-esteem. This form of "confidence" borders on bravado, bullying or arrogance. A confident mask may fool people most of the time but, in a crisis, it is no real substitute for the genuine article.

There is no magical trick that will help your child develop the kind of confidence that is born of a solid sense of self-esteem. It is simply a matter of being able to take the long view, to be patient and consistent.

It is not easy to pass on a feeling you do not have yourself; and, as a first-time mother, you may not feel wildly confident. It is sometimes difficult, also, to remember that doing the best you can is good enough when you feel pressured on all sides to be the "perfect" mother.

Being a perfect mother seems to include being an accomplished housekeeper, an energetic, sympathetic and interested mate to your partner, a dutiful daughter and possibly an efficient career woman as well. It cannot be done. In the first few months of motherhood, no one can keep high standards in all these areas, at the same time as they are coming to terms with being a parent and dealing with their mutinous hormones.

You may feel a crushing sense of failure; guilt may rear its ugly head and your confidence may hit rock bottom. So you'll be doing both your baby and yourself a favour if you get your priorities sorted out before your child is born. It is very important that you do everything in your power to keep your own sense of self-esteem intact. Only by doing this will you be able to pass this priceless gift on to your child. A sense of self-esteem is far more important to your child than a spotless kitchen or several sets of clean clothes a day.

Hanging on to your own self-esteem is just the first step in helping your child gain confidence. The next step is to set up and maintain good channels of communication with him. This process starts soon after birth, when you respond to his cries, smiles and gurgles. This is a sign to your child that he is an interesting and worthwhile person in his own right.

When your child begins to talk it is very important to listen to what he is saying and to answer him. This may seem an obvious thing to say but it is not all that easy to do. Very few people listen well. Counsellors spend a great deal of their training learning to listen properly and to give those they are trying to help their undivided attention. They recognize what a rare talent it is.

It is particularly hard to listen to young children, because so much of what they say is boring and repetitive. Mothers are often preoccupied with a thousand pressing problems, and childish chatter can be very low on the list. However, what your child has to say to you is important to him. If you take the time to listen this will help him to feel that what he has to say is important to others, too.

Try to make space during the course of your busy day to talk with your child. Bedtime is a good opportunity for a long chat. If you can manage it, take time out to have several short conversations with him during the day. Ideal opportunities for this are when he is eating or having a bath or when you are playing together. At all times, the most important thing to remember is to really pay attention to what he is saying. This will pay huge dividends in terms of his self-esteem.

Your child may make you very cross by interrupting while you are talking to someone else. The best way of dealing with this is to take a second to ask him quietly, but firmly, to wait a moment and then you will listen to him. Then keep your promise.

It is an essential part of building your child's confidence to establish rules and to be consistent in enforcing them. Not interrupting is a good rule for your child to learn early on, but his reward must be your undivided attention in return.

Children who are allowed to run riot are not necessarily happy children. They see this lack of parental control as a lack of caring. You may have to face tantrums and sulks when you set firm rules, but this is where it is important for you to take a long-term view. Research clearly shows that children brought up within clear-cut boundaries, whose lives are managed by consistent, established rules, are far more likely to grow up with an inbuilt confidence. Troubled adults are very often those who experienced childhoods where the boundaries were constantly shifting or virtually non-existent.

Obviously, over-zealous discipline can be as bad as none at all. It is a question of striking a balance. If you explain why you have made certain rules it will help your child to understand the need for them. If you negotiate some rules with him, it will make him feel that he has a part to play and will encourage self-control.

Bear in mind also that everyone needs privacy and the space to be alone. Children are no different. It is just as important to your child to have his privacy respected as it is to you. When he really needs to be by himself, respect it; he is not just "being silly".

If you show your child this kind of respect he will, in time, learn to respect himself. Self-respect is the vital ingredient of confidence. Allowing your child space and privacy is just one of the many ways you can help him to gain confidence.

Fear of change

It is very tempting to try to protect your child from the harsher realities of life. Death is a particularly tough one. Many people fall into the trap of rushing out and buying another rabbit or kitten when a much-loved pet dies. This, although understandable, can be a very big mistake.

Your child needs to experience loss, grief, sadness and a whole host of other difficult feelings to become a complete person. So, however painful things are, resist the urge to make it all better by trying to fill the gap with an instant new pet. Allow your child plenty of time to experience loss and grief, because they are an essential part of life. If he is protected from these things when he is young, he will grow up to fear them. This fear may be disabling. Never tell your child that he is silly or stupid to feel fearful (or any other feeling). Talk about feelings but never condemn them.

Fear of loss becomes a fear of change. In order to affect any change, however good, you must lose something. If you move house, you lose the old one, the neighbourhood, its people and familiarity. What you gain may be exciting and better, but loss is also an essential part of the move.

This is true of all change. Where there is change, there is loss and where there is loss, there is grief. A person cannot dread change and be confident at the same time. Helping your child deal with loss will give him the courage to face up to life.

Bad behaviour

There will be occasions throughout your child's young life when he misbehaves. He will get into rages, he will throw tantrums and he may even be violent and aggressive. Two-year-olds are notorious for this kind of unreasonable behaviour.

Later, your child will probably experiment with the effects of being downright rude, especially to you. This kind of appalling behaviour is tricky enough to deal with at home, but in public it can be humiliating and embarrassing. It is never easy to keep your cool at times like this, especially if you are feeling harassed already.

It is all too easy to give your child the impression that you do not like him when he is being naughty. Phrases such as "you are a bad boy" or "you naughty boy" spring readily to the lips when what you really mean is "you are being a naughty boy now, but the rest of the time you are lovely". However, your child may not know this.

When disciplining your child, make it very clear that it is his behaviour you don't like. When things have calmed down a bit, it is a good idea to explain to him that you love him dearly, but that you don't love bad behaviour. A reassuring cuddle will help a lot.

Coping with "failure"

Your child needs to understand that he is really good at some things and has difficulty with others. If he is made to feel ashamed of his failures, he will be unable to take pride in his achievements.

It is obvious that praise will help him towards success in certain areas, but it is equally important to acknowledge that he finds some things hard. He must understand that success in everything is neither vital, nor even realistic.

He needs to know that doing the very best he can is achievement enough. Truly confident people are those who recognize their limitations and who know that it is their strengths and weaknesses that make them the valuable and unique human beings that they really are.

It is important for your child's self-esteem and confidence to know that he is loved because of who he is. Your unconditional love for him is the backbone of good self-esteem.

Conjunctivitis

Conjunctivitis, commonly known as pink eye, is an inflammation of the conjunctiva – the membrane covering the white of the eye and the inner surface of the eyelids. It frequently occurs in babies and young children, who get it from rubbing and so infecting their eyes. This type of conjunctivitis is not serious and usually responds quickly to treatment. However, some conditions that resemble conjunctivitis can cause blindness, so it is important for the doctor to check any inflammation of the eye in order to have the infection correctly diagnosed.

The most common cause of conjunctivitis is infection by bacteria. When a child rubs his eyes, he may transfer bacteria from the fingers on to the eye surface. Children with runny noses caused by a cold often develop conjunctivitis in this way. Bacteria from the nose are rubbed off on to the hands and transferred to the eyes.

Bacteria may also be transferred to the eyes from infected face flannels or towels. Occasionally, a fly or other foreign body that gets in the eye leaves behind germs that cause conjunctivitis, even if the offender is removed almost immediately.

Some viruses also cause conjunctivitis. Chlamydia trachomatis, for example, gives rise to the very serious form of the disease called trachoma, which occurs in tropical countries. This kind of conjunctivitis is spread by touch, especially in overcrowded living conditions. In cooler climates, the Chlamydia virus gives rise to a less severe form of conjunctivitis.

Between 5 and 10 per cent of young adults carry Chlamydia in their genital tract, where it is responsible for the most common type of sexually transmitted infection. Chlamydia is present in the semen or vaginal fluid, so there is danger that parents may transfer the virus by touch to their child's eyes, either directly or via a flannel or towel.

A woman carrying Chlamydia in her vaginal fluid can pass the virus to her baby during the birth. Within a few weeks of delivery, the child may develop conjunctivitis as a result; this form of the infection is called ophthalmia neonatorum. Another, even more serious, form of ophthalmia neonatorum is gonorrhoeal infection of the eyes.

Allergy is another cause of conjunctivitis. Children who suffer from hay fever often develop conjunctivitis when the pollen count is high. Grains of pollen from the air get into the eye and set up an allergic reaction. In some children, industrial dust, for example from wool or cotton, can have a similar effect, and chemical fumes can cause conjunctivitis too.

Conjunctivitis usually affects both eyes, but babies occasionally become infected in one eye only. This usually happens when a tear duct leading from the eye to the nose becomes blocked. As the liquid from the eye cannot trickle down into the nose in the normal way, the eye becomes too moist, and tears run continually down the face. As a result, the baby frequently rubs the eye, which soon becomes infected.

The first symptom of conjunctivitis is usually a gritty feeling in the eye, with irritation just under the eyelids. The eye becomes red because blood vessels in the conjunctiva become enlarged and inflamed, and pus forms, producing a discharge.

If the complaint is caused by a bacterial or viral infection, large quantities of pus may be produced. This clouds the child's eye, causing a sticky feeling and blurring vision. Overnight, the discharge may dry on the child's eyelashes and eyelids, temporarily sealing the lids together. In most cases, a doctor can tell from a brief examination whether the conjunctivitis is an infective or an allergic type. In cases of infective conjunctivitis, the doctor may use a swab to take a sample of pus from the eyes for examination in the laboratory. This can determine whether the infection is bacterial or viral, and thus help in determining the most appropriate treatment.

For infective conjunctivitis, the doctor usually prescribes antibiotics. Drops may be prescribed for use during the day, with an ointment for the night. This is particularly helpful in preventing the eyelids from sticking together. If there is a lot of discharge, it is advisable to bathe the child's eyes, or to wipe the surfaces of his eyelids with cotton wool dipped in warm, slightly salty water (about one level tablespoonful to half a litre/one pint of cooled boiled water).

Chlamydial conjunctivitis is usually treated with the antibiotic tetracycline in the form of eye drops. In addition, the child is often given an antibiotic to be taken by mouth, such as tetracycline or erythromycin, as the infection may be slow to clear with local treatment alone. Chlamydial conjunctivitis occurring outside the tropics does not usually cause severe infection and generally clears without producing permanent eye damage. However, in the tropics, trachoma caused by a chlamydial infection should be treated quickly. Otherwise the eye may require surgery and could perhaps sustain permanent damage. Gonococcal infections respond well to antibiotics, but these must be given early

Allergic conjunctivitis is treated with drops containing anti-allergy drugs. Antihistamine eye drops are useful for short-term treatment in older children but for long-term use, cromoglycate drops may be prescribed to counteract the allergic response.

Always ensure that a child suffering from conjunctivitis has his own soap, flannels and towels. These should be stored separately from other people's. It helps to prevent various kinds of infection spreading if each member of the family has their own, perhaps each in a particular colour.

It can also be helpful to teach your children as soon as they are old enough that dirty hands can cause infections, so it is important to wash the hands before touching the eyes. Even if the hands look clean, they are never free from bacteria.

Constipation

Constipation is an interference with the process by which food passes through the intestines. It causes long, often highly irregular gaps between bowel movements – sometimes as long as one week.

However, all children have their own particular patterns of bowel movements. These may occur several times each day or only once every two or three days. So if you have a child who defecates at quite long intervals, do not automatically assume that he is constipated. There may be nothing at all wrong with him.

Actual constipation may be recognized as follows. The abdomen of a constipated child will be enlarged, and he may complain of discomfort. This condition is often accompanied by flatulence (wind), a furred tongue, bad breath and headaches. And the child may experience pain while eventually passing motions because his faeces will have hardened, as the moisture from them is absorbed into the blood.

Probably one of the most common causes of interference in peristalsis (the process by which solid food normally passes along the intestines) is the food itself. Once the child's digestive system has fully developed, it is able to break up most kinds of solid food material eaten and extract the nutritious substances. However, the human digestive system cannot break down plant cellulose, which commonly occurs in fruit and vegetables and in the outer husks of corn grain, a form called bran. Plant cellulose in food is generally referred to as roughage, or fibre.

Although it is not digested, fibre plays an important role in the body because it stimulates peristalsis. So a diet lacking in fibre is a common cause of constipation. Some foods, such as meat, eggs and cheese, contain no fibre at all, whereas whole grain bread, bran, dried fruit and beans are all high fibre foods.

Another cause of constipation is simply a lack of food in the intestines. If a child has an illness that causes loss of appetite, his condition may become complicated with the onset of constipation. Also, lack of exercise, caused by a prolonged period in bed, can lead to constipation. The diseases of colitis and diverticulitis are sometimes a direct cause.

Some children experience pain on defecation because of damaged veins (piles) or cracks (fissures) in the anus. This condition makes the child reluctant to defecate, so the faeces accumulate in the body and become hard because water from them is absorbed into the bloodstream. In turn, this makes them even more painful to pass from the body.

Sometimes, the cause of constipation is psychological, rather than physical. Like breathing and the heartbeat, peristalsis is controlled by a part of the brain that works without our direct control. However, a child soon learns to control when he defecates, and this ability to hold back a bowel movement sometimes causes a problem. Almost in an absent-minded way, the child may overlook signals from the intestine indicating that the bowel is full and a visit to the lavatory is now due.

If constipation occurs along with some other illness, then consult your doctor, as it could be dangerous to treat your child yourself. In other cases, the best treatment is a commonsense one.

If your baby is bottle-fed, ensure you are making up feeds exactly as instructed. Keep a relaxed attitude if potty-training a toddler. Anxiety-based constipation can result from training that is too strict or has begun too early. Make sure that your child eats foods containing fibre regularly, and give him plenty to drink as this will help to soften the faeces. Encourage your child to exercise in order to tone up the abdominal muscles and also to relieve stress and promote relaxation.

Avoid giving your child laxatives, except as a last resort. Some laxatives work by irritating the nerves of the intestine to encourage peristalsis, which sometimes causes pain and even diarrhoea. Once the child's intestine has been cleared out by the use of a laxative, it tends to hold the next lot of food for a fairly long time. Do not be tempted to give your child another dose of laxative. Simply give his digestive system time to return to normal, and make sure he has plenty of fibre in his diet and takes some regular exercise. Repeated doses of laxative may condition the intestinal nerves to the artificial stimulation so much that they fail to work without the laxative.

If you do feel it is necessary to give your child a laxative, lactulose (Duphalac) should be suitable. If you are unable to find a remedy for your child's condition, consult your doctor in case it is caused by some undiscovered underlying disease.

Conversation

◆ See **Baby Talk**, **Speech**

Cooking

You probably never thought of yourself as a magician but that is how you appear to your child as you cook, say, scrambled eggs, transforming them from a runny, slimy mixture to a hot meal, golden and delicious. A three-year-old will be intrigued by this miraculous transformation and will want to take a closer look at what's going on – and why not let him? If he beats the yolks and whites he will learn how the "yucky" parts mix together; watching you heat them, he will soon grasp the rudiments, not to mention the magic, fun and creative possibilities of cooking.

As your child gets older he will be able to do more complicated tasks like rolling pastry and making sandwiches, but don't expect too much from him too soon. After all, even an apparently simple movement like whisking will be new to him and he is bound to find it difficult to start with. To give yourself an idea of how tricky it is, try using your left hand to beat an egg. (If you are left-handed, try using your right.)

Before you do any sort of cooking or mixing with your child, always:
● Put away all sharp objects – forks, knives, skewers, graters – before you start work; make sure that breakable plates and bowls are out of reach.
● Organize yourself so that you don't have to turn your back on your child while he is preparing something.

● Do all the chopping and grating yourself. When he is about five, your child may be able to cut certain things with a blunt knife but even then you should keep an eye on him.

● Keep your child away from the cooker or microwave at all times. If he wants to have a look, then lift him up to see when you have a spare minute.

● Keep electrical equipment – and flexes – well out of harm's way. When he is four or five, you can let your child switch a mixer on and off for you, under supervision.

Mix and learn!

By the time he is three, your child will have long since learned that shaking objects can produce some interesting noises. And what could be more rewarding than shaking something that produces both an exciting noise and a favourite drink?

Making a milk shake will help your child learn about how foods mix together and will help him to discover new tastes. To make a milk shake all you need is milk, flavouring, and a plastic screw-top jar. The flavouring can be crushed fruit – fresh or canned – a fresh fruit juice or a teaspoon or two of honey, but for deliciously thick, frothy shakes, experiment with yoghurts or ice cream. Prepare the ingredients and place them separately into large plastic bowls. Let him pour the milk into the jar until it is about half full and then let him add his chosen flavouring. Make sure you tighten the top of the jar, then let him shake for all he is worth.

Encourage your child to choose and experiment with different flavourings. Some of his suggestions may sound utterly revolting to you – peanut butter with mashed bananas, for example – but he will not know how they taste mixed together until he has tried them for himself.

Encouraging culinary effort

As your child becomes more adept at handling objects, he will be all the more eager to give you a hand with "proper" cooking. And the more you let him do, the more confident he will become. At first, he will inevitably spill ingredients and knock bowls flying, but these mistakes will most likely upset him more than you, so boost his ego from time to time and assure him that he is doing well.

Start by giving him small chores to do, like brushing pastry with oil, milk or beaten eggs before baking. Not only will he derive great pleasure by painting the pastry but when it comes out of the oven he will be proud of his contribution. You can emphasize his efforts by asking him to brush a face or other design on the pastry: when the pie is eventually lifted from the oven he will be able to see the difference between the glazed and unglazed parts.

Tossing a salad is another small task that is marvellous fun for a young child. After you have washed and chopped all the ingredients, ask him to put them in a large bowl and let him add the dressing, then hand him a pair of wooden spoons. Bits and pieces will probably be scattered everywhere but it is hard to enjoy yourself without making a bit of a mess!

If your child likes muesli for breakfast, why not let him mix his own? All you need is wheatflakes, or rolled oats, wheatgerm, chopped nuts, and chopped dried fruit. Let him choose his own ingredients and then pour the mix into a large, screw-top jar. One way of making his muesli mix extra-special is to encourage him to make his own label for the jar.

Once he has got the hang of mixing muesli and salads, let him try something a bit more sophisticated like a tuna stuffing for eggs. First, prepare the ingredients – peeled hard-boiled eggs sliced in half, tinned tuna, chopped parsley and some mayonnaise – and place them all in separate bowls. Then let the mixing begin, starting with the egg yolks and the mayonnaise. As he adds each new ingredient to the bowl, let him have a small taste so that he can experience how the flavours change. When he has finished stirring, let him spoon the mixture into the hollows in the egg whites, using a teaspoon. If he does not like hard-boiled eggs, he can mix up a similar recipe of cream cheese, tuna and chopped herbs and use this to fill celery sticks or hollowed-out tomatoes.

At about four years old, your child will like nothing better than to crack eggs for you. Be warned: it can be a messy experience. Allow him the chance to feel the texture of the yolks and egg whites. His reaction will probably be an extremely loud "yuck" but if he enjoys scrambled eggs or omelettes, he will know that eggs are delicious, once cooked. Let him whisk up his own dinner and guide him as he adds the pinch of salt, knob of butter or grated cheese. If you can spare a moment, lift him up to have a look at the eggs as they cook.

Unless you have a couple of dozen eggs to spare, there is little point in letting your child try to attempt separating the yolks. If you are making something like meringues, do that task yourself, showing him what you are doing, as you do it. Beating and whisking yolks or whites, however, is something he will really put his heart into.

Meringues are a perennial favourite with children. So, with that in mind, let your four-year-old whip up the whites – another piece of egg magic where slime turns to fluff. However, don't forget that whipping up eggs by hand will be tiring for him and you can always let him finish off the beating when the whites are nearly ready and you are about to fold in the sugar. Don't let him loose with an electric mixer, but he can help turn the handle on a mechanical beater and he will love dolloping spoonfuls of mixture on to a baking tray.

As your child approaches five, he will revel in taking on more advanced projects like kneading dough or rolling out pastry. If you are making dough, either for bread or for a pizza base, help your child to measure out all the ingredients. If you have old-fashioned weighing scales, he will enjoy balancing ingredients against the weights. Let him sift the flour – another favourite pastime – and then help him to mix in the water, yeast, sugar and salt. Most children adore kneading dough with their fingers, although it can be tiring, so you may have to come to the rescue after a few minutes.

When the dough is no longer sticky, wrap it in greased polythene and place it in a warm place to rise. Children find this the most exciting stage of bread-making and they invariably want to have a peek at the dough every five minutes to find out how much it has risen. Having a look once or twice is fine but as dough can take several hours to rise, it is not a bad idea to get on with another project or to go for a walk to take his mind off it. When the dough is ready, let your child knead it again before placing it in bread tins. If you are not using non-stick tins, let him grease them with a little butter or margarine and explain to him why he is doing it. When the dough has proved (doubled in size), pop the tins in the oven and wait for the magic moment when the bread is ready and can be lifted out.

A similar project that your child will enjoy is making pastry. He may like seeing the change in textures as he rubs the fat into the flour, but the best bit is undoubtedly rolling out. However, his skills will be tested to the full when it comes to using a rolling pin and you will have to show him how it is done. He will also be intrigued by the little things you do, like first sprinkling flour over the work surface so that the pastry does not stick. Show him how to roll out from the middle and encourage him to try to get an even thickness. (It might even be an idea to let him practise using play dough first.) His first attempt will probably be lumpy and uneven but his judgement and dexterity will improve with practice and he will be immensely proud the first time he gets it right. If you are making a pie, he can cut out shapes from the pastry trimmings, using biscuit cutters, to decorate the top. Finally, let him wipe down the work surfaces after his session, to give a complete picture of what working in the kitchen is all about.

When it comes to helping prepare for a tea party, you will probably have to fight your child off as he will be only too eager to help. He will certainly be capable of stirring the ingredients together for cakes and cookies but will probably enjoy making sweets most of all. One simple sweet recipe uses marzipan, plain chocolate, icing sugar and food colouring. The first stage is to roll the marzipan into marble-sized balls – let him do this with the palms of his hands and encourage him to try to get each ball the same size. Let him watch as you melt the chocolate in a microwave or on a stove but don't let him get too close.

When the chocolate is cool enough to touch but still runny, let him dip in the marzipan balls before placing them on a cold plate. Use cocktail sticks to spear the marzipan and avoid messy fingers. Once the chocolate has set, he can decorate the sweets with coloured icing drizzled from a spoon or piped from a small cone of greaseproof paper. Other things can be coated in chocolate, too. Try glacé cherries, fresh mandarin segments, strawberries, raisins, nuts or pieces of candied peel.

You may not relish the idea of washing up after a cooking session, but luckily most children do, so why not make the most of the opportunity and let him do it for you! Only let him tackle non-breakable objects and do check that the water is not too hot. Of course, the standard of the washing up may not be up to scratch and you may end up doing it anyway, but persevere and encourage – one day it may pay off.

Coughs

A cough is the forcing of air from the chest in a sudden, usually noisy, action. Coughing is the body's way of helping to clear the air passages of obstructions or other irritants that may cause harm. It is a reflex action triggered by the presence of the foreign material. In the case of an obstruction, such as a piece of food lodged in the throat, coughing stops as soon as the item has been dislodged and coughed up. But usually, coughing is associated with infections, and is more persistent.

Coughing is a sign that something is wrong in the air passages, but more important than the cough itself is the material (if any) coughed up. A productive cough is one that brings up phlegm, and this may be white, yellowish or, if blood is present, pink. A dry cough is one that does not bring up any material from the air passages.

Other important features are the frequency at which the coughing occurs and whether there is any accompanying pain. The child may also suffer from hoarseness, a certain breathlessness and fever.

In the early stages of a cold, the lining of the breathing passages becomes inflamed, and this may cause a dry, irritating cough.

A persistent dry cough associated with a fever may be the first sign of a lung infection such as pneumonia. If there is hoarseness as well, there is a possibility of laryngitis – an infection of the larynx, or voice box.

Coughing that brings up a little clear, white phlegm is common in the later stages of a cold. But thick, yellow phlegm usually indicates an infection, such as bronchitis, which may also cause wheezing.

If the child has breathing difficulties as well as a cough, the cause may be more serious.

Persistent coughing is commonly one of the first signs of asthma in children, and may occur long before a child has any difficulty with breathing. The coughing is often worse at night, and the child may later develop chronic nasal catarrh and a characteristic wheezing, finding it more difficult to breathe out than in.

Croup usually gives children a cough that is initially dry, later becoming productive and then noisy, with laboured breathing.

Violent coughing that occurs in spasms, with vomiting and sometimes a crowing noise, may indicate whooping cough.

Coughing accompanied by pain may indicate that the child is suffering from a serious condition, such as pleurisy. This infection of the lung and its covering membrane produces a sharp pain in the chest whenever the child coughs or breathes deeply.

Coughing that produces blood may be caused by lung infections, such as tuberculosis.

Most coughs, especially those accompanying colds, are not dangerous and get better on their own within a few days, without any treatment. Using medicines to suppress the cough can be harmful, especially if it is a productive cough, and may delay recovery.

A productive cough may be eased by using the type of medicine known as an expectorant. It will help to liquefy the sputum, thus making it easier to cough up. However, if your child is old enough to use a steam inhaler, this may prove to be more effective as a remedy.

For a cough associated with a cold, the child may get relief from decongestant drops or a spray to relieve nasal catarrh. Otherwise, this may trickle down the back of the throat and cause more coughing. A warm, soothing drink, such as honey and lemon, often helps. Some children may prefer a fruit-based medicine, although this may be no more effective than an ordinary drink.

A dry cough in a child over 3 months may be treated with a suppressant, such as pholocodeine linctus. Call a doctor if any type of coughing persists, and seek medical advice immediately if a child has a painful cough, is having difficulty breathing or is coughing up blood.

◆ See also, **Common Cold**

Counting

Most of us assume that our children will learn about "sums" and numbers when they go to school. Very few parents believe that pre-school children can cope with numeracy, that is to say, an understanding of numbers. Yet you can easily give your child a basic grasp of numeracy which will help him to develop skills, not only in maths, but also in logical thought and planning.

You will quickly become aware of how observant your new-born baby is, and how fresh is his view of the world. What seems boring and routine to you is new and exciting to your growing child. It is because your baby is so alert and receptive to new ideas that it is easy and fun to teach him about numbers through play.

Your baby delights in his hands and fingers, and already a sense of numbers, formed through a sense of groups of similar shapes, is developing in his mind. You can help by talking to your baby and telling him what he can see. "Here is one hand, here is another hand, now we have two hands," or "This is one foot, and here is one shoe." "Look at the white cat and look at the black cat. We have two cats in our family."

This simple repetition of naming and numbering what a 12-month-old baby can see will pass on a sense of both language and numeracy. It does not matter that he himself will only begin to talk when he is around two years old – his mind will have taken in some of these ideas.

As your child reaches his third year, he'll be able to talk quite a lot. You can ask him to do things, and he will respond with questions and actions. He can help you to lay the table, and with this simple task you can again introduce him to numbers, and show him ways of making a group or "set" of objects. One plate, one knife, one fork for Daddy; the same for Mummy, and another set of plate, knife, fork for him. Now he has three places, each with its own table setting. As he helps you, remember to explain and count everything.

Another everyday household job is sorting the washing. Show him how to put all the white things together, then all the dark things. Let him help you sort items into simple pairs. He can match socks, and gloves, then he can tidy pairs of shoes, and pairs of slippers. Tell him exactly what he is doing and praise him. "Well done, you found one of Daddy's slippers. Where is the other one? Good. Now we have a pair of slippers." Even getting dressed can be turned into a numbers game as one foot goes into one wellington and two boots make a pair.

He should also be able to grasp what the word "three" means. He has learnt that "three" is mummy, daddy and himself. He now knows that when he goes to bed with Teddy and Pink Rabbit there are "three" in his bed. He is beginning to understand that three is different from one and two.

From the ages of three to five, children begin to enjoy simple games. Many of these games are related to numbers and sets. Snap, the ever-popular card game is a perfect example. The child has to sort out and recognize sets, he has to respond to them quickly and he must understand when a set is complete.

There are other card games designed for children such as Memory or Pairs but you can invent other fun games with a standard pack of cards. Show him how to sort them into red marks and black marks. Then you can lay out a row of cards showing a heart, a spade, a diamond and a club and he can match the other cards to these. Or you could make a small pack of cards yourself showing sets of symbols.

One of the most ancient methods of counting – sliding beads along an abacus – is still helpful today, and it's attractive and colourful, too.

Jigsaw puzzles can also provide hours of fun, and one that combines numbers and pictures turns counting into an absorbing pastime.

As your child is learning to talk and to count, he is also becoming aware of the shape and texture of things. Again, you need to name things and explain to him as he experiments with toys and objects, to help him understand shapes and sizes.

When you give him play dough, tell him you are making a ball, or a sausage. Make things of different sizes and explain them to him. Point out the "big" ball and the "little" ball, the long, thin sausage and the short, fat sausage. Tell him which shapes are fat, square, round, thin or long – and repeat everything many times.

In everyday conversation, concentrate on size: "Daddy is big, baby is small; a big mummy cat, a little baby cat." You can play the same game with toy animals. Ask your child to match the mummy cow with little baby cow. An excellent toy for understanding space and size is the traditional Russian doll, with a number of different-sized dolls fitting one into the other. The child opens the big doll to find a small one inside. He opens that one to find an even smaller doll. It is a toy that fascinates and intrigues any child.

By listening to you patiently repeating and constantly explaining sets of numbers, your five-year-old should be well equipped in basic numeracy. He may thrill you by counting to 20, but you will feel true satisfaction when you realize that he really understands that one is different from three.

It is quite enough for a pre-school child to grasp the concept of three although, because our fingers are obvious objects to count, he may also understand five. This means he has a solid grounding in basic numeracy and will not be confused when he is given his first lessons at school.

Crawling

Probably somewhere between the ages of six and nine months your baby will begin to crawl, and this new-found mobility will be very exciting to him. Until now, he has been dependent on you to give him toys and entertain him. His view has been from the cot or your arms, but now, as he rolls and crawls across the floor, he can see all sorts of strange things and he can chase after them, hold and investigate them.

Help to make his journey across the room an adventure by giving him some soft, fun toys to play with. He can roll on them, cuddle them and even clutch them in his hand as he crawls along. He will enjoy reaching out and grasping things, so give him rattles or similar playthings which have moveable parts inside them or make a noise when they are shaken.

Simple games such as passing the rattle backwards and forwards, or shaking it rhythmically will stimulate his interest. Play little games with him which encourage him to crawl and fetch – but don't tease him.

Let him grasp the toy the moment his hands reach it, because it is important he feels a sense of achievement and confidence in this new, enlarged world.

Push-along toys and balls are also excellent in encouraging him to crawl and stretch. Some balls are made of clear plastic with bright coloured objects inside – such as ducks – and these always fascinate a small child. Your baby will examine them, with his mouth and his hands, and will delight in pushing them away and chasing after them.

The important thing to remember when you have a crawling and inquisitive baby is that he is quite unaware of danger, or even what he is playing with. Try not to be cross when he spills the sugar or topples flour all over the place – he doesn't know it is food, he just thinks it has a wonderful texture and looks amazing. Be careful that he doesn't pick up bleach or detergent containers, and that you keep all sharp edges and breakable items out of his reach. Constant supervision is essential.

Once your baby starts to crawl, he will soon learn to move round the house at speed. He will be enjoying his new-found freedom but his natural curiosity is going to create some difficulties for the rest of the family. Make your older children aware of the danger of leaving things around which the baby can pick up and chew. For example, if they play with construction kits, they must be very careful not to leave any small bits lying around.

Your baby is at the stage where you may find a playpen very useful, although it might be an idea to get him used to it before he becomes mobile. They are ideal for short periods of time when you cannot be watching your child but you need to be quite sure he is safe. Do make sure it is placed away from draughts, from the window or a door, and you must take special care to put it far from objects he can pull over, such as the ironing board with the iron placed on top.

Give him a few of his favourite toys to play with and take him out of the playpen as soon as he cries. A playpen is a very useful piece of equipment, particularly for you, the mother. Be very careful that your baby does not feel confined or trapped inside his playpen. He must feel happy, not lonely, when he is placed inside it.

It is not difficult to make a game out of being in the pen, and as long as you toss balls over the edge, and talk to your baby so that he can hear your voice, or call to him and sing to him if you have to leave the room for a moment, he will think it's fun rather than feeling isolated.

Your baby may have the oddest reactions once he is out of his pushchair and able to explore the garden. Grass, pebbles, and stones will intrigue or puzzle him. Let him explore with his fingers the feel of twigs and the texture of stones, but be very quick if he picks up tiny pebbles and stalks. He will naturally put them straight in his mouth.

Give him a pile of pebbles which are small enough for his hands but too big to swallow. Show him how to build them into a pile, or how to break the pile using a spade. Let him dig into the earth, or, rather, show him how the spade is used. He will not yet have the strength or co-ordination to do it himself but he will have fun learning.

A small bowl of water and a mug or two, and a toy sailing ship will entrance your eight-month-old in the garden, but any play involving water must be closely supervised. Mostly, your baby will enjoy being able to explore with you beside him, naming the new things he finds on his little journey and showing him how to squeeze the earth between his fingers and smell the flowers.

If you have a pool or a pond you will need to put a fence around it once your baby is on the move.

Some of the best games for your baby do not require toys. He will love to play peek-a-boo, and shriek with delight when he learns to "hide" from you behind his hands or behind the chair. Remember, for him, all these actions – the crawl behind the chair, putting his hands over his face – are new and exciting.

Some babies skip the crawling stage altogether and there's nothing worrying about it. Often these babies start to sit steadily at an earlier age and proceed to pulling themselves to stand and cruise. Rather than being unable to crawl, many babies choose alternative ways of getting around, such as: sliding around on their bottom, rolling over or wriggling, moving forward on hands and elbows with legs dragging behind, or a "bear walk" – moving on hands and feet together.

Croup

Croup is the common name for various conditions that cause the larynx (voice box) or trachea (windpipe) to become partially blocked, resulting in breathing difficulties and a harsh cough. The term is also used to describe the characteristic sound heard when the child breathes in. Children are most likely to suffer from croup when aged between six months and three years.

Croup is more serious in a very young child because there is a danger that the child's windpipe may become completely blocked as a result.

Attacks of croup usually start suddenly and occur mostly at night. The child has difficulty in breathing in, and makes a growling or wheezing noise. The cough sounds like the bark of a small dog. These unusual sounds often frighten the child, causing panic and making it even more difficult for him to breathe properly.

Various childhood infections, especially the common cold, can give rise to swelling of the larynx and trachea, thus causing a partial blockage. Another possible cause of swelling is an allergic reaction. Occasionally, croup is caused by the child inhaling a small object, such as part of a toy or a piece of food. The foreign body may itself cause sufficient blockage to give rise to croup, or it may irritate the air passage and cause inflammation and constriction later.

Comfort and calm your child and call a doctor immediately if you are worried about coping with the problem. Keep your child in a warm room and increase the humidity by boiling some water in an electric kettle and allowing the steam to fill the room. The moisture will help to relieve your child's discomfort.

Alternatively, take your child into a warm, steamy bathroom. Sit him up on your lap, as he will find it easier to breathe in this position.

If the symptoms do not disappear by themselves, call your doctor, who will try to ascertain the cause of the croup so that he can determine the best treatment to prescribe.

You should seek medical help immediately if:
● your child has severe difficulty in breathing
● you suspect that he has inhaled a small object
● the lips appear blue, indicating that he is not getting sufficient oxygen
● the skin is unusually pale or even grey
● your child seems distressed or very unwell
● his temperature is abnormally high
● any other symptoms cause you concern
● you are unable to calm your child or relieve his suffering.

Crying

Crying is sometimes a natural and often involuntary reaction caused by an emotional state, such as anxiety, or produced in response to pain. In such cases, the purpose of crying is to release tension. At other times, it is a way of expressing grief or need.

Tears consist of a watery, salty fluid, which is produced continuously by the tear, or lacrimal, glands. These are situated above the outer corners of the eyes. The flow of tears keeps the eye clean and free from germs. It also lubricates the eyeballs, to let the eyelids move smoothly over them during blinking.

Each time the eyelids blink, the fluid drains away into small holes in the inner corners of the eyes. From here it passes down the tear ducts to the back of the nose and throat.

When your child cries, or if an eye is irritated by dust or grit, the flow of tears increases.

Besides having tears running down his face, your child may appear flushed in the cheeks and his forehead may become wrinkled. The corners of the mouth often turn down and there is a marked change in the breathing pattern. The general rate of respiration gets much faster, and a deep initial breath may be followed by sobbing or wailing.

The most common causes of crying in young children are hunger, wind, general discomfort, pain (especially during teething), boredom and loneliness. A frightening noise can also set off crying, as may over-stimulation and tiredness. Rough handling, and dressing or undressing can bring on tears very easily although, strangely, wet or dirty nappies are unlikely to cause much distress. Another possible reason is the onset of illness.

Crying is, in fact, inevitable because it is the only way a newborn baby can communicate, the only way of telling you that he has something to be upset about. Whether he is unhappy for some obvious reason, like hunger or overtiredness, or for some unfathomable reason of his own, the same unhappy face and nerve-curdling wail will be struck up. While you're trying to work out exactly what the problem might be, a gentle cuddle to let him know you're there is never going to go amiss. But realistically, you may feel more like abandoning him than giving him a hug, especially when you are tired and your nerves are frayed.

You may be accused of "making a rod for your own back" if you always comfort your child when he cries, but actually your instinct is to comfort a distressed baby – if only in an attempt to stop the noise. In fact a baby's cry is designed to produce that very response – for mum or dad to come running to "turn it off". And if you do turn a deaf ear to your baby's prolonged crying, your baby soon learns that its cries go unheeded. Research suggests that leaving a baby to cry may stop him crying eventually but in doing so, he is actually learning to stop asking for attention, which in turn can damage his ability to form loving relationships – so vital is this learning experience in the first year of his life.

Whether you agree with this theory or not, it's quite probable you wouldn't be able to stand the noise while you "sit it out" anyway. Happily though, going to your baby seems to be a good thing for both you and your baby. It actually makes your life easier because if you respond promptly and reliably to his crying, he will end up crying less than if you ignored him. The reasoning behind this is that beyond the first few weeks of his life, your baby cries more out of a need to communicate than out of unhappiness or discomfort. So if you go to him when he cries, and you soothe him, talk to him, smile at him or even frown at him, he quickly catches on to these as more effective ways of telling you what he wants and starts copying them. He's probably as relieved as you when he doesn't have to keep relying on one cry to express his every need.

There is a theory that babies have different cries for different needs. If you think you can distinguish between an "I'm hungry" and an "I'm tired" cry, then you may find your life slightly easier, but most people just have to rely on trial and error together with some commonsense to find out what the problem is.

Hunger is the most common cause of crying and therefore a good starting point. Your baby has been used to having a constant food supply while he was in the womb, so it's no wonder he seems to cry a lot for food. Experiments have shown that having a full stomach is what brings most comfort to a baby, more than sucking or being held, which suggests that a baby fed on demand is more likely not to cry than one who has to wait.

While waiting for a feed, however, or when suffering some distress that you can't work out, a baby may well derive comfort from sucking his thumb or a dummy. He won't be fooled by a dummy if he's hungry, but it can be a good stopgap to quieten him while you get ready for a feed.

Heat and cold are also often the reason for a baby becoming upset. Because a young baby cannot regulate his own body temperature he can easily get cold. The ideal temperature for his room is 24°C (75°F) for the first month and between 18°C (65°F) and 20°C (68°F) after this.

If you find that heating the house to this temperature is too much for the rest of you, keep your baby at the right temperature by adjusting the number of blankets on him. You can check whether he is too hot or too cold quite easily by feeling the back of his neck: if it is sticky with perspiration, take some covers off; if his skin feels cool he needs some more blankets.

Swaddling a baby in a shawl or cotton baby blanket is another way of making sure he is warm and snug while giving him a lovely feeling of security, which is often what all the tears are about.

In fact, close contact with anything, whether he's asleep or awake, often stops the crying. The trouble is that you can't hold him all day and rocking can be very tiring. Carrying him around in a sling on your chest is a good alternative – it leaves you all your mobility, so you can still function while your baby is soothed by the closeness and movement of your body.

Overtiredness is something to be aware of as it can stop your baby going to sleep and can set off the "screamers". Again, swaddling quickly soothes his nerves, and consequently soothes yours too.

A baby left to cry himself to sleep will often simply wear himself out and become even more upset and difficult to comfort. If your baby cries try checking on him without picking him up straight away. Try laying a hand on his body to give him the comfort of contact, rock the cot if it soothes him, sing or talk gently to him, or try a soothing music tape or musical cot mobile.

As your baby gets older he will sleep less and may often cry simply because he is bored. If you leave him alone to contemplate the ceiling, don't be surprised if he cries out for company and something to entertain him.

Your baby can often start crying when a change in his small world gives him a shock. If he cries when you undress him, this is probably as a reaction to being naked rather than your lack of gentleness. The best way to avoid the wailing at this point is to keep talking to him in a calm way while you undress him and to have a warm soft towel ready to wrap him up in, so that he's not left feeling exposed.

With all these "stop-the-crying" activities, it is a great help if you can share the responsibility with your partner, as the rocking, humming, soothing, swaddling and cooing can be exhausting. And if you're feeling frazzled, you won't actually be a very good soother.

Some babies cry because they are suffering colic. This condition causes great distress in the baby and his parents. He is not crying because he is hungry or cold. He appears to be suffering terrible tummy ache, although the causes of colic are not fully understood by medical experts. Nothing will stop him crying, but cuddle him anyway. Don't let him feel that he is alone and rejected. Be patient, take heart – usually colic ends very abruptly when the baby is three months old. Overnight, he will stop screaming, become calm and only cry to tell you he is cold, wet or hungry.

If you have run out of options and your baby has still not stopped crying, you may want to try one of the following, however odd they may sound:

● Driving round the block with the baby (but he may wake up when you switch off the engine).

● Going out with the baby – fresh air and a change of scene often helps.
● Switching the vacuum cleaner or the hairdryer on for a soothing hum.
● Flushing the toilet repeatedly.
● Putting on a tape of a beating heart or of "white" noise (such as static interference on the radio).
● Pretending you're on a television programme where you're showing the viewers how to be the "perfect" mum coping with a crying baby.

For most people, then, a crying baby is one of those things that just has to be borne with as much patience and good humour as possible. Babies do grow out of it and often, there is a perfectly good reason for them doing it. Finding this reason may feel like looking for a needle in a haystack sometimes, but keep trying – the relief of the quietness when the crying stops is well worth the effort. And remember, if your baby is suffering from colic, it will all be over in three months.

Cuts and Abrasions

An abrasion is an area of skin that has been torn away by force. Light scuffing of the skin is called a graze, but sometimes a large, deep area of skin is affected and the abrasion is more like a burn.

Abrasions sound less dramatic than cuts, but can be much more painful as millions of tiny nerve endings are exposed. Abrasions can become full of dirt or grit, so the main problem in dealing with them is to get rid of infection.

Small cuts can be caused by anything sharp: glass, razors, kitchen knives or even paper. Even small cuts tend to gape slightly, so to help them heal faster they should be taped up in some way.

The body is very efficient at dealing with wounds, at staunching the bleeding, fighting infection and healing the skin, but it often needs help. Whenever the skin is broken, blood vessels may be torn and germs can enter the body, so all wounds need to be cleaned.

When the bleeding has stopped and the wound is clear of infection, a fibrous scab begins to form. The scab shrinks over the next few days and forms an extremely strong bond between the cut surfaces.

To stop bleeding

You can staunch the flow of blood from a small wound quite quickly by pressing on it with a clean pad – a folded bandage or clean handkerchief. Hold it there without lifting it off or changing it for about five minutes, until the bleeding stops.

Cleaning the wound

It is essential to clean every last bit of dirt out of any contaminated wound, as dirt causes infection. Antiseptics can reduce the risk of infection but are no substitute for thorough cleaning.

Wounds can be cleaned with a variety of liquids, from mild antiseptics to soap and water. Tap water is quite clean, so you don't have to boil water in a kettle before using it to clean the wound. If you use any antiseptic, make sure you dilute it as instructed. By using too strong a solution you may damage the tissues and make the wound even worse.

Removing grit

If there is any grit in the wound, a quick scrub with a clean brush under running water will get it out, but it will hurt. If you cannot remove all the grit, seek medical advice. Large pieces of grit can be picked out carefully with tweezers.

Brush any last bits of dirt from the wound with small swabs of gauze or cotton wool soaked in antiseptic. Use separate swabs for each stroke, and always work from the centre of the wound outwards.

Applying a dressing

A small, clean cut can be covered with a plaster. A larger cut will need a non-stick dressing held in place with a cotton or crêpe bandage. Never use cotton wool or the woolly side of lint against the wound, as it will stick to it and harm the scab when removed.

◆ See also, **Bleeding**, **Dressings**

Dancing

From the first rocking back and forward in your arms your baby will be introduced to rhythm and movement.

As with so much of a child's development, he will copy you in what he does. So if he sees you dancing to music the chances are, he will join in.

In Africa children of two and three years old are already dancing in a very rhythmical and co-ordinated way, simply because they see and hear dancing around them as so much of their daily life and have been carried on their dancing mothers' backs.

Children are born with a sense of rhythm. Even as they learn to crawl and walk, they are, in a sense, moving to the rhythm of their own bodies, their breathing and their heartbeat. Later, when a toddler hears music with a strong beat he will respond quite spontaneously by moving his body and "dancing". As he gets older, different types of music may suggest certain movements and, particularly with your encouragement, his dancing will become more varied. Dancing can also be a way for a child to express himself.

Learning to dance properly and practising moving to music not only helps children to develop their natural feeling for rhythm and expression but also teaches important physical skills such as balance, control and co-ordination.

There are so many different forms of dance to choose from that the most important factor will most likely be whether your child finds it fun as an activity and is eager to move on and learn more.

From the age of about two, your child will begin to make stepping movements to music. Playing different kinds of music and encouraging your child to stamp like a giant, march like a soldier or fly like a bird allows him to use his imagination and to recognize the mood of music. Giving him a simple shaker or some rhythm sticks will provide him with the means of making his own rhythmic music.

By the time he is three he will be able to follow simple instructions and so be ready to join one of the babies' classes, whether for ballet, tap or folk dance. Such classes are not geared towards working for exams or following a demanding routine but aim to give a gentle, fun introduction to a particular form of dance. Whatever the type of dancing, classes tend to involve encouraging simple movements to music. Nursery rhymes are used and dolls may be taken along for certain routines.

Many parents choose ballet for their children's first taste of dancing. It may be a good choice because classical ballet has a system of training that is well established and has long been adapted for children, from the very youngest upwards.

If your child begins classes around the age of three, do not expect instant results. The benefits at this early stage are really recreational. He will gain confidence and concentration and enjoy being with children of the same age.

The physical training in dance classes is equally as useful for boys and girls. Although far fewer boys than girls take dancing classes, there will be schools in your area that have boys among their pupils.

If your son is keen to dance don't tell him it is not masculine; lots of boys like to dance, taking up ballet, tap or other styles. Boys are star competition disco dancers, too, and breakdancers seem to be predominantly male.

If your son learns to dance he will gain confidence and co-ordination, may become a better sportsman and will perhaps even grow up to be a famous dancer one day.

Having decided that you want to send your child to dancing classes and made up your mind which kind of dance you think will most appeal, the best way to find a suitable class in your area is to contact the appropriate governing body to get a list of local schools. The Imperial Society of Teachers of Dancing is a worldwide organization with associate teachers taking classes in ballet, tap, modern, ballroom and many types of national dance.

It is worth being aware that anyone can set up a dancing school but good teachers are usually affiliated to the governing body of their particular discipline. Before enrolling your child in classes, you will most likely want to go along and see for yourself how they are run. A good dancing school can still be recognized by the way it encourages appropriate dress – or even uniform – and good grooming. Premises should be properly heated, clean and well lit. The classes may not be held in a proper studio with a sprung floor – but beware of draughty, dirty halls with rough, splintery floors.

Some teachers allow a parent and prospective pupil to watch a class, while some will even let the child go along for a trial class. The best schools come recommended by friends and often have a waiting list, so you need to sign up early.

Most teachers do not allow parents to sit in on lessons – it is too disruptive – but at the start your child may need to be reassured that you are waiting outside. A child who is already happy to be left for a morning at playgroup will probably adapt well to attending a half-hour structured dancing class.

Girls usually wear a leotard, crossover cardigan and tights or socks for ballet, while boys normally start in shorts and a T-shirt. Both wear appropriate shoes. Many schools sell equipment more cheaply than the shops and some keep second-hand items. It is not advisable to buy all the clothes before your child seems keen to stay. Teachers are usually happy for beginners to wear shorts and a T-shirt and to dance in bare feet until they settle in. Clothes should allow for freedom of movement, and long hair should be tied back.

Very few children who join a dancing class will go on to become professional dancers, but they will nevertheless gain a lot from the experience. The discipline, physical expertise, strength and suppleness gained through dancing helps them in every type of sport. Children who take up dance early and continue past the baby stage develop a sense of rhythm and co-ordination, balance and good posture.

◆ See also, **Exercise and Fitness**

Death

Helping your child cope with death

If someone close to you dies, your first reaction is likely to be one of shock, numbness and confusion. You may still be in this state when you tell your children. Of course breaking the news is never easy, but it may be of some consolation to know that, if your children are very young, the idea of death may be less disturbing for them than it is for you.

One reason for this is that young children are not really able to understand what death means. Even so, they are sensitive to other people's feelings and may react to anxiety, sadness or sombre moods in members of the family perhaps by developing problems or becoming more clinging.

It is not until he reaches the age of three to four that a child can start to understand the idea of death. At about this age some children develop a strong curiosity about death. Perhaps they have seen a dead bird in the garden, or they may wonder where meat comes from. Death may be a puzzle for the under-sevens, but it is often one which they treat fairly matter-of-factly. Parents are often perturbed and shocked at the apparent indifference and callousness of young children over a death in the family. Your child may well say, "Was there a lot of blood?" when told of a road accident, or may be clamouring for sweets within hours of sharing in the news of the death of a close relative.

As hurtful as it is try not to be angry or scold your child for this – what to an adult appears callous is only natural for a child, who has not yet learnt the accepted "protocol" of reacting to death, and whose understanding of it is not nearly complete.

A four- or five-year-old child struggling to make sense of the world will often demand a reason for why somebody has died, especially if it is an accidental death, or the death of a young person. "Did he die because he was naughty?" might be a typical question from a four-year-old.

Another common idea about death is that it means someone has "gone somewhere else" – that they haven't really stopped living, or that they will be back. The idea that someone – or something, perhaps a cherished pet – a child holds dear could really cease to exist is very hard. If children simply do not understand the finality of death, it is because they don't yet have a sense of time. Many children will be used to their grandparents, for example, being away from them for long periods, so they might think, why shouldn't death be just another long spell away?

It is generally agreed that before the age of eight or nine a child cannot understand death in the way adults do. Just because they do not share our idea of death, however, it does not mean that little children don't have very great needs when someone close to them dies.

Children, like adults, need to be able to express their emotions, whether it is sadness, anger or just confusion. Without sharing grief with people who will offer comfort and support, the process is bound to be more painful. Fortunately, between the ages of three and six or seven, children are usually very open about how they feel.

How any child reacts will depend partly on how those around him are behaving. If the whole family is subdued and quiet, with little crying or talking about the event, a child will soon learn what is expected of him and may well develop his own "stiff upper lip" if he thinks that sharing his feelings would not be welcome. It is not uncommon for children to feel guilty if someone close dies. A four-year-old might think that an older sister has died in an accident because he was rude to her or wished she would go away for some reason. If you are helping a child to cope with death and there is the slightest sign he might feel guilty, make a point of telling him it was not his fault.

If one parent dies, a three- to five-year-old is likely to think, "Will the other one die? Who will look after me?" Young children need a lot of reassurance that they will not be abandoned and that there will always be someone there to love them.

The reassurance a child needs for a sense of security does not come only from kind words. Try to make sure that – as far as possible and as far as is appropriate – the regular rhythm of ordinary life continues. The golden rule for grieving is to be available, to be around and always prepared to answer questions. Try to talk about the person who has died, look through photograph albums together, and listen to the child's feelings. If the person who has died was particularly close to you then you may feel you need to enlist the help of a close friend or relative. They can help by listening to your child's feelings while you attempt to cope with your own.

Telling a child that their brother, sister, father or mother has died must be one of the most difficult tasks facing any adult, but there are a few basic guidelines that will help you to help your child eventually come to terms with the loss.

Firstly, do not be afraid to show your grief (within reason – hysterical anguish will only serve to upset and worry them even more).

When your child first hears the news, hold him and cuddle him. Throughout his grief, one cuddle will probably be worth a thousand words.

Telling him the real cause of death may seem macabre, but try to explain in the best and most honest way you can, as it will help to diminish the bewildering and mysterious ideas he may have about death. Make it clear to him that whoever has died cannot feel anything now, that he or she did not choose to go and that it was nobody's fault. Phrases like "your brother's gone away" suggest that he chose to go and that, perhaps, he will be back soon. The phrase "gone to sleep forever" could conjure up fears of going to sleep.

A lot of what you say when answering a child's questions about death will depend upon your own views. Try at least to be reassuring. Whatever your religious views or lack of them, there is no harm in saying that the dead person is peaceful and feeling happy now. Such a reassurance will be sure to comfort a small child.

Whatever you say, try to get across the message that people should not be ashamed to talk about a death and that there is nothing wrong with crying or showing your emotions in any way when someone you love has died.

Losing a baby

Stillbirth – the death of a baby before birth after the 28th week of pregnancy – happens in approximately one birth in every 200 in the UK. Cot death, or Sudden Infant Death Syndrome, occurs to one baby in every 500. And there is one neonatal death – death in the first month of life – in approximately every 130 births.

Most countries collect the statistics, which put together all the stillbirths and early neonatal deaths (deaths in the first week of life). They are expressed as a perinatal mortality rate, or PMR, and worked out as the number of deaths per 1000 live births. In most Western countries, the figure is between 10 and 16.

All of these figures hide a real family tragedy. There is much research going on into why some babies die, and though progress is being made, mainly because tiny babies born very early are now surviving, mysteries remain. Even when the cause of death is known, it may not have been possible to prevent it happening.

Stillbirth

This can be a mystery. Sometimes, it happens because the baby is tiny and weak, perhaps with a heart defect or a handicap that is not survivable. It can also happen, however, to a baby who seems to have been growing well and who has no impairment to health at all. The placenta sometimes becomes much less efficient than it should be – for no apparent reason – and this deprives the baby of vital oxygen, and as a result he dies. The mother may suspect there is something wrong, because her baby stops moving.

Movements that slow down in the last week of pregnancy, or even stop, are not unusual. In most cases, it simply means the baby is sleeping, or that there is less room in the uterus for athleticism now the baby is getting bigger. But if you notice no movements at all for 24 hours, then it is a wise move to ask your midwife, doctor or antenatal clinic for advice. If necessary, you can be examined, and the baby's heartbeat can be checked.

Neonatal death

Babies who die in the first week or month of life – the neonatal deaths – are almost always born pre-term and very small. In fact, much of the improvement in perinatal mortality rates over the years has been due to two factors: fewer babies are born pre-term because mothers on the whole are healthier before and during pregnancy than they used to be, and of those babies that are born too early, more can now be saved due to good medical and nursing treatment in special care and intensive care baby units found in hospitals.

Some babies who die after birth are born with a handicap that means the baby cannot survive very long. The handicaps like this include anencephaly, when the brain has not developed, serious heart defect, or other defects of the major organs. Not uncommonly, babies like this are also born pre-term. Some defects are operable, and when the operation is successful, the baby can survive. But, unfortunately, surgery for tiny, weak babies is hazardous and presents a risk in itself.

The experience of support groups connected with baby deaths indicates that for many parents, having a photograph of their baby gives an important source of comfort in the months and years ahead. Many hospitals now are happy to take a photograph, even after death. They will also ask if you want the chance to hold your baby. This can help you to say goodbye and to acknowledge your little baby as a real person, who'll always live on in your heart.

Cot death

Also known as Sudden Infant Death Syndrome, this is the phenomenon of baby deaths without any obvious cause. In most cases, the babies who die in this way have shown no sign of serious illness, no congenital defect (that is, a handicap present at birth) – in fact, there seems to be nothing wrong with these babies in the weeks and days leading up to death. Although many babies are discovered to have died while apparently asleep in their cots (hence the name), a few actually die in their parents' arms.

There are many and various theories about the cause of cot deaths. Most experts feel that if we ever find out why babies die in this way, there will turn out to be a lot more than one single cause. It may be that a combination of factors can somehow overwhelm the baby's immune system, and make him or her vulnerable to a virus, that would otherwise be shaken off – but, as yet, no one really knows for sure.

Latest ideas include advice to parents to place the sleeping baby on his back, rather than tummy, and to prevent the baby from becoming too hot. It may be that sleeping on the tummy prevents the baby from staying cool, and encourages covers to ride up and over the head and shoulders, making the baby extremely hot. Duvets may not be the best sort of bedding for a baby in the first months of life. Instead, sheets and blankets allow the parent to control the temperature of the bedding (by removing or adding a layer).

The loss of a baby carries a second sadness in its wake – the desperate fear that it will happen to another, future brother or sister of the dead baby.

If your baby dies, and the cause is known, then ask the doctor about the chances of recurrence. It may be that you can have genetic counselling – a discussion with an expert who knows the risks of certain conditions happening again in the same family. Taking folic acid before and during the first few weeks of pregnancy can prevent anencephaly and other defects of the neural tube.

Most families who suffer the loss of one baby do go on to have healthy babies without any problems, but the anxiety is bound to be there until your new baby passes the age at which your previous baby died.

You will always remember, and love, your baby who died. That is right and normal. Grieving is a process that must not be hurried and a couple must learn to come to terms with their loss together. It is also right and normal, however, that in time, the grief you feel will no longer be the main focus of your life and thought, though the anniversary of the day your baby died will always be a special day, and one you will remember for ever.

Diarrhoea

Diarrhoea is a symptom of a disorder, usually an infection in the intestines, although it may sometimes indicate a more serious problem. It can be dangerous in babies and young children if it lasts more than a day or two, so it is important to seek advice from a doctor in such cases.

Diarrhoea is an uncomfortable symptom, and may be accompanied by pains in the abdomen. The stools are much more fluid and less well formed than usual. In severe cases of diarrhoea, the stools are very watery and may be passed very frequently. In some cases, the child may also have attacks of vomiting.

Persistent diarrhoea causes considerable loss of water and salts, and may lead to dehydration which, if untreated, can be fatal. Babies are particularly at risk as they can become dehydrated much more quickly than older children, and vomiting may make it very difficult for them to absorb the fluid given by mouth to replace that lost in the diarrhoea.

Diarrhoea occurs when the lining of the intestine becomes irritated. This may be due to an infection, the presence of a poisonous substance or some other cause. As a result, the lining of the intestine becomes unable to absorb water and salts from the food. In consequence, food and water pass through the length of the intestine much faster than usual and the stool becomes watery. In addition, the inflamed condition of the intestine walls may cause them to release water, thus increasing the amount of fluid lost in the stools.

Acute diarrhoea

One of the most common causes of acute diarrhoea is food poisoning; in this case diarrhoea often starts within a few hours of eating contaminated food. The most frequent causes of food poisoning are bacteria that grow on contaminated food, producing toxins (poisons) in the process. This kind of food poisoning is often caused by toxins from Staphylococcus bacteria.

In other types of food poisoning, the bacterium itself may cause the infection. For example, the Salmonella bacterium causes diarrhoea, with pain and vomiting. The Campylobacter bacterium also causes diarrhoea, often with fairly severe stomach pains. This bacterium can spread by touch between members of a household, or may be spread in contaminated food or water.

Viruses sometimes cause diseases whose symptoms include diarrhoea. Gastroenteritis, for example, may be a viral infection. It causes diarrhoea, vomiting and abdominal pains. This complaint is also known as gastric flu and summer diarrhoea.

Gastroenteritis is a common affliction in babies but, to avoid making a wrong diagnosis, it is important to distinguish between loose stools and diarrhoea. Breastfed babies often have very loose motions, and they may pass several stools each day. Bottle-fed babies produce stools with a consistency more like those of adults, but the colour varies greatly.

In spite of the appearance of the stool, a breastfed baby is less likely to have gastroenteritis, as the breast milk protects the intestines from infection, and in breastfeeding there is no risk of infection from unsterilized bottles and teats.

Highly spiced foods, or large quantities of fruit or shellfish can also cause acute stomach upsets and loose bowels.

Infections completely unconnected with the bowels cans cause diarrhoea in children. This typically happens to toddlers with ear and throat infections.

Diarrhoea also accompanies various epidemic diseases, including typhoid, dysentery and cholera, which, however, have practically disappeared from Western countries. Typhoid and dysentery are spread by bacteria, often ingested with food, whereas cholera is spread by drinking water that has been infected with faeces. The difference between food poisoning and dysentery is that the symptoms of dysentery can take up to 24 hours to develop and are longer lasting than in food poisoning.

Traveller's diarrhoea occurs when new strains of bacteria replace the normally beneficial ones residing in the large intestine. Such bacteria are commonly acquired from the water supply, and do not affect local people, who have built up an immunity to them through long exposure.

Chronic diarrhoea

If parasites get into a child's food and water, they may cause diarrhoea. One such parasite is the amoeba, a single-celled organism, which causes amoebic dysentery, a common disease in the tropics. The diarrhoea alternates with periods of constipation, and the condition may persist for some years.

Diarrhoea also occurs when some other disease of the intestinal wall prevents the proper absorption of foods. These malabsorption problems also leave patients badly undernourished.

Although the course of action for treatment of diarrhoea depends on what the cause of the trouble is, the basic treatment is very simple. The priority is to keep up the level of fluid intake by getting your child to drink plenty of liquids. Eating is not essential and, if he isn't hungry, he shouldn't be forced to eat, especially if he has been vomiting.

Diarrhoea may be serious for a baby, particularly if the stools are abnormally loose and watery, and solid food should be stopped immediately although breastfeeding should continue. In either case, your baby should be given extra fluids, best of all a mixture of 4 teaspoons (20 g) of sugar and ¼ teaspoon (2.5 g) of salt in half a litre of water. If you are bottle feeding, give your baby half-strength milk (half as much powder or liquid for the usual amount of water).

If, apart from having diarrhoea, the baby appears to be well and is taking fluids, then keep a careful watch for the next 24 hours. If he develops other symptoms, such as vomiting, or if the stools are tinged with blood, then call your doctor. Retain a soiled nappy for the doctor to examine when he calls.

Your doctor may advise stopping all milk and giving your baby only clear liquids. He may prescribe a balanced sugar/salt solution to make up for the salts lost in the diarrhoea and restore the normal absorption of water from the intestine. It is unlikely that your doctor will suggest a medicine to "dry up" the diarrhoea in small babies. Mild attacks will soon be over, while seriously ill babies should be treated in hospital.

Drugs may reduce the level of activity in the intestine and slow down the passage of its contents but this will not reduce the duration of the illness. Antibiotics, usually sulphonamides or erythromycin, may be prescribed for some forms of food poisoning, especially if the cause is found to be bacteria such as Salmonella and Campylobacter.

◆ See also, **Food Poisoning**, **Gastroenteritis**, **Vomiting**

Disability, Diagnosing

The moment when you are either told or you discover yourself that your baby is not normal is one you will not forget easily. The most common handicaps are cerebral palsy, which can affect both brain and body, and Downs syndrome, which is genetic in origin. Whilst a condition such as Downs syndrome can be diagnosed at birth, there are many disabilities whose symptoms may take some time to manifest themselves.

Often medical staff are reluctant to share their worries with new parents, especially since their concerns may prove to be unfounded once tests have been carried out. Most parents do sense that there may be a problem, however, and usually prefer to be informed. With problems that are not immediately obvious it is often the parents who are first to notice or suspect disability. In some cases parents try for years to bring such problems to the attention of doctors before being taken seriously. Regular developmental check-ups are particularly important in such cases as there is more chance that any problem will be picked up sooner rather than later.

The most important cause of physical handicap is damage to the central nervous system (the brain or spinal cord) during fetal life, at birth, or in the first few years of childhood. At this stage the central nervous system develops very rapidly so that any damage is likely to have a profound effect causing delays in normal development of body control, speech, vision, hearing, social, emotional and learning skills. The extent of damage can vary, and where a disability emerges slowly, parents have to cope with a long period of doubt about their child which can be extremely stressful.

In the case of mental handicap, the diagnosis is formed very slowly over the first few years of life, or even as late as when the child first starts school.

If your child is handicapped you need to be told what is wrong with him, its cause, how it can be treated, and what to expect of his future. If the disability is the result of a chromosomal abnormality or other genetic defect, genetic counselling can be very helpful. It can alleviate the feelings of guilt that many parents experience by showing them that nothing could have prevented what has happened. It can also help to assess the risk to future children.

If your child's problem is a severe one, confirmation of the diagnosis will probably cause you to experience a range of emotions beginning with numbness, then disbelief, anger, despair and finally acceptance. If the problem is less severe, and is diagnosed after a long period of doubt, there may even be a sense of relief at the prospect of finally getting help. In either case, support groups who can give you information and put you in touch with other parents in similar situations can be invaluable at this stage, helping you to realize that you are not alone.

Discipline

It is often only when you are confronted with the control and guidance of a small, new person that you and your partner may come to realize that there are enormous differences between you. How will you react if your partner wants to send your two-year-old to his room for having a tantrum? Does one of you insist on good table manners while the other thinks that they aren't particularly important? Or is one partner the lenient one? Does one of you get angry and shocked if the other smacks your child? It is essential that you recognize your differences and arrive at a compromise on them if you wish to create a happy family life and maintain harmonious personal relations.

Unfortunately, in most homes differing views on how best to handle children only surface during a crisis, when a child is being difficult or irritating. It is hard to be calm and in sensible agreement when your little boy is refusing to go to bed at the end of a hectic day, or when he is howling in the middle of the night for no apparent reason.

If one of you is taking a tough line on some aspect of discipline, it will help you both to discuss why this is. If the answer is, "My father always made me and it never did me any harm," it will not help to shout back that your own father was quite different and that you grew up fine.

An understanding, gentle, sympathetic exchange of views with your partner may reveal deep childhood fears and anxieties. Sharing your emotional problems will help you both to decide on the sort of discipline you want to give your children.

Many people who have been brought up very strictly are determined not to copy their parents, but it can be surprisingly hard to grow from a repressed child to a trusting and kindly parent. If your partner comes from this type of home you may need to show him that affection is all important – far more important than obvious discipline. But perhaps your own background, too, was unnecessarily strict and in revolt you have become rather slack and undisciplined yourself.

You should understand, then, that it is possible to be too "soft" and that, although your partner may be an exacting parent, it stems from good motives.

However, even if you both accept that as parents you can achieve more through love than through fear, this does not mean that any attempt at discipline has to be seen as repressive or too tough. No child is going to have his spirit squashed because you teach him to be co-operative and considerate. You are right to believe that praise can achieve more in a small child than punishment, but when childish tantrums rage, and home is dominated by a yelling child, your partner may be right to insist on discipline.

There comes a point in the life of every family when parents have to discuss ideas of discipline and what each of you expects from your children. If you do not sit down and seriously exchange ideas, and share the problems of parenthood together, the disruption caused by your children may well break your own loving relationship.

Many parents can become victims of their children, and of their own empty threats. We have all heard fathers growl, "Do that again and I'll ..." or mothers shout, "I'm telling you for the last time ...". Your children soon learn that such warnings are meaningless and therefore disobey both of you. This, in turn, causes both of you to grow angry with each other, with accusations such as, "It's your fault he's naughty – you never mean what you say."

Real problems arise over serious disagreements waged in front of your child. If one of you constantly undermines the other's efforts at discipline or you belittle your partner's values, your child is left in the nasty position of choosing sides, or playing you off against each other. Your child will learn to manipulate you and may well destroy the relationship between you and your partner.

Looking after your marriage will help you to look after your children with more patience and understanding. Thrash out your problems as parents. After all, this is something you are in together; you both created this family; you share this family and it is sad to let the demands of your child separate you from each other. The happiest homes are those in which the parents support each other.

Imagine how confused and angry we would be if the laws of the land changed from day to day or hour to hour, and you will have some idea of the way constantly changing the house rules affects your small children. If they feel insecure and always uncertain and bewildered, they will become more difficult to manage.

Of course, you are not expected to be perfect and, of course, your child accepts differences in his parents. Dad may be tidier and is irritated by mess, Mum may demand more help about the house. These things are not difficult for a child to understand, but constant bickering over him and his behaviour will upset him very much. Children who feel they have caused their parents to fight often display symptoms of withdrawal. It may be better to be direct and show that you are angry with your child, rather than turn on your partner.

If you feel that you and your partner are growing further and further apart, and having horrible quarrels over your child, it might be a wise move to try to sit down calmly and have a serious discussion about it without resorting to angry accusations or recriminations. Try to pinpoint those areas where you disagree and try to identify how important they are. If you cannot compromise by meeting your partner half-way on a particular issue, it may be that you can learn to accept his view on one aspect of discipline, and that he will accept your ideas on another.

You should also make an effort to consider your child and his needs and responses. Much of your fury and anger is quite unnecessary if you as parents realize that very small children have mysterious needs – and a logic all their own. What may seem irrational and downright naughty to you may make perfect sense to your son. It is when you impose your own values and timetables and totally ignore those of your child that stress and tension occur.

For instance, you spend hours dressing your little boy, while your partner is hurrying you because you all need to keep an appointment. As you get the child to the door, he starts crying because he wants to wear his red shoes. You get cross, your partner shouts at you to go upstairs and change the wretched shoes, and you yell that you've spent hours dressing the child. Meanwhile your little boy sobs even louder in his distress.

Now, if you both accept that your very small child has a right to approach the world in his own way, you will allow him to have his red shoes. It may delay you by five or ten minutes, but so what? It will save an unpleasant scene and more important, your child will absorb kindness and consideration from your behaviour.

Another frequent cause of anger is a child's inability to concentrate for more than a few minutes at a time. A two-year-old finds it very difficult to sit quietly for 20 minutes and eat his food. He may need to look around, play and perhaps even sing between every mouthful.

This kind of behaviour can drive impatient adults crazy. His father may start shouting at you for not "teaching" the child to eat properly; you may feel inadequate and upset. But why not try to understand your child instead of blaming each other? You should agree to let the little one eat at his own pace, and you should understand that he will learn, slowly, from his parents' behaviour that, during mealtimes, a person sits down to eat, not play.

You and your partner may have grown so far apart because of the unexpected ways of your baby that, for the sake of keeping your family together, you may have to resort to a programme that you both accept and which will guide you both. It is vital that you also recognize that your child will not understand your programme, but that he will absorb discipline from your behaviour, and he will gradually begin to follow your programme. Remember, he is unlikely to gain much benefit from your quarrels.

For instance, you may agree – as parents – to start at a simple basic level: a family timetable. Admit that it will take time and patience, but you will work together towards the same aim.

Both of you will be amazed at the soothing effect this simple shared discipline will have on family life. First, the joint decision to follow regular times for meals, baths and bed will bring you closer as parents and, secondly, your child will come to welcome the routine.

Surprisingly, perhaps, children respond well to a routine. They feel secure with a controlled and predictable pattern and it helps to calm and relax them. They become easier to manage, and you will find that you as parents have fewer occasions to become tense and irritated with your child and therefore you are not continually yelling at each other. What appeared to be huge differences between you may disappear when the family has accepted a regular timetable of sleeping and eating.

Remember, you are no longer just a couple, but parents. The happiness and stability of your family depends on both of you. Your abilities to make mature decisions, and loving compromises, will bring you and your children the pleasures of a closely bonded family, and the affectionate friendships which exist in a happy home.

Key factors in effective discipline

● Try to minimize conflict by agreeing a mutual stand on key conflict issues such as bedtime.

● Determine to back each other up over discipline and not to allow the children to play one of you off against the other.

● Make time for each other so that you can discuss calmly and out of earshot of the children your misgivings over discipline or any problem behaviour in your children that worries you.

● Agree together to adopt a positive approach, rewarding and praising good behaviour, rather than a hostile negative approach.

● Set a good example by adopting standards of behaviour yourselves which you want your children to copy.

● Childminders and nursery groups bring different disciplines to bear in your child's upbringing. Look for stability when choosing.

Try to ensure that your childminder does not have views on discipline which differ markedly from yours. Try too to ensure that your child has consistent care and is looked after by one person regularly, rather than being moved from one to another.

Discipline in a nursery or playgroup will be different from that at home. But when choosing, visit several groups and opt for the one that seems to match your own ideas most closely.

◆ See also, **Smacking**

Divorce

No matter what the reasons for separation or divorce, it is important not to burden your child with your doubts and anxieties. Rehearse what you are going to tell him and try to anticipate the questions he is likely to ask so you can deal with them sensitively, and honestly.

Break the news at home, not while out on a special treat planned to lessen the blow – as it almost certainly will not. In fact, it would be cruel: one moment your child is having a happy time and the next his secure little world is in ruins. If possible, you and your partner should tell him together, because however bitter either of you may feel, your child needs you both.

Research has shown that even where there are tensions in a household, the child usually prefers that to "losing" one parent.

If your child is scarcely out of babyhood, sit him on your lap where he can derive immediate comfort, and say simply that Daddy is going to live in another house, but he will be coming to see him often. Very young children cannot cope with much detail. Just answer any questions as gently and truthfully as possible.

With an older child, be prepared for a variety of reactions. Let him express his feelings freely, and always listen carefully. He will almost certainly do his utmost to persuade you to stay together. There may be tears, pleading, anger, or even threats, such as "I don't want to live with either of you. I will run away." He may try to be brave, even defiant: "I don't care, because you don't care about me or you wouldn't do this."

Such reactions are hard to take but your child has just had an enormous shock and this is his way of coping. It would be unwise, and cruel, to stem the tide with false assurances such as, "Don't be upset. It is just for a little while so that we can sort things out. Then everything will be alright." All too soon he will see that you lied.

When your child calms down a little, say that you do understand that the news is very upsetting but Daddy is only moving out of the house, not out of his life. Explain when he will move and how often he will come to see him. Assure him also that you both still love him just as much – and always will.

Even where the child has been the unwitting cause of the separation, do not burden him with the fact. If you decided, for whatever reason, that his safety or general well-being is at stake if you remain with his father, then that is your concern. Try not to apportion blame to anyone involved – and that, of course, includes yourself.

If you handle this stage well, your child will not be shattered by the experience. Children can be very resilient if they are treated honestly and openly.

However low you feel in the first few weeks or months, never complain to your child about his father. Such confidences are inappropriate and say loud and clear that you don't like Daddy, and want him to take your side. The child needs you both and, whatever his age, he is already having to cope with rapid growth and development, without having to experience divided loyalties, too.

It could have serious long-term effects on your child, however bitter the break-up, if his father completely disappeared from his life – even if that is what you would prefer. "Why did my father abandon me?" he will ask himself, and you, over and over again. So do encourage his father to maintain regular contact wherever possible.

Even if he insists that he must get right away and cannot be relied upon even to write, try to keep in touch with his family. Grandparents can play a vital role in your child's development and many do not want to be cut off from a loved grandchild. Uncles, aunts and cousins can also help to fill the void. However, be careful not to voice anger or bitterness at the way things have worked out, or try to make them take your side. Simply show that you appreciate and value the relationship.

Ideally, agree access without recourse to the courts. If you can do this, all future negotiations between you will be much easier and are more likely to be fruitful. It will also place less strain on your child.

It is important, too, that visits are as frequent and regular as possible. This will restore your child's confidence in you both. If, occasionally, his father cannot visit, perhaps because he has to go away in connection with his work or is taking a holiday, tell him beforehand. It will help if he also writes to him or telephones him frequently while he is away.

Try to agree a mutual code of fair play as parents. If, for instance, his father indulges the child with expensive presents or treats while you struggle to buy essentials, that is clearly going to make life difficult. And when you are angry and upset, it is even harder to understand that he may simply be trying to show the child that he loves him too. Because he sees him less often, he over-compensates to ensure that he does not start to grow away from him. So agree at the outset that while occasional treats are a good thing, a spoilt child is not.

It is also mutually helpful if you and your partner can pre-plan and discuss all relevant issues in a matter-of-fact way. If, however, you are abruptly abandoned, contact your local authorities (locate them through the area telephone directory). If you have a local Citizen's Advice Bureau, visit that too. Along with free advice, you can collect leaflets on entitlements.

Another excellent source of information is your library. Apart from useful books, you may find a noticeboard detailing local childminding facilities, playgroups and even any support groups which have been started by parents in similar circumstances.

These groups offer the friendship and support of other single parents, advice and assistance, shops, a free newssheet and opportunities for personal development. They should also help to encourage your confidence and self-reliance.

However sensitive you feel about the break-up, do notify your child's teacher or head of school that your child is now living in a one-parent household, and explain how well or badly he is coping with the changed circumstances.

One in three marriages fail these days, so schools are used to the effect this can have on children and try to help them through this difficult time. If your child seems inattentive, unusually silent or even disruptive, he will receive a more tolerant reaction if they understand the cause.

Often, the most difficult problem that you have to face is the sudden and dramatic drop in income, even if the parting was amicable and the father has made an allowance or is giving some support.

If you have as job, think twice before giving it up to spend more time with your child as a compensation. If you make good provisions for his care during your absence, he may benefit more from the extra income.

Perhaps you could arrange for a close relative, friend or neighbour to collect your child from school and look after her until your return home each evening. Agree some financial arrangement or offer return childminding one evening each week.

Alternatively, your local social services department may put you in touch with a registered childminder or nursery. Now that women's importance in the workplace is gaining wider recognition, a few employers are providing crèche care, so this may be another option.

You might also consider working part-time until your child is older. Job-sharing is a common arrangement now in areas such as banking, teaching and some large department store chains. Shops often welcome Saturday staff so, if your ex-partner has your child on Saturdays, this could be an opportunity for you to earn extra money – and make new friends.

If your child is under school age and you feel you cannot leave him in anyone else's care, however well qualified, you could perhaps work from home, or set up a child-care group yourself. Keeping busy is a sure way of keeping despair at bay – and if you are happier your child will be happier too.

Doctors

In recent years there has been a move away from the individual family doctor, working alone or with one partner, towards group practices. Your doctor is now much more likely to be one of a group of doctors working in partnership, sometimes with a trained nurse to help with routine matters. These people, together with health visitors and district nurses are collectively known as 'the primary health care team'.

You will probably find that your doctor (or the doctors in your local practice) prefers to treat everyone in a family to get an overall picture of the pattern of health in the family, and you will in any case probably prefer this. Usually in a practice with several doctors you will be allocated, or be able to choose, a particular doctor who is the one you normally see, except in an emergency.

The doctor's work is to resolve all the medical (and often emotional and psychological) problems that are brought to the surgery. Many of these problems can be dealt with immediately, but sometimes another opinion or special tests may be needed, and you may have to take your child for an X-ray or blood test, to a specialist, for out-patient treatment, or for admission to a hospital as a result of seeing your doctor.

Make sure that you know your practice's routine for making appointments and visiting the surgery or clinic. For example, your group practice may have a special "Well Baby" clinic for routine checks, immunizations and so on, so you may only need to visit the surgery for appointments when the child is ill. If you are not sure whether a visit is necessary, remember that many doctors are happy to give advice over the phone, and may have times of day allocated for this. They may also prefer to telephone you back rather than receiving a call from you. Check this out with the receptionist, and arrange to be available at the appropriate time.

Remember, too, that the receptionist can often give advice on whether it is necessary to see the doctor, and if so, how urgently. As a general guideline, however, you should see your doctor without delay if your child has:

● high temperature (over 39°C/102°F, or over 38°C/100°F for over two days)

● difficulty in breathing, with wheezing

● severe pains in the abdomen

● fits, or unconsciousness

● diarrhoea or vomiting in a baby or young child, if the attack carries on for more than a few hours

● persistent headaches or dizziness or disturbed vision

● prolonged loss of appetite.

If the condition seems life-threatening then call an ambulance or take the child straight to hospital yourself. If the condition is serious (for example if a baby or small child has been vomiting for several hours, or if any child has a temperature of 40°C (104°F) or more which you cannot reduce by sponging and paracetamol), call your doctor urgently, but take the child to hospital if the doctor can't be contacted.

If you are worried about your child yet feel reluctant to call the doctor out it may be possible to arrange to take the child into the surgery and be seen without waiting. This has the advantage that all the doctor's facilities are at hand for any tests, and, especially if you have a car and live not too far away, it is often the best solution. Some practices even have a special waiting room for anyone who may be infectious, or who needs to be kept comfortable.

But do not hesitate to call the doctor out if you feel it necessary. He or she would rather be called before an emergency sets in, which can often be in the middle of the night.

Children over the age of five can often speak for themselves and answer the doctor's questions about what is wrong with them, but for younger children you will need to tell the doctor about the symptoms.

The doctor will also want to know all the details of the illness from you, and it may be a good idea to make a note of all the details you think relevant beforehand, to make sure you don't forget anything. You should be able to say how long the symptoms have been observable, whether there have been fluctuations in temperature, or any swellings of glands, puffiness, changes of skin colour; whether there has been vomiting, diarrhoea, lack of appetite, headache, pain, loss of consciousness, blurred vision, convulsions. Other questions that may be relevant are what and when the child has eaten, whether you have tried any remedies, and to what effect; whether the child has been in contact with anyone ill, and any relevant family health matters.

In turn, you may want to ask the doctor some questions, and again, it may help to have these written down. Questions may include: How long can the illness be expected to last? Can the child mix with other children? Will you need to bring your child to see the doctor again? If medicine is prescribed, should the treatment be continued until the end of the prescription or only until the child is better? Should medicine be taken before or after meals, and is it crucial to take it at regular intervals?

Make a note of any advice the doctor gives you as it is surprising how easy it is to forget, because of your anxiety about the child's health. If the doctor gives you advice only rather than a prescription, don't worry, but do make sure that you understand the advice and follow it carefully. Make sure too that you get from your doctor an idea of the course the illness will follow, and don't be afraid to seek his or her advice again if it doesn't go as predicted.

Dog Bites

◆ See **Bites**

Dressing Babies and Children

There's no more tense combination than a new, inexperienced mum, a new, frightened baby and a pile of clean baby clothes. Young babies feel scared and vulnerable when the comfort of their clothing is removed, allowing the air to touch their little naked bodies. Screaming is the natural reaction and one guaranteed to turn an already difficult situation into a fraught one.

As you, a shaking wreck, wrestle with an unco-operative, howling infant, an impenetrable vest and an obstacle course of fasteners, this is when you discover that the smart and costly layette you lovingly bought is a nightmare to get on and off. Clothes that open down the front or with wide envelope necks are always best, because babies hate having their faces covered or being turned over to be done up at the back. Also, clothes that mean you can change the baby's nappy without stripping him completely and with raglan sleeves so that you don't have to force tiny fists through tight armholes will be better for everyone involved.

A newborn baby will be reassured by a hands-on technique. Tuck your hands underneath him for a few moments and talk to him before lifting him up or putting him down. Remember that the changing mat can be a bit cold and hard.

Managing clothes and a baby who has no muscle control takes practice. In the meantime, dress and undress him on a flat surface because it is easier than using your lap. Keep the time he is naked to a minimum, wrap him in a soft shawl and talk soothingly to him. Stretch the neck and armholes of vests and then guide your baby's head and arms gently in without squashing his nose or getting his fingers caught up.

It is easiest to put on a front-fastening babysuit if you lay it out first and put the baby down on top of it. Another tip is, if you concertina the sleeves, you can gently ease in little arms.

As your baby gains some muscle control, you will find it easier to dress and undress him on your lap, especially if you sit with your legs crossed. This will support his lower back against your crossed knee, and with one arm around his shoulder and his head against your body, you have a free arm to ease clothes on and off. Your closeness will also make it easier.

Try to change nappies before they leak and tuck a soft bib or terry nappy under your baby's chin when burping him at feeding time. This way you will avoid having to change all his clothes with the nappy.

Once your baby can crawl, he can escape, so changing happens on the move, with you crawling about after him. Nappies hang lop-sided and battles are fought as the baby tries to get away and you try to get him dressed. Frustrating though it is, keeping calm, humouring and distracting him is likely to work more than holding him down while you dress him by force.

Once he is on his feet, the chase gets more difficult, but at this age he can be distracted by games of peek-a-boo and a hide-and-seek of head, hands and feet as they emerge from the clothes. This should amuse rather than annoy him. Tantrums can often be deflected by using dressing as a time to learn new words.

When your child starts asserting his independence there will come a time when he will insist on trying to dress himself. At this stage, a good deal of diplomacy and tact will be needed as he insists on taking on more than he can manage.

While his furious refusals of help may try your patience to the limit, remember that time spent helping him to help himself means that he will learn skills that will save you time in the long run. It can help to buy clothes that are manageable for a toddler: trousers with elasticated waists; tube

socks without heels; sweatshirts and T-shirts with a picture on the front so that a youngster can tell front from back; coats with toggles or big buttons, rather than difficult slot-in zips; and shoes with easy Velcro fastenings.

Morning battles over clothes are a regular feature in many homes with young families. They're particularly stressful if you work outside the home or need to get your child to playgroup or nursery on time. At a very early age a child develops a preference for some items and an aversion to others. Midwinter mornings will find screaming toddlers intent on wearing a swimsuit, while on summer days they will choose a treasured snowsuit. By the time you are ready to leave the house, everyone is exhausted by the clothes war.

There are several solutions to this. It can help to put away unseasonable garments and party dresses. Another idea is to offer two or three outfits at bedtime so that your youngster can decide for himself what he wants to wear the next day.

Another way to help the mornings run smoothly is to be organized. Five minutes spent arranging clothes in the morning will save fifteen minutes dealing with tantrums. Lay out clothes so that your child can get them on easily. Roll up legs of trousers and put them on the floor so that your toddler can step into them. With his feet in the right holes, you can show him how to bend down and pull the trousers up.

Another solution is to keep clothes accessible. For instance, put coat pegs at child height and keep shoes and wellingtons paired and in a tidy row at floor level. Keep extras simple and to a minimum, mittens on tapes threaded through coat sleeves, rather than gloves, and top coats with hoods rather than woolly hats.

While a parent may find getting a child dressed fraught with confrontation and like taking part in a very trying game of beat-the-clock, for a child it is an important part of his learning process.

If your child simply hates getting dressed, try:

● Turning it into a race with mummy to see who can dress themselves first.

● Offering a game, a book, or a special treat as a reward.

● Putting a star chart on the wall, with stars awarded for prompt dressing.

● Making it all a game, with silly made-up songs like "John can put his vest on" and peek-a-boo.

● Giving lots of praise, applause and cheers for each item put on.

● Buying clothes with nursery or cartoon characters on them, for easy back-front identification.

When shopping for childrenswear, try involving your youngster in making the choice, but don't just turn him loose in the store, otherwise he may end up in tears when you refuse to buy the frilly dress or the garishly multicoloured Bermuda shorts that he's set his heart on. If you select two or three suitable items and let your child make the final choice from these, you will both be satisfied. Taking your child's tastes and choices seriously will instil confidence in his decision-making abilities, tempting as it may be to impose your own preferences.

If a special occasion or particular pursuit calls for particular clothes, don't force the issue. Discuss with your child what he thinks everyone else will be wearing or what clothes he thinks best for the occasion. If he is not easily persuaded and clings to his unsuitable choice, drop the matter for a while, let him wear what he wants and then give it one last try before you go out.

Discovering how to put on a pair of shoes or how to button a coat, or the freedom to select a dress or jumper is all part of learning co-ordination, independence and self-confidence. Such skills take time and parental patience. Ultimately, a child marching proudly down the street in a jumper worn back to front or in brightly clashing clothes is truly a well-dressed child.

Dressing Up

Why do children dress up? The reasons for it change as the child's understanding and interpretation of the world develops and changes and his horizon widens. Children begin to "pretend" more as their language skills improve, and you will find your child plays more sophisticated dressing-up games during the late pre-school years, when he has mastered simple sentence construction and has a fairly extensive and varied vocabulary.

Children start dressing up long before this time, however. As soon as they have developed the physical skills to put things on their heads, you will find them using all sorts of objects as hats. At this stage they will have little concept of being someone else, but they will enjoy the idea of being in control of their environment, and the physical achievement of this activity. They can make the world go dark by putting on a large hat that covers their eyes, then make familiar surroundings reappear by taking the hat off.

Children of just one year find large "saucepan" hats quite hilarious, but do watch that they don't get stuck. Also, don't force young children to put things over their heads – the fun for them is in controlling the situation themselves, and forcing them into it could be counterproductive and even quite frightening. And make sure that there are no plastic bags in reach when your children are at this stage to avoid the risk of suffocation. In fact, plastic bags should not be given to children of any age for the purpose of dressing up.

During your child's second year his dressing-up games will blossom into quite complex scenarios. This type of pretend play should be encouraged as it helps your child to learn and develop in a number of beneficial ways.

The most obvious benefits of dressing-up games are the physical skills required to put on and take off clothes. Putting on shoes – usually mummy's or daddy's to begin with – is the first step towards being able to put on his own shoes. Children love wearing big shoes, not only because they like to pretend that they are grown up, but also because they're easier to slip on and off. Tottering about in mummy's shoes develops balance as well, but keep an eye on young children who can easily trip and fall.

Although most pre-school children will not be able to do up buttons or tie laces properly, you will find that they attempt to do so during dressing-up games. Frustration can result, however, when they fail to complete the task, so select some dressing-up clothes with Velcro fastenings that are easy to fix together.

Just as the one-year-old enjoys the sense of control when putting on and taking off a hat, so the older child uses dressing-up games to acquire control that he does not usually have. In his imaginary world he can be "boss" – directing events and making anything happen. Most young children will start by pretending to be mummy or daddy, using shoes, make-up, a hat or bag as props. Dolls and teddy bears may take on the role of the child himself, and you can't wish for better entertainment than watching your little one telling off teddy, putting him to bed, feeding him, and so on.

By imitating adult behaviour, your child is developing language and social skills – by dressing up he is literally learning how to be grown up. Although "mummies and daddies" is usually the favourite game, pre-school children also love cowboys and Indians, doctors and nurses, firemen, policemen, shopkeepers and, of course, he-man and other cartoon characters.

The most important aspect of his dressing-up game is the idea of being grown up and inhabiting the world at large, but your child is also learning how to put himself in someone else's place. He imagines what it is like to live in the world outside his home, and the clothes and props help to create this environment.

Similarly, characters from books, films or the TV allow the child to create an imaginary world, not necessarily restricted by actual people and places, although you may find that even these fantasy worlds reflect your child's more intimate experiences and their life at home.

You may also find that girls find it easier to adopt feminine roles than boys do masculine ones. This may be because many little boys do not see what Daddy does during the day if he goes out to work, whereas if Mummy is at home all day her role is more clearly defined.

Try not to enforce sexual stereotyping on your child when he is playing these games. Sometimes, we try to slot our children into rigid sex roles at a very early age, which can adversely affect their emotional development. For instance, telling a small boy off for wearing mummy's shoes, but allowing a girl to do it is unnecessary and unfair. And allowing a boy to play a doctor while encouraging a girl to be a nurse is simply reinforcing old sexual stereotypes. Most children who have reached the age of three will have learnt that boys are different from girls. And they are more likely to develop a balanced view of their role and potential within that world if sexual stereotypes are not forced upon them.

Language skills and dressing-up games develop side-by-side. As your child's language improves, you will find speech format and tone become very important in dressing-up and pretend play.

Children will use different voices and speech patterns when they are pretending to be someone else. For instance, "Daddy" will talk in lower tones and speak about things that daddies do. "Telephone talk" is another example. Your child will notice and copy tiny details of speech and behaviour.

He may also pretend to be a few different characters all at the same time, changing clothes, hats and props, as well as his tone of voice to denote different roles. A high, squeaky voice may be "baby" and a controlled, authoritative voice may define a doctor.

Children not only love to dress themselves, but they also like to dress (and undress) others. Pretending to be a parent and putting clothes on a younger sibling is a common game, and because it is often easier to take clothes off than to put them on, children love "undressing" games too. So don't be surprised if you leave two little ones alone for a few minutes and return to find the one with the more advanced manual skills has stripped the other down to nappies – in his capacity as doctor!

Dressing-up also encourages children to care for one another – the "nurse" bandages his friend's cuts, and "Mummy" looks after her babies, cuddling and comforting them.

Dressing-up games sometimes provide an outlet for emotional problems. If he doesn't understand why he has been told off, or if he's upset by a particular event, you may find your child acting out the situation with his teddies. By doing so, he is trying to take on the role of the one doing the scolding and in that way attempts to understand and explain to himself what has happened.

Dressings

A dressing is a protective covering that is applied to a wound. It is used to absorb blood or pus, to control bleeding, to prevent infection or dirt from entering a wound, and to protect it from further damage.

Dressings must naturally be clean, sterile, non-irritant and porous, so that air can enter and sweat can get out. They must also be large enough to cover the wound completely. Dressings are held in place by bandages or adhesive tape.

Usually a dressing is made of layers of gauze, and is applied dry to a bleeding wound, helping the blood to clot. Dressings for burns, which heal to form a crust that would stick to a dry dressing, are impregnated with paraffin, and there are also more complex dressing, which involve layers of packing, and medicated dressings for ulcers, discharging abscesses and large wounds. These complex dressings are usually applied by a nurse or doctor.

Keep a supply of adhesive dressings (known as plasters or sticking plasters) in your medicine chest for use on the small wounds that children get so frequently. These dressings consist of a pad of absorbent gauze or cellulose on an adhesive backing which is perforated to allow sweat to evaporate.

For larger wounds, non-adhesive dressings can be bought in sterile packs for use with bandages or sticking plaster. In emergencies a clean, ironed handkerchief or piece of cotton sheeting can be used to stem the flow of blood while waiting for medical treatment. It is important to apply pressure on the wound through the dressing to help stem blood flow.

Wash your hands thoroughly, and put on thin plastic gloves if available. Use a cotton cloth to clean the wound by dabbing it from the centre outwards, using a fresh area of cloth for each stroke. Do not use cotton wool as this leaves "hair" that may stick to the wound and become infected.

Ensure that the wound looks clean and healthy and that any major bleeding has stopped. Dry the wound with gentle dabbing movements, and decide whether to use adhesive dressing (better for a small wound) or non-adhesive dressing (better for a larger wound).

Your child should not go swimming with a dressing as wet dressings delay the healing process.

Adhesive dressings

Make sure that the dressing is large enough (i.e. that the adhesive part is not on the wound), and that the skin around the wound is completely dry. For a new wound it should not be necessary to apply any antibiotic cream, but if for any reason this has been used, wipe off any excess or it will prevent the dressing from sticking.

Hold the dressing over the wound and slowly peel off the strips while pressing the dressing on to the wound. Smooth down to make sure that the dressing adheres.

Non-adhesive dressings

Use a dressing pad large enough to cover the wound completely, and gently lay the dressing over the wound. Secure a small pad with strips of sticking plaster, or hold a larger dressing in place with bandaging. To make your own dressing, apply to the wound pieces of gauze which have been taken from a sterile pack and cut to size, and on top of these put cotton wool padding, all held in place by means of a bandage.

Dry dressings covering small wounds can be changed every three days, or whenever dirty, uncomfortable or wet. If the wound seems to be infected, change the dressing frequently, and ask your doctor for advice. (Signs of infection are increasing discomfort, swelling or discharge.)

Wet dressings, meant for infected or discharging wounds, and impregnated with an antiseptic or antibiotic substance or with soft paraffin, are usually used only on medical advice. They are replaced daily or more frequently if stained or wet.

◆ See also, **Bandages**

Drinking Liquids

There is usually no need for parents to worry about a child's fluid requirements. No healthy child is likely to take insufficient fluids, thanks to an inbuilt mechanism in the brain – the hypothalamus – which stimulates the need to drink by making the mouth feel dry whenever the body needs more fluids. Equally, it is almost impossible for a child to take in too much fluid.

More than two-thirds of a person's weight is accounted for by water. Part of this water is circulating in the blood plasma, part of it is carried in the body tissues as tissue fluid, and part of it helps to make up the body cells.

A proportion of the water in the body is lost every day, mainly through urine and perspiration (even when the child is not visibly sweating). Some fluid is excreted in the stools, helping to make them soft and easy to expel, and some moisture is breathed out in the breath. Fluid lost in all these ways enables to body to do the vital job of getting rid of its waste products.

The amount of fluid in the body is kept under control by the kidneys, which filter the blood and extract wastes to be passed out in the urine. If there is too much fluid, the kidneys create more dilute urine, and if there is not enough the urine is more concentrated, so that fluid remains in the body. This is when the hypothalamus in the brain steps in and causes the mouth to feel dry so that more fluid is drunk.

Of course, children do not always drink simply because they need fluid. They may drink because they like the taste of a particular drink, because their friends are drinking, or to help their food down, just as grown-ups do. Excess fluid is soon passed out of the body, and the body's fluid content, with its finely balanced salts and sugars, remains the same.

Although it is almost impossible to have too much fluid, not enough can be dangerous, especially in children. This is not likely to happen when the child is healthy and able to satisfy his thirst, but it can arise if the child is ill, either with an infection, especially in the tummy, or with a condition that affects the functioning of the kidneys or the nature of the urine.

Nerves can make a child urinate little and often, but passing an unusual amount of urine, together with abnormal thirst, may mean something is wrong – check with your doctor to be sure.

A child with sickness or diarrhoea and fever loses body fluids. If these fluids are not replaced without delay the child will rapidly become dehydrated. This is dangerous because it means that not enough fluid is circulating to maintain the body's chemical balance and to get rid of wastes, and there is not enough blood to carry essential nutrients to the tissues.

Dehydration can lead to unconsciousness, convulsions, and even death. The smaller the child, the more rapidly this can happen, as such a large proportion of the body's fluids, together with their vital salt content, can be lost in vomit, watery stools and sweat. The first signs of dehydration are general lethargy, irritability and dry mouth. Later worrying signs include sunken, lifeless eyes, dry skin that lacks its usual "springy" feel, and lack of urine. In severe cases there may be drowsiness, coma and convulsions. Give more fluids at the onset of these signs and call your doctor for advice.

A child who is ill does not always automatically feel thirsty and want to drink, and you will need to watch your child's fluid intake very carefully if he is ill. Apart from not feeling thirsty, he will probably not be feeling hungry either, and since a large proportion of fluids usually comes from food, he will need to drink even more to keep the level up.

Try feeding a sick baby on boiled, cooled water, and give an older child frequent small drinks of water or well-diluted fruit juice or squashes. To make sure that lost salts are replaced, use a rehydration mix, such as Dioralyte, which you can buy at the chemist's. Dioralyte can be given to toddlers at your discretion, but not to very young babies without medical advice. Call your doctor if the child is still ill after six hours of this treatment, or sooner if you are worried.

Sources of fluids

Milk provides complete nutrition and fluids for babies before they are weaned. There are many reasons for choosing to feed your baby yourself, not least because breastfed babies acquire their mother's immunity to infections, and seldom have tummy trouble. Remember, if you are breastfeeding you need to drink at least six pints of liquid daily, but be guided by your own thirst.

If you are bottle feeding your baby, you will have to be very careful to mix up the formula milk exactly as advised so that the nutrients are in the right concentration. You must also make sure that you buy "modified" formula, so that your baby does not get too much sodium and phosphate. Your health visitor will advise you on choosing and preparing the milk.

The quantity of milk you give is important. Breastfed babies may sometimes need supplementary bottles. Normal (non-formula) cow's milk should not be given until the baby is at least a year old.

Milk continues to be important long after the baby is weaned, as it is an excellent source of protein and carbohydrates. Your child may happily drink up to a pint (500 millilitres) of milk a day, and this is very healthy. Children need all the nutrients in whole milk and must not be given low-fat milk.

As the child begins to absorb more protein from meat, eggs and cheese, his milk consumption will fall, and you will find that he wants other drinks. As a drink to satisfy thirst between meals, pure water is best, and this can also be given to babies (not, of course, instead of milk). Until the baby is at least six months old, the water should first be boiled and cooled.

Many people prefer not to give their children drinks containing colouring and other additives and some people insist that there is a link between these and hyperactive behaviour. Get into the habit of reading the label when selecting drinks. Remember that the first ingredient listed is present in the highest quantity, and so on to the bottom of the list. Also, "strawberry flavour" does not mean that the drink is made with real strawberries, and look out for unwanted sugar, sweeteners, flavours and colours. You may choose fruit juices instead, but it is not a good idea for your child to drink juice in large quantities, as the natural sugars it contains will encourage him to develop a "sweet tooth" and set up bad habits that may last a lifetime.

Try diluting fruit juice with water, or give the child water with ice cubes in it and call it "juice". A pretty cup or a coloured straw will also help to make water more tempting. For a really nutritious and appetizing picnic drink, combine milk and fresh fruit in the blender. Add crushed ice to the flask before setting off.

Do not give young children salty drinks (such as meat extract or diluted savoury spread), or mineral waters which are not explicitly stated to be suitable for babies (because of their mineral content). Avoid stimulants such as tea and coffee, and never give alcohol to a child – apart from breaking the law, his liver and kidneys are unable to process it, causing a dangerous build-up of toxins.

◆ See also, **Bottle Feeding**, **Breastfeeding**

Drowning

Accidental drowning claims between 700 and 1000 lives each year in the UK alone. Many of the young children who have drowned would still be alive if they had been taught how to swim, the dangers to avoid, and what to do when in trouble in the water. However, even children who can swim should be supervised by someone who will be able to assist if they get into difficulties. For, contrary to popular belief, most people who drown are swimmers. And the majority die within ten metres of the shore.

Often, parents are unfamiliar with a particular stretch of beach and do not realize that the current is too strong for a young child. If a toddler paddling in shallow water slips over, he may be quickly carried out into deep water by the tide.

Most of the deaths occur in inland waters, and this has led many people to assume that it is more dangerous to swim in fresh water than in salt water. It is true that fresh water is less buoyant than salt water, but the main reason for there being more cases of drowning in fresh water is the lack of rescue services in most of these areas. Canals, lakes and rivers are rarely adequately guarded, whereas many holiday beaches are protected by lifeguards employed by the local authority. Even on beaches with no lifeguards, there are usually plenty of other people around who can assist a swimmer in danger or can go and fetch help.

Although swimming accidents account for most cases of drowning, it should be remembered that a young child may easily drown in a paddling pool, or even in the bath, if left unattended.

Drowning can occur so quickly that the child may not be able to call for help or wave to attract attention. So anyone in charge of a child who is swimming should watch for any changes in behaviour. A swimmer in trouble will usually face towards the shore and use the breast stroke, which will cause the head to bob up and down. If the rate of bobbing becomes slower, this may indicate that the child is tiring. As he slows down, his body will become nearly upright in the water. And, if he becomes exhausted, he will stop swimming and float vertically, with the head just above the water. He may be unable to raise his arms to attract attention as this would make him sink. Difficulties with breathing may prevent him from calling out. At this stage, he may also become disoriented and no longer be facing the shore.

In most cases of drowning, the victim panics and as a result loses control of his breathing. What then happens is that water enters the lungs and the victim suffers from a lack of oxygen. Technically, death results from asphyxiation.

A child who has got into difficulties in the water can be saved by prompt, effective resuscitation. As soon as the victim has been brought to the shore, he should be turned on one side so that the mouth can be cleared of any obstruction. He should then be rolled on to his back with his head tilted backwards to prevent the tongue from obstructing the passage of air. Then he should be given five rapid breaths of mouth-to-mouth artificial respiration.

This may be sufficient to ensure that the child continues breathing normally. To check, put your cheek in front of the child's mouth. The skin of the cheek is fairly sensitive and will normally detect even weak breathing. If the child is breathing, he can now be turned on to his side again and nursed in that position. However, if he is not breathing, artificial respiration should be continued for at least an hour. Children should be given one breath every three seconds – a faster rate than the one which is recommended for adults.

To check that the heart is beating, place your ear against the centre of the child's chest. In the event of a cardiac arrest, firm intermittent pressure on the chest must be given alternately with artificial respiration. This makes the task of resuscitation very tiring for a single person so, if possible, two people should be employed. The layperson can learn these skills properly only by attending a course and practising on a dummy. Trying it on a healthy person may cause harm.

Even if the child seems to be recovering well, he should be taken to hospital. There a doctor will check the child's temperature, heartbeat and level of oxygen in the blood. The oxygen level is often low in such cases, so the doctor will probably give the child oxygen to breathe.

The doctor will also check the lungs to see how much water has been inhaled. A child who has inhaled water runs the risk of developing a form of pneumonia several hours after the accident in the water. Some years ago, this was nearly always fatal but, with a better understanding of the physiology of the lungs and with the development of improved hospital equipment, this rarely occurs today.

Drowning accidents may be prevented by bearing in mind the following:

● The human body floats naturally in water until a large quantity of water is swallowed. Consequently children – and adults – should be taught how to float on their backs with their mouth, and nose, kept above water. If a child is in difficulties in the water he should roll on to his back with arms and legs outstretched until he is spotted and rescued.

● Never let young children out of your sight when you are near water.

● Make sure that your children learn to swim as early as possible – preferably before they start going to school.

● Don't let children float on a lilo in the sea. They may easily be carried away from the shore by the wind or tide.

● Don't let children swim after a beachball that is floating out to sea. A child can quite easily be swept out too.

● Never let a child go swimming straight after a heavy meal. (A light meal should cause no harm.)

● On beaches, look for any signs or flags warning of dangerous swimming conditions.

● Teach children never to stray out of their depth until they are strong swimmers.

● Make children wear life jackets when they go boating.

● Tell children not to panic if they get cramp while swimming. They should float on their back or dog paddle until the cramp wears off.

● Keep garden ponds fenced in while small children are about. Even a few centimetres of water could cause drowning.

● Never leave a baby alone in a bath, even for a few seconds.

● Ideally, try to ensure that all adults in the family learn resuscitation techniques.

◆ See also, **Artificial Respiration**, **Cardiac Massage**

Dummies

If you put a finger in your small baby's mouth, you will be amazed by his powerful sucking ability. All but the most premature babies have a sucking reflex at birth. It is not learnt – it is instinctive and the reason for it is clear. In order to eat, a baby has to suck, whether from the nipple or the teat of a bottle. But many babies also find sucking gratifying even when they are not hungry. It is common knowledge that a crying baby is often comforted by being given something to suck.

But you can't give your baby an empty bottle to suck, because that causes wind, and he won't want a full one when he isn't hungry. He may love to be at your nipple all day – but that's not much fun or very convenient for you. A dummy may be the perfect alternative.

Once you decide that your baby really needs the comfort of a dummy, take care in choosing one and be prepared to try several different types.

A newborn baby has a smaller mouth than a toddler, but even so, he can accommodate a standard bottle teat which is about the size of most dummies. A more important consideration is the size of the plastic mouthpiece.

This must be small for your newborn, so that it does not obstruct his nose. If you are buying for a toddler, make sure it is large so that he can't put the whole dummy in his mouth and choke on it.

Orthodontic dummies have a flattened teat, but the more conventional types have a round shape. You can try both to see which your baby prefers, although the orthodontic ones are thought to be better for the gums and

teeth. The shape of the plastic mouthpiece is a matter of your personal choice but make sure that, whatever you choose, it has ventilation holes to guard against suffocation.

Nowadays, dummies come in a variety of colours, and prices range from the cheap to the very dear. But remember that more expensive does not necessarily mean better. It is not a good idea to buy a dummy with fancy trimmings, such as rattling noises. Buy your baby a rattle instead! You will need to buy at least three dummies for your baby so go for the type that suits your budget. Just make sure that it conforms to the approved safety standard. This means that they have been tested for strength and durability, and to make sure that they cannot fall apart or be chewed up during use.

Beware of buying cheap imports which may not have been thoroughly checked and stick to reputable shops or department stores. Never hang a dummy around your baby's neck, and always discard one as soon as its teat is at all perished.

There are no hard and fast rules about how, when or where to use a dummy. It is for your baby's pleasure so use it whenever he wants it. There are some things to consider though.

Your newborn baby's dummy, like his teats, should be sterilized. Follow the methods advised for sterilizing your bottles. Once your baby reaches the stage when he is putting his fingers – and other objects – into his mouth, sterilization is no longer necessary. Obviously, if the dummy falls to the ground, you should wash it before re-use.

Storing the dummies in a container will not only keep them clean but it also makes it easier to find one when you need it. Some dummies come with their own container, but any jar or box will do providing you clean it regularly. Keep a good supply, and put some in strategic places, such as the car, your handbag, at grandma's, and with your childminder.

You can give your baby his dummy whenever he needs comforting, because it satisfies his instinctive urge to suck. Dummies are not a kind of stopper in your baby's mouth, in order to stop him crying. If your baby is crying because he is hungry, wet, cold or in pain, he will spit the dummy out and carry on crying.

Dummies can also help you to establish a routine. If you give your baby a dummy when he is going to sleep, he will associate it with sleep and this will help you to settle him down to a sleeping routine as he gets older.

Some experts even argue that dummies can also help your baby to develop skills with his hands. This is because babies become very attached to their dummies and will rummage round in their cot or pram to find them, and try to put them back in their mouths. This kind of stimulation is an important part of your baby's development.

There are few valid reasons for considering a dummy to be a bad thing. If you use it properly, to soothe your child and comfort him when he's tired, a dummy can be very useful. Do not be frightened off by "horror" stories from friends and relations. As long as you follow simple hygiene care and throw out old, worn dummies you should have no hesitation in using one.

You may dread the idea of your child walking round with a dummy in her mouth when he's four or five years old, but don't despair. Your child will probably discard his dummy himself before this. If, however, it doesn't happen and it does bother you, you can start to limit use of the dummy. Give him a new toy and ask him to give up his dummy in exchange. Distract him with a story, or a drink, or an apple when he asks for his dummy. You can draw comparisons and point out that no one else at playgroup has a dummy – but don't embarrass him. Try and make it seem a fun thing to go to playgroup without a dummy. Gradually, you will reach a point when your child will only need the dummy at bedtime, and then, not at all.

But don't feel you must wean him off the dummy. Remember, small children do become attached to odd items such as a piece of blanket or an old toy, or a dummy, and you should not worry about it. As your child develops, he will naturally drop the old habits and attachments of babyhood, and he will feel happier to do it in his own good time. After all, nobody "weans" their child off an attachment to a teddy bear. The child simply grows out of his need to carry his favourite toy about. The same process will happen to his need for the comfort and habit of sucking his dummy.

◆ See also, **Comfort Habits**

Ear Infections

There are three kinds of ear infection (otitis), depending on which part of the ear is affected. These are known as: otitis externa (outer ear), otitis media (middle ear – this is often known as middle ear infection) and otitis interna (inner ear).

Otitis externa is not usually very serious; but middle ear infection, although it usually responds to treatment, can become serious if it is not treated in time, as it can spread to the inner ear, to the mastoid bone behind the ear, or even to the skull-cavity, as well as occasionally causing a perforated ear drum. This is quite a common complaint in young children. Otitis interna is more serious, but also much rarer.

Otitis externa is an inflammation of the ear canal which causes discharge from the ear, and earache. The flap itself may also become red and feel sore, and it may be dry and itchy. This complaint is particularly common in children who swim a lot. In babies the ear may be red and hot, and the baby will be fretful and restless, and will probably rub at the affected ear or ears.

Otitis externa may be caused by a bacterial or fungal infection, and it can be brought about by an abscess or boil in the ear, a foreign body in the ear or damage caused by probing the ear to clean out wax. Children who spend a lot of time at the local swimming pool may be prone to infection as the skin is more susceptible when wet, and there can be infection in the water.

Otitis media causes severe earache, and, sometimes, temporary deafness. In babies and very young children there may also be feverishness, vomiting and diarrhoea. Sometimes there is a sudden discharge from the ear, which may make it feel better. Although the attack of middle ear infection is usually preceded by a cold, sometimes a child is subject to chronic infection (attacks that follow on from each other and never clear up properly).

Middle ear infection can be caused by an infection travelling inward from an infected outer ear, but is often a secondary infection resulting from a cold, sore throat, or enlarged adenoids. The bacteria or viruses responsible pass down the Eustachian tube, which links the back of the nose and the middle ear cavity.

Young children are particularly prone to middle ear infection because their Eustachian tubes are short and narrow, and infection can easily pass down them.

Especially when it is bacteria that are responsible for middle ear infection, the infection can become chronic if it is not treated successfully. This means that it lingers and recurs, and this can lead to glue ear.

Otitis interna is a much rarer condition that occurs only in conjunction with other diseases. It may spread inward from the middle ear if the child has middle ear infection, or outward from the meninges (the lining of the skull) if the child has meningitis. In either case the symptoms already present with the primary illness will worsen and there will be severe ear pain, but there should be no danger of the symptoms going unrecognized, as the child will already be treated for the primary infection.

Treatment

The treatment of otitis externa will depend on the cause. The child should always be taken to the family doctor, but in the meantime you can gently wipe away any discharge with a clean flannel dipped in warm water. Look inside the child's ear in case there is an obvious foreign body which you could easily remove, but do not try to remove anything that you cannot get hold of easily and do not put anything in the child's ear as this could damage the ear as well as pushing the object further down the ear canal.

While waiting to see the doctor you can give the child paracetamol to soothe the pain, and fix a pad of cotton wool over the ear, using adhesive dressing, to absorb any discharge. Alternatively a wad of warmed cloth or a hot water bottle wrapped in a towel can be placed against the ear to ease pain.

Your doctor will then remove any foreign body, lance and drain an abscess or boil, and clean the ear. If the condition is caused by an infection, he or she may prescribe antibiotics or other ear-drops or antibiotics to be taken by mouth.

The child will not be allowed to go swimming until the inflammation has cleared and will be advised to keep his ears dry when bathing. It will also be as well not to wash his hair until the condition has cleared. This may take up to a week or ten days, although if the trouble is caused by a fungal infection it may be more persistent and a further course of treatment may be necessary.

For middle ear infection, the home treatment is the same as for otitis externa. Any pain can be eased by paracetamol or by a warm cloth or wrapped hot water bottle being placed against the ear, and the child should be taken to the doctor.

The doctor will probably prescribe an antibiotic to clear up the infection if it is caused by bacteria, or to prevent bacterial infection from developing if the cause of the otitis media is a virus. Additional drugs may also be given as nose-drops or nose spray, to help unblock the Eustachian tube. It may also be necessary to make a small surgical incision, under anaesthetic, to relieve the pressure on the eardrum and prevent the eardrum from becoming perforated. This will involve a short stay in hospital.

Sometimes the pressure relieves itself as pus perforates the eardrum. If this happens the pus will usually drain away to the outside of the ear, the eardrum will soon heal, and the child's hearing will return to normal. The doctor will keep a close check on the child's progress to make sure that complications are not developing.

If the child has otitis interna as a complication of another disease the strong antibiotic treatment being given for the main disease will also treat the otitis. There is, however, a slight risk that permanent damage may be done to the ear.

◆ See also, **Earache, Glue Ear**

Earache

Earache can be caused by impacted wax or a bad cold, by tooth decay or even a boil. The outer ear infection, otitis externa, can also sometimes result in earache. But severe earache in children is usually caused by middle ear infection (otitis media).

Often a child or baby with earache will be very distressed, and there may be a high temperature. Babies with earache may rub their ears, or be obviously in pain.

Children under five are particularly prone to middle ear infection, and the main symptom is bad earache. This is usually preceded by a sore throat or a cold, as the infection starts in the throat and travels up the Eustachian tube. Discharge from the ears and some loss of hearing can also sometimes occur.

Always seek medical attention for these symptoms, as untreated middle ear infection can spread, causing perforation of the ear drum and infection of the inner ear, which can lead to permanent deafness.

If the earache is caused by an infection the doctor will prescribe a course of antibiotics.

A warm cloth held over the ear can help to soothe pain, and a cold one will help if the ear feels hot. The doctor may advise you to give paracetamol to control the pain.

Earache caused by impacted ear-wax should be treated by a specialist. If the pain is caused by the child having pushed something into his ear, it should be better when the object has been removed.

The ears are very complex and sensitive, and you must treat a child's ears with special care:

● To clean a child's ears, wash them gently with soft cotton wool. Never insert any object (including cotton buds) into the ears.

● Any discharge, pain or loss of hearing should always be reported to your doctor straight away.

● If a child has pushed any object into the ear, see your doctor. Do not attempt to remove the object yourself.

● Remember that it is easy to inflict serious damage on children's ears.

◆ See also, **Ear Infections**

Eating Problems

As a parent you naturally want your child to eat healthy nutritious meals. Just like adults, children need food for energy and to fight off infections but they also need it to fuel the amazing amount of growing they do – by the time he is two years old, your child will weigh roughly four times his birthweight. A diet with a lot of variety is an almost certain way to make sure a child gets all the nutrients he needs.

It's not surprising, therefore, that parents become concerned and anxious when all their child wants to eat is, for example, chips, peas and chocolate milk. Two or three days of this as a steady diet won't have a greatly adverse effect but when days stretch into weeks or months and concern mounts, it can be hard to stop your worry coming out as anger and frustration against your stubborn child.

The most common reason for unhappy eating is attention-seeking and a first show of independence. It does not take long for a three-year-old to realize he can be the centre of attention of the whole family by refusing to eat or insisting on eating in front of the television rather than at the table.

The simple cure for this type of unhappy eater probably doesn't have anything to do with food or family meals. Try to work out why he is seeking extra attention. It may be his way of crying out for one or both parents to spend more time with him, for a number of reasons: from jealousy of a new brother or sister to disappointment at changing to a new childminder.

If there is a new baby in the house, your older child may well be put out now that he is having to get used to the idea of his parents sharing their affection rather than showing it all to him. Mealtimes particularly can be a major source of unhappiness, as they reinforce the fact that he is no longer the baby, but expected to behave more like an adult.

It is small wonder that he feels jealousy as he sees his mother cradling the new arrival while feeding him, looking into his eyes and generally excluding him, the older child. If you think this may be the cause of your child's mealtime misery, try to give him lots of attention while he is eating. Spoonfuls of food can be delivered into his mouth in a fun "here's-the-train-going-into-the-tunnel" way, and he may need help with cutting things up. Don't expect him to be all grown up just because he is on to "grown-up" food. The cause of his unhappiness may be quite difficult to work out: he may simply be off his food, just as you would be if you were feeling down, or it could be something more deep-seated. If this is the case it is better to try and find out what the problem is, rather than make food a focus for power struggles and tantrums, in the hope that if he ate properly everything would be all right. In short, if your child feels secure away from the table, he might not make such a fuss and seek attention at the table.

When trying to get to the root of the problem, don't overlook the possibility that your child's loss of appetite or limited food preferences may be due to illness. Some of the most common ailments which affect appetite are: swollen glands, which make it difficult to swallow; a cold, which generally reduces the appetite and often makes food tasteless; very rarely, a more serious problem such as a malformed jaw, can make a child want soft foods only; lack of energy or "slowing down" which can be the first signs of any illness.

If you have any concerns about any of the above, consult your doctor, who will be able to diagnose any real problem.

Often less easy to deal with is the situation when a three- or four-year-old is beginning to feel independent and he wants you to know it. This is when the real battle of wills begins: you insist he eats a "proper" meal or meat and two vegetables, and with steely willpower he insists he isn't eating anything other than ice cream or whatever the current favourite is.

Before the situation develops into a daily confrontation, put yourself in your child's place. As an adult, nobody forces you to eat anything you don't want and you probably eat foods that are far from being considered good for you. Just imagine what your reaction would be if every evening a dish of your least favourite food was placed in front of you, and you were told you had to stay at the table until it was finished.

A small child cannot analyze his feelings easily, and does not have much power over his situation, and has certainly not learnt all the complicated social graces and accepted ways of behaviour that you have. Also, remember that the attention span of a three-year-old is not long, and that sitting still is very difficult when there are so many other exciting things to be doing. Your child, unlike you, is not going to be able to sit tight during supper, eating his food politely and exchanging small talk.

Just as no two children are exactly alike, there are no hard and fast rules for dealing with unhappy eaters. Most childcare experts agree that "mealtime moodiness" is an inevitable phase of growing up and parents must try to remain calm when dealing with it. Your child will almost certainly outlast you if you let a daily battle develop over what he will or won't eat.

There are, of course, some children who just are fussy, or small eaters, just as there are some children who will eat practically anything. And they wont necessarily change as they grow up, either!

As alarmed as you are with your child's unhealthy diet, health problems are unlikely to develop. Before anything serious to his health develops, he may well become bored with his limited diet. A child who is active from morning to night and constantly growing out of his clothes isn't suffering. And what may seem to be "junk food" might not be as lacking in nutrients as you fear.

Even the ever-popular burger and chips has a fairly good range of essential nutrients. The burger is a source of protein and fat, the potatoes provide carbohydrates and protein, the salad garnish will give a small amount of vitamins C and A, and the bun is a source of protein, B vitamins and minerals, and is a good source of fibre too.

A painless, if slightly crafty way of getting your child to eat a variety of foods is to enter into a conspiracy with some of his friends' mums. A child's desire to be like his friends will usually have him copying his friends in no time.

Often, a child who "copy-eats" in this way takes to something his parents have offered him without success for weeks. Rather than be maddened that he wouldn't touch spaghetti when you were trying to tempt him with it, however, try to see it with relief as one battle over, however it was fought.

Sometimes, of course, other adults can thwart your plans for your child's healthy diet. Grandparents, particularly, seem keen to indulge big eyes with sweets, chocolates or ice cream.

If this starts to be a problem, you must explain to the sweetie-giver why you are not happy and ask them to limit the gifts. It wouldn't be fair to expect your child to refuse a tempting present.

One of the worst things you can do when meeting resistance from your child at mealtimes is to get angry even though it can be difficult to keep your self-control. Swallow hard, and when your child announces he has finished (even if he hasn't) and wants to leave the table, quietly take his plate away, rather than entering into a screaming match about him finishing his food. If you can be matter of fact about it, the pressure will lift from your child and yourself and you may be able to avoid a confrontation.

Being positive is another, often difficult, but effective way to get results. Children respond so much better to a positive suggestion than a negative one. "You can have some jelly after you've eaten some more dinner" is much more likely to persuade your child to eat some more of his first course than, "You can't have any jelly until you've eaten your dinner."

Once you have established some ground rules, such as one sweet a day or always sitting at the table to eat, explain them clearly to your child, make sure you stick to them and tell everybody else concerned and ask for their co-operation. An obvious example of a rule to enforce is, if he doesn't eat his lunch there won't be any more food until teatime.

Think carefully however before you announce these rules. Don't impose rules you don't have the time or patience to enforce. It doesn't do any good to tell a child he has to sit at the table until he eats something if you and your partner don't have the necessary hours of spare time to make sure the rule is enforced.

Even if your child is determined not to eat anything, insist that he takes his place at the table together with the rest of the family – eventually he will probably want to join in.

Before you put an overall ban on snacks, think about how active your child is – even the best eaters may become hungry between meals and need an energy top-up, but, equally, be aware that small tummies don't need much to fill them up, so a snack just before a meal can play havoc with your child's appetite.

If you do allow snacks, make sure they are as healthy as possible to make up for the nutrients your child might not be getting at meals. An apple cut into segments can be presented as "boats" and a carrot can be sliced into sticks – making fresh fruit and vegetables look attractive, fun and less daunting for a child. Small boxes of raisins are usually very popular, too, as are cubes of cheese. All these snack ideas are much better for your child than cakes, biscuits, chips, chocolate or ice cream.

When your child becomes obsessional about a favourite food, take time to find out how nutritious it is, and if there are any hazards of eating too much.

Obviously you can't let a young child grow up on a diet of just ice cream but a steady diet of it won't hurt him for a couple of days. Also, ice cream made with whole milk is a good source of calcium; and if you make your own ice cream, you can add fresh fruit and eggs to add protein and various vitamins and minerals.

Fish fingers, another childhood favourite, are actually a good source of protein; and if you make your own, with fish, mashed potatoes, an egg for binding and coat them with fresh breadcrumbs, you can avoid the additives and colourings of bought ones.

The important thing to try to do is to encourage your child to eat lots of different foods and to make food as attractive and tasty as possible. This gives them the best chance to get all the nutrients necessary for healthy, growing bodies.

Try to think positively about what your child will eat, and use this as a basis for making sure he gets as much goodness as you can help. A lot of food's nutritional goodness depends on your cooking methods: steam or boil vegetables in a small amount of water until just tender; cut down on fat in cooking by using non-stick cookware; serve oven-baked chips rather than deep-fried; bake or grill fish fingers rather than pan-frying; scrub vegetables instead of peeling to preserve the nutrients under the skin.

Finally, take heart from all the mothers of healthy, strapping teenagers who still cannot quite believe that their child grew up so tall and healthy on what seemed to be a diet of cola and chips!

Eczema

Many babies and young children suffer from eczema and it tends to fade away as the child gets older. It usually runs in families, although often only one child in the family is affected. Eczema can be precipitated by an allergy but may be brought on by emotional upsets. Often, there seems to be no obvious cause.

Eczema is characterized by inflamed patches of skin, which soon become dry and cracked or covered with tiny red pimples or blisters. This is accompanied by severe itching, and scratching the rash makes it worse, causing wet, bleeding sores and encouraging it to spread.

Eczema usually starts on the child's face and scalp and spreads to the hands and limbs. It is at its worst in the skin-folds, or where clothing rubs against the skin.

Babies who suffer from eczema are sometimes allergic to cow's milk. In families where the allergy is known to exist, breastfeeding will give the child a good chance of avoiding the complaint. If this is not possible, or when the child is weaned, artificial milk based on soya is a nutritious alternative. Exposure to household pets can also, unfortunately, bring on attacks and should be avoided if it is suspected.

Eczema is often associated with dry skin, so the most important part of the treatment is to keep the skin moist. It should not be washed too often, and soap should be avoided as it dries the skin and can also cause allergic eczema.

Ask your pharmacist for an alternative to soap, such as aqueous cream or emulsifying ointment, or add an oil containing liquid paraffin to the bath water. Use bland baby moisturizing creams and keep the skin well covered in cold weather to prevent it from drying.

Doctors sometimes prescribe creams or ointments based on coal-tar extracts or, for short-term use, steroids. These help to soothe the rash but there is no known cure. The main concern is to stop the child from scratching, which makes the rash worse and may lead to skin infection.

Little children can be protected from hurting themselves if they wear cotton mittens, and cotton underclothing and socks will help to stop the rash from getting worse. Wool in particular should be avoided as it can irritate sensitive skin.

Note: It is essential that children with eczema do not come into direct contact with anyone with cold sores (herpes simplex). This is because eczematous skin is vulnerable to the herpes virus and liable to widespread infection if exposed to it.

◆ See also, **Allergies**

Electric Shocks

Electric shocks can be fatal and it is vital to try to eliminate every risk of their happening. Check that you have taken all possible precautions to guard children from danger (*see* Safety).

The effect of an electric shock varies from a mildly unpleasant tingling to severe muscle spasms, destruction of tissue, shock, and failure of heartbeat and of breathing. Even low-voltage electricity can kill in some circumstances.

Although in some cases the severity of the shock can throw the victim aside, usually he is unable to let go of the appliance. In this case, the first thing to do is to switch off the current. If this is impossible, use a broom handle or a wooden chair to separate the child from the appliance. You must act quickly.

Treatment will depend on the severity of the case. If the child is not breathing, artificial respiration is urgent and can take an hour or more. If possible, get someone to call an ambulance while you do this. (*See* Artificial Respiration.)

Do not move the victim unless you have to, as there is a danger of fractures if he fell or was thrown. If there are obvious burns or wounds, get someone to cover them with dressings while you continue to give resuscitation.

If the child is breathing, put him in the recovery position – lying on his front with lower arm behind his bottom, upper arm and leg bent at right-angles at elbow and knee, and with head to one side to prevent choking.

Keep the child warm and reassure him (if conscious) while you are waiting for the ambulance to arrive.

Note: Electric shocks can cause damage to the nervous system, so always get medical attention for any severe shock other than one causing only a brief, mild tingling and leaving no visible mark.

To prevent electric shocks from occurring always:

● Be sure that the wiring in your house is up to standard. If in doubt have it checked by a qualified electrician.

● Use shuttered or covered sockets so that young children cannot put their fingers, or poke objects, into them.

● If you have a standard fuse box, make sure that the fuse wire or cartridge is of the correct rating.

● Switch off, and unplug, any equipment not in use.

● Keep flexes as short as possible and away from children's reach. Do not run flexes under carpets.

● Make sure that plugs are correctly wired and earthed, and replace any damaged plugs straight away.

E Numbers

A food additive can be defined as a substance that is not normally consumed as a food by itself, and one not generally used as a typical ingredient of food. Since the beginning of January 1986, most foods have carried a full list of additives, as well as flavourings and these are described on their packaging as E numbers. High-technology food production and distribution have created a situation in which these additives are necessary, and as a result it has become important for us to be informed about these hundreds of preservatives, artificial emulsifiers, anti-oxidants, colourings and more.

There are known to be links between food additives and various childhood problems, and while at first these theories were treated with some scepticism, evidence is mounting that E numbers can be at least in part responsible for tooth decay, stomach problems, eczema and asthma. It may also surprise you to know that even learning difficulties, diabetes and hyperactivity have been linked to additives.

Some of the additives known to trigger off hyperactivity or allergies include E210, E211, E220, E250, E251, E320 and E321. Another group that is potentially harmful are the "azo dyes" which include E102 (tartrazine) used as a colouring in foods ranging from orange squash to pie fillings and salad cream to fizzy drinks.

The 'E' of an E number in fact denotes that the additive has been deemed safe by the EEC. This does not necessarily mean, however, that they are safe beyond reasonable doubt for all children. While some are essential to keep food fresh and are therefore preferable to the alternative of eating tainted foods, many are used solely for cosmetic purposes, simply to improve the food's appearance. If you suspect that one or more additives may be responsible for your child's allergy or behavioural problems, you might find it helpful to keep a diary of all the food he eats and when. Decide on those you are going to eliminate, and make a note of any changes when you do this.

If in doubt, it is best to stick with fresh, unprocessed, wholesome foods, especially fruit and vegetables when planning meals for a growing child. Most of these will help to boost development and build long-lasting health. Beyond this, always read the small print on labels, and while there is no need to go to extremes, it is best to avoid feeding your baby or child on a steady diet of manufactured foods.

◆ See also **First Foods**, **Food Allergies**, **Healthy Eating**

Exercise and Fitness

Most parents assume that their young children are naturally fit and that they do not need to worry about the amount of exercise they take. Sadly, this is not always the case. Recent research has shown that many of today's children are heading for serious health problems in later life.

Youngsters as young as ten years old have been found with the first signs of heart disease and, although these cause no outward effects at that age, they significantly reduce the child's chances of a healthy future.

In many cases, these early signs of trouble have been linked to unhealthy diets and inadequate exercise – bad habits that are formed in the first few years of life, but which continue on through adulthood.

The good news is that in most instances these problems can be avoided, and preventive measures will not only keep your child in good health, but they may also help to get you into better shape too.

So why are children today generally nowhere near as fit as children were, say, 30 or 40 years ago? One of the main reasons is that they are simply not given as much opportunity to exercise as before. Nearly all of us own a car and transport our children to playgroup, school and the shops without them having to take more than a few steps.

Television has also played a large part in the trend towards inactivity. Young children will often sit passively for hours in front of the box and may find the TV a far more attractive option than playing outside.

As you can see, many of the conveniences we now enjoy and which have supposedly made life so much easier have, in fact, made it more difficult to keep our children and ourselves fit and healthy.

One important factor to bear in mind is that healthy children usually belong to healthy parents, so the first step is to get your own exercise programme into action. Play with your child, walk with him instead of taking the car, go for cycle rides together if he is old enough. If you make sure that you and your toddler are physically active, you will both reap the benefits.

We all need to exercise regularly if we are to stay fit, and although the type and extent of the exercise required varies throughout our lives, it is important that old and young alike keep as supple as possible.

Exercise performs similar functions in children and adults. It increases the strength of muscles, including those of the heart, makes us more supple and improves the capacity of the heart and lungs to carry oxygen around the body. A plentiful supply of oxygen is particularly important to the healthy development of growing bodies. In addition, exercise increases stamina and helps to increase immunity against infection and disease.

Exercise also has an additional, special significance for children because their physical and mental development are very closely linked. Young children learn about the world around them and about their own abilities through physical movement and activity.

Babies and toddlers require different forms of exercise as they grow. A child of five will obviously have greater strength and flexibility than a toddler of three, so it is important to recognize your child's physical limitations and not to push him too far, too soon.

Despite his limited ability to move by himself, a newborn baby is still quite active. Gently massaging his body and limbs will help him relax and keep his body malleable.

By about three or four months your baby will be rolling from side to side, and kicking his legs and waving his arms when he is on his back. Even at this age he is enjoying his physical skills and learning how his body works. Encourage him to move by tickling his tummy and make his legs and arms wave, and try gently bending his legs, then letting go and allowing him to extend and kick them.

As soon as he starts to crawl or move independently, encourage him to use his new-found skills. Do not give him toys but place them just in front of him, or call him to you from a couple of feet away. Before long, his strength and balance will have increased and he will be up on his feet.

At first he will use the furniture and you for balance. Place your furniture around the room so that he can walk from one piece to another. This will give him independence and help him to develop good coordination and balance. When he is ready, try placing some furniture a foot or so apart to encourage your baby to take a few steps without support.

Once your baby is toddling, invest in a toddle truck to help increase his mobility. This will allow him to pull himself up without the truck tipping over, and once up, he can use it as a support as he pushes it along.

If possible, take your toddler for at least one short walk every day, but do remember that he will tire quite easily at this age. Always take a buggy with you so that he can ride if necessary.

Walking hand in hand with your toddler will be very awkward, so invest in some reins. They will allow both you and him to walk more comfortably, and will prevent him from running into the road. He will not be able to control his speed or to manoeuvre around obstacles very easily either, so avoid walking around shopping centres and other areas which may be potentially dangerous. Slippery floors should also be avoided if possible. A walk to the park will give him more freedom to run around and will be less trouble for you too. The air will probably be cleaner here as well.

Some children may demand to be carried home, even when they are obviously not tired. Do not mistake this for laziness. All children have a natural instinct to stay with their parents. He knows that you can walk faster than him and is afraid that he will be left behind. Scolding him or walking ahead, hoping that he will catch you up, will make matters worse and he may then become reluctant to go for walks if this happens, so carry him or take a buggy with you. Many of these are lightweight and easy to carry.

By your child's third birthday, he will be confidently running, jumping, climbing, skipping and hopping. Make the most of this time and encourage him to practise using his whole body to perfect co-ordination and balance, and to increase suppleness, stamina and strength. It will be good for you, too.

Contact your local sports centre and enquire about toddlers' exercise classes. These are becoming increasingly popular and offer a good opportunity for your child to meet others of his own age in a safe, active environment.

Gymnastics and dance classes are open to children of about three and over, and, as well as being great fun, will help children who are not naturally well co-ordinated to learn greater body awareness.

If your child obviously dislikes a particular activity, do not force him into it, but do encourage him to take up a different one.

You will find that toddlers use physical activity to express their emotions. They will jump, run and squeal when they are happy and stamp their feet in anger when they are upset. Try not to suppress your child's physical outbursts – you may risk repressing his emotional development and his enjoyment of physical activity. For instance, he may not understand that he can be happy, without running about.

Try to ensure that your toddler is physically active every day, and don't expect him to play boisterous games on his own – he will need you or other children to stimulate activity. He will also require close supervision when playing strenuous games to guard against overtiredness or injury.

Remember to get into the habit of warming up with your child before exercise with gentle, stretching movements. Do the same to cool down after the activity. An instructor at your local sports centre will show you how to warm up if you are unsure.

You might consider some of the following activities, all of which can contribute to your child's physical well-being:

● **Cycling** – improves muscular strength and co-ordination. Ensure that any bicycle you purchase meets the British Standard, and don't let your child cycle unsupervised – he will not be able to control his speed easily until he is older.
● **Swimming** – buy him some arm bands and ask at your local pool about lessons for toddlers.
● **Walking** – get to know your environment. Make your walks more interesting by pointing out different birds, insects, flowers and animals.

● **Exercises at home** – lie together on your backs and "cycle" with your legs, or try frog jumps by crouching down and then springing up.

● **Racing** – race your child to the nearest tree or marker, allowing him to win occasionally of course.

● **Jumping** – try jumping holding a soft ball between the knees. This will strengthen leg muscles and increase co-ordination and balance.

And these are games for toddlers will help increase stamina and strength.

● **Tag** – your child will love to be chased and to chase you, but do remember that he will want to be caught after a very short while.

● **Jumping beans** – increases co-ordination, balance and stamina. Jump in the air from standing with both feet, bending the knees as you land. Encourage your toddler to imitate you.

● **Football** – a young toddler will not yet be able to catch but he will be able to kick a ball, although not very well. Nevertheless, he'll enjoy the game and it will help to increase his co-ordination, balance and stamina.

Try not to overprotect your child – he may fall when physically challenged, but over-anxiousness on your part may raise unnecessary fears and prevent him from fulfilling his true potential. Don't leave him unattended during exercise, and stop him if he shows tiredness, stress or pain. Don't allow others to egg him on and force him beyond his physical limits, and if your child is completely fearless and attempts dangerous feats, don't congratulate him if he succeeds. Firmly explain that his tricks are dangerous and that he will hurt himself – he may lean this lesson on his own, but don't tempt fate.

Note: If your child has breathing difficulties, a heart complaint or physical handicap, consult your doctor before any strenuous exercise. This applies to children of all ages (and parents, too).

◆ See also, **Dancing**, **Gymnastics**, **Swimming**

Eyesight

Imperfect eyesight is technically known as refractive error. It is usually due to physical defects in the eyeball, in the lens, or in the muscle which adjusts the lens.

The image on the retina will not be properly focused if the cornea is imperfectly shaped, so that light rays are distorted by it, or if the lens is insufficiently elastic or the muscles controlling it do not change shape sufficiently. If the eyeball is too long or too short the image will not be accurately focused on the retina, and will be blurred.

Short sight

If the eyeball is too long or if the cornea is too steeply curved there will be good close-up vision, but poor distant vision. This is easily corrected by spectacles.

Long sight

This is also frequently caused by the imperfect shape of the eyeball, with the eyeball being too short from front to back. This too can be corrected by spectacles. A child is usually born long-sighted, and diagnosis often follows complaints of eye strain or fatigue.

Astigmatism

This is a very common defect, caused by the cornea on the front of the eye being imperfectly rounded, so that a distorted image is formed on the retina. Again spectacles can cure the problem by compensating for the defective cornea.

See a qualified optician for a professional opinion if you suspect that your child is having any problems with his eyesight.

Fainting

Fainting, known medically as syncope, is a sudden loss of consciousness, usually preceded by a feeling of weakness and giddiness, and sometimes nausea as well. A child of any age can have an attack of fainting, but it is quite unusual except in adolescence.

A child who is about to faint will feel weak and giddy. His skin will look white and feel clammy, and his breathing will become quick and shallow. When he faints, he will fall to the ground and will usually regain consciousness within a couple of minutes. One cannot faint in a lying position – only when sitting or standing.

Fainting is caused by a reduction of the blood supply to the brain triggered by a reflex in the vagus nerve that slows down the rate of the heartbeat. It can also be caused by low blood pressure and by a low blood sugar level. In some children (and adults) the reflex in the vagus nerve is particularly sensitive, causing them to faint more readily.

Fainting can be caused by standing still for too long, which makes the blood accumulate in the legs rather than circulating in the body. It can also be brought on by standing up suddenly, if the blood vessels fail to adjust quickly enough as the body changes position.

As in adults, fainting in children can be caused by a stuffy room, which can affect the supply of oxygen to the brain. Emotional shock can cause fainting, triggering the reflex in the vagus nerve; as can excitement, for example at a pop concert or a party.

There can be a lack of nutrients, especially sugar, in the blood before breakfast, and it is wise to make sure that all children always eat something before rushing off to school, especially those prone to fainting.

Any parent concerned about fainting in a teenage girl should make sure that her daughter has plenty of iron in her diet by giving her liver, meat, cereals and green vegetables. Fresh fruit and vegetables supply the vitamins without which red blood cells cannot function properly.

If you are worried by your child having frequent fainting attacks and you know that he has a good diet and regular meals, see your doctor.

In most cases fainting treats itself. Once the body is flat, blood reaches the brain and recovery is fairly rapid. Keep the child flat with the legs elevated while he recovers consciousness. Also discourage your child from getting up too quickly after a faint, to prevent another one. If you see that a child is about to faint, encourage him to sit with his head between his knees or to lie down for five minutes.

Falls

As they begin to walk, young children fall constantly, and rarely come to much harm. Even children from about three to seven almost never hurt themselves seriously when they fall down because their joints and bones are very supple.

Older children are less prone to falling but when they do, their injuries are often more serious. This is partly because they are taller and heavier, and partly because their bones are not as supple as those of a small child. Furthermore, with older children, accidents often occur when they are involved in fast-moving athletic activities such as football, climbing or horse riding.

Even if there is no visible injury, any child complaining of pain some hours after a fall should see a doctor. Although a young child's bones rarely fracture, it is possible for them to be bent (this is known as "green stick fracture"). Moreover, the main part of the thigh-bone is surprisingly brittle, even in a young child, and can easily be broken.

Head injuries

These are perhaps the most serious injuries resulting from a fall, and often need medical treatment. Again, any child who has had a bad blow to the head should be seen by a doctor, even if there is no visible sign of injury.

If you did not see the fall (and so do not know how hard it was) danger signs to look out for in your child are loss of memory about the accident (this could mean that the child was knocked out), persistent headache, drowsiness, or nausea, giddiness, a squint, lack of balance or a staggering gait.

All these symptoms could indicate concussion. Blood from the ear or nose or a straw-coloured discharge from the nose are signs of possible skull fracture. A child with any of these symptoms should be seen by a doctor at once.

Fractures

In older children, injuries often take the form of a fractured wrist or fractured neck of femur (the part of the thigh-bone between the ball of the hip joint and the main shaft of the bone).

Both these injuries will cause severe pain and swelling, and they are not likely to be overlooked.

Cuts, grazes and bruises

The most common results of children falling are cuts, grazes and bruises, which can usually be dealt with at home.

Treatment of injuries from falls
Serious head blow

See a doctor – the child may be kept under observation for 24 hours.

Unconscious and not breathing

Get someone to call an ambulance. Start mouth-to-mouth resuscitation at once, moving the child only if absolutely necessary.

Unconscious but breathing

Do not move the child. Cover with a blanket (or coat) and call an ambulance.

Suspected spinal or neck injury

Do not move the child. Keep him warm and call for an ambulance.

Suspected arm or wrist fracture

Support the arm in the most comfortable position and take the child straight to a doctor or hospital.

Suspected leg fracture

Call an ambulance and keep the child warm while waiting. Allow the child to move his leg into a more comfortable position, but then keep him still. Do not give him anything to eat or drink in case an anaesthetic is necessary.

Bleeding

For serious bleeding get someone to call an ambulance immediately. Hold a clean pad over the wound, applying pressure, while waiting. For less serious bleeding, hold a clean pad over the wound until bleeding stops. If bleeding is from an arm or a leg, keep the limb elevated to reduce the outflow of blood from the wound.

Bumps and bruises

No treatment strictly necessary. A gauze pad soaked in cold water and applied immediately may minimize swelling and witch-hazel has a soothing effect.

◆ See also, **Bandages**, **Bleeding**, **Concussion**, **Cuts**, **Dressings**, **First Aid**, **Fractures**, **Head Injuries**

Family Gatherings

Before you invite your guests, whether it is to an adult party in the evening or a party for all generations at lunchtime, think carefully about the kind of occasion you want. Do you want it to be for all the family, or would you welcome a chance to see your friends without the children?

When planning the event, try to have a clear idea in your head of how you want the occasion to be and whether this will be practicable if there are young children around. Think of ways the children can be entertained and kept happy – for instance, you could set aside a room in the house for children to use, clearing out furniture, putting cushions on the floor, providing children's snacks, drinks, toys and perhaps a children's video.

If, however, you want an evening party of the type you used to have when children were not your prime consideration, then the chances are that your guests will organize a babysitter and come without their families. But what of yours?

You have two alternatives for your child. The first is to tire him out so that he goes to bed early and sleeps through it, or you can let him have a long rest in the afternoon so that he can stay up and make an appearance at the party or join in the fun. This, of course, depends on how you feel and also how likely your child is to co-operate.

If he is unlikely to go to sleep, or is likely to be woken up by the noise, you might do better to resign yourself to it and let him rest in the afternoon so at least he'll be in good spirits.

For family occasions, such as weddings, christenings, birthdays and Christmas, it's best to assume that children will be included and cater for them accordingly.

Remember that some family members can become very put out if they feel excluded from family occasions by not being able to bring their children. Better to ask a few friends to help, or a nanny or au pair to be on hand to supervise the smaller guests. Organize a play area and special tables for children's food so that toddlers do not get trodden underfoot.

At an occasion, such as a christening, the children are certainly going to be the centre of attraction. Christenings are often noisy occasions with lots of young family members around. They are often held in the afternoon and a tea-time party can be reasonably short and easier to cope with for the children – sandwiches and cakes, some party games and balloons, and the children should be happy.

Christmas is the ultimate in family occasions and probably the most difficult to cope with for small children. There is a tremendous build-up to Christmas, with schools and playgroups starting to make Christmas decorations as early as October, and the shops getting ready months in advance. Children often have such high expectations of the occasion that the reality cannot match up to it, with the result that there are tears and tantrums on the day itself.

Even if you are not a Christian yourself, it's worth giving the children something to think about other than presents, chocolates and mince pies. The idea of celebrating the birth of a special baby is one that children respond to, and that this person grew up to be a good man and teacher who helped others to behave better to one another. Some churches have special services for young children, or perhaps grandparents would like to take children to church on Christmas morning to give you all a welcome break from tripping over presents and from one another!

In summer, if the weather is fine, you might like to hold large family gatherings outside. If it is a special occasion and you feel like pushing the boat out, you could hire some equipment to keep the children busy. For a large occasion you could hire a bouncy castle, and for a small occasion, a trampoline, slide or climbing frame. A local toy library or playgroup will either be able to lend out their equipment or tell you where you can hire from.

If you feel you want to make it very much a day for the children to remember, then why not provide some entertainment too? You can think of some simple children's games, such as apple bobbing, a treasure hunt, musical chairs or cushions. And for a really grand occasion, you could even hire a children's entertainer.

Regardless of the type of occasion, you'll need to work out numbers and decide how much food you are going to need.

● If you are serving alcoholic drinks, allow one glass of champagne (for celebrations) per person and half a bottle of red or white wine each. In summer, allow for more white than red wine.

● Provide enough squash or fruit juice for the children and about a quarter of the adults.

● Remember that you will need more alcoholic drink for an evening party than for a lunchtime occasion. As a rule, people tend to drink less alcohol in the middle of the day.

● When preparing food, always over-estimate the amount you will need. You can always finish it up later.

When you send out invitations, make it clear whether you are going to provide a meal or just snacks – there's nothing worse than preparing a delicious feast only to find no one eating because they all ate before they arrived, or to find people wandering around looking hungry.

For a lunchtime party, for example, a variety of salads, with perhaps one or two hot items is likely to be best. Include some rice, pasta or potato salads, which can be delicious and are quite filling. Unless you have plenty of seating areas, choose foods which can be eaten with a fork. Juggling with a knife, fork, plate and glass is too much, even for the most dextrous of guests. For children, sausages, sandwiches and crisps are likely to go down well and should be provided in addition to whatever else you are serving. Slices of quiche or pizza are easy to handle and popular with children.

Always provide a decent alternative to alcoholic drinks for guests who are driving, are pregnant or who can't or don't drink – not just one token bottle of mineral water or orange juice. Try making an alcohol-free punch or fruit juice cocktail, with ice and chopped fruit, served in an attractive bowl or jug, for adults and children alike.

Preparing food in advance can be a problem if you have young children around. You can either prepare it the evening before, while they are in bed, or try to get someone to take them off your hands earlier in the day.

Shopping should also be done well in advance, and preferably without the children, to give you time to think and choose what you really want, rather than having to rush round because the children are misbehaving.

Again, it is important to be realistic and not to try to do something so elaborate that you are going to panic and fail to achieve what you intended. Simple food, well-prepared, is likely to go down better than an elaborate meal which is has been hurriedly prepared.

On family occasions, enlist the help of relatives in advance, if you can. For example, ask grandparents to come early to keep the children occupied while you're making last-minute preparations. You can also enlist people to collect hired glasses, take drinks around, bring items of food, or help with clearing up afterwards.

Remember that children often get very over-excited before parties or big occasions, so it helps not to build up to it too much and to remove your children beforehand, so they aren't too fizzed up when people start to arrive. If you want to dress the children up or have them looking especially nice, keep their smart clothes to one side and put them on only just before the party. And don't forget that some children hate wearing smart or fussy clothes. If your child is one of them, don't spoil the occasion by insisting on dressing him up. Just put on ordinary clothes which your child looks nice in and leave it at that. There might be an outfit that he's particularly fond of – be prepared to compromise for a quiet life.

Once things are in full swing you must:

● Keep objects which are dangerous to children out of reach. This includes peanuts, on which small children can choke, ashtrays and cigarettes, and alcoholic drinks.

● Remember that small children underfoot can get trodden on or can trip up older people, especially the elderly.

● Make sure spills are quickly wiped up – a slippery floor can be dangerous for children and adults alike.

● Make sure babies left sleeping in carry cots upstairs are safe. Keep cats, dogs and other children out of the room and make sure somebody can hear them if they start crying.

● Keep an eye on children if they are playing upstairs or out of sight – when a group of excited children get together, they may get up to tricks you wouldn't dream possible!

Finally, when entertaining, remember to give some thought to yourself, too. You might take time off the day before to go to the hairdresser's or go shopping on your own to buy something new for the occasion. At the party itself, try to find a bit of time to talk to people and relax in between – you can do this by delegating some tasks to others.

Above all, don't expect too much from yourself. You won't be able to escape from having sticky fingers on your clothes or dribbles on your shoulders if you have young children or a new baby. Your parties won't be quite so stylish and you'll also be likely to be a lot more tired. On the other hand, the best parties are often those which have a mix of generations and if you plan things well, the occasion will be one for everyone to enjoy.

Fatherhood

It used to fall to the mother of a pregnant woman to provide a lot of support, but today more and more couples are living away from the extended family. The modern father has therefore in many cases taken over some, or all, of her role.

Understanding the physical changes a woman undergoes during pregnancy can help her partner give her the support she needs. It is important that he is aware of morning sickness, tiredness and backache in particular. He should know when visits to the antenatal clinic are due and even try to attend a few. If he is unable to organize this, he should make a real effort to be at the ultrasound examination at the hospital.

This usually happens in the 17th week of pregnancy, and ultrasound scans are done as a routine to confirm the stage of the pregnancy and that the fetus is alive and normal. Should something unexpected be revealed, such as twins, then it is preferable for both parents to hear this information together.

As the pregnancy progresses and later is more visible, it will be easier to realize its reality. This may not be easy in the early stages when to all intents and purposes you look just the same as before. Your partner will be able to feel the uterus (womb) growing by pressing your tummy. Later on he will also be able to feel the baby kick and hear his heart beating.

At some stage, you will both need to decide on the type of delivery you would like to have and where the baby is to be born. The options will be determined by the progress of the pregnancy, whether it is a first delivery and what facilities are available locally. During the course of the pregnancy most of these things will be explained to you, however, and it is essential that your partner is included in any discussion about the birth itself.

This is the time for your partner to think seriously about attending you in the labour ward. There is a fair amount of pressure for fathers to be with their partners at this time, although 20 years ago it was a rare occurrence. The father must be very careful and honest about his decision. Will he be able to cope with the pain you experience; will he faint at the sight of blood; and will you have to worry about him or do you need him very much? He should discuss all these aspects with you.

Very few men are prepared for the personality changes which you may reveal in pregnancy. The great hormonal upheaval in your body may cause depression and periods of listless fatigue. You may also develop anxieties about the well-being of the baby and very little will reassure you – least of all reasonable, logical talk.

The father will have to learn to tolerate these changes and he must know that these new attitudes are not permanent but simply a result of pregnancy. He will have to call on his own resources of patience and humour. However, if he is aware that this change may occur, he will not feel so depressed or despairing himself.

Once a baby is expected, there are many practical considerations which need attention and the man can certainly find his "fatherhood" role here. The proud and happy young man may rush out and spend a fortune on equipment but he should try and remember that the needs of a new baby are minimal.

Expensive purchases like cots and prams demand some "market research", and it can be quite difficult to find out what the baby will actually need as opposed to what the shops would like to sell.

A DIY enthusiast will come into his own as an expectant father and create a nursery for his new baby. He might also check the safety features of the house before the baby is born, because any major changes must be made during the pregnancy. There is very little time afterwards for even the keenest DIY man to practise his hobby.

As the pregnancy enters the last few weeks you should have your bag packed and ready to take to the hospital, and your partner should know where it's kept. At this stage, you may well be feeling rather miserable and uncomfortable, and backache is a common complaint now, which he can help with massage. You may also be frightened and anxious about going into labour and will need your partner's care and reassurances.

If anything goes wrong with the pregnancy you will both rely on each other for comfort and sympathy. Miscarriages are common but that does not make it less painful when it happens, and the discovery that the baby may be handicapped can be worse in some ways as the parents are forced into very difficult decisions.

For the actual birth, the father should make the arrangements for getting you to hospital when you go into labour. If he plans to take you himself, the car must be in working order and he should organize to leave work at short notice. He will need to arm himself with a pile of coins and a list of phone numbers so that he can use the hospital's public telephone. And he'll kick himself if he forgets the camera for those first pictures of the baby.

When the big day finally arrives, the father must be prepared for his own feelings of stress and emotional turmoil. It is distressing to watch a partner in pain, and hard to cope with the anxious hope that she and the baby will be all right.

You may be far too distracted to even notice your partner. This does not mean that you don't need him and whatever has gone on before, you will long for your partner to be with you after the birth. Most hospitals are very good about allowing parents some time together with their baby.

It can be very strange for the father to return home alone after all the excitement, especially if it is the middle of the night and he cannot share his emotion with anyone.

He will realize very soon, however, that his time is cut out while you are still in hospital. He will probably have to ferry relatives to and from the hospital, and then supply them with tea and cakes when they decide to soothe his loneliness by visiting him at home. No doubt you will give him little lists for this and that, so he will also have to find time to fit in this shopping.

It is an extremely difficult period for a man when he brings his partner and child home. The bond between the mother and the tiny, helpless baby is very intense and intimate. He will struggle with feelings of rejection, and even jealousy. Many fathers feel excluded and left-out and even irrelevant in their own homes.

But he can forge his own bonds with the baby. He should try to take at least two weeks off after the birth, allowing him time for "bonding" with the baby. By frequently holding the baby, bathing and changing it he can feel closer to it. If the baby is bottle fed, he can take his turn at night feeding. All this will give you a chance to rest, and by taking care of the baby and tending to it your partner will not feel so excluded from the closeness of mother and baby.

If your partner is away from home a lot or does shift work, you may need to make greater efforts to encourage him to be involved with the care of your child when he is around. The level of involvement you should aim for is very personal to you both – too much or too little will lead to dissatisfaction.

Whether your partner is the main breadwinner or not, remember that he is not just there to provide material things for his child. He has an indispensable contribution to make to your child's social and emotional development.

The kind of close relationships your child will be able to have when he is older will depend on whether he forms close relationships with people of both sexes in his early life. And you and your partner can help ensure this part of his social development together.

Your partner may be away from the home for much of your child's waking hours. So try to make good use of the time they do have together and encourage them to play together as much as possible. Remember that it's the quality of their time together that's crucial, not the quantity.

Just how much your child is affected by your partner's work schedule will depend on whether or not he has known anything else. If, for example, your partner starts a job which keeps him away from the home longer or means that he works irregular hours, after he has formed a close relationship with your child, then your toddler may find it difficult adapting to this new routine. The daddy he saw each evening is now only around at weekends or less often. But as long as he knows that he does have his own special time with Daddy, he will soon adjust.

Knowing that he is a valuable and irreplaceable member of the family will help give your partner the sense of identity and personal value he needs. But in order to feel indispensable, he must be involved in the day-to-day care of his child.

You may find that the major advantage of shift work is that your partner spends more time at home when your child is awake and in need of care and stimulation.

If, however, your partner's hours do not coincide with your child's waking hours, or if he is away from home a lot, it will take more thought and ingenuity on your part. Start by making use of his time when he is at home. Often it is far simpler to get the baby bathed and ready for bed before you know your partner is due home. By all means do this once in a while if you have a special evening in mind. But otherwise, it will do your family's relationship a power of good if you can share this "end-of-the-day" experience together.

Fathers should take comfort in knowing that although you may be very absorbed by the baby, you still have a desperate need for the security and support of your partner. After all the excitement, the flowers and congratulations, the reality of the new baby may bring you down to earth with a bump. You will again be having changes in hormone levels as your body returns to normal, which might make you weepy. You may be sore from stitches and you may feel distressed about your appearance. Your partner's loving comfort and encouragement will be more important to you than ever before.

Favouritism

Many parents worry before the birth of their second or subsequent child about whether they will love them as much as their firstborn. In reality, there's seldom a problem: it seems that parental love can – and does – stretch to embrace each child, but maybe not as equally, or fairly, as parents ideally would like. All too often, there will be one child who is "special" to one or both parents and when this happens deep resentments and jealousies can develop within the family.

Favouritism is both common and understandable, but it can be destructive if not recognized and faced up to. Many children grow up still feeling the effects of favouritism from their childhood and yet most parents, if asked, would find it difficult to admit to preferring one child above another.

Recognizing that you do have a favourite and admitting those feelings to yourself is, however, the first vital step towards helping the situation. You may not have admitted your favouritism to yourself because you feel guilty about it. You may only be aware that you're more critical of one child than the other, or that you tend to make frequent comparisons.

Once you can admit that you do have a favoured child, you can begin to try to understand why he means more to you. For example, it's often assumed that the first child is likely to become the favourite, but this is often not the case. First children often carry the burden of their parents' expectations, and if they don't turn out exactly as their parents hoped, they can easily become the butt of unfavourable comparisons with brothers or sisters.

Sometimes, favouritism expresses itself as much in your reaction against one child as it does in your favouritism towards another. So it may be that because you see in one child those very traits you dislike in yourself, you find it easier to get on with your other child. Some parents quite simply find it easier to love one child because he or she looks like a cherub, or has a placid, affectionate nature. One of your children may develop similar interests to you, or show similar talents, so that you tend naturally to be drawn to him and do more together.

The factors that make up a very close emotional link are subtle and deep, however, and you may only be partly aware of why you respond in the way you do to a particular child. It

may be that you feel especially protective towards one child because he or she seems vulnerable – maybe he's less handsome than his brother, or she's more frail than her sister. Maybe your partner clearly prefers your firstborn, in which case you compensate by feeling more loving towards the one who's "left out". You may even find yourself cherishing your youngest because he's mischievous and cheeky, even though he causes you more work and effort. Surprisingly, the cause of favouritism can lie in things not directly to do with the child. For example, both parents may find difficulty in bonding with a child who was not planned or whose arrival coincided with a difficult phase in their relationship.

Families in which there is a chronically sick child are particularly prone to the effects of favouritism. If you have a child who is disabled or often ill and delicate, it's difficult not to be especially protective. In this case, your feelings are compounded by guilt and you may find it impossible to say no to the child – you may even demand that your other children give into the sick child's wishes.

Although the explanations of why favouritism occurs are sometimes hard to uncover fully, the effects it has on the children in a family are obvious, deep-felt and often long-lasting. Resentment is perhaps the strongest feeling among the brothers and sisters of a favoured child, and this often expresses itself in sibling rivalry.

Another very common response is for the other child or children in a family to rebel against everything the "favourite" stands for – and in so doing, they may alienate themselves still further from their parents. In very young children, this rebellion is likely to express itself in difficult behaviour, ranging from open defiance and attention-seeking to being withdrawn or fearful of incurring the parents' disapproval in any small way. A classic reaction is for the unfavoured child to become as naughty as the favoured one is "good".

What is often overlooked is how deeply parents' preferences can affect the favoured child, too. Although some children may bask in preferential treatment, for others it is a source of guilt. They may become anxious to shift attention away from themselves and may even begin to feel they can't live up to their parents' expectations. Bearing the brunt of parents' hopes can be a heavy burden for young shoulders and can make your favourite child over-responsible and over-anxious. In the long term, living up to your high expectations could come only at the cost of stress and fear of failure for your growing child.

What you can do about your own favouritism is to look carefully at the everyday situations in which it might show. Mealtimes are a classic example: they provide a setting in which, if you're not careful, you may well play off one child against another without realizing it. Remarks such as, "Why can't you eat up your dinner like your brother?" or "Your sister ate so well when she was your age," can cause resentment and, to your children, reveal underlying preferences.

It's also a common trap for parents to label their children – and then to interpret all their behaviour in this way. By saying, "He's the naughty one," or "She's such a good little girl," you are, once more, holding one child up as a model. Take some time to think about each of your children individually and in a positive way, reminding yourself of their individual qualities and strengths. Learning to accept the differences between your children and respecting them for what they are – even if this doesn't match up to your picture of what you expect them to be like – will make a tremendous difference to their sense of self worth and confidence.

Sometimes it's difficult to recognize when you are treating one of your children less favourably than the other. If you feel you do favour one child, check that you're not falling into any of the following traps:

● turning a blind eye to squabbles in which your "favourite" gets his or her own way

● not being absolutely fair about rules, i.e. enforcing rules about sharing, or behaviour, with your less-favoured child but relaxing them when your favourite child protests

● being quick to point out the mistakes or failings of one child and not the other

● being more prepared to give in to requests for treats from your favourite

● listening to tales about the other child from your favourite child.

Remember each child is bound to bring out a different reaction in you and if you take the trouble to make time for each one and show interest in their particular enthusiasm or talent, then you're more than likely to produce self-respecting individuals who can tolerate differences and live together with the minimum of resentment and maximum enjoyment of each other.

Fears

Fear is an essential part of a baby's survival instinct. His basic fear is of being attacked, hurt or killed; he will react with fear to loud noises or sudden movements, crying and grasping for his mother. Babies and children also react with instinctive fear to everything unknown or strange.

A small baby may become extremely upset if he is not picked up at once when he is crying from hunger, or he may show signs of distress if you put him down in a strange place. A baby knows that he cannot survive without an adult's loving care. If you are holding your baby securely, he will remain calm, not jumping at loud sounds or showing fear at something strange. An older baby, when shown something potentially alarming, will often look into your face to see your expression before reacting – if you smile, he will look again and even reach out for the object; if you look worried or afraid, he will cling to you and cry.

One of a baby's or a child's most basic fears is of being separated from his mother or other loving carer. Many babies display some kind of "separation anxiety" from the age of about nine months, crying as soon as their mother pops out of the room and reacting with fear to strangers.

When your child reaches the age of two, he is able to express himself through language and use his imagination in new ways. While most of this development is positive, allowing your child to express his needs for instance, and to carry out more complex activities, many parents notice that their child suddenly starts to express fear about things they previously took for granted. A picture in a book, a mask hanging on the wall or a tree on the way to the shops may frighten him or he may suddenly want his light on at night or reassurance that you are still nearby.

Some children, especially those not used to being cared for on a regular basis by a person other than their mother, remain very clingy for some time, and are obviously afraid of being deserted by their mum each time she leaves the house.

Young children need frequent verbal and physical demonstrations of your love for them. They need a regular routine, cuddles, companionship, and a chance to talk about the things they consider important to them. It is the sense of security they gain from you which helps to banish other fears. Constant nagging, on the other hand, telling a child off, saying that he is naughty and punishing him may make a child very anxious, and indeed engage in worse and more attention-seeking behaviour to try to prove to himself that you do love him even if he is naughty.

However, even the happiest and best-loved child has fears – either real, or irrational. Many of the "real" fears are understandable as they are based on an unpleasant, frightening experience. For example, a child who is attacked by a dog is likely to become afraid of all dogs, and a child who has fallen from a climbing frame and has hurt himself badly may well be nervous about climbing things for some time.

Irrational fears are much more difficult for a parent to understand, though often the explanation is a simple one. In some cases, children pick up fears which a parent is trying to conceal; for example, a child may sense that the parent is terrified of spiders and become afraid of them himself, even if the parent tries to pretend he is not.

Fear of the dark is very common and many, if not most, young children like to sleep with a dim light on in the room or a light shining in from the hall or corridor. Waking up in complete darkness can be a confusing or terrifying experience for a young child. Small children dream a great deal and may occasionally have quite alarming dreams, often before they are old enough to put words to them.

Children may dream about monsters, ghosts or other scary things. Recent research has shown that television may have a harmful influence here, as children frequently seem to think or dream about television programmes while in bed. Most children watch violent and frightening images daily in television cartoons and programmes, often from a very early age if older brothers and sisters are viewing. While they may not seem alarmed at the time, some of these images may disturb them when they are trying to sleep.

Some time around the age of three or four your child might become aware of death. This may come about because of the loss of an elderly relative or even a well loved figure, or from the death of a pet. Children usually accept a down-to-earth explanation, and parents can reassure children that death usually comes only at the end of a long and happy life.

A child will be much better able to cope with his fears if his parents answer his questions about difficult areas such as death openly. He will also tend to be less fearful if his parents are positive about life and do not constantly worry him with their own fears. Sometimes a protective mother will tell her child repeatedly, "Don't do that, you'll fall and hurt yourself," or "Don't go near the road, you'll be run over and squashed," or "Don't eat that, it could be poisonous." The child will come to perceive the world as an overwhelmingly dangerous place and will lose any desire he might have had to explore and try things out.

On the other hand, you won't help your child to become braver by scoffing at his fears or forcing him to do things that frighten him as some kind of therapy. Many parents do this, especially with their sons, because they want them to seem confident and fearless, and to grow into movie-screen macho men. However, being fearless is not the same as being brave: a child is fearless when he has no fear, brave when he feels fear but overcomes it.

Children learn to face their fears by approaching things a little at a time, not by jumping in at the deep end. A child who is afraid of heights will gradually learn to climb a climbing frame if you help him to go just a little bit higher each time – or even better, if you allow him to go a bit higher himself.

There are fears which have a welcome protective quality. A child who is afraid of traffic is less likely to run out into the road; a child who is more timid and clingy is less likely to run off in a crowded shop or in the park and get lost. Remember that your child's fears are often a survival mechanism, and deserve your respect.

A phobia is different from a fear in that it has an existence in the child's or adult's mind independently of the feared object. A child who is afraid of dogs may run when he sees one; a child with a phobia will be frightened at the mention of a dog, will avoid parks in case there is a dog there, or will refuse to look at books which might possibly have a picture of a dog in them. Although phobias are relatively common in children, they should not become severe enough to make the child's life a misery or prevent him from taking part in normal activities; if this is the case, you should see a doctor.

When dealing with your child's fears, never threaten him with something he is afraid of, or send him to bed as a punishment if he is afraid of the dark or bad dreams. Build up his confidence in himself – don't constantly run him down or tell him he's cowardly. Always be sympathetic to his fears and take them seriously, whatever they may be. The child who is afraid of crocodiles hiding under his bed at night will not be reassured by you telling him this is nonsense. He is much more likely to be reassured if you tell him either that you'll shoo them away for him, or put them in the garden at night. Similarly, blowing bad dreams away out of the window, or "killing" ghosts quite impressively with a fly-swat will help your child understand that you believe him and want to do something about his fears. Trying to give rational explanations that ghosts do not exist or that crocodiles don't live under beds will only frustrate him; he will just feel that you don't understand him and may decide not to mention his fears next time around – but he'll still be afraid.

Try to help your child talk about his fear – if he starts hiding and suppressing his fears he may never learn to trust people in later life. And try not to show your own feelings of panic in a frightening situation – set an example and react calmly.

Children do, in fact, often find their own ways of dealing with their fears and overcoming them in their mind. They might make up scary stories of danger and torture "just for fun", or play fantasy games in which they are the hero fending off the much-feared villain. Bravely "investigating" the source of their fear (walking up to dogs, flushing the toilet themselves, etc.) can help, or playing doctors or dentists before a visit to the doctor or dentist, using a doll as the "victim".

Ultimately, if your child feels secure within the home it will help him cope with change in the outside world, especially at times when things seem too much for him, as they can when he is starting playgroup or school and everything seems strange and intimidating. A child explores and deals with the world best if he has a stable base when things get rough. He will then be able to deal with his fears and anxieties so that he can set off confidently into the wide, complex world,

Febrile Convulsions

Convulsions are violent, involuntary and irregular movements of the body. Also known as fits or seizures, convulsions are among the most distressing symptoms that the parent may have to deal with.

The most common cause of convulsions in young children is a high body temperature. The tendency to react to high temperatures by having convulsions is often present in other members of the family, but the child usually grows out of this condition and, after the age of five, febrile convulsions (those caused by fever) rarely occur.

In the newborn, convulsions may be caused by brain damage, and in premature babies, a common cause is low blood sugar or calcium.

Febrile convulsions may start with the child becoming unconscious and falling down. He usually twitches uncontrollably, and writhes and shakes. The teeth may be clenched violently at times and, if the tongue gets in the way, it may be bitten. The eyes roll upwards, breathing becomes laboured and there is sometimes frothing at the mouth. He may also spontaneously empty his bladder and bowels.

Convulsions of this kind last for only a few minutes, after which the child may briefly regain consciousness. He then falls asleep, and may make peculiar facial expressions while snoring.

Stay with your child if he starts to have convulsions, as you will be able to prevent him from injuring himself. Kneel beside him on the floor and lay him on his front so that, if he vomits, there will be no danger of him choking.

If possible, place a clean pad, such as a folded linen handkerchief, between the child's teeth. This will prevent him from biting his tongue. But, if the teeth are clamped shut, do not try to force them apart.

Loosen the child's clothing, especially around the neck and waist, and while the convulsions are occurring, try to prevent him from striking his head or limbs on nearby objects. If possible, pull him away from such hazards, but do not try to restrain him, and do not try to arouse him by slapping.

When the writhing stops, move the child into the recovery position (*see* First Aid) and contact your doctor, staying with him all the time. Try to cool his fever by mopping with lukewarm water, or wrap a damp cloth around his head.

Other types of convulsion may be caused by a disorder of the central nervous system, such as epilepsy. And sometimes a child's temper tantrums are so severe that he has convulsions. In some children, certain drugs may cause convulsions, especially if the stipulated dose is exceeded.

Epileptic convulsions may be similar to febrile convulsions, but they can take many forms. Sometimes only one part of the body is affected and the child may remain conscious throughout.

It is likely that if one of your children has had convulsions caused by fever, then the same may happen to any brothers or sisters, as this problem tends to run in families. Any child suffering from a fever needs to be cooled, but particularly one known to be susceptible to febrile convulsions. If you spot the temperature rise in time, bathing the child's skin with tepid water may be sufficient to prevent him from having convulsions. Too many febrile convulsions can increase the likelihood of later epilepsy.

Feet

During childhood, the bones in the feet are soft, like gristle, and they do not harden completely until the feet have stopped growing when your child is in his mid-teens. The nerves in the feet develop slowly, with the result that your child does not feel pain if his feet are cramped, so it is up to you to check and recheck that his feet have plenty of room for movement and growth. If you do not, the bones and joints may become distorted and in serious cases will need surgery to correct them later.

When your baby is very small, get into the habit of checking that the toes of his stretch suit are not too tight or they will make his toes squashed and curled up. Always err on the side of caution – too big is fine, too small is not. You can always get a few more weeks' wear out of a stretch suit by cutting off the feet and using socks if the weather is cold, but you may not want to do this if you think you might want the suit for a subsequent baby. Check socks and tights in the same way and if in doubt choose a bigger pair. It is also important that cot blankets and sheets are not tucked in too tightly as this can squash his feet for long periods of time while he is asleep.

Your young baby does not need shoes until he is walking outside, so resist the temptation to buy those beautiful pram shoes you see in so many shops. In cold weather keep his feet warm in stretch suits, socks or little cloth or wool bootees. Slipper socks with non-slip soles are ideal once he has started walking indoors. Exercise is vital for the healthy development of the muscles in the legs and feet, so let him kick his naked legs and feet as often as possible.

When your baby starts to walk, do not rush out to buy shoes. As he walks more the shape of his feet will change slightly as they carry his weight. He will learn faster and feel more secure if he is allowed to walk in bare feet and can feel the floor beneath him. He will also fall less often. Going barefoot also helps the bones and tendons develop healthily. Once your child is walking outdoors, you will obviously need to buy him a pair of shoes, but barefoot is still best in the house and garden.

Hand-me-downs and second-hand bargains are fine for your child's other clothes, but not for shoes. As a child wears shoes he moulds them to the shape of his foot. That shape is unique so wearing shoes that have previously been worn by someone else means that your child's foot is being forced into an unnatural shape.

Once your child is ready to walk out of doors, take him to a reputable shop that employs trained fitters to be measured for that all-important first pair of shoes. Look for certificates on the walls of the shop or special badges on the assistants.

Children do not need fashionably shaped shoes – a good shoe follows the shape of the foot and allows for natural growth. It should have a rounded front with space that allows the toes to move freely, and offer good support to the ankle, instep and heel. It needs to be adjustable, and therefore laces, buckles or velcro fastenings are best. At first, the type of fastening does not matter too much, but for an older child velcro is usually easier to manage.

The upper should be made of natural material – leather or canvas – to allow the foot to breathe and the sole should be flexible enough to bend with the foot. Width is as important as length and most reputable makes are sold in a range of widths.

The fitter will measure both feet for length and width. It is quite normal for a child to have one foot slightly longer than the other and the fitter will offer shoes that fit the larger foot. If there is a big difference your child may have to wear an insole inside one shoe.

The foot gauge offers only a rough guide so the fitter will then check the shoes on your child. She will fasten them and ask your child to stand up as his feet will spread when they are carrying his weight. She will feel round the foot to check that there is room for movement and growth at the front, and that the shoe is wide enough and deep enough not to press down uncomfortably. Too much room is as bad as too little and your child's foot should not slip around in the shoe.

The shoe also needs to fit the contours of his foot under the arch. Once the fitter is satisfied that the fit is correct she will ask your child to walk in the shoes and check them again. Listen to your fitter's advice – she will know which shape and style is best for your child. A well-fitting shoe has a slight space between the heel and the back of the shoe (but not too big or it will cause blisters); a snug fit on top; laces at least 5 mm (¼ in) apart; if buckled, a bar long enough to adjust; no slippage at the heel; and no excessive creasing at the front or gaping at the sides when your child walks in them.

Your child will also need rubber boots and slippers and these need to be changed as soon as his feet grow. However, these can be saved for subsequent children or given away as they do not mould to the shape of the foot in the same way as shoes. Although most come in single sizes and one width fitting, these do vary from make to make so expert advice is essential.

Children's feet grow fast and this growth occurs in fits and starts. You may sometimes find yourself buying new shoes every six weeks, while other pairs may last for several months. To ensure that you do not miss one of these spurts, have your child's feet measured regularly, ideally every 8 to 12 weeks. A good shoe shop will be happy to do this and will not put you under pressure to buy new shoes if they are not necessary.

Try to keep trips to the shoe shop happy. A small child will be delighted with a new pair of shoes, but an older child may have very definite views as to what he wants, which may not coincide with yours.

If you can, discuss the subject before you go shopping, bearing in mind that no shop can stock every style in every size and width, and that certain styles and makes may be more suitable for his feet. If you do fall out, try to find the plus points of the style of shoe that does fit – the fitter will back you up. In really bad cases, it may be worth going to another shop to see if their range is different rather than end up with a pair of shoes that will never be worn.

Look out for socks and tights as well – if these are too small they can undo all the benefits of a well-fitted pair of shoes. Check and keep checking that these are not too small, and get into the habit of replacing them regularly. Natural fabrics like cotton or wool are best as they let the feet breathe. The very stretchy synthetics can squeeze your child's foot even if they appear to fit and will make his feet very hot.

Try to choose socks and tights with a shaped toe and heel and no thick seams as these can rub on the foot. And do not try to economize by buying too big – this can do just as much damage as the extra material will fold under the toes and put pressure on them.

Foot abnormalities
Club foot (talipes)
This is a malformation of the foot and ankle that is present at birth. If the doctor can move your newborn's foot to the correct position, no surgical treatment will be needed, but surveillance and manipulation will probably be necessary. If this is not possible and the foot points either inwards with the toes pointing down or upwards with the toes pointing out, treatment will be required. If there is no nerve or muscle disease the doctor will manipulate the foot into a more normal position and strap it with adhesive tape. Your baby may need to wear special boots at night. You may also be encouraged to manipulate your baby's foot. In very serious cases an operation may be necessary.

Flat feet
Many parents worry unnecessarily about flat feet. The apparently flat feet that babies have are due to their having a large quantity of fatty tissue in the soles of their feet and a pad of fat filling up the arch in front of the heel. The arch develops as the foot is used and gains strength.

If you are worried about your toddler's feet, look inside your child's shoes. If they are markedly worn along the inside edge, it could be that the arches of the foot have not developed properly. Have this checked by your doctor or a foot specialist who may recommend remedial exercises to correct it.

Pigeon toes
The medical term for pigeon toes is "in-toeing" and it describes the condition in which the fronts of the child's feet are turned inwards. It is common for children learning to walk to turn their feet in, and the problem usually corrects itself.

In-toeing can be to do with the feet but it can also be due to an inturning of the whole leg.

When the in-toeing occurs in the feet only, the problem usually resolves itself by the time the child is about three, without any treatment being necessary. If this does not happen, the condition can be corrected by plaster casts, or, occasionally, by means of surgery.

An inturning of the whole leg also usually puts itself right, by the time the child is six or seven. In earlier days, children were put in splints to treat the condition, but this method of treatment is no longer considered necessary. In the few cases where the child does not grow out of the condition, an operation is sometimes performed to realign the bones of the upper leg, with excellent long-term results.

Crossed toes

This is very common in children; some grow out of it while others may grow into it. Don't worry too much about them but be extra careful when buying shoes to check that there is plenty of room around the toes. If they cause any problems, see your doctor.

Common foot problems

There are a number of common problems which can affect your child's feet, some of which can be avoided if he always wears correctly fitting shoes.

Athlete's foot

This is a fungal infection that leads to redness, soreness, itching and cracking and peeling of the skin, usually in the soft skin between and under the toes. It is often picked up from public places such as swimming pools (*see* Athlete's Foot).

Blisters

These are fluid-filled gaps in layers of skin which are usually caused by shoes or socks rubbing on the feet. Professionally fitted shoes should avoid the problem, but if your child does develop blisters, buy new shoes. Never pop a blister, as infection may get in, but put a plaster on it and try to prevent shoes rubbing in the same place. Wearing two pairs of socks for a while may help prevent rubbing.

Chilblains

These shiny red swellings usually occur on the toes. They are caused by the feet becoming chilled and damp. Chilblains do not hurt when the feet are cold, but when the feet warm up again they become painful and itchy.

Chilblains clear up on their own, but do not let your child scratch them as in extreme cases breaking the skin may cause ulcers. Soothe them with witch hazel or calamine lotion and either cover them or put mittens or gloves on your child to stop him scratching. If a chilblain does ulcerate, apply a sterile dressing and see your doctor or chiropodist. You can prevent chilblains by making sure your child wears warm socks or thick insoles in his shoes and boots in winter. Never warm his feet directly in front of a fire or on a hot water bottle.

Corns

These are a build-up of hard skin in small round areas, often on the toes. Corns are caused by badly fitting footwear when the pressure pushes the skin inward and a hard core forms in the centre. This core then presses on the nerve endings under the skin. Well-fitted footwear should avoid the problem, but if your child does develop a corn, do not try to treat it yourself; see your doctor or chiropodist.

Ingrowing toe-nails

The name is misleading. The toenail is normal but the adjoining skin is inflamed and swollen and over-rides the edge of the nail. It is most common in the big toe. Usual causes are shoes, socks, tights or stretch suits which are too tight or when the toe-nails are cut too short or too far down the sides.

You can prevent them by being careful about the size of footwear, and cutting your child's toe-nails straight across and not too short. If one does develop and you notice any redness or pus around the nail, see your doctor or chiropodist.

Plantar warts

These are warts on the soles of the feet that are pushed inwards by the pressure of standing. A layer of skin may form over the top. They are caused by a virus and are highly infectious. Some people call them "verrucas".

Plantar warts may disappear of their own accord but it is always advisable to consult your doctor. Do not try to treat them yourself and do not let your child scratch them. Cover them with a plaster if your child is going swimming as they can be passed on in warm, wet environments.

Sweaty feet

We sweat all over and fresh sweat has no smell but it may start to smell if it cannot evaporate so that bacteria can break it down. Sweaty feet are uncommon in children, but make sure your child's feet can "breathe", wash them and change socks daily.

Healthy feet

Exercise can help to keep your child's feet healthy – but remember to keep it fun. Try some of the following games, but follow your child's lead and stop if he shows signs of boredom.

The Clock Game

This helps to restore the balance of muscles controlling the ankles. Ask your child to sit down and imagine that his big toe is a piece of chalk with which he is going to draw a circle. He should stretch his leg out straight and make a complete circle in a clockwise direction moving his foot only. Try six circles in each direction for each foot.

Walking the line

This shows children how to walk with toes straight. Chalk a line on the floor and ask your child to walk along it without "falling off". Check his posture as well.

Reefing the towel

This strengthens the foot muscles. Ask your child to stand on a small towel with feet turned in and heels touching the edge of the towel. Then, using the toes, roll up the towel under his feet.

Pony pawing

This exercises the ankle. Ask your child to stand on one foot and paw the ground like a horse with the other with the toes pointing downwards. Try it 12 times with each foot.

Marble race

This develops flexibility of the toes. Put some marbles on the floor, near a small dish. Ask your child to pick up a marble with his toes, hop to the dish and drop it in. Makes a good race for two or more children.

Fever

Fever or raised body temperature usually indicates that a child has an infection of some sort, but the cause may not always be obvious. People often refer to fever simply as "a temperature", meaning an abnormally high temperature.

The normal body temperature is 37°C (98.4°F) but this varies from person to person, from day to day, and even from one time of day to another. Some healthy children have temperatures as low as 35.6°C (96°F) or as high as 37.2°C (99°F).

Normally the body temperature rises during the day, reaching its peak at about 6 in the evening. A temperature of 37.7°C (100°F) or more is considered to be a fever.

The body temperature is kept fairly even by the region of the brain called the hypothalamus. When the body temperature goes up, for example after strenuous activity, the brain causes the heat to be lost by diverting blood to the skin; the skin surface cools through evaporation of sweat, and this brings the temperature down again.

A mild fever may have hardly any symptoms, but the higher the temperature the more the child is likely to be "feverish". Symptoms will include sweating, restlessness, hot skin, flushed cheeks, and often the desire to sleep (which can be very beneficial).

Very high temperatures can cause hallucinations. They can also cause convulsions (*see* Febrile Convulsions) and can be fatal. Call your doctor if your child's temperature is 39.4°C (103°F) or above or if your baby's temperature is 37.7°C (100°F) or above.

Bacteria multiply best at normal body temperature and may not reproduce at all when the body is fevered. A raised temperature can also promote immune system activity. The white blood cells multiply and become more active when there is an infection. Both viral and bacterial infections can cause a rise in body temperature.

Viruses cause such common illnesses as flu, measles, mumps, chicken-pox and whooping cough, while bacterial infections cause colds, sore throats, infections of the bowel and bladder, and abscesses, as well as more serious infections such as typhoid fever and tuberculosis, which are now rare in the developed world. All these illnesses are accompanied by a raised temperature. Finally, tropical diseases such as malaria which are caused by parasites are accompanied by very high fever. And, extremely rarely, fever can also be an indication of a tumour.

Very high temperatures can accompany quite minor illnesses, so temperature alone is not an indication of the severity of the illness. Symptoms such as loss of appetite, vomiting and the child being miserable and lethargic are a much better guide to his general health.

Bacterial infections can be treated with antibiotics. This is not necessary for most infections, which can soon be overcome by the body's own defences.

A child with a high fever need not be kept in bed, but should stay resting comfortably indoors. He should not be forced to eat if he has no appetite, but it is important to encourage a feverish child to drink as much as possible to make sure that he doesn't become dehydrated.

In most cases unduly high temperature can be brought down by sponging the child all over with tepid water. If the child is in bed, he should just be covered by a light sheet, which will need to be changed frequently as it will absorb a lot of sweat.

If you have a baby with a high temperature and sponging with tepid water does not bring it down, call your doctor. Do not let an older child's high temperature worry you too much if the child seems otherwise well, but call the doctor if the child's temperature is 39.4°C (103°F) or above, or if it remains high despite home treatment.

Paracetamol lowers a high temperature by blocking the messages to the brain, and this can be given to a feverish child if sponging has not made a difference. Never give aspirin to children under 12.

Fighting

◆ See **Aggression**, **Bullying**, **Sibling Rivalry**

First Aid

Specific first aid entries are given under separate headings. The key entries are as follows, and ideally should be looked at before any specific problem occurs:

- Artificial Respiration
- Bleeding
- Burns
- Cardiac Massage
- Choking
- Concussion
- Drowning
- Electric Shocks
- Febrile Convulsions
- Head Injuries
- Poisoning
- Shock
- Swallowed Objects
- Unconsciousness

◆ See also, **Bandages**, **Bee stings**, **Bites**, **Bruises**, **Dressings**, **Fainting**, **Grazes**, **Heat Stroke**, **Sprains**.

First and foremost, remember that the risk of accidents other than cuts and scrapes can be kept to a minimum if you are aware of danger and observe safety codes (*see* Safety).

All parents need to know how to deal with cuts and grazes, but also what to do in the case of choking, burns and poisoning. For serious accidents, an ambulance should be called straight away, but it is as well to know what to do while waiting for the ambulance to come.

Doing the right thing could save a child's life. You should know how to administer artificial respiration; check the pulse and give cardiac massage if there is no pulse; and put the child in the recovery position (see below).

Cardiac massage can only be learned properly under instruction, but it is worth trying in an emergency if a child's heart has stopped beating, even if you have not been trained or the training took place a long time ago.

The recovery position

It is a good idea to practise putting a child in the recovery position, and children themselves can learn how to do this in case they ever have to look after an accident victim.

This position should be used if a child is unconscious or semi-conscious after an accident, while his heart is still beating and he is breathing regularly. In this position the child can breathe easily and will not inhale any vomit if he is sick.

The recovery position is for use in circumstances where there are not likely to be broken bones or internal injuries, for example: after a fit, after being saved from drowning, after asphyxiation, after a severe electric shock, after poisoning and after a deep faint.

To put your child into the recovery position, lay him on his front with right leg and arm extended and the head turned to the right side. Make sure that his mouth is clear of any obstructions.

First-aid kit

Every household should have a first-aid kit kept in a securely closed box in a safe place, high enough to be out of the reach of children. Many chemists sell first-aid kits complete with box, but if you make up your own it should include: sterile packs of gauze, lint and bandages, adhesive dressings, adhesive tape for securing your own dressings, cotton wool, safety pins, scissors, tweezers, antiseptic ointment, small bottle of disinfectant, calamine lotion and infant paracetamol (tablets or liquid).

What to do in an emergency

1. Keep calm.
2. Eliminate danger (for example, separate child from electrical appliance in case of electric shock; turn off gas and open window in case of gas poisoning).
3. Check that the child's airway is clear with your finger.
4. If possible, get someone else to call an ambulance to prevent delay while you attend to the child.
5. Check breathing (watch for chest movement and place your face close to the child's nose to feel for breath). Give artificial respiration if the child is not breathing.
6. Check pulse at side of Adam's apple with fingertips. Give cardiac massage if you are sure that there is no pulse.
7. Staunch any bleeding, starting with the worst wound, or attend to any severe burns. If blood is pumping from the wound indicating that an artery has been cut, use firm pressure with a pad directly over the bleeding.

8. Place the child in the recovery position and keep him warm to prevent shock.

9. Call an ambulance if this has not already been done.

Note: To save yourself vital moments in an emergency, keep the telephone number of your doctor's surgery and the local accident and emergency unit by the telephone.

First Foods

The right time to start giving your baby "solid" food varies from baby to baby, and it is a decision you should make together with your doctor or health visitor who will have been keeping track of your baby's development and weight gain.

There are no advantages in starting to introduce mixed feeding too early. Milk provides your baby with all his nutritional needs until he is around six months old. In fact, in the first few weeks your baby's digestive system is too immature to cope properly with any other food, and starting him on solids too early can spark off an allergic reaction.

Your baby's growth and appetite is the best guide to what you should do. If he is putting on weight and seems content with the amount of milk he is getting then he may not need anything else for the time being. Some babies can go right through to six months needing nothing more than the breast or the bottle, whereas others show fretful signs that a tummyful of milk just isn't keeping them happy for very long, and they need to be given something more substantial.

The old rule of thumb was that a baby was ready for weaning when he was four months or weighed 6.5 kg (15 lb) and that is still a good rough guideline to go by.

Most babies make the start on a mixed diet between three and six months old. Even a baby who is thoroughly contented with a milk-only diet and who is putting on weight satisfactorily should be given extra food by six months. By this time he is quite capable of chewing food and needs the practice. Waiting too long may also make him rather suspicious and fussy when you do introduce the new flavours and textures of solids, because he has become too accustomed to milk and too set in his ways.

Weaning is a gradual process and it will take several months before your baby is fully on a mixed diet. There is no need to hurry it. Milk will continue to be the most important part of your baby's diet until he is well over a year old and the other food you give him is just a useful extra.

The aim to begin with is to get your baby used to taking his food from a spoon instead of the breast or a bottle and to find out his personal likes and dislikes. It is a slow process too because you must be careful to make sure that the foods you are offering your baby "agree" with him.

Moreover, your own approach to weaning can set the pattern for mealtimes for years to come. If weaning is a miserable experience for your baby, because you rush it or don't take account of his feelings or preferences, you may find you have started a battle royal about food which you will regret in the future.

Once you and the doctor or health visitor have decided that it is time to introduce solids you must choose which food you are going to start your baby on. At this stage, when you will be giving tiny tastes, the nutritional value of the food is neither here nor there. The important thing is to start with a food that is easily digestible – it will be months before your baby's system is mature and robust enough to deal with many of the good things you would like to give him. That first food will be his only food for a short while. You have to see how he likes it, and how his body reacts to it over a period of days before trying anything new.

The best first food is a sweet ripe fruit either served raw or lightly cooked, for instance apple, pear or banana. Cooked vegetables are also a good first choice, for instance potatoes, cauliflower, carrot, peas, parsnip or swede.

Baby cereals have been traditionally the most popular weaning foods as they are bland and taste similar to milk. Remember to start with a rice- or oat-based cereal, as wheat is known to cause allergies (see Food Allergy). Small quantities of a wheat cereal can be tried when your baby is a little older – after about seven months – as long as you monitor his reaction to it carefully.

Up till now your baby has been used to the taste, texture and temperature of milk. The first new food you give him will seem very strange indeed, and he won't know how to eat it. Until your baby has had some weeks of practice with other foods, your best move is to make what you offer him as close to what he knows as you can.

All his foods will need to be puréed to begin with, even those that mash easily like banana or boiled potato. The puréed food will still seem too thick and "sticky" to your baby, who is used only to sucking, so it should be mixed with his usual milk – formula, or expressed breast milk – to make a sloppier, smoother texture. Try to keep the temperature close to the lukewarm milk he is used to. Anything too cold or too hot is likely to give him a shock and may well put him off the whole business of eating "grown-up" food.

The first tastes should be just that – tastes. Look at it from your baby's point of view: from being used to a warm bottle teat or nipple dispensing his favourite milk, he suddenly has a hard spoon pushed into his mouth with something that tastes and feels very odd to him. He has no way of knowing that this is food, which will fill him up; he doesn't even know yet whether he will like it or how to swallow it properly. For at least a week or two he needs to accustom himself to this strange new experience.

Give the first tastes when he is still a little hungry but not starving, for instance halfway through his midday bottle. If you start to try feeding him from a spoon when he is crying with hunger this new method will seem like an insult. When he is a little full and more contented he will be more likely to give it a go.

Put a little of the chosen food on the tip of a small spoon and touch it to his mouth. What he will do is suck at the spoon, and some of the food will make its way in. Be prepared for a look of great surprise, and perhaps a grimace. He will be thinking about what he is feeling and tasting, and he will soon let you know what he has decided. If he seems not to like it, don't despair – it might be the novelty of the experience that is upsetting him and once he knows what he is doing he may well find he likes the food. You will probably also find that much of the food will come out again – he doesn't yet know how to swallow this different texture, but that doesn't necessarily mean he is rejecting it. If he indicates pleasure, give him a little more in the same way. But don't get over-confident and tip a whole spoonful into his mouth. He won't like this and it may put him off. Let him take control of how much he eats and when. As soon as he loses interest or turns his face away from the spoon, offer him the bottle again.

The next day, if he has had no adverse reaction to the food, try again. Always let him decide whether he wants it or not and be patient with his inexpert sucking technique. In his own time he will learn how to eat from a spoon properly and it doesn't yet matter how much he actually manages to get into his stomach.

Your aim at this stage is to get your baby accustomed to the whole process of eating solid food and make it seem a pleasure. You also want to lay the foundations for a mealtime habit that will gradually turn into a normal eating pattern.

After a few days, start to give your baby tastes three times a day – morning, midday and afternoon. Gradually increase the amounts to two or three teaspoons if he seems to enjoy it. Once you are happy with the way he is reacting to his first food you can add the next one. But always wait at least 24 hours to be sure that he has no adverse reaction to each food.

Don't immediately decide that he doesn't like a certain new food because he rejects it once. It could be because he wasn't hungry at that meal. Wait a day or two and try him with it again – he might be delighted this time. He might also have been put off by the texture of the food the first time around. Try it smoother next time, and see if that makes a difference.

While your baby is at this stage of eating small tastes of sloppy purée it makes sense to prepare a normal quantity and store or freeze what you don't need at once.

Purées will keep a day or two in the refrigerator. Using a clean spoon each time, spoon out the quantity you need and warm to the correct temperature.

Alternatively, freeze home-made purées in an ice-cube tray. This allows you to press out just the amount you need each time.

Once your baby has tried a range of fruits, vegetables and cereals and is becoming enthusiastic about the process of eating, you can add other food. Try him with egg yolk, yoghurt, cottage cheese, puréed steamed fish and chicken, and lentils, introducing each one on its own to begin with. Once you know that his digestive system can cope with all these varied foods you can start mixing them together and creating interesting combinations and flavours.

From about six months your baby is ready and able to chew. Start by making the texture of his food a little coarser. You can do this by mashing the food well with a fork rather than puréeing it, so that it is not so smooth. Having to work the odd soft lump of vegetable around his mouth gets him ready for even firmer textures.

When he's sitting up and can hold things in his hands you can start giving him "finger foods". Rusks are an obvious choice as are breadsticks or fingers of toast. Cubes of cheese and large pieces of fruit are also good. Avoid small, hard foods, such as peanuts, on which he could choke, or which could go down the wrong way. Never, of course, leave him alone with any food, as he could have trouble even with food that you consider to be safe.

Although allowing your baby to start feeding himself at this stage may mean more mess for you, it pays off in the long term. A child who is allowed to try even before he is any good at it will be feeding himself properly long before the one who is discouraged from doing so.

Steaming is the best method of cooking food for your baby as it retains most of the goodness. Don't be tempted to make the dishes you prepare for him "nicer" by adding sugar. Your baby will only think it is tastier this way if you get him used to it. Letting him develop a sweet tooth is not good for his teeth or his health. Seasoning with salt is also bad: your baby's kidneys can't deal with extra salt at this stage. Don't use extra fat in the dishes either: the fat that naturally occurs in food and milk is all he needs.

Once your baby is on a mixed diet similar to your own you can start to give him a mashed-up version of what you eat yourself. But remember to take his portion out and mash it before you have added the extra flavourings that you and the rest of your family like.

When he is starting to eat more substantially at mealtimes you can get into the habit of serving him his solid food before he has filled up on milk. This way he will naturally increase his eating and decrease his drinking. This is a good time to begin giving him his milk or juice in a cup at mealtimes though he may still want the bottle or the breast in the evening or morning.

Fontanelles

Fontanelles are the soft spots on a baby's skull. If you run a finger gently over a baby's head you will feel two of these indentations and even a pulsing in places, but this is absolutely normal.

The largest fontanelle is positioned at the top of the baby's head. It is diamond-shaped and measures roughly 4 cm (1⅛ in) across and is known as the anterior (front) fontanelle. The anterior fontanelle pulsates noticeably to the baby's heartbeat, which can seem alarming to parents, giving the impression that the brain is more exposed and consequently the baby more vulnerable than he really is. There are five more fontanelles, one on its own and two in pairs, but these are usually too small to be felt easily. The other single fontanelle is known as the posterior (back) fontanelle. It is smaller than the front one and is situated about 5 cm (2 in) behind it, at the back of the head. The mastoid fontanelles are located at the back of the head behind the ears, and the sphenoidal fontanelles lie at each side of the skull, just above the baby's cheek bone.

In the skull of a new-born baby the bones are completely separate, but joined together by tough sheets of fibrous tissue – the fontanelles. This enables the baby's skull to change shape during the birth.

If the baby's head is large or the mother's pelvic opening very small, the bones of the skull actually overlap during the birth, and the baby is born with a very narrow head. The bones resume their normal position within 24–48 hours without harming the brain at all.

As the baby grows, new bone is laid down and the fontanelles gradually close, although very occasionally the anterior fontanelle does become larger and more noticeable during the first three months or so. At about three months the sphenoidal and posterior fontanelles close and by the time the baby is about a year old the mastoid fontanelles are closed. The child can be up to two years old before the anterior fontanelle finally disappears completely.

New mothers sometimes worry that they could damage the baby's brain by touching the fontanelles, but this is not so. The tissue between the bones is very firm and it is perfectly safe to wash the baby's head, although not too roughly.

Food Allergies

Any allergy is a sensitivity to a substance that does not normally cause any harm. The substance that causes the allergy is called an allergen. Food allergens are rare but include cow's milk and fish, especially seafood.

Food allergies can be triggered off by any number of foods, and the allergen can often be difficult to track down. Food allergies may run in families (although without affecting all members of the family) and are often linked to the incidence of eczema and asthma. There is a whole range of symptoms that can be caused by food allergies and they always arise a few hours after the food has been eaten.

Skin

Some food allergies result in skin irritation. This ranges from a red, flushed rash to an eczematous condition, with a scaly rash on hands, face, neck and limbs; or hives, in which there are red, irritated swellings on the skin, with small white, very itchy points at their centre.

Digestion

Upset stomach with diarrhoea, vomiting and nausea can be symptoms of food allergy. These symptoms usually become apparent within an hour of eating the food responsible, making it easier to identify the cause and eliminate the culprit from the diet.

Other symptoms

● Asthma is often caused by allergies, and food allergies are sometimes responsible.

● Swollen tongues and lips may be symptoms of food allergies, and again can generally be traced to the food responsible.

● Migraine headaches are thought to be caused by allergic reactions to food in some cases, but these seem to affect adults more than children.

● Some specialists think that certain behavioural problems, and in particular hyperactivity, are reactions to substances in the diet, although these may not be, strictly speaking, allergic reactions.

Food allergens are absorbed into the bloodstream and can therefore cause reactions in almost any part of the body, and this is why it is often difficult to track down the precise cause if your child is suffering from a food allergy – and even, sometimes, that it is an allergy that is causing the symptoms at all. Swollen tongue and lips, and digestive disorders are usually more obviously linked to the particular foods that have caused these reactions.

An allergic reaction is the result of the body's defence mechanism coming into play when confronted with what should be harmless substances. The body produces antibodies to these harmless substances and these antibodies cause certain cells to release histamine. It is the histamine, produced by the body itself, that provokes the symptoms of allergy.

Normally, the body is able to tell the difference between a dangerous foreign protein and a harmless one, such as a food protein. But in an allergic person the body treats a harmless protein as if it were harmful.

Since, once a child is weaned, the diet normally contains so many different elements, it can be very difficult to isolate the foodstuff that may be triggering off an allergic reaction. An elimination diet is one way of diagnosing the cause.

At first a very plain diet is provided, often consisting of little more than water, one vegetable (usually potato) and one meat (usually lamb) (*see* First Foods). If the child has no symptoms while following this diet, it is considered likely that food allergies are to blame for the condition. After this, different foods are re-introduced, little by little, and any reactions noted.

Another approach to an elimination diet is simply to remove those substances (wheat and cow's milk, for example) most likely to be responsible, one by one, and keep a note of the results. Often nowadays the substances responsible are food dyes and additives, and if food allergy is suspected in children it may be worth feeding them fresh food without any additives for a while to see if the symptoms diminish.

To speed up the diagnosis, some doctors now use an alternative test in which a weak solution of various possible allergens including preserving agents is injected under the skin or dropped under the tongue to see if symptoms are provoked.

Unfortunately there is no effective treatment for food allergies other than avoiding the food that causes the problem. This means that parents must select food with care, reading packets and labels to check on the contents of pre-packed food.

Allergies to shellfish or a particular kind of fruit are relatively easy to cope with, but allergies to wheat or dairy food do demand a major revision of the normal diet. Your doctor will help with suggestions.

Sometimes suitable substitutes can be found fairly easily – for instance cow's milk can be replaced with goat's milk or soya milk, and potato flour or cornflour can replace flour from cereals to some extent.

Drugs can control some food allergy symptoms. Corticosteroid drugs have an anti-inflammatory effect and can be prescribed as a cream or as tablets for skin rashes and in liquid form to be taken by inhaler, for asthma. Asthma attacks can also be controlled by drugs known as bronchodilators. Both drugs may be given by injection in particularly serious asthma cases.

However, these drugs are not cures – they simply relieve the symptoms. And usually they are not suitable for long-term use. So avoiding the allergen is really the only solution, difficult though this may be.

It is best not to make a fuss and to try to give the child the same diet as his brothers and sisters as much as possible. It is surprising how even quite young children can learn what they can and cannot have, and adapt to it.

If allergies are known to run in your family, it may help to breastfeed for as long as possible and not give solids for at least four months. Avoid wheat, citrus fruits and eggs in the early stages of weaning and watch for reactions to new foods.

◆ See also, **Asthma**, **Eczema**, **Hyperactivity**

Food Poisoning

Food poisoning usually takes the form of tummy pain, vomiting and diarrhoea. This can be extremely debilitating and cause dehydration. The pains are usually violent cramps that come on quite suddenly. They can continue for a few days, often becoming worse just before an attack of vomiting or diarrhoea. Vomiting tends to stop after a few hours, but diarrhoea can continue for a few days.

Especially in young children, diarrhoea and vomiting can lead to the loss of relatively large quantities of fluids and salts. This causes dehydration and affects the body's delicate chemical balance. In some extreme cases, when not treated promptly, they can lead to coma and even death, and this makes food poisoning potentially serious. The early signs of dehydration are: dry mouth and lips; a sunken fontanelle (if the child is under 18 months); sunken eyes; dark yellow urine, or no urine being passed at all; drowsiness, lethargy and irritability in older children.

Call a doctor in the case of children under two who are vomiting for two hours or more or who have bad diarrhoea.

In an older child, if the symptoms of dehydration appear, take the child immediately to the nearest hospital accident and emergency department.

Food poisoning comes about as a result of the child eating contaminated food, and this contamination can be caused by bacteria, by toxins or by chemicals. Usually everyone who has eaten the same food is affected to some extent.

Bacterial food poisoning

In this type of poisoning the cause is, as the name implies, bacteria (germs) which either were present in the food from the beginning or have been introduced, and which then multiply on the food before it is eaten. Once ingested with the food these germs continue to multiply inside the stomach or bowel.

Salmonella bacteria are often found in poultry and eggs, particularly duck eggs, and are killed by thorough cooking. The bacterium Clostridia contaminates food through dirt or flies, and Shigella and Escherichia coli can contaminate food through poor hygiene.

The interval between the contaminated food being eaten and the symptoms developing is an indicator of the type of poisoning. If the cause is a bacterial infection symptoms can take from 12 to 24 hours to develop.

Toxins

In toxic food poisoning the problem is caused by toxins released as germs multiply on the food, rather than by the germs themselves. Perhaps the best known form of toxic food poisoning is botulism which, although very rare, is very dangerous. It can be caught from badly tinned or bottled food.

Germs known as Staphylococci can be transferred to food from infected boils or cuts. Once they are on the food they grow rapidly and produce Staphylococci toxin, which quickly affects anyone eating the food.

Toxic food poisoning usually occurs almost as soon as the contaminated food has been heated. If the toxins are from Staphylococcus there is vomiting and pain, but there is no diarrhoea. However if the cause is botulism, symptoms arise after an interval of about 12 hours, and include vomiting, abdominal pain, paralysis and coma.

Chemical poisoning

A few foods contain chemicals which are poisonous to people, as in the case of poisonous mushrooms and toadstools. Sometimes this type of food poisoning can even result in death, and children should be warned against tasting or even touching mushrooms while on walks.

Some nuts contain small quantities of chemicals that can be poisonous if eaten in very large amounts, and the green parts of potatoes also contain poisonous chemicals.

Finally, foods that have been treated with pesticides could in theory cause food poisoning if the pesticides have not been used in accordance with official advice, if fruit skins are not washed or if the food is eaten in very large quantities.

Treatments

The most important treatment in most cases of food poisoning is to replace the fluid that is being lost as a result of vomiting or diarrhoea. If the child is over 12 he can be given plenty of water to which a little fresh fruit juice has been added.

Babies and young children should be given a mixture of two level teaspoons of sugar and a generous pinch of salt in 200 ml (7 fl oz) of water, or for severe fluid loss the doctor will prescribe powders containing a balanced mixture of salts and sugars which are mixed with plain water.

For a baby who is being breastfed as well as receiving solids, the breastfeeding should continue. The child should be given additional clear fluids by bottle or spoon.

Depending on the type of poisoning, antibiotics may be prescribed by your doctor to clear up the infection but they are not needed in all cases.

For fungus poisoning an antidote may be given, and the patient is taken to hospital for care and treatment. In serious cases intensive care may be necessary.

Paralysis and death can occur if botulism goes untreated – a swiftly administered antitoxin and intensive nursing are necessary to counteract it.

The child's stomach is washed out, and he may be put on a ventilator. Once the acute stage is over, the outlook for a complete recovery is excellent.

The best way to prevent food poisoning is through good general hygiene. Training a child to wash his hands after the toilet is important as it reduces the number of bacteria on them, lessening the chance of transferring bacteria to the mouth and reducing the risk of many forms of food poisoning. Do not accept food from food handlers with dirty or infected hands.

Other points to note are that frozen meat must be defrosted thoroughly before being cooked. When meat is being cooked from a partially defrosted state, large parts of it will be warm rather than hot during the cooking, and this causes Salmonella and other bacteria to multiply rapidly. Also, cooked and uncooked meats should be kept separately in the fridge. All uncooked meats have bacteria on their surface, which are normally killed when the meat is cooked. If the uncooked meat comes into contact with cooked meats bacteria can be transferred to cooked meat, where they will quickly multiply.

It is also important not to use a knife that has been used for uncooked meat on any other food without cleaning it carefully first.

◆ See also **Poisoning**

Foot Odour

◆ See **Feet**

Fractures

Fractures are broken bones, and they are usually caused by falls or car accidents. Fractures are fairly unusual in young children, as their bones are very supple. They are most likely to occur if the child is the victim of a car accident. It takes a great deal of force to break a healthy child's bone in a fall, but some bones are more vulnerable than others.

Very young and supple bones are most susceptible to a type of fracture known as a greenstick fracture. This gets its name from the way in which a willow sapling breaks when it is bent too far. A greenstick fracture is a crack that goes part-way across or part-way along a young bone.

Sometimes these cracks are so small that they do not show up in an X-ray. Their presence is diagnosed from the pain the child feels when using the bone. These are known as stress fractures, and heal with rest.

In a simple fracture the skin is undamaged, while in a compound or open fracture part of the bone is driven through the skin, and a comminuted fracture is one in which the bone is splintered. In a complicated fracture there are other internal injuries. Finally, there are so-called pathological fractures, which are rare and occur only when there is an inherent weakness in the bone, usually due to disease.

The most likely cause of a fracture will be a bad fall, and the hand and wrist are most likely to be injured in breaking the fall.

In older children fractures occur more frequently, partly as the bones become less supple, and partly as the children become involved in sport. Ideally children should be supervised by a trained adult when they are playing sports, so that injuries will be recognized and properly attended to. But of course this will not always happen, and it is as well to teach children about the dangers and symptoms of fractures (and other injuries) and what to do if they occur.

The most serious fractures of all are caused by road injuries. Even if one of the vehicles involved is not moving, the speed of the other intensifies the impact of the accident.

Perhaps the most obvious symptom of a fracture will be that the child is in great pain. He will probably be pale and sweating (signs of shock), due to loss of blood from the broken bone.

If a limb is fractured, it may be in an unnatural position, it may look bent or swollen and the child will be unable to move it. But some fractures, especially in the ribs or hand, may be almost unnoticeable and may take time to be recognized. Very young children have difficulty in explaining where the pain is, making it more difficult to spot what is wrong.

Bones are not necessarily displaced in a fracture, and sometimes an X-ray is necessary to identify the type of fracture.

The chief danger from a fracture is shock, due to pain and loss of blood, especially if the broken bone cuts through surrounding blood vessels. If the skin is broken there is a risk of osteomyelitis (infection of the bone).

Fractures of the skull can cause damage to the brain, due to increased pressure from internal bleeding. If a fractured skull is suspected the child will automatically be taken to hospital and put under observation for 12 hours or more.

A rib fracture can cause a ruptured lung or liver. Again this will result in severe loss of blood. Likewise a fractured pelvis can cause damage to the bladder or urethra.

A fractured spine needs particularly careful, skilled handling to avoid damage to the spinal cord, because if this happens, permanent paralysis can be the result.

A special danger for children is fracture across the end of a bone, close to the joint, which can stop the bone from growing properly. If this happens, the affected limb will not reach the same size as its opposite partner.

Nevertheless, most fractures in children are not particularly serious, as long as loss of blood is controlled and infection prevented. As well as being more supple, children's bones also heal much more quickly than adult bones if they do fracture. If your child has sustained a fracture, keep him warm and reassure him. Handle him with care, only moving him if absolutely necessary for safety. Cover an opened wound with sterile gauze and bandage and call an ambulance. You should not move the child unless you really have to, or give him anything to eat or drink in case he needs an anaesthetic. Don't transport the child to hospital yourself unless it is impossible to get an ambulance, or move him before immobilizing the injured limb.

At the hospital shock will be treated first (see Shock) and a blood transfusion given if necessary; the pain of the fracture is relieved with drugs. Only then is the fracture itself attended to. Muscular spasm usually pulls apart the broken ends of the bone, and the child will probably have to be given an anaesthetic so that the ends can be realigned. When this has been done, the break is encased in plaster to hold the bone in place while it heals. Fractured ribs do not need to be immobilized in this way while they heal.

In comminuted fractures, where the bone is splintered, it may be necessary to join the bone by screwing a metal plate along it to act as a splint. This often has to be done if the thigh bone is broken. A plaster cast is then applied to keep the bone still while it heals.

If it is impossible (when the pull of the muscles is too strong) to stabilize the broken bone by using plaster, then the child has to be put in continuous traction. This means that he has to be kept in a hospital bed with the broken bone held in place by weights adjusted to counteract the pull of the muscles.

The speed at which healing takes place depends on the blood supply at the site of the fracture. A fractured leg usually has to be kept in plaster for about 12 weeks, while a broken arm may take only 6 weeks to heal. Bones possess remarkable healing powers.

During the recovery period the child will be encouraged to do exercises to keep the muscles strong.

Friendships for Children

Even when your child is ready to make closer contacts with other children – possibly around the age of two – he will still need you to guide him towards friendly social behaviour. Toddlers can learn from each other and enjoy being together, but unless you are there to act as a support they will each be confused by some of their mutually "antisocial" actions. Your child may snatch another's toy, or have his taken. He may hit out as he becomes frustrated, or he may be whacked by a toy being swung round by another child. None of these actions is intentionally spiteful in very young children, but you may need to mediate and kiss the occasional bumped brow. You will have to show your toddler patiently that there are alternative ways of playing together which allow you all to have a more enjoyable time. Direct him away from conflict – show him a toy he can play with instead, or introduce both children to a toy they can play with together or alongside each other.

One of the best ways of introducing your child to other children is through mother and toddler groups. Your local clinic, church or community centre may each run and your library will probably have information on all of them. Perhaps the first benefit from these groups is that you can meet other mothers and your developing friendships may give positive encouragement to the toddlers. Also by watching other children you will learn more about your own child, and you will learn as much as he does about the ups and downs of first friendships.

Mother and toddler groups are good because they provide "neutral" territory for the toddlers to meet in. Although they are not old enough to play with each other, they are happy to play alongside one another. Away from the all too familiar home territory, the toddlers may be more relaxed together and less possessive about toys.

Certainly your child will seem to make fewer demands on you because in these surroundings your relationship is obviously less concentrated. Also, the groups provide toys that will be different from the ones at home, encouraging your child to share from the start, even if he is still too young fully to understand this idea.

A large space gives him room to wander off and come into contact with the other children. Though these encounters may not produce much response at first, they are steps towards the pleasant familiarity that allows a young friendship to develop.

At this toddler stage, much of the communicating between your child and other children is done through you. Even if he speaks a lot at home, your child will be quieter among other people, possibly not understanding someone at all if they are unfamiliar. So, from time to time, he will come up to you at these early playgroups to tell you something about another child or toy as a signal for you to re-introduce him into the "game" again.

He also still relies on you to make suggestions for play; toddlers' imaginations are just beginning to develop, but at this stage it is too early for them to make imaginative suggestions to one another and they cannot sustain any constructive game.

Children learn from copying one another, however, and if your child ventures into the playhouse in the corner, he may be followed in by one or two other toddlers. You can join in and try to encourage the group activity. Or your child may disappear into the playhouse with some building bricks and be followed in there by another toddler, also with bricks or another toy. They may play quite happily in there side by side for some time, but then emerge only to pursue separate activities again.

Sometimes older toddlers will follow each other round and round the room, until a sort of chasing game develops. It may be these physical games that mark the beginning of a real interaction between your child and others.

Often it is girls who make friends earlier and more easily by sharing the same close space and playing constructively alongside one another, while boys will play chasing games but show a certain wariness about sharing toys or playing with each other.

However these first attachments are made, friendship is an important discovery for your child and you can encourage it in several ways. Perhaps you and other mothers from the group could arrange further meetings, taking turns once a week in each other's homes. That way, your child has a chance to develop new friendships with the added stimulus of different settings. He also has the chance to play with his friends in his own home environment.

Organizing these mini "parties", or a picnic, or visits with other familiar children to places such as an adventure playground or the local children's pool may provide another basis for early friendships. Discovering new experiences with other children often intensifies the experience and strengthens the friendship – and it is something you can talk about later.

Use these experiences as subjects for stories or paintings that include his playmates so your child will feel that his friends are an important part of his whole life – someone he can refer to when he is alone with you, or when talking about his activities to other members of the family.

By the age of three your child is probably ready for nursery school, or a pre-school playgroup. It is likely that this is the first time he finds himself among other children without your reassuring presence, or the support of another familiar adult. Even if he has been used to mother and toddler meetings, you cannot be sure how easily he will settle into the new environment.

Despite initial anxieties at being left without you, he is now at an age where making friends is part of his natural development. He is beginning to look outward and the structure of the playgroup activities will steer him towards playing and learning with other children. The whole group may be divided into smaller groups, sometimes pairs, for certain activities and your child's social skills will probably develop quickly once he has settled in.

By this stage your child's imagination is opening up and friends help him to expand it. He is more articulate and is more able to hold his own in an argument. He is gradually becoming less reliant on an adult to resolve disputes, though he is still not able to reason well and needs you to teach him a sense of what it must be like to be in another person's shoes.

Take the opportunity to find out from teachers and helpers how your child reacts to other children when you are not there. It is important to know this, so that you can help to iron out any anxieties or problems your child may have. Relating your child's behaviour at home to how he reacts within a group of children is not always easy. You may decide that you will have to modify your own behaviour and give in less readily to your child's demands.

If, for example, your child throws a tantrum at home, you may have a way of pacifying him quickly or you may leave him to shout it out. Either way, if your child has a fit of temper at nursery or playgroup, you will not be there to sort him out and he will soon have to learn that he cannot always be the centre of attraction.

Before this frustration alienates him, try to explain at home that he would think the other children silly if they were behaving like that and now he is grown up enough to go to playgroup he should try to tell the teacher when he begins to get upset about something, before he gets too cross about it. He wouldn't like it if another child hit him in temper, so he shouldn't hit out either.

Of course, growing up with an elder brother or sister at home will give your child a head start in social behaviour. He will have, subconsciously and by experience, absorbed a lot of basic rules that make or break another child's "friendly" attitude towards him. He may have learnt how to make up after a fight, how to behave in order to be included in a game, and how to share or wait for his turn.

There may be one or two adults outside the immediate family whom your child has befriended – an elderly neighbour who has time to spend with him, and who may be lonely, will have a host of stories for your child. He will enjoy talking to somebody with time to devote to him and both will benefit. Friends of yours, too, may enjoy taking your child on a special visit to the zoo or park. Whoever these grown-up friends are, you will have to feel that you trust them completely yourself, before letting your child go off with them on his own. But once established these friendships can be valuable and add a different dimension to your child's concept of "friends".

Learning about making friends will be full of small dramas for your child and he may be surprisingly fickle in his affections. He may come home from nursery school talking about one particular child all the time – then suddenly that child is forgotten and another is constantly mentioned instead.

But this is all part of the shifting changes of childhood. By the age of four-and-a-half or five, when he is ready to start school, your child is able to play constructively and imaginatively with other friends, inventing games, acting out roles, and first squabbling then hugging one another as arguments come and go.

◆ See also, **Imaginary Friends**, **Nurseries and Playgroups**

Friendships for Parents

A new baby results in more than just joy and excitement. It also means many changes in your life with new pressures and demands on your time. For months, it will be difficult to find just a few quiet moments for yourself, let alone time to see friends. Even the best friendships suddenly become difficult to maintain.

Yet, the months after your baby's birth are a time when you may need the support and companionship of loyal friends more than ever. It's also a time when you'll make friends with other new mothers.

When you become a mother you automatically become a member of a sort of club. When you are walking in the street with a pram or pushchair, women will smile at you. You will strike up conversations with other mothers in the supermarket, at the nursery, at the clinic. Some of these women, if you let them, will become your staunchest allies and your greatest support.

You will make friendships that may last a lifetime. And you will meet people you would not normally have been in contact with before you became a mother.

Existing friendships provide continuity in your life while everything else is changing, and new friends will share your changing anxieties and interests. Both types of friendship are valuable, and it's important to overcome any obstacles to keep friendship alive. Just remember, life will not be the same as it was before your baby was born.

One person you will see regularly after you and your baby come home from hospital is the health visitor. When the community midwife stops visiting, your health visitor will keep in touch over your child's first five years, providing vital support and companionship.

The Health Visitors' Association suggests using your visitor as a fund of knowledge. She will be able to tell you about local mother-toddler groups as well as childcare and baby-minding facilities. She'll also be able to put you in touch with other mothers in the neighbourhood with children about the same age who have similar interests and hobbies to your own.

Isolation can be a real problem for mothers of young children. Women who have been used to going out to work can find themselves suddenly deprived of contact with adults. And with a new baby and, perhaps, a toddler or two to take care of as well, you'll certainly be less mobile than before. Going out for an afternoon visit isn't just a matter of picking up the baby and locking the door – a carrycot, extra nappies, bottles and formula (if not breastfeeding) and a change of baby clothes will all have to be taken. It's not a light load, especially if you're carrying an active baby as well.

Having local friends is a good way to keep up contact with the outside world without having to make each visit an exhausting whole day's outing. If your baby was born at a local hospital, you're bound to make new friends with other young mothers living nearby. You'll also meet other women when you take the baby to the clinic or the doctor's surgery. Check at local leisure centres for postnatal exercise classes and mother-and-baby swimming lessons. When your child gets older, you'll also meet mothers at library reading mornings and playgroups.

If you are shy and find it difficult to make friends, your health visitor will help. Also, many countries have national childbirth organizations – in Britain there is the National Childbirth Trust – which organize support groups and other social events. There are actually many sources of support and help for lonely new mothers.

New local friends will be worth their weight in gold. Not only will you be able to give each other mutual support and exchange experiences, you'll be able to babysit occasionally for each other. This will give you a chance to get together with other friends.

Even the oldest friendship can become strained if your friend doesn't have a baby. As much as she might adore your child, she will probably not be as fascinated as you with all the small details of the baby's day. Likewise, you might not be as interested in the office politics that once fascinated you. To prevent the gap between you from widening, try and have a little chat on the phone about once a week to keep abreast of what's happening in her life.

When you get together with your childless friends, you've simply got to forget about your children for a while. Make sure you see them somewhere other than in your house. Friends get terribly annoyed if they are pouring out their hearts to you only to be constantly interrupted by a baby.

For a new mother suffering extended postnatal depression, that is, beyond the first few days after delivery, friendships are one of the vital links along the road to recovery.

According to counsellors, depression sufferers often become isolated as they are unable to talk to anyone because they fear people will think they are going "potty". In this situation, friendship and companionship can really make a difference.

One of the most important friendships that can be strained with the arrival of a baby is the one you have with your partner.

Young fathers, too, find parenthood a daunting experience, and are often uncertain how to cope with all the new pressure. Your partner will also be tired and, like you, will find there just isn't enough time to see old friends. Try taking turns at babysitting so you can each have an evening out with your own friends.

It's important to understand that strains are inevitable. Try to work out compromises both of you are comfortable with. If, however, after several months the strain doesn't seem to lessen, don't hesitate to seek professional help. Again, your health visitor will help, or, if things are bad, you can look for marriage guidance counsellors in the telephone directory.

Of course, if you gave up work when the baby arrived this is a time in your life when "money is no object" applies less than ever. And going out with a working friend in the evening usually involves spending money.

The bill at the end of the evening can come as a shock and it can make you feel incredibly guilty when you should be enjoying your night out. It's worth saving up a little in advance – if you can find cash to spare!

Both you and your partner are entitled to a certain amount of spending money. Maybe you can agree on allocating part of your monthly household budget to a "fun fund". Equally shared, this fund may save arguments, guilt feelings and having to ask each other for "pocket money"!

◆ See also, **Postnatal Depression**

Frostbite

Lengthy exposure to extreme cold can damage the tissues by affecting the blood circulation. But frostbite proper causes ice crystals to form in the skin as circulation ceases altogether in the affected parts, and this is even more serious.

Through exposure to extreme cold the circulation gradually fails to carry blood to the extremities, and the parts of the body that are frostbitten become lifeless, void of any sensation and literally frozen. Frostbite is most likely to occur in the extremities: the nose, ears, fingers and toes. The skin starts to become red and hard, and gradually becomes pale grey. The frostbitten area has no feeling, and a rash of little blisters may develop.

Frostbite is an emergency, and correct treatment is essential. The most important thing is to get the child out of the cold and wrapped up in blankets or coats.

It is equally important not to rub the affected areas – by doing this you are not improving the circulation, for it has stopped altogether in the frostbitten parts. Rubbing will make the damage worse.

The aim is to thaw out the frostbitten areas, and the way to do it is by applying warm – never hot – water. The water should be kept at blood heat, and if the hands or feet are affected they can be immersed in water. The face or other parts of the body can be warmed by your own body heat, as can hands and feet if warm water is unavailable. (You can put hands or feet in your armpits, or the child's face against your face or body.) If possible, feed the child sips of a warm drink.

When the damaged skin is pink again it should be covered with sterile dressings, just as if it were burnt. The child should then be taken to hospital, still warmly wrapped and preferably lying down to keep the frostbitten areas level with the heart.

FROSTBITE

In hospital the child will be seen by a doctor to check that blood circulation has been restored, and if necessary drugs will be given to improve the circulation. The affected areas will be properly dressed and the child may be kept in for observation or further treatment.

g

Gardening

Just as children respond with delighted curiosity to animals, so they seem to have an instinctive interest in nature and the outdoors. Fresh air, movement, colour, variety – all these can be found outside and at no cost at all.

Walks in the park or a pram parked outdoors are enough for a baby. Lying on his back, he happily absorbs his "worm's-eye-view" of clouds, branches, leaves and birds. However, as your baby becomes an active and curious toddler, he will demand more from the park or garden.

As you walk through the garden, show him a flower and describe to him the colour; find a furry leaf and let him feel the texture. Talk to him constantly, describing the shape of the plants, or the feel of them. "A yellow daisy, a slippery leaf" – no matter how often you repeat these descriptions, they will intrigue your child. This kind of descriptive trip through the garden is also an excellent way to show your child the meaning of words. He will learn to distinguish colour, he will begin to know what "rough", "prickly" or "smooth" mean. These words will not simply be learnt by him, but he will soon connect them to the real sensations. This kind of insight can be given to your baby even if you live in a flat.

All young babies take a while to learn to sniff and smell but they are stimulated by very positive scents. Crush mint, or sage, or lavender between your fingers and show him how to "smell". As you do so, describe the smell, name the herb and even tell him that mint is great with lamb, and sage with onions really makes a good chicken stuffing. Remember – his little mind is not really little, but a wonderful learning machine, full of curiosity and capable of absorbing an enormous amount of information.

This instinctive love of the natural world will become more obvious as your child learns to run and talk. All children adore the freedom of whizzing across a lawn, rolling on grass and skipping round trees. You can harness this genuine pleasure in the outdoors by introducing your child to a knowledge of plants. Show him how grass and flowers and trees start their life; show him the miracle of growth from seed to leaf and flower and fruit.

Your two-year-old will be entranced when the dull mustard and cress seeds, which you scattered over a wet flannel before he went to bed, have burst into little sprouts when he wakes up the next morning. You can also put beans and peas on damp cotton wool and your toddler will observe their rapid change into plants. Of course, at this stage, it would not be wise to let him hold or touch these seedlings because he's bound to pop them into his mouth. You can put the beans on damp cotton wool in a glass jar which he can hold and so enjoy the seeds without much danger.

However, at about three years of age, a child can really start to enjoy the process of gardening. He will love to have his own little spade and his own watering can, and to help you in the garden or with the window-box. He is too small to understand the time lapse between planting a seed or bulb, and its emergence from the soil. But he will love being busy, and it is important for him to feel the earth, and pebbles, and water dampening the soil.

There are certain seeds and cuttings which do show fairly rapid results and which you and your child can prepare in a simple way. Pineapple tops and carrot tops can be placed in jars of water, and over the following days and weeks the changes in growth can be seen. Avocado seeds and citrus seeds can also be observed as growing forms in jars in the kitchen. They all take a little while to show changes, but if you keep an eye on them, you can show your child each obvious stage of development.

Do try and connect these "kitchen gardens" to the flower beds and plants you pass in the park or in friends' gardens. Explain the process of growth, and tell the child that all these lovely flowers and trees started from tiny seeds, his plants in the kitchen. Start teaching him the names of the flowers you encounter – marigolds, sweet peas, roses, snapdragons. These sorts of conversations will deepen his knowledge and extend his vocabulary.

A four-year-old can be given his own plant or garden bed to look after. Provide him with a small patch of garden, or tub, or pot and label it with his name. Of course, he will need your help and supervision, but he will be very proud of his own pot plant or little patch of beans.

An ideal gardening "tool" for small children is a "growbag". These are available from major nurseries and can be used on balconies, patios or in the garden. The growing method is very basic and the growbags are designed for minimum effort with maximum effect. Show your child how to plant the seeds and ease him into a routine of watering. His delight as his tomato plants grow leaves, and then fruit, will be intense. And the whole family will be proud when they actually eat the fruits of his labour.

If you do not have a garden or balcony, give him a pot plant to care for. There are now many miniature fruit and vegetable hybrids and these may be ideal. Spread newspaper to protect your carpets and put the pot in a saucer. There are watering cans with a minimum spill design, and both you and your child will appreciate one of these.

There are few activities, or hobbies and crafts, which bring the feeling of deep satisfaction that growing plants brings to your child. The care and routine required for even a simple pot plant are all part of the gradual process of accepting discipline and responsibility. A gentle and cheerful, but never forced, introduction to caring for seeds and plants will add a special dimension to your child's life.

If you are yourself a keen gardener, you may find yourself growing a little impatient with his clumsy efforts but do try not to take over. First, he will lose confidence if you never let him finish his job, and second, he will lose interest because the activity seems to cause anger in his parent. It does not really matter if he makes an awful mess and gets himself covered with earth, or if he doesn't dig a proper-sized hole. What is really important for a small child is a slow and carefree introduction to gardening.

Many adults who are not keen gardeners are surprised to rediscover, through their child, the pleasures of nature. If you copy your baby and regard the world, even the tiniest flower, with the same wonder and concentration as he does, you will start to enjoy talking to him about plants and seeds. There will also be immense satisfaction for you in improving your baby's vocabulary and understanding of the world around him.

Constant contact with the outdoor world – walks in the park and trips to the country – is very healthy for growing children. If a child is given encouragement to observe plants and trees, and to involve himself in the growing process, his view of the world will be enriched. He will become aware of colours and shapes. He will know about the changing seasons. His vocabulary and practical manual abilities will also improve. And yet these qualities develop through the easy pleasures of gardening.

Not all plants are "fun", however. Make sure that you keep your child away from poisonous plants, such as:

- Aconite – the whole plant
- Broom – the seeds and pods
- Daffodil and narcissus bulbs
- Daphne – only the berries
- Honeysuckle – berries only
- Laburnum – seeds and berries
- Lupin – seeds and pods
- Rhubarb – berries only
- Yew – berries.

In fact, nearly all plants have some parts that are "poisonous", so the safest thing to do is impress upon your children from an early age that they should never put any plant material in their mouths.

Remember that even domestic pets can transmit disease, so caution is necessary when they share a garden with small children. Ponds must be totally inaccessible to small children, and the garden must be enclosed, especially if there is a main road or river nearby. If there are trees, walls or fences, children will climb them, so make sure your little ones are supervised.

Finally, keep all tools out of reach and store pesticides and fertilizers safely and dispose of the containers with care.

As well as growing their own plants, children can use a garden or park creatively in other ways. Let him make pictures with leaves, berries, acorns, chestnuts and cones. He will feel the knobby cone, the prickly holly leaves and the smooth berries, and incorporate these textures into his creative work.

Gastroenteritis

Gastroenteritis is an inflammation of the lining of the stomach and intestine which causes diarrhoea, vomiting, stomach pains and sometimes fever. It is a fairly common infection in both children and adults but should be treated as a serious illness when babies and young children become infected, since it can lead to complications. Children under the age of four are most at risk from fluid loss which in turn can lead to brain damage if the illness is not treated promptly.

The most common cause of gastroenteritis in children is a virus that is inhaled, rather like the common cold. Outbreaks, which usually occur in winter, can often spread rapidly in nursery schools and kindergartens and in other places where groups of children congregate.

Gastroenteritis can also be caused by bacteria on contaminated food which may be ingested or may be transferred to the mouth by dirty fingers. Contaminated food is often the result of poor hygiene in the kitchen. Your baby, for example, may become infected because of faulty cleaning and sterilization of bottles and teats; it is less common, of course, in breastfed babies. Also, by not washing your hands thoroughly after going to the toilet or changing nappies, you or a member of your family can spread infection when handling food or feeding bottles.

The main symptom of gastroenteritis is diarrhoea with greenish, watery stools but children may also be vomiting, have a fever and show signs of drowsiness and general illness. Older children and adults usually complain of loss of appetite and "gripeing" pains in the stomach. Your child may have the symptoms within a few hours of eating contaminated food but if it is a viral infection symptoms may take a couple of days to develop.

Dehydration is a danger when a child – and more seriously – a baby is losing a lot of fluids through vomiting and diarrhoea. The sick child is usually very thirsty but can only suck, or sip, feebly and then is unable to retain even small amounts. If your child's condition does not improve within 24 hours, or if his skin and mouth look dry and warm, and his eyes are sunken, call a doctor immediately. Bear in mind that babies are much more vulnerable to fluid loss than older children; if your baby has vomiting and diarrhoea for more than 6–8 hours you should always take him to the doctor.

In gastroenteritis, the first aim is to restore fluids to the body. If a baby is not able to retain liquids he may need to be treated in hospital with an intravenous drip until the water balance is restored. Often an older child can take a salt and sugar solution (*see* Diarrhoea) or apple juice in small sips until the diarrhoea settles. Your doctor may also suggest giving a balanced glucose and salt solution. Some children continue to have diarrhoea after the infection has passed and this can be due to damage to the inflamed intestine by sugar or protein, especially milk protein. If this is the case, talk to your doctor. In instances where the attack has been caused by bacteria, antibiotics may be prescribed to make sure that the infection is completely eliminated.

Your child should rest in bed until he is completely recovered. Give him an easily digested diet of mainly bland foods and liquids, but beware of acid drinks such as orange or lemon which can cause irritation. Yeast extract or clear soups are more suitable fluids.

Given that gastroenteritis can be caused by poor hygiene, it may be prevented by taking a few simple precautions:

● Be especially careful about preparing food and washing hands after going to the toilet.

● Make sure all food from the freezer is thoroughly thawed and thoroughly cooked; heat kills bacteria.

● Be particularly vigilant about cleaning and sterilizing feeding units and bottles.

● Always follow manufacturers' instructions about dates by which foods should be used.

● Keep work areas scrupulously clean.

● Do not allow pets near where food is being prepared.

● Keep food in the refrigerator, especially in summer.

● Get rid of flies in the kitchen.

● Keep waste bins covered, and do not allow your children to play near them.

Genitals

The genital organs in men and women are those that nature designed for the purpose of sex and reproduction. They are fully formed at birth but only function as reproductive organs from puberty onwards when hormonal development makes this possible.

Male genitals

In boys and men, the genitals consist of the testes and the penis which lie outside the body; the prostate gland, seminal vesicles and various tubes linking the genital system are found inside the lower abdomen. The two testes, which lie on either side of the penis, are each enclosed in a pouch of loose skin called the scrotum. After puberty the testes produce sperm and the male hormone testosterone (which is responsible for the sexual changes of puberty, such as the growth of body and facial hair and the breaking and deepening of the voice).

At birth a boy's genitals are larger in proportion to the rest of his body than at any other time until puberty. They may even look red and inflamed. This is perfectly normal and is caused by the mother's hormones. The doctor or midwife checks for any abnormalities and in a few days the swelling dies down.

The penis is a tube-shaped organ which has a collar of skin at the tip known as the foreskin. The penis provides the exit for urine and, after puberty, for the ejaculation of sperm. The foreskin is sometimes removed for cultural or medical reasons by an operation called circumcision.

Circumcision is medically necessary in only a small number of babies but when it is desirable for cultural or religious reasons, it is best done soon after birth. If you want your baby circumcized in the hospital, consult your doctor about this.

In some baby boys when the scrotum is touched – usually by cold hands – the testis retracts back into the abdomen. This condition usually rights itself within the first couple of years, with the testis becoming fixed in the scrotum and the passageway to the abdomen closing over.

Occasionally one or both testes do not descend before birth but in most cases this too rights itself within the first few years. You can test that the testicles are descended and fixed by feeling for them as separate, walnut-shaped objects inside the loose scrotal skin. Your doctor will check for the presence of both testicles on your regular visits to the clinic and later in routine medical examinations. If one or both have not descended or become fixed by the time your son is seven or eight, a simple operation may be necessary, since an undescended testicle will not be able to produce normal sperm and is more likely to develop cancer later.

Female genitals

The female reproductive organs – the ovaries, Fallopian tubes, womb and cervix (neck of the womb) lie inside the body. What we call the genitals consist of the vagina, a muscular canal situated below the neck of the womb, and the external genitals known as the vulva which protect the entrance to the vagina. The vulva consists of two folds of flesh called the inner and outer labia. The inner labia join together in front to partly cover a small fleshy organ, the clitoris, which is covered by a flap of skin called the clitoral hood. The vagina is the vessel into which sperm is deposited in the reproductive process.

Like a baby boy's genitals, a girl's labia may appear swollen and red at birth. A small amount of vaginal bleeding or a clear or whitish discharge is also quite normal in the first few days after birth. These are the result of the oestrogen hormone being passed from mother to baby.

There are few things that go wrong with the female genitals during childhood. If, however, there is any discharge, it is important to see a doctor as this could be a sign of infection, possibly as a result of a foreign object in the vagina. It is not uncommon for little girls to poke a bead or small object into the vagina when they are exploring their bodies.

Handling genitals

Babies usually become aware of their genital organs within their first year; when their nappies are left off it is only natural that they will explore these areas of their body. Later they discover that touching or fondling the genitals gives them a pleasurable sensation. Nearly all boys handle their penis and most girls also masturbate. This is perfectly normal and there is no need to discourage it. Above all, do not scold your child or stop him from masturbating; this could lead to problems with relationships in later life when sex and pleasure could be seen as something furtive and unhealthy.

Masturbation in public is embarrassing and the best you can do with a young child is to distract him. An older child can be told that it is simply bad manners to touch the genitals in public, like picking his nose – it is something not done in front of other people.

When you are washing or changing your baby, never pull back a small boy's foreskin for cleaning or for any other reason, and do not try to open the lips of your baby girl's vulva to clean inside; it is unnecessary. Always wipe from the front backwards to the anus; this minimizes the risk of bacteria spreading from the bowels to the bladder.

◆ See also, **Masturbation**

German Measles (Rubella)

German measles is an illness caused by the rubella virus. It is fairly common in both children and adults and is often undiagnosed because the symptoms are so mild. The rubella virus can, however, have a devastating effect if a woman catches it in the early months of pregnancy. Fortunately, however, vaccination is now available which gives women who are not already immune life-long protection against the disease.

An attack of rubella in the first four months of pregnancy can severely damage the growing fetus, causing a range of defects which include deafness, eye and heart defects, mental backwardness and bone deformities. Sometimes these are so severe that the baby is miscarried or dies soon after birth.

The reason for this is that the virus attacks the fetus at a crucial stage in its development, and while it is growing the fetus has no defences, or antibodies, to protect itself against the onslaught. It is ironic that an illness that is hardly noticed by children and adults can have such dreadful consequences for an unborn child. Children are most likely to get rubella in the spring or summer; it also appears to run in four- to six-year cycles of minor epidemics. Like the common cold (and many other viruses) it is passed from person to person by airborne droplets. After an incubation period of about two to three weeks, your child may develop symptoms similar to those of measles, only less severe.

The two most noticeable signs are a rash of fine pink dots which first appears on the face and neck but spreads to the trunk and limbs, and swollen lymph nodes behind the ear and the back of the neck. The child may also have a slight fever. The rash disappears within four or five days and may even go unnoticed.

Many cases of German measles pass undiagnosed since it seems hardly worth bothering the doctor over such a minor ailment.

There is no treatment which will cure the disease but you can relieve some of the symptoms if your child is feeling unwell or suffering discomfort from, for instance, a sore throat, for which rest at home and liquid paracetamol gargles will help.

In theory, your child is infectious for seven days before the rash appears and for up to eight days after it has gone. In fact, once the rash appears, the child will be highly infectious for up to five days.

You should inform your child's school and your place of work if anyone in your family has rubella, and mention the risk to any pregnant women. Also be especially sure to avoid your doctor's surgery or antenatal clinic if you or your child has rubella. There is no need for strict isolation but it is best to stay at home for four or five days if you have rubella.

Mention you have rubella to all new contacts, especially female ones.

Since 1988, the MMR (measles, mumps, rubella) triple vaccine has been given to all children at the age of 14 months in many countries. Before then, a single dose was given to girls between the age of 11 and 13. If your daughter was born before the MMR vaccine became available, ask your doctor about her immunity before she reaches puberty.

Gifted Children

Parents of gifted children know that it can be very hard going answering the constant demands of an extremely inquisitive, active, often sleepless child. As if this were not enough, super-bright children can find it hard to live with their own brightness and experience feelings of intense frustration. Behavioural problems and emotional problems sometimes result, leaving parents feeling exhausted and inadequate.

IQ used to be the only criterion used to judge whether a child had special abilities, but now it is recognized that children can shine in so many varied ways that pure intelligence is no longer regarded as the definitive key. What has also become clear is that outstanding ability is really not that rare, with 4 out of every 200 children born meriting the "gifted" tag, although sadly, the potential of half of these may never come to be recognized or stimulated.

So what happens if early potential fails to be recognized? For many children, the true extent of their ability just stays hidden, either because the child has been labelled awkward or stupid or shy. The good news is that research now shows that many of the signs of giftedness are present in babyhood and toddlerhood, and these signs can be picked up by parents and clued-up health visitors or nursery teachers. Knowing what to look out for and being aware enough to foster your child's budding talents can make life easier for families all round.

Although there are no hard and fast rules, there are various characteristics which can show up in the first two years in a child who later turns out to be extremely able. Some of these characteristics may even be evident as early as the first few weeks after birth. For instance, from just a few days old, your baby may seem to need conversation, stimulation and entertainment from other people and when this is not forthcoming he may cry from apparent boredom. He may also strike you as needing a great deal less sleep than babies of a similar age. Physically, early head control is said to be common among gifted children. Later on learning to crawl, walk and run at an earlier age than the average may be another sign of high potential, together with well-advanced manipulative skills.

Once he's mobile he may show a vehement determination to investigate new surroundings, sensations and experiences, despite your own determination to keep him away from danger. Another common pointer is well developed language – gifted children often learn to talk sooner than other children, and beyond the second and third birthdays, can be far ahead of the usual level for the age group both in length of sentences and words used. Having said this, it is known that Einstein didn't say a word until he was three years old (although he was extremely good at jigsaw puzzles).

Along with advanced use of words comes advanced levels of understanding. Gifted toddlers seem to be able to follow fairly complex instructions and latch on to new ideas quite early on. Another characteristic is the ability to understand abstract concepts. For instance, a child may quickly start to appreciate the notions of past, present and future, and learn the difference between "tomorrow" and "next week". He may learn songs, words and tunes easily, have a good sense of rhythm and have an excellent memory generally, remembering incidents and conversations even you have forgotten and which you thought meant nothing to him at the time.

Whatever signs of early brightness a child may show, remember that not all gifted children will fit these profiles in every way, and that most normal, healthy children with average, or above average intelligence will share some

of the above characteristics. Virtually all children will be driven to explore their surroundings relentlessly and all toddlers, once they can speak with confidence and fluency, will have a period of asking question after question.

Likewise, all children need entertaining, talking to and singing to, but gifted children need so much more; they are hungry for stimulation and keeping up with their voracious appetite for new activities and pastimes can test parents to the full. Finding ways to occupy your bright child will be your main objective from day to day. It can be exhausting catering for a child that needs a lot going on, but persevere and you'll get better at it.

Apart from joining the usual parent and toddler groups, investigate other ways in which you can get together with other parents and children – swimming sessions at your local pool, toddler gymnastics (to use up all that energy) and even storytime at your library.

At playgroup or nursery, check that there are a variety of stimulating activities and that the adult teachers and helpers involve themselves with the children's work and play. Don't be afraid to let the playgroup or nursery know that you feel your child is bright – there are ways of telling the staff without sounding as if you're bragging. You could perhaps indicate that home life is especially demanding because he's easily bored, and that he enjoys fresh challenges.

Formal teaching of skills such as music and dance is certainly possible for the pre-school age group, but do check that the teacher you choose has experience with young children. Even gifted children need to enjoy what they're doing, and to learn primarily through play and discovery. Properly organized team sports are probably beyond your child – after all, he's still learning about sharing and co-operating. But gymnastics and sports such as roller or ice skating are great fun, and most importantly, they remain a challenge, as they increase in difficulty. Other sports to consider for this age group include horse riding, cycling and short tennis (played with soft balls on a small-sized court).

It's essential to remember, though, that even gifted children need time off to be just children. They still need to run round the park, play on the beach and potter about. These are the times when their imagination will have free rein – they'll begin to resent it if every moment is directed towards learning or doing a specific activity.

For many parents, having a gifted child can be very much a mixed blessing. Some experts go as far as to say the problem presented is as difficult to cope with as a physical or mental handicap. There are now strong arguments for gifted children to be recognized as having "special needs" that should be addressed by the education authority – in the same way that disabled children, or children with emotional disorders, can have a tailor-made educational programme that matches their particular needs and abilities. Problems can start when the sheer frustration and boredom experienced by a child leads to bad behaviour and fluctuating emotions. For instance, an exceptionally intelligent young child who's yet to develop the maturity to cope with his anger and boredom at not being given enough to do may appear to be extremely naughty, aggressive and destructive. A few may be diagnosed as hyperactive or as having communication difficulties. So, it's always worth considering whether your child's frequent temper tantrums, disobedience and violent behaviour may be due to an active, enquiring mind that's not being recognized, or properly stimulated.

Sometimes, the frustration may come from not being able to put all his big ideas into practice. For instance, if your child enjoys very difficult puzzles but lacks the dexterity to put all the pieces together quickly he's likely to explode with rage! Later, at school, he may be reading well long before the other children and have lots of super ideas for stories – but not be able to write them down quickly enough for his liking. Strangely, it's very common for bright children's writing skills to lag way behind their reading ability. Quite simply, when intellectual age far outstrips emotional development, it's not surprising that a child will feel confused, even frightened by his own extraordinary abilities.

To cope with this as a parent, patience and love, rather than discipline, will be your greatest allies.

Some parents resent their children for being cleverer than they are, others feel embarrassed about their prodigy's abilities.

Try to remember though that it's wonderful that your child's intelligence could possibly make a contribution to the world when he's older, and that his talents could benefit himself and his future family. Let him know you understand that it might be difficult feeling "different", but you'll always support him in getting the very best out of life.

Parents of school-age gifted children often report how unsympathetic the school can be to a high flyer. It's true that it can be difficult for some teachers to engage the interest of all the children in the class no matter what their abilities. However, the best teachers manage this by concentrating on group work, and what's become known in secondary schools as individualized learning. A good school will cater for all its children, including the gifted ones, by being flexible and responsive to their differing needs. Try speaking to your child's headteacher if you feel the classwork isn't stimulating enough.

In some areas, special weekend schools have been established to give extra learning time to gifted children. Here, there may be the opportunity to work with computers or other advanced technology, or to learn other languages.

Children who excel at sports might benefit from extra coaching out of school – though there are plenty of cautionary tales about focusing even highly talented children too closely on their chosen sport. It's possible to peak too soon, like the string of American tennis starlets in the seventies, many of whom had to retire because of chronic injury. Or resentment may lead the child to switch off from the sport, as a protest against too much parental pushing.

Early promise doesn't always mean you have a child prodigy on your hands. Children develop at very different rates, and the apparently advanced, inquisitive and precocious four-year-old may end up perfectly intelligent and happy, yes, but perhaps not especially academic or intellectual.

Some talents – especially artistic or sporting – don't really come into their own until the school years. Once your child is older, able to express himself well, aware of what's on offer and able to make use of the equipment and the opportunities available, he may suddenly develop special skills in team games or music or other areas.

As a parent you need to be aware of your child's needs and to always be on the lookout for new interests and new sparks of curiosity in him so you can foster and encourage them. This is part of being what has been termed "a gifted parent" – something we can all aspire to.

Interestingly, until recently most people believed that intelligence was something that you were born with – you either had it or you hadn't. But controversial theories have emerged that it is possible to deliberately expand any child's brain power with intensive teaching if it's given right from infancy. The method, known as "hothousing", involves bombarding babies with information for several hours a day – a process aimed at making the most of the enormous potential of the young brain.

The results can be dramatic: by the age of two a typical hothoused baby can solve complex maths equations, and read encyclopedias by the age of four. Many five- or six-year-olds can play a musical instrument outstandingly well. However, many educationalists believe that such high-pressure learning could be damaging and stunt the ability to think creatively. What is clear is that stimulation and one-to-one communication can accelerate a child's mental development.

Glandular Fever

Glandular fever is a viral infection which mainly affects adolescents. Outbreaks often occur in schools and colleges where young people spend a lot of time in each other's company. Although babies under two have been known to get it, it is very rare; it is also uncommon in adults who are over the age of 30.

The virus is passed from person to person by close or intimate contact, including kissing (in fact, glandular fever is often known as the "kissing disease"). Some people are more susceptible to the virus than others but most cases are mild. Even so, it can take young people up to eight or more weeks to recover fully from the disease, during which time they may be moody and depressed.

The first symptoms are listlessness and fatigue, which many parents dismiss as simply problems of adolescence in an older child. However, the youngster soon develops headaches and chills, followed by fever, a sore throat and swollen lymph nodes in the neck and armpits. Sometimes a rash appears and, in severe cases, the liver may become inflamed and jaundiced. A blood test will confirm the disease.

There is no special treatment for glandular fever except rest and relief for the sore throat and headaches. With mild cases the child may not need to take time off school but most patients need a couple of weeks at home since they feel generally unwell and any exertion can make them feel very fatigued. Glandular fever can be debilitating and it may take several months before the child feels really well again. Depression and listlessness can last for many months and it is important that you – and your family – are aware of this.

Glue Ear

Glue ear occurs when the middle ear fills with a sticky mucus. The condition can affect one or both ears. It is common in young children and is usually the result of enlarged adenoids or of swelling of the lining of the Eustachian tubes from an infection or allergy. Either of these conditions can cause a build-up of fluid in the middle ear. Although the fluid itself is harmless, it may cause discomfort and it muffles sound from the outside world so that the child does not hear distinctly.

The child may complain of earache, and there may be a feeling of fullness in the ear and a sensation of clicking on swallowing or moving the jaw. Often, though, there is no pain with glue ear and the first signs are usually backwardness in speech. You may notice that your child is not repeating sounds correctly or that he turns one ear towards a sound in order to hear clearly. You can test your child by asking him to repeat certain sounds or words. If he cannot repeat them accurately, something is wrong and the problem needs to be diagnosed by a doctor. Hearing difficulties are common in young children but it is very important that they are treated promptly or learning and speech development could suffer, particularly when the child begins school.

If you or your child notice any of the above symptoms, take him to the doctor, who will look into the ear to see if fluid is there. He can also test the child's hearing. For a first attack, the doctor may prescribe decongestants and nose drops or antihistamines. If the problem recurs or becomes chronic, a simple operation may be needed to drain away the fluid via a hole made in the eardrum, and a grommet – a tiny plastic tube – is inserted in the hole to keep the channel open. Later the grommets may be taken out by the doctor, or they may fall out on their own, leaving the small hole in the drum to heal up. Hearing should then be normal.

After the operation it is necessary to keep the ears dry, so ask your doctor's advice about ear plugs to wear in the bath or shower and in swimming pools.

Grandparents

Nearly all grandparents revel in the new role they have to play and often seem to be having a better time of it than you. Indeed, most problems tend to arise when grandparents embrace the idea of "grandparenthood" over-enthusiastically and make plans involving your new baby without discussing them with you first.

It is important to establish clearly defined roles early on so that as the child grows older he can benefit from having an easy and relaxed relationship with his grandparents.

Many ideas regarding bringing up babies and children have changed dramatically over the years, so when your views clash with those of the grandparents don't be surprised. The trick is to listen to the advice offered and then decide whether or not you wish to take it.

If you don't like the idea suggested, just point out in a firm but humorous way that you're going to try your own idea first. Your main priority is caring for your child as best you can, so don't let yourself be bullied or made to feel guilty. At the same time, it can make grandparents feel hurt and left out if you keep dismissing their ideas.

Attitudes to working during pregnancy and early childhood have also changed enormously. Nowadays, most women continue to work up to the later months of their pregnancy, and there are always stories of women who manage to run a business up to an hour before they give birth!

Returning to work after the baby is born remains a hotly controversial topic. Grandparents will doubtless have their views on this, but, again, you have a perfect right to do what you think is best. You may work to supplement the family income or because you enjoy it and want to continue your career, or both.

Grandparents may find this difficult to understand and accuse you of neglecting your child. If this is so, it will be very hard for you not to feel guilty, as you have probably thought about the pros and cons yourself, and few decisions come with a "you-have-done-the-right-thing" guarantee. In other words, their fears and worries about you going back to work probably echo your own fears and worries. But stick to your guns and remind yourself that it is your decision, and your child may well benefit from the situation – after all, a happy mother makes a happy baby.

Once your toddler starts going to a playgroup, you can encourage the grandparents to come with you to collect him. They may not be used to the idea of pre-school education, but by involving them like this they will feel they are helping in your child's early learning years.

Grandparents have an infuriating habit of pointing out that they have done it all before and therefore must know best. Whereas you cannot dispute the fact that they have brought up their own children, you can point out that this is your child and you must be allowed to do things your own way, and make your own mistakes, too.

You may also tell them that trends change and medical research has advanced at an amazing rate so that what was considered good for baby then is not necessarily good for baby now. You might soothe them by saying that you want to see what suits the baby best. This is a tactful way of saying that you won't always follow their advice, but that sometimes you will.

Nutrition is one of the old chestnuts that mums and dads and grandparents fall out over. A lot of it stems from a basic change in attitude to children's eating habits over the years. Rigid mealtimes and "force feeding" are now considered unnecessary and unhelpful; and if the grandparents bristle when your one-year-old covers himself and all available surfaces with food, remind them that the sooner he gets this out of his system, the sooner he will become bored with it and will want to become a neater eater in his own good time.

Contrary to stereotyped opinion, some grandparents present a problem by not seeming interested enough in their grandchildren. Perhaps you look as if you're coping so well that you don't need or want any help. Or, they are so over-anxious not to interfere that they end up never coming near you and their grandchild. They may just feel that at this stage in their lives they are unable to relate to little babies or very small children. Or they may be feeling neglected themselves, and you have to try and include them more in your life – ask them to help with nappy changing, mealtimes, days out, and so on.

Try not to feel resentful towards them. Be positive, and try to involve them in your family life. You will probably find that your children adore them.

At times you will be irritated by comments from grandparents, who will tend to compare everything you do with what happened in their day,

naturally enough. To be fair, their comments may be well intentioned and the grandparent may genuinely want to help. Remember, too, that following the birth of your baby you may be oversensitive to remarks, as you may be tired and are overwhelmed at how busy and demanding your life has suddenly become.

Spoiling a child is what many parents dread most, and they often assume that grandparents will do exactly that. But being nice to children doesn't spoil them, so let everybody enjoy themselves. The only time that this indulgence creates problems is when your child expects you to behave in the same way. Just say firmly: "When you go to see Grandma and Grandpa you are allowed to do such and such, but at home we have different rules." Your child will understand the difference, and happily accept two sets of rules if they are set out clearly and stuck to.

Grazes

Children regularly graze themselves in falls and minor accidents and although grazes can be painful they are hardly ever serious. A graze usually results from a sliding fall which damages the superficial layers of the skin, leaving a very tender raw area. This may bleed and ooze pus. A graze or abrasion only affects the outer layer of the skin, the epidermis, which is largely made up of dead cells. When the epidermis is damaged in a graze, cells move up from the dermis to replace the damaged ones, so no scarring occurs.

However, because millions of tiny nerve endings are exposed in a graze, young children find the intense stinging pain quite distressing and so deserve sympathy plus a little fuss over treating the wound.

Most grazes are covered with dirt and grit and the first thing to do is to clean the wound. Soap and warm water are as good as anything but you can use a mild antiseptic instead. As it is impossible to get rid of all the germs, avoid rubbing the graze too harshly and making it even more raw.

Ideally, the graze should be left exposed to the air; within a few hours a tough scab forms over it, acting as a natural protective dressing. In practice it may be better, where young children are concerned, to cover the graze with a dressing to prevent it from rubbing on clothing or becoming dirty. Also, children tend to pick at unprotected scabs, and so delay the healing process.

For a large graze, cover with a dry gauze strip and hold it in place with surgical tape. Never apply any adhesive dressing directly on to a graze as it can be extremely painful to remove. Change the dressing daily and leave the graze uncovered at night to allow the scab to dry hard.

Although grazes rarely cause problems, some do become infected. If there is redness beyond the area of a graze which seems to be slow in healing, or if it is oozing moisture or pus after a couple of days, take the child to the family doctor.

◆ See also, **Bandages**, **Cuts and Grazes**, **Dressings**, **First Aid**

Growth

Growth is an amazing process which is characterized by rapid development of the body in the first few years of life, after which the rate of growth slows down before a sudden spurt towards maturity in adolescence. Although every child follows this basic pattern of growth, there are wide variations in what is termed "normal growth"; children, like adults, come in all shapes and sizes, very few of them abnormal.

The most important factor for growth is adequate nutrition. Very occasionally hormone deficiencies or genetic defects can cause growth problems, but these are rare and will almost certainly come to light early on in your child's life as your doctor monitors his height and weight. Nowadays, even these unusual growth problems can be successfully treated, so that a child grows in the normal way.

The birth size of your baby depends on several factors, including inheritance (the parents' size), the sex of the baby and place in the order of birth (second and subsequent babies in a family tend to be born bigger that the first baby), and the health and circumstances of the mother during her pregnancy.

The factors which influence birth size carry on affecting growth until the age of two or thereabouts. It is only after this that a child's individual growth hormones come into play. One of the few possible pointers to eventual height and stature is the size of your baby's hands and feet. Large or long feet can mean that your baby or toddler is destined to have a big frame as an adult.

Whatever your baby's birthweight, you can expect him to lose a little weight within the first five days of life. He will regain it within about ten days and then gain weight steadily. Your baby's weight will be monitored at your regular visits to the clinic, and you will be able to see this pattern for yourself.

There are a few exceptions to this pattern, such as premature babies or babies who have been ill in the early weeks of life. These frequently have a "catch-up" spurt of growth, although premature babies may well remain slightly smaller than average throughout their growth period.

The method of measurement preferred by doctors and health visitors to chart expected growth is percentile charts. These charts do not show just the average height and weight for your child's age, but give the 100 bands of expected growth for children of different sizes from birth. The graph on which you plot your baby's development will show the average weight, height and head circumference of children at given ages.

Often, these graphs are simplified so that they have three bands of growth for boys and girls separately, representing light, average and heavy babies. You'll find that your child's growth will fall within one of these bands, although there will of course be fluctuations on the curve, according to the particular circumstances and factors affecting your child's growth.

What these charts do is to allow you to see that your child is developing within the range of growth expected from his or her birthweight: some flexibility is built in, but a sudden jump into a different band could be a sign that you should watch your child's weight or height gain more closely. As long as your child's weight gain is in proportion to his increase in height, then there's no need to be concerned – he may naturally be a small, medium or extra large child. Only when there is a dramatic weight increase not matched by a growth spurt upwards, or vice versa, need you feel bothered.

Growth is rapid in the first six months (approximately 20 g/0.7 oz) a day) and then slows down towards the end of the first year (when it is approximately 15 g/0.5 oz a day). In general a baby of average weight will increase its length by a quarter during the first six months, and double its weight.

It is sensible not to be too anxious about your baby's weight. What matters is the overall regularity of his weight gain, not the amount gained at each weighing. Parents who keep a record of their baby's growth will see how quickly a baby tends to get over minor setbacks.

Once he has passed his first birthday, your baby's weight gain begins to slow down. The average child gains about 2.5 kg (5½ lb) in weight and 12 cm (4¾ in) in height during the second year. At this stage he needs to be weighed and measured about every three months to check his progress. Although he may still seem ill-proportioned and baby-like in appearance, this soon changes when he begins to walk and develops the sturdy little body of a toddler.

Between his third and fifth years your child's growth rate will slow down even more (to 2 kg/4 lb 6 oz and 7 cm/2¾ in, on average per year); his body will lose much of its stockiness and he will become more elongated. He may even look quite thin but this is normal and nothing to worry about. At this stage of growth he needs to be measured and weighed roughly every six months.

From the age of four or five, your child continues to grow at a fairly steady rate until the growth spurt of adolescence; on average this will be 10 cm (4 in) for boys and 8 cm (3⅛ in) for girls.

Children need to be measured and weighed about once a year throughout their childhood, to determine whether they are within the normal range – percentile – for their age. The majority of children are, but with the few who are outside the limits, doctors will look for an obvious cause such as bad nutrition, or simply whether the child has very tall or very short parents. In rare cases, the child may have a growth deficiency and this will be diagnosed and treated.

Adolescence

There is tremendous variation in the ages at which the adolescent growth spurt starts and this can cause anxiety in parents (and children) who see classmates and friends of a similar age developing into adulthood while their own child seems to lag behind. In fact, the growth spurt may be anywhere between the ages of 9½ and 13½ for girls and between 10½ and 16 for boys. Between the ages of about 11 and 15 a child's muscle growth rate almost trebles.

The adolescent growth spurt actually starts before the other changes associated with puberty in both sexes. This is particularly so in girls who may grow up to very near their full height without much change in the shape of their breasts and hips. The degree of sexual development varies greatly from individual to individual and the single factor that seems to have most influence is the age at which puberty occurred in the parents. If both parents had a late puberty, then the children can also be expected to be late.

Growth in height takes place through an increase in the size of the bones of the arms, legs and back. Bones grow through new bone being added along their width and at both ends. By studying X-rays of their bones doctors can arrive at children's "bone age". This may differ from a child's real age by a couple of years, which is not unusual. Bone age is a useful way of detecting any growth abnormalities early in a child's life when there is still time for treatment.

Hormones

Growth is controlled by a number of hormones, of which the most important is growth hormone, produced by the pituitary, a gland attached to the brain. A very few children do lack this hormone, which can be replaced if its lack is detected early in the child's life. Thyroid hormone is also essential for normal growth and if this is lacking, growth will fall away from the average but this too can be rectified with hormone therapy. At puberty the sex hormones are responsible for the bodily changes that take place in boys and girls.

Growth problems

If a child's growth rate does not seem normal, particularly in the early years, you should take him to the doctor who will probably measure the child's bone age. If it lags more than two years behind the real age, the doctor may recommend that the child be taken to a "growth clinic" to be given growth hormone. This will restart normal growth but it may not be able to make up for the height the child has already failed to gain. This is why it is important to get advice from the doctor early before much growing time is lost.

A very small number of girls are born with a faulty gene which results in a condition called Turner's syndrome. This affects only one in 3000 girls who remain small and who require sex hormone replacement in tablet form in order to acquire normal female characteristics.

Occasionally, poor growth starts in the womb. This can happen when the mother is in bad health, has a disease when pregnant or is undernourished. Smoking and alcohol can also cause poor development. Although children suffering from this will be born small and remain shorter than would be expected from their parents' height, they often grow up quite healthy and there is usually no need to worry about their overall development.

Gymnastics

A healthy, curious baby will roll over, sit unsupported, stand erect, walk, run, jump and tumble with no extraordinary help. The force of his own development will see to that and a child does all these things as soon as his body is ready. He may walk earlier than the little boy next door, or even a few months later, but do it he will, following a predictable sequence governed by his own inner clock. So why exercise?

There are some very good reasons why a more conscious approach to your baby's development and well-being can be a source of joy and benefit to you both. In itself, exercising with your child is a fun and stimulating way of spending time together. Through simple and gentle movements you can increase your baby's awareness of his body, help build strength and control of joints and muscles and, as he grows into a toddler and small child, improve his sense of balance and co-ordination.

In working through exercises with your child you act as his partner, lending him your own strength and co-ordination for balance and support. Guide him through a series of carefully chosen movements that are fun and appropriate to his abilities.

Although you can't speed up your child's natural pattern of development simply by exercising, you can give him every opportunity to practise his muscle control. Infants gain control over their bodies from the top downwards. Before they learn to sit they have to be able to hold their head well. Once the muscle control has moved downwards they learn to straighten their back, crawl and eventually walk.

Whatever happens, try not to hurry this process along or you may put your baby's little body under undue strain. For instance, if you pull your baby up unsupported before he's ready, you'll see his little back curved forward under the weight of his head which will droop or sink backwards into the spine.

Instead, give him the chance to strengthen his upper body by placing him on his tummy once in a while. Instinctively, he will try to push himself up with his arms so that his head, neck and upper chest are off the floor. As he gets better at balancing he may turn his head to look from side to side. Some babies are really miserable when in this position so don't let him stay there long if it's making him unhappy.

From about three months, your baby may try to pull himself up using his hands to grip yours and will enjoy being given the opportunity to swing up gently towards you. Try supporting him firmly under the arms and sit him on your knees or on the edge of a table to get him used to being upright.

At around six months, when his back is stronger, but when he still tends to swing forward at the hips when sitting, encourage him to support himself on his arms by placing his hands flat on the floor in front of him. If he's happy in this position, try putting a small cushion on his lap and stretch his arms out on to it, encouraging him to lean forward. This leaning does several things; it helps his balance, relaxes his back, allowing it to gain strength gradually and it prepares him for crawling.

Your baby's legs will also benefit from gentle exercise. Left to his own devices he will happily kick away when lying on his back. You can extend the possibilities by guiding his legs in a bicycling motion. If your baby is enjoying one of his regular kicking sessions, take hold of his ankles and gently rotate his legs first in one direction then in the other. Then let him push the soles of his feet up against your hands too.

At around seven to eight months, babies begin to want to straighten their bodies and stand up in your grasp. Soon, you'll find they won't miss an opportunity to bounce. Put your baby facing you on your lap, give him your finger to hold and let him bend his knees and move his body up and down, up and down, over and over again. It's what he wants to do instinctively and it's all-important preparation for crawling and walking in the coming weeks and months.

Once your baby is crawling (and even if he misses out this phase altogether), he'll soon he pulling himself up into a standing position using your hands, legs or anything else he can clutch. Then soon afterwards, he'll be taking his first steps – or "cruising" – between pieces of furniture. When you sense he's almost ready to walk alone, stand up and take his hands from behind, raising his hands to about shoulder level. Let him lead you forwards. He may delight in this, but if he's afraid or not yet secure, increase the way he walks like this very gradually. Many children take their very first independent steps between two adults, so give him the opportunity to launch himself excitedly from the arms of one parent to another by squatting just two or three baby paces apart.

Your toddler and energetic pre-schooler will gradually demand other and more vigorous forms of physical activity, some of which you can provide even in a limited space. Walking practice can be made more fun by giving him something to do at the same time. Begin quite simply with fetching and carrying games, perhaps by giving a small basket to collect objects in. As he becomes steadier he'll enjoy pulling a toy which follows him about. Walking backwards can be another game and is a good exercise for improving balance and co-ordination. The pull-along toys will come in useful here too. Encourage your child to grasp the handle or cord with both hands in front of him and to step backwards while pulling the toy towards him.

Climbing is the next important skill to learn and this will be no problem if you have carpeted stairs in your home. If you don't, let him develop this ability in a friend's house, then he won't greet this common obstacle with fear or recklessness. Most crawling babies will gleefully scale a flight of stairs on all fours. Keep close behind him and teach him how to come down by crawling backwards. After this he should soon be able to do it the other way, lowering himself from one step to another on his bottom.

As he grows he'll want more challenging activities. Here you can use your imagination – and his – and a few simple objects to transform your living space temporarily into a mini gym. Large floor cushions, air beds, an old cot mattress or even a duvet are great for rolling, jumping, or tumbling on to. Move any furniture to the sides of the room and make sure that your exercise area is quite safe.

Using cushions to break your toddler's falls, guide and support his body through a sequence of swings, forward and backward bends and somersaults. Bending and rolling exercises work on the arms, shoulders and spine and will strengthen and relax the whole body.

Use a ball or a bean bag (made from 13 cm/5½ in squares of fabric and filled with dried beans) as props for your exercise routine.

Show your child how to grasp a ball between his feet, raise his legs into the air and lower them again without dropping it. A child's trampoline is a sound investment which can be used for endless bouncing and imaginative exercises. If nothing else, it may persuade your child not to bounce so much on your bed!

Babies who can crawl, toddlers and young children all enjoy tunnels. These can be simple or complex. A cardboard box laid on its side with the flaps taped back can fascinate a little baby for whom it offers a chance to orient himself in a new kind of space. Combine boxes with furniture for a toddler, and for an older child create a system of tunnels as a complicated obstacle course. If you work together you'll find he's constructed low passages through which only he can slither and platforms which may be the secret entrances to a castle. It's all good exercise and fun too.

He'll be working on his balance and co-ordination all through these early years and many simple games can help him. One of the easiest involves chalking a line on lino, or pinning a string taut on a carpet, and asking him to walk along it placing one foot directly in front of another. Show him how extending his arms out to each side can help him balance. Later you can place a board securely on a couple of bricks and let him walk the length of it. In fact, one long board, 30 cm (12 in) wide, by 4 cm (1 in) thick, and 150 cm (5 ft) long is a very good investment.

At around the age of five, or maybe even slightly younger, your child may be ready to join a formal gymnastics class. This will help him to develop existing skills further, and learn new ones. Above all, it should be a fun way for him to explore the way his body moves and to keep growing bones and muscles supple.

◆ See also, **Exercise and Fitness**

Hand-eye Co-ordination

Babies start life using their hands and eyes separately, but in order to become an active participant in life, the baby has to put the two together and learn to reach out and touch the things he sees. This process is known as hand-eye co-ordination.

At around ten to twelve weeks, a baby finds his hands by eye, as well as by touch. He knows where they are and will play with them and watch them all the time. He will bring them together, move them apart, then bring them together again, learning to control them as he does so. He will also begin to follow a moving object with his eyes. When he is about three months old he will start to explore his hands with his mouth as well as his eyes, putting individual thumbs and fingers in and inspecting them.

Reaching out to touch objects is actually a very complicated task for a baby of three months. In order to do this he has to see it, want it, estimate how far away it is, then use complex movements of his arms and hands to get it. You cannot actually teach your baby how to do this, but you can help things along. Toys he can swipe at are excellent at this stage, and things suspended from his cot or pram will encourage him to reach out and try to judge distances. A light rattle is particularly good as the noise it makes will encourage the baby to try to repeat what he has achieved. It also helps him to make a connection between what his eyes are seeing and what his hands are doing.

At around four to six months your baby will be able to focus on objects at almost any distance and follow them with his eyes in any direction. He will gradually stop having to look from his hand to an object and back again before grasping it and by six months he will be able simply to lift his arm and move his hand straight to the thing he wants. During this period he will also learn to get hold of what he touches: he will keep his hand open until it makes contact, then close it around the toy. Remember that at this stage he will grab hold of anything and everything within reach, so keep anything unsuitable in a safe place.

The development of hand-eye co-ordination is a crucial part of your childs first six months, and will remain important throughout his life, helping to perfect skills such as driving for example.

Handicaps

◆ See **Disabilities**

Hay Fever

Hay fever is caused by an allergy to one or more of various substances in the air when inhaled. The most common allergen (substance causing an allergic reaction) is pollen.

The nose, sinuses, eyes and upper throat react in hay fever because these are the parts that are most exposed to the air-borne allergen. Although pollen from grass and trees is the most common allergen, the same symptoms can be caused by fungus spores, animal hair and scurf, and house mites; and such attacks are still loosely referred to as hay fever.

A child with hay fever sneezes a great deal, often particularly in the morning. His eyes feel itchy and are watery, the head feels heavy as the nose and sinuses become blocked, and the throat may be sore too.

Hay fever caused by pollen is seasonal and occurs only when the particular type of pollen responsible is in the air. The first pollens to appear each year are tree pollens. Plane trees and silver birches in particular are often responsible for cases of hay fever occurring in mid-March.

In mid-summer, grass pollens are released into the air, followed by nettle pollen, and from mid-summer until late autumn, fungus spores are abundant in the air. House mites and animal fur can cause trouble at any time of the year. A child can be allergic to more than one of these substances, so that hay fever can continue through the seasons.

Hay fever develops because of a genetic error in the body's immune system. This error affects the receptors on cells called mast cells for an antibody called IgE. This is produced in unusually large quantities in people with allergies. The error causes IgE to attach more firmly to mast cells.

The antibody attaches itself to mast cells, which contain, among other chemicals, histamine. The attachment of the allergen to adjacent IgE molecules strains the mast cell membranes, and they release histamine. This release of histamine and other chemicals from the mast cells causes the blood vessels to dilate (increase in diameter) and this makes the mucous cells in the nose and sinuses become overactive. Children whose bodies manufacture a great deal of antibody in response to allergens tend to develop asthma and eczema, rather than simple hay fever.

By far the best treatment for hay fever is prevention – making sure that the child is not exposed to the allergen that brings on the symptoms. This means that if a family pet causes hay fever, the pet will unfortunately have to find a new home. House mites can be kept under control by means of frequent vacuum cleaning and by using synthetic materials, as opposed to feathers and down, in the bedding.

Unfortunately there is no foolproof way of making sure that the child is not exposed to dust containing pollens or spores. Keeping away from trees and grass as much as possible helps – a day out at the seaside being preferable to a day in the country during the pollen season.

Antihistamines

Antihistamines are often prescribed to stop the allergic reaction of hay fever, but these can tend to cause drowsiness. Your doctor may prescribe a succession of types until a suitable one is found. Steroid injections can bring dramatic relief, but they are prescribed only if the condition is really incapacitating, since they usually have undesirable side-effects and are considered to be unsuitable for long-term use.

A low-dose steroid preparation may be prescribed to be puffed into the nose three times a day, or a solution of sodium cromoglycate may be prescribed to prevent the mast cells from releasing histamine. Both of these treatments have to be administered every day throughout the hay fever season to stop the symptoms developing, and have no effect once symptoms have occurred.

Do not be tempted to treat a child who has hay fever with decongestant nose drops. These are intended only for short-term use, when the runny or blocked nose is caused by an infection. Prolonged use can cause further inflammation of the mucous lining of the child's nose and sinuses and make the problem worse.

If your child suffers badly from hay fever your doctor may decide to do a patch test. In this test, small patches of skin are exposed to the various possible allergens to see which one causes a reaction.

Following the result of this test, the child may receive a course of injections of minute quantities of the allergen in the hope that the immune system will learn to react normally to it. This desensitization treatment is always carried out by a specialist, as there is a danger that the child will have a severe reaction. The specialist will make a careful observation of the child for about two hours after each injection to make sure that no allergic reaction occurs, and will always be equipped to deal instantly with reactions.

◆ See also, **Allergies**

Head Injuries

The brain is the most important organ in our bodies, since it controls everything we do. This is why it is vital to protect a child's head from injury as much as possible and to seek medical help at once in the event of an accident in which the head is hurt.

There are two ways in which the head can be injured, and these are known as deceleration and acceleration. In deceleration the head is moving and is suddenly brought to rest – as when a child falls and hits his head on the pavement or when he is flung against the windscreen in a car accident. In acceleration the head is still, and receives a violent blow – as when a child is hit by a moving swing or by a flying cricket ball.

In either type of accident, if the blow is violent, the soft tissue of the brain can be severely shaken inside the skull. This may cause unconsciousness (see Concussion).

The critical factor is whether damage has been done to the blood vessels. Bleeding in the brain rapidly causes pressure to build up, since the brain is encased within the inflexible shell of the skull and has no room to expand. Serious damage to the skull is caused if the bleeding does not stop or if the pressure is not quickly relieved.

It is also possible for the skull to be fractured as a result of a head injury (*see* Fractures).

Of course it is not always the case that a head injury results in serious damage to the brain or skull. In many cases there will just be cuts and bruises or a short episode of concussion with no lasting effects. Cuts and grazes on the scalp look worse than they are, because they bleed a lot, but they usually heal quickly. However, any injury to the head should be treated as potentially serious.

If the child is bruised and bleeding after a blow to the head, but has no other symptoms, it is unlikely that any serious damage has been done. But even so it is important to keep a close watch on the child over the next 24 hours to make sure there is no dizziness, loss of memory or blurred speech. Medical attention should be sought at once if any of these symptoms begins to develop.

Concussion

Following a blow to the head, perhaps if the child falls heavily and the head hits something hard, the child may experience concussion. When concussion occurs, the child may be briefly unconscious, may feel dizzy and perhaps have a headache on recovering, and sometimes has no recollection of the events leading up to or immediately after the accident. If the child has these symptoms he should be seen by the family doctor or taken to hospital straight away. Usually the only treatment needed for concussion is rest, but the child will probably be kept in hospital for observation for at least 24 hours after the accident.

Fracture of the skull

This is not always as serious as it sounds. Strictly speaking all the bones of the face are part of the skull. Injuries here will usually be obvious. But if the base or lower part of the skull is fractured the only symptoms apart from dizziness, perhaps with a brief spell of unconsciousness, may be a straw-coloured liquid trickling from the nose or blood or discharge from the ear. Such leakage of cerebro-spinal fluid calls for specialist management in hospital to avoid infection (meningitis). As long as there is no bleeding in the skull a full recovery is most likely. But it is essential to call an ambulance at once for suspected skull injuries.

Fractures of the bones of the face are repaired by being wired together for support until they have healed. Nursing care will be given in hospital while the child is recovering unless the injury was a minor one (perhaps to the nose). The cranium heals itself, and once it has been established that there is no damage to the brain, the child will be kept under observation in hospital for a while as the healing takes place.

Bleeding in the brain

If your child is knocked unconscious and does not regain consciousness an ambulance should always be called. A symptom of bleeding within the brain in these circumstances is one or both pupils being dilated (enlarged) and failing to constrict (get smaller) when a bright light is shone into the eye.

Another symptom of bleeding in the brain is the big toe moving upwards if a blunt object is rubbed along the sole of the foot (normally this would make it turn down). Permanent brain damage can be the result if the child is not given immediate hospital treatment.

Bleeding in the brain can stop by itself. If there is bleeding between the skull and the brain a surgeon will try to stop the bleeding and relieve pressure in the brain to avert serious brain damage. The child may be put into intensive care to make sure the essential bodily functions continue while attempts are made to stop the bleeding, or while the body is trying to heal itself if nothing can be done surgically. There may be a long period of unconsciousness, but recovery is still possible.

Epidural haematoma

This is an injury in which an artery within the skull is damaged, causing bleeding between the skull and the outer membrane of the brain and damage to the brain. The symptoms of this are a child relapsing into unconsciousness. This injury is usually caused by a blow to the temple, and needs immediate medical treatment.

What to do

The following are basic guidelines for action in the event of a head injury:

● Minor injuries should be cleaned and dressed (*see* Bandages, Dressings) and will soon heal. Stitches may be needed for large cuts.

● Always take your child to see a doctor after a head injury which made him unconscious for more than five seconds, even if there seem to be no after-effects.

● Be on the lookout for symptoms of brain injury after a child's head has been knocked – signs to watch for are headaches, dizziness, forgetfulness, drowsiness, confused speech, unsteady walk or further periods of unconsciousness. These may even occur several days after the accident.

● Always call an ambulance for a head injury when in doubt.

◆ See also, **Bandages**, **Concussion**, **Dressings**, **Falls**, **Fractures**

Head Lice

There are three types of lice – head lice, body lice and pubic lice. Children are most likely to be affected by head lice. It has now been established that head lice, once thought to be associated with poor hygiene, thrive in clean hair. Many children suffer from an infestation at some stage, as it is so easily passed from child to child in group situations, and there is no shame involved.

The eggs of the head lice are laid in the hair, close to the scalp, and secured to it by a cement-like substance. After about eight days the eggs begin to hatch and the new lice feed off the scalp by sucking blood. If left untreated the young lice moult three times over a period of about nine days, and after this they are fully formed adults with the ability to reproduce. Female lice lay up to ten eggs a night.

An infestation of head lice is the result of head-to-head contact with someone who is already host to the lice.

The main symptom of head lice is an itching scalp. If you inspect the child's scalp you should be able to see either the eggs, which are about 1 mm long, or the "nits", which are actually the discarded egg casings, still cemented to the hair.

Since lice are not put off by cleanliness, washing the hair frequently doesn't help. Keeping the child's hair short, or pinned back, so that hair-to-hair contact with other children is less likely, may help a little, but there is not a great deal that can be done to protect a child from infestation.

The safest way to deal with head lice is to use emulsions of benzyl benzoate, or lotions of carbaryl or permethrin. They are sprinkled on to the scalp and rubbed into the hair. They have an alcoholic base and are inflammable, so must be used carefully, and in a well-ventilated room.

Ask your doctor's advice before buying a treatment for head lice, because the lice and eggs can become resistant to particular forms of treatment. Your doctor will know which treatment is being used successfully in your area at the particular time of the infestation. And as lice move easily from head to head, it is sensible for every member of the family to be treated once any child in the family has lice. Parents and grandparents can carry head lice too!

Always look regularly in your child's scalp every week, under a good light, especially around the ears, crown and neck line. An itchy scalp is a suspicious sign and you should be on the lookout if you hear of an outbreak in your child's class. Equally, you should inform the class teacher if your own child has head lice so that other parents can be told to check their children's hair.

Remember that regular combing, brushing and checking may help to prevent infestation, and always discourage your children from sharing brushes and combs.

Healthy Eating

It is ironic that while many of the world's children are malnourished because of a lack of quantity, or even variety, of food, children in the wealthy countries may be going short of vital nutrients because of too much choice. Every parent wants their child to have a well-balanced diet but not everyone knows what this actually is or how to encourage their children to eat what is good for them instead of what is not.

Research has shown that, left to themselves and presented with a variety of fresh, nourishing foods, children will, over a period of time, eat the quantity and kinds of food they actually need. The problems begin when they are allowed to fill up with highly processed, sugar-rich foods which provide only so-called "empty" calories. Not only does this reduce their appetite for other foods which may be more nutritious, but it also discourages them from eating things with different, more subtle tastes and a variety of textures.

Eating a well-balanced diet means taking in a wide enough variety of food to provide all the essential things that the body needs to function and grow. There are six basic nutrients that we all need – carbohydrates, protein, fats, vitamins, minerals and water.

Carbohydrates

These are made up of starches and sugars which are broken down to provide energy. Sugar occurs naturally in many foods and in itself is not harmful. Refined white sugar, like white flour, however, contains no vitamins or minerals and should not be eaten in excess. It can lead to obesity and is also very bad for teeth, so it's best to discourage a "sweet tooth" from the very start. Cereals, bread, pasta and pulses all provide useful carbohydrates.

Proteins

These are needed for energy, growth and tissue repair. They may be classified as "first class" – meaning complete – or "second class". Animal proteins such as meat, fish and dairy products are all first class because they provide all the amino acids we need. Vegetables, cereals and pulses are also good sources of protein – but because not all amino acids needed are present they are known as "second class". However, combining different plant foods can easily solve this problem, as can adding some dairy produce – so cauliflower cheese or lentils with brown bread, for example, make up combinations which provide necessary amino acids and are satisfactory alternatives to meat.

If you are bringing up your child as a vegetarian, or if your child simply refuses to eat meat, you will need to bear this in mind, and perhaps seek the advice of a dietician. If your child likes fish encourage him to eat it; fish is a wonderful source of protein and minerals. Otherwise eggs, cheese, milk and nut spreads are all very valuable foods for a growing vegetarian.

Fat

A small amount of fat is an essential element of everyone's diet, not least because it helps keep the body supplied with the fat-soluble vitamins A, D, E and K.

Vitamins and minerals

Children will glean a whole range of these directly from their food if they eat a good variety. Iron, one of the most important minerals in our diet, can be found in meat, bread and cereals. Other sources plentiful in iron are pulses (such as lentils, split peas and chick peas), dried fruits, spinach, brown rice, tofu and dates. Iron is absorbed by the body more efficiently when Vitamin C is present so that a drink of fruit juice with a meal can boost your child's iron intake.

When planning nutritious, well-balanced meals for your child, it can help to divide everyday foods into four categories. If you try to include something from each of the categories below each day there will be little doubt that your child will be eating healthily.

Category 1 – Protein Foods
Red meat, poultry, fish (white or oily), egg

Category 2 – Dairy Produce
Milk, yoghurt, cheese

Category 3 – Cereals and Grains
Breakfast cereals, bread, pasta, pulses, pastry, nuts (in the form of nut spreads)

Category 4 – Fruit and Vegetables
Fresh and dried fruits, leafy and root vegetables. Serve some fresh and some raw every day.

A toddler weighing 10–14 kg needs about 1200 calories a day, and 30 g of protein; the exact amount will depend on how large and how active he is. A toddler who drinks a pint of milk a day has a flying start; this provides over half the protein requirement, all the B vitamins except thiamine, three-quarters of vitamin A and all the calcium. Two to three slices of wholemeal bread provide about 8 g of protein; with peanut butter spread on it this would be higher. Add two sausages, fish fingers, slices of ham meat and this is already much more than your child's daily protein requirement. One small carrot provides all the vitamin A your child requires; the juice of a single orange provides three times the requirement for vitamin C. If your child doesn't like green vegetables, as many don't, there is no need to worry; fresh fruit can easily provide all the vitamins a child would get from eating their greens.

If your child dislikes some foods, there are usually simple alternatives or easy ways to "disguise" the food. Eggs provide protein and iron, but protein is also found in meat, fish, cheese, bread (especially wholemeal) and milk. Eggs can be eaten (in moderation) in cakes and custards. Milk is often seen as a child's main source of calcium. If yours won't drink milk, try giving yoghurt or cheese instead. Baked beans, green vegetables, apricots, dates, figs, wholegrains and pulses are some lesser-known sources. A child who doesn't like meat may dislike the texture, but may eat meat ground up in soups or sauces for pasta.

If your child doesn't like fruit he may drink fruit juices, or like fruit cooked in puddings such as apple crumble (very good made with oats or wholemeal flour in the crumble and not much, preferably brown, sugar). Some children enjoy nibbling dried fruit such as apricots or apple rings.

Certain foods which parents think of as "bad" for their child can in fact be nutritious or useful. Ice cream, if it is good quality or home-made, can be a useful source of protein and energy. High calorie foods such as chips can be good for a child who doesn't eat much and needs to increase the number of calories he gets. A child who eats enough protein and not much carbohydrate will actually have to break down the proteins and use those for energy, so additional calories in the form of biscuits or cake might actually be valuable so that the protein is not "wasted".

If there is any doubt about your child getting enough vitamins, supplements may be recommended. For a child who is eating a well-balanced diet, such supplements are unnecessary; some experts are concerned that it is even possible to consume too much of certain vitamins, so don't automatically assume that your child needs a supplement.

Many young children cannot last from meal to meal without getting hungry, and a child who is too hungry will often not eat well when mealtimes come. It helps to realize this and to have a routine of a mid-morning and mid-afternoon snack.

A mid-morning snack can consist of an apple, a banana, a slice of bread with some vegetable extract or cheese, biscuit, and a drink – perhaps orange or another fruit juice. A mid-afternoon snack could consist of a biscuit and piece of fruit, also with a drink. Serve the snack at a regular time, for instance when you get in from collecting children from school. It is better to get into the habit of giving a healthy snack when you get home rather than buying sweets, chocolate or crisps from the newsagents on the way.

You don't have to stop your children enjoying sweets or chocolates but it's best to limit the amount they eat. One way is to try to give sweets or chocolates only occasionally and always at the end of a meal. A child who has eaten a healthy meal is likely to eat fewer sweets, while appreciating them just as much.

Many commercially prepared foods contain a great deal of sugar, even savory foods in which you'd least expect it. The average pot of yoghurt contains over five teaspoons of sugar. A tin of baked beans also contains a high level of sugar, as do tomato soup, tomato ketchup and some savory pasta meals.

Convenience foods are also often high in salt. Apart from the fact that salt makes children thirsty so they fill up with drinks which then reduce their appetite, too much salt is bad for the kidneys because they have to work overtime to flush it all out of the body. Many such foods contain artificial flavourings such as monosodium glutamate, colourings, and preservatives, which may have harmful effects in the long term if eaten in large quantities. Artificial sweeteners may also have harmful effects; many allowed in Britain are banned in the US and the rest of Europe.

Many drinks such as colas, blackcurrant syrup and orange squash are high in sugar. Others contain alternative sweeteners; however, these may not be safe for children in large quantifies and parents may want to avoid them. Unsweetened fruit juices, diluted with water, are the most healthy drink for young children.

Knowing what's good and what's bad for your child to eat is half the battle. No mother can expect to be a supermum, serving up piping hot, nourishing meals for her children three times daily. Nor can she expect that each of her children will gratefully eat everything that is provided. Your child may eat little and often throughout the day; he may scorn food one day and then eat voraciously the next. It is helpful therefore to know that children need surprisingly little of the right things to thrive. So as long as your child has a zest for life and all the usual signs of well-being, then there's no cause for worry.

◆ See also, **E Numbers**, **Eating Problems**, **First Foods**

Hearing

Babies can hear from the moment they are born. In fact, they can sense sound vibrations when they are still in the womb and react with pleasure to recorded heartbeat sounds or other rhythmical sounds after birth. Loud, sudden sounds will make your baby jump, and the sharpness of the sound will be reflected in the reaction.

You will also note that your baby seems to have a seemingly built-in interest in, and capacity to listen to voices and the sound of people talking.

You may not be aware of this at first since he will not turn his head to listen to you, but you will begin to notice that he may stop crying as you approach his cot, talking. He may start moving excitedly at the sound of your voice, or alternatively stop moving and kicking in order to concentrate on it. He will also react to the different tones in your voice even though he cannot understand the words you are saying.

By around just 4–5 weeks your baby may start to make a connection between listening and looking, and will begin to search visually for the source of your voice. Soon after this he will start to react to a wider range of sounds than before so that those in between soothing music and a loud crash will become important to him.

There is a direct link between hearing and learning to speak. Your baby will "babble" more fluently if he is talked to a lot, but probably less so if he is neglected. Having said that, a baby will babble even if he is deaf, and hearing loss or deafness will not show themselves in a child's voice until the second half of his first year. Hearing loss can only really be spotted at such an early stage by watching a baby's reaction (or lack of) to sounds produced without visual clues.

Older children can become temporarily partly deaf after a middle ear infection or a heavy cold which blocks the eustachian tubes. Repeated infections can cause permanent damage to hearing so any acute pain in the ears should never be ignored, and should receive medical attention.

◆ See also **Baby Talk**, **Ear Infections**, **Earache**, **Glue Ear**

Heat Stroke

Playing in the sun is usually beneficial to children, but overactive exercise and too much heat (especially when combined) can affect the body processes and lead to heat exhaustion. The problem is made worse in humid conditions where the body's sweat cannot easily evaporate. Heat stroke (also known as sun stroke) can be the result in extreme cases.

Heat exhaustion is brought on by prolonged exposure to heat, especially if the weather is hotter than usual and the child has not been gradually acclimatized to the heat. The situation is made worse if the child is very active in his play, for this temporarily increases the body temperature and causes further sweating and loss of fluids and salts.

In these circumstances the loss of body fluids as the body sweats to cool itself down, and the loss of salts in the sweat causes an imbalance between salts and sugars in the bloodstream.

In extreme heat, the body's heat-regulating mechanism cannot cope at all and this is when sweating stops, high fever develops and the child may collapse with heat stroke.

A child who has heat exhaustion because he has been exposed to too much heat will feel weak, sick and dizzy. He may also suffer from cramps in the legs, he will certainly look pale, and he may have a raised temperature.

In the more serious form of heat stroke, the body temperature is always raised up to 40°C (104°F), and there may be fainting or even complete collapse. The most important symptom is that sweating ceases completely. When this happens the pulse will be rapid and the skin feel dry. Heat stroke can be very serious, and can cause coma, brain damage, and even death if left untreated.

Minor cases of heat exhaustion respond well to treatment at home, but if the child is actually verging on unconsciousness or has become unconscious, and if his temperature is at 40°C (104°F) or above, he should be given medical treatment at once, either by your doctor, or in hospital. If the child collapses artificial respiration must be applied.

To treat heat exhaustion at home, put your child to bed in a cool room, with windows and door open to encourage a draught, and with the minimum of clothing and covering. Give him a large intake of fluids with salt to restore the salt-sugar balance. The best way to do this is to mix one teaspoonful of salt (5 ml) to 1 litre (1¾ pints) of water or squash and get the child to go on sipping it.

To reduce body temperature, sponge the child with tepid water, leaving the water to evaporate on the skin. Take the child's temperature every half an hour or so, and as long as it is returning to normal all should be well within an hour or two.

If the child does not respond to home treatment within a couple of hours, or if his condition is more serious (as described above) your doctor will decide on suitable treatment. Drugs may be given to help cool the body down and fluids and salts may be given by intravenous drip feeding rather than by mouth as in less serious cases.

Herpes and Cold Sores

The most common form of herpes in children produces cold sores. These are painful blisters on the margins of the lips, nostrils or, rarely, eyelids, which can be recurrent and troublesome.

Cold sores are caused by a strain of the virus Herpes simplex known as Type 1. There is also a strain known as Herpes simplex Type 2 (which causes sexually transmitted diseases), and another form of herpes known as Herpes zoster (which causes chickenpox and shingles). These have nothing to do with "herpes" cold sores.

Herpes simplex is an infectious virus transmitted through physical contact. About one in five children has contracted the virus from a relative or playmate by the age of six.

Direct contact through kissing is the most likely way to pass the virus on, so anybody who has a cold sore should avoid kissing until the sore has completely healed. As with all infections, scrupulous hygiene should be observed, as it is thought possible that the virus can be transmitted on towels and cutlery used by an infected person.

The first attack of Herpes simplex is usually the most severe. Small, painful blisters erupt on the child's tongue, inside the cheeks and on the lips. The whole of the affected area can be so painful that it makes eating and drinking difficult, and the child may also have a fever. Five to seven days after appearing, the blisters burst, and then heal, with a crust like that on a graze developing as this happens. Occasionally, symptoms affect the area round the eye rather than the mouth or nose.

Although a first attack gives the body some immunity, the herpes virus then lies dormant in the body and can attack again. Subsequent attacks are usually less violent and cover only a small area at the edge of the lips or nose, but they are nevertheless a nuisance. They often seem to appear when the child has a cold, or at other times when his resistance is low, but they may be brought on by exposure to sun or strong wind.

Herpes can cause severe complications in babies with eczema. The cold sores do not confine themselves to the baby's face but erupt wherever the eczema rash is present, and cause infections to set in. If your baby suffers from eczema take extra care to keep him away from anyone with cold sores, and take him to the doctor straight away for early treatment if he does happen to contract the disease.

As herpes is a virus, antibiotics do not help, but this family of viruses can be treated by drugs such as aciclovir (Zovirax) in ointment or tablet form. Aciclovir must be used at the earliest stage possible if it is to be fully effective.

Sometimes herpes sores can develop into secondary infections which are caused by bacteria. If this happens the doctor may prescribe antibiotics such as penicillin. In minor attacks no treatment is necessary and the sores soon clear up.

Occasionally the first attack is so virulent that hospital treatment is needed. This is the case when the inside of the mouth swells so much that swallowing becomes difficult. If this happens, drip feeding can be necessary while drug treatment is having an effect.

◆ See also, **Chickenpox**

Hiccups

Like adults, children of all ages get hiccups, and some babies seem to get them after every feed. Usually they do not last for long and no action is needed for them.

Sometimes hiccuping is brought about by eating or drinking something too hot or too cold, by eating too much or too quickly or by running about too soon after a meal. Suddenly gulping cold air can also upset the smooth breathing process and bring on an attack of hiccups. It is also thought that some people get hiccups when they are nervous because anxiety can set off abnormal impulses in the part of the brain that controls breathing. But often there is no apparent cause.

Normally as you breathe, air flows smoothly in and out of your lungs in time with the regular contractions of the muscular diaphragm, which moves up and down beneath the lungs, and the expansion and contraction of the ribs, which move in and out around the lungs. When something goes wrong with this smooth pattern, hiccuping can be the result. So in a child who has hiccups the diaphragm, and usually the intercostal muscles that control the movement of the ribs, begin to move in twitching spasms.

This makes the child unconsciously gulp for air, and as this happens the epiglottis (a little flap at the top of the windpipe which prevents food from entering it) and the glottis (the opening between the vocal cords) both snap shut. This causes the flow of air being forced up through the windpipe to be cut off and produces the hiccuping sound.

This lack of muscular co-ordination is caused by an imperfect working of two sets of nerve mechanisms. There is disturbance either in the nerve impulses sent out by the brain to control the rhythmical activities of breathing or in the impulses set off by one of the two phrenic nerves which serve to regulate the contractions of the diaphragm.

Hiccups are a symptom in themselves. They usually cause no problem and it is rare for them to continue for more than a few minutes.

Medical treatment is rarely needed for hiccups. You only need to take your child to the doctor if there are other symptoms of illness (even if they do not seem to be related) or if a bout of hiccups refuses to stop. For babies with hiccups there is little you can do, and usually they do not seem to worry the baby. If the hiccups go on for more than an hour, try giving a teaspoon of gripe water.

For an older child one of the popular cures may help, even if they work only by causing a distraction. He should try holding his breath to the count of 20 or sipping water out of the wrong side of a glass.

Another remedy is to breathe in and out into a brown paper bag (holding it over the nose and mouth) for a minute or so. This is thought to be effective through causing the child to breathe in carbon dioxide from the air which has been breathed out, which depresses the activity of the nerves responsible for the hiccups.

Hideaways

Once your child can walk he will tend to follow you around the house while you work. If you stay in one room, he will play alongside you, often squeezing himself into an awkward corner, or under a table – happy to be hemmed in in his little hideaway as long as he knows you are close.

As he grows more independent he will then quite deliberately choose to play in these enclosed spaces from time to time and if you have a garden he may prefer one particular corner of that, too.

Small spaces give your child close contact with his surroundings, and their "confined" nature produces a sense of security. But the physical closeness may also be achieved by overcoming real obstacles – he may have to scramble between chair legs to get under the table, or through the branches of a bush to reach the space beside a shed. All this adds to his sense of adventure, fun and territorial achievement.

Your child's choice of location for a special place of his own will depend on his personal ingenuity or adventurousness, as well as the layout of your home, but whether he is a toddler or a pre-school five-year-old, he will prefer not to be too far away from you.

Dens made by children under five are not the same as the escapist "camps" of a seven- or eight-year-old, so your child will want to be able to see out of the den and to know you are still close. You should still respect the den as his territory however, as – even at this early age – building a den is part of exploring his independent identity.

Probably the best and most exciting dens for children are those that seem most out of bounds to you, but there are some potential hideouts that should be out of bounds to your child:

● Cupboards that cannot be opened from the inside, that have loose shelving or contain dangerous implements or materials.

● Freezers – especially if they are in a garage or outhouse. Keep them locked at all times.

● Any derelict or tumbledown outbuildings or any neighbouring building sites.

● Any deep holes in the ground.

Also, do not let your child use collapsible household items as building materials – ironing boards, deck chairs and some clothes-horses could damage fingers.

Your child's den might serve as a scaled-down copy of real life, in which case it will probably represent a house. He may create a kitchen area where

he can provide tea for teddies with toy cups. Alternatively, he may want to make the den into a garage for his cars, a shop or a hospital, a school, an office or a police station.

Younger children may rely on you to make suggestions for play in the den, as their imaginations are just developing. If you suggest building a den where he can make tea for his teddies, for example, then to him, the creative play has an obvious function, and you can help and encourage him to make play dough cakes and sandwiches to serve in his toy tea set.

This early introduction to entertaining also helps along the first moments with visiting children. It is not always easy to get young children to play together in each other's houses, but a den is a good focal point. It scales things down, allowing them to build, explore, and create their own miniature world.

So, what do you and your child use to build a den? Your toddler may decide for himself the particular area or corner that he feels to be his own. If you have provided cushions on the floor since his earliest days, then he may already regard this area as a kind of den, just wanting it to be built up a little so that it is more enclosed. You could place two or three chairs around the cushions, then drape a rug or sheet over them to form a backdrop, leaving the front open, so that he can still see you. He will probably rearrange this himself – in fact, pulling the sheet down on top of him may be part of the whole fun. You could join in this game of hide-and-seek.

Another space that provides an opportunity for den building is under a table. Clambering between chairs and around table legs is part of the attraction. Once again, throw a large sheet or rug over the table to form a kind of screen.

Building materials sometimes come unexpectedly to hand. If you buy any relatively large household item save the box it is delivered in. If it is a really large item such as a washing machine, the box will make a good enough den without too much alteration – but do check for dangerous staples and rough edges. Otherwise, you can open up the box to make a flat piece of card – an ideal wall or fence for a cosy space between two pieces of furniture. The folds of the dismantled edges may be flexible enough to act as hinges so that part of the board forms a door or gate.

A den need not involve the use of elaborate building materials or special construction skills, but if you do the building, your child needs to understand how it is done so that he feels he can join in. After that, the inside should be left up to him. He might have his own small chair or stool which he can drag inside, if the space is big enough, or he can improvise with cushions.

Both girls and boys will be happy to play "house", organizing and caring for dolls and soft toys, like little parents.

Ready-made dens are available in the form of Wendy houses or playhouses. These take up space, but you could put them up for just a few days at a time – perhaps during a spell of bad weather, or when you know your child's friends will be visiting. At night they can be a temporary storage space for toys, dolls and teddies that usually clutter up the rest of the room.

If you put up the Wendy house for a short period, try to give your child a different den activity for each day. As well as playing pretend houses, there are other forms of creative play with play dough, colouring books or face paints. Collect together some old clothes and hats to make a dressing-up box, and put this into the Wendy house for some of the time.

For four- to five-year-olds you could make the game of matching pairs. Collect up old postcards and greetings cards (tearing off the greetings side) and cut the pictures, diagonally, into two halves. Put one set of halves in the Wendy house and hide the matching set around the room. Your child and his friends may not always be able to match perfect pairs, but they'll have fun trying to find the cards and you can help fit them together afterwards.

Your child's den is his territory, but explain to him that animals also have dens where they sleep, or bring up their babies. For animals, a den is usually a hollow in a tree or a hole in the ground, or sometimes a cave in the side of a hill. Mountain lions have dens, and so do foxes.

This could be an opportunity to encourage some play acting. Ask your child to pretend to be a certain animal in its den. You can join in by trying to guess which animal he is.

Of course, a Wendy house can be put up in the garden, if you have the space, as most are fairly weatherproof. Other ready-made dens for the garden are playtents and wigwams. These tend to evoke the "fantasy" world of the den because rather than serving as a scaled-down house for your child, they belong to a different, "wild" outdoor environment.

In a tent your child can "camp out", but he will still want you close by, so put it up when you know you can spend time in the garden too. If your child can be outside for most of the day, make him some den snacks to eat inside the tent (though avoid leaving food inside it for too long as there is a danger that it will attract insects). Sandwiches or cut-up fruit and vegetables are all healthy and portable.

If you don't have an outdoor playhouse or tent, your child will have just as much fun (maybe more!) building his own garden den. From early toddling days he may have a favourite corner of the garden. If you give him a gardening set consisting of a spade, rake, sieve and bucket his favourite place will probably be somewhere he can dig. An earthy patch beside the shed or behind a bush could be ideal. If the corner is sheltered in this way you won't need to do any constructing; nor will you need to buy or build a sandpit.

Provide him with a few objects that can "furnish" his corner: old plastic flower pots and jelly moulds make good utensils for making mud pies, while a stone slab provides a good flat surface for turning out these concoctions and a small plank of wood or a log makes a seat. The space may even be big enough for a child's small garden chair.

A garden den has a life of its own and is different from anything your child builds inside the house. To you the small corner in the garden might appear to be a scruffy patch of earth. But your child is small enough to notice aspects of the plant and insect life that you probably don't see. Certain branches of a bush may provide ideal hanging space for pots or pans; certain niches in a log make ideal shelf space or seats for soft toys. He may happily play alongside a familiar ant trail and be fascinated by the bugs that live under a particular brick. So try not to disturb this corner and certainly don't give it over to planting unless you are sure your child has lost interest or grown out of the space.

If he sticks to the favourite corner, your child may want to make improvements as he grows older. If you go to the seaside for your holiday, encourage him to collect pebbles and shells that he can later use to border his corner of the garden.

You may find the den a very useful deposit point for many of the interesting things that your child insists on bringing back from walks and holidays. Feathers, eggshell, pieces of seaweed, bits of wood can all have a place – and a use – in the den. The den may also provide an opportunity for an introduction to gardening, as you can plant bulbs, seeds or young seedlings where he will be most likely to follow their progress.

In a den your child creates a real world of his own. He may be influenced by the reality of his daily domestic life but in the den he has a chance to re-enact and explore the social and natural life he sees around him.

As he gets older and he understands more about his surroundings, his imagination plays a greater part in his play so that the den may hold a fantastic world of imaginary friends – and now and then, you may be invited in as "guest of honour".

Hives

Also known as nettle rash or urticaria, this skin complaint is a common allergy symptom. Usually, attacks do not last for long and there is no need for treatment. Hives is often triggered by an allergen (the substance responsible) which can be something that comes into contact directly with the skin or it can be something in food or breathed in from the air.

There is a wide range of culprits, including wool, plants, eggs, strawberries, shellfish, perfumes, house mites, pollens and dyes. In some children, no independent substance is responsible and heat, cold or pressure – or even emotional stress – can bring on the same rash. Sometimes a child will get hives from sitting in a hot bath. In each case the skin over-reacts.

The rash is caused by a release of histamine in an allergic reaction which is fully described under other headings (see Allergies, Food Allergies, Hay Fever). A hives rash looks very similar to insect bites or nettle stings on the skin. The spots of the rash are raised blisters, linked together to cover an area of skin which can vary a great deal in size. Sometimes the spots hardly differ in colour from the rest of the skin, but sometimes they form large red weals. The skin around the blisters often becomes red, and the whole area is burning and itchy, just like nettle stings.

Sometimes the rash appears in places where the child's skin has been in contact with the substance causing the allergy but in other cases it can appear on almost any part of the body. It also has the odd habit of disappearing in one place only to reappear elsewhere.

As with all allergies, the best treatment is prevention, by identifying the allergen and trying to make sure that the child is not exposed to it. If the allergen is something that touches the skin the causal link will probably be apparent, and if it is a food that the child rarely eats the connection between eating it and having the rash will be noticed. But quite often, pinpointing the allergen is not an easy task.

Fortunately the attacks are usually short-lived and not troublesome, and in these cases treatment is not necessary, although calamine lotion can be applied to soothe the rash. A doctor will treat a child who has frequent and long-lasting attacks by prescribing anti-histamine ointment or tablets.

Occasionally hives can take a more severe form known as angio-neurotic oedema or giant hives. This produces large swelling on the lips, eyelids, back or throat, and may cause difficulties in breathing. It is treated with adrenaline or corticosteroids, both of which are initially given only under strict medical supervision. People with severe allergic reactions now commonly carry their own adrenaline syringes.

Holidays

The key to a successful holiday is to have realistic expectations. Once you accept that you have lost your pre-parent days of lying for hours on the beach, strolling through museums and galleries or energetically trekking around ancient ruins, the less disappointed or frustrated you will be. See this as an opportunity, when you are free from the demands of everyday life, to enjoy a part of your child's development.

Taking the first holiday after the birth of a child can seem a daunting task but there's actually much to be said for getting back into the holiday habit sooner rather than later. For one thing, you'll both need some time to relax after the months of pregnancy and the excitement of the birth. And although you may feel your new baby is too "fragile" to travel, parents are generally amazed at how resilient their newborn is – and how very portable, too.

Although it may seem to require great organizational skills, it is actually much easier to travel with newborn babies than with older children, particularly if they are being breastfed. You can pack all a baby's needs in one bag as, at this early stage, there will be little in the way of toys to carry with you. And if you are bottle feeding, it is quite simple to make up enough feeds to see you through the journey.

Of course, you can't just dash off without any other considerations. You'll need to be discharged from postnatal medical care first and be quite confident that you are fit enough for the inevitable stress that planning and packing for a holiday entail – as well as the rigours of the journey itself. If you are in any doubt, ask your doctor or midwife for advice. But, provided you're not likely to be embarrassed by your new baby crying inconsolably in public, the earlier you and your partner get some time away, the better.

Travelling with a slightly older child has its advantages too, however. For example, he'll be more aware of where he is and what's going on and will participate more in the fun – although you'll need to consider his needs more too.

Whether to holiday in your own country or go abroad is perhaps the first decision to be made. Staying at home for a holiday can be fun as long as you

accept the weather risks, and it means you won't have to do without your everyday "comforts" – from your favourite cereal to the latest TV soap. You also won't need to struggle with a foreign language. However, if your budget can stretch to it there's nothing like a holiday in another country to broaden your horizons and make you feel you've had a complete break. Taking a child abroad is something that you may find worrying but basically the same precautions apply to children as to adults – have the necessary vaccinations, use bottled or boiled water if you are at all uncertain about the quality of the drinking water and make sure that all food is freshly prepared and thoroughly cooked. And don't forget to update your passport after each new family addition!

As far as you and your child are concerned, adequate facilities for him are the most important thing. Remember, what is good for him is good for you because you'll never get a moment's relaxation if you're forever having to find things for him to do.

Types of holiday
By the sea
With little waves splashing on to a gently shelving beach, plenty of other children playing nearby and perhaps a rockpool or two for added entertainment, parents can be sure that their children are having a good time. Naturally, they cannot be left unattended, but at least each partner can take it in turns to watch over them (and renew their skills at building sandcastles and hunting for elusive crabs and fishes).

But if you're thinking of a seaside resort, look out for alternative attractions to the beach especially for days when the weather is not at its best. Aqua-parks, zoos, cinemas and funfairs are all handy stand-bys.

In the countryside
Children can be slow to appreciate the merits of fine scenery but depending on their age, may enjoy nature walks and features such as rivers and lakes.

Holiday camps and villages
Holiday camps have always been popular for their abundance of entertainment and "minders" for the children. They were traditionally sited near to seaside resorts so that holidaymakers could have the best of both

worlds – plenty of fun things to do plus the joys of the beach – although there are now new types springing up in many countries, often situated hours from the nearest coast but offering just as much fun.

These holiday villages are designed for the whole family. Traffic-free roads guarantee safe cycling and a variety of water chutes and rides thrill the young and the young at heart.

Like the traditional camp, these villages provide most of their facilities as part of the all-in cost of holidaying there. This is a boon to parents who want to keep within a set budget as there are few unforeseen extras once they have left home. They also often offer childminding services.

Theme/activity holidays

Keen to diversify away from uneconomical crops, many farmers now offer accommodation on their holdings with wonderful opportunities for children not just to meet the animals but also to see a farm at work.

Camping too is an option offered by many a farmer with a spare acre or two and can give you the best of both worlds – the freedom to organize your own accommodation but with something to keep the children occupied close to hand. Needless to say this type of "rough" camping is unsuitable for a small baby but can be most rewarding children of pre-school age.

Even the more physically demanding activity holidays need not be dismissed by the new parent. Ski resorts are increasing their crèche facilities all the time with some even taking very young babies. And even three-year-olds can learn to ski. Pony trekking is good for slightly older children and provides fun for the whole family. Activities like these, started at an early age, can provide a child with an interest for life.

Camping

You may be interested in a rather more organized camping holiday, on a designated well-maintained campsite with facilities such as showers and a launderette. And nobody will blame you as any convenience counts when travelling with young children!

Joining one of the camping organizations is perhaps the best way to get the most out of planning such a holiday as it will be able to provide you with up-to-date information on the best sites to visit, the facilities offered and current charges.

Accommodation

One crucial aspect of choosing the ideal holiday now you are a family is the type of accommodation you decide on. Very often partners have different ideas about what they would prefer in a holiday situation – whether it's maximum privacy or maximum service. Even though much will depend on your budget, try to reach a compromise with your partner on this question as the type of accommodation you stay in can make or break a holiday with children.

Caravans are much loved by young children as they feel they're being master of their own home in compact form. On poor weather days, however, lack of space can be a problem, so plan to take plenty of toys, games, crayons and paper for the younger ones. The same applies to a tent, which is even more fun in fine weather but worse in the wet! Also remember to take extra care with little ones when you have cooking facilities in a tent.

A self-catering cottage or villa can be a true home away from home and an ideal holiday base – at a price – if you want your privacy and daily routine disturbed as little as possible. It may be less fun and less exciting for children but at the same time they can play more freely and you don't have to remind them constantly to be less noisy and clear away their toys.

If you opt for hotel accommodation you'll be able to enjoy full service, and often entertainment for the children will be provided, especially with larger seaside hotels. You may so much appreciate the feeling of "being spoilt" and served around the clock that this more than makes up for the lack of freedom, privacy and flexibility.

Travel

Consider the following when planning how to get to your holiday destination:

Car

A very flexible option and the more passengers you have, the cheaper the transport becomes. Space is limited, however, and long journeys can be tiresome for children.

Coach

Someone else does the driving, and the children are likely to make friends on the journey. Stops for meals and breaks are restricted.

Train

A fast means of transport with space for children to run around and great novelty value although costly. Avoid too many changes of train.

Boat and hovercraft

These are usually combined with other forms of transport and are every child's dream – unless they are seasick! Usually there are good facilities for you and the children to while away the time.

Plane

A fantastic adventure for older children who will even tolerate some flight delays if they make friends in the departure lounge. On many flights children under two years old fly free but do not get their own seat.

Going with friends

Even before you decide on where and when to go on holiday it's worth thinking about whether you would prefer to go with friends who perhaps have a child or children of similar age to yours. When such an arrangement works it can double your holiday fun and halve the problems of childminding. As well as having a ready set of known playmates for each family, you can be sure that your children are in good hands if you take the occasional night off.

To get the best out of this pairing however, try to talk about anything you would particularly like to do or prefer not to do while on holiday before you go. It is also important to discuss in advance how you are going to divide all the costs, for example, the food bought for a self-catering holiday or group trips to the zoo or a meal at a restaurant. Friends have been known to fall out over basic matters like this because money issues hadn't been sorted out in advance. Last but not least, don't be afraid of planning some time apart from your friends while you're on holiday – all families need some time to themselves occasionally.

Questions to ask

If you have never visited an area before it can be difficult to make a decision based on brochures alone. This is where your travel agent or tour company comes in. Ask them about the suitability of beaches for families, and whether cots, linen and other equipment such as a highchair can be hired. They should be able to inform you of any nearby building work, or noisy discos, close to your accommodation. If your travel agent cannot satisfy your queries, ask friends for recommendations. Finally, don't forget if you are driving or hiring a car that the motoring organizations will be able to advise you on anything from safety seats for your child to the best routes for you to take.

Sensible precautions
In the sun

Babies should never be left in strong sun and never in a car, even with the windows open. Always park the buggy in the shade and check that the canopy is properly positioned to keep the sun at bay. If necessary drape something such as a dark-coloured beach towel from the canopy to give complete protection. On the beach find a shady spot or use a big umbrella.

Do not dress a little one in too many clothes, as he will become overheated. Keep them to a minimum in the heat and always use cotton, which is coolest. While it is hot, babies enjoy being freed from their nappies for a while but remember a toddler's tender bottom is less accustomed to sunlight than the rest of his body. It will not take long to produce painful sunburn if he crawls around bottom up. A pair of cotton pants will give protection.

For baby's first summer, he should not be deliberately exposed to strong sun at all. Toddlers and older children will also burn easily in the hottest part of the day, between 11 am and 3 pm, even when it is overcast, and they are particularly at risk on, or near, the sea or lakes, when the sun reflects off the water. Also fair-skinned children take longer to build up a protective tan and are more susceptible to sunburn.

As a very general guideline, you may expose your child to the sun for five minutes on day one, increasing the exposure by five minutes on each subsequent day. Make sure that maximum protection sun cream is applied, and stop exposure if your child has any ill effects.

You do not actually see sunburn until it has struck so do not rely on checking your child's skin for redness while he plays. Cool breezes also bring false security as they may keep a little one feeling chilly while he is being burned.

Cotton shirts or T-shirts, cotton pants and a wide-brimmed hat will keep the sun off. High factor protective creams will help too, but in the fiercest sun they will not give enough protection. Reapply creams when your child has been in the water, or use water-resistant creams which will give better protection while your child is bathing. Also remember that early or late in the day is the best time to allow young bodies to be exposed to the sun.

It is always a good idea to limit time on the beach especially in the middle of the day, so look for some entertainment inland. And in hot climates youngsters need extra fluids so ensure that they have lots to drink. Sunburn is, of course, a burn and should be taken seriously. In milder cases the skin becomes red and hot; in more severe cases blisters form, which if they break, weep and leave the skin raw.

If a child gets sunburnt you can soothe the pain and limit any damage done by putting him in a tepid bath or shower. Junior paracetamol will help the pain and in milder cases, inflammation can be reduced by a hydrocortisone cream, which you can buy from a pharmacist. Calamine or an antihistamine will help the itching. Keep the affected skin out of the sun as further exposure will make it very painful.

In more serious sunburn cases unless there is only a very small area of blistering and your child is perfectly well, he will need the attention of a doctor. If he is feverish or ill seek medical attention immediately.

On the sand

Don't automatically expect your toddler to love the beach – many children simply hate it at first. One way to avoid this problem is to gently introduce your child to sand prior to a trip to the beach, by putting a plastic sand pit in your garden. Or you could provide a sand-free zone on the beach by bringing along a small paddling pool that packs flat. This will also come in handy for water play if your tot is terrified of the waves.

On the beach, gritty sand can get everywhere. If it gets inside your baby's wet or dirty nappy this can bring on nappy rash. Cotton pants will keep sand out.

Canvas shoes are also better for older children than rubber flip-flops, which can chafe the skin and it becomes even more sore when sand and sea water aggravate it.

In the water

Playing in water may be tremendous fun but always remember that it is fraught with danger for children. Tiny tots can easily drown in just a couple of inches of water and every year children die in baths, paddling pools, rivers, the sea, or even after toppling into buckets or garden water butts.

Babies and toddlers do not put their arms out to save themselves when they fall and do not hold their breath when they tumble into water. They open their mouths to scream and take in water instead of air.

Never allow a tiny tot to be out of your sight or even out of your grip while in a swimming pool or the sea. Older children should also be constantly supervised. Arm bands and floats are only swimming aids not life preservers.

Inflatables are also extremely hazardous and can be quickly swept out to sea by winds and tides. They should be kept on a line and only used with extreme caution.

The only way to avoid tragedy when you are in or near water is to be constantly vigilant. Even when your youngsters have learnt to swim they must always be under supervision. When warning flags are flying obey them and keep the kids out of the sea.

Other dangers

Always be alert in crowded departure lounges; a small child can easily wander and rapidly become completely concealed in the crowds. If this happens, keep calm and get official help to mount a search.

Dehydration in a hot country can be a problem: make sure the children drink plenty of fluids and give them some juicy fruits (though not too much, as fruit can cause tummy troubles).

Do not allow your children to stroke or be licked by stray animals. The animal may be vicious, and there is also a risk of rabies.

Tips for the journey

You need to pack, and keep at hand, a bag or two to deal with hunger, thirst, boredom, sickness and general mess and stickiness. If you are usually nervous about travelling, try to relax and the whole experience will be more bearable. If you are not overwhelmed by the very early days of childcare, but you are travelling with a young baby, you have probably got the easiest option of all.

Older children have more complicated feeding needs, they need to go to the toilet and they get bored and/or sick! If you are embarking on a long car journey, for instance, it is best to take it in stages, stopping every couple of hours for a stretch, a visit to the toilet where necessary and a change of driver if possible.

Of course, if a miracle should occur, and all your little darlings fall asleep, you will fit in a good, long drive without frequent breaks.

Plan to stop frequently for meals, but take a supply of food in a cool-box to fill in gaps, to stave off boredom, and to cope with unexpected delays, breakdowns or inconsiderately closed restaurants.

The main problems with journeys are boredom and restlessness. It is tempting to offer food to take the edge off these feelings but try to avoid foods that may cause sickness or be too messy.

For cleaning-up operations you'll need a supply of wipes, damp kitchen cloths (rinse or keep them moist from your drinking water supply), kitchen paper and plenty of bags to dispose of the rubbish.

A good book of travel games will save you from five thousand repetitions of "I spy". A wipe-clean drawing board is a good tool, as are ordinary drawing pads and plenty of pens and pencils.

Flying, though it may well be your only option, brings its own stresses and strains. Cramped conditions, especially if your child is sharing your seat, can be a real difficulty. With any luck, you will not be on a long-haul flight in such circumstances.

If you are travelling by train there will be plenty to look at, and there's always the possibility of a stroll to the toilets or the restaurant car. Many more time-passing games are possible when you can sit side-by-side or facing one another than when you are strapped into a car.

◆ See also, **Car Journeys**, **Dehydration**, **Drowning**, **Heat Stroke**, **Sunburn**

Hospital Stays

Many hospitals try to make wards bright, cheerful places. The walls are decorated with posters of favourite cartoon characters, there are books and toys stacked on shelves and in some places, the nurses do not wear uniforms. These changes from the traditional hospital ward have occurred quite recently, within the last 20 years or so, and they are all designed to create a cheerful and reassuring atmosphere for children.

However, the fact remains that going to hospital is still a strange and alarming experience for a small child. He has probably never spent a night away from home before, and certainly hasn't been placed in a large "room" with a lot of strangers for company. He is ill and vulnerable, and does not want to be separated from his family or taken out of his home. However, if your child is hospitalized because he is ill or has to have an operation, you will have time to allay his fears by explaining what a stay involves. Try to establish a belief in the doctor, so that your child trusts him and understands that this person will make them better, or take the pain away.

You can do this in an unobtrusive way, by pretending that teddy or dolly is ill. Your child will observe how gentle and loving you are towards teddy when you are playing doctor, how good teddy is when he has to take medicine and he will learn that a sick teddy has to stay in bed.

Story books and hospital games are also available, and it is advisable to let your child learn when he is very young that hospitals are part of everybody's life. In this way, if he has to go to hospital, it will not be an entirely new idea to him but something he already knows about through play and acting out stories.

This kind of awareness is essential because there may come a time when your child has to be raced into hospital and you will not have a moment to talk to him or explain where he is going. This, of course, is not likely, but children do have accidents or develop unexpected symptoms which require emergency treatment. In such circumstances, the child who knows about hospitals will not feel so frightened, and he will have some understanding that doctors and nurses are there to help, not harm, him when he is ill or hurt.

If your child does have to undergo an emergency operation, do make sure that when he comes out of anaesthetic he wakes up to a loved and familiar face and sees that one of his parents is there. If you have had time, try to gather a few of his very favourite possessions together. Fetch his teddy or his security blanket or other favourites, so that he does not feel totally isolated from home and the things he loves.

Most hospitals have facilities for parents to stay with their ill children. In fact, in guidelines laid down by the British government years ago, it was strongly recommended that the parents be allowed to visit their child at any time of day or night, or be allowed to stay overnight. You know your child; you know if he is timid or shy or boisterous; and you know just how much – or how little! – he needs you. If you feel that your child will be secure and brave only with you, insist on your right to stay with him. Take a sleeping bag if necessary, but, generally, you will find that your hospital will be co-operative and even encourage you to stay in the ward.

Hospital staff are quite glad of your help and they are aware that an ill child is happier when his parents nurse him. You can bathe and feed him, or just quietly cuddle and soothe him. Also, if you stay in the hospital, you may feel more reassured about the kind of treatment your child is receiving. You can talk to the nurses and doctors and learn what sort of follow-up care you can give your child once he is discharged from hospital.

When you have proper warning of your child's admission to hospital, you and your family can make proper preparations. Your child can help pack his own things and this can give him a sense of going on an adventure, rather than fearing that he is being taken away from home. Check with the hospital what your child is allowed to bring into the ward. Will he wear his own pyjamas and dressing gown? Can he bring books and toys? Should be bring in a toilet bag with soap and towels as well as his own toothbrush?

Don't forget to pack for yourself if you plan to stay in the hospital (are you expected to bring your own bedding or sleeping bag?), and take lots of change for coffee machines and the public telephone.

If neither parent is able to stay in the ward, do be honest with your child. Explain that you will be there at certain times, and make sure that you keep to these hours. Find out if you can speak to him on the phone and if you can, keep your promise to do so. Let him take his comforters with him; explain that he will meet lots of other little children and that he can ask the nurse for anything he needs. Explain to your child that if he is really unhappy and needs you, the hospital will call you.

If no one from the family can stay with your child, the staff who will be looking after him must be given detailed information. Prepare a list of phone numbers for them to contact you or your family, and explain to the ward sister any special needs your child may have, such as his favourite bed-time drink, his need for a particular comforter and the words he uses when he wants to go to the toilet. You should tell her if he has particular food likes or dislikes.

You should also find out exactly what sort of treatment your child will undergo. Ask if he is going to have blood tests, X-rays, scans, and whether he is going to be in an isolation ward. You should know whether he is going in for observation or whether he will be given heavy medication. It is worth asking if and when your child is allowed visitors. Can you bring his brothers and sisters or can only adults visit?

It is not often that a child is put in an isolation ward as many of the infectious diseases of childhood can now be prevented through inoculation programmes. However, when a child does suffer chickenpox, whooping cough or measles, and the illness is having a serious effect, he may be admitted to hospital for observation. He will be put in his own room, isolated from other patients for fear that the virus may infect them. Your child should know that he will be on his own, with very few visitors allowed. This may be the kind of situation that does demand that the parents spend a lot of time in hospital with the young patient.

Armed with all the information you can obtain about the medical treatment planned for your child, you can prepare him for his stay in hospital. Warn him that he may have injections or medicine. Explain that he may have to be "photographed" by a big machine called an X-ray or a scan. He should be prepared to suffer some pain or discomfort and do not pretend to him that he won't. This is a delicate problem because, although you don't want to fool him and send him off without any anticipation of pain, neither do you want to frighten him. Perhaps teddy can be called in again, and by playing "hospitals" with your child, you can gently prepare him for the pain and discomfort he may experience.

You can take comfort from the fact that hospitals try to keep medical examinations and tests on children to a minimum level.

There are times when parents feel quite helpless and find themselves very dependant on the medical staff. Very small babies are taken over by the close attention of the doctors and nurses, while the parents stand by feeling anxious and useless. There are children who require long-term hospitalization, which will seriously alter the domestic routine of their entire family. In both these situations, parents and hospital staff have to develop a special relationship tailored to the circumstances.

Just as you spoke to the staff before the hospital visit, so you must consult them before you take your child home. Does he need to take any medicines and how often? Must he return to the hospital for outpatient treatment, or have a check up with his own doctor? The hospital doctor will write or talk to your doctor, and your health visitor may be informed of your child's discharge. You will feel much more secure if you know who is there to help you if you are anxious about your child's recovery.

If your child is not seriously ill, but is having a routine operation or observation, you can feel fairly confident that he will have an interesting, rather than miserable, time in hospital, for he will probably be surrounded by kind nurses, new friends and a warm, friendly atmosphere. And he will, no doubt, be a healthier and, therefore, a happier child after his stay in hospital. He will have lots of stories to tell you about his experiences, so do listen and discuss them with him. Teddy may also become a patient again, with your child playing doctor!

Housework

Even if you're fortunate enough to make a rapid recovery after the birth of your baby or are helped by having a baby who is a good sleeper, you simply will not find time to do all the work there is to be done around the house.

Your baby takes precedence over everything, so once you have finished feeding, washing and changing him, washing his clothes and bedding (possibly even his terry nappies) and washing and preparing bottles, you hardly have a moment for yourself, let alone the house. You may find yourself still in a dressing gown at midday because you had no time to get dressed. Even going to the toilet is something you tend to put off for hours on end in the first weeks.

So where should you begin in the effort to get to grips with what seems to be wave after wave of things to be done? At first you will simply have to lower your expectations of how you would ideally like things to look. You will find that suddenly there are always things lying around on the floor and surfaces. Just tidying these away can make an instant difference to the look of a room – and make you feel a bit better. Obviously there is no point in putting bibs and blankets back in drawers if you will need them again when the baby wakes up.

On the other hand it is a good idea to lift toys and rugs off the floor when they are not in use, chiefly for safety reasons. A household obstacle course is not what you need when you are carrying a baby around.

If you can, try to have one room or one area that looks relatively untouched at the end of the day. This is not in order to pretend to yourself or your returning partner that life at home is a piece of cake, but rather to maintain an area of "adultness" – a tidy little sanctuary – for both of you to relax in.

Use one of these moments together with your partner to discuss how you can streamline the housework a little. When you have a new baby, feelings of guilt seem to dominate many of your actions. Because he depends so much on you, you feel responsible for his every joy or sorrow. Too easily, you can extend this guilt into other domestic areas so that you feel guilty for not hoovering, for not washing up and for not having prepared the evening meal. To make things worse you may feel that your partner is a member of the silent jury that is condemning you.

Talking about the new burden of tasks is the first step towards making things easier for yourself. After all, the housework has to be done in order to provide a healthy environment for you and your baby. You are not doing it to prove your moral worth.

Can you share out the chores? As the person who is at home all day, most of your energies are absorbed by the constantly present and "invisible" jobs, such as keeping the baby clean and doing the family washing. Your partner can help by doing the "one-off" jobs at the beginning and end of each day. For example, if you are bottle feeding he can make up a batch of bottles each morning, wash and sterilize them in the evening and then make up the night's batch. Of course, you will probably end up having to make extra bottles during the day, but having a few at the ready cuts down on a lot of stress.

Your partner can also help by taking out the rubbish, doing a weekly vacuum and helping with shopping and meals. In fact, it is over the baby's feeds and your meals that most co-operation and compromise will probably occur. You may well find that the worst time of day is the early evening when you are trying to get your baby to sleep for the night, as well as tidy up a bit and prepare the evening meal. To ease this "rush hour" you could agree to eat later for a while and decide on a weekly menu so that you keep your daily decision-making to a minimum.

Allotting tasks and drawing up menus may sound very regimented, but you do need some sort of structure to help you win through. On the other hand, too strict a routine for these early weeks may be unrealistic because your baby's demands will be changing all the time and your own sleeplessness can leave your energies at unpredictable levels.

Apart from your own feelings of exhaustion and disorientation, the other obstacle on the path to hassle-free housework may be the baby himself. While he sleeps you can get on with the basics but when he wakes up he will want to be near you. Even though he can watch you from his cot, the floor, a playpen or bouncy chair, he may not be happy unless he can make close physical and eye contact. Some parents find it easier to do the housework by strapping the baby in a sling.

Coping with a new baby can be lonely at times, so ask a friend round to keep you company or to keep the baby entertained while you get on with a few jobs. Or form a mini-co-operative with two or three other new mums and take turns to visit one another's houses each week. It gives each of you a chance to do jobs like ironing while the babies are kept happy.

If any members of your family live near by, do not hesitate to ask them for help. Family ties seem strongest when a new baby arrives and parents, in-laws, sisters and brothers are usually keen to become involved, though they may not know the best way to go about it. Asking them for help will please them and is essential for you. The early weeks are a sensitive time however, and you will tend to feel very susceptible to apparent criticism or outside interference – so ask for the kind of help that won't leave your nerves jangled.

Usually the best help is for visitors to keep the baby amused while you rush round with a carpet sweeper, duster, mop or whatever you have been meaning to use for days but have not had the chance to apply.

When things get tough and all about you seems chaotic remember that this only lasts a few months. Once your baby's sleeping pattern improves, your energies become recharged. At a certain point you will get used to being a parent and suddenly you will realize you are on top of everything. If you occasionally feel nostalgic for this time last year when life seemed simpler, think instead about this time next year when, believe it or not, you will feel like an old hand. From a place where you and your partner spent evenings and weekends, your house will have remoulded itself into a working family home.

◆ See also, **Hygiene**

Humour

Laughter and humour are very important social skills, and they go a long way towards enhancing the quality of life in general. An appreciation of the ridiculous makes acceptance into groups much easier and it helps children to co-operate with parents, teachers and other children. The stresses and strains of life are also a lot more bearable if one can have a good laugh now and then. There is plenty of evidence that humour aids memory and learning.

It is tempting to believe that a sense of humour, like a sense of smell or sight, is something you are either born with or without. This is not entirely true. It would seem that the seed is there, but that it needs the right conditions in order to grow. Your child's inborn sense of fun needs to be encouraged in order to help it to develop.

The first outward signs that your child has the tools to develop a lively sense of humour are smiling and laughing. Smiling comes after the first few weeks of life.

Laughter comes a little later, sometimes as early as five weeks but more usually at around three months old. The first chuckles may not be in response to anything in particular, he may just be trying it out. It is at this stage that you should actively begin to encourage your child's giggles by introducing funny games and activities.

An important ingredient of these early games should be that your child can look forward to the fun part. Rhymes and repetition help to build this anticipation. There are several tickling rhymes including "Round and Round the Garden" and "This Little Piggy" that are old favourites, but it is also good to make up your own little tickling rituals when your child is very young.

"Here Comes Mummy" is a good game to play when dressing your child or changing his nappy. Begin very simply by saying "Here comes Mummy to stroke that tummy"; soon he will chuckle before you stroke him. Once he recognizes the catchphrase "Here comes Mummy" add things like "to nibble those knees" and "to tickle those toes" until you have a patter that you both enjoy.

As soon as your child is able to support his head, "peek-a-boo" is ever popular and always produces squeals of delight. Enlisting the help of teddy will add variation to this very simple game. You can make him pop his head up in some very odd places and say "boo". Not only will your child enjoy teddy's strange behaviour but it will help him to develop his visual skills as he looks about him to see where teddy will turn up next.

Slightly older children are delighted by a little controlled mayhem. Your child will go through the stage of hurling his toys out of his pram or highchair, which may irritate you but will have him squealing with glee. Perhaps it is best to bow to the inevitable and turn this activity into a game called "dropping a clanger".

Simply place a large metal tray beside his chair and give him a heap of unbreakable toys to drop. Drop one or two yourself to show him what a satisfactory clang they make and retreat. There are several benefits to this game. The wonderful crashes will distract him so that you only have to retrieve for him when he has run out of ammunition. His hand to eye co-ordination will improve because he'll have to aim, and last, but not least, wreaking such havoc will amuse him enormously.

Another good mayhem game involves building a wall of wooden bricks and bringing it crashing down again by rolling a ball at it. Skittles is another variation. You can add to the fun by being sure to make as much noise as possible by playing them on a hard surface. When your child is older he will enjoy doing the building and destroying himself.

At about three years old, your child will laugh uproariously at your misfortunes, like tripping over or dropping things. Amuse him still further by pretending to have these disasters. Soon he will begin making deliberate mistakes to make you laugh. It is important to be a good audience and laugh in the right places.

Clowning will be amply rewarded by your child's squeals of delight and his attempts to copy you. Silly walks and grotesque faces never lose their appeal. Simply walking like a penguin can be enormous fun. It will not be long before your child has developed clowning routines of his own. Your child will love silly voices and noises during story time, and he will try to mimic them.

The attraction of some kinds of comedy is that it allows the audience to feel superior to the buffoons on stage. Children love this feeling of superiority and adore "getting one over" on Mum or Dad. There are many opportunities to set up these ridiculous scenes and they will not only amuse but they will improve your child's powers of observation.

Encourage this sense of the ridiculous by setting up a situation comedy like this one.

Announce that it will be boiled eggs for lunch and solemnly drop an old watch into the pan and attempt to time it with an egg. Feign astonishment when your child tries to tell you, through his chortles, what you've done. Next, try to cut the bread with a fork and spread the butter with a spoon to add to the fun.

When your child's language is developing he will enjoy nonsense words and rhymes. There are many books available full of nonsense poems, songs and stories to appeal to young listeners. Most have lovely pictures to add further interest.

As time goes on your child will enjoy plays on words and puns. You could make a book of your family's puns or a book of silly sayings, like "it's raining cats and dogs", or, to appeal to the gory side of children, "keep your eyes peeled".Another idea is your own silly alphabet book with sentences like "tiny Trudy ties toes together" or "soppy Susan sucks sardines slurpily". Of course "x" is troublesome but you could go for the "stick it in the middle" option as in "Trixie Baxter boxes foxes".

Making your own comic book is fun for the older child. Photographs of your child and his friends performing silly actions are useful for this. Add to the interest by providing dressing-up clothes and finger paint make-up or masks. Stick a series of pictures in a book and add a funny text with plenty of sound effects so that it is good to hear when read aloud.

Children love slapstick but it is messy, so the chance to indulge this love is rare. Try it at a children's garden party and urge the guests to bring swimming costumes to wear for a "custard pie" fight. Blancmange makes good pies when allowed to set on small cardboard plates. Provide plenty of ammunition. Save the pie fight until near the end and provide a paddling pool or garden sprinkler to clean everyone up. Supervision is essential and be prepared for plenty to be thrown at you.

Most children find the antics of puppets very funny and much laughter can be had from them. Your child will enjoy puppet shows when he is as young as a year old. At the toddler stage, he can make his own plays. Simple tubes of paper with faces drawn on them will do for finger puppets, and he can use silly voices for each character. Glove puppets can be made from old socks with bits of felt for eyes and tongues.

All children go through the stage of being fascinated by "naughty" words. This can be a trying time for parents because such words are repeated endlessly amid paroxysms of laughter. It is difficult for a parent to find "bum-bum" rib-achingly funny, especially if they are uttered in public in clear, ringing tones.

To the average four- or five-year-old "toilet" words are hilarious. "Wee-wee" or "poo-poo" will have your toddler and his friends rolling on the floor in uncontrollable mirth. The differences between girls and boys and the words associated with them will also cause extreme merriment. Some parents may be bored or upset by this obsessive stage. The good news is that it passes quicker if you don't make an issue of it.

There is no doubt that childish humour is repetitive and often very boring to adults, but it is definitely worth encouraging by being a good audience and joining in. Shared smiles and laughter are a vital part of the bonding process between mother and child. They provide great pleasure and satisfaction to both parties. Shared laughter is also an important part of social development. Groups of children often erupt into fits of giggles all at once and sometimes laughter spreads from child to child until the whole group is convulsed in merriment. Laughter, like measles, is catching. Group glee appears to help both children and adults to relax and feel a part of things. A well-developed sense of fun is a priceless gift.

Hygiene
Teaching your child personal hygiene

The basic rules of cleanliness are so simple that they should be second nature by the time your child is five. By then, he should automatically wash his hands before meals and after using the toilet as well as brushing his teeth after meals, taking a daily bath or shower, washing his hair at least once a week and keeping his fingernails clean.

These routines are important for a number of reasons and involve more than just washing off the surface dirt all children pick up from playing. For one thing, cleanliness helps prevent disease. Washing hands stops bacteria being passed from fingers to your child's mouth; brushing teeth cuts down on tooth decay; bathing keeps the skin's pores unclogged, preventing acne and other unsightly skin conditions; shampooing prevents scalp diseases and helps keep your child's hair looking healthy.

Every parent has to expect their young child to get dirty constantly. Some children only have to walk out of the door, and they seem to be covered with dirt from head to toe. This is in no way a reflection of bad parenting. What is important, however, is that you don't leave your children unwashed and that you make sure they have clean clothes every day. This is how to establish the habits of a lifetime as – with a bit of luck – your child will gradually become "sensitized" to looking, feeling and "smelling" clean.

The best way to teach your child cleanliness is to set a good example yourself. Instead of just telling your child to wash his hands before a meal, say "It's time to eat, let's wash our hands first," then go off to the basin with him. This way he will start to think of it as a very "grown-up" thing to do.

Try the same approach with brushing teeth. Likewise, if he isn't comfortable taking baths, let him see you enjoying a relaxing bath at regular intervals and encourage him to join you or your partner occasionally. It may seem time-consuming to take such an active approach to teaching your child cleanliness but be assured it will pay off.

Good standards of cleanliness will also be important when your child starts mixing with lots of other children at playschool. Toddlers aren't very tactful, and if your child doesn't have good personal hygiene habits it won't be long before his playmates nickname him "Stinky-poo" or "Greaseball". This can be most upsetting for young children and, in extreme cases, make them feel uncomfortable to be around other people for many years to come.

Of course, with a young baby, it will be up to you and your partner to make sure he is clean. But by the time your child is walking and potty-trained, he should start learning to take some of the responsibility for his personal hygiene himself. He will still be much too young to take a bath on his own but he can be expected to wash his hands before meals, brush his teeth and comb his hair as part of his daily routine.

Repetition and patience will be the keys to success. Also, don't forget that all children are different. Some toddlers take to baths like ducks to water, while others will fight with all their might to stay out of the bath-tub.

Other children won't want to have their hair washed because they get soap in their eyes, or they won't want to brush their teeth because they don't like the taste of the toothpaste. You may have to resort to all kinds of tricks, like offering your child strawberry-flavoured toothpaste or using non-sting shampoo.

To avoid bathtime battles, try to make bathing as much fun as possible. Let your child have as many waterproof toys and even unbreakable kitchen utensils as he likes with him, and allow a few minutes for just playing. Novelty soaps and bubbles are other inducements. Few children can resist the fun of a bubble bath and many shops sell it in plastic cartoon-character shaped containers.

Children's skins react differently to the chemicals in soaps and bubble bath. If you notice a reaction on your child, such as red patches or dry, flaky skin, ask your chemist for a milder brand. If the reaction continues, consult your doctor.

Although you may have to coax your child into the bath with a sense of fun and frolic, don't forget the purpose is to get him clean and teach him how to clean himself. With younger children, you will have to wash them. As they get older, they'll enjoy playing with the soap and working up a lather. Don't forget to remind your child to wash the back of his neck, under his arms and between his legs.

Have a big fluffy towel ready for when your child steps out of the bath. Having his skin rubbed with the towel not only feels good, but also stimulates the natural oils so his skin doesn't dry out.

If your child isn't enthusiastic about taking baths, always give him some positive feedback when the bath is over. Be sure to tell him how good he looks, and how everyone likes clean children. Also, you could play games with him or read him books after his bath to make it into a special time. This will help to develop a positive attitude towards taking baths.

While in the bath, your child could also have a go at brushing his fingernails. If dirt builds up under the nails, it becomes a breeding ground for bacteria, as well as looking bad. Many shops sell inexpensive novelty-shaped brushes with extra-soft bristles that are ideal for children.

If your child's nails get too long, he can easily scratch himself or other children while playing. A good time to cut finger-nails and toe-nails is after a bath, when they are at their softest. Use blunt-edged scissors, and always supervise older children when they are learning to cut their own nails.

Bathtime is also a good time to wash your child's hair. However, if he strongly dislikes either (the bath or the hairwash) try to keep them separate routines as your child may come to associate one with the other. There are two reasons why children often fight against having their hair washed – shampoo gets in their eyes and stings, and they are afraid of having water run down their faces.

Be sure to use a "tear free" shampoo, specifically made for children. It is milder, and, as well as cutting down on the stinging in the eyes, it won't be too harsh on your child's scalp. If shampoo in the eyes continues to be a problem, you can always let your child wear a pair of swimming goggles, or a specially designed headshield. Both might look foolish but can save tears.

For the best results, follow this simple routine so your child will know how to wash his own hair when he is older. If it is long hair, first brush it forward from the roots to the ends. This helps to loosen any dirt and take out any loose hairs. Wet the hair, then rub in the shampoo, piling long hair up on his head and away from his eyes. Instead of putting the shampoo directly on to your child's head, it is best to rub a small amount in your hands, then rub it into the hair. This helps to distribute it evenly.

To help your child get into the habit of washing his own hair, let him rub the lather into his scalp. Not only will this be fun, especially if he can admire his frothy hairdo in a mirror, it also helps stimulate the glands in his scalp. These produce a natural oil that makes hair healthy and shiny.

Make sure you always use clean water to rinse your child's hair. If you don't have a hand-held spray attachment, fill a saucepan or jug with clean water and use that. Continue rinsing until the water runs clean. This is important because any shampoo that remains in the hair will dry and flake off like dandruff.

Take care that the water runs off the back of your child's head, not down his face as most children find this frightening. Also, always check that the rinsing water isn't too hot because the skin on your child's scalp is even more sensitive than the skin on the rest of his body.

Not washing your child's hair and scalp regularly or often enough can result in cradle cap, which affects all youngsters, not just babies. If this irritation of the scalp does develop, your chemist or doctor will advise you to switch to a special antiseptic shampoo that will clear up the condition after a few days of using it. Don't use adult anti-dandruff shampoos on your child without seeking advice first.

For the first couple of years, you will have to look after your child's teeth yourself, and you should supervise him brushing his own teeth until he's at least five. Even though the baby teeth, or milk teeth, will eventually fall out, good dental care is essential from the start.

If one of these first teeth has to be removed because it is decayed, your child's permanent teeth might not grow into the correct position. This can cause him problems for years to come. Make sure he doesn't eat a lot of sugary food as sugar causes tooth decay.

When your child starts developing co-ordinated hand movements, you can start teaching him how to brush his own teeth.

Let your child hold the toothbrush and take his hand to guide him through the motions. Starting on the top row at the front, hold the brush at a 45 degree angle and gentle brush up and down, only covering two teeth at a time. Continue around to the teeth on both sides, then repeat with the bottom row of teeth.

Do this with your child after every meal to establish the habit. It may take several months, or even a year, before he can do it by himself but it is important he learns the proper way.

Along with this education in physical cleanliness, your child should be learning about the importance of wearing clean clothes. After all, what's the point in keeping body and hair in healthy and attractive condition if your clothes could do with a wash? Make sure your child wears clean underwear and socks every day and don't let him go to bed with his underwear still on – even though young children hate that cold and uncomfortable moment before they slip on their pyjamas.

You could encourage your child to take an active part in all aspects of personal hygiene and his appearance by making a cleanliness chart. The chart should have a column for each day of the week with individual boxes for bathing, washing hands, brushing teeth, and washing hair. When your child has satisfactorily completed one of the tasks, he can put a tick on the chart. When all the boxes for a day have been ticked, stick a gold star at the top of the column. After a whole week has been filled, for example, reward your child with a special treat, perhaps a new novelty toothbrush. Don't forget to put the chart somewhere where your child can easily reach it.

Hygiene in the kitchen

Look around your kitchen. The worktops, table, highchair tray and sink may look clean to the naked eye, but even the smallest trace of food on them can harbour bacteria that will multiply if left.

Wipe all surfaces thoroughly with a damp cloth after every meal, making sure every trace of food is removed. Do not forget the underside of the table or highchair tray – sticky fingers get everywhere. Once a week clean with a mild disinfectant solution.

Sinks and taps should be wiped over to remove any particles of food and grease each time you finish washing up, and disinfected once a week. You can also flush soda crystals down the plughole with very hot water once a week to remove any grease or food trapped in the U-bend.

Wooden spoons and chopping boards should be scrubbed after every use, and wiped with a mild disinfectant solution once a week. The sterilizing solution you use for your baby's bottles is ideal, or choose one that is recommended for use on items that come in contact with food.

If you do not own a dishwasher, wash your dishes in hot water using a washing-up liquid to remove grease and food particles. Wash glasses first, followed by cutlery, plates and finally pans, and rinse them in clear water after soaping to remove any traces of detergent. Change the water as soon as it becomes cool or dirty.

Either leave the dishes to drain in a special rack (which also needs to be kept clean and disinfected) or dry them using a fresh tea towel each time. Never use a tea towel more than once without thorough washing – if you leave it to dry in a warm place it produces a bumper crop of germs.

Never leave dirty dishes lying around after a meal as they will attract flies and the bacteria will multiply. If you are not going to wash them immediately, put them in the sink and leave them to soak in cold water.

If you have pets, wash your pets' food bowls separately from your own dishes, using a special cloth or brush, and disinfect them once a week. Remember babies will taste anything – including pet food.

Be careful also with rubbish. Keep the lid of your bin closed and empty it frequently in hot weather. Wash and disinfect it once a week. And do not neglect your floor, especially if you have a crawler on the loose. Pick up dropped food and mop up spills immediately. Wash the floor once a week using a mild disinfectant solution.

When buying food, always choose the freshest you can from a shop or stall that has a rapid turnover and keeps its produce clean and protected from flies.

Raw meat, especially chicken, contains bacteria which are killed off by thorough cooking but you can avoid spreading these bacteria around your kitchen before the meat is cooked. Keep a separate chopping board for meat – plastic is better than wood as it is easier to keep clean and sterile – and wash it carefully after each use. If you are not going to cook meat immediately, freeze it or keep it in the fridge on a plate on the bottom shelf so that any juices do not drip on to cooked food below. Always keep cooked and uncooked meats separately.

Fruit and vegetables may also contain bacteria as well as pesticide residues. Fruit and salad vegetables should be thoroughly washed and scrubbed and you need to be particularly careful with those you are going to give to your baby. Store vegetables in a cool place or in the vegetable container at the bottom of your fridge and use them up as quickly as possible.

Packaged convenience foods are a great help in the kitchen but also need to be handled with respect. With today's interest in healthy living, many contain fewer preservatives than they used to. While this may be good for our health, it does mean that they might not keep as well or as long as you would think. Follow the instructions on the packaging, especially those concerning storage in a fridge or freezer, and always use by the date indicated.

When you buy frozen food, get it home and into your freezer as fast as possible. Look on the packaging or check with your freezer handbook for the maximum storage time and do not risk keeping it for longer. The low temperature in the freezer does stop bacteria multiplying, but it keeps them in a state of suspended animation rather than eliminating them.

Try to defrost meat in the fridge, even though this does take longer and pour any juices carefully down an empty sink. Make sure the meat is thoroughly defrosted before cooking as otherwise only the outside will be cooked through – the inside will be just warm enough for bacteria to thrive. When meat has defrosted, do not refreeze it without cooking first.

Fridges do not kill bacteria, although many multiply more slowly than in the warm atmosphere of the kitchen. Once again you need to observe safe storage times, and keep the inside of your fridge clean, defrosting it regularly if it is not self-defrosting.

Cooked meat and dishes containing meat should be covered, cooled quickly and kept in the fridge until you need them. If you do forget and leave a dish out for some time, reheat it and boil for two minutes before cooling and refrigerating.

When you are serving a meat casserole that has been cooked earlier and refrigerated or frozen, merely heating it through will not kill off any bacteria. Bring it to the boil on the top of the stove or in the oven and boil for two minutes.

If you use a microwave be sure to follow the manufacturer's instructions. Stir the food well to get rid of any "cold spots" and leave it to stand for the recommended length of time. To be on the safe side, do not reheat food more than once. Be just that little bit more vigilant when you are cooking for your baby to avoid upsetting his immature digestive system.

Baby foods which are sold in tins or jars are produced in a way which ensures they are sterile and are safe to use straight from the container. If you baby is unlikely to eat the whole tin or jar at one sitting, transfer the amount for one meal to a plate or bowl and put the remainder in the fridge immediately. Once you have put a licked spoon into the food it is no longer sterile.

Always throw away any food your baby does not eat immediately after a meal – the same goes for bottles or cups of milk or yoghurt-based drinks. Warm milk is the perfect breeding ground for bacteria.

When you are cooking for your baby use fresh ingredients – never use left-overs that have been lying around for any length of time. Cool the food rapidly and if your baby is not going to eat it at once, cover it and put it in the fridge or freezer until it is required. When you are defrosting home-made meals for your baby, always boil them for two minutes and cool them again before serving. A quick way to cool food is to put a large plate in the refrigerator until it is thoroughly chilled, then spread your baby's meal on it.

Hyperactivity

The term hyperactivity is widely used but has not been strictly defined. It is used to describe a child's behaviour rather than a definite medical condition, and many parents are tempted to describe their child as hyperactive at one time or another.

Hyperactivity usually starts in children when they are still babies, but the symptoms become more obvious as they begin to walk, when they tear about in a completely disorganized way, unable to concentrate on anything, even for the short time of a normal toddler's attention span.

Not every hyperactive toddler becomes a hyperactive child, but those that do may show a complete lack of attention, while other children are becoming able to occupy themselves happily in their own activities. Inability to concentrate makes it difficult for hyperactive children to get on with other children. They cannot see the point of any game and cannot concentrate on it for any length of time, so that other children do not enjoy playing with them. The hyperactive child responds by being aggressive and so makes matters worse.

A hyperactive child often seems of below average intelligence, and has difficulties with learning. He also finds it hard to distinguish between left and right and cannot understand the relationship between shapes or different sizes.

In addition to this the child is usually clumsy and can also be destructive. He has sudden, violent changes of mood, rapidly turning from rage to joy to misery, and he will frequently not sleep well. While normal

children may show some of these characteristics from time to time, with hyperactive children they are always in evidence.

Hyperactivity can be caused by brain damage or epilepsy, or may be associated with psychiatric problems such as autism (a mental condition which prevents the child from communicating, even with his own parents) or schizophrenia. But hyperactive behaviour can also be found on its own, without any apparent cause or associated condition, and some doctors refer to this as the attention-deficit hyperactivity disorder (ADHD)

Some doctors believe that hyperactivity must be caused by a brain disorder or something in the genetic make-up, but there are therapists who believe that it is caused by problems in the child's relationship with the parents and with the rest of the family.

Other doctors believe that hyperactivity is a reaction to certain foodstuffs, and particularly to what are termed additives – artificial flavouring, colouring or preservatives (*see* E numbers) – whereas some go as far as to blame the child's general diet for the condition. However, these theories are far from proven.

It is important for parents and other children in the family to remember that the hyperactive child is not being deliberately difficult. He needs tolerance and patience, combined with firm handling on the part of the parents. The more secure the child feels the better he is able to cope.

Parents should talk about the problem to the child's teacher and head teacher. It may even be decided that he needs remedial teaching because of learning difficulties.

It is important for the child to have plenty of opportunity to run about and let off steam in the fresh air. He will also benefit from all the attention you are able to give him. With your quiet encouragement he should be able to develop better concentration and to get satisfaction from finishing something, whether it is reading, drawing, putting toys away or making something in the kitchen.

Your doctor may decide that the child needs drug treatment. Hyperactivity responds well to tranquillizers, but oddly enough, nervous system stimulants such as methylphenidate (Ritalin) or dexamphetamine (Dexedrine), which speed up adults, can have a calming effect on hyperactive children. It may be necessary to try various drugs under medical supervision until the best treatment is found. It is very dangerous to give your child drugs without medical supervision.

The doctor may also refer the child for psychological therapy, which could help improve his attention span. Some therapists believe that the condition involves the whole family and will want to involve everyone in their treatment.

Some doctors recommend a strictly controlled diet, eliminating all additives, and a number of parents have found this helpful.

Parents themselves will find dealing with a hyperactive child exhausting, but it is not helpful to get angry and impatient. What will help, if possible, is for parents to be able to take time off regularly to free them from pressure. It is reassuring for parents to know that in most cases the child eventually grows out of hyperactivity, although he may continue to have social problems through having found it so difficult to relate to other children for so long. Equally, learning may still be a problem after these difficult years, and remedial teaching or special support from teachers may continue to be necessary.

Illness (in Children)

Never be put off seeing a doctor if you are worried about something, however small it seems. Also, do go back to the surgery if you are still worried a day or two after the doctor has seen your child and pronounced him well. It is right to be persistent. If, for instance, you call the surgery and get an unsympathetic response, consider whether you need to go to the casualty department of your local hospital.

As a rule of thumb, the younger the child, the sooner you should call the doctor. In addition to the all-important behaviour changes, you should also watch for signs of illness.

Recognizing signs of illness

Gastro-intestinal infections are not uncommon in babies or small children, though breastfed babies are less likely to suffer from these. If your young baby is vomiting frequently or has diarrhoea you should contact the doctor immediately, as small babies can easily become dehydrated. Don't confuse a normal breastfed baby's stools with diarrhoea. Even though they are fairly liquid or frequent, diarrhoeal stools are normally greenish and much more watery. If you are unsure, save a soiled nappy in a plastic bag to show your doctor.

If you are worried that your child has a temperature, you can check it with a thermometer held under the arm for two minutes. Alternatively, use a "fever strip" which you place across the forehead. Trying to take the temperature of a wriggling baby is not easy, but you can do it more easily while he is asleep or feeding.

If your baby or young child has a temperature, he will need to be kept cool. Put him in cotton garments which will breathe easily and try to keep your child at an even, warm temperature – don't move him backwards and forwards between a hot living-room and cold bedroom, for instance. You can try sponging a baby with tepid water to make him feel more comfortable, but you should call a doctor if your child is hot enough to need this.

Bear in mind that a "normal" reading may give false reassurance. What is important is whether your child is unusually hot for him. Also, watch out for a subnormal temperature as this equally needs attention.

At some time in the first few months of life your baby is likely to catch his first cold. He may be fretful and difficult to settle, his breathing may sound alarmingly noisy, and he may feel feverish, as well as having a runny nose. Some small babies seem relatively unbothered by a cold, while others get quite distressed because they cannot breathe through their mouths if their noses are blocked. A breastfed baby may find feeding difficult if his nose is blocked and become angry and frustrated.

If your baby has a cold and is having trouble feeding, is off his feeds and seems listless or otherwise unwell, you should contact your doctor. If your baby has had a cold and appears better, but then seems unwell again, you should always see a doctor, because it is possible that the baby has a secondary infection, perhaps of the ear, throat or chest.

A child with an ear infection may be in a lot of pain, crying and sleeping fitfully. A baby may pull at his ear and an older child may keep putting his hand to his ear. Sometimes your child may not give a particular clue that he has earache.

A baby or young child with a throat infection will be off his food and may be sick, sometimes refusing to eat or drink much at all. This is because with a sore throat babies find sucking very painful. A baby with a chest infection may breathe noisily, but look at the baby's chest when he is breathing – if the ribs are being drawn sharply inwards with each breath, you should call a doctor at once.

Although many of the common childhood diseases such as measles, rubella and mumps can be prevented by vaccinations, children can still catch them. If your child develops a rash, especially with a temperature or other signs of being unwell, telephone your doctor for a diagnosis.

As a general rule, you need medical help for your child if:
- you think your child is not his usual self
- you think your child is ill, even if you cannot put your finger on what is wrong
- your child has a fit or seems pale or bluish in colour
- your child has a fall and is unusually quiet or drowsy, looks pale, seems unco-ordinated or loses consciousness
- there is bleeding from the ears, nose or mouth after a head injury
- there is any difficulty in breathing or it seems quick or sounds grunting
- your child is drowsy, hard to wake and does not seem to recognize you
- your child is burnt or scalded
- your child has a hard cough with noisy breathing
- your child seems unusually hot or cold or floppy
- there is diarrhoea and vomiting
- if your child seems off his food or is refusing his feeds
- your child cries for a long time or in an unusual way
- your child seems in pain.

A sick child at home

A small baby who is unwell will probably sleep more lightly than usual and want to be carried around by you – in fact, you may find yourself carrying him around all day. Keep him in a sling or nearby in a Moses basket so that you can easily soothe him.

An older child will need your company and cuddles, too. If he needs to rest, it may help both of you to make up a day-bed in the living-room.

Boredom is likely to be a problem for a sick child, so give him lots of your time. Stories, story tapes, puzzles and crayons and gummed paper shapes, together with plenty of scrap paper, are acceptable diversions in this situation.

Illness (of Mother)

Once you have children there is little or no hope of being able to retire to bed for the day when you are feeling unwell.

If you have a small baby and are breastfeeding, you will have to carry on getting up in the night and feeding whether or not you feel up to it. While your partner is at work, you will find yourself with a temperature, pushing the baby round the block in the hope of lulling him to sleep so that you can throw yourself on the bed for an hour or so.

Worse still is when you have two children or more. Do you stagger off to school so at least you can lose the eldest for the best part of the day, or do you keep them all at home because you really do not think you can make it there and back? Is it better to go to the mother and toddler group so that your toddler amuses himself, or to stay at home where your bored child might make more demands on you?

There is little benefit to anyone if you let yourself reach the end of your tether, so always turn to neighbours, friends or relations for help. If you have fed the neighbour's cat every time they are on holiday, you will feel more justified in asking them to collect your eldest from school or come in and read stories to your children for an hour while you go to bed.

Feel free to ring up friends to beg them to have your child for an hour or two – you can do the same thing for them when they have gone down with flu next week. In a crisis, grandparents and other relations are also invaluable, so make the most of them too.

One problem with a family is that, because young children are so prone to coughs, colds, tummy upsets and common childhood ailments, they are constantly passing them on to you, so that parents get ill more often than other people. When you know you may be ill at least three or four times a year, you hesitate to ask your mother to come and stay or your partner to take the day off work because you have a cold or a headache, as you might need them more desperately later on. In any case mothers often find that their bout of flu clashes with a day when their partner has an important meeting at work or when grandparents have gone away on holiday.

With all this in mind, it is important to do what you can to prevent illness in the family by eating a healthy diet or, failing that, taking vitamin supplements. Avoid seeing friends who are in the early stages of colds or flu, and make sure you and your children are immunized against diseases like measles, mumps and rubella. Good hygiene in the house – like keeping the toilet clean and washing hands before meals – will help prevent stomach upsets in particular from spreading (see Hygiene).

Even if you take great care, illness is still bound to occur. If you are seriously ill – bad enough to be unable to get out of bed or even to have to go into hospital – someone usually rallies round. There are problems, nevertheless – if you have a small breastfed baby, the baby may have to come into hospital with you, and you may find yourself having to make all kinds of difficult and perhaps not very satisfactory arrangements for other children. Mothers in this situation also find that they come out of hospital sooner or are on their feet again much earlier than they should be.

Try to avoid launching straight back into the mother routine. Ask your partner to take the children out for an hour or so while you take some rest. If he is not available, call on the help of friends or family. Just a brief daily respite from the energy and noise of children until you feel you are on the mend will help to speed recovery.

Feeling ill is often worse if you are pregnant. Severe morning sickness can reduce a mother to misery for weeks on end, especially if she still has to keep on caring for a toddler. Most pregnant mothers with small children feel exhausted anyway for the first few months and then again in the last one.

A high fever can be dangerous while you are pregnant and, because a woman's immune system is less effective in pregnancy, you are more likely to catch infections and find it harder to fight them off.

There is also the risk of developing high blood pressure or pre-eclampsia at the end of pregnancy, a condition which necessitates bed rest as it can be dangerous for mother and baby alike. Bed rest with a toddler in tow is almost impossible to achieve for more than a day, but if the condition is serious, hospitalization will be necessary in any case.

Perhaps the most difficult situations for mothers to cope with are those illnesses where you feel really terrible but can just about manage to carry on. The problem is that while you continue to cope, nobody will believe you are as ill as you really feel.

It often helps to create a distraction for your child when you are feeling like this. Try to keep a box of things for the children to do hidden away in a cupboard. Colouring-in books and felt-tips, a jigsaw puzzle, play-dough or plasticine, or things to cut out are all good for an afternoon when you just want to sit still on the sofa. A new story tape to listen to or a new video also work wonders. Failing that, see if you can dig out some old toys that they have forgotten.

Sympathy is something which is hard to come by when you are an ill parent. You are likely to feel nothing but irritation at your sick partner when he lies in bed all weekend groaning, and he is likely to feel the same when you go down with it on Monday morning forcing him to stay at home. Other mothers, with memories of staggering around with flu a couple of weeks ago themselves, may have more sympathy and take a child off your hands for an hour.

Your doctor will probably tell you to "take things easy" and "rest" for a day or two. If you explain that you have small children, the doctor may nod with sympathy and tell you to forget about the housework or "let things slide". If you are feeling terrible, however, the last thing you want is to have your home looking like a disaster area. This will just make you feel even more ill and miserable, and give you even more work to do at the end of the day, so it may be best just to carry on as best you can.

However, always remember that you can take short cuts. For example, give the children a picnic on the lawn in summer, and open tins of beans or spaghetti rings instead of making a nourishing stew. For once, let them watch too much television and give them a reward if they will play quietly for an hour.

◆ See also, **Doctors**

Imagination and Imaginary Play

Until he is about two years old your child will be more concerned with the solid, real things in life than with the abstract or pretend world. "What's that?" will remain his theme tune and you will be fully occupied introducing him to the objects he meets every day. He will be thrilled with his achievement when he can name a potato, a sock, a girl or a boy.

But even though there is little outward sign of imaginative life (except perhaps the odd "brmm, brmm" as he pushes a stray shoe around the room), this accumulation of practical information forms the foundation on which his imagination will develop. The imagination needs a solid base of practical experience as its starting point, and it's important that your child should discover as many real things as possible, and experience as much as possible through all his senses. He needs to know that a chair is for sitting on before he can start to think that it could just as well be used for a delivery van or flying to the moon. An active imagination can bring an enormous amount of pleasure. As adults we know the joy of escaping into fantasy worlds for a few moments' respite from the humdrum real world – and young children show signs of the same feelings.

As if pleasure weren't reason enough, using his imagination helps a young child get to grips with the wider world around him by sorting out his limited bits of knowledge and putting them together slightly differently, to try to make sense of things. He tests out "theories" of life and tries to extend his understanding; he role-plays situations that he knows something about – being a mummy, a daddy, a doctor or a nurse.

Just as with the more practical aspects of life, it's never too early to encourage and help your child to develop his imagination. Prepare the ground well by offering a wide range of play situations. Almost all types of play provide opportunities for both practical and imaginative development. You don't need to set aside physical space to let the imagination play. All you need do is recognize the "pretend" potential of all those cars and trains, dolls and teddies or even cardboard boxes and saucepans, and make some suggestions.

Do be careful not to get too carried away at first. There's no point deciding that "today we are going to be imaginative", come what may, and trying to push your child into it. Make suggestions, float ideas, and be prepared to postpone them if they are not readily taken up.

If left to his own devices, your child's imagination will start to come through anyway; your part is to be alert to the emerging signs and do your best to encourage rather than discourage them. But you must also know when to take a back seat; if you see your child happily engaged in some fantasy play, don't butt in just because you feel you've had a better idea.

Some children invent an imaginary friend to keep them company, or through whom they can more safely be naughty or controversial. You may have to provide food and clothing for this friend, and you will certainly have to take his feelings into account.

Remember this friend won't be around for ever so accept his temporary presence. Provide social opportunities so that the friend doesn't become overwhelmingly important to your child. But don't try to dismiss him; this is just as much a childhood comforter as a dummy or a blanket, and when he is ready, your child will just leave his friend behind.

Encourage drawing and painting and be prepared to believe that your child's scribbles are, in fact, buses, animals, or spaceships.

Children of all ages love to take on the character of another person, animal or even an object. You can help by collecting hats and shoes, bags and belts as basic props but don't be overly concerned about this. Even without props toddlers will enjoy roaring like lions or purring like kittens. Encourage pre-school children to take a better look at domestic pets or at pictures of large animals to refine their attempts.

Trains, cars and submarines are all favourite subjects for pretend play, but why not try being a chair, a door or a pair of scissors? In this way the imagination is helping the child to gain a better understanding of the real things around him.

Show your child how to attempt different ways of walking, talking and facial expressions to create someone else. Let him feel different emotions by encouraging him to pretend to be fierce, timid, angry or sad.

Pretending can provide hours of fun, whether alone or with a friend or brother or sister. All you need do is to suggest the idea, add the occasional encouragement or give a virtuoso performance of your own. In fact, your willingness to join in will be the best encouragement of all.

Try to avoid traditional sexual stereotyping in these situations. There is no reason why your son should not pretend to be Mummy or your daughter a firefighter. In this way you can allow your child to experience a little of what it feels like to be something or someone else.

Imaginative play can be used to prepare your child for a traumatic event such as going into hospital or a new baby.

Suggest "Let's play doctors". Take it in turns to play each of the roles of doctor, patient, nurse and visitor. In this way you can familiarize your child with the idea of going into hospital, and you can use the opportunity to reinforce information that you have already given him (that Mummy will be staying with him all the time; that some nurses wear uniforms; that they frequently tend to stick a thermometer in your mouth when they come by, and so on).

Role-play also helps you to find out a little more about how your child is feeling. While he may not be able to put it into words if you simply ask, "Have you any worries about going into hospital?", he may express his anxieties in the course of the game.

One of the best ways to engage the imagination is through story-telling. But don't worry, you don't have to be a prize-winning author to delight your child – so long as you cast him in the starring role.

Young children love to hear stories about themselves. Even "Tom was a happy little boy who lived with..." will be enough to engage Tom's attention. Fairly ordinary details of Tom's domestic life will be enough to start with. Encourage your child to join in and tell you what happens next. Always be ready to encourage the story along and to comment on how Tom must feel about whatever is happening.

For slightly older children, story-telling on car journeys is a good idea. Begin with "Mummy, Daddy and Tom were going to the seaside when suddenly the car broke down", and let each person take a turn at adding one or two sentences to the story.

Older children can also combine story-telling with pretending to be someone else; in other words, they can start to act. But even at four or five, although the desire to perform might be strong, an adult will have to help keep things simple.

Making up stories is fun but reading from books is no poor relation. Traditional stories and legends require imaginative listeners and by the time he is around three years old your child will be enthralled.

Don't forget the world of fairies, witches and wizards, monsters, ghosts and goblins. All children like to imagine a world beyond their own – a world of magic and mystery, with perpetual parties and gloriously good things to eat.

Most children enjoy being scared or excited, so long as they are in a relatively safe context. No child enjoys being seriously frightened, but being chased by a ghost-playing older brother might just thrill and excite them both. However, bear in mind that two- and three-year-olds especially can be easily worried, so keep an eye open for real anxiety, especially if an older child is setting a more demanding pace.

Life without a little fantasy would be unbearably dull. Luckily, every child has the potential to imagine and to create. Help your child to enjoy his creative powers by joining in and encouraging his efforts.

Having said that, it can be both worrying and infuriating when a child withdraws into a fantasy world. Although this is perfectly normal, it is nevertheless worth considering whether your child has some hidden anxiety. Observe him closely to get a better idea of any possible problems – a new baby or starting nursery school are the obvious stress points, or perhaps you are pressing him too hard to do too much for himself. Offer more reassurance and ease up on your expectations, and encourage physical games to take his mind of his worries. If you feel that he is suffering or missing out on valuable play or social skills, seek expert advice.

Impetigo

Impetigo is a highly contagious skin infection which mainly affects children. Although some people associate it with eczema it can equally affect skin where there are insect bites, scabies or cold sores, and it affects perfectly healthy skin as well. In newborn babies it can be serious, even life-threatening, but otherwise it is not a threat and can easily be cured.

Impetigo is caused by the staphylococcus bacterium, which is found in the nose. It can be transmitted by breathing or sneezing, particularly on to damaged skin.

Impetigo first appears on the face, scalp, hands or knees. It begins as little red spots which soon become blisters and quickly break, exuding a pale yellow, sticky liquid. The blisters then dry to form large, irregularly shaped, brownish-yellow crusts.

If only a small area of skin is affected, there are usually no other symptoms, but if large areas are involved, or if the surrounding skin is also infected with other bacteria, your child will feel unwell, and will have a high temperature and swollen lymph nodes (for example those in the neck).

Unless precautions are taken, impetigo can quickly spread to other members of the household or school, either through infected flannels and towels, or by direct contact. As always when a child is ill, it is very important to keep flannels and towels used by the affected child away from other members of your family. If possible these should be boiled after use, as should your child's bed linen and clothes.

Children with impetigo should be told not to scratch the crusts, which can cause the infection to spread as well as running the risk of scarring. They should also be kept away from school until the infection has cleared.

The earlier treatment begins, the better. If the area affected is small the doctor will prescribe an antibiotic cream to be applied to the blisters three or four times a day until the crusts have healed. For larger areas additional antibiotics will be prescribed, to be taken by mouth or occasionally by injection. Thick crusts may have to be soaked off with liquid paraffin or salt water.

If left untreated, impetigo can cause abscesses elsewhere in the body, and very occasionally may even be responsible for nephritis (an inflammation of the kidneys). But as long as your child sees the doctor and starts the treatment straight away there is usually no problem. Very young babies may need to be treated in hospital.

Independence

Once he passes his fourth birthday, home will no longer be the centre of the universe for your child. He may already have adjusted to starting nursery school or playgroup and will be approaching his first full day's separation from you when he starts primary school.

This milestone will mean a great deal to you as well as your child. If you have prepared him well for this major change, then hopefully neither of you will see it as a trauma, but as an opportunity for him to achieve his full potential.

As your child grows more confident in his body, it is essential that he gets the chance to exercise his developing muscles. At this age, muscle growth accounts for 75 per cent of weight gain. Games such as climbing trees, swimming, and ball games will give him stamina, suppleness and strength.

Cycling is another excellent form of exercise and will give your child added mobility. From being an expert tricycle rider at four, he is likely to be able to ride a two-wheeled bicycle with stabilizers at five.

Hopping, skipping and jumping are skills your four-year-old has mastered with the increased control over his body. Balance and co-ordination allow him to walk on a narrow line without falling off, stand on one foot, and hop forwards on each foot separately. Skipping is also a great game for developing jumping and balancing skills, as well as being a favourite social activity for your child to play with his friends.

Your child will still not have fully perfected the fine use of muscles, especially skilful use of hands. He will, however, be adept at threading small beads to make a necklace and threading large needles. He will be able to use a crayon or pencil, held in adult fashion and his drawings will be much more recognizable. He may well be able to tell you what it is he is going to draw before he draws it, showing his new ability to plan ahead. But don't take his paintings too seriously, by placing too much emphasis on the finished product rather than on the pleasure he had in making it. This could encourage him to do the same thing over and over to "improve" it, or to gain compliments, and he will see it as a way of pleasing you rather than a way of expressing his own imagination. Wait until you are asked for help.

By four and a half, your child should be able to take much more responsibility for his own care. Dressing and undressing should be part of his routine, and choosing his own clothes is important, as he is developing his own taste and is gaining independence.

Laces, ties and back buttons may still pose some difficulty, so try to make life easier by going for front buttons, elastic waists and slip-on shoes where possible.

The friendship with other children becomes increasingly important between four and five years old. Your four-and-a-half-year-old is likely to choose his own friends and will be co-operative with his companions most of the time. You will need to allow him to develop these new friendships and not expect him to find all his pleasure at home.

As he becomes less dependent on you and far more dependent upon his playmates, this will enable him to adjust to being away from you all day at school. To reach this position, however, he needs to be totally confident in you as a secure base who will always be there when he needs you.

Between four and five, your child will start to gain control over his strong emotions. The vivid expression of the four-year-old, for example, when expressing affectionate feelings for a favourite aunt by pinching her, will give way to the greater self-control of the five-year-old, who is learning to express his feelings constructively. And feelings such as physical aggression are curtailed as he discovers that his peers retaliate and hurt him back.

Jealousy is an emotion he will be coming to terms with. He may well have experienced the pangs of jealousy if a new baby sister or brother has arrived on the scene. Although he wishes to be grown up, his babyish side will not easily be left behind. He needs to be allowed to be the little boy as well as the big boy. For example, he will enjoy being tucked up in bed, and actions such as this will mean he is then less likely to become jealous of younger children.

At this age your child has a rapidly expanding vocabulary. By five he will have about 2,000 words and be using most of the basic rules of grammar to make quite complex sentences. He will be able to have fully intelligible conversations with people outside the home, and if he got lost he should be able to tell them his name, address and his age.

He will love riddles and jokes, as he shows you his developing sense of humour. Listening and telling long stories where fantasy and facts intermingle will give you both pleasure and demonstrate his increasing creativity.

As he approaches school age, you may find that he begins to pick out words as you read to him. If so, it is worth showing him some simple first reading books. Do not push him too hard in this direction; let it come naturally. The most important factor in this early learning is that success, overall, outweighs failure.

If he enjoys building and constructing these are the years when he will fill every spare minute making things. He can progress from puzzles of a few pieces to jigsaws that may even initially challenge you.

Give him more difficult puzzles as he is ready for them. The ability to concentrate on a task in hand is a priceless asset for a child approaching school age and should be encouraged whenever possible.

At five he is still discovering, and making certain of the difference between reality and fantasy and generally extending his grasp of the outside world. Watch you don't stifle his imagination. It can be easy to do this unintentionally. Children at this age are very amusing in their first attempts at doing things. To laugh or point him out to another adult, however, may make him feel useless and "stupid".

His greater sense of reality makes it easier to tolerate some frustration; he has learned that in the real world he cannot make things happen at once, when he wants them to. He has a better understanding of how one thing leads to another, a greater ability to remember people and places, and to realize that many things are permanent and do not disappear.

All of this makes it possible for him to wait for things to a much greater extent than he could ever tolerate before, and is an indication of growing independence.

Insects

Many children grow up fearing and disliking creepy-crawlies and flying insects, and this can persist into adult life and cause problems. Of course, there are many creatures that could be harmful to a small child and as a parent you will naturally wish to protect them from stings and bites. But by introducing your child to the delicately balanced insect world you will stimulate his natural interest in tiny creatures and their behaviour, while teaching him all he should know about those that are harmless and those he should approach with caution.

Your child's first experience of the insect world will probably be the butterflies and bees he sees fly past his pram. But it won't be long before you both discover the many ways you can explore insect life styles together.

As you sit in the garden or walk through a park, look for signs of insect life around you and show the clues to your child. You may not see any insects immediately but you will soon learn to read the tracks and signs they leave as they feed and grow around you.

Look at leaves: sawn off edges or holes in leaves are the work of caterpillars. Explain to your child how the bendy caterpillar chewing his way across a leaf will eventually turn into a colourful butterfly. You may also see some butterfly eggs on the underside of a leaf.

Bright red and spotted, ladybirds are always a delight to a child. Ladybirds are safe to touch and handle and a child will love counting the spots on its back.

Easy to see at night when they are attracted to the bright lights indoors, by day moths will provide a good game of hide-and-seek. Masters of camouflage, they blend into leaves and bark. Some moths, such as the peppered moth, settle on lichen-encrusted bark, while the angle shades moth makes itself look like an old leaf and settles on branches near other leaves.

Embark on the snail trail and track down slugs and snails. In the early part of the day you can show your child the shiny tracks they have left on paths or across large leaves. By day the snails take refuge under leaves, on shady walls and under garden sheds. As soon as dusk falls they can be seen crawling over lawns and greenery. Slug activity is at its peak at night too, but by day you can find slugs resting under empty flower pots and in damp shady places.

Collect a few and place them in a glass jar with several lettuce leaves and watch them grazing. Use a magnifying glass to show your child the rasping, sand-paper thin tongue that chews its way through the lettuce leaves. Watch and listen to bees as they buzz about in a herb patch. Tiny thyme flowers are particularly attractive to bees – and while the bees are busy gathering pollen and nectar, you and your child are not in any danger of being stung. The bees are just too busy working.

As you watch them collecting pollen and nectar to make honey, you can explain that the bee is helping the flower to make its seeds and produce next year's plants or fruits. Also show your child the bright yellow stamens filled with pollen and the guidelines on a flower that direct the insect to the sweet nectar-filled parts of the flower. Explain how they make honey to feed their young.

Interaction and observation of the balance between man, insect and plant life is an important part of a toddler's gradual entry into the world at large. And as part of your observation of nature you can tell stories about the life of the insects and bugs you find. Your child will also love to count legs and spots and look at the different markings and colourings on wings of moths and butterflies.

At a later stage your child will want to move closer to this small-scale world and will actively seek out water bugs and beetles in ponds and at the seaside. He will turn over stones to discover the top of an ant nest or woodlice at rest. If you have explained to him early on that some insects sting and bite, and have taught him which ones are safe to get close to, at this stage you can point out how to handle the insects gently and safely.

You can catch insects for short-term inspection using a clean glass jam jar. Your child will have to be patient and quiet and wait for the insect to walk or fly into the jar. If you cover the jar with a piece of muslin and an elastic band, the insect will have adequate air and will not be able to escape until you are ready to return it to the spot where it was found. If the insect your child wants to examine is feeding on a leaf or on clusters of other insects (for example, ladybirds feeding on aphids on leaf and stem shoots), place a leaf or stem tip in the jar before trapping the insect.

It is particularly fascinating for children to watch the ordered, seemingly untiring activity of a colony of ants. Place some bread and jam on the ground near where you see a line of ants. Your child will be mesmerized as they carry off tiny crumbs and follow each other in straight lines back to the nest. If you happen to disturb an ant nest in a stone flower pot, for example, show your child how the army of ants immediately starts to scurry around in all directions moving their white eggs to a safe place.

If your child does seem to show more than a passing interest in the insect and bug life around him, you will find a magnifying glass invaluable. Lie on a rug or blanket with your child and hold the glass over grass or soil, or on to the surface of flowers and enjoy the close-up view that you will get. Look at ants on the ground and ladybirds on leaves through the glass. As your child grows up stimulate his interest by buying a junior microscope. It will not be sophisticated, but will offer him the chance to look at tinier forms of life in the soil, in drops of water and on leaf surfaces.

But even with simple everyday utensils and containers and the right sort of encouragement, you can help your child develop a sensitive understanding of the delicate insect world.

Mini Habitats
A caterpillar hatchery
Your child will be fascinated to watch a caterpillar turn into a moth or a butterfly. The whole process takes several weeks but it will involve him in daily activities of observation, cleaning the hatchery and picking more leaves to feed the caterpillars. And then finally, when the butterfly or moth emerges and flies off to freedom, your child will have had a very special insight into the insects' life.

Make a caterpillar hatchery using a litre-sized plastic drink container. Cut away the narrow top end of the bottle. Prepare a muslin cover so the insects can breathe. Lie the bottle on its side and line it with moist kitchen paper. Gently place the caterpillars or eggs in the container. Add several leaves from the plant where you found the caterpillars or eggs. Place the muslin cover over the open end of the bottle and tie it up with a ribbon or string. Take care not to tip the bottle over. Add new leaves every day and remove any that have dried out or simply don't look fresh. Keep the hatchery in a cool place.

Every few days your child should gently remove the paper, replace it with fresh and then, equally gently, return the caterpillars. After a week or two add a few bare twigs to the container.

As the caterpillar feeds, it grows and gets too big for its skin. It sheds this several times and eventually attaches itself to a twig. The last time it sheds its skin it develops a hard skin in its place. Then it hangs motionless, not feeding for several weeks until a magical moment when the hard case splits and the creased and folded butterfly or moth emerges. The new insect's wings straighten and take on colour as they fill with blood and the outside surfaces dry out. Now is the moment for your child to release his "pet" to the wild.

Knowing what he does about the wonders of the insect world, will help him understand why he has to let go of something he has grown to care for.

A wormery

Use a glass jar or unused goldfish bowl to view the underground world of garden soil. Fill the container with alternate layers of ordinary garden soil and fine sand, moisten it slightly and place a layer of leaves on the top. Cover the container with a dishcloth or brown paper to keep the wormery dark. The earthworms in the soil will gradually drag the leaves down into the soil to use as food. As they eat the leaves and move them through the soil they also digest soil and soon the layers will lose their definition and become mixed. On the surface of the soil you can show your child the ruffles of soil (worm casts) that the worms have digested. Garden soil is full of worms but if you want to make sure that there are worms in your underground habitat pop in a few more. Sprinkling soapy water on to grass will attract worms to the surface.

Insomnia

Insomnia – not being able to sleep – is usually associated with older people but children can suffer from it too. Insomnia really means habitual sleeplessness over a substantial period.

Reasons for insomnia are legion but only a few of them need medical treatment, especially as far as children are concerned.

Babies tend to evolve their own sleep patterns which may not, unfortunately, coincide with yours. It is perfectly natural and normal for a baby to wake up in the middle of the night and this should not be misconstrued as insomnia.

However, a two-year-old who is familiar with a routine should go to sleep readily and should sleep for at least 8 hours out of 24. He may wake up in the middle of the night, possibly several times, but again this is not considered unusual. The cause may just be a bad dream that has disturbed him and all he needs is some comforting. Most children go back to sleep again without too much trouble.

A sick child may sleep soundly if he is on medication, but a mild illness like a common cold will be more likely to keep him awake as breathing and relaxing can become extremely difficult. Anybody with a fever, whether child or adult, is prone to waking up in the middle of the night bathed in sweat. This can be extremely distressing and scaring to a child and he may even be reluctant to try and go to sleep again.

Another common reason for children being unable to sleep at night is a change in routine or a change in surroundings. A new cot or strange wallpaper can make a child feel scared or insecure and going to sleep is the last thing he will want to do until he is convinced that he is safe.

A heavy meal before bed-time can make children wakeful. And so can a badly ventilated bedroom that lacks fresh air. If your child is listless and complains of no sleep one morning, either of these could be the cause.

Anxiety is the most common cause of insomnia in adults and it can also keep children awake at night. Children are remarkably quick at picking up family tensions that create doubts about their security and will sleep badly when this happens.

The symptoms of sleeplessness are obvious enough. But diagnosing genuine insomnia (being unable to go to sleep on a regular basis) in children is not always so easy. It is only when the problem recurs night after night, week after week, that you should take the matter in hand. The older your child is, the more you should take note of the problem. A two-year-old is bound to be wakeful for short periods during most nights but a five-year-old should be able to sleep more consistently through the night (except when ill).

There are essentially two forms of insomnia. As with adults, some children find it hard to go to sleep, but others wake up in the middle of the night and only then find it hard to nod off again.

Of the two, the latter is more significant as it usually betrays signs of deep anxiety – something that should be tackled quickly before it becomes a problem.

As far as babies are concerned, there are, broadly speaking, two ways of coping with disrupted sleep patterns. On the one hand, you can let your baby dictate his own routine – sleeping when he wants to, for as long as he wants to – or you can impose a regime. For many parents, imposing a regime is the most practical option.

Whichever option you adopt, it is imperative that you are consistent – a change in routine will almost certainly lead to restless nights. If you go away on holiday or stay with relatives for a weekend, make sure that you take a supply of teddies, dolls or other familiar toys as well – they will help to provide the necessary comfort in an otherwise strange environment.

Older children also need reassurance at night, which can be a frightening time, especially if they have vivid imaginations and can see monsters looming out of the curtains or wallpaper. Try not to ridicule your child's perceptions. Although they may seem silly to you, they may be extremely frightening to him – to the extent that they will keep him awake night after night.

Comfort your child by reading him stories and if need be, show him that there really is nothing sinister under the bed or in the cupboard.

If your child goes to school and persists in waking up in the middle of the night, it may be something at school, rather than at home, that is making him panic. Try to find the cause and act on it immediately, if necessary with help from teachers.

The one thing to bear in mind is that drugs (sleeping pills or depressants) should be used only as a very last resort. Consult your family doctor if the problem becomes unduly worrying and never give your child drugs unless they have been prescribed for him.

In general, it may be helpful to use the following guidelines to try to help your child sleep better:

● Try to ensure that he gets plenty of exercise and fresh air during the day – this will encourage sleep later on.

● If your baby has difficulty in getting off to sleep, don't keep him up late in the belief that this will make him more tired and therefore more likely to get to sleep. He will undoubtedly get tired but this will probably make him bad-tempered and upset, so instead of going to sleep, he may end up crying.

● Check that your child's nightwear isn't restrictive in any way. It should be soft and loose all over. Some nylon garments can irritate children's sensitive skin.

● Some fresh air at night encourages sound sleep and an open window or a door left ajar is always a good idea even in chilly weather.

● Avoid giving your child a late-night snack last thing before bed as this will stimulate rather than pacify. A hot, milky drink at bedtime, however, is a good idea.

◆ See also, **Fears**, **Night Frights**

Left-Handedness

Fortunately, the times when left-handedness was seen as a problem, if not actually a disability or a handicap, are well past.

Stories from Victorian and Edwardian school rooms of left-handed children being forced to write and draw with the right hand, are still part of everyone's folk-memory. Maybe you yourself had to undergo that kind of rigid "conversion".

It's almost certain that left-handers who go through this sort of pressure are at risk of ending up with problems such as stammering, disturbed behaviour and distress.

Left- or right-handedness is controlled by the same area of the brain that is involved in language, which is why confusing the issue can cause difficulties. Research has shown that stuttering occurs more frequently in countries whose rigid school rules don't allow left-handed children to actually draw and write with their left hand.

Left-handedness is not the norm, but it's not at all rare. Most estimates conclude that about 8 per cent of people are left-handed – about 200 million people worldwide – and more of these are male than female.

On the whole, it's likely to be an inborn, possibly hereditary characteristic. There are theories that what seems to be the hereditary aspect – a left-handed parent producing a left-handed child – is at least partly a result of the child imitating what he sees his parent doing. The chances of your producing a left-handed child are greatest if both you and your partner are left-handed, less great if only one of you is but it is impossible to be precise.

Most left-handed children, however, are born to a pair of right-handed parents. But because left-handedness is so relatively uncommon and such a distinctive trait, it usually doesn't take long to trace a left-handed member in either family among preceding generations.

Identical twins are more likely to be left-handed than single babies or non-identical twins.

The hereditary issue still causes controversy among the experts – with some maintaining that worldwide, the incidence of left-handedness would be a lot higher if left-handedness had not been, over generations and in many cultures, actively discouraged and even viewed with suspicion.

In fact, there are many unanswered questions about left-handedness that continue to fascinate the scientists. Why, for example, is left-handedness more common among people of genius, both artistic and scientific? And why is it more common among criminals? And among children who had a stressful birth? Research still goes on, but it's likely that we'll never have the complete picture.

How do you know which hand your baby is going to prefer? Most babies swap "favourite" hands at first, and many younger toddlers don't demonstrate any preference. It's not until your child reaches two that you can begin to recognize whether he is left- or right-handed.

Look at the hand he uses to pick up a cup, to hold small pieces of food such as peas, to manipulate bricks and jigsaw pieces. It's perfectly possible that he shows a high degree of "ambidextrousness" or "mixed-handedness" – the ability to use either hand – with many tasks.

Firmly-established left-handers sometimes continue with this useful skill throughout their lives, without ever having to practise it in any conscious way. A classic example is the tennis player who by moving the racket from the left to the right hand saves himself a lot of running.

When your child is three or four, his preference will be clearer, and it will probably be set for life from then on.

In some studies, left-handed children have been shown to be more likely than right-handers to have speech delays and some other learning and behavioural difficulties, but the relationship between all these factors isn't at all clear. Don't assume that because your child appears to be left-handed that he'll have problems in talking or at school. The majority of left-handed children have no long-lasting difficulties at school or later.

That doesn't mean, however, that the fact that your child is left-handed should be ignored. Learning to write may need a little more time and practice in holding a pen or pencil comfortably, and your child's school needs to know he's left-handed for this reason.

Writing can be awkward, unless your child is helped to discover a position that's comfortable for him and which allows him to see his writing as he does it. Some left-handers "hook" their left hand, with the pen facing the body, so the hand is actually above the line of writing.

A very simple way of encouraging your child to write, so he can see what he's doing without holding his hand in an awkward position, is to slant the paper to the right (for right-handers, it slopes to the left).

There's no way of avoiding the slight difficulty of having to learn to "push" the pen rather than "pull" it – that's because many languages are written from left to right – but at least writing becomes more natural this way.

To ensure that your child is able to see what he is writing, try to persuade him to grip the pen further away from the point, at least three or even four centimetres. This will also prevent smudged writing.

If your child grips his pen or pencil too tightly when drawing or writing remind him from time to time to relax his grip. You might find your child is happier writing with a good quality fibre-tip pen than with a ball point. Ball-point ink may smudge if it's touched by the hand before completely drying – and it's impossible for the "learner" left-hander not to touch the writing as he writes and his hand moves on across the page.

Later on, once your child is writing confidently, he can use a specially made fountain pen for left-handers, where the pen nib slants down from left to right. Generally speaking, the broader the nib the easier your child will find writing with it, so do avoid an extremely fine nib which will slow down his writing and may cause him to jab holes in the paper.

Although some musical instruments, such as the guitar and the violin, can be adjusted to suit left-handed players, this requires complex string and internal alterations, and in most cases left-handed children are taught to play musical instruments in the same way as right-handed children. The reasoning behind this is that learning to play an instrument is a fairly unnatural action for any child and requires the same amount of effort and skill from both right- and left-handers.

If your child shows a very early interest in playing a musical instrument or if you're very keen on him starting, go ahead with it – there's no reason to envisage problems or to delay just because he is left-handed.

As in the case of writing, experts nearly unanimously agree these days that children are best allowed to follow their natural preference when it comes to physical play or sport activities. Being told to throw the ball with his right hand or kick it with the right foot can cause extreme frustration.

A left-handed child may "see" differently. Play games that strengthen his eye-to-hand co-ordination, such as rolling balls, stringing beads, throwing bean bags at targets and using wind-up toys.

Parents today take comfort from the interesting statistics involved in left-handedness. Rather than view this preference as a "disability", it is now seen as a positive factor that may even indicate that your left-handed child will express an extra skill or determination later in life.

This should not mean that you swing to the other extreme, and begin to expect special achievements from your child. Such pressure could cause as much harm as trying to stop him from using his left hand.

Apart from warning his teachers that writing may be more difficult for him than it is for the right-handed, there really is no need for special care and precautions. After all, to the person who is left-handed it is a perfectly natural way to function. It is only the right-handed majority who think it is "odd" and difficult to use the left hand.

Legs

From the waist to the end of the toes there are more than 60 different, interlinking bones. The femur (thigh bone) is the longest bone in the body; and the second longest is the tibia (shin bone), the main bone at the front of the pair of bones in the lower leg.

The femur and the tibia meet at the knee in a hinged joint which is protected at the front by the patella (kneecap). At the bottom of the tibia and fibia (the bones of the lower leg) are the complex bones of the ankles (tarsals), the foot (metatarsals) and the toes (phalanges).

Corresponding to the bones, the muscles of the leg include some of the largest in the body. In the lower leg are three sets of muscles, the peroneal muscles on the outside of the leg, the flexors or calf muscles, and the extensors – the muscles in the ankle and foot.

The upper leg also has three sets of muscles: the quadriceps and hamstrings at the front and back of the thigh respectively, and the adductor muscles of the inner thigh. The muscles of the buttock connect with the upper leg and the pelvis.

All the tissues of the legs, and particularly their large muscle systems, need to be supplied with blood to provide oxygen and nutrients.

Blood circulation is perhaps at its weakest in the legs, and blood can easily collect in the veins, since it has to work against gravity. However, in growing children they do a lot of work, quite apart from taking the weight of the body when standing.

But because of their flexibility they are surprisingly rarely injured. Cuts, bruises and grazes are the most common types of injury. As children grow up and begin to use their legs fully, one of the most vulnerable spots is the shin, which is easily bruised as the shin bone is protected only by a thin layer of skin. The malleolus – the part of the shin bone at the outer ankle – is another vulnerable spot, and the kneecap is prone to dislocation and fracture.

Leg pains

Usually there is nothing really wrong when children complain of leg pains. Adults may refer to these as "growing pains", but they can be quite a problem for the child – and worrying for the parents. So-called "growing pains" are most likely to affect children from four to eight years old. They are felt in both legs as a dull, aching pain, sometimes down the whole length of the thigh, or, more usually, all down the lower leg. Often these pains are worse at night, when they can disturb the child's sleep. The normal aches and pains may become worse after the child has been taking part in sporting activities.

Although most generalized leg pains will be simply growing pains, there are a few, quite rare, conditions, which also cause pains in the legs.

Certain distinct types of leg pains, sometimes linked with other symptoms, can be an indication of more serious illness:
● Severe pain in one area, deterring the child from using the leg. This could be a fracture if the child has recently had an accident, or it could be a symptom of osteomyelitis (infection in the bone marrow).

● A painful knee, with swelling could be a dislocation if it follows an accident, or it could be Still's disease or arthritis.

See your doctor if your child has leg pains other than generalized pains, and if generalized pains last continuously for longer than a day.

It is not really known what causes generalized leg pains. Some doctors believe that they are connected with growth spurts and that they may be the effect of the muscles not growing at quite the same rate as the bones. Others argue that there can be no medical reason to explain why growing causes pain.

In some cases, of course, aching in the legs is a natural consequence of taking an unusual amount of exercise and giving the muscles more work than usual, but in this event the connection will be obvious.

As long as there is no medical reason for pains in the legs, the only treatments are the old-fashioned remedies of warmth, relaxation and sympathy. A warm bath or a hot water bottle may help to take the pain away, and soothing massage can help to relax tense muscles. While there is no need to make a fuss, you may find that a cuddle and a show of concern do wonders for your child.

Finally, if there seems to be any chance that he is tense and anxious about something that is happening to him at the time, uncovering the cause and getting your child to talk about any worries may solve the problem. Reassurance may be all that is needed.

Lungs

The lungs occupy most of the thorax or chest cavity, where they are protected by the rib cage. The air we breathe passes into the lungs, and from them oxygen is absorbed into the blood stream, while waste carbon dioxide is breathed out.

The right lung is larger than the left, since the heart takes up some of the space in the left side of the chest.

The lungs themselves are made up of a dense network of little tubes, some containing blood (blood vessels) and some containing air (bronchi).

The right lung is divided into three separate parts (lobes) and the left lung into two, and each lung has one air passage or bronchus, connected to the windpipe which divides and subdivides, somewhat like the branches of a tree.

The subdivisions of the bronchi are known as the bronchioles and at the end of the tiny final branch of each of these are little air sacs known as alveoli. The lungs are surrounded by membranes in two layers, known as the pleura, and the bronchi are lined by a self-cleaning mucous membrane which causes invading particles of dust, smoke and bacteria to be coughed out.

When we breathe in, our chest muscles and diaphragm (the band of muscle separating the upper from the lower chest) cause the ribs to rise and expand and air is drawn in. The air passes via the bronchi into the alveoli, where oxygen is taken up by the red cells of the blood to be transported to all the tissues of the body. Carbon dioxide, a by-product made when the body produces energy, is carried back in the blood to the lungs and breathed out.

Naturally, a baby does not use its lungs while it is still in the womb and surrounded by fluid. All the oxygen the fetus needs is obtained from the blood in the mother's placenta, so the alveoli are flat, like tiny, deflated balloons.

At the moment of birth a startling change takes place as the placenta separates from the uterus and ceases to supply oxygen to the baby, and the baby spontaneously takes his first breath.

Breathing starts with little gasps, followed by a prolonged cry, showing that the alveoli and lungs are expanding. It takes several months before all the alveoli have expanded and the baby's lungs are fully in use.

Lung disorders
Asthma
A constriction of the bronchial tubes, often as an allergic reaction to something breathed in.

Bronchitis
An inflammation of the lining of the bronchial tubes, with or without an infection.

Pleurisy

An inflammation of the pleura (the membranes surrounding the lung), usually caused by an infection.

Pneumonia

Inflammation of the bronchi and lung tissue caused by an infection.

Pneumothorax

A result of injury to the chest or of a lung disease in which air escapes from the lungs into the pleural cavity.

◆ See also, **Asthma**, **Common Cold**, **Coughing**

Lying

Most children try to trick their parents now and then. Perhaps the commonest situation is when they are trying to pass the blame on to someone else for something that is, in itself, quite trivial, such as an accidentally broken mug or a biscuit taken without permission.

One of the most unpleasant things about discovering your child lying or stealing is the thought that, at the tender age of three or four, he has lost his innocence, as there is something underhand and deceitful about lying and stealing that is not a part of the more open kind of childish naughtiness you may be used to. The first time you catch your child telling a lie or taking something that doesn't belong to him, however, the chances are it is not a sign of lost innocence, but just the reverse. It may be that he or she is truly innocent of the conventions adults try to live by.

For young children, imagination and reality are often mixed to the extent that they can easily confuse the two. When a cardboard box becomes a car or a broomstick becomes a pony, that "fact" can become so important to them that they forget that it's all a game and they are only pretending.

There can be a series of small, linked steps between childish fantasy and outright adult-like lying. So, if your little ones run in and tell you "we are playing hunt-the-monsters in the garden", it could be perfectly true. Then "I saw a monster behind the dustbin but it got away," wouldn't worry the mothers of most four-year-olds. Similarly, if one child said, "After the monster escaped we flew to see Granny in Australia because we wanted some sweets," you might just mutter a knowing "Oh did you?"

What if, however, later that afternoon, your three- and four-year-olds hardly eat any of their favourite tea? They explain it's because of all the sweets that Granny gave them and you begin to change your attitude. What should you do – interrogate them as if they were criminal suspects, or laugh it off?

Usually it is quite easy to know when a young child is fibbing, but if you challenge your child over something when you don't really know the truth about what happened, try not to get into a pointless battle which neither of you can ever win. Rather than have a repetition of "You took it from him," "No, I did not!", "Yes, you did!", it might be better to act as if you really did know the truth, even when you are not certain. This is an example where a little dishonesty might be justified if it encourages your child to think that he cannot get away with lying.

When your child admits to being dishonest it's pointless trying to shame him by telling him what a terrible person he is. This will probably only

make him less likely to own up in future and become more devious to avoid getting caught.

It is important to make it clear that it's the behaviour which is bad, not the child himself, who is (you hope) capable of acting honestly most of the time.

Almost regardless of how you react to any one incident, the most important thing is to be sure your child knows that you care about how he behaves.

Remember that whatever rules you give young children, the simpler they are, the more likely they are to be obeyed. But "always tell the truth" is not an easy rule for a young child to follow. A four-year-old might have to learn to hide the truth when his big sister asks him what he's got her for her birthday, or else it won't be a surprise. There may also be occasions when you'll need to explain that there are lots of different ways of telling the truth. It's possible to be honest without being blunt and hurtful. If you don't mind, allow the occasional "white lie", pointing out it has to make someone else feel better, not just the person telling it.

Even if what's literally true is not always appropriate, children have to acquire a sense of what it means to behave honestly. The most powerful source of that picture of honesty will be the attitudes and behaviour of the parents themselves. What you say may be important, but children are very observant and quick to notice if what you say doesn't match up to how you behave.

The rules for when to take things that don't belong to you, or even whether or not they belong to you, are, for a young child, almost as confusing as when and how to tell the truth. You walk round a supermarket picking things off shelves. Why shouldn't your three-year-old help himself, too?

The link between money and ownership has probably always been something of a mystery to little children. Now, with electronic shopping, you can just hand a banker's card over to the person at the till. As far as your child is concerned, no money changes hands, unless you explain it to him.

It's not easy for adults to explain the rules they follow for telling the truth or for not taking things that don't belong to them, however, and detailed explanations aren't always the best way of getting a message across to children. Young children who pick up so much through imitation can also be affected by the world of television and stories. If they are old enough to watch television, is honesty respected and deception punished in the programmes they watch?

You can use children's innate love of stories as a way of pointing out right from wrong if you want to help get your values across. Lots of traditional fairy stories deal with people who lie or steal so you could use these as a starting point for discussion. For a three- or four-year-old child you could make up your own stories. If your child has done something particularly naughty, like repeatedly taking and hiding someone else's toy, you could make that episode into a very simple story, perhaps with the characters of your son and his friend disguised as a cast of teddy-bears or dolls. The "naughty bear" need not be punished harshly. All that would be needed would be for the mummy bear to have found out the truth of the situation, and perhaps be a little sad. A telling off in story form can sometimes work at a deeper level than an everyday scolding.

Even before they get to the age of five children begin to realize that other children don't want them lying or stealing either. The odd occurrences that do crop up in almost any family are, like so many childhood problems, best dealt with by persistent reminders of what's right and wrong combined with a joint parental effort to set good examples.

◆ See also, **Imagination and Imaginary Play**

Manual Skills

Your new baby will wave his arms about in an excited but helpless fashion. His hands flap, his fingers move and wriggle, but he has very little control over his muscles.

Gradually, with a combination of instinct and experience, this small human begins to discover the power of his hands and to develop his strength and skill. It is fascinating to watch his steady progress towards what is called manual dexterity – the ability to control and use the fingers and wrists.

By his ninth or tenth month your baby will learn to use his thumb and forefinger to pick up small objects with the so-called "pincer" grip, rather than scooping them up with his whole hand. At a year old, he should be able to pick up a cup by its handle and even drink from it, and he will hold an object in each hand and bang them together. Now is the time he excites the whole family because he can clap his hands and wave goodbye.

From his first birthday onwards his skills develop more rapidly. He delights in pulling things apart, then with some frustration tries to fit them together again. He enjoys pushing small objects inside larger ones, and he will be very busy taking things out of boxes or bags. In using his hands and his eyes as he does these simple tricks, he is beginning to understand different shapes, sizes and textures. As he explores the things around him, he develops better and finer control over his finger movements and develops strength in his hands and wrists. Let him play and explore without interruption – just make sure that all sharp and dangerous objects are well out of his reach.

Bricks make an excellent toy for one- to two-year-olds. If you make a tower of bricks, he will enjoy knocking them down. He will get pleasure from taking bricks out of a box, then putting them back again. By the age of two he may be able to balance two or three on top of each other. You can show him how to put bricks together in a line and he will be very excited to realize that the bricks can be built into a structure such as a garage or house. You will be delighted to see him carefully – and with some difficulty – put a small car or doll inside this structure.

Balls are excellent toys for small children although they have no skill in using them in the first years of their lives. When your baby is a year old, he will enjoy holding a small ball in his hands and throwing it; and will feel very clever as he races to retrieve it. His ball control, at this stage, will be quite clumsy but it is important that he is unaware of this. It would spoil his confidence.

Stacking beakers, which are graduated so that they fit inside one another or can be built into a tower, stimulate him into thoughtful concentration and greater control of his finger action. At first, he will be able to stack one or two beakers, the largest ones first, but gradually he'll be able to do more and more.

Other stacking toys are rings or discs of wood or plastic which fit on to a central pole. These are frequently designed to form brightly coloured figures such as a clown or policeman when they are put back in the right order. Figures which stack on top of one another and pop into the air when a button is pressed not only bring forth squeals of joy from your child, but extend his understanding of mechanical effects. Now he can build and create on his own, and even press a button to make something new happen.

Nesting toys are another great favourite. The traditional Russian dolls, the old-fashioned nesting doll, will be difficult for a two-year-old to manage but he will be fascinated by the ever smaller people fitting inside the largest doll. In fact, even by 18 months your toddler will be fascinated with things that fit inside one another. "Peg people" which fit into holes and keys which fit locks will keep him busy and he will enjoy posting-box toys. Young toddlers also love opening things and taking lids off to see what's inside.

There are, of course, endless toys to develop your child's dexterity, and to cater to his level, but your toddler will be perfectly content with ordinary kitchen pots, shoe boxes and handbags at this stage. He needs to learn to use his wrist so give him the opportunity to practise unscrewing movements on taps, door-handles and knobs.

"Activity centres" – toys designed for babies – encourage many of these skills. You can buy shapes which screw like a nut on to a central screw, which often come with a complete toddler tool-set. Once your child learns to control his wrist in this way, he will twiddle every knob within reach – washing machine dials, television and radio knobs, the central heating control switch – so beware!

After his first birthday, he may take an interest in simple jigsaw puzzles. The "play-tray" sort where you lift out shapes with a small peg handle are best for beginners. Your child will enjoy lifting the shapes out, then trying to fit them back again.

From about 18 months your child will take a great interest when he sees you write or draw, and will want to copy you. Now is the time to buy some bright, chunky crayons and sheets of paper and let your child have a go. At first he will only be able to make scribbling movements – moving the crayon backwards and forwards. After this he will make more deliberate lines, and then learn to make curved lines and circular shapes.

Your one- to two-year-old will touch any object just to explore and enjoy its feel and texture – especially messy things like food, sand, water, clay and play-dough. Inevitably, while he's learning to feed himself he will make a mess. But feeding himself is an important skill – he may prefer to use his hands to scoop up food and put it in his mouth, but shortly after his first birthday he should be able to handle a spoon and feed himself in a haphazard way. You will have to help, but you should encourage him to eat with a spoon. Give him the chance to scoop up sand and let it run through his fingers. Let him draw marks on the ground with a stick, or put wet sand into shapes. Sand gives your child practice in filling and emptying containers, and he can build sand-castles and mudpies. Visit sand-pits in the park, or just give him a bucket or washing-up bowl filled with suitable clean sand in your garden, on your balcony, or even in a corner of the kitchen.

Kneading and making shapes with dough, clay, plasticine or playdough is very good for developing strength and manipulative skills from 18 months onwards. Also, you can get your child to help with making bread, biscuits, or pastry, letting him roll out or pat the dough, cut shapes, and put them on a tray or into a baking dish. At first your child will only be able to make simple shapes – like an egg, sausage, or worm – but you can show him some other shapes or make little animals to inspire him.From the age of two onwards your child's manual skills will develop more rapidly. By now his hands should be strong enough for him to turn door handles, and to unscrew a lid off a jar. He may be able to put on mittens or shoes, but not be able to deal with gloves or the buckles and laces on his shoes. He will now draw careful and deliberate lines on paper, and will also be able to wield a brush. His hand-eye co-ordination should be good enough to allow him to put together the pieces of a simple jigsaw puzzle. Also, he will start to build his own simple constructions with bricks. He'll also enjoy fitting together large toy construction sets like sticklebricks.

Your child of three will begin to draw his first shapes on paper. It is important that he has a lot of practice in holding crayons and pens, as this is a vital part of his future ease and ability in writing.

The muscle control in his fingers is now well advanced. Playing with miniature toys, such as a dolls' house or toy farm, are excellent aids in helping him learn to use his fingers with steady accuracy. At first his little toys will fall over constantly, but resist the temptation to help him. It is important that he learns through his own efforts. He'll soon get the hang of standing them up. His skill with bricks will be fairly advanced and he should be able to create quite sturdy walls, bridges and houses.

Ball games are now becoming less clumsy. Your child's growing strength will make him better at throwing a ball. You can start to play throwing games and show him how to hit a large target, and to land the ball in a large container.

Your child will be able to undress himself at the age of three and to undo simple fastenings like zips or the catches on dungarees. He may be able to manage large buttons, too, especially on a woollen garment where the buttonholes stretch a little. It is unlikely that he will cope with buckles or laces until he is past four years old. He will, however, also manage to thread objects on to a string, and many children of this age enjoy threading a shoelace through a card to make the outline of a picture – a useful precursor to lacing up their shoes. His drawing skills will develop tremendously. He will be able to draw "real" pictures now. Give him colouring books – colouring is an activity he will enjoy and it will help him to develop his finger and wrist control. By the age of four he might even be able to copy the letters of his name. Also, by this age your child should have mastered the use of scissors, but only give him blunt "child" scissors. He will not be skilled and he may injure himself with sharp blades. He won't be able to cut round a shape accurately, but he will enjoy the cutting out process and sticking his efforts on to paper. Give him old Christmas cards or magazine pages to cut up, or strips of paper which he can cut into shorter lengths or squares.

Tracing off pictures and using templates improves your child's potential drawing and writing skills, but often your pre-schooler will need you to hold the tracing paper or template steady. Children vary enormously in their drawing skills. Even if your child doesn't seem to have a great talent, he is gaining confidence in his manual skills all the time.

Your growing child will become increasingly competent in handling everyday items. Before he has turned four, he will be able to pour out a drink for himself without spilling it too often. In the kitchen you should encourage him to handle some basic utensils. He can even help you in certain tasks such as weighing out flour and sugar, and mixing and stirring ingredients. He will particularly love rolling out dough and cutting shapes in it.

As your child approaches his fifth birthday he may well be able to dress and undress himself, put on shoes and his coat, hold a pen, draw with confidence and use a pair of scissors. You can pride yourself on the encouragement you gave him to do these things for himself, and that you were patient and did not always step in to help if he was clumsy or slow. Remember, however, that there is no absolute progression in a child's manual ability. What one toddler can do at 18 months, another may achieve at 20 months. The development of your child's dexterity will happen naturally simply because life teaches him to use his hands. But you, his parents, can help strengthen his wrist muscles and improve the skill of his fingers. Don't force him, but do give him the opportunity to use his hands regularly by constantly giving him tasks which extend his ability.

◆ See also, **Hand-Eye Co-ordination**, **Paper Play**

Manners

Developing a pattern of good manners in a child is one of the most difficult tasks that face the new parent. It is a slow and laborious process that must be worked at carefully and with great patience over the years.

First, we have to be very clear in our minds why we think manners are important. Essentially, good manners make everyday life easier and smoother. They are the oil of the social machine. Life is, quite simply, nicer when it is conducted in an easy, polite fashion. Courtesy on the bus, between you and shop assistants or waiters, or the person who serves you at the post office, makes all these transactions cheerful and pleasant. Rudeness in any of these situations can upset not only you and the person serving you, but all the other people around you.

Every day, all of us are caught up in these aspects of public life, and if we can conduct them smoothly, we feel calm and peaceful within ourselves.

Courtesy at home is, perhaps, a less obvious need, but if we, as parents, can give our children a thoughtful, calm and well-mannered environment we will have reason to feel quite proud, because we will also be creating a peaceful, happy home.

But it is not easy. Small human beings are by nature demanding and selfish, and it can take years of care to make them well-adjusted, co-operative members of society. And we would do well to remember that our children will always learn more from what we do than from what we say.

The first lessons in manners for our very small children are the habits of saying "please" and "thank you". You will find that these lessons have to be repeated frequently from when your child starts to speak and for the next two or three years after that. You may have to ask him, and remind him, every time you give him something that he must say "thank you". And if he wants anything he should use the magic word "please". But he will learn these phrases much more quickly if you, his parents, also say please and thank you not only to him, but also to each other.

He will be absorbing other levels of consideration from you. When you ask him if he is cold or hungry, or if he would care for a glass of water, he is learning by your tone and manner that it is right to be thoughtful about other people's needs. You can observe him copying your behaviour when he starts talking to his teddy bear and cuddly toys. Listen carefully to him – you may hear a good imitation of yourself. Is he being kind to them? Is he worrying about their comfort and is he saying please and thank you at the right moments?

Hospitality

Another early lesson is that of attitudes to guests. You can easily teach your toddler to be polite to his granny or auntie when she visits, because he will love the feeling of importance he derives from playing host. Let him ask Granny if she would like to hang up her coat and he will race to show her the right place to put it. He can ask if she would like some tea or coffee. From his childish delight in being so clever, and in the warm approval that his behaviour brings from his parents, he is learning to be polite. You are also showing him that it brings pleasure to those around him.

Even when he is quite little – say, nearly three – he can pass plates of biscuits or cakes to your guests. All the time he is absorbing habits of hospitality and generosity. Remember not to be cross if he drops or spills something – this will only cause him to lose confidence and his willingness to perform these social tasks.

Of course, there will also be times when he is grumpy or shy, and he will refuse to greet visitors. Try not to force him. It is better to ignore him than to embarrass him in front of guests. Perform these little rituals of hospitality yourself and he will learn to accept that this is the right way to behave in front of visitors. By the time he is six or seven, he will be in the habit of being polite to your friends and family.

Table manners

Many parents long for their child to learn table manners, but this is a very slow process. This is due partly to the fact that a small child's manual ability is not well developed. He cannot handle his knife, fork or spoon easily, and occasionally finds it easier to eat with his hands. Again, it is no good hurrying this process of learning to eat "properly". Gradually, as his hands grow stronger and he has more control over them, your child will learn to handle the cutlery correctly.

Other aspects of good behaviour at the table he will learn from a mixture of your teaching and your example. He must be aware by the time he is four that it is better to eat with his mouth shut, though you will probably have to remind him of this many times. He will learn, again more from example but also under your instruction, that he should wait to be offered more food and not to just grab and yell for it in greedy style. Of course, in his own home he should feel free to ask for more food but this is not acceptable when he is visiting and you will have to teach him the difference. His patience and good behaviour at table depend on your manners. Do you remember to offer him seconds or to pass him the gravy?

Again, he will copy you, his parents. This can be quite alarming – suddenly you have to be on your best behaviour at the supper table because you really do not want your child to stretch across the table or gobble down his food. And how can you ask him to behave nicely when you find yourself leaning across to grab the sauce? Children do have an uncanny and disturbing talent for imitating their parents for better or worse.

Social events

These days, children are taken to parties at a very early age and these social events can be a nightmare for the parents and demanding for the children too, especially if there is a bad-mannered child among the guests. However, most three-year-olds want to be "good" and want to please, and you can prepare your child to behave at parties by having little tea parties with his toys. In this way, he can learn through play that when you give presents you do not open them yourself. He should also begin to understand that he cannot use other children's toys without asking – and that even then he needs a "please" in his request.

It is best if mothers do not leave their small children alone at parties, but hover in the background, not so much to nag their offspring, but to watch that the natural selfishness of the child does not take over.

Politeness and consideration

As your child reaches the age of five, he can be taught telephone manners. You can teach him how to answer the phone with a polite "Hello", and to give his name, or to say "this is the Jones' house". He will know to ask who is calling and then to request that the caller hold on while he fetches you. You could train him to take a message, but don't expect him to get it right every time.

Simple habits of tidiness and help around the house are also lessons in good manners and consideration. At first, when you show him how to put his dirty clothes in the laundry bin, to put his slippers away and to hang up his coat, he understands that it is clever to do these tasks. Later, he will understand that it also pleases his family, and from this he learns that it is a good thing to do.

Doing simple tasks round the house will lead, eventually, to the happy time when he offers to help you. Through helping you, he will have learnt consideration of others too. You and his father have offered to help your child when he needs it; you have been gentle when he is tired or poorly and sympathetic when he is upset. This kind of patience is probably the most difficult part of parenting a small child, but it does pay dividends in the end.

As your child grows older, he will naturally be more clear and open about what he likes and what he wants to do. This self-assertion will not be such a problem if you have managed to give an example of kindness and patience. But if you have been irritable and impatient towards his needs when he could not voice them properly, the only lesson he will have learnt is that it does not matter whether or not you think about other people's needs.

After all, your child is small for a very short period. It may not seem so when he insists on wearing his thick coat on the hottest day, but be sympathetic to him. He is at a stage when he cannot explain his needs, but he feels your kindness and consideration. As time passes, you will be very glad that you gritted your teeth and practised patience with your toddler. You have to live with him for a long time as he grows up, and it will be that much easier if he is a person who has a basic understanding of kindly manners.

This foundation in good manners will also make his life in the outside world smoother and easier. Habitual good manners will go a long way in ensuring that your child is respected and liked by the people he meets. He will not feel awkward or resentful among strangers because you have shown him to consider the needs of other people rather than just his own.

Marriage/Relationship Problems

There can be no question that the birth of a child can put an enormous strain on the relationship of his parents. They will, of course, experience the obvious delight and pleasure a new baby brings, but there may also be conflicting views on feeding, sleep patterns, spoiling, money matters, physical intimacy and countless other issues. Coupled with feelings of sheer exhaustion which can blow smaller problems way out of proportion, this can be a recipe for disaster. Many parents are unprepared for this and can be quite shocked when what they thought would be the happiest time of their life seems to become a battle of wills.

Remember that children, even babies, can sense tension and disharmony and will react with crying, or difficult behaviour which will in turn play havoc with the already frayed emotions of his parents. This can create an endless cycle of stress, blame and unhappiness for all concerned.

It is important therefore for new parents to discuss their views on child care as far as possible before their baby is born, and to get an idea of how they both want to bring up their child. Whilst nothing can prepare you for the at times overwhelming tiredness and frustration you may feel, you must make time for each other, and tackle new problems as they arise. Don't bottle things up or allow them to fester, and if your problems do not seem to be ones you can solve yourselves, try consulting a marriage counsellor. In most cases when a couple disagree each feels that the other is to blame, yet an outsider can often rationalize a situation in a way that those directly involved cannot.

◆ See also, **Divorce**, **Fatherhood**, **Motherhood**

Massage for Babies

Massage is one of the oldest forms of healing, and many parents do actually massage their children instinctively without realizing it, by stroking them, or gently squeezing their hands, for example.

In the early years touch plays a vital role in the healthy development of babies and children. Research into care for premature babies shows that those who are gently stroked are more likely to thrive than those deprived of touch. Massage works in the same way as cuddling and stroking, helping to strengthen the bond between parents and children and to increase a child's feelings of confidence and self-esteem. It also relieves tension and restores a sense of calm and balance.

The best time for a massage is before or after a bath for babies, and just before bed for toddlers and older children. Make sure it is a good time for you too otherwise your child will sense that you are rushed or tense. Your hands should be warm, your nails short, and you should remove any sharp rings or jewellery.

To massage a new baby, sit on the floor with your legs stretched out in front of you. Place your baby on a soft towel on your lap with his head facing your tummy and turned to one side. Rub a few drops of massage oil into your hands (vegetable oils such as sweet almond, grapeseed, avocado and sun-flower used individually or as a base for essential oils are all suitable), then place them on your babys buttocks. With your fingers pointing away from you, draw your hands towards you, bringing them gently up to the baby's shoulders. With your middle and ring fingers only, return down the baby's sides to the buttocks and repeat several times. Next, lift your baby up and draw your knees up towards you. Supporting his head with your knees, start to work on his tummy drawing clockwise circles gently with your fingers.

For a slightly older child you will need to adapt your technique as he will be more fidgety and impatient. Try concentrating on different areas each session, rather than attempting a full body massage.

Massage has been found to help all sorts of problems ranging from insomnia, headaches and breathing difficulties, to poor circulation, skin conditions and digestive problems. It can also speed up recovery after illness. You should not, however, massage a child who has a fever and should avoid cut or bruised areas and scar tissue.

Mealtimes

◆ See **Eating Problems**, **Healthy Eating**, **Manners**

Measles

Until recently measles (medically known as rubeola) was a very common childhood illness, but it occurs less frequently now that many children are immunized against it. This is usually done in a child's second year and provides a high level of immunity for life. Although measles is a highly contagious illness, it is very rarely serious in developed countries. The most likely age for contracting the disease is from one to six years, and a baby is protected by inherited resistance, which wears off after about six months. Having the disease once confers immunity for life.

Measles is caused by a highly contagious virus which is passed from child to child in airborne droplets. A child who has not been immunized or has not gained immunity by having had the disease is almost certain to contract it if he comes into contact with it. Since there is an incubation period of from 7 to 14 days, children can pass the infection on without their parents knowing they have it.

Although measles is commonly recognized by its rash, the first signs of the disease are a high temperature (about 38°C/100.4°F), with a runny nose and eyes. These symptoms are often mistaken for a cold, and this is known as the catarrhal stage because the virus is confined to the mucous membranes of the eyes, nose and mouth.

A cough soon develops, together with a sore throat. Sometimes a red flush appears at this stage and disappears again after a few hours. The child is usually upset and off-colour, with a loss of appetite, and there may be sickness and diarrhoea, but symptoms can be very mild. Usually the inside of the child's cheeks are lined with tiny white spots, known as Koplik's spots, which are unique to measles. These may be difficult to notice as they are so small, and you may not think to look for them, since you are likely to think that your child merely has a bad cold or flu.

After anything from a couple of days to a week, the child's temperature drops temporarily, and then the measles rash appears. This consists of raised, dusky-red spots, grouped together in patches to give a blotchy appearance. It appears first behind the ears, then spreads to the neck and forehead, eventually covering the face and trunk, and, in severe cases, the limbs. Any itching accompanying the rash is usually slight. Over the next three days or so the rash disappears, leaving a brownish stain on the skin which usually disappears with a peeling of the skin.

Complications are rare in cases of measles. In a few instances, however, the appearance of a rash is accompanied by a new bout of fever, and the eyes can be very irritated by the light. This indicates that complications have arisen.

Middle ear infection (otitis media) is the most common complication of measles, and is especially likely to attack a child who is already prone to ear infections. Some children develop croup – a harsh, barking cough. Chest infections such as bronchitis and even pneumonia are also possible complications. Any ear problems, coughing up of phlegm or wheezing should always be reported to your doctor without delay so that they can be treated properly.

The eye irritation and sensitivity to light often found with measles can become serious and may develop into a severe form of conjunctivitis, with a thick, sticky discharge from the eyes. This too needs to be treated urgently.

Finally a tiny minority of children develop encephalitis as a result of measles, with headache, high fever, drowsiness and a pain in the neck. This is potentially fatal and must be given urgent medical attention.

Mild forms of measles can be treated at home, without the need for a doctor to see the child. The doctor must be called, however, if the child shows symptoms of any of the complications described above. The more severe cases of measles may also require medical attention. The doctor will, if he or she believes there is a threat of complications, prescribe antibiotics to prevent them; if other illnesses have already developed they will be treated as necessary.

Meanwhile, in normal cases your child will almost certainly need extra rest, although not necessarily in bed, and should drink plenty of fluids. If he has a high temperature, it can be brought down by sponging with tepid water, and it is safe to give paracetamol in the dose appropriate to the child's age to help bring down the temperature and subdue the feverish symptoms. Gargling with a mouthwash bought from the chemist will help soothe a sore throat. If the child's eyes are irritated he will need to have the curtains closed.

The child will probably have little appetite for a while, but glucose drinks will help to provide energy until he is able to eat again, when you should give him a light diet.

The measles rash is usually not particularly itchy, but if it is, it can be soothed with calamine lotion. It goes without saying that since measles is highly contagious the child should be kept away from school – and, where possible, other children – until all the symptoms have disappeared.

Memory Games

Memory is one of the most important functions of the brain. It is essential to the development of language, which is, in turn, necessary when learning to read and write. When your child is learning to read he brings his whole life experiences, his memories, to the job. The richer his experiences and the broader his vocabulary, the easier reading will be for him. However, memory is not just a matter of words or sounds. All of the senses have memories attached to them.

Although there is evidence that some children can remember things from their time in the womb, the memory only really begins to develop at about eight to ten months. From this time on you can help your child's memory to develop with simple but enjoyable games and routines.

Very young babies, less than a year old, are beginning to develop their short-term memories. Your child will be able to remember where you have just hidden a toy. A game can be made of this – a very simple treasure hunt.

A game can also be made out of everyday routines such as getting up, bathing, nappy-changing, eating or dressing. For example, there is the getting-up game, "Fox and Rabbit". This begins with you saying, "Here comes fox looking for that rabbit, where's that rabbit?" While saying this, you make a show of hunting under the cot and rummaging through the blankets. Then, with great delight, you discover the rabbit – your baby – with the exclamation "Ah, there he is, time for breakfast", and with plenty of lip-smacking you nibble some toes or a knee.

A variation of this is "Bear and Cub" which begins, "Here comes mummy bear looking for her cub, now where is that cub?" Again there is the search and delighted discovery. When your child begins to join in the fun, hiding from you under the covers, it is a sure sign that his memory is developing. Another indication will be the delighted squeals of anticipation that greet your approach.

Similar games can be made up for any activity. The important thing is to stick to key words and phrases in the same order. These kinds of games help to develop both a memory for language and the order (or sequence) of things. These skills are vital early preparation for reading and writing.

Long before your child is ready to learn about letters and sounds you can help prepare his memory by associating sounds with pictures. Put aside some "quiet time" just before bed and sit cosily with your child on your lap. Choose a book with clear pictures and make the story-telling more exciting by making sounds to go with the pictures – of animals, for example.

Soon, your child will remember what comes next and make the sounds for you. Allow him time to do this by pausing before you make the appropriate sound. "Here is a dog, the dog says (pause) woof, woof." When your child shows signs of boredom with the same book, offer a new one.

At about 20 months your child will begin to enjoy stories about himself. Make them very simple to begin with. For example, "When you were very little you used to suck your toes. Wasn't that a clever thing to do? Daddy can't suck his toes." Your child will love these stories and later, between two and three, he will begin asking for them. They will help your child gain a sense of time, past and present. Once a story is well established, try changing the words. Your child's sharp corrections will soon show you how well his memory is developing.

It is a good idea to create your own picture books. Make series of pictures of an everyday routine, bathtime or bedtime for instance. Take photographs of each stage of the activity, then stick them in a scrap book, one to a page, and write a brief sentence under each. Make several of these books and read them often. Soon your child will be able to tell you what comes next.

A much-loved addition to the bookshelf is "My Book" filled with pictures and photographs of your child's favourite things and people. Allow him to help select pictures and stick them with a glue stick. Then you can ask your child to show you a picture of teddy, Grandma and so on. Stick a photograph of your child on the front cover. Such books help to fix the ideas of time and the sequence of things. As his memory develops he will learn to predict what comes next – a very important skill when learning to read.

You have been talking to your child since he was born but from about 14 months onward his stock of remembered words will be growing rapidly. Help him built it up with language games. "Show Me" is an easy game for a very young child. Put a pile of clothes in front of him and ask him to show you a shoe or a jumper. Try a pile of farm animals or a tea-set. Keep it brief as he will get bored quickly. Remember to name the things for him first. These games help to add to your child's store of words and they introduce the idea of "sets".

Each evening, make a point of talking your little one through his day. Remind him of each thing he did during the day. He will probably find this easier working backwards through the day. As he begins to talk, encourage him to repeat your conversation, or offer his own thoughts. This kind of conversation not only develops your child's ability to remember, but can also help to sharpen his observations.

Between the ages of two and three, introduce your child to "feely bags". Simply put an item into a cloth bag (for safety reasons, never use plastic bags when playing with your child). Make a great show of feeling it and, saying "Is this is a shoe?" then draw it out and with astonished delight, exclaim "Yes, it's a shoe!" Encourage your child to pop something into the bag while you close your eyes. Feel and guess again. Soon your child will be feeling and guessing, too.

As your child masters the "feely" game, try the "smelly" game. Choose three or four pleasant-smelling objects and talk about each one. Then cover your eyes, and ask your child to choose one of the "smellies" and waft it under your nose. After much sniffing, guess what it is. Make the odd mistake to allow a few superior giggles from your child.

Now let your child have a go at sniffing. Give hints at first to ensure success. These games add descriptive words to the memory bank. They can be enjoyed by older children, too.

You can also try a sound version of these games. Half fill a yoghurt carton with sand, another with dried pasta shapes and a third with buttons. Let your toddler help.

Get him to shake one of the cartons and listen to the sound it makes. Allow him to check what is inside. Repeat the process with each carton. Then ask your child to cover his eyes and listen while you shake one of the cartons. See if he can pick out the one you shook. Give him plenty of help, then take your turn. Later, add more sounds.

When your child is between three and four you can play "Kim's Game" using the same sort of objects as "Show Me". Place a few things, three to begin with, on a tray and ask your child to point to and name each item. Then get him to cover his eyes. Remove one of the objects and ask him what is missing. Always allow him plenty of time and give clues where necessary. You can slowly add to the things on the tray as he improves. Always take your turn.

"Pelmanism" or "Pairs", a game of matching cards, will be enjoyed from about the age of three. Cover a surface with the cards, face downwards. The object is to make as many pairs as possible. This is done by taking turns to turn two cards face up. If they match, they are removed and the player tries again. If not, they are replaced face down. The players must remember the cards they have seen, and their position, in order to make pairs. The player with the most pairs wins. It is probably best to buy this game, as the pictures are clear and it is sturdy enough to withstand enthusiastic young players. Both "Kim's Game" and "Pelmanism" help improve your child's visual memory in particular, being based on observation and concentration.

Always remember when playing memory games that they should be fun; they are not tests. Don't rush your child. Allow him plenty of time to do what is required of him in the game. Give plenty of clues and hints when needed. Success is the name of the game when it comes to learning anything. And remember to praise and show your delight when your child achieves something new.

Money Matters

A baby changes your life in many ways and, for many couples losing one income has a major effect on their standard of living. Even if you decide to continue working after your baby is born you will still have to budget for child-care costs. And the best way to cope with all these changes is to think seriously about your income and outgoings now, before the baby arrives.

It's sometimes worthwhile to try living on one income while you are pregnant, so you have time to adapt to a tighter budget. However, to allow for a minimum amount of discomfort, do this gradually over a few months if you can manage. Begin the first month by putting aside a quarter of your second income. The next month put aside half and the third month three quarters. Finally put all of your second income aside, so you are managing on one income. This may seem like you are being unnecessarily thrifty but it should give you a useful nest egg of money saved up to cover the costs involved in having your baby.

As well as the initial costs, the baby will have some effect on regular outgoings, for example increased heating bills, and extra laundry costs, so allow for these in advance. Wear and tear on the house also increases once your baby is mobile – one energetic toddler has been known to spill bubble bath on the landing carpet, spread chocolate mousse on the living room wallpaper and cause a flood in the bathroom all in the same week!

Child-care

Types of child-care vary and so does the cost, though many working mothers estimate that their income divides into three; a third for tax and work costs such as travel, a third on child-care costs and a third left over.

Childminders look after your baby in their own home. They often have a child or children of their own so your baby has company. There are drawbacks, however, as they may not want to care for your baby if he is ill, and you may not want to take your baby there if the minder's own children are ill. But for many women working part-time, a childminder who lives nearby is the ideal solution. (*See* Work, Going Back To)

Nannies either live in your house or come to work in your house and they care for the baby, clean his room and wash his clothes, but do not generally do housework. They usually cost two or three times more than a childminder, and you may well have to pay tax and national insurance on their behalf. (*See also,* Nannies.)

A nursery or crêche provides group care for babies and children. You may be fortunate enough to have a subsidized crêche attached to your workplace. Nursery costs do vary, but in any event, they usually cost a little less than a nanny. (*See also*, Nurseries and Playgroups.)

Clothes and equipment

Kitting out your baby always appears to involve a huge outlay of money, but you may well receive many gifts of clothes when the baby is born, so don't buy too much yourself. Hand-knitting also saves money as wool and a pattern are much cheaper than the finished garment. If relatives or friends are willing to knit for the baby, ask for some second size clothes, as first sizes are often outgrown in three or four months.

Nappies can take a large chunk out of your budget. Disposable ones mean a regular outlay. Remember that a small baby will need six to eight nappies a day – which amounts to a staggering 200 a month. Towelling nappies may seem cheaper, but you have to take the cost of buying them, and then add the costs of soaking, washing and drying and, of course, the extra work. Most parents find they use a mixture of the two. If you do decide to opt for towelling nappies, then buy the best quality you can afford as cheap ones rapidly become thin and will not remain absorbent for long. (*See also*, Nappies.)

Some items of baby equipment make good second-hand buys as they get little wear and tear. These include prams, cribs, baby baths, slings, first seats, first-size clothes, party clothes, robust sit-and-ride toys, or push-along toys. Shoes, cot mattresses and pushchairs are best bought new, however, if possible. If you are not buying second-hand, and you are not lucky enough to have family-owned items that can be passed down to you, why not buy the simplest basic versions and add your own touches by painting and using transfers? You can also save costs by making cot sheets and quilts, and by lining a crib yourself. Hand-made versions are about half the price of shop-bought ones.

At about six months many parents find that there seems to be another mini spending boom. The baby has grown and many new clothes are needed. This is also the time that many babies move from a pram to a pushchair, outgrow their first car seat and need a high chair – seemingly all on the same day. Also, by around nine months most babies can crawl around and you will need to invest in stair gates, cupboard locks and other safety equipment.

Holidays and eating out need not become a thing of the past. Remember that babies under two years usually fly at 10 per cent of the adult fare on scheduled flights (though you may have to pay full fare for them on chartered flights). In most hotels babies stay free. Look out for hotels that offer special family rooms with up to two children staying free. Some hotels, particularly those in popular resorts, make a cot charge, so double-check before booking. Many restaurant chains will heat bottles for free, and many also sell jars of baby food very cheaply, or in some cases these are free. And, the Pay-Once-and-Help-Yourself type of restaurant usually allows under-fours or fives to eat for free.

Planning ahead

Essentials as well as luxury items can be very expensive, so it's worth putting aside some money, if you can, to cover these expenses. First shoes at about 14–18 months, for example, can be pricey, as can large sit-and-ride toys which are usually needed at about 18 months.

By the time your child is two and a half to three he may well be quite sociable and you may want to allow for the cost of activities such as swimming classes, gym classes or nursery. At about this time – if you have access to a garden – you may also want to invest in a couple of large-scale garden toys such as a sandpit, climbing frame or paddling pool. Garden toys usually get plenty of use and last for several years, so they are well worth the high initial cost.

To set against all these costs most families receive some form of child benefit or state grant and, in some cases, a tax allowance. This can make a major difference and contribute towards the cost of feeding and clothing your child. If it is paid weekly or monthly you may find it a useful way of saving for major items.

It's wise to plan ahead for your child's needs. Life insurance schemes allow you to pay a small weekly sum to insure your child's life over a set period. If you take out such a scheme when your baby is born, to mature when he is 10 or 20, you will be able to give him a sum of money at some stage in the future.

If a generous relative wants to wet the baby's head with a lump sum of money do make sure that you get advice on how to invest it. There are some schemes that are particularly tax-efficient for children. Relatives such as grandparents may also be able to give the money in tax-efficient ways through a covenant, so do consult an expert.

Moodiness

Mood changes in children are more sudden, more intense and more extreme than in adults, who disguise and hold back feelings which they know are unacceptable. Not so with children – if they feel it, they'll make sure you know about it!

The good side, of course, is that a child's mood can be altered far more easily than that of an adult, and the secret, as usual, is to keep one step ahead so that you stand a better chance of diverting or dissipating the disaster.

Moods can be affected by too much or too little sleep, sustenance or stimulation; by pain or discomfort; by the moods of others (especially the mother); by minor successes or failures; or even by the weather. However, as with adults, the extent to which an external factor will affect your child will depend on his individual temperament. While some children will be badly affected by gloomy weather, a minor frustration, or anxiety in the home, others will remain quite placid in these situations.

Boredom can be a problem early in your baby's life. Just when you thought things were settling down into a pattern of sorts, you find that your baby is restless, or he is crying and fretful. If he is not hungry, wet, or in pain, he may be just plain bored.

Give him interesting things to look at or to explore with his hands and mouth. Prop him up with pillows so that he can watch you as you move around. Put him in a baby bouncer so that he can move round and change his view or lie him flat on a playmat and give him different shapes and textures to investigate.

Chat to him as you go about your own business, but at some point you will have to give him your full attention and agree to entertain him. A bored baby will quickly become an unhappy, fretful baby.

Once you realize that your baby can and does get bored, plan a varied rhythm to your day. Your baby – and you, too – will benefit from having some quiet time, some activity, a change of scene, and if possible a change of people to listen to and watch.

Babies and small children are not able to cope with boredom. They do not know how to entertain themselves and a bored toddler needs to be given attention instantly or else he may use disruptive tactics to make his life more interesting or to attract you.

A bored toddler will do anything to get your attention or to force you to change course. A tube of toothpaste down the sink or cornflakes in the toilet are not naughty acts, because he does not know how to treat things; they are simply interesting things for him to do. But once you know that it's boredom and not a major personality defect that you are witnessing, solutions are easy.

If there are things you simply must do in the home, the best way to contain your child's boredom is to enlist his help. And try not to feel frustrated by the slowness of his assistance – dusting, sweeping (with a small brush), washing up (plastic cups), won't get the housework done, but it will fascinate your child, and he will be absorbing constructive ways of using his time. If you make a real effort to keep your toddler busy and interested, he is less likely to behave badly. And, when he does, you will know that his naughtiness is not boredom but has another cause.

Life with a toddler is full of drama. He has been engaged since birth in the struggle for independence, but at 18 months to two years the struggle reaches a peak, and it may stay at this level for some time. His inner turmoil is great as he seeks to gain control of himself, and this manifests itself in wildly fluctuating moods.

Make the most of cheerful moods to let him know that you like him. Keep him company and harness his energy to some activity appropriate to his age, such as tower-building for the younger child or looking at letters and numbers for the pre-school child.

However, at this age, he may often be in a difficult mood. Frequently, the mood is simply negative – a blanket resistance to all proposals, from what to have for tea, to a reluctance to enjoy a party or even consider a walk to the park.

An understanding of what's going on inside your child will help you realize that he is neither a brute nor a social misfit. He is learning to exercise some control for himself: he must make decisions; he must stand alone, but at the beginning, he thinks that he can never say "yes" even though what's proposed is exactly what he wants. Sometimes the "no" is automatic and simply a way of giving him time so that he can think more about a decision which he feels is difficult to make.

You can help him by not giving him too many choices until he is ready for them. Give him practice at decision-making that doesn't cost him too much. Say "Let's go to the park today, and visit Sarah tomorrow," rather than making him choose outright. If he has to make the decision, he will believe that he can only have one pleasure. He is not able to plan a trip to the park and a visit to a friend at a later (abstract) date.

It is tempting to break this mood by simply overpowering him and forcing him to misery. Again they are suffering from underdeveloped inner controls. When friends come to visit, and boisterous play begins, small children cannot decide when it's time to calm down. They will simply carry on rushing around becoming more and more out of control until someone else steps in. It's up to you, the adult, to understand what is happening and to control the mood. A story, a drink, a simple distraction of some sort is what is needed.

When Daddy comes home at the end of the day, just when you might be calming your child in preparation for bedtime, excitement will take over again. It is cruel to deprive the child and his father of this time together, but let your partner's contribution be positive, taking the pressure off you at the end of this long and tiring day. As parents, you will both learn that it is essential to calm your child and give him a peaceful preparation for bed.

A tired child can be completely unco-operative: he can become a dead weight in your arms or he can thrash around wildly; he can refuse to walk or to eat; he may scream and shout or pull his own hair – or yours. A bath might soothe him, or he might be beyond it; it really doesn't matter if he goes to bed unwashed occasionally. You will soon learn to recognize the warning signs, and discover how to avoid the distress of an over-tired excited child.

Avoid tears before bed by sticking as far as possible to a set routine of, for example, supper, bath, story, bed. Do give fair warning that you are soon going to embark on the bedtime process.

A tantrum may ensue but it is more than likely that your child is simply too tired to exercise control for himself and he is simply testing you to make sure that you are in control.

It is not only the emotional conflict within a growing child that causes his many moods. The moods of others around can also affect him. For example, a baby responds fretfully and anxiously to a tense new parent. It is no use telling the mother that she is communicating her fears to her baby – she knows that, and it's one of the things she is most worried about. What the mother needs is more support and reassurance so that her worries can be lifted, then she can start communicating peace and tranquillity.

Fathers, grannies, friends and professionals should all be called on to support the new mother in those first difficult, nerve-wracking days with her new baby.

The mood of a parent will always have an effect on a toddler or pre-school child, and as an adult, you can exercise some control, presenting a relatively even mood to your child even when you're not feeling very inwardly calm. When you are feeling very low or angry with the world, however, do not be proud – enlist the support of others rather than burden your child unnecessarily with your "dark mood". Abandon the washing and visit a friend to take the pressure off both you and your child. It won't put the world to rights, but it may lighten the mood. On the other hand, you should not feel guilty if you do have bad moods. It is important for your child to see that you, too, have different emotions, and to observe how you deal with them, for this is one of the ways he will learn to gain control over himself – by imitating you. Childhood is a turbulent time, and moodiness is not surprising, but there may also be factors in the family which are adding to a child's distress.

● Problems between parents rarely escape the attention of young children for instance. If there are problematic home circumstances that you can control, do so. If not, protect your child from scenes which may disturb him or explain the problem in terms that he can understand.

● Illness may be the cause of an unusually grizzly period. Mild earache, for example, won't make him seriously unwell but may badly affect his mood.

● A tired child does not always just go to sleep. Instead, he can give up exercising control, so that he swerves from one wild action to the next.

● Hunger is often the cause of irritability and moodiness. A suddenly lowered blood sugar level can affect behaviour, but your child may not equate his feelings with the need to eat. Try to make sure he eats regularly.

● Food additives or an unbalanced diet may cause behavioural problems.

Motherhood

When to become a mother

Early motherhood may be bought at the cost of a career, yet delaying parenthood to climb the top ladder may leave us feeling robbed of the joys of child-rearing in what is considered to be our "prime". But with parenthood marking the major turning point for women, what is the "prime time" to become a mother?

Women under 20 are at their most fertile age but they do not necessarily have the best chance of having a healthy baby. Reports on perinatal mortality (covering babies who are stillborn, or die during the first week) have revealed that there are more deaths involving mothers under the age of 20 than for those aged between 20 and 30.

The schoolgirl mother, under the age of 16, also has an increased risk of having a baby with congenital abnormalities. And, under the age of 18, there is an increased risk of premature labour and pre-eclampsia – raised blood pressure, swelling of feet, ankles and hands, and protein in the urine.

Studies have shown that, as far as the health of the baby is concerned, the safest time for a baby to be born is when the mother is between the ages of 20 and 24. Coincidentally or not, for a large part of the population this is also the most popular age for getting married. But however mature a couple may be, marrying in their early twenties and having a baby soon afterwards, means that they will probably face the additional stress of money worries, parental responsibilities and, especially for women, loss of freedom and the feeling of enforced change.

The birth of a baby figures high on what experts term the "life stress scale". And for women, the arrival of their first child often changes their lives more than any other event. The high stress value of having a baby is borne out by the fact that, statistically, divorced couples are more likely to have had a baby early in their marriage.

So while becoming parents in the early twenties may be safer for the baby, it can have an adverse effect on a new marriage and on the job prospects of a woman not firmly established in her career. And while most women now see motherhood as only a career break, and something like half the mothers of pre-school children work, surveys suggest that women still give a higher priority to their children than to their jobs.

The late twenties – between 24 and 29 – is the second safest age group, as far as babies are concerned, to give birth. Medical experts also now advise that if possible a woman should have her first baby before she reaches the age of 30.

But it can be a case of swings and roundabouts: if a couple married in their mid twenties, their relationship will still be in its infancy and if a woman's career is not yet established this may not be the best time to take time out to have a child.

They may not have reached a secure stage financially either. However, this must be weighed up against the fact that the woman's level of fertility reduces as she grows older.

According to one expert, parent-child relationships are, on average, better when parents are in their thirties.

A couple is more likely to be financially able to cope with a family by this stage, and many women will have established their careers and feel able to take a break to have a child. But emotional and financial security have to be weighed against the increasing risks. Loss of elasticity in a woman's pelvic tissue after the age of 30 and other problems are more common when having a first baby after that time.

The length of labour increases with age, too. Most women in their early thirties will have a healthy pregnancy and a healthy first baby. But as they move into the more risky age group it becomes even more important to take proper care of themselves, co-operate in medical supervision and follow antenatal advice.

Women who have delayed having a child to follow a career often find the mid-thirties decision time. They have reached what has been termed the "deadline decade".

They have passed the early thirties, identified in surveys as a time when people, particularly women, are least satisfied with their marriage. They are likely to make good relationships with their children, to be more secure in terms of career and finances. But, while the biological clock ticks away, there may be doubts surrounding the decision about whether to have a child.

Fertility declines faster past the age of 30, and it is at 35 plus that a woman having her first baby takes on the label of an "elderly primagravida", a term covering women in the last third of their reproductive life.

It should be remembered, however, that good antenatal care and supervision in labour render the risks negligible and that age alone should not deter a woman from having a child. Many older first-time mothers have an easy labour but pregnancy and labour do present more risks for them. There is a higher incidence of pre-eclampsia and placental insufficiency, and also a higher risk of Down's Syndrome.

The now-or-never age for first-time mothers means the likelihood of longer labour, an increased perinatal mortality rate and the highest risk of having babies with a congenital abnormality.

On average, the length of labour increases by one or two hours for every ten years, although many women having their first child over the age of 40 have an easy labour.

And although fertility continues to decline, experts have noticed an unexplained feature in the fertility of women around the age of 40, sometimes called "the last fling of the ovary", which results in some unexpected late pregnancies.

As they are identified as a high-risk category, 40-plus mothers will receive the most stringent monitoring and the most careful antenatal care throughout their pregnancy and labour. Their welfare and that of their unborn baby will be better ensured by the fact that they are likely to have better living conditions and finances and will be only too eager to follow antenatal advice.

If you are contemplating when or whether you should have a baby, you might find it useful to ask yourself the following questions:

● Is work going well and is your career important to you?

● Will your accommodation and finances take the strain?

● Are you involved in the upheaval of moving home?

● Is your marriage new; is your relationship secure?

● Are you coping with serious family illness or the recent death of a loved one?

● Do you feel confident about coping under stress or ambivalent about having a child at this time?

Of course the "right" time for you, is when both you and your partner feel ready, whether you are 20 or 40.

Life after a baby

Sometimes becoming a mother can seriously shake your sense of identity, especially in the early days. Many women feel that their whole life has been turned upside-down and that they have lost touch with themselves.

It is very important to realize that you are changing. This does not necessarily mean losing the old you: motherhood can mean that you grow as a person. You develop new skills and attributes to add to your old ones. You can become even more accomplished.

During the first few days after your baby is born you are likely to have a great sense of pride in your achievement. You may have had a great deal of support from your partner, family and friends. But, there must come a point when your partner goes back to work and the flock of visitors becomes a trickle.

Suddenly, you and your child are alone together for most of the day. This is a difficult time, probably the most difficult of all. Between you, a routine that suits you both will eventually be worked out. However, this can take quite a long while and the adjustment is not always easy.

You will still be aching a bit from the effects of labour. You will be feeling very tired. Your child will be demanding your attention for what feels like 24 hours a day. You will almost certainly be struggling to keep up with household chores. And on top of it all your partner may be expecting the same level of attention and care he received before your child was born.

You may feel guilty that you are not Superwoman, able to cope with all these demands with ease. Professional carers find it very hard to reassure women at this stage, try as they might. The sense of failure, of being neither a "good" mother nor a "good" wife, can be very strong.

During this period of adjustment you may expect to be subjected to sudden and dramatic mood swings. You may go from blissfully content to extremely unsettled in a matter of moments. The birth of your child may feel like your greatest achievement one minute and the biggest mistake of your life the next. All of these conflicting feelings will be utterly convincing when you are experiencing them.

It is important, therefore, to make time for yourself. In early motherhood, you are giving so much of yourself to your child it is vital to remember that you must allow yourself time to put something back.

Remember that you need nurturing, too, and make time for it, however difficult this may seem at first.

Some women come into their own when they become mothers. This is often true of young mothers who have, up until this time, still been regarded as little girls by their families. Somehow, becoming a mother is a passport to joining the big girls. This can be a very liberating experience for a young woman. She seems to step out of the shadows of her own mother and older siblings and gain her autonomy.

For older women, who have gained a sense of their own identity through careers and independent lives, motherhood is more of a mixed blessing. On the one hand they feel they have fulfilled their womanhood by having a child. On the other hand they may feel the loss of career and independence very deeply. They may be torn between the need to care for their child personally and the need to get back to work. Whichever they decide to do, some pretty difficult compromises have to be made.

Your feelings for your partner

Another important conflict that often faces new mothers is her new role as both mother and lover. Having a baby is bound to change your relationship with your partner. It may not be a case of "worse" or "better", but it will certainly be different and it helps if you are aware of this. For a start, motherhood changes you, and your relationship inevitably reflects these changes. You and your partner must try to recognize and face up to any problems.

Before having a baby, most couples relate to each other chiefly as lovers. Their main area of concern is their relationship with one another. In a way, this is a luxury only to be appreciated in retrospect, after the baby is born. It is a good reason for delaying having children for a few years, until you have settled down as a twosome.

Becoming a parent adds new dimensions to both your lives. Your man, as a father, will have real responsibilities, perhaps for the first time in his life. With a baby to support, he will have to think more carefully about his life.

Continuing as a couple will be more than just a question of how much you love each other and want to be together; with a child to care for, there will be an element of duty involved too. This readjustment can be somewhat alarming for a man, who may look to you for extra love and comfort at this time of change.

Becoming a mother can make quite an impact on a woman. Physically it will probably be the most strenuous and tiring period of your life. Giving birth is equivalent to undergoing a major operation, but instead of getting lots of rest and cosseting afterwards, your time will be taken up with struggling to cope with the demands of your newborn baby – on very little sleep.

While you grapple with all the changes, both physical and psychological, something has to go, and in the early days that may be your role as your partner's lover.

Before the baby your body was yours alone; it was also something you chose to share with your lover. But pregnancy changes that: for a while your body is physically occupied by your growing baby. After your baby is born you have to be available for the baby at any time of the day or night, especially if you are breastfeeding him.

This can alter the way you perceive your body, and sometimes alters the way your partner sees you, too. A man who has witnessed the birth of his child can feel differently about his partner's body for a while too.

Feeling exhausted and fraught, as most parents of young babies do, you will not be in the right mood for sex. It is more than that, however. Libido – your sexual urge – is often still low well after things have settled down and you are getting enough sleep.

A change in the hormonal balance of the body after childbirth is, in part, responsible for this diminished sex drive. You're producing prolactin (which makes breast milk); and your production of the hormone progesterone, massively increased during pregnancy, falls dramatically. It is known – although not in precise detail exactly how – that these changes affect us emotionally and physically.

Aside from physical exhaustion, it can also be very difficult to relax when you have a new baby. Your mind fills with worries, and you can feel you're always on red alert, waiting to hear the slightest noise or cry. This can apply to both partners, though it's probably more acute for the woman. The link between a mother and her baby keeps her protective instincts well-honed. Sexual longings can have a hard job breaking through.

For some women, sex is physically uncomfortable, or actually painful because of stitches after a tear or episiotomy. The stitching can cause problems: too-tight sewing, a knot of scar tissue, or a persistent infection, all of which can make intercourse unpleasant. And if it hurts, you certainly won't want to do it. Caesarean scars can also cause problems as they are likely to be tender for some weeks after the birth.

Even if you're physically fine, you may have bad memories of the birth – and it can take a while to feel in charge of your body again. You may feel protective towards your body and not want to share it with anyone, not even your partner. You may feel inhibited about making love when your baby is in the same room with you, even if he's fast asleep. Or you could feel strange about being both a mother and a lover, and need time to come to terms with your dual role.

There are also some very practical reasons why sex is less of a joy after childbirth. Who likes being interrupted by a hungry cry just as you're getting into your stride, for example? If you have an older child as well, the unpredictable demands of two children can make grabbing a bit of privacy, let alone enough time for regular sex, extremely difficult.

All these short-term problems often resolve themselves when the emotional relationship is basically a good one, especially when you understand why sex can be less frequent after a baby. However, if you think your problems are linked to the way you feel about each other, or if they don't seem to be getting better as time goes on, then do seek professional advice, whether it turns out that all you need is basic reassurance, or a series of therapy sessions.

Either way, one of the most important things to remember during these difficult times is to show each other physical affection, even if sex is out of the question for the time being. Lots of cuddling and kissing will help. For some men this is a new lesson to learn, as denial of sex can seem like withdrawal of love. Sexual intercourse, however, is not the only way to demonstrate physical love or satisfy sexual desire. Sex play that doesn't finish in conventional intercourse is a good way to satisfy both partners.

There comes a time, sooner or later, when desire returns, dealing with the baby becomes a pleasurable routine, and you can both give proper attention to each other. Although it is not easy to go back to the way things were before the baby, it is still possible to combine your roles of mother and lover. Rediscovering your relationship with your partner is a pleasure, especially with the extra dimension of shared parenthood, which should make for a deeper relationship than you had before.

◆ See also, **Bonding**, **Postnatal Depression**, **Work (Going Back To)**

Mouth

The cavity of the mouth is lined with mucous membrane. The roof and the lower part of the mouth are rigid, but otherwise it is surrounded by muscles. We use the mouth to speak and sing, to chew, yawn, whistle and make facial expressions. It is linked to breathing and digestion, the back of the mouth connecting with the entrance to the digestive tract and the respiratory tract.

Even though the mouth is full of bacteria and prone to minor injury it is surprisingly resilient at all ages and recovers fast from injury and common ailments. In a healthy child or adult the membrane lining of the mouth has a remarkable capacity for regeneration, so that any form of mouth infection is usually a sign of poor general health.

The lips are made of soft muscle fibres interspersed with elastic tissue. They have a generous supply of nerve endings, which is what gives them their essential sensitivity – after all, the major part of a baby's experience is gained via the mouth and lips.

The lips are covered by a modified form of skin, which, unlike true skin, has no hairs, sweat glands or oil-secreting glands. (This is why the lips easily become dry and chapped.)

The mucous membrane lining of the mouth has glands which produce mucous – a slightly sticky, clear fluid. The action of these glands, helped by that of the saliva-producing salivary glands, keeps the mouth moist.

The roof of the mouth is known as the palate. The front of the palate is the hard palate, against which the tongue presses in the first stage of mixing and softening food, and in making certain consonants (known as hard consonants) in speech.

The back of the palate, known, appropriately, as the soft palate, is mobile, and closes off the naso-pharynx (the entrance to the respiratory system) when food is being swallowed. This is to prevent the food from being forced up into the nose, which is linked to the back of the mouth.

The piece of tissue you see hanging down from the soft palate is known as the uvula, and some anatomists think that it helps to form a seal at the top of the air passage to help prevent choking while eating. The tongue strikes against the soft palate in making the sounds that are known as soft consonants.

The tongue consists mainly of muscles, which children learn to control in the most intricate way as they master the skills of eating and speaking. It is attached to the base of the skull, to the lower jaw, and to a bone called the hyoid bone above the larynx, and is much bigger than the part we see. Our tongues are very sensitive to touch and heat, and confer our sense of taste through the many taste buds which cover them. Together with the teeth (once they are through) the tongue plays a vital part in the first stage of the digestive process.

We all depend on our mouths for survival, but particularly when we are babies. A baby is born with the instinct to suck, and for a baby the sensitive mouth and tongue provide most of the information necessary about the outside world.

This is why, until the age of about two, babies and toddlers tend to examine things by putting them in their mouths. Although worrying and irritating to parents, it is inevitable. All parents can do is keep objects that would be dangerous to swallow away from children while they are at this stage.

Food is chewed before being swallowed. Chewing, technically known as mastication, involves the tongue, as well as the teeth. The tongue places the food first to the teeth, which mince it, and then to the back of the mouth to be swallowed. This, of course, is why babies have to be given puréed food when they are first being weaned, and why they have to graduate to adult food via mashed food and food that has been cut up into small pieces.

In the mouth, the food is mixed with saliva produced by the three pairs of salivary glands. The saliva reaches the mouth through small channels or ducts and is produced in response to the sight and smell of food, as well as to food being put in the mouth.

Saliva is slightly alkaline and contains an enzyme called ptyalin. This begins the breakdown of starchy foods, and is the first stage in chemical digestion.

Once the food has been chewed and softened, it is ready to be swallowed. It is pushed up against the hard palate, and the soft palate dilates to allow it to pass.

A flap of tissue known as the epiglottis, positioned down behind the tongue, closes off the passage to the lungs to prevent choking as the food is swallowed and transferred to the oesophagus (gullet). Contractions of the oesophagus then move the food on to the stomach for the digestive process to continue.

Mouth problems

Most problems arising in the mouth indicate poor general health or poor dental hygiene. However, since the mouth is closely linked to the ears, nose and throat, an infection such as a cold can also produce symptoms in the mouth.

Dribbling

This is usually caused by teething, but it can also be associated with mouth ulcers and colds. Certain types of mouth ulcers can be caused by viral stomatitis, and the condition is usually associated with poor general health.

The treatment of dribbling will depend on the cause. In itself it is not, of course, a problem. Babies who are dribbling because of teething may find it soothing to have a hard rusk or a cool spoon to suck.

Ulcers

These are little white or yellowish patches in the mouth, surrounded by an area which is red and sore. They can also cause bad breath, and are often linked to cold sores.

For mouth ulcers the doctor may prescribe soothing lozenges or ointment. The child should not eat chocolate or acid foods such as oranges or tomatoes which will make the ulcers more painful.

Thrush

This is a fungal infection caused by the fungus Candida albicans, which is always present in the mouth and intestine, but which is normally kept under control by other bacteria. It is a common problem in babies.

Thrush is indicated by white patches on the tongue and also on the roof of the mouth and inside the cheeks. This is particularly common in babies.

Thrush will probably be treated by anti-fungal cream or gel, and children with sore and swollen lips (cheilosis) may be prescribed an analgesic ointment to soothe the pain. The doctor may also give antibiotics.

Cheilosis and stomatitis

Both of these are caused by bacteria. (Stomatitis may be triggered by anaemia, vitamin deficiency or gastro-intestinal diseases.)

Cheilosis and stomatitis are characterized by swelling and inflammation of the lips and mouth respectively. In the latter, the tongue is coated with a white substance.

In the case of stomatitis, the doctor will probably want to do some tests to uncover the underlying cause, as this can be a sign of a more serious complaint. In mild cases, stimulating the flow of saliva by sucking sweets or chewing gum could be all that is needed, but the doctor may prescribe a mouth rinse, or swabbing the child's mouth.

Cold sores

Cold sores, or herpes, are inflamed blisters on the lips. These are caused by the virus Herpes simplex, which is usually caught in early life, and which then remains dormant in the body, flaring up from time to time. It is especially virulent in babies and young children with eczema.

A child with cold sores need only be seen by a doctor if these are large and painful or if they occur frequently. Ointment may be prescribed to soothe and treat the sores. Preparations available from the chemist are all that is required in many cases. Make sure that the child has a healthy diet, with plenty of fresh fruit and vegetables, and is not allowed to get over-tired.

Gingivitis

Gingivitis is caused by a bacterial infection of the gums, and this seems to be related to poor dental hygiene and the build-up of plaque around the teeth. The symptoms of gingivitis are bleeding and soreness in the gums, especially when the teeth are brushed; the child may also have bad breath.

Children with sore gums (except teething babies) should be taken to a dentist at once. Gingivitis can cause loss of teeth. The dentist will probably scrape the teeth and give advice on good dental care.

◆ See also, **Teeth**

Mouth-to-Mouth Resuscitation

◆ See **Artificial Respiration**

Moving Home

Moving house is one of the more stressful events you'll have to face, and with a child in tow it's even more difficult. There are ways, however, to minimize the tension and upheaval.

Once you have a definite removal date you will need to start planning for the day itself. To a certain extent you will have to plan around your child so that his routines are not totally disrupted. As you will know from other big occasions like birthday parties or Christmas, the less ruffled your child remains, the calmer you will be. This is something of a vicious circle, however, as you obviously won't be able to avoid showing that you are preoccupied with all the extra arrangements.

However young your child, it is worth explaining to him what you are planning, and why. Both babies and toddlers quickly pick up our moods, and will realize that something is afoot. If the operation is conducted like some secret mission, they could quite easily, and understandably, get the wrong end of the stick, and possibly even think that you are moving without them. An open and honest manner right from the beginning is the best policy. There is no need, however, to unsettle your child unduly with all your house-hunting worries. He need only be involved once you've actually got a moving date, not before.

If the new home is nearby, you may find it helpful to pass by with your child. By chatting about – and even seeing – a new house, your child's world of here and now incorporates the notion of moving house. He may resist the idea at first, but you can divert his energy towards making his own preparations, an activity which will quickly persuade him that this could be fun after all. For example, try giving him his own special box or packing crate so that he can pack his favourite toys himself. He'll probably want to unpack and repack every day, but if he regards the whole operation as a game, he will have fun and you'll have a little more peace of mind.

Packing always takes longer than you would imagine, and packing with a toddler around can be an absolute nightmare. If you have a baby, try to do your packing while he's asleep. If your child is older, try to leave him at a friend's house before you start the serious business of sorting things out and loading up packing crates. It always helps to be organized – start by making lists of what rooms or items you can pack up first, then those that have to be done later and those that need to be left to the last minute. Try to weed out and throw away as many unwanted things as possible. You'll have so much to do in the new house that you'll regret any extra sorting out once you've moved in. But don't throw out familiar toys from your child's room, even if he seems to have outgrown them. In new, unfamiliar surroundings those old things will be reassuring to him.

Label your boxes so that you know which rooms they come from and which rooms they will be going to. Leave your child's things to a late stage in packing and make sure that they will be among the first off the van so that you can set up his room as soon as you get there. If you are moving with a baby, you will need to keep his changing equipment, bottles and possibly his pushchair or carry cot with you; so don't expect to have much room to spare for your own things on the journey!

If you can, try to arrange for both you and your partner to have a day off work on the day before moving, as well as the day itself. However brilliantly organized you've been, the day itself is likely to be chaotic and totally exhausting. Again, if you possibly can, try to spare your child your frayed nerves and also limit your worries by finding someone to look after him. You and your partner will have more than enough on your minds without trying to deal with a fractious little person who wants a glass of milk when all the kitchen stuff has just been packed away or wants his long-forgotten teddy which is at the bottom of a crate somewhere.

If your child has a favourite auntie or grandparents, you could ask them to look after him for the final packing stages as well as for the move itself, so that you can get on with all those last-minute things without too much panicking. There are benefits for all of you; you and your partner will be able to approach the big day with calmer nerves and your child will be having a treat – a couple of days being spoiled rotten.

Before the actual day, try to get your toddler used to the notion of moving. For example, make up a few moving games to familiarize him with the idea. Load up a toy truck with wooden bricks and "move" these, or pack up some of teddy's belongings and take them, with teddy, to a "new house". You could even buy your child some small overalls, like those used for painting in playgroups, so that he can join in even further, pretending to be a removal man. And your local library will almost certainly have books about children moving house which will help get the idea across even more.

It will be far less upsetting to leave familiar surroundings if he knows that moving is a normal, if infrequent, event in most people's lives.

Another thing you should do before you actually move is to find out whether there is a zoo or city farm near your new house and tell your child about it. You can then make a special treat of going there once you've moved in or perhaps you can promise to visit the local toy shop, the park or the swimming pool.

When you arrive at the new house, organize your child's things first – highchair, cot and changing unit for a baby; your toddler's bed, toys, "special" box, and potty. Try to set up your toddler's room in a similar way to the old one – you can make changes later. If you are planning to move a new baby out of your bedroom, it may be worth continuing the discomfort of all sleeping in the same room just until your baby has settled into the new surroundings. On the other hand, you may want to take advantage of the situation and put him straight into his own room.

One of your first jobs in the new house may be to childproof it. Before you move, buy a supply of plug socket covers and cupboard door "kiddilocks" so that you can cut down any immediate hazards for your crawling baby or curious toddler. If you are moving from a flat to a house, make sure you have the necessary stair gates.

On your first night in your new home, leave a night light on for your child at bedtime; this will make him feel cosier and unafraid of any new shadows. It will also prevent everyone crashing around in the dark. Show him where your room is, so he can find you easily in the middle of the night, or in the morning. And try to spend a bit longer on the bedtime story, and go through what happened in the day with him, untangling any worries he has about his new, unfamiliar home.

Once you have finished the unpacking you can start to enjoy the process of settling into a new house and neighbourhood – but don't be over-ambitious. Just as packing takes longer than you think, so your attempts at getting things straight will take much longer than you imagined.

Mumps

Mumps, medically known as epidemic parotitis, affects mainly children from 4 to 14 years old, although it is slightly less infectious than some of the other common childhood illnesses such as measles or chickenpox. It can now be prevented by immunization. Mumps causes general symptoms and, characteristically, swelling of the salivary glands (six in total) situated around the mouth. A child who has had mumps gains lifelong immunity to the disease as a result.

Mumps is caused by a virus which is passed on through coughs, sneezes and the breath of someone who has the disease. The germs are breathed in and begin to act on the respiratory system.

The symptoms of the disease do not begin to show until from two to four weeks after it was contracted. Then the child with mumps may have flu-like symptoms, with a slight fever, sore throat and shivering. He may also feel pain around his ears and find swallowing difficult.

Soon the large salivary gland just in front of the ear (known as the parotid gland, from which mumps gets its medical name) becomes tender and swollen. Sometimes only one side of the face is affected, but usually both sides of the child's face become noticeably swollen round the jaw, and the child finds it very painful to open his mouth wide or to swallow.

At this stage the temperature may rise further, often as high as 39.4°C (103°F). All six salivary glands can be affected, making the whole jaw area swollen and painful at once, but sometimes only one gland is affected at first, with the infection gradually passing from one gland to another.

At the height of the attack the child with mumps can feel quite unwell. Apart from being tired, hot and cold and shivery, and probably a little tearful, he will usually have no appetite, and will not be inclined to eat because of the pain on swallowing.

Two to three days later the swelling begins to subside and the temperature begins to fall. The child will soon feel more perky and his appetite will return. In some cases a child can have mumps while hardly showing any symptoms at all, and without noticeable swelling of the face. Even such mild cases confer lifelong immunity to further attacks.

Although mumps is not a serious disease, it is slightly more likely to cause complications than other common childhood illnesses, and parents need to be on the look out for signs that complications may be arising.

The most frequent of these is pancreatitis, or inflammation of the pancreas. This causes tummy-ache and sickness, which usually last for a day or two.

Orchitis (inflammation of the testes in boys) and oophoritis (inflammation of the ovaries in girls) are also possible developments. Orchitis causes pain and swelling in one or both of the testicles, and this occasionally occurs even when the child's face is not swollen. It is not unusual, and in all but very rare cases everything returns to normal within a week. Oophoritis in girls is less common. It causes severe pain in the lower abdomen, accompanied by bouts of vomiting, and usually lasts for two or three days. It has no long-term effects.

Two other possible complications can be very serious – encephalitis and meningitis. The former is characterized by severe headache, high fever and vomiting and the latter by neck stiffness with headache and, often, vomiting. Both complications must be treated urgently by your doctor as they can be fatal, especially in very young children, if left untreated.

Although it is very unusual for any of these complications to develop, it is as well to be on the lookout for them, and it is important to let your doctor know at once if any worrying symptoms arise.

Your family doctor should be called to confirm that the child is suffering from mumps, and if this is the case treatment will depend on the severity of the mumps. The child should be kept at home for about ten days after the symptoms appear, but need not necessarily stay in bed.

Fever can be reduced by tepid sponging, or by paracetamol, which will also help to calm any aches and pains. The throat will be very sore for a few days, and the child will probably be unable to eat solid food. He will need plenty of cool drinks, and you may be able to tempt him to eat soups and purées. A wrapped hot-water bottle placed against the sore face may be soothing.

Musical Awareness

Babies and children love to respond to rhythm in music from the earliest age. Indeed, even babies in the womb, it seems, are aware of music. In one recent study, a group of babies whose mothers had watched a TV "soap" each day towards the end of their pregnancies were soothed by hearing the theme tune in the first weeks after birth. The researchers suggested the "soap" babies had learnt to associate the theme tune with a period of peace and quiet – when Mum put her feet up for half an hour in front of the TV –

and calmed down as a result. The same sort of response has been shown in babies whose parents regularly played the same music in pregnancy and afterwards.

As soon as your baby is able to focus and concentrate on your face for more than a few seconds at a time – any time from five or six weeks old – grab his attention by singing songs and rhymes to him – do the actions too. Babies and toddlers love these, right up to school age. Try the familiar ones from your own childhood, such as "Round and Round the Garden Like a Teddy Bear" and "This Little Piggy". As your baby gets older he'll try to sing along with you. He'll be delighted when he repeats one or two words, and claps his little hands together, or grabs his own toes.

Let your child know he can be part of the music and encourage him to join in. When you're singing to him or with him, clap your hands against his. Hold his hands and show him how he can clap too. Don't expect him to do it without help until he's coming up to his first birthday – and even then, it will be some time before he makes a proper clapping sound. That doesn't matter. By encouraging him to join in you're helping him to see that music is a source of fun.

Don't forget his legs and feet! Lie him on his back and move his limbs so he can "dance" while you sing to him. You can jiggle and rock him on your lap chanting other nursery rhymes, such as "This is the Way the Ladies Ride" or "Ride a Cock Horse".

Let him use some "musical instruments" as you sing and act out the rhyme – a small bell, a rattle, a wooden spoon and a pan lid, an empty coffee tin with plastic lid, or whatever you have handy that he can hold – and which is safe to use. Most babies and toddlers love musical toys, especially ones they can operate themselves. The simplest toys have a string to pull; more complicated ones may have to be operated by you.

You may long for your toddler to learn to play a musical instrument, but this may not be a good idea although experts differ in their opinion on this subject. Most music teachers are not trained to teach tiny children and, besides, the instruments are not designed "child size". You can find small violins manufactured in Japan but these are not designed for music lessons. Your child is just encouraged to carry it around while music is played, and the idea is that he will begin to connect the sounds of the music to the sounds he can make on his little violin.

If you have set your heart on your child learning early, it's vital to check that the teacher you have in mind has experience with very young pupils. Otherwise, it is a good idea to wait until your child is at least seven.

That doesn't mean you can't put together a few simple homemade instruments before then, to help your child experiment with new sounds.

Probably the simplest of all is to put a few dried beans or split peas into a balloon before blowing it up – blow it up and you have an instant and enormous rattle. The balloon naturally amplifies sound, so water-filled balloons sound like waves breaking. Experiment with rice or flour filled balloons.

Other simple instruments include comb and tissue paper – it might take a moment to master the lip-tingling technique but it is worth the effort. Jars of different sizes with different amounts of water inside give different notes when tapped gently with a spoon. By adjusting the level of water you can tune your notes and invent your own signature tunes. Stretch elastic bands over an empty cereal packet, a cup or an empty tin for simple twangers. Or turn your flower pot upside down and suspend it from a chair and you have a sweet sounding bell. Several flowerpots of different sizes will give you an interesting peal of bells.

If you feel like going a step further, there are several books available that give instructions for making simple xylophones and so on.

Playing home-made instruments will provide great sound effects for musical story telling. You could also combine it with dressing-up by making musical costumes – try hanging threads of beer bottle tops to the brim of a hat, bells to wrists and ankles, or making a hole in walnut shells and sewing them in loose clusters to sleeves. And small saucepan lids or small cymbals tied between knees can be lots of fun. These are just a few ways of bringing old clothes alive with sound.

Try to choose instruments that you yourself like the sound of, or at least find tolerable. And join in and follow your child's ideas. It is actually much less stressful and it is good for your child's musical ideas to be listened to. Having a child offers you a wonderful opportunity to discover new sounds and new skills, or even dredge up old ones. Maybe you have an instrument you have not played for ages – your child is going to be an appreciative audience. Encourage friends and relatives who play to bring their instruments over. And check out children's concerts and outdoor events in your area. Festivals, fairs and fêtes are usually full of music. Your child will love seeing musicians perform and even loud music does not seem to upset babies, though they should not be too close to the speakers.

Try to listen to all sorts of music with your child, and extend the range beyond the usual scope of radio and television. Visit your local library; many have music sections, some with music specifically for children which includes music from around the world. The rhythms and songs from other countries might well appeal to your child. Look out for panpipe music from South America; Eskimo singing with its extraordinary vocal sounds; African drumming and singing; Spanish flamenco; salsa from Central America and Greek dance music. You can always order records that are not in stock. There are also records available of children's music and musical games from countries around the world. Never before have there been so many different types of music available to us, so take advantage of this for yourself as well as for your child.

You can buy good quality tape-recorders made especially for children. Your child can then choose when and what music to play, which is

particularly good for long car journeys. Most portable radio/cassette players also have a built-in microphone, making it very easy to record. You could record your child's first sounds as a keepsake. Later he will delight in hearing his own voice played back.

Children's electronic keyboards have become very sophisticated. They are expensive but even the cheapest have up to 100 sounds, a variety of pre-set rhythmic feels (jazz/rock/latin) and a record/play-back facility, which means it records what you play on the keyboards and stores it in a memory. Your child can then enjoy playing back his own compositions, played by a full orchestra at the touch of a button.

Music is of added importance as a source of enjoyment and means of communication to babies and children with special needs. Blind children often have an exceptional love of, and gift for music. Deafness does not necessarily preclude enjoyment of music as much music is transmitted through vibrations that a deaf child will be particularly sensitive to.

Children with learning difficulties and speech problems can also benefit from music; singing and rhythmic work help the child to develop speech, and can also be offered to the child as an alternative means of expression, by-passing the problems they meet in using words – so it is both a learning tool and a way to relax.

Instruments can be adapted or suitable ones chosen for children with physical handicaps, and joining in musical activity often provides the necessary motivation for a child to develop motor skills and co-ordination.

There is an increasing awareness of the usefulness of music in special needs education, and research work is being undertaken on the importance of music with very young handicapped babies and their families and carers, as a means to improve relationships and strengthen bonds.

◆ See also, **Dancing**

Names

If there is one subject that is bound to set expectant parents squabbling, it is the choice of a name for their soon-to-be-born child.

Often, social or religious customs can make the choice easier. Ashkenazi Jews, for example, often name their children after relatives who have died. If it is an uncle they wish to remember, but the child is a daughter, then her name will simply begin with the same letter, so that Lionel, for example, is transformed to Laura. Many Hindu couples consider the baby's horoscope before choosing a name, while Eskimos believe that taking a new name in middle age restores their youth. In aristocratic families the same name is passed from generation to generation.

It is also quite common in many cultures, even among young parents, to name the baby after a favourite aunt, uncle or grandparent. You may choose a name on this basis because you want to please that particular relation, or you want to show your affection for them or, in the hope that your baby will share qualities you admire in the person whose name you have chosen.

It is an ancient belief that a name bestows special traits upon a person. For centuries, we have called our children after the Apostles and the saints, and even if modern society has forgotten the meaning, these Christian names are still widely used. So "John" has always been popular all over Europe, because John was supposed to be Christ's favourite disciple and was chosen to look after Mary, mother of Jesus. By the same token, Andrew, Simon, Mark and James are still widely used, and these names have survived because, long ago, parents hoped that their children would be as good and as noble as these Apostles.

Many cultures also believe that a name has magical qualities and for that reason should be used very carefully. The Ancient Egyptians gave their children two names. One was the "Good Name" and was only used in private and in secret. They thought that no evil or harm would fall on the child as long as his "Good Name" was a secret.

Fortunately, we do not attach these difficult ideas to the names we give our babies, but perhaps this is the ancient and forgotten reason why so many of us are given two names. It is more likely, however, that two names was a simple compromise for the squabbling family.

You may like to choose a name that has a special meaning, so that a longed-for baby girl is called Gemma, meaning "jewel", or a baby you've waited and waited for could be called Zoë, "life", or Kevin, an old Irish word for "dear birth".

A practice, not so fashionable nowadays as it was earlier in the century, was to name daughters after flowers. There is a whole language of flowers, and Edwardian mothers pored over plant books or beautifully illustrated flower books to find names which meant "faithful" (Ivy), "innocence" (Daisy), or to signify purity and sweetness they would choose Lily.

Boys were often named after heroes like Richard (the Lionheart) or Peter (the Great) and today, parents might call their sons after great boxers, tennis players or cricketers. In this way, their admiration for these sportsmen can be openly expressed.

Many parents also have a special attachment to their favourite characters from books, or the authors they most like to read. Nowadays, a girl called Colette is quite likely to be named after the famous French author and not, as in earlier centuries, after the saint Colette. During the late 1960s, numerous "hippie" parents named their sons Sam to recall a character in *Lord of the Rings* by J.R. Tolkien.

Pop stars and movie stars have also played their part in creating fashions for names. The Royal family has strongly influenced the nation's choice in names, so that Victoria, Charles, Elizabeth and Diana have all been fashionable at one time or another.

There are also very individual reasons for choosing particular names for your children. Immigrant parents may recall their homeland by giving their children names familiar to Greece or Poland, but which are quite strange and unusual in their new country of Canada or Australia.

There are also, of course, marriages which cross racial and cultural lines. So the children of a British man and a Russian woman might have names like Tanya and Natasha to show the world that their children are the products of two traditions, as well as two individuals.

Often other children in the family are keen to name the new baby. This can make for much hilarity and originality. Your ten-year-old romantic will take the task very seriously and give you a long and impossible list of names like Hecate and Magnolia. The logical child will offer a sensible choice of alphabetically arranged names – and there are parents who, in desperation, will resort to this method of choosing.

There are individual responses to names and these may have no logic. Some may hate the name Judy because they had an "enemy" at school with that name; or they refuse to call any child Roger because they knew a dog with that name. One couple startled all their family and friends by giving their daughter a totally unexpected and unfamiliar name. It took an uncle to observe that the child's name was the same as a nearby street. The parents had, quite unconsciously, read the name frequently and it had stuck in their minds.

Whatever name you decide on, do bear in mind the fact that your child must carry it with him for the rest of his life. Think of how he may be teased at school if you give him a really outlandish name, and try, also, to not choose a peculiar form of spelling, otherwise he will be forever having to spell out his name for people. You might also consider whether or not you like the shortened form of a name you are thinking of giving your child, as this will inevitably be used – William might become Bill, Victoria will be Vicky, and so on.

Another consideration is to match the first name to your surname. Does Joanna sound right with Atkins, or perhaps Susan sounds better? Would you match Christopher to Irwin if you thought James Irwin came more easily off the tongue?

If you are completely at a loss as to what name to choose, there are name books available containing endless names and their meanings.

It is a curious fact, however, that once you have stopped squabbling, and poring over books, or you've decided which grandparent will be honoured, the name you choose will be exactly right for your baby, and will give him a unique identity to grow into.

Nannies

A nanny's or a mother's help's job is to ensure that the baby or child in her care receives all the physical, emotional and intellectual stimulation he needs, whatever his age. This, of course, has to be achieved in a way that works not only for the nanny, but also for you as a parent.

A good nanny will display kindness, discretion, willingness, patience, stamina, "unflappability" and flexibility. An ability to plan and think ahead, and good organization skills are also essential.

Some parents do not want a fully trained nanny for many reasons, but having said that, most will agree that attendance at a course can indicate a certain level of maturity and more than just a passing interest in the subject. Trained nannies will have been exposed to many different theories about child care and should emerge with clear ideas as to what is best for a child. There is always the worry, however, that a little knowledge can be a dangerous thing, especially when it has not been backed up with practical experience. There are many different courses and qualifications for nannies, and if this is something that is important to you when selecting the person who is going to care for your child it may be worth looking into exactly what different courses cover and from what angle.

Your choice of nanny will depend to a great extent on your needs and also your finances. You may choose a live-in full-time nanny, a full-time daily nanny, a part-time nanny, or perhaps a "nanny share". When it comes to actually finding your nanny, you will again be faced with various choices: you may decide to advertise for one, or use an agency. The latter should, in theory, save a lot of time, frustration and hassle. This is not always the case, however, and the agency service does also come at a price. Often the best way is to follow your own instincts as they rarely steer you wrong; if something about an existing or a prospective nanny does not feel right, don't ignore it, however silly it may seem.

When you get to the interview stage you will need to allow time for discussion. Find out about previous experience, whether she has children herself, and try to show interest in her as a person. Always ask for at least two referees, and follow these up, rather than relying on written references. Watch her as she talks to you. How does she treat your child? How does she talk to him? Does she seem genuinely interested? Does she seem to display patience and consideration for him? And how does he respond to her?

Once you have reached a decision and have offered somebody the job, you will need to define precisely the terms of the job – for example do you expect her to do cleaning, cooking, washing and ironing, or is her sole duty to look after your child?

You will also need to discuss arrangements for holidays, sickness pay and what will happen if either she or your child is ill. The question of tax and National Insurance contributions must also be addressed. Other matters you may want to discuss at this stage are time off, a period of probation, notice on both sides, house rules, a discipline procedure (for both nanny and child!), overtime, dress and car arrangements.

Nappies

Your baby will have to wear nappies, day and night, at least until he is toilet-trained. It is therefore a good idea to try to minimize any inconvenience, and the best way to do this is to be prepared.

You will need a safe place ready to lay your baby while you are changing him, and a cloth or flannel, cotton wool, tissues and baby lotion or oil for wiping him clean. You may also need nappy rash cream and barrier cream to protect his skin. But first you need to decide what type of nappies you are going to use.

Choosing nappies

The variety of nappies available may seem a little bewildering, but basically the choice is between washable (fabric) and disposable ones. Most people end up using a combination of both types, though they may rely more heavily on one or the other. Each type has some advantages and some disadvantages. You will need to take into account your own circumstances – for example, how much time and space you have for washing and drying nappies – as well as your own child's needs (such as his age and whether he has any skin problems or allergies) before deciding what's best for you both.

Buying terry towelling nappies may seem expensive at first, especially since you will need at least 24 (and preferably more if you want to avoid frequent washing). You will also need to buy at least a dozen nappy pins. Terry nappies certainly involve more work than disposables, and they need to be the best quality you can afford, because they will have to stand up to frequent rinsing, sterilizing, washing and drying. But they can actually work out cheaper than disposables over time. They also have a number of other advantages. The thickest ones are more absorbent than most disposables, and are good for use at night. They also come in useful in other ways: you can put one over your shoulder when you burp your baby, use one to catch the dribbles and sick when he's feeding, or tie one gently round his neck as a bib. If you do use terries, don't forget to wash them before you use them for the first time, to soften them for your baby's skin. If his skin is very irritated or sore at any time, you can use a gauze or muslin nappy inside the terry for extra softness. Some areas have nappy-washing services that pick up your soiled nappies and deliver clean ones to you.

Standard terry nappies are square-shaped, but they also come in other shapes, the most common being T-shaped. Some shaped terries have fasteners, so you don't have to bother with nappy pins, and shaped terries are generally simpler to put on than terry squares. They are also less bulky so your toddler will find them easier to walk in. However, they can be expensive, and they don't usually come in different sizes so you may find them too bulky for your very young baby.

You can stop fabric nappies from getting badly soiled – and cut down on the washing – by using disposable liners inside them. These look like extra large strong paper tissues, and come in packets or rolls. They can be flushed away down the toilet. "One-way" liners allow urine to pass through to the fabric nappy, keeping the surface of the liner which is next to your baby's skin relatively dry. This helps to avoid nappy rash or soreness due to moisture or rubbing. If you want to avoid changing your baby's entire outfit every time he needs a nappy change, you can put waterproof pants on over his terry nappies.

There are different ways of folding towelling or fabric nappies. The best method for your baby will depend on how big he is, so you will need to experiment. Make sure that the nappy doesn't bunch up too much between his legs, keeping them wide apart, but make sure that it doesn't fit too tightly, either.

Fabric nappies need to be thoroughly washed to get rid of any traces of ammonia or bacteria. You can buy special nappy sterilants which reduce both time and effort. All you need to do is soak your nappies in sterilizing solution for the required length of time. Then only soiled nappies need to be washed. Wet nappies can simply be rinsed in hot water and dried.

Disposable nappies may work out more expensive than fabric nappies in the long run, but you may well find they're worth it. They are much easier to put on, since they don't need to be specially folded or held on with pins – and above all, they don't need to be washed. They are designed to be used and then thrown away. Even if you use fabric nappies as a rule it is a good idea to have a stock of disposables on stand-by. They are ideal for travelling and visiting, or any other situation when soaking and washing can be a problem.

The two main types of disposable nappies are "two-piece" and "all-in-one". Two-piece nappies are made up of a pad in special plastic pants to hold the pad in place. These pants are usually T-shaped, designed to be tied at the sides, or fastened with poppers. Pads come in different shapes, degrees of absorbency and sizes, so you can choose the type that caters for your child best. Like disposable liners, they are also available in rolls. They are designed to be torn in half and flushed away, but if you don't want to risk a blockage it is probably better to dispose of them properly in strong plastic bags.

All-in-one disposables are like a nappy liner and pair of plastic pants all rolled into one. They are very popular because they're so easy to use. An all-in-one consists of an inner absorbent layer with a plastic backing on the outside and a one-way liner on the inside. Some have elasticated legs, which can help to protect against leaks, and most have resealable tapes. They come in various sizes. Some are designed to be more absorbent for night use, and some are designed differently for boys and girls, so that the thickest and most absorbent parts are where they are most needed. All-in-one disposables cannot be flushed away and need to be disposed of hygienically in plastic rubbish bags.

You might want to take the "green" factor into consideration when making your final choice: nappies are made from trees and for every 500 disposable nappies one large tree has to die; before your baby is potty trained he is likely to use around 5,000 nappies; and disposables are only about 70 per cent biodegradable as they are plastic-coated.

However, the use of electricity and detergents when using cloth nappies must not be overlooked when entering the "green" debate.

Changing your baby

Whatever kind of nappy you choose, your basic nappy changing procedure will be the same. You will need to change your baby's nappy whenever you notice that it is wet or soiled. In the first couple of months, your baby will probably wet his nappy every 2–4 hours. If you are breast feeding, he may soil his nappy after every feed, and if you are bottle feeding, he will probably soil his nappy 3 to 6 times a day.

As a general rule, you will find that you change his nappy when he wakes in the morning, after bathing and before putting him to bed, as well as after every feed. If he falls asleep immediately after feeding, try changing him in the middle of his feed. This way you won't have to disturb him later, and you won't be tempted to leave him to sleep in a soiled nappy either.

Once you have got everything you need, lay your baby on the changing table, and unfasten his nappy. If it is soiled, use the front of the nappy to remove as much of the faeces as possible from your baby before removing the nappy, always wiping away from the genitals to prevent the spread of bacteria. Once removed, fold the nappy over to stop the faeces from falling out, and place it to one side. Gently use a wet cloth or cotton wool to wipe all the urine from your baby's genitals. With a baby boy, don't pull his foreskin back, and never pull back a girl's labia to clean inside her vagina.

To clean your baby's bottom, lift up his legs with one hand, keeping a finger in between the heels. When you have finished washing your baby, dry him thoroughly. If the nappy was soiled, use baby lotion or oil on cotton wool to wipe your baby clean, using a new piece for each wipe.

Never forget when you are in a rush that: nappy pins are dangerous – make sure you slip your fingers between your baby and the nappy when fixing the pin; lotion or cream on your fingertips will prevent the tabs of disposables from sticking properly; you must wash your hands after cleaning baby; and you should never leave your baby unsupervised on a raised surface.

Nappy rash

Sometimes your baby's skin may become red and sore around the areas covered by his nappy. This can often happen when he sleeps through the night without a nappy change. Most babies get nappy rash from time to time. But using the following guidelines may help to protect your child.

- Always clean and dry your baby thoroughly.
- Leave his bottom to "air" as often as you can (but watch out for accidents).
- Use a special nappy rash cream at the first sign of broken skin.
- Change nappies frequently.
- Use one-way nappy liners.
- Avoid plastic pants if there are signs of a rash.
- Apply a good barrier cream overnight.

Protect his skin from harsh products and allergic reactions:
- Wash and rinse nappies thoroughly.
- Use non-biological powders and avoid fabric conditioners.
- Use unscented products, and avoid soap or talcum powder on your baby.

Once your baby starts to walk, you don't want his nappy to be too bulky, especially between his legs. Bulky nappies not only make walking more awkward but if worn all day, they may also put long-term pressure on his legs and affect their development. Your child may naturally be bow-legged, but this inborn tendency could be increased by wearing the wrong size or shape of nappy. So give your toddler less bulky, disposable nappies to encourage him to move about freely. You can still put him in towelling nappies at night.

When your child's nappy stays dry from time to time during the day, you may think of trying to do without one, but be prepared for accidents. Even if he can let you know that he wants his potty, he may not be able to wait while you pull his clothes down. Trainer pants can be the answer. These are a kind of plastic knickers with a towelling lining. They are "safe" in case of an accident, they are comfortable to wear and they can be pulled down quickly when necessary, although there is the argument that the child still feels as though he is wearing a nappy, and will therefore act accordingly!

Nappy-changing will soon become a part of your natural routine. Once you've got all the practical details worked out, you will be able to relax. And that's when nappy-changing can become a special time for you and your baby to share. Relax and don't rush it. He'll enjoy having a good kick without the restrictions of a nappy, and he'll love those few precious minutes of extra attention you can give him. So enjoy playing with him, talking to him and tickling him – and generally having fun.

◆ See also, **Potty Training**

Nature Study

By the age of two, your child's spontaneous curiosity and eager observation have begun to find expression in language. He is also increasingly confident in his ability to move around and explore. Now you can encourage him to extend the limits of his small world and develop his awareness and enjoyment of the natural world that he sees about him.

Access to animals and nature can be as easy in a town as in the country. Birds and insects are found everywhere – you may even come across a spider, moth or earwig in your own home. Parks are often a richer source of wildlife for a toddler than open fields or woodland, because the animals may be a little tamer.

Ducks on ponds are an ideal introduction to birdlife as they are gregarious, colourful and responsive when you throw food for them. They also form distinctive family groups. Males and females often bob about in pairs and you can point out the usually brighter drakes from the less showy "mother" ducks. Your child may be especially thrilled by ducklings as they swim after their mother in early summer. Ducks are also funny, especially when they land on water or when they waddle on to solid ground, so highlight your child's observations by letting him indulge his natural sense of humour. Swans may also be fascinating, but don't let your child too near them, as they can turn aggressive unexpectedly.

Apart from water birds, parks are often a good place for your child to see familiar birds at close hand. Many will come very near if you scatter breadcrumbs for them, and all are noisy. Point out their various sounds so that your child will recognize them again and encourage him to mimic their calls.

Squirrels in parks are often very tame. They may come right up to your child and sit up to "beg" for food. Like any animal, they react nervously to sudden movement so show your child how to move slowly to avoid frightening them, and teach him not to touch them. This is a useful lesson for him to learn in any case, whether it be for squirrels in the park or unfamiliar pets. Try to teach your child caution without making him frightened.

A country walk is another small adventure for your toddler. Even if you already live in open countryside, your child's interest will be stimulated when you help him discover what to look for. If you can, familiarize yourself with the types of wildlife you may find in the kind of countryside you will visit. For example, footpaths through farmland may take you close to hedgerows, the site of small birds' nests, while at the edges of fields which border woodland, you may find rabbit burrows and other animal homes.

Fallen logs in woodland will shelter all sorts of bugs – pick up a small one to show your child the insects and beetles underneath. You will almost certainly find ants working away among the fallen leaves – show him one that is carrying a piece of leaf back to its "home". By telling little "stories" about what you see, you will help him relate the natural world to his own experiences.

However you decide to explain these discoveries to your child, keep them on a small scale and at an accessible height for him. Pointing way up to the tops of trees will only frustrate him. He needs to explore physically the new things around him and be able to touch, pick up or at least see at eye-level. Don't stop him getting messy – it is all part of the fun and the freedom of outdoor spaces. You'll need to be patient. A clump of grass or a square centimetre of bark can hold him entranced for ages, and you should not hurry his observation.

To your child, discovering nature can be part of play, and a walk in the country will be as physically stretching as time spent in a playground. Encourage him to walk along fallen tree trunks and to jump over puddles – it will help him develop his co-ordination too. Repeat the visit several times so that your child will feel at home in those surroundings, but vary the incentives for the day out – take a picnic for instance. Ask your child whether he would like to take home some of the natural objects he finds. A small collection of stones and feathers can be arranged and labelled. This will help extend his learning.

You can make more sophisticated collections with an older child. Pine cones are ideal for demonstrating one of nature's mechanisms – place them in the garden or on a window-sill and watch how they open in sunshine and close with rain. If you take some plain paper and a soft pencil on your walk, your child can try taking bark rubbings. He can put these in a scrapbook when he gets home, along with any other special objects.

If your child is approaching school age, you can show him some of the "systems" of nature as well as the individual creatures. If you find a spider's web, show him how it attaches to the bush and explain that the spider waits outside the web until a fly is trapped, that the spider knows when this happens because it can feel the web's vibrations and will crawl across to eat the fly. Visit the same place in different seasons, so that your child sees the changes that take place in trees, or flowers, or ponds. You can begin to use more specific names: "chestnut tree", rather than "tree"; "blackbird", not just "bird".

Of course farms are an obvious location for finding all the domestic animals, but it can be difficult for your child to get near them. It is best to avoid taking him through fields occupied by livestock – cows and horses tend to gather round you and even sheep can be frighteningly large for a toddler. Farm animals may be more accessible in city farms, which are open most days. Here your child can see and touch most types of domestic animal and, depending on the season, there may also be new calves or lambs for him to look at.

As well as more exotic creatures, zoos often keep farm animals, which are usually found in a special "kids' corner". Zoos may be expensive for a family outing, but pre-school children usually enter free, and they are often the only way of introducing your child to animals that may be familiar to him in picture books. You can ask for a list of the day's activities that tells you about feeding times or special events.

Don't forget that your child has a short concentration span. Aim to see just a few animals and leave on a positive note, before he starts to get fed up. Many zoos organize tours for school groups, and these may cater for nursery schools or young infants. There may be a "story time" for very young children, telling the story of one animal that they can see there. You may like to give a special treat to your child and his little friends by organizing a zoo birthday party. Ask your local zoo if they make arrangements for such events.

The seaside is another place where the world of nature is very easily introduced to your child. Point out the seagulls which swoop and call, or take him to paddle in rock pools and look for crabs. Pick up the slippery seaweed on the shore and let him collect all the different shapes and sizes of shells. As the tide goes out, you might find tell-tale signs of other animals' presence such as worm casts, or sea birds' footprints. In fact, for most small children, these little explorations on the beach, peering into rock pools and picking up shells, are far more fun than the sea itself. And, of course, he can make wonderful collections of the strange things to be found on seashores. Whether you visit the park, spend a day in the country or explore the beach, your child will delight in the discoveries you make in the natural world. All his senses will be used to the full and his own natural curiosity will be stimulated and satisfied.

◆ See also, **Gardening**, **Insects**

Newborn Behaviour

◆ See **New Babies**, pages 5–16

Night Frights

There is a big difference between the emotional power struggle that goes on between you and your child when he plays up at bedtime, or cries out for you after lights out, and the involuntary night terrors and nightmares that have him screaming and sweating in the middle of an otherwise ordinary sleep. The difference is important. The first situation shows your child being wilfully manipulative, whereas the second sees him completely out of control. It is useful for you to recognize the usual pattern of these strange sleep disorders and to know what to do to help calm your child when he is suffering from one of them.

The following scene is typical of the sudden, scary, sleep phenomenon known as a "night terror". You've been into your child's room. All is well. Your child is fast asleep, his body is deeply relaxed and his breathing is slow and regular. You couldn't wake him if you tried. A little later you go to bed, too, and slip exhausted into a deep sleep. Forty minutes pass and you awake to the sound of screams. "A bad dream," you think. But in his room your three-year-old is moaning, sobbing, and thrashing wildly about in the bed. He has a strange look on his face, like one "possessed". When you try to put your arms around him he pushes you away and doesn't seem to recognize you at all.

You feel terrible – worried, inadequate, even angry. You are aware of yet another broken night and you feel hurt because he won't let you help him.

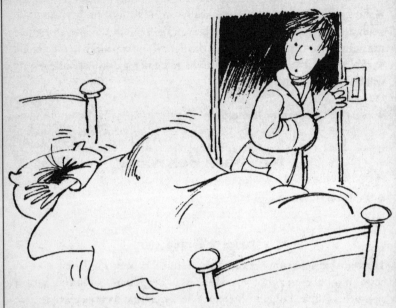

He doesn't even seem to hear your voice. You try to shake him awake. The thrashing gets worse Finally, after ten, 20 or even 30 minutes your child visibly relaxes. He stretches and yawns, then lets you settle him down under the covers and is quickly asleep. The night terror has passed. In the morning he seems his usual self and doesn't remember anything about the incident.

It was early when he woke screaming – between one and four hours after he fell asleep. Dreaming occurs later, in the hours before morning; this type of sleep is also known as REM (Rapid Eye Movement) sleep and refers to the "activity" that goes on behind your dreaming child's closed eyelids. Non-REM sleep, deep dreamless sleep, occurs in the earlier part of the evening. It is during the change-over between the two types of sleep that dramatic episodes like a night terror take place.

When you are dealing with a child who is suffering from a night fright, try to remember the following:

● He is not awake, and does not know what he is doing or saying, so don't take any notice of any hurtful words he may come out with.

● It will pass, but until it does there isn't really much you can do to help it go away.

● Turn the lights on if it helps you to cope with the rather eerie situation. If your child is running around you will need to clear the way of toys or anything he may trip over.

● Don't try to wake him or hold on to him against his will. If you are desperate to calm him, try wiping his face very gently with a warm, wet face flannel.

● Although nobody truly understands why a child gets night terrors, there does seem to be a relationship between their occurring and the child being over-tired, so make sure your child is getting enough sleep.

● It is very tempting in the morning to tell your child all about the night before, if he has had a night terror. You may think he will be comforted or even amused to be told what he got up to in the middle of the night. But it is better not to mention anything to him, especially if it involves a "tease". Children find it quite alarming to hear that they were doing things without knowing about it. Also, if the restlessness he shows in his sleep is a result of subconscious worry, it will not help to make him worry about this as well.

Nose

The nose, sinuses, mouth, throat and ears form an interlinked system of air passages along which infections can easily spread. For this reason you should see your doctor if any symptom in the ear, nose or throat lasts longer than one week.

The nose's primary function is for breathing. The lining has a rich blood supply which warms the air as it is breathed in. It also contains mucus-producing glands which humidify the air and trap airborne particles such as dust and bacteria. The nasal passages contain hairs which help to filter the air. Finally nerve endings in the roof of the nasal cavity provide our sense of smell.

The nasal passages, the ends of which can be seen at the bottom of the nose (nostrils), continue backwards into the nasopharynx, which lies above and behind the mouth. The adenoids, a raised ring of tissue, lie to the rear of the nasopharynx. The nose is self-cleaning and you should never put anything into it.

Nature intended the nose for breathing and the mouth for eating and drinking. However, it is possible to breathe through the mouth and many people do so. A cold often causes mouth breathing as do enlarged adenoids and tonsils, especially in children of four or five years old, the age at which both adenoids and tonsils reach their full size. If a child has enlarged adenoids, they may block his nose, and this will force him to breathe through his mouth.

Snoring and night-time coughs are also associated with mouth breathing. Coughing often happens when mucus builds up in the throat or is a result of post-natal drip, when mucus drips from the back of the nose into the throat.

Structural abnormalities of the nose can also cause mouth breathing as can allergic conditions such as hay fever. If your child persists in breathing through his mouth when he does not have a cold or any other nasal obstruction, see your doctor to find the cause.

Stuffy or runny noses often accompany colds. The common cold is a viral infection which enters the body through the nasal passages and throat and causes inflammation of the mucous membranes lining these passages. There is no specific cure for a cold and it should normally be left to run its course. However, if any discharge changes from clear to yellow, this may be a sign of secondary infection and you should see your doctor, as you should if your child has catarrh or a runny nose for more than six days – this could be a sign of chronic sinusitis or chronic infection of the nose or throat.

A blocked or runny nose in a baby needs to be taken more seriously as it can cause feeding problems and there is a greater chance of complications. Your doctor will give you nose drops to use before each feed.

Sniffing usually accompanies a cold but it can become a habit and sometimes indicates an underlying problem such as enlarged adenoids. See your doctor if you are worried.

If you do, for any reason, have to give your child nose drops, use the following guidelines:

● Warm the drops before applying by standing the container in warm, not hot, water for a few minutes so your child doesn't get a shock when they enter his nose.

● Lie a baby or very young child on a flat surface and enlist the help of an adult or older child to keep him still and hold his head steady. Ask an older child to tilt his head back to give him drops.

● Do not let the dropper touch your child's nose as you will transfer the germs back to the bottle. If the dropper does touch his nose, wash it thoroughly before putting it back in the bottle.

Nosebleeds can occur as a result of a bump on the nose, nose-picking, or continued nose-blowing. Some children seem to be more prone to nosebleeds than others, possibly due to the fragility of the blood vessels in their noses.

If your child has a nosebleed help him lean forwards over a bowl or sink and pinch his nostrils together for ten minutes. Encourage him to spit out any blood rather than swallowing it. If after ten minutes the bleeding has not stopped, try holding a cold, wet cloth or an ice pack over your child's nose for two minutes, then pinch again. (Avoid blowing his nose for four hours after the bleeding has stopped.)

If bleeding persists for more than half an hour consult your doctor. You should also speak to your doctor if your child's nosebleeds are frequent or severe.

Children are naturally curious and will inevitably stuff small objects into their own or others' orifices such as noses and ears. Neither you nor your child may notice it at first but after two or three days your child may have a nosebleed or foul-smelling discharge from the affected nostril.

If you can remove the object easily with tweezers, do so, or if your child is old enough to blow his nose properly, ask him to blow down the affected nostril as you hold a finger against the good one. Do not ask a young child to do this as he may sniff the object back into his air passages.

If you cannot dislodge the object or if it moves further up the nostril, see your doctor or go to the nearest accident and emergency department. If your child shows any signs of breathing problems, call an ambulance or go immediately to the accident and emergency department. Do not allow a child under three to play with objects small enough to swallow or put up his nose.

◆ See also, **Catarrh, Common Cold, Sinusitis**

Numbers

The pre-school years, from three to five, are a good time to begin to introduce numbers – and this is where a simple toy telephone will come into action.

As he gets older you can incorporate the learning of numbers by making a little telephone book with his toys' numbers in it. Draw a picture of each toy, one toy to a page, then write the name of the toy and its telephone number underneath, for example Teddy 234. His doll can have the number 567 and so on. It's best to avoid real three-figure numbers in case your child decides to experiment with the real thing!

Make a show of looking up teddy's number then lift the receiver and dial it. Remember to say each number as you dial it. Then suggest that your child might like to call teddy for a chat. Obviously he will not really understand these numbers at first. This doesn't matter at this early stage. You are teaching him the sequence of making a call and introducing numbers and the order they come in.

Encourage your child to look out for numbers in his daily surroundings – on houses, car number plates, buses and so on. If you start with his own house, or car, or things that have his age number on them, you will increase his interest by relating numbers to him.

Show him plenty of number books, where the number is printed alongside corresponding pictures. This will help with learning to count as well as with number recognition. Remember that at first he will recognize but not understand the numbers he sees, so don't expect him to become a mathematical genius at this stage.

◆ See also, **Counting**

Nurseries and Playgroups

Deciding whether or not to put your child into some kind of pre-school care or education will depend to some extent on your own particular situation. If you decide to go back to work, all-day or part-time care becomes a necessity and has to be organized down to the minute. But if you are not working, you will have more freedom to choose where your child goes, at what age he starts and how long he attends each week.

Begin by considering your own needs and those of your child, and what you can both gain from the experience. Spending time with other children may help your child to learn to share and to co-operate in his play, especially if he doesn't have younger brothers or sisters or friends in the neighbourhood. He will also get the chance to meet new adults. Leaving you for a short time each day will help him gradually to increase his independence. It may also give him the chance to play with a wider range of toys and equipment than you can provide for him at home.

Furthermore, he will have the opportunity to learn and develop new skills, many of which may form the basis for later learning at school. He may also be introduced to daily routines – such as tidying up, or sitting listening to stories – which prepare him gently for what goes on at "big school".

From your point of view, caring for a young child can be very demanding, especially if your child is constantly on the go. Having time to yourself can provide a welcome break and help you to re-charge your batteries. You may simply be glad of the chance to stay at home and put your feet up or to catch up with household chores. But it can also allow you to take up a new interest or hobby, to join a class or go back to college. Going back to work can also boost your confidence in yourself and introduce another dimension in your life outside the home.

Of course, you may decide to keep your child with you at home. This may be because you want to make the most of these early years together, and feel that you can provide him with a wide range of friends and experiences without sending him somewhere else.

If the first stages of your relationship with your child have been unsettled for any reason – for example, if you or your child have been unwell or if there has been friction or an upheaval in the family – then it may be better to keep your child at home until he has got over this period and feels more secure.

Similarly, it may not be a good idea to start your child at a pre-school group too soon after the birth of a younger brother or sister. It is natural for your child to be jealous of the attention you give to the new baby, but this will only be increased if he feels he is being sent away. So wait until he has got used to the new arrival before making any other changes in his life.

Unless you are working, you will probably start thinking about finding a nursery or playgroup for your child when he is about two. Most pre-school provision is part-time for children between the ages of three and five. However, at what stage you should start thinking about it will depend on your own circumstances, and on what is available in your area. If there are not very many places on offer where you live, then you may need to think about it slightly earlier, and it might be necessary to put your child's name on a waiting list.

Different types of pre-school provision have different procedures for obtaining a place. Some may not allow you to register your child before he has reached a certain age, while others may be happy to put his name down as soon as he is born. You may need to think ahead to make sure that you and your child don't miss out later.

The most common pre-school provisions include playgroups, day nurseries and nursery schools and classes – though not all of these may be available in your area.

The main differences between the various types of pre-school care are in the hours that they operate, the type of service that they provide (for example, whether or not they provide education or simply physical care), the extent to which you will be expected to join in and help, the training of the staff, the number of places available, and the costs involved.

All in all, most parents opt for the local playgroup when it comes to choosing their child's first schooling, although the exact proportion varies from area to area, depending on what is available.

Playgroups cater mainly for three- and four-year-olds. Some playgroups may take your child when he is only two and a half, but you will probably have to go with him. Playgroups are often organized in church halls or community centres and are usually run by the mothers of the children. There is a small charge for each session.

The emphasis is on encouraging children to play and develop their social skills. Playgroups offer a wide range of activities, and you will be encouraged to join in. Some playgroups are combined with parent-toddler groups, so they can provide a service for all children under five. If this is the case, you will be able to stay with your younger child, while leaving your three- or four-year-old in the playgroup.

Day nurseries may be private or state-run, and are an ideal solution if you intend to go back to work, as most of them offer flexible hours. They are usually open all day every weekday throughout the year, though they may close for a couple of weeks in the summer. Most of them provide care for children between the ages of two and five.

Local authority day nurseries are usually run by qualified nursery nurses, and are regularly checked by the authority for hygiene, safety, and the care they provide. Some local authority day nurseries are free, but many charge a small fee which may vary depending on your income.

Private day nurseries are run as businesses and charge for their services. Their standards may be more variable than those of state-run nurseries, and their staff will not necessarily be qualified.

If you want your child to be in a group setting that puts more emphasis on learning opportunities, then you may want to choose a nursery class or school. Nursery education is provided for three- and four-year-olds, and is controlled by the local education authorities. Nursery schools are independent establishments, while nursery classes are usually attached to an infant or primary school.

Nursery education is free, and is usually provided on a part-time basis during school term times. Your child will attend for two and a half hours each weekday, either in the morning or the afternoon. Nursery schools are generally well equipped and are staffed by trained teachers and nursery nurses.

Private nursery schools are also becoming increasingly popular. Many claim a high standard of discipline and stress an early introduction to reading and writing. But their educational aims vary widely – Montessori nurseries, for instance, encourage free expression and individual learning and exploration, whereas Rudolph Steiner kindergartens favour arts and crafts, avoid any pressure, and don't push reading or writing. The expense, however, is considerable and the hours are usually limited to morning or afternoon sessions.

Before deciding which kind of place you want for your child, you will need to know what is available in your local area. Try and get a list of facilities for pre-school children from the local education authority and don't forget to ask around among friends. Word of mouth is often the most successful way of finding out more about individual places in your area.

Once you've got a shortlist of possibilities, the best way to make your final choice is to go and visit. Before you do, it's worth sitting down with your partner and talking about your own feelings and expectations in the matter and trying to place yourself in your child's position. How will it change his little life and what is he likely to feel and think about it all?

Starting playgroup or nursery is a very important stage in your child's life. In many ways it's his first step out into the world where he will be learning to be sociable, to share and to be part of a group – without you protecting him and holding his hand. Even if he has been looked after by friends or a childminder previously, he was probably always in some kind of home environment when you left him. Now, of course, he will have to get used to "neutral territory" – usually at least twice the size of your living-room – and an organized hour-by-hour routine.

You yourself may want continuity in his upbringing more than anything else, with the playgroup set-up being an extension of home. If your child is used to a very warm atmosphere, lots of cuddles and you giving in to his requests, you may look for the same kind of environment with a high adult to child ratio, when choosing a nursery or playgroup. On the other hand, you may feel a few hours a week of structured activities and rather more discipline will do him a lot of good.

If your main concern is that your child gets a good educational start and will be encouraged to develop some reading and writing skills, a private or state-run nursery school will probably be your best bet. A state nursery class – by its very nature and location – will also help make the transition to big school as smooth as possible. Your child will already be familiar with the school and some of his classmates.

You may want to visit first on your own or perhaps with your partner or a friend. But do try and take your child with you before you make a final decision. After all, he is the person who will be spending most time there. Watching his reaction may help you to decide between different options, and the visit will be his first step towards feeling at home in his future surroundings.

Just use your common sense as you look around. If the place is too tidy, your child may not be allowed to play freely. On the other hand, if you feel worried about the general hygiene, then your child's health might be at risk. Watch how the staff deal with other children and you'll be able to judge if that's how you want your own child to be treated.

Inside, activities to look for include puzzles and building materials; books; drawing and painting; clay, sand and water; dressing-up clothes, and so on. Outside, space and equipment should encourage children to run around freely, to ride, climb, and play games. Observe whether the children are clean, well fed, and well supervised. The environment should be safe for your child, and free of obvious hazards.

Finally, do talk to the staff yourself. This way, you will find out whether or not you have the same ideas about looking after children, and whether or not they think it is important to talk to parents about what is happening both in the nursery and at home.

Once you've chosen a place for your child, it will be important for both of you that he settles in happily. Talk about your visit together, and reassure him about any new routines, particularly mealtimes or group activities. Things won't be so strange for him if he knows what to expect. If you possibly can, stay with him until he is settled. If this is really impossible, and there isn't another family member or friend who could go, you can make sure that he has something familiar with him, like a favourite toy or teddy bear.

Above all, reassure him that he will be coming home, and tell him who will be collecting him and when. He may need a bit of time before he feels secure in his new routine, and realizes that you haven't abandoned him for ever. But once he's settled, you should both be able to relax into your new, and challenging, way of life.

Nutrition

● See **Healthy Eating**

Observation

A newborn baby can see, but only gradually learns to focus and make sense of what his eyes perceive. As your child grows, the changes that take place are more to do with his ability to interpret what he sees – to name, describe and draw what he's looking at.

You can help your child to make these connections between his eyes, brain, body and the world outside by providing him with stimulating things to look at, toys, and activities. Pathways are being laid down in your child's brain and the more practice you give him in drawing and painting, looking at books and relating what he sees and does to words and ideas, the better he will become at doing these things by himself.

Your child may be interested in looking at books from the age of one, but at some time before his second birthday you will notice that he suddenly relates things in books to objects in the world outside. He may be confused at first; many children aged around 12-18 months try to pick objects out of books with their fingers or cannot recognize what a picture represents. Sometimes there is a sudden moment when a connection is made and a child gazes from a picture of a cat in a book to your pet curled up on the rug with great excitement.

Looking at books with your child gives you a wonderful opportunity to talk about shapes, colours, numbers and size. Your can do this with toys and objects all around you, too. When looking at a book, ask your child lots of questions: where is the monkey? how many birds are there? what colour is the apple? what is the witch going to do? Also let him point to things and tell him what they are, what colour, how big, and so on.

You can show him things he sees in books in real life too. Show him a teddy in a book and his own teddy, or look at a mug and then give him a drink in one. Make up stories about the objects in the picture or do some drawings based on the book.

At the age of one, your child may still be confused by the sight of himself or of you in a mirror. You will see him looking at himself, at you, then at both of your reflections. He is obviously wondering if there are suddenly two of you. He will reach out to touch the mirror and may be confused by the slippery surface where he expects to find a person. However, by the age of 18 months your child should have sorted out reflections and reality, although many children are confused if they see a reflection in an unexpected place – in a glass door, in a crowded shop, in a lake or pond.

You can play games with mirrors to help your child sort out what is happening. Put your finger on his nose in reality, then on his nose in the mirror. He can feel one but not the other! Games with multiple reflections in a dressing-table mirror, or with two mirrors, can also be fun. Once your child is two, he will be able to understand and say a great deal more about what he sees. He will be able to start sorting objects into different types and colours and sizes. This can be a game you play together; take a box of farm animals and select a cow, saying "Find me a cow like this". Then look for other animals, putting them in different piles. You can do this with fruit, with bricks of different shapes and colours, or many objects around the house. Talk about the differences between them; perhaps one cow is brown, the other black and white, but they are both cows!

Many toys have differently shaped or coloured components which you can sort out. Playing "shops" is a very good way of making sorting out objects fun – all the yellow bricks can be bananas, the red ones apples, the long ones sausages, and so on. You can also use counters or buttons or toy money. Your child can sort these into "pennies" and "pounds" at two or three, and by the age of five should be able to distinguish between different real coins.

From two onwards your child will be interested in drawing and painting. Let him experiment with finger paints, with thick paint and with runny paint, with wax crayons, (washable) felt-tips and pencils. Your child will also enjoy colouring in; help him choose which colour is most suitable for each part of the picture – often your child will fill in red grass and a purple sky! At two or three, don't expect your child to paint anything which you will recognize, to colour in accurately or, indeed, to concentrate for long; the whole point is simply to enjoy it.

By five, your child will probably draw people and objects and do much more detailed drawings, as he is now able to concentrate for much longer. At this age you can suggest he tries to draw certain things familiar to him or that he uses certain colours, but don't be tempted to stunt his spontaneous creativity in the pursuit of realism.

While a one-year-old has probably had fun with very simple jigsaws and play-trays where wooden pieces can be lifted out of a wooden tray by a small peg, by two he is ready to tackle proper jigsaws. Start with bold, simple designs which your child can fit into a wooden surround. You can progress to larger floor puzzles with larger pieces and then to those with more, smaller pieces. At two or three, ten-piece puzzles will probably be enough; at three or four, 25-piece puzzles will be more fun; and by the age of five your child may enjoy tackling more complex puzzles with up to 80 pieces, though you will probably need to help.

Help your child to tackle jigsaw puzzles by asking him to look carefully at each piece, at the lid of the box, and at the rest of the puzzle. It's usually easiest to start from the outside so you could ask him to look for the corners and the pieces with straight edges. Then you can help by asking questions like, "Where is the fireman's hat?" or "Which lady doesn't have a head yet?" Use colour and shape too and ask "Where is a piece with lots of red on it?" or "Is there a round piece anywhere?" Your child wants to feel that he has done it himself, so whenever possible let him put the piece in place, even if you have pointed out to him which piece fits where, and which way it goes.

At four or five your child will probably love those books of simple puzzles and activities which contain colouring-in, join-the-dots and spot the difference. You can buy a good supply cheaply, or even draw your own. "Spot the difference" is a good way of helping your child look at a picture carefully, as is looking for objects hidden in a picture. You will soon notice that the more your child practises these kinds of activities, the faster his eyes will solve them.

Children love memory games of any kind, and memory card and board games are just as popular now as they were with previous generations. Always start off with just a few cards to be identified and paired as young children get easily impatient and discouraged.

Alternatively, make up your own memory game by placing a few familiar objects on the table. Have your child look at them carefully, naming them one by one. Make him turn away, cover the objects with a cloth and then ask him how many he remembers. Or leave them uncovered, add or remove an object, and ask questions to find out if he's noticed.

Many young children spend quite a lot of time watching television and many parents worry about this. Watching too much television obviously means that your child has less time for other activities, and many very young children do become bored with TV, yet reluctant to switch it off.

However, television can be educational and can show children things it might be difficult – or expensive – to show them in real life. Just think of exotic wildlife and animal documentaries which most children – and adults – find fascinating. Try to select the programmes you think your child would enjoy and learn from though, and sometimes watch with him so that you can talk about the programme afterwards. It's best to switch off the television at the end of a programme, as research has shown that children quickly forget a programme if they immediately watch something else and don't have time to mentally digest and file away what they have just seen.

Out of doors, there are lots of ways you can encourage your child to look around and notice things – and make a game of it too. Talking to your child about everything you see will encourage him to take an interest in the world around him: show him the aeroplane in the sky, the bird in the hedgerow, the numbers on garden gates. When waiting at bus stops, you can make a game out of counting how many people go past with something blue on them – perhaps a scarf or a pair of shoes – or with older children they could each pick a different colour and see who gets the most numbers of passers-by in that colour before the bus arrives.

"I spy" is a great favourite, and an excellent way of passing an idle half-hour on a park bench. If you go shopping, you can ask your child to look out for certain things as you go round the supermarket, or ask him how many goods in the trolley begin with a "B". Or you can make "shopping cards" – take pieces of postcard-sized paper or card and draw or stick a picture of something you need on them – bread, yoghurt, tea, apples and so on. Your child can help you find the pictures in magazines, cut them out and stick them on, and then he can search the supermarket and match his picture with what's on the shelf.

You can help your child to get a lot more out of special treats like trips to the zoo or to the seaside if you spend a little time in preparation. First, talk to your child, perhaps read him a book with seaside scenes or zoo animals in it, and decide in advance what your child particularly wants to look at or do. Take a drawing book and crayons with you, so that when your child is tired from walking or playing you can sit down and do a drawing of a favourite animal or something that takes his fancy.

You can also write down some "quiz" questions before you go, relating to some of the things you will encounter during your outing, and see if your child can guess or discover the answers. At the zoo, you could ask questions like: what do penguins eat? can polar bears swim? are lions sleepy or do they run around all the time? are snakes wet or dry to look at and touch? By the sea, ask what can you find in rock-pools? what colour is seaweed? what does the white crest of the wave remind you of?

At the same time as encouraging your child's powers of observation, you should be on the look-out for any possible eye problems. These are not always obvious, so it's worth taking him for regular check-ups at an optician since the earlier a problem is detected, the better.

Colour blindness is less noticeable than short-sightedness (myopia) or a squint, and is very rare among girls, but some colour blindness occurs in about 8 per cent of boys. However, it is only with severe red/green colour blindness that there is usually any problem, as your child won't be able to read traffic lights or recognize other important "stop-go" and safety signals.

Most parents do not notice colour blindness with young children, thinking their confusion may be verbal rather than visual. If you're not sure and want to find out, make an appointment with the optician or raise the subject at your child's next developmental check-up.

Acquiring a child's-eye view of your surroundings will be just as much fun for you as discovering a continually new and exciting world is for your child. Some children are almost born scientific observers but if yours isn't, there are numerous ways in which you can stimulate and sharpen his awareness and his visual senses so that he makes the most of his potential.

◆ See also, **Eyesight**, **Memory**, **Painting and Drawing**, **Television and Videos**

Only Children

In the past, small families were the exception rather than the rule, but nowadays, effective contraception, a lower mortality rate in newborns and changing lifestyles have put an end to the vast families of the Victorian era. We now no longer need to have plenty of children to ensure some survive to adulthood and we do not, on the whole, rely on children to support us in our old age. So all the arguments for large families have gone and many couples choose to have just two or three children.

Families who opt for only one child, however, still tend to be at the receiving end of criticism because many people believe that an only child cannot be happy. Suggestions that they will be spoilt or over-indulged tend to be put forward along with hints that they may never learn to share toys or will be timid and shy as a result of never having to experience the rough and tumble of family life. Studies have shown that many of these old wives' tales are not true. What matters is how much love and attention any child receives.

Research has shown that only children are, in fact, very good at making friends. So are eldest children, but second and subsequent children are more likely to argue and refuse to share. This may be because only children do not have to share all the time and sharing occasionally is easier for them. It may also be that making friends is a skill we have to learn and only children may have more opportunities to observe their parents making friends.

Some only children do find it hard to cope with rows and disagreements. Brothers and sisters soon learn that rows have to be patched up, and however angry they are in the heat of the moment, it soon passes. This experience allows a child to understand and express his anger. Sometimes an only child can find it hard to find a safe way to express anger as friends may not be as tolerant as brothers and sisters.

It is important, therefore, that the parents of an only child find ways to allow their child to express his feelings and learn how to control emotions such as anger and hate. Adults argue and make up, and so do friends, but you may find you need to handle the situation with some care so that an only child does not feel threatened by his own strong emotions.

Language development is usually quite advanced in only children. Plenty of adult conversation seems to be essential to the development of language, so much so that twins, who often talk most to each other sometimes develop language more slowly than single children, and some even develop their own special form of language.

Even if an only child spends all his time with adults he will still apply the rules of language structure in this way and only learn the differences by hearing the language spoken around him. So he may well develop language faster than children in large families but he will learn it in the same way.

In some ways, only children and firstborn children are very similar. A firstborn is an only child for the vital first months or years. He is the centre of the family and, as such, benefits from the attention his parents can devote to him. This tends to make him feel confident and secure. Firstborn children often find the shock of the arrival of a second baby very traumatic. Some experts have suggested that they never quite recover from this shock and spend the rest of their lives striving to achieve just to please their parents and regain their place as the centre of the family.

This theory sounds a little extreme, but research has shown that high achievers tend to be the firstborn and only children. It may simply be that all that love and attention gives only children and the firstborns a great deal of confidence, so as they grow up they cope well with the world and all the challenges they meet.

First-born and only children tend to have a slightly higher IQ than younger brothers and sisters. There have been many theories put forward for this. It may well be because mothers are younger and usually fitter and well nourished when conceiving their first child. It may also be that an only child receives more attention and stimulation which can affect the IQ levels attained later in life. Certainly advocates of intensive learning programmes for children tend to suggest spacing a family widely.

Only children do not have to be old beyond their years or babyish – two accusations sometimes made. Given plenty of opportunities to play with other children and the emotional space to develop at their own rate, they can be perfectly happy, normal individuals.

There is no doubt that you can smother an only child, but this applies to individual children in larger families too. Many brothers and sisters will say that one sibling was "mummy's favourite" and it is very easy to spoil or over-indulge one child, often the youngest.

The parents of an only child may well find they need the company of other parents just as much as their child needs friends. Comparing your child with others helps to make you realize that even if he is going through a difficult stage, it is a perfectly normal difficult stage.

It is easy to fall into the trap of blaming every behavioural difficulty on the fact that your child is an only child, but remember your friends may well be blaming the same problems on the fact that they have just had another baby, or that their "problem" child is a first, middle or last one.

Painting and Drawing

Children love making things – and they particularly enjoy making things that they can keep. In this respect, drawings and paintings are different from other forms of creative play. They don't get knocked over or cleared away, like towers made with building blocks. Instead, they can be treasured. As your child learns to draw and paint, he will be able to see what he has done, show his pictures to you and his friends, display them proudly on the wall and perhaps even keep some of them for years to come. There are lots of things you can do to encourage and stimulate his interest and efforts (and do keep the "masterpieces" in a safe file or box to look back on as he grows older).

Long before he can draw as such, your child will love to scribble. Although his efforts may seem fairly aimless to you, he will be gaining experience at holding and manipulating a crayon, and he will be building the foundations essential for later drawing and writing. He'll also love seeing the effect of different colours on the paper.

Give him big, chunky, non-toxic crayons that he can hold easily and plenty of scrap paper. Don't worry if he doesn't hold them properly straight away. Most very young children start with a "fist" grip and only later move on to a proper "pincer" grip, using their thumb and index finger. And don't worry which hand he uses. He may seem to use one, then the other, before settling on the one that comes most naturally to him.

The important thing whenever anyone is painting or drawing is that they enjoy themselves and have the freedom to develop their skills. This is just as vital for children as for adults. But make sure your child has lots of paper available, otherwise he may be tempted to scribble where you'd rather he didn't!

Don't expect your child to produce a recognizable picture straight away. He will probably be able to make a mark on a piece of paper with a crayon, if you show him how, when he's about a year old, and later he'll love to scribble vigorously, making strokes and circles – but he may not be drawing and painting pictures freely until he's about four. Whatever he produces in the early days however, you're still likely to think of them as great works of art.

When he's three, his pictures of people will probably show a circle for the head and a couple of other parts of the body. But don't be surprised if his first portraits of you show your legs or arms growing out of your head! With practice, by the time he's about five, he will be including about half a dozen parts of the body fairly accurately.

You can help your child to develop pencil control by drawing him simple shapes to copy and giving him pictures to colour in. But don't forget to give him lots of opportunity to make his own pictures, without any help from you. Creativity means finding his own way, rather than doing what you want him to do.

Remember, drawing doesn't have to be confined to oblong pieces of paper and pencil or crayons. The greater the variety of materials you can provide, the more your child wil feel excited about experimenting. Encourage him to draw standing at a makeshift easel or a proper child's version if you can afford one. For an improvised easel, you can always use clothes pegs or a large bull-dog clip to fix paper to the top of a children's blackboard.

As your child gets older, he will also love to draw on different shapes of paper – try long thin strips, or shapes like circles and triangles, for a change. Different types of paper may also encourage him to experiment or develop his drawings in different ways. Watch how he uses lined or squared paper, compared with plain paper, and give him different coloured paper too from time to time.

You can also give your child different things to draw with. Chunky wax crayons are best when he's first learning how to hold things and practising scribbling. But once he's got a reasonably firm grip, he'll enjoy being more adventurous. You'll find there's a whole range of materials available to choose from, including felt-tips, pastels, chalks, pencils, crayons and even charcoal, but remember to check that anything you give your child is non-toxic. And try to encourage him to put the tops on felt-tip pens to prevent them drying out.

You can also encourage him to use some of these materials in different ways. For example, wax crayons, chalks and charcoal can be used to make rubbings of all sorts of objects. You can take them with you on a walk or a visit to the park, and make wonderful rubbings of tree bark or, at home, make rubbings of leaves and coins.

Although painting can be messy, as long as you're prepared it can be great fun. Once your child is two, he will enjoy painting simple pictures. He'll need a big brush with a long handle to start with. Small thin brushes of the type provided in traditional paint boxes are much too fiddly at this stage. He also needs to be able to see the results of his efforts if he's going to be encouraged to continue. Give him bright colours – yellow, blue, green and red – and only give him a few colours at a time.

It will be easiest for him to paint standing up, either at a low table or an easel. To avoid spills, you can buy paint pots which have lids with a hole in the top for his brush. Or you can try making your own out of old cottage cheese containers.

If you use pots without lids (perhaps the bottoms of old washing-up liquid bottles), don't forget to put only a small amount of paint in each one in case of accidents. To keep the pots upright you can make a holder to stand them in by cutting a hole for each pot in a large piece of foam rubber.

To begin with, providing a brush for each pot is the best way to keep the colours from getting mixed together. As your child gets older, he should be able to use an extra pot of water to clean his brush between colours. Then he'll be able to use a palette or a paint box.

Don't be disappointed if you find it hard to interpret your child's first attempts. Sometimes, he may just be experimenting with different shapes, and watching the effect of one colour on another. At other times, he may have a definite subject in mind, but it may be hard to make this out.

Often pictures that start as one thing turn into another halfway through. Although you may be curious to know what he's painting, beware of forcing him to describe or label it unless he wants to. He may give you an answer just to please you – "It's a plane" – but he may just have been making a pretty pattern. Whatever it is, do take an interest and give him lots of praise for his efforts. And if he does want to tell you what it is, then it's a nice idea to write a simple description – for example, "My Mum" – at the bottom of the picture.

Your child may use some of his paintings to describe the world around him. He is likely to paint people (and animals) who are important in his life, his home, the places he visits regularly, and any familiar activities – shopping, travelling on the bus or by car, and playing in the park. Favourite TV programmes also rate highly along with well-known fairy stories.

Sometimes, children can express themselves better in drawing or painting than in words. If a particular incident has distressed or confused your child, he may use his paintings to try to understand it better or express how he feels. Painting has long been recognized as a useful outlet for emotions, and this is the basis of art therapy with both adults and children.

Sometimes just making a picture – or even a series of pictures – about an incident may help him to understand it. You may find that talking to your child about his painting, rather than about the incident it describes, will help you to understand how he feels, while helping him to work it out.

Don't just associate painting with brushes. Paint can be put on to paper using lots of different things, and your child will have fun trying out a whole variety of objects such as small rags, bits of sponge, or string. Fill up a roll-on deodorant bottle with paint for your child to use as a giant ball-point pen. Or introduce him to the idea of printing.

Printing can be done using natural objects, such as leaves, potatoes, carrots and other root vegetables, and household objects, such as cotton reels, jar lids, and anything with an interesting texture or surface. If you use vegetables, slice them so that they are easy to hold and have a good interesting surface for stamping on paper.

One of the easiest ways to organize printing is to place a sponge (or several sheets of kitchen paper) on a shallow container, like a biscuit tin lid, and pour a bit of paint over it. Give your child another tray with objects for printing. Then show him how to press each object on to the paint pad before stamping it on paper.

Many children love exploring different substances with their hands. Finger painting is fun, because it allows your child to discover the feel of paint at the same time as creating different pictures with it. You can buy ready-prepared finger paints, or mix your own. Thick finger paint can be used straight on to paper, plastic or even a glass window. And it is easy to wash off.

You can make your own finger paints using ordinary wallpaper paste (without a fungicide) and dry powder paint. You can mix them in advance, storing them in a jar ready for use, or make the preparation part of the fun. First, mix the wallpaper paste following the instructions, making it thin enough to just run off the spoon. Place a tablespoonful of paste on to the painting surface, then sprinkle a teaspoonful of dry powder colour on the top. Then simply let your child's hands do the rest!

Bubble painting is another interesting paint technique. First make sure your child can blow – rather than suck – through a straw. Then put an inch or so of thin paint in the bottom of a small bowl, adding a couple of drops of washing-up liquid. Give your child a straw, and show him how to hold one end in the paint while he blows gently through the other. He will be amazed at the way the paint bubbles up higher and higher. When he's made a good cluster of bubbles, help him to place a piece of paper carefully on top of the bowl. The bubbles will burst on to the paper, leaving a beautiful and unusual pattern. Use bowls holding different colours of paint, one after the other, to make multi-coloured bubble pictures.

Your child will be proud to see his favourite paintings and drawings displayed on the wall, fridge or cupboard door. Putting up new ones at regular intervals will add variety to the display and stimulate him to produce more. Let him help you choose which ones to keep and which ones to throw away and he'll feel involved from start to finish.

Paper Play

Even the youngest toddler will enjoy playing with a soft, scrunchy ball made from crumpled-up newspaper, rolling it along the floor and throwing it up into the air. And an older child will discover that paper is not just a surface for drawing and painting on, but that it can be cut, folded, stuck and manipulated in a variety of interesting ways. If you show your child how to fold a simple paper aeroplane this will give him hours of fun.

If you have an older child who is good with his hands, you may want to buy special paper for him to use. Investigate large stationery stores, department stores and artists' materials shops – they all stock a wide variety of types of paper in different sizes, weights, colours and textures and as long as you avoid hand-made paper, most art papers are not too expensive. You could make the outing into a treat, perhaps to buy "that special piece of yellow paper" for a particular project.

You will have to supervise your child when he is working with paper and adhesives, helping him plan and carry out his ideas. Scissors with rounded ends are a must for safety reasons, but there may be times when a sharply pointed pair and your assistance are needed. Never leave a child alone with a pair of sharp scissors.

Crumple several different coloured papers into balls of various sizes, then have a competition with your child to see how far each ball goes when it is rolled along the floor. Does the yellow ball roll further than the red ball?

Line up several empty cardboard packets on the floor, pretend they are skittles and try knocking them over with paper balls. To make the game more fun, you could cover the boxes with plain paper and draw a face on each one, or stick cut-out magazine pictures on the front.

If your child is beginning to recognize numbers, draw a large number on each covered box with brightly coloured markers, then play the game by asking him to knock down one of the numbers.

Young children love to make music and they will delight in playing the following strange instruments.

Roll a small sheet of paper into a tube, fasten with sticky tape down the edge and show your child how to blow down it to make a tooting noise. Roll more tubes, making some narrower or wider in diameter and longer or shorter than the first one and compare the different sounds they make. Try making the tube wider at one end, like an ice-cream cornet, and let your child blow down each end in turn.

Fold a piece of tissue paper over the teeth of a small comb (choose one with rounded teeth) and show your child how to press his lips to the paper and blow to make a buzzing noise. Complete the orchestra by taking a couple of small empty cardboard boxes, add a few dried peas or beans and seal the tops with sticky tape to make a pair of impromptu maracas!

Your child's cutting out techniques can easily be improved with repetition, but you will have to make this into a fun activity.

If your child has an interest in a particular subject such as animals, flowers or cars, for example, either buy or make him a large scrapbook and suggest he cuts out the picture he likes from old magazines or birthday and Christmas cards. He can stick them in the scrapbook himself using one of the lipstick-type paper adhesives. Emphasize the fact that this is "his" book and encourage him to try and cut round the pictures as neatly as he can.

To make a special scrapbook, perhaps as a birthday present, add a sheet of folded card to the outside of the pieces of paper and then sew through all the layers. You could decorate the cover with your child's name and some cut-out pictures and cover it with self-adhesive, transparent film to make the scrapbook more durable.

From sticking pictures into a scrapbook it is a natural progression to making collage pictures, where your child is beginning to learn how to combine isolated images to make one complete picture. Suggest he makes a picture of somewhere he knows well: his house, the inside of a shop, or a local garden or park. Help him choose and cut out pictures from magazines and greeting cards. Use a stiff piece of coloured paper for the background and encourage his creativity by suggesting he adds details to his collage with felt-tip pens or paints. He could also stick down scraps of fabric, lace and ribbon; lengths of string and knitting yarn; drinking straws and corrugated card as well as brightly coloured gummed paper shapes.

Three-dimensional tissue paper collages are fun to make and can be attempted by quite young children with a little help.

Begin by painting the shape of a tree trunk and several branches on a large piece of paper. Use a big brush and make the shapes strong and bold. Then tear pastel shades of tissue paper into small pieces and show your child how to crumple each piece into a loose ball. Put a dab of adhesive on one of the tree branches and let him press a ball of tissue into the blob of glue. Repeat all over the branches to make the tree blossom. Use this technique to make pictures of his teddy, a bowl of hyacinths, the family pet or mummy wearing a tweed coat.

Rows of dancing dolls are always fun to make, but you will need to offer some help with both folding and cutting until your child is more dextrous and can easily manipulate a pair of scissors himself. The end result is always fascinating, whether a first attempt cut roughly out of newspaper or a special present made from cartridge paper.

Begin by cutting out a long strip of paper, the stiffer the better. Then show your child how to fold the strip backwards and forwards to make a concertina, pressing each fold in place with his hand. Then help him draw half a doll shape against the folded edge, making sure the arms and legs stretch right across the paper, and cut round the outline.

Let him unfold the row of dancing dolls himself and see how they all hold hands and their feet dance along together. Encourage him to colour in their clothes and faces carefully with felt-tip pens. As well as doll shapes, try making a row of houses, animals or trees instead, but take care that the shapes will join up at the top and bottom when the strip is unfolded.

Snowflake patterns are made in a similar way to dancing dolls, but this time you begin with a large circle of paper. Fold this in half three or four times, press the folds firmly in place then show your child how to cut large and small v-shaped notches into the folded edges and along the top. When the circle is unfolded, he will have made a snowflake. Encourage him to make several, as each one will have a different pattern. Small snowflakes in a range of bright colours make attractive Christmas decorations – make a hole near the edge, thread with of gold or silver yarn and hang on the tree.

An older child can make a piece of "stained glass" by cutting a snowflake out of black paper then sticking small pieces of coloured tissue paper over the holes. Display this on the inside of a window and it will look really effective when the sun shines.

Papier maché is another very popular form of paper play. There are two types of papier maché, but the pulp method is the most suitable for young children to use. The pulp can be used as a modelling material; it will harden when dry and can then be painted and varnished. You will need to prepare the pulp in advance, and make sure you cover your work surface and surrounding floor with newspaper.

The following papier maché pulp recipe will make enough for two or three children to use in an afternoon and it needs to be prepared about three hours in advance. Make less or more according to your needs.

You will need
1¼ litres warm water
250 g plain white flour
2 or 3 newspapers

1. Tear up the newspapers into rough strips about 2.5 cm wide, then tear the strips across into small pieces.

2. Put the flour into an old plastic washing-up bowl and gradually add the water, stirring vigorously to break up any lumps.

3. Stir in the torn newspaper and leave to stand for about three hours, squeezing it with your hands at intervals.

When the pulp is ready (when the paper is really soft and the mixture has a clay-like consistency), spread a piece of polythene sheeting on the work surface and give your child a large handful of pulp. Show him how to model with it and shape lots of different objects: a plate of cakes and buns for a doll's tea party, a chunky bracelet for himself, a model of the family cat or dog.

When he has finished modelling, carefully transfer the objects on to a clean piece of polythene and leave them in a warm, dry place for at least two days to dry out and harden off completely. You can speed this process up by baking them in a cool oven. Then help him paint them and you can finish them off with one or two coats of non-toxic paper varnish. One of the easiest varnishes to use is PVA medium thinned down with water. Although playing with paper is much less messy than painting or printmaking (with the exception of papier maché modelling), the following simple precautions will help you avoid problems and ensure that you and your children have a thoroughly enjoyable and successful paper play session:

● Make sure you have an adequate supply of paper, a suitable adhesive, safety scissors and sticky tape before you begin. Nothing is more frustrating for a child than to run out of paper or adhesive right in the middle of creating a collage. You should try to find a supply of inexpensive paper – rolls of lining paper from a DIY shop, unwanted computer printouts from a friend who works in an office, cheap unlined pads in different sizes from your local printer or photocopy shop.

There is also a wide range of paper adhesives suitable for young children. These are non-toxic, difficult to tip over or spill and will wash out of clothes without leaving a stain. The easiest ones to use are either shaped like a giant lipstick or come in a chunky plastic bottle with a brush fitted inside the lid.

● Whichever type of adhesive you choose, always put the lid back on when it is not in use – this will prevent it from drying out and make it last longer.

● When using adhesive, cover the surface of your table with a layer of old newspaper. You may also like to cover the floor to catch spills and pieces of surplus paper.

● Although the paper adhesives made specially for children are washable, dress your child in old clothes, play apron or smock just in case, and mop up spills as soon as they occur.

● Buy safety scissors with rounded ends which are specially designed for young children. Never leave your child alone with a pair of sharp scissors, even for a moment.

● Allow plenty of time for each session and let your child help you tidy away when the session is finished, then admire his efforts.

● Work outside during summer if you can, although this will be less successful on a breezy day.

Party Entertainment

Children acquire all sorts of skills – physical, social and intellectual – not just from strictly "educational" activities but also from playing games with other children. Party games are no exception and, although designed for sheer fun and entertainment, they will challenge your child's abilities just as much as an everyday routine such as getting dressed. With practice and repetition, he'll soon learn to anticipate what the next stage will be and what will be required specifically of him.

Long before "fair play", "team spirit", or "competitiveness" mean anything to him, he will enjoy the chance to pit his wits and skills against others. From as early as two years old, party games offer any child the opportunity to learn game skills that will see them through their childhood and beyond.

A lot of early party games highlight one particular skill or ability. You'll be amazed at your little one identifying voices from a mere squeal when blindfolded and playing "Squeak-piggy-squeak" – even though you know he can recognize voices normally; or at his powers of observation when he spots the smallest toes peeking out from the curtain while playing "Hide-and-seek".

The all-time favourite for the very young, "Pass the parcel", on the other hand, will put your little one's manual dexterity to the test as he quickly tries to remove layer after layer of paper from the parcel. To play the game, seat all the children in a circle and make them pass the parcel round from one to the other until the music stops. Whoever has the parcel at that moment has to start to unwrap it, and continue passing it around as soon as the music starts playing again. The winner is the child who removes the last layer – and gets the present. To keep young children happy during this game it's a good idea to place a small sweet in each layer: this way everyone gets something.

Party games provide children with more than a bit of fun and the opportunity to test and display their social skills too. In joining in with their friends, and probably some children that they have not met before, they will learn the subtle codes of behaviour, such as fairness, patience, and sensitivity towards others. These qualities will serve them well throughout their lives.

In party surroundings, a child may well realize that having a tantrum achieves little once he is outside the circle of his own family and that displaying a virtue such as sharing toys or sweets is a happier way of getting along with people and gaining their friendship and respect.

So, whether you are giving a party for your own child or helping with the organization of someone else's, it can be as well to have a working knowledge of a few of the staple games for such occasions and the particular skills they require.

There are several different ways of categorizing children's games – there are moving-around and sitting-down ones, team games or "fight-for-yourself" games, some that require props, some that don't. When planning a party make sure that you have a good mix of all the different types and that they are suitable for the age group you have invited. Four- to five-year-olds may well be able to remember and play by a few simple rules but you'll need to keep things a lot simpler for the younger ones.

This is where "do as I say" or "do as I do" games such as "Simon says" come into their own. From an early age, children show themselves to be great mimics of those around them – indeed this is one of the principle ways in which they learn how to do things in life, and it is this ability that the game relies on for success. An adult master of ceremonies announces that Simon says to put hands on heads for example, while doing it himself, and the children all follow suit. The only rule is that any child who puts his hands on his head when the all-important words "Simon says" have been omitted from the command is out.

As with all games, have a trial run first to let everyone see how the game is played and then start for real. Even the two-year-olds will display remarkable concentration when it comes to listening for the key phrase although you might like to give those under three an extra "life".

Blindfold games rely on touch, hearing or memory. "Squeak-piggy-squeak" is a good test of the last two of these although you can put a player's memory off balance (literally) by turning them round two or three times before they set off to seek their first "piggy".

To play the game, seat all but the child who is "it" around the edge of the room. Blindfold the remaining player, give him a cushion and tell him that he has to put it on another player's lap, sit down and ask them to "squeak-piggy-squeak". If the blindfolded player guesses correctly whom he has sat on, that person becomes "it" and once he or she is blindfolded everyone moves around. You'll need to indulge younger players a little, especially when it comes to climbing up on laps, but all children love the game.

For "Blind man's buff", allow the children to walk slowly around the blindfolded player calling to him. When the blindfolded player touches another child, he has two or three guesses at whom he has captured. To keep the pace of the game going, you can always "sacrifice" yourself once or twice and give a clue to the blindfolded one.

"Musical chairs" is another old party favourite and a great test of a child's powers of anticipation. You'll see the tension in the room rise to fever pitch as the chairs vanish one by one and the remaining players nervously eye the remaining chairs, each other and the hand at the cassette or record player. (Chairs can be a bit cumbersome for the younger members of the two to five age group so you may prefer to use cushions instead.)So that the prize-winner is not only the person at the end of the game left sitting on the sole chair or cushion, suggest that players dance around while the music is playing and then, at the end, award a prize or points to the best dancer regardless of when they were disqualified from the game. You can use this kind of tactic as a valuable "handicapping" system so that no one falls too far behind, or gets too far in front, of anyone else.

Dancing is also one of the key elements of a game that tests a child's concentration and patience – "Musical statues". In this game, children dance around until the music stops and then they must "freeze" in position until it starts again. Anyone moving before then is out.

But it's not just tests of their individual skills that children love. Team games that require co-ordination are popular too.

For "Pass the balloon", line the children up in two or three teams, depending on the number of children and the space available. The child at the head of each line is given a balloon and, on the command "go", has to pass it over their head to the next child. This goes on until the balloon reaches the last child who then runs to the front of the line and starts the whole process off all over again. The game is over when the first team has their original child at the front of the line once more.

You can also organize a game of indoor "football" with a balloon and exercise everyone's hand-eye co-ordination. To play, the two teams sit facing each other on opposite sides of the room and try to hit the balloon over the heads of the other team. So that everyone has a chance of hitting the balloon, seat the children a little way apart and tell them not to move from there.

The heady mix of party games and party food will send most children into raptures of delight but the two do not always go together successfully. Little tummies full of sandwiches and jelly need time to recover before activities start again. To keep them still during the "after-tea" lull, try performing some magic tricks, or an improvised "Punch and Judy" show. Play sitting still games such as "I spy", or if you have one, show a video for half an hour or so.

Although an hour or two of good fun should be the central aim of any series of party games, they inevitably bring into play a whole wealth of social behaviour that will be required throughout your little one's life. Taking turns and being a good sport are just two of the characteristics of a contented child and a contented adult too. And learning to lose gracefully is hard in the beginning but it plays a vital part in getting on with playmates.

Most two- to five-year-olds will take part in party games and never question that the referee's decision is final. For the benefit of those who have not yet learned to be good losers, however, you should always be ready to start the next game quickly. Many children will forget their loss as soon as the fun starts again. Use a system of forfeits for bad temper. You could deduct a point from their overall score or "award" a silly hat to wear. It's also a good idea to keep spare "props" for your games so that you can carry on if someone decides that "it's my ball and I'm not going to give it back!". This avoids fuelling the issue and keeps the party going.

Although it is traditional to award sweets as prizes, there are other prizes that little ones will like just as much and that will do more to help preserve their teeth. Try mini packets of raisins, or individual items of fruit such as apples and tangerines. Large balloons on which you have written the children's names go down well, as do individual toys taken from inexpensive cut-price gift sets.

When you have a large number of children running around the house, for safety's sake as well as your own peace of mind, it's as well to declare some places "no go" areas. These might be the kitchen, the bathroom, and if possible, whichever room the TV and other expensive breakables such as hi-fi equipment are kept in. Otherwise move these items into an out-of-bounds room. Of course children may need to use the bathroom but make sure they are supervised if possible.

At any party there is bound to be at least one shy child. If you suspect that a particular child will be shy, ask their parents to stay for as long as necessary to get them involved in the games. Many slightly older children have a natural caring disposition towards younger ones, and you may be able to "pair off" shy and caring children. Always be prepared to act as companion for a shy child. Your duties may not last long – it's quite likely that you will be abandoned in the first rush of excitement, but make sure you have the telephone number of any absent parents just in case their child simply isn't happy.

As long as you prepare games (and any "props") in advance, and you ensure that there is at least one prize per child, there is no reason why your child's party should not be a roaring success.

◆ See also, **Family Gatherings**

Penis (Caught in Zip)

Little boys who are not quite used to grown-up trousers with zip fronts do risk getting their penises caught when they are zipping or unzipping their trousers in a hurry.

This form of accident happens most often when the child is in a rush after going to the lavatory and is rapidly trying to get zipped up and back to what he was doing. Equally, if he is not paying attention when he gets dressed or if he is hurrying because he is late when going out, he may catch himself in his zip.

It makes sense not to dress your little boy in zipped trousers until he is old enough to handle a zip competently. Make sure he knows that he must take care when fastening a zip, and never hurry him when he is in the lavatory or dressing for school. It is much better to help him with dressing if there is a need for speed.

Having his penis trapped in a zip's teeth is painful as well as alarming for the child. Stop him from panicking by being calm and reassuring. It can help to put an ice cube wrapped in a clean handkerchief on the penis to numb it while you check to see what has happened. If you think you can safely deal with the problem yourself, get the little boy to sit or lie comfortably while you do so.

When the zip's teeth have safely been extracted gently apply a soothing antiseptic ointment to the injury, and continue to do this several times a day until the penis is no longer sore. If the child complains of pain it is safe to give him paracetamol in the correct dosage for his age. He will probably feel more comfortable dressed in pull-on trousers or shorts for a few days afterwards.

If you think that you cannot free the penis yourself, get the child to your doctor's surgery or the nearest accident and emergency ward, holding some wrapped ice over the injury to numb it. If you do not have your own transport, it may be necessary to call an ambulance.

In the surgery or hospital, the child will be given a local anaesthetic and then the zip will be removed. Afterwards he will be quite sore for a few days, especially when passing water, and you will be advised if any further treatment is necessary.

Pets

Any parent of a toddler will tell you how much their child loves dogs and cats, and older children are often enthralled by trips to the zoo. One of the most delightful experiences for a parent is to watch the intense curiosity and joy on her baby's face whenever a dog wanders past, or the family cat washes itself. These creatures are fascinating to a small child because they move and "talk" in a way that is so different from himself, or his mummy and daddy.

We all know children who treat their dog as their best friend, and have long talks with – and even confide their secrets to – this four-legged pal. But by keeping a pet in the family, we can also develop a sense of loving care in our children.

As every parent knows, pets do add to their own work load and to the household budget, and they can cause some irritation and squabbles in the family.

You must think about the long term and whether or not you want to be committed to a pet for its lifetime. Yet, don't be put off by the possible hassles caused by a pet. Instead, choose the animal most suited to you, your home and the age of your children.

Dogs

Like humans, every animal has its own personality, and some are more gentle than others. There are thousands of breeds of dog and certain characteristics have been specially bred in each breed. Everyone knows that there are working dogs, like collies, and that there are those often bred for guard duties like Alsatians. If you are choosing a dog for your home, ask a local vet or the local RSPCA to advise you.

Generally speaking, a small or medium-sized dog, such as a cocker spaniel, is a good choice for a family with small children. They are not as alarming as a large dog, they are cheaper to feed and – usually – they make less toilet mess to clear up.

If you are choosing a new puppy it is a good idea to spend an hour or so with the litter before you pick out the one you want. You will find that one puppy will be livelier and more interested in you than the others appear to be.

It takes a while to house-train a puppy, and if you are coping with a small baby and a toddler, you are not going to enjoy teaching a dog to be clean too. Not only that, you will be faced with the problem of hygiene because your toddler will take time to learn that he must stay away from the dog's toilet area.

You may also encounter problems from a dog you owned before your baby arrived. All dogs have a strong sense of territory and, also, devotion to you. Take care that your dog does not feel completely neglected or ousted by the baby. This can be a serious problem, and you and your partner should discuss your dog's needs. Both of you will be absorbed and exhausted by the demands of your new baby. Will either of you have the time or the energy to give the dog the attention he is accustomed to and actually needs?

Remember, even a little and cheerful dog must be trained. It has to learn to respond to orders; to come in, go out, sit and stop, and, to get the best out of your dog, it is a very good idea to attend dog discipline classes with the animal. You will find that your older children will be eager to go to such classes, and it will be part of their pleasure in getting to know their dog.

Generally speaking, if you do not already own a dog, it is probably better to look for another kind of pet for your small child. Wait until your child is five or six before bringing a new puppy home. When he is that old, he can learn more quickly how to cope with a dog and also your own workload will not be so heavy.

Cats

Cats are popular pets in most homes because they involve less work than a dog, and they are, in many ways, safer with small children. True, a cross cat may give a small and careless hand a scratch or two, but most times a cat will not turn fierce – it will just stalk off from an irritating human. Many people believe that cats are stand-offish and aloof but this is not altogether a true picture of the domestic cat. If you give your kitten a lot of attention – hold it in your lap, stroke it often, scratch its ears – you will find that it will grow into an affectionate and playful adult.

Your toddler will get an enormous amount of pleasure from a cat with this temperament. He will love rolling a ping-pong ball and watching the cat leap after it, or pulling a piece of string for the cat to chase after.

It is up to you to make sure that your cat is warm and friendly, so that when a new baby arrives, the cat will not retreat to its own aloof world. If you introduce a kitten to your toddler, you will still have to spend time giving the kitten a lot of physical attention to make sure that it will grow to accept the attentions of your child. If you leave the kitten to fend for itself, it may well develop into a private creature and your child will not get much pleasure from this particular pet.

As with dogs, there are numerous cat breeds such as the beautiful Burmese or the very intelligent Siamese, but most of us are happy with an ordinary household moggy of no particular class. Besides, we do not need to worry so much about cat breeds. They are often developed for fur length, colour or appearance and not, as with dogs, for their strength and ferocity.

Birds and fish

If you have limited space and feel at ease with caged birds, a budgie or canary will please even a very small baby. Remember, just the sight of a bird can thrill and entertain your baby. Some of these birds, which are bred to be caged, are gorgeous in colour and they can be very active and comical. Give your bird a large cage, with "toys" like a mirror, little swings and stepladders. Hang the cage where your child can see and hear the bird.

Fish are also colourful and lovely to watch. Even a small aquarium or the traditional goldfish bowl will allow your child to watch and enjoy the colour and movement of the fish. Again, you will find a wonderful variety of colours and shapes among the fish on sale at pet shops. These are, of course, ideal pets for flat dwellers with no access to gardens or parks.

Ideal first pets

When your baby starts growing into a walking, talking person and is coming up to his third birthday, animals like rabbits, hamsters, guinea-pigs and gerbils are an ideal introduction to pet ownership.

Their great advantage as pets for small children is that they are not very time-consuming and they can be safely contained in a hutch or cage. With dogs and cats, however, you would have the nagging worry of whether your child was safe alone with them, or indeed vice versa. You must make sure your child treats the family pet with respect.

You can develop a "care routine" with these animals and your toddler will soon learn the routine and enjoy being part of it. So, the rabbits are fed at the same time every day; their play time when you let them out to hop about is also regular, as is the cleaning of the hutch. Your little one will enjoy those times when he can trot after the rabbits, or hold them in his little lap. He will be entertained watching the hamsters or the gerbils racing round their cage, playing with the wheels and tunnels you have given them for exercise.

Your child will help with the routine and he will absorb all the basic lessons in the care and responsibility of a pet. This is an important step towards that great moment when he will own a dog or a cat and have to take care of it. Even among these smaller animals there are a variety of breeds. Do some research, for there are breeds which are extra docile and gentle.

Hygiene

Whatever pet you choose, do find out exactly what sort of hygiene precautions you must take. There are some diseases which humans can pick up from animals and although these are comparatively rare, it is important to keep your animals clean Dog faeces must be picked up and disposed of efficiently. There are now chemical loos, which you can install in your garden, and safely throw any mess into.

Cats are by nature much cleaner and more modest than dogs, but if you keep a litter box indoors for your feline friend, it must be cleaned regularly and your toddler must not be allowed near it. (Pregnant women should not handle soiled cat litter as an infection may be passed on to the unborn child.) Your rabbit hutch, hamster cage or the like, must be regularly cleaned and aired, as much for the animal's comfort as for your own and your family's health concerns.

Feeding dishes should be cleaned as soon as they are empty, and must be washed separately from the family dishes. Make sure your animal has a regular supply of water and always keep your toilet lid closed in case a thirsty or curious animal should investigate it.

Grooming is essential. Keep brushes and combs scrupulously clean to avoid spreading any fleas. Though both cats and dogs should be brushed regularly, only dogs need to be actually bathed.

Whatever animal or bird you choose, take it as soon as possible to your local vet for a health check-up. Find out what inoculations and injections, if any, your pet should have and ask your vet for advice on the general care of the animal. If you have chosen a cat or dog, it may be wise to take out insurance against vets' bills. This health insurance is usually quite inexpensive and most vets carry advertisements for the service in their waiting rooms.

Although an affectionate dog is fun to be around, it is best to discourage it from licking anybody's face. And always ensure your child washes his hands after touching a pet, and if he is scratched or bitten, take him to the doctor in case an infection sets in.

Death of pets

Before choosing a pet it is useful to know, and take into consideration, the average lifespan of various animals:

Mouse	2–3 years
Hamster	2–3 years
Budgie	5 years
Rabbit	4–5 years
Cat	10–15 years
Dog	12–18 years

It is quite likely, and inevitable in some cases depending on the animal, that a family pet will die when your child is still quite young. Coming to terms with the cycle of life is an important part of growing up, and in a sense, the death of a loved pet can help this. When this happens, always let your child grieve. Allow him to sob and talk to him about the pet. Remember your child's memory is fairly short. If he is allowed to express his emotions, he will soon forget his pain. If you can, give the pet a burial with a little ceremony of flowers and a few thoughtful words, but if not, hold a little memorial ceremony, also with flowers.

As your children grow, they will learn a bit about life in general from the animal world. A pet will prepare your child for future relationships and responsibility, but, apart from all this, pets give an endearing and comical note to many aspects of family life.

Photographs

No matter how automatic your camera is, taking good pictures requires a little concentration, thought and time. You cannot hope to be a great photographer and a brilliant party organizer, too. So, if you want a good photographic record of a special event, let someone else do a share of the organizing while you concentrate on your camera-work.

Even when armed with the latest equipment, your vision and skill behind the lens are the most important elements in taking a good shot. Not everyone has an artist's eye, but don't worry; following a few straightforward tips can make anybody into a competent photographer. You will still make mistakes, but your success rate will be much improved.

Good composition is crucial; all too often, family snaps feature a small child and an awful lot of confusing background – chairs and the like. Much better to fill the frame with the child. Either get in close with the camera or use a larger lens from further away. Focus in on just the head and shoulders for a strong, detailed portrait.

Get down to the child's level too. If a baby can see you, he or she will respond more readily. If they are at the crawling stage, lie down on the floor with them.

Keep backgrounds simple so they do not detract from your real subject. A plain wall or sofa is generally more effective than a patterned background.

The right background can enhance a shot. Plain brick walls are a good choice; while a wall with a mural can produce an amusing picture. Foliage is another good background but make sure it doesn't appear to be growing out of someone's head.

The contrasts between the child's small size and the adult-sized world can be telling. A shot of a toddler in front of your parked car might well produce a good picture.

The key to good action shots is to use a fast shutter speed (if your camera is adjustable) that will freeze the action. If your child is carrying out a repetitive action, for example on a swing, you should have time to select your shot. Focus on the swing at the bottom of its arch when it is coming towards you. The hair flying in the breeze will be enough to suggest a sense of movement.

If the game is a more unpredictable one, focusing can be difficult. If you have a 28 mm or 35 mm wide-angle lens, move right in close and snap the picture. Accurate focusing is much less critical with a wide-angle lens.

With group shots the difficulty is holding everyone's attention. A tripod can help, as you can more easily do or say something that will get them all looking at the camera. Alternatively, get someone to stand behind you and attract their attention. Pulling a face at the right moment should get them all laughing.

A wide-angle lens is useful for dramatic hand-held shots. Get in among the children, so they are all crawling around the lens. They will enjoy it and you will almost certainly get a lively shot.

Two interesting variations, once again with a wide-angle lens, are worth a try if you want an unusual picture. Lie on your back and get them to peer down over you. Alternatively, stand on a chair and have them look up at you – this goes down well at parties.

Though they may loathe you for it in later years, shots of your children in their less agreeable moments can make an interesting addition to the family album! The next time one of them throws a tantrum, reach for the camera and get snapping. If nothing else, it will probably make you feel better. Children can be beautiful – and funny – when they are angry.

The key to taking good candid shots is patience. Keep the camera to hand and wait for your opportunity. Children tend to go through a period of being camera-shy, but later they become quite precocious and want to appear in every shot you are taking. Their attention span, however, is quite short and they will soon lose interest and get on with something else. This is the moment to take those natural shots. It helps if you have a long lens and can shoot from some distance away, where they are unaware of your interest.

Professional photographers are almost obsessed with lighting, and rightly so – it can make or mar a picture. The most flattering light is soft light, the sort you find outdoors in the early morning, late afternoon and early evening. It brings out the best skin tones and casts a warm glow, whereas a harsh midday sun bleaches out features and casts hard shadows.

If you are shooting when the sun is high in the sky – and you are bound to want to take pictures at a lunchtime picnic or on the beach – then here are a few pointers that will improve your pictures.

Use a slow film – ISO 64, 50 or even 25 in very bright sunlight – as this will bring out more detail in an otherwise sun-bleached scene. If your camera is adjustable, use the fastest shutter speeds to get action-stopping shots of children playing. Take shots in the shade where possible, under a café awning or a beach umbrella, for instance. Hats, too, can help to reduce the sun's glare on the face.

Another useful tip is to do what you were always supposed never to do: that is take the picture while facing into the sun. The sunlight will produce an attractive halo of light in the child's hair and the face will be in a degree of shade. Sand throws back enough light to illuminate the face gently.

The important thing when taking shots into the sun is to meter from the face, not from the sun-drenched background. If your camera takes its reading from the bright background, your subject will be under-exposed and too dark.

Using the light from a window is a good way to get atmospheric pictures indoors. Try a mother and baby shot by a sunlit window. Once again, soft morning or evening light is best. In bright sunlight, shade the window with a net curtain or filter the light through a partly-closed blind to produce an interesting dappled effect.

Using a flash can produce a harsh, unflattering light that casts strong shadows. It can also arrest movement and can drain a picture of atmosphere. Taking good shots with a flash requires some skill and practice, so avoid it if you can.

One way round the problem of poor light is to use fast film – anything from ISO 400 up to ISO 800. Fast film allows you to shoot in poorer light conditions but the drawback, and this is especially true of extra fast films of

ISP 1000 and upwards, is that the colours will be weak and the image will be noticeably grainy with less sharp detail.

A tripod is an indispensable aid in bad light as it allows you to take pictures at slow shutter speeds (too slow to hand-hold) that make the most of available light. But a tripod will be far too cumbersome to use with active children and you will find a camera with a flash unit indispensable in many situations. If your camera does not have a built-in flash and you are planning to take a lot of indoor shots, it is worth investing in a flash unit with a tilt head. This allows you to bounce the flash off a wall or ceiling, rather than firing it directly at the subject. The shadows will generally be less harsh and it avoids the problem of "red-eye", which is caused by the flash reflecting off the back of the retina of the eye. The latest compact cameras have a double-flash option which help reduce this problem.

To avoid dark shadows that tend to merge with your subject's hair, giving them an out-sized head, make sure your subject is a metre or so away from any background. Bounced flash will also minimize this effect.

Shots taken indoors often have a greenish hue. The culprit here is fluorescent light. Without using filters, the problem cannot be avoided. Unless you want pictures of bilious-looking children, avoid taking shots in rooms with strip lights.

Camcorders – portable video cameras that record a moving image with sound – are great for special occasions. They provide a lasting record of what the children were really like at a certain age. Fairly straightforward to use, they have a zoom lens so you can focus in close or take a wider picture. You need to perfect the technique of panning – tracking your subject and keeping him or her in focus and in the picture. But even bad home videos can be great fun to watch later. Try hiring a camcorder from a camera or video shop before buying.

To avoid building up a mountain of photographs, try to sort them all once they are developed. Decide straight away which ones are to go into an album or frame, which ones can be sent to relatives or close friends, and which ones can be stacked away (or thrown out).

By being fairly selective you won't be overwhelmed by a large pile waiting to be stuck into an album. If you put them into the album as they're developed you won't have trouble remembering the appropriate date or how old your child was in each photo. Buy some plain stickers for the head of each page and write the date on that, along with other details such as the names of other people in the photos, or the location.

For special events, such as religious festivals or your child's birthday, it is often rewarding to ask other relatives or guests for copies of some of their photos. That way you see another perspective and are more likely to get pictures including whichever one of you normally takes the family photos.

The significance of photographs changes with the passage of time. For the present and immediate future you will keep photographs of your child for your own pleasure. When your child is older, however, he will be intrigued by his own past, so include shots of your house, car, the local area and his small friends. He will be able to see how styles, places and people change and gain a sense of his own family history – especially if you compare the photos with others from your own childhood.

You can also share your memories by helping your toddler to make up a photo album or scrapbook after a holiday, or a visit to the country, zoo or amusement park. You can include other mementos such as postcards, dried leaves or tickets.

When a second baby arrives start a separate photo album for him and let your toddler choose some of the photos. This is a good way of including your first child in the arrival of a sibling.

Planning your Family

When you are planning your family there are many factors to take into consideration. Finances can dictate when you do or don't have another baby, your older child's (or children's) personality comes into play, your own state of mind, whether or not you want to return to work, and so on. Assuming that your circumstances seem to favour your having another baby, however, what would be the pros and cons of having children close together?

Many parents seem to prefer getting the nappy, bottle and sleepless night stages out of the way as soon as possible so that they can move on and enjoy the benefits of family life sooner. For older mothers it can also be safer and less exhausting to have babies bumper-to-bumper. There is also the fact that having got used to the limitations of life with a small baby it is less of an upheaval to have another one, rather than getting life back to normal, only to have it disrupted again a few years later.

As far as the children themselves are concerned, they will enjoy the benefits of having playmates in situ, and a first child is far less likely to remember a time when he was an only child and had his parents' undivided attention. He will have had long enough with his parents to have acquired a certain self-confidence, but not so long that he expects to be the centre of everyone's universe. This can make rivalry less of a problem. The children will also find it easier to share toys, and even friends, as they get older and will enjoy growing up together.

On the minus side, life with a small family may be intolerably exhausting at times. You may find that you put unreasonable demands on your first child, expecting them to grow up long before they should. He may feel left out and resentful towards the baby or his parents (or both) and these feelings will need careful handling if they are not to remain with him. Second and subsequent pregnancies will be particularly tiring as you will be expected to cope with the demands of your other children during the day, and broken nights as well. When you are caught in the middle of it all there will be times when you will find it difficult to keep your cool and to meet everybody's needs including your own.

All these factors should be carefully considered when planning a family in order to achieve the dynamics that will work for you.

◆ See also, **Only Children**, **Sibling Relationships**, **Sibling Rivalry**

Play

The value of play, particularly during the pre-school years, cannot be overestimated. Though your child may not be aware of it, nearly all forms of play, whether it be physical, creative, competitive or scientific, is part of a valuable learning process, making a positive contribution to your child's development both intellectually and socially.

◆ See also, **Cooking**, **Dressing Up**, **Hideaways**, **Imagination**, **Memory Games**, **Painting and Drawing**, **Paper Play**, **Playgrounds**, **Sand Play**, **Science in Play**, **Toys**, **Water Play**.

Playgrounds

Fun is the element that attracts children to playgrounds. But beyond their sheer enjoyment, their minds and bodies are undergoing a huge range of learning processes. For example, important codes of behaviour are learnt as children jostle for position on the slide or play at families in the wooden Wendy house. And, without even knowing it, from their first crawl towards their favourite piece of equipment to the day they horrify their parents with a death-defying leap off the roundabout, children are exercising their bodies so that muscles, co-ordination and balance begin to work in harmony.

It matters little to your child what type of playground you first introduce him to. In terms of overall entertainment, stimulation and safety, however, some are much better than others, so it is worth finding a good one and using it as often as possible.

Along with the traditional roundabout and swings, the kind of facilities to look for include:

● Integrated climbing frames with little "rooms".
● Walkways and slides (in sizes suitable for the unsteady toddler as well as big children).
● A well-kept sand-pit for creative play.
● Equipment that a child can use alone if he wishes.
● Barriers to prevent little ones running across the path of swings.
● A safety surface beneath each piece of equipment (a layer of wood chippings or a springy cork-tile-like surface).
● Some equipment that can be used quite safely when damp. Wooden equipment is best. Plastic can be wiped dry but can be dangerously slippery when wet.
● A full-time attendant.
● A fence to keep dogs out. (Dogs are now excluded from many playgrounds in order to allow little ones to play free from the dangers of Toxocariasis canis – a parasite species of roundworm whose larvae, hatched in dog excrement, cause an infection which can result in tumours, blindness and even death. The condition affects mainly toddlers, who are highly mobile and likely to put their unwashed fingers in their mouths.)

You'll find good playgrounds everywhere these days, however. Because the baby population has increased, it is noticeable that more and more playgrounds have sprung up, containing an ever-increasing range of imaginative equipment.

Dashing around a playground, children gain ever-greater control of the various muscle groups in their bodies, used for kicking, running and jumping, and more intricate movements such as buttoning a coat. The pace of development, and degree of sensitivity of both the larger and smaller muscle groups, is stimulated constantly in a playground, whether your child is playing "tag" on the climbing frame or making castles in the sand-pit.

The refinement of your child's skills of balance, foot- and hand-eye coordination, muscular strength and stamina, and reactions go hand-in-hand with his emotional development and increased independence. It is your child's growing sense of balance that provides the key both to his fun in the playground and to much of his development as well. Compare him at six months, gamely struggling to sit up on his own, with his masterful display of this skill once he is just a few weeks older. Later, see how he strives to walk unaided and then, after weeks of bumps, falls and joyful toddles across the room, he is an expert at this and is starting to run.

As his sense of balance matures, he will explore with success more of the equipment in the playground. Although he will be safer using the baby swings for several years, he will soon master climbing the steps of the slide, easing himself into a sitting position and letting himself go – all without your help! And he will run across suspended walkways with positive relish, hardly noticing how they sway as his sense of balance instinctively compensates for their unpredictable movement.

But balance alone is not enough. Much of the equipment in a children's playground requires strength; an hour pushing the roundabout, scaling the climbing frame and swinging from horizontal bars will give him as good and thorough a "workout" as any.

As he gets older, you will see his physical proficiency progress. Not only is his body using all the nutrients in his diet to build new muscle tissue all the time, but his bones are growing too. He discards the baby swings in favour of the ordinary ones, propelling himself vigorously backwards and forwards, now sitting, not standing, leaving you breathless just watching!

Where once he may have skipped impatiently from foot to foot waiting, under your command, for the roundabout to stop before clambering aboard, he will now leap on long before you feel he is ready. He is not necessarily being naughty – it is just that his body's nervous system has now developed to the point where his hands, eyes, feet and brain can work together at lightning speed so that he can judge for himself (usually) when to jump aboard.

Interestingly in this area of physical and sensory development, boys and girls often make progress in different directions. Girls seem to gain balance and poise faster than boys. They outshine their brothers in any activity requiring a hop, skip or a jump. Boys, meanwhile, seem to gain strength and speed at a greater rate and excel at pushing, throwing, catching and kicking.

When at the playground it is interesting to consider the particular skills your child is developing as he uses each piece of equipment.

Swings are good for sense of balance, rhythm, and co-ordination, while roundabouts develop muscular strength and stamina. The slides are a great confidence builder as your little one learns that he is quite safe – and has fun too – when he lets go at the top. And of course, climbing up the steps demands a fair amount of strength, co-ordination and concentration. Climbing frames exercise muscles and co-ordination abilities. Along with the roundabout, climbing frames are often the focal point of much imaginary play too. Sand-pits are great for running and jumping into, but also for quieter moments. The sand feels great between fingers and toes.

The playground is a great place for your child's emotional development and sense of independence to blossom. You will feel yourself become less of a hand-holding guide and companion and more of a mere spectator as, once in sight of a playground's delights, your little one runs ahead with barely a backward glance.

It can be difficult for parents to "let go" at these times, particularly as they are all too aware of the potential dangers of the playground. Their imaginations run riot as their little ones race heedlessly towards the swings. But it is essential to any child's growing sense of self that he begins to "go it alone" as soon as he is able. It must be a watchful distancing, however. Mum or Dad must always be there to lend the occasional helping hand. If you find yourself wondering whether you should allow your child total freedom to do as he wants in the playground, ask yourself the following questions. Are you being over-protective? How many times did you come to harm as a child from such activities? Do you know what to do if he does hurt himself?

This growing sense of independence – both emotional and physical – will be evident when your little one plays with other children as well as on his own. As his confidence grows he may start to "show off", performing for his proud parents and helping other children master what he has learnt.

The other side of this coin is that a child who is not allowed to or is unable to develop his physical skills may well shy away from such activities. But don't worry if your child is not one of the more adventurous ones, however, as he is bound to acquire other valuable skills.

Cautious children often prove able guardians of children younger than themselves. They will make sure that each gets a fair share of rides, particularly younger brothers and sisters. And they may also become great organizers, directing games rather than starring in them, as their vivid imaginations and early managerial skills outstrip their physical skills.

Pneumonia

Pneumonia is an infection of the lungs. It can affect children of all ages but is most common in the first year. There are three types: bronchopneumonia, hypostatic pneumonia and lobar pneumonia. Bronchopneumonia occasionally occurs as a complication of measles. If your child is suffering from measles and does not appear to be getting better two or three days after the rash has developed, or if he is very short of breath and has a persistent cough, consult your doctor. Similarly bronchopneumonia can occur after an attack of influenza, whooping cough, diphtheria, bronchitis or even a severe cold when the child's resistance is lowered, but again this is very rare. It can also occur after a child has come close to drowning if he has inhaled dirty or polluted water.

The other two forms of pneumonia arise quite suddenly, sometimes preceded by vomiting or convulsions. All forms of pneumonia are caused by a bacterial or viral infection affecting the alveoli (air-pockets in the lungs where oxygen seeps into the blood and carbon dioxide escapes from it). The infected alveoli become blocked with fluid that in time forms a solid clot. The position of the blockage varies with the type of pneumonia. With bronchopneumonia, the blockage affects the small alveoli and is scattered all over the lungs. In lobar pneumonia the whole of one segment of the lung, called a lobe, is involved, while hypostatic pneumonia affects the lowest parts of both lungs. The more severe bacterial pneumonia is, fortunately, now much less common than it was and seems to be giving place to the less dangerous viral pneumonia.

If your child has pneumonia he will probably have a runny nose, a high temperature and fast breathing. He will feel very ill and will be listless and show no interest in anything. He may also be flushed or, in severe cases, his skin may appear grey and sweaty and he may make little grunting noises as he breathes. In some cases he will also have a cough which is generally dry (i.e. not producing phlegm), and if the pneumonia is affecting the outer surface of the lung, the pleural membranes may be affected and breathing will be painful.

Always consult your doctor immediately you suspect pneumonia. Pneumonia used frequently to be fatal but today it is easily cured by modern antibiotics. While you are waiting, prop your child up in bed with pillows to help his breathing, keep him warm and keep the air moist by boiling a kettle in the room. (Never leave your child alone in a room with a boiling kettle.)

Mild cases may be treated at home with antibiotics given by mouth but in more severe cases the child will need to be admitted to hospital. Your child will need a larger amount of antibiotics than can be swallowed and these are given by injection, either intravenously (into a vein) or into the thigh muscle. Injections into the muscle are painful and leave a dull ache so some doctors prefer to give them intravenously to avoid this.

Your child will also be given physiotherapy to help clear the infected parts of the lung. A child with pneumonia usually recovers within two or three days.

Although pneumonia does not normally recur, if your child has inhaled a small object, perhaps a toy or nut, he may suffer repeated attacks of pneumonia. This is because the swallowed object causes an infection which leads to pneumonia and although the pneumonia responds to the antibiotics each time, the underlying cause has not been removed. If your doctor suspects this is the problem, he will arrange an X-ray. If the diagnosis is proved to be correct the doctors will give a general anaesthetic and pass a tube down the airways to find and remove the object.

Poisoning

Many household substances contain poisons and with small children about it is important for parents to be aware of the dangers in the home and keep potentially harmful substances out of reach. Several common plants in the house or garden also have poisonous effects and children should be trained not to put any part of any plant in their mouths. With very young children it is advisable not to grow poisonous plants or to grow them only where children cannot get at them.

As soon as a baby begins to crawl, he takes a delight in exploring his surroundings and it is natural for him to put things in his mouth. Young children from crawling age until about five or six are particularly at risk of poisoning unless all danger is kept out of their reach preferably in a locked cupboard.

Older children may deliberately put themselves at risk, sometimes simply due to peer pressure. Glue sniffing, drug taking and alcohol abuse are all worrying possibilities.

The symptoms of poisoning will differ according to the poison your child has taken. Corrosive poisons such as household cleaners have a burning action and a child who has swallowed them will scream with pain. Sleeping tablets and many other drugs will cause drowsiness. Solvents inhaled from lighter fuel, dry cleaning fluid and glues causes mental confusion. Many poisonous plants cause vomiting and nausea, stomach pain and diarrhoea.

Some common poisonous plants

Castor oil plant
Lily of the valley
Monkshood
Oleander
Yew
can all be fatal

Cherry laurel
Cuckoo pint
Deadly nightshade
Dieffenbachia
Laburnum
Lupin
Privet
Snowberry
Woody nightshade
are all dangerous

Many types of poisoning can led to unconsciousness or convulsions. The effects of paracetamol are usually delayed (even up to three days) but can be fatal. Always seek medical advice even if you think the drugs swallowed are harmless.

It is important to know what your child has taken. Keep any bottle or container so that you can show the doctor what the poison was. A sample of any vomit or diarrhoea should also be kept to help identify the poisonous substance involved.

Seek medical aid for any kind of poisoning, but first do what you can to protect the child from further harm. If the child is unconscious, place him in the recovery position (*see* First Aid). Check that he is breathing normally and give artificial respiration if necessary. Wipe the child's face with a dry cloth and then rinse with plenty of water to remove any of the poisonous

POISONING **P**

substance that may be round the mouth. Now telephone for an ambulance.

If you know what the child has taken, tell the hospital staff so that you can be given advice on how to treat the child while waiting for the ambulance. The more information you can supply the better. If the child is unconscious or semi-conscious, keep a check for breathing and heartbeat and be ready to administer artificial respiration or cardiac massage.

In the case of gas poisoning, turn off the gas, open doors and windows, or better still, take the child outside if possible. Give mouth to mouth resuscitation if the child is not breathing. (Lay the child on his back, close nostrils with one hand and hold jaw with other hand, and gently but firmly breathe into the child's mouth.) Give cardiac massage if the heart is not beating, and meanwhile, get someone to call an ambulance.

If the child is in pain from having swallowed a corrosive substance, do not make him vomit. A corrosive substance does further harm to the oesophagus (gullet) if it is regurgitated. Instead, give the child plenty of milk if it is available, or water.

Corrosive poisons
Bleach
Caustic soda
Weedkiller
White spirit
Turpentine and turpentine substitutes
Paint stripper
Ammonia
Washing soda
Cleaning fluids
Detergent
Dishwasher powder
Polish
Petrol

Medicines do not have a corrosive effect, and if you know for sure that the child has taken a large amount of a medicine, and if he is conscious, it is safe to make him sick. Do this by putting a finger down the child's throat rather than by giving mustard or salt which can aggravate the situation. It is not vital to make the child sick, however, and it is best to follow the advice given by the hospital.

Once in hospital, the child may be given a drug to induce vomiting or may have a gastric washout. In certain cases an antidote to the poison may be administered, and if the child is unconscious he may be put on a ventilator.

Usually plenty of fluids will be given to help flush the poison through the kidneys, and in some cases the child may be put on a kidney machine. He may be kept under observation for a few days, but will usually be allowed home after 24 hours, with no further ill effects. You will need to continue to give plenty of fluids and a bland diet for a few days until the child's digestive system is fully recovered.

● See also, **Food Poisoning**, **Toadstool Poisoning**

Postnatal Depression

Postnatal depression (PND) is far less easy to define than the "baby blues" most women experience a few days after giving birth. One woman in 20 may suffer from PND which happens after the birth of a baby and frequently affects women who have never experienced depression before (and do not re-develop it later). However, the symptoms are similar to those of any depression, and there may be an overlap of ordinary depression in some people. It may not happen immediately after the birth, but over half of the affected mothers have the symptoms within three months and almost all within six months.

The symptoms vary, but there is usually a feeling of tiredness which is out of proportion to the amount of physical activity you have been doing. Perhaps you feel that you can't be bothered to get out of bed in the morning, or can't make the effort to make yourself look nice. You may feel more irritable than usual, and not able to laugh at the things which usually make you laugh.

While depressed mothers often feel terrible in themselves, they are still physically able to care for their baby even if it is a struggle. Sometimes, however, their feelings towards the baby alter, and this may take the form of being over-anxious about the baby's well-being, or imagining that their love and feelings for the baby are not as strong and positive as they were in the beginning, and they may even experience anger and resentment towards the baby. Very occasionally, these feelings spill over and it is these very rare cases that need urgent medical treatment.

There are several probably causes of postnatal depression. It may be due to hormonal imbalance, or it may also result from stress when a person is particularly vulnerable – which a new mother certainly is. This possible cause is backed up by the fact that it is more common in mothers who are in some way isolated or have few people to turn to for help and advice. Research indicates that it is more common if the pregnancy has been difficult, if labour was long and complicated, when a Caesarean section was needed, or when the baby was ill after the birth and had to be separated from the mother. In this respect, it is like a normal depression – a reaction to difficult times.

Postnatal depression has also been seen in women who adopt babies, which shows that it is not just a hormonal problem. Having a new baby can be quite hard to adjust to. You may not have been prepared for just how much time and energy, both physical and mental, it would take. You may not have bargained for the extent to which you would have to adjust your life to the baby's needs rather than the other way around and you probably won't have time to do the things you want, as the baby seems to absorb you completely.

You may feel that you have changed, and your self-esteem is lowered – not long ago you might have been holding down a responsible job but now you never seem to achieve anything apart from feeding the baby. As a result, you can't help feeling that the relationship with your partner is suffering because the baby takes up so much time. This can also cause stress and make the situation worse.

If you have never been depressed before, these feelings may come as quite a shock, especially since you will have been looking forward to the baby for some time. You may feel like brushing the feelings to one side and trying to pretend that they don't exist. This usually doesn't work.

You must tell someone if you are feeling depressed. Don't think for a moment that depression is something to be ashamed of, that it is somehow self-created, or a sign of weakness. It is a recognized medical condition and one which should be treated as such. Talk to your midwife, health visitor, or doctor about it. It may be tempting to pretend that you can cope on your own, but the pretence adds to the problems. It is essential for your own sanity to get it out in the open and if necessary have some form of treatment.

You must tell your partner, although it will be difficult for him to deal with it too. Having a baby puts a lot of strain on a relationship. He may feel left out because the baby is taking up so much of your time. He may feel quite threatened if he suspects that you are unable to cope, and confessing your fears to him may confirm the worst of his suspicions, but it is important that you do talk to him about it. It helps a great deal if he understands the condition, but you should get extra help as your partner, yourself, and the baby are an interdependent unit and if one needs help, you all do.

If you are suffering from a more severe depression, or the more physical signs of depression such as extreme tiredness and lethargy are present, your doctor may suggest anti-depressants. There are a few side-effects, such as a dry mouth or slight drowsiness, but neither of these should be severe and the effect usually wears off after a while. The tablets can take up to three weeks to have a full effect, but they will usually help you to get some sleep.

If you are breastfeeding, make sure your doctor knows so that the tablets will be of a type designed not to affect the baby through your milk, and will not be addictive. Any drowsiness that they may cause should not be severe enough to interfere with your care of the baby. It is important to go back to your doctor with a report on how the treatment is working.

Since it is felt that postnatal depression may have a hormonal cause it may help to try hormone treatment. The hormone used in the treatment is progesterone, which is usually given either rectally or vaginally as it can be broken down by the stomach – but you can use tablets if you don't like the idea of suppositories. Hormone treatment is worth trying, particularly if your depression is of an up-and-down type. Some people feel much better with progesterone treatment, and it can do no harm. With or without medical treatment, postnatal depression can last for a variable length of time, but usually no longer than six months or so.

There is no need to feel a failure if you have had a period of depression. When it lifts you often feel wonderful and enjoy motherhood all the more, and you may be able to understand and help other people in the same situation. And if you suffered postnatal depression with your first baby, do not automatically assume that it will happen again with your next one. A lot of stress factors will be eliminated the second time round – you'll be feeling more confident as a mother, you've come to accept the routine and, through your first child, will have made a lot of contacts for company and support.

Potty Training

The "right" age for potty training is only when your child is ready. As a rough guideline, the majority of children aren't ready to use the potty to move their bowels before the age of 15–18 months, and before about two years to control their bladder. Even when toddlers are using the potty most of the time they will still be having accidents until they are at least three

years old or more. Some children take longer; a few manage earlier; boys are usually slower than girls, but they are all individuals.

Before your child is ready to use the potty at will he needs to be fully aware of what is happening when he wets and soils his nappy. The first sign that your child is nearing this stage is when he starts signalling that he has just wet or soiled himself – either by showing you, or by making signs or noises you will soon learn to recognize, or even by using your family word for what he has done.

Leaving your child without nappies as much as possible helps during this stage to make him aware of his bodily functions.

Soon after this stage, your child will know he is about to wet or soil before he does so. This is a sure sign that he is ready to learn to use the potty.

Most parents feel tempted at some point to fit potty training neatly into their plans or a time when it just seems so convenient to get it over with. A hot spell may inspire you to take your toddler's nappies off for good and let him play in the garden for hours on end – hoping that by the time the rain comes the "training" will be finished and the carpet saved.

You may decide to take a long holiday to spend a lot of time with your toddler, be relaxed and do a "crash course" to get him clean and dry. Or money matters may urge you to do away with the weekly expense and bulk of nappies.

Provided that your child is, indeed, ready for it and sufficiently aware of his bodily functions, this kind of concentrated effort may well be successful. But do not be too disappointed if you realize that the time is not right yet.

Starting playgroup (sometimes as early as two-and-a-half years) could be another factor weighing on your mind. Although most playgroups expect children to be basically clean and dry when they start they do make allowances for accidents – don't be extra strict or try and rush things with this date constantly in mind.

Pressures from outside – whether from other parents, or grandparents – should not influence your timing. Potty training is certainly not an area for competition. The more relaxed you are about it, the more likely you are to get the training process over with quickly and easily.

It is a good idea to buy your potty early and let your child become familiar with the sight of it around the house. You can explain to him what it is for and that he will be using it when he is a little older.

A child learns to control his bowel movements before his bladder. There are usually a few useful seconds' delay between the moment he knows he is about to move his bowel and the moment it actually happens.

If your child moves his bowel at predictable times, it is worth leaving him without nappies around these times. Make sure the potty is near by at the first signs and ask if he wants to use it.

However keen you are that he should do so, try not to show it and be matter-of-fact about it. In the same way, if your child does not want to use the potty just yet, try to hide any impatience or disappointment you may feel.

Getting to the potty in time to catch urine takes a few months longer, usually some time after your child is two. He may know in advance that he is about to pass urine, but the action follows on a split second after the knowledge.

Don't let the occasional "off" day, when your child just doesn't want to co-operate or even know about the potty, get you down. He may not be feeling well and it's best to forget the whole issue for a day or two. A philosophical attitude to stains and puddles on carpets and kitchen floors is all-important. Your child may well lose heart or motivation if you expect him to be able to use the potty successfully all the time too soon after he firsts gets the hang of it.

Once your child is eager to use the potty and is managing to do so at least half the time, it is worth taking him one step further from the "bare bottom" stage.

Trainer pants are ideal for this period as they will catch dribbles, if not a full flood. Either lined or with PVC covering on the outside and soft terry towelling inside, they are comfortable to wear and help make the transition from nappies to underpants.

If struggling with pants is met by initial resistance, try to make them more attractive to your child by pointing out that he is "big" now and showing him that you are wearing something similar yourself. Let your child get used to this new routine of pulling pants up and down before you go over to real pants.

Unless your child has been consistently dry during a number of naps, you may want to continue using nappies during any sleep times, and certainly at night. Even a child of two-and-a-half can still find it difficult to hold urine for more than four or five hours.

For your own convenience as much as your child's undisturbed sleep, do not rush to overcome this final hurdle. Again, it pays to wait for the sign that your child has outgrown night-time nappies – a succession of nights when he has woken up with a dry nappy.

Sooner or later your child will have to start using the lavatory, rather than a potty. Once he can control his bladder for long enough to be able to reach the bathroom, the potty can stop following him around and be given a permanent place in the bathroom or next to the lavatory. You may want to buy a child's seat to fit over the normal toilet seat which your child can start to use when he wants to. Once boys are using the lavatory regularly, they should be encouraged to lift the seat and aim carefully. You must still be prepared to mop up after them for a long time to come, however.

Children should be using the lavatory at least part of the time after the age of three, particularly if they are starting nursery school or playgroup where a lot of children will have given up potties, and they will be suddenly faced with this large-size facility.

Even once your child is perfectly competent at using the potty – or later on the lavatory – at home, going out to the shops or on trips is a different matter. A visit to a friend's house (who may happen to be house-proud and not used to small children) may end up in embarrassing puddles if you overestimate your toddler's reliability. To begin with, you should take a potty with you at all times. Your child will be very discouraged (if not outraged) to be put back in nappies for a trip out, and will equally be mortified to wet or soil himself just when he is so proud of his progress. Instead, you could continue to use trainer pants when out, even if your child is using ordinary pants at home. Always carry a couple of spare pairs of pants with you in case of accidents.

It is also worth getting your child used to urinating in a discreet place without a potty. This is easier for little boys who are starting to stand up to pass urine, while girls will need to learn to do so being held by you.

Always make sure you wash your toddler's hands if he has touched the potty or any of its contents, and teach him to wash his hands after going to the toilet. You will need to continue wiping his bottom yourself for quite some time after he is going to the toilet on his own.

◆ See also, **Penis (Caught in Zip)**

Rashes

Babies and small children often develop rashes, which frequently disappear as quickly as they came, without the child's having felt ill at all. A rash can be a symptom of an infectious disease such as chickenpox, or can be due to an allergy or a fungal or other infestation.

You should take your child to the family doctor for a rash that does not disappear within a day or two or if the child has a fever or other symptoms of illness. If it seems likely that the child has an infectious disease, call the doctor out even if the child is not too ill to go to the surgery, so as not to expose other people to the possibility of infection.

If a rash flares up when the child is taking medication you should let your doctor know at once. Consult your doctor or health visitor if the child seems prone to getting rashes.

Infectious illnesses

The most common infectious diseases of childhood cause their own distinctive rashes.

Chickenpox

Chickenpox causes small, pimply spots which appear in fresh outbreaks at intervals of a few days, starting on the chest and back and spreading to the face and the rest of the body. The spots develop into blisters which then dry to form crusts, causing intense itching. Before the rash begins to appear the child usually feels off-colour.

German measles (rubella)

German measles (rubella) causes a flush of tiny pink spots, all over the body, sometimes starting behind the ears, and spreading to the forehead first, and is sometimes very mild. The rash is short-lived, lasting two to three days. The child might have a fever, but may just feel slightly off-colour.

Measles

Measles causes dark red spots which start behind the ears and spread to the face and body. This usually follows the child having symptoms of a bad cold and sore throat, and the appearance of small white spots inside the cheeks.

◆ See also, **Chickenpox**, **German Measles (Rubella)**, **Measles**

Scarlet fever

Scarlet fever causes a flush of tiny red spots which spread from the face and chest to the rest of the body, and which always leave an area round the mouth unaffected. The child will have a sore throat and enlarged tonsils, and may also have a fever and vomiting and feel very poorly.

Contagious rashes
Cold sores

Cold sores (herpes) are itchy or painful blisters which develop round the mouth and nose and dry to form a crust – similar to the rash of chickenpox. Some children seem prone to attacks of cold sores.

Impetigo

Impetigo causes red spots on the face, scalp, hands and knees. The spots blister and exude a sticky, yellowish fluid which dries to form a thick crust.

◆ See also, **Cold Sores**, **Impetigo**

Scabies

Scabies (caused by a mite) is an itchy, red rash occurring in small areas usually between the fingers, or on the palms of the hands and soles of the feet, and itching more at night.

Other rashes

Cradle cap

Cradle cap is a yellowish brown or grey crust which forms on the scalps of young babies.

Eczema

Eczema is a sore, red rash usually affecting folds in the skin or areas of the face. These become infected if the child scratches them, and the skin is dry and scaly.

Heat Rash

Heat rash occurs especially on the face and neck, elbow creases, backs of knees and in the groin, usually when the child gets too hot. It causes irritation and feels hot.

Hives

Hives or nettle rash looks very much like nettle stings, with pale, raised spots surrounded by red and linked to cover an area of skin anywhere on the body.

Allergies

Allergies, including allergies to food, can cause various types of skin rashes and flushes. Sometimes the link between the allergen and the rash it causes may be obvious, but often it can be difficult to track down.

Prickly heat

Milia or prickly heat is a rash of tiny, white pimple-like spots which particularly affects young babies.

Nappy rash

Nappy rash causes red skin in the nappy area or in the folds of the skin at the top of the legs. The skin may be broken and spots may develop.

◆ See also, **Allergies**, **Eczema**, **Hives**

Reading and Writing

Between the ages of one and two your child will begin to follow the stories that you read to him. As well as story books and picture and word books, you can show your child colourful alphabet books. You don't have to worry about teaching him the alphabet at this stage, but it is useful if he becomes used to the shape of the letters alongside familiar pictures. Emphasize the sound of the letter, rather than the name ("a" as in "apple", not "ey" as in "a, b, c") and check that the book you use shows letters as they are most commonly pronounced ("g" for "goat" and not "giraffe").

You could play an adapted version of "I spy", using sounds for the beginning of words, rather than the letter. And when you use the alphabet, you don't have to stick to the strict order of starting with "a" and ending with "z". It may be easier for your child to learn contrasting sounds first – "b" and "s", "m" and "t", for example. Teach him a few sounds at a time. Gradually he will learn the whole range; later he can learn the alphabet by letter name and order.

By three years old, your child will be showing good shape and picture recognition. He uses and understands language well and chatters continually to you. You can talk about stories together and he can also listen to stories on the radio or television. When you are reading him a story, guide his finger along the words on some of the pages. This way he learns that you are following them to tell the story and he learns that, in English, you read from left to right and from top to bottom. Point out words which occur often, such as the name of the main character, or an action word which may be well illustrated. Telling him rhymes – tongue twisters such as "she sells sea shells on the sea shore" or "hairy Harry had a horrible hat" – is a great way of playing with words and exploring the fun you can have with letters and sounds.

You can now start to familiarize your child with separate words, outside the usual setting of his story books. Write his name on the fridge door using magnetic letters. You could make name settings for each member of the family that your child can place on the table. Or you could label one or two things in his room, so that the look of the word is immediately associated with the right object. If your child likes using these word cards, you can develop games such as word and picture snap. For this, write some names of things on separate pieces of card and draw or stick cut-out pictures of the corresponding objects on other cards. One of you should turn over the picture cards as the other turns the words – if two of them match, it's snap!

For a more active game, write out action words like "jump", "run", "skip" on word cards and ask your child to pick a card and then act out the word. If he gets it right, he can ask you to do the same. This form of reading is known as whole word recognition and is useful up to a point. However, the method means that your child will always rely on you to teach him the word in the first place. If you haven't told him the word, he won't be able to work it out by himself. Learning the sounds, or "phonics" of a word will allow him to do this. Just as you have begun to introduce him to the sounds of the alphabet, so you can now show him how to join these sounds when reading a word.

Continue your "I spy" game using sounds for the beginning of words. Or you can play "odd one out" by naming a series of objects which all begin with the same sound, except one. You can make a letter scrap book by writing a letter at the top of a page and then cutting out pictures of things that all begin with that letter. Gradually, your child will link the written sound with the pictures.

You can play many variations of the initial letter game. For example, collect together a variety of everyday objects in a bag and then write the letters of the alphabet on cards. Ask your child to find the object in the bag that corresponds to each of the letter cards laid in front of him. Or stick envelopes on to a cardboard box and draw letters on each one. Collect or make picture cards which you can hold up for your child to place in the right envelopes. Talk about each picture or object in the games and ask him to say the sound it begins with.

From the initial letters, you can progress to the combination of sounds in each word. Tell him about common pairs of letters – "sp", "st", "ck", "ch", "th", and so on. Tell him these are "good friends" who like to be together and make word cards that use them – "sock", "rock" and so on.

All these activities pave the way for your child being able to follow the words of a story that's being read to him; and to him being able to read out short bits on his own. Your child will have learnt some of his favourite stories by heart, so as you guide his finger over the words on some of the pages, you can stop to let him complete the sentence. Praise him as this will give him confidence. There will be a transition from knowing by heart to actually recognizing the word and as your child's ability to work out sounds increases, he may be able to work out an unknown word for himself.

Soon you can let him fill in the gaps. Read aloud together then let your child continue for a while on his own. After a few words, join in again. This is rather like learning to walk, or to ride a bicycle. At first your child needs support, but he then gains the confidence to do it on his own. Don't tell your child that he is wrong if he makes a mistake as he learns. For example, he may try reading the story in a favourite picture book and say "the dog goes to sleep" when the text says "the dog goes to bed". Agree with him, then read the written version. In this way you correct your child without any sign of criticism. Praise and warmth are the best teaching tools.

As your child becomes familiar with reading letters, you can introduce him to writing. Painting and drawing are the first steps towards manual dexterity, so introduce writing as part of this activity. Teach him to write his name on his pictures: write out his name with a thick felt-tip pen, showing him the strokes used to form the letters. Then help him write over the name himself. When he has mastered this, write out his name again in pencil, then he can go over the letters with a thick felt-tip pen. After this, write out his name again and ask your child to copy it underneath, or on a separate piece of paper. Encourage him to "talk through" the letters, helping him to memorize them. Then encourage him to label other objects or people in them. You can make scrapbooks together, labelling each cut-out, and you can model letters in play dough. Your child will only be able to learn a few words at a time, so make a "special box" for him to keep the cards of the letters and words he has mastered. As he forms each letter, encourage him to speak it out loud. If he has problems with certain ones, think of a shape it resembles – a "p" is a pea on a stick, an "o" is an orange, and so on.

Children love computers, so if you have one at home that isn't too precious, let your child bash out letters on it, as every method of producing words should be fun for him, and hitting a key may be a less frustrating way of finding out that he can make written words than grappling with pen and paper. There are some wonderful CD Roms designed to help children learn to read by linking words and pictures.

Keep reading and writing fun. Only introduce your child to new stages of learning if he seems willing and ready, and be prepared for a very short concentration span. It may be better not to tell too many people that you are teaching him to read. He may be put off by having to "perform" his skills in front of others. Best of all, don't let him know that you are "teaching" him anything – let it all seem like a game.

Of course, your pre-school child need not master all or any of these games or stages towards reading and writing. He may show absolutely no interest at all in labelling or spelling. If this is so, don't worry, and don't push him. He'll get round to it in his own time.

Religion

Religion can be a sensitive and emotive issue especially in families where the two parents hold conflicting views. It is a good idea for both partners to discuss their views before their child reaches the "Why?" stage, when he will ask endless questions they may find difficult to answer in a consistent way. How you choose to answer such questions (about God, life, death and so on) will depend on your own beliefs, but remember that he may be exposed to, and quite possibly strongly influenced by, other views at playgroup or school and you will need to know how to reconcile these different opinions.

You should try to be as open-minded as possible, and this need not mean compromising your own faith. You could perhaps take your child to the library to look at books on different religions and cultures and compare and contrast them with your own (or simply discuss them objectively if you have no strong religious convictions). In this way you will encourage your child to value family religious traditions whilst being sympathetic and tolerant towards people of other faiths.

Restaurants

It is only to be expected that most children will become restless whilst waiting to be served at a restaurant. In most towns there are perhaps a couple of establishments (besides fast-food restaurants) that provide special activities and equipment for children, such as colouring books, toys, highchairs and baby changing facilities. However, the majority do not, so if you plan to eat out with your child it is as well to take one or two small toys or books with you that you know will keep your child occupied and prevent him from running around other people's tables wreaking havoc. This will make the outing a more relaxing and enjoyable one for you without the danger of accidents or the worry of annoying other diners.

It may be worth looking through restaurant guides to find those that are more, rather than less, child-friendly since even the best-behaved child may not be welcome in certain establishments.

Ringworm

Ringworm is a fungal infection that can affect the skin on the scalp, trunk and feet, fingers or groin and, less frequently, the armpits. It is intensely itchy and the infection develops in the shape of a ring, particularly on the scalp, which gives the condition its name. (It is, however, nothing to do with worms.) Children can catch it from each other or from dogs or cats in the family. Country children also frequently catch it from cattle. Different varieties of the fungus responsible for the infection affect different parts of the body and cause slightly different types of attack.

Ringworm is caused by one of several closely related fungi. In most cases it thrives on moisture and warmth, and all forms are highly contagious.

Ringworm of the scalp often causes a bald patch or patches. It usually spreads outwards in a ring, which is red, itchy and scaly. As the centre of the ring heals the ring itself grows bigger. The hairs within the ring are often broken off, and they begin to regrow from the centre of the ring as the skin starts to heal again.

On the trunk, ringworm is similar in appearance. An itchy patch is formed, which heals from the centre but grows larger in diameter as it heals. The skin is red and scaly, and within a few weeks small new patches may form.

The equivalent of ringworm on the feet is athlete's foot, which causes itchy, red patches between the toes. After a bath, or if the feet are sweaty, the skin can look soft and white, and dry crusts may form. The infection usually attacks the area between the toes, but can spread under the toes, and may also lodge under the child's toe-nails, causing them to be hard and ridged, and sometimes discoloured. Athlete's foot is more frequent in older children. Ringworm on the hands or in the groin or armpit also causes red scaly patches which itch and spread.

All other forms of ringworm should be treated by your doctor and as the infection is highly contagious, the child should be kept out of contact with other children as much as possible. He will have to take time off school for ringworm of the scalp or hands, and within the home he should not share combs, brushes or towels with the rest of the family.

In most cases the child will be treated with an anti-fungal cream, and it will also be important for you to make sure that the affected area is washed and carefully dried two or three times a day. When the armpits, trunk or groin area are affected loose clothing, made of cotton, should be worn to keep the skin cool and dry.

In severe cases an antibiotic drug – griseofulvin – may be prescribed. This is nearly always given when the child has ringworm of the nails and will cure even the most persistent cases.

If you suspect that a family pet has ringworm (signs will be scratching and bald areas) take it to the vet for treatment. Your pet will be grateful, and this will also prevent the infection from being passed round the family.

◆ See also, **Athlete's Foot**

Routine

For many new parents, the most important goal is the establishment of a routine. This will incorporate feeding, sleep and play, and getting it right can often be the key to relieving stress and the return to a settled lifestyle.

◆ For more detailed information on different areas see **Bathing Babies and Children**, **Bottle Feeding**, **Breastfeeding**, **Mealtimes**, **Playing** and **Sleep Patterns**.

Rubella

◆ See **German Measles**

Safety

Wherever your child is, his safety is of paramount importance, and needs to be carefully masterminded by you.

Nobody can make a home completely safe but you can always make it safer. You don't have to turn your house or flat into a prison with locks on every door, but you can concentrate on making the most dangerous objects and areas inaccessible to your youngster – both to protect him and bring you peace of mind.

Some safety precautions rely on common sense – such as moving bleach out of harm's way – but others depend on equipment which you may have to buy. Special safety gadgets can be expensive and so you may be tempted into buying second-hand. This is fine in principle, but you should check that any second-hand item is in good working order and that no parts are missing.

Unless you know exactly what you are doing, it is best to steer clear of DIY projects where child safety is concerned. Each year, hundreds of children are injured because of DIY ideas that didn't work properly. It is always best to stick to products that are made by a reliable manufacturer.

If it's hot, it's dangerous. The kitchen is potentially the most dangerous room in the home, packed with alarming hazards. But for the child the kitchen is also one of the most fascinating places in the home, full of curious noises and wonderful smells. And most intriguing of all is the cooker. Which child hasn't reached up eager to see what's on the menu for dinner?

You can prevent your child's inquisitive fingers from pulling hot pans down from the hob by installing an adaptable cooker guard which forms a barrier around the top. The guard may confine your cooking space but that's a small price to pay to avoid the potential dangers of a pan of boiling water or hot fat. Always turn pan handles inwards and use the back burners whenever possible.

The other main source of scalding water, your electric kettle, can be held firmly in place with another type of guard which is screwed to the wall. A good investment that goes hand-in-hand with a kettle guard is a curly flex which will coil up out of reach of your child's hands.

Many horror stories are told of children playing with fire. Most people find fires, particularly open ones, entrancing to watch, but children often try to go one step further and want to explore what a fire is by touching it. To prevent nasty burns, fit guards around all your fires whether they are open, gas or electric. (The fixed grilles already in front of many fires are not sufficient when it comes to protecting your baby.) The best type of fireguard is box-like and is clipped to screw-eyes driven into the wall. Many types are adaptable so that they can fit small and large fires alike, but although they keep your child away from the fire, they can't reduce the heat output.

More people die or are injured by the smoke from a household fire than from the flames. A smouldering cigarette end can cause some types of cushion or upholstery to erupt into clouds of black, poisonous fumes. As smoke can be so lethal, it makes sense to install smoke detectors around the home.

How many detectors you fit will depend on how large your home is but one near the kitchen and one in your child's bedroom is a good idea. Smoke detectors are extremely sensitive so if you have a small kitchen, you may find that the toast you burn every morning sets off a shrieking alarm. If so, move it just outside the kitchen.

Children find electric sockets and switches some of the most interesting things invented. While it is a good idea to steer children away from sockets, it is an even better idea to blank them off so that fingers and toys can't be pushed inside the holes. Special blanking plugs are cheap and effective, but what happens when you want to use the socket? You push a plug in and your toddler pulls it out – exasperating for you but a great game for him!

A socket cover, which hides plugs underneath a plastic box, will make it extremely difficult for a plug to be pulled out but it won't stop you from using the socket. In theory, socket covers are simple to fix, but if you are fearful of anything to do with the electricity supply, it is best to get someone in to help you.

The flexes that lead from sockets can be a hazard if they trail across the floor, as much for you as for your child. If necessary, exchange a short flex for a long one so that you can lead it along the skirting board, out of harm's way. Conversely, if an appliance has an unnecessarily long flex, swap it for a shorter one or better still, a curly flex.

To avoid tiny fingers meddling with video controls you can get transparent screens that slot over them, but be sure that the type you buy is suitable for your type of machine. As for the tapes, either keep them in a cupboard you can lock, or out of reach on a shelf.

Cupboards fascinate children and they like nothing better than to remove all the contents and then play hide and seek. However, if all your cupboards are systematically vandalized, why not try a compromise? Leave one low cupboard in the kitchen as a play area and fit childproof catches to the others. Catches come in a whole range of designs so you should be able to find something that suits your particular set-up. You can get door slam protectors if you have any cupboards with doors that close automatically and might trap small fingers. Similar catches can be attached to refrigerators and freezers.

Bathtime is a time to relax and have fun, but here again you need to take some precautions. A slip-resistant mat stuck to the floor of the bath with suction pads will make it safer for your child to stand up in the water and splash around. A child can drown in just a few centimetres of water, and to make matters worse, baths are slippery which makes it all too easy for a toddler to fall over.

The taps in a bath can also cause problems, especially the hot one. Protecting bath taps isn't easy and, if your child is intrigued by them, the safest thing to do is to have a bath at the same time, making sure that you are at the tap end. Run cold water last to cool the tap down.

To prevent experimental toddlers from going on excursions up or down the stairs when you are busying yourself with other things, fit special gates at the top and bottom. Most types can be expanded or contracted to fit wide and narrow staircases. Opening and closing stair gates behind you may seem a chore to begin with, but you will soon get into the habit and start closing them automatically.

If you have a glass-fronted door or window that can be reached by your child (or a football), a simple precaution is to cover the vulnerable panes

with transparent sticky-backed plastic. The sheets can be trimmed to size and are simply rubbed on to the glass with a squeegee. Although the plastic covering may not stop the glass from being broken by a hearty blow, it will stop it from shattering into dangerously sharp shards.

Most children love peanuts but many parents don't realize that toddlers can easily choke on them, quite apart from sticking them in their ears and up their noses.

All small objects that can be swallowed are potentially lethal, so keep pen tops, buttons and the like well out of reach. Also keep cigarettes, matches and lighters out of reach and don't forget to clean out ashtrays.

Before giving a toy to your child, test that it is safe. Squeeze soft toys to make sure that there is nothing sharp inside, and firmly tug at eyes in teddies and other soft toys (eyes are notorious for coming loose and getting stuck in children's throats). Pull at the fluff on soft toys. If it comes away easily, discard the toy – fluff can easily cause a baby to choke if it gets stuck in the throat. Keep an eye on older children who may give your toddler a dangerous toy to play with, such as a truck with broken wheels.

When choosing a cot, check that the mattress is not inflammable, that it fits properly and is not covered with a protective sheet of plastic which could cause a very tiny baby to suffocate.

Also, look at the bars on the cot – ideally, they should be about 2.5–6.5 cm apart so that your child can't get his head stuck between them.

Many children kick off bedclothes at night, but don't be tempted to use an electric blanket. Not only could your child become too hot, he could also get the flex caught around his neck.

If you are worried about your child getting cold at night, place a convector heater with a thermostat in the nursery to regulate the temperature.

It takes time for older children to get accustomed to the expanse of an open bed and they can easily roll off in the middle of a dream. You can prevent this by fitting a side barrier. Keep it in place until you are confident that your child can cope with the freedom of an ordinary open bed.

Small babies have very little control over their neck muscles so they find it hard to sleep on pillows. In fact, a pillow can be positively dangerous as it could suffocate a baby. However, once your child is about a year old, a shallow pillow is fine.

Children love animals but the reverse is not always true. Your Alsatian may put up with your child swinging on its tail, but your neighbour's labrador that has "never hurt anyone" could turn nasty. Don't take chances. Also, dog dirt is both unpleasant and dangerous. Sweep up dirt from the garden before your child gets close. Similarly, place a cat's litter tray well out of reach. Cats have been known to suffocate babies by curling up on their faces, thinking that it is a nice warm place. Keep your cat away from your baby and use a cat-net on cots and prams.

Safety in the garden

All children love playing in the garden on a nice, warm day. But even the garden is not completely free of snags. Hide away any cans of insecticide and fertilizer where they cannot be reached, and put unused pots and tools away in a lock-up shed or in a safe cupboard indoors.

Ponds can provide great pleasure but they are a major hazard for babies and toddlers. If you have a pond, no matter how small, either drain it until your child is old enough to recognize the dangers, or cover it with sturdy nylon netting that is securely anchored all round. And always keep your garden gate shut, especially if it opens on to a road.

A very young child should not be left unsupervised in the garden as he could hurt himself falling on steps or eat earth or poisonous plants. Teach your child not to eat anything from the garden without checking with you first, as many common garden plants including yew and holly berries, laburnum seeds, daffodil bulbs, lupins, rhubarb leaves and privet hedging are either very poisonous or can lead to upset tummies if eaten.

Never let a child play unsupervised in a paddling pool and always empty it after use and store indoors. Rain can collect in the base if it is left upside down. Be very careful where you position climbing frames and swings to make sure that the surface where your child may land or fall is soft – grass or bark chippings are best.

Do not buy equipment that is too advanced for your child's age, as he is bound to want to test it out. Make sure younger children do not use the equipment unsupervised or wander too near when older children are playing – they are not yet mature enough to get out of the way of a moving swing or a jumping child.

Follow the instructions for fixing carefully – some large items need to be cemented into the ground. Check them frequently to make sure that no nuts and bolts have worked loose or ropes become frayed. Always buy from a reputable manufacturer and beware of second-hand bargains – they may be missing vital components or have lead in the paint.

Safety in the car

Over 3,000 children under five are killed or injured in car accidents every year and car restraints are one thing that it is not worth economizing on.

From birth to about nine months (10 kg) your baby is safest in a rear-facing car seat, held in place by existing seat belts and, preferably, placed in the back. For an older baby and toddler (10–18 kg) you will need a forward facing car seat which is fastened to the back either by a special anchorage kit or by an approved seat belt. Incorrect fitting is dangerous so check that the seat is correctly installed.

A convertible car seat which adapts to your child's growing needs is a wise investment. These are initially rear-facing but can be refitted in a forward-facing position when your baby reaches 10 kg.

Always look for the British Safety Standard number when choosing a car seat (or any piece of baby equipment), or better still, an ABSI Kitemark.

Children learn fast how to undo the restraining straps of their car seat or safety belt, so teach him from the start that he may not do this until you tell him it is safe to do so. Also, remember that a very angry or upset child will forget or ignore the rules so have childproof locks fitted to the rear doors of your car to make sure that there is no risk of him ever escaping into traffic.

Safety Outside the Home

When you are crossing the road, do not be tempted to nip across at places you know are not necessarily the safest. And never let the pram or buggy leave the edge of the pavement until you are sure the road is clear. Many accidents happen when a car or motorbike comes sweeping round a corner and either hits or has to swerve to avoid a pram or buggy. If you cannot find a safe place to cross with a good view of the road and you have to cross between parked cars, always step in front of your baby to check that there are no cars coming.

A very young child has no sense of danger and also cannot remember what you told him a couple of minutes ago, so once he is walking you will have to watch him all the time. At one moment he will be walking quietly beside you, the next he may spot something interesting on the other side of the road and dash off to explore – right into the stream of traffic. Always hold a young child's hand firmly.

You can begin to teach your child road safety as soon as he can understand simple explanations. Tell him that people go on pavements and cars go on roads and that the kerb marks the boundary between the two. Do not trust him to stay on the kerb though and never let him walk alone on the pavement at any distance from you until you are absolutely sure he is safe. Teach him to walk on the inside of the pavement with you between him and the traffic. When it comes to crossing the road, explain the drill to him (and follow it yourself at all times). When he knows it, let him give the instructions and tell you when he thinks it is safe to cross. Make road safety fun by letting him press the buttons on the crossings and look out for the green figure that mean it is safe to cross.

Never, however, let a child under five cross the road alone. Even if he is concentrating, a child of this age still muddles right and left and cannot judge accurately how far away approaching traffic is, how fast it is moving, or if a car is moving at all. Even when your child is older it may be a long time before he is mature enough to cross a busy road alone, so keep stating the rules and watch him until you are absolutely sure he is safe.

Even in the park you need to be careful. Traffic sometimes drives through parks, and there is also danger from older children on fast bicycles or skateboards. Let your child run around in safe areas only and teach him to treat the roads running through parks as he would any other road. Keep an especially careful eye on him when he is near water.

In the play area, keep your child in view at all times. Do not let him go there accompanied only by an older child who is likely to let his attention wander and be inclined to show off himself. If you cannot go yourself, make sure your child is with an adult you trust.

Most accidents affecting children over two years old happen when they fall, usually off play equipment, over their own feet or through bumping into another child. So while you want your child to mix with others, do not let him get caught up with an exceptionally rowdy group. If you can, choose a park where the play area has an impact-absorbing surface such as bark or sand as this will reduce the chance of head injuries should he fall.

Warning your child about strangers

While you do not want to give your child the idea that all the people he meets are potentially unpleasant, you do need to teach him that he simply cannot trust everyone.

With a baby or very young child, it is best to keep him within your sight at all times and only to leave him with someone you know and trust. Once your child is slightly older, you can talk to him about potentially dangerous situations.

You may find it easiest to start by taking examples from real life and asking him what he would do in certain situations, if, for example, someone were bullying him into doing something he did not want to do, such as taking biscuits from the tin when you have told him not to. He will probably answer that he would tell you. If not, explain that this is the best course of action and that you will not get angry. You can lead on from a familiar situation to talking about adults or older children touching him and kissing him and asking him to keep secrets he is unhappy about.

Teach your child his name, address and telephone number and tell him that if he is separated from you or another adult he should go either to a police officer, a shop assistant or a mother with children to ask for help. Explain to him what to do if he is frightened by someone, for example if a man he did not know came up to him and spoke to him. Get him to practise saying "No, go away," and to shout if necessary.

Always keep the lines of communication open and encourage him to tell you about anything that he is at all worried about but do not make him nervous by harping on about vague dangers. Always give clear examples of what you are talking about. As your child gets older and can understand more, you can elaborate the rules as he gains more independence.

Here are some useful guidelines to follow to avoid potentially dangerous situations:

● Encourage your child to talk to your about all his experiences – good and bad.

● Be precise in what you say; vague warnings can worry your child without telling him anything concrete.

● Tailor your warnings to suit your child's age and the amount of freedom he is allowed.

● Always believe what your child tells you, and listen to him when he is unwilling to stay with a particular adult, for example a childminder or babysitter.

● Never leave your child with strangers or accept a babysitter without personal recommendation or references.

● Teach your child that certain parts of his body (the areas covered by his swimsuit) are his alone and he need never let anyone touch them if he does not want to.

● If your child needs to be collected from somewhere by someone other than yourself, have a family password to let your child know that the person is safe.

● Never leave your baby alone outside a shop; always take him with you.

Sand Play

Playing with sand is an important learning experience for your child. Almost every playgroup, nursery school and infant reception class will have access to sand, either in a specially designed sand-pit or sand-tray. Children learn a great deal about the behaviour of substances, weight, size, movement and balance from using sand, as well as enjoying themselves thoroughly in the process.

Your child will soon discover that dry and wet sand behave very differently. Dry sand is less messy and will pour like liquid. He will enjoy letting it run through his fingers or seep through his toes and pouring it from one container to another. Your child may also be surprised by how the same quantity of sand poured into a small container seems to be much less when poured into a large one. A child under four will have difficulty understanding that there is the same amount of sand in the large cup as in the small one. This kind of play helps a small child understand about volume.

If you have some scales, you can let him pour sand into the pan and balance it with weights. This will teach him about quantities and balance.

If you wet the sand a little, it will become firm and he will be able to mould it into shapes. He can use a specially designed mould, a jelly mould or a small beaker to do this himself. You can then show him how to make sandcastles using a bucket and spade – at first he will knock them down, but gradually he will get the idea of how to make one himself. He will enjoy slowly filling up a bucket, patting the sand down with his spade to make it smooth and then tipping it out.

If you make the sand really sloppy and wet, it will become like a liquid once more, pouring from one container to another. Your child can let it drip through his fingers and make sand pies by patting it out on a firm surface. Many parents think playing with sand is only possible on the beach or in a sand-pit in the local park, but it is an activity that is perfectly suitable in the home. You can keep a tub or plastic box filled with sand on a balcony or patio or even in the kitchen or bathroom.

If the sand is outdoors, you will need a lid to the container to keep the rain off and cats out. If you keep the container indoors, you will need to put down newspaper or a groundsheet to protect the floor. You will also need to stay with your child to make sure he does not spread sand around the house.

If you have a garden, you can make a sand-pit. A sunken sand-pit needs to be dug out and lined with bricks, concrete or polythene and involves a great deal of work. More easily, you can make a raised sand-pit using bricks or wood. You can even improvise by using an old tyre to contain the sand.

Choose a spot which is sunny, otherwise the sand tends to get damp and stay that way. It also helps if you choose a spot which is not too far from a tap so that loose sand can be washed away and not trodden into your carpets.

You can also buy plastic sand-trays, sometimes with a seat at either end for your child to sit on, and sometimes with a paddling pool incorporated. These can be good value, though they may get broken if children are too boisterous. These sand-trays usually come with a cover which you may need to weight down to keep animals out of the sand.

When it comes to buying the sand itself, the type of sand you buy is important. You can buy play sand in small sacks from toyshops, but this is usually quite expensive. Silver sand used to be recommended for sand-pits, but it has been found that sharp pieces of silver sand in the eye can cause damage, and that a coarser sand is safer.

You can get sand cheaply and in large quantities from a builders' merchant, but check that the sand has been washed, otherwise it will stain everything dark yellow, and the stain can be hard to remove. Unwashed sand is usually quite dark in colour, while washed sand should be pale.

You will also need to provide some equipment to help your child experiment, but this does not necessarily mean that you need to buy a lot as many household implements will do the job. You can use sieves, colanders, empty washed yoghurt pots, bottles, spoons, rolling pins, jelly moulds and slotted spoons. A bucket and spade and a watering-can will be useful and you can also buy stacking beakers, some of which have moulds on the bottom or different sized holes.

Sand in the eyes can, of course, be very painful. Never let children throw sand about, especially in people's faces. Also, beware of dry sand blowing into the eyes on a windy day.

If your child does get sand in his eyes, they will water profusely and the sand will be washed out naturally. Crying is actually good, as this will help the process. Once the sand is washed out, check your child's eyes to make sure there is nothing left behind to cause further irritation. Try to stop him rubbing his eyes as this will make the discomfort worse. If his eyes remain red and sore, or look infected, see a doctor.

Sand will usually find its own way out of a child's ear if left alone; you can turn the child's head to one side and make him shake his head to encourage it to fall out. Do not be tempted to poke things into your child's ear to try to scoop sand out, as this is likely to cause more damage than the sand itself, especially with a child wriggling. If your child gets sand in his mouth he will usually spit it out himself. If you have a drink at hand get him to rinse his mouth out with it, telling him not to swallow. Babies or small children often repeatedly eat sand; while this will not do any harm if the sand is clean, it's best to try to prevent it by giving him plenty of other distractions.

Scalds

◆ See **Burns and Scalds**

Science in Play

By playing with simple stacking bricks, your child is quite naturally discovering the basic principles of design – how to build a tower or wall, and soon a bridge or a house. Within this, he is exploring symmetry and dimensions, balance and support.

There is lots of fun to be had with balloons. If your child is over three (it is dangerous for children younger than this), let him put small beans or split peas into a balloon before you blow it up and tie it as usual. You now have a huge rattle which, when held close to the ear and shaken, sounds like a thunderstorm. The balloon is acting as an amplifier, making the sound louder. Experiment with different contents and listen to the effects – try paperclips or water, but beware!

Show your child how to rub the balloon against his woollen jersey to make static electricity. Sometimes it needs quite a vigorous rub before it is charged, but once it is, it will stick to his jumper.

If your child enjoys painting, he might like to use his artistic creativity to experiment with colour. Together, make some circles out of thick card and decorate the discs with bright squiggles, scribbles and patterns. Make a small hole in the centre of each disc and push a used match through it. Spin the disc on the unburnt end and watch how your patterns and colours change.

This next experiment relies on making very solid blocks of colour, so you may have to help. Take another disc of card and, with a pen, mark it into quarters. Paint two opposite sections red, and the other two sections yellow, so you have alternating red and yellow segments. Make it into a spinner as above and watch the colours merge to give orange as the disc spins round and round. Using primary colours (red, yellow and blue), try the same, using different pairs of colours.

Now, for another experiment, mark six equal segments on a disc and paint the colours of the rainbow, one in each segment, in the following order: blue, violet, red, orange, yellow and green. Put a large nail through the centre of the disc and fix it into a hand drill. Turn the drill and watch the colours disappear. White light is made up of the spectrum of colours seen in a rainbow. By colouring the disc in segments, the light is broken up. The spinning motion puts white light back together again.

Playing outside, in the garden, the park or on the beach on holiday, provides good contact with the natural world. Back indoors, you can set aside a special shelf for him to use as a nature corner. Here he can put his special finds – an interesting stone, shells, a feather, autumn leaves, conkers, acorns and sticky buds or pussy willow placed in water. Some children love collecting and all sorts of things take their fancy – the nature corner can accommodate anything. (*See* Gardening and Nature Study.)

There is always a scientific explanation for the magic of tricks. Here's one explained by the greater density of salt water over ordinary water so objects, including people, float more easily in salt water. Your child will enjoy performing this trick for an admiring audience:

1. Find two ½ litre jars and one 1 litre jar.

2. Add 6–8 heaped tablespoons of salt to ¾ litre of water and stir until the salt dissolves.

3. Put the salty water into one of the ½ litre jars and ordinary water into the other ½ litre jar.

4. Now your child can very carefully lower an egg into first one, then the other jar. To everyone's surprise it floats in one jar and sinks in the other.

5. Remove the egg and pour the ordinary water into the larger jar. Lower the egg into the jar.

6. Slowly empty the salt water into the big jar and see the egg rise, as if by magic, to sit suspended in the middle of the jar.

Changes in the climate are another interesting area for observation, and weather can provide a stimulating area of study for even the youngest scientist.

Look at the sky each day when your child is getting dressed, discuss what sort of day it will be and what to wear. Discover how the clouds move by taping a black paper frame to a window that looks on to the sky and see how the clouds move across the frame, sometimes fast, sometimes hardly at all.

Explain to your child that it is the wind that is moving them, and show him how the wind also moves trees, leaves and grass.

Self-Esteem

◆ See **Confidence**

Separation Anxiety

◆ See **Shyness**

Sex After Childbirth

◆ See **Motherhood**

Sex Differences

Recent research suggests that the differences between the sexes which are so clear by the age of five are a complex mixture of biological factors – that's to say the influence of sex hormones – and the effects of environment and upbringing. Woven together, these inborn and learned distinctions affect the interests and attitudes of boys and girls from babyhood onwards.

Even before the birth, the future sex of a baby is a matter of great interest and endless debate. Few parents escape the constant speculation of friends and relatives and many now choose to be told the sex after an antenatal scan.

It is now thought that boys are more innately physical and aggressive than girls because of the male sex hormone testosterone. Any parent with young boys knows how much pleasure they derive from rough and tumbles; again, research shows that four-year-old boys spend far more time romping and fighting than girls, for whom craft activities and pretend domestic scenes take up much of their play.

Girls tend to play in small groups or in pairs where "best friends" are important. It's unusual for girls to play competitively and quarrels don't usually end in aggression. Boys, on the other hand, are more likely to show rivalry, and they play in larger groups with "leaders" who have more status.

Boys are generally more keen on vigorous games and sport than girls and take far more interest in competitive team games. Sometimes, though, it's hard to tell whether it's the child or his father who really enjoys kicking a ball round a field every Sunday afternoon!

That boys seem to spend much of their time thinking and doing, and girls in feeling and relating, was shown in an experiment carried out among a group of ten-year-olds. Pairs of children, who didn't know each other before, were put into a room for ten minutes with several toys to play with. When two boys were in the room together, communication was confined to exchanges about the toy they were trying to construct, and their attention was focused mainly on their mutual interest in the toy. After ten minutes they knew each other's name and age. The pairs of girls, on the other hand, communicated in much greater depth. For them, the toys seemed almost an excuse to get to know each other and by the end of the time they had learnt a good deal about each other – family backgrounds, descriptions of homes and favourite activities.

Toddlers don't appear to show any preference for one type of toy or another. One study showed that when provided with a choice of playthings, 18-month-old girls spent as much time as boys playing with a large truck which, for slightly older children, is usually regarded as a masculine toy.

Your 18-month-old may not be fussy but by the age of three or four your child may well be quite certain about what are "suitable" and "unsuitable" toys for their sex.

As well as differences in the ways girls and boys play and relate to others, there is research to suggest that:

- As babies, boys tend to cry more and sleep less than girls.
- Later on, girls are better at counting and make fewer mistakes than boys.
- Girls tend to talk more fluently than boys in the first four years of life.
- Boys tend to be physically more affectionate than girls.
- Girls in general dress themselves and feed themselves earlier than boys.
- Boys can throw much farther and more accurately than girls.
- Boys tend to be more confident and agile in learning to walk and run.

● During the pre-school years girls develop faster in terms of language skills and intellectual learning.

● Boys tend to develop co-ordination and agility faster than girls.

◆ See also, **Sexual Stereotyping**

Sexual Discovery

Babies, especially boys, usually become interested in their genitals at the end of their first year. They may discover their penis at bathtime or when their nappy is being changed and handle it out of curiosity; babies often find this handling quite pleasurable, but not in the way an older child or adult would. Small boys often pull or tweak their penis in quite alarming ways and it is not uncommon for them to have an erection. Girls too, find handling their genitals pleasurable.

It's best simply to ignore such behaviour. If it makes you feel uncomfortable or if you feel it happens rather too often, you can easily distract a child by giving him a toy to hold, tickling him or otherwise attracting his attention – but don't let him know that you find his behaviour upsetting.

Never scold your baby or child or slap his hand for handling his genitals as this will spoil his new-found enjoyment of his body. If you try to pull his hand away or stop him, it is likely to make him more interested and more determined to do it.

When your children are a little older, they may experience more intensely pleasurable feelings from touching their genitals and may masturbate in a more obvious way. If your child does this when you are present – for example, while snuggling down for his bedtime story – you can either choose to ignore it or gently distract him. It is best not to tell your child that this behaviour is wrong or punish him as this will give him a bad feeling about his body and may encourage him to conceal masturbation, and perhaps even become preoccupied by it.

Children of different sexes frequently have the opportunity to see one another in the nude – for example, in the summer, splashing in a paddling pool in the garden – and will soon notice that boys have a penis and girls don't. And around the age of five or six children often play games like "doctors and nurses" which involve exploring one another's bodies. Let your children carry on with such games while keeping an eye on them so things don't go too far. Of course it is inevitable that questions will soon follow.

A girl may feel deprived that she doesn't have a penis, so you may choose to tell her that one day she will have breasts to make milk for a baby and she will be able to grow a baby in her tummy, which boys cannot. A boy may fear that a girl has lost her penis, and that this could happen to him, so it is important to explain to him at an early age how boys and girls differ. A good time to start talking about this is at bath or nappy changing time.

Children will inevitably ask questions about their parents' bodies too, especially if they are used to seeing them undressed. You can use this as a way of talking about sexual matters. Some parents are able to feel very relaxed about their bodies and happy to discuss them with their children; others want to retain more privacy. It doesn't really matter which attitude you take, as long as you are honest with your child and do not make him feel that sex or nakedness is something to be frightened or ashamed of.

If you are expecting a baby and your other child is two or more, you can use this as a good opportunity to explain about how babies grow and develop and how they are born. The earlier you tell a child and the more simple you make your explanation, the easier it will be to add to it later on as your child's understanding grows.

Sex is as much to do with feelings and emotions, however, as it is to do with bodies and physical differences. Your emotional relationship with your child is very important for the development of his attitude towards sexuality later in life.

Your own relationship with your partner will have a bearing on how physical your relationship is with your child. If you and your partner are openly affectionate and loving with one another and make it clear to your child that you have a strong emotional bond, he will feel secure in many ways.

Not only will he be reassured that your inevitable rows and disagreements do not mean you might separate, but he will also feel free to enjoy his "love affair" with the parent of the opposite sex because he knows it will not threaten your relationship or get out of control in some way. He will also pick up subconscious "signals" from you that it is all right to kiss and cuddle.

Obviously not all children are lucky enough to have happily married parents, and an increasing number live in one-parent families. If this is the case in your situation, it is very important that you give your child plenty of attention, tell him that he is loved and give him the opportunity to see caring adults of both sexes.

It is, however, important that your own and your partner's sex life remains private. Your child might be disturbed by seeing or sensing you making love – he will be aware that this is something very powerful that he cannot be a part of and being totally excluded may be very hurtful to him. What is, in fact, a passionate embrace may look aggressive and frightening to a toddler.

Quite apart from actual lovemaking, most parents find that there are other things they want to keep private from their child, even if this is difficult at times. You may, for example, want to conceal your periods from your child. You may decide this partly because children almost always associate blood with being hurt and may find the explanation difficult to understand. Keeping young children out of the loo can be very difficult at times, however, and they are also likely to come across tampons and sanitary towels and ask what these are for. Every parent has a limit to what they feel they can share with their child and it is quite all right to say you'll tell them another time or discuss it when they are older – and change the subject. Be firm but pleasant and don't make it sound as if you are concealing something really interesting.

Telling your child the facts of life can be fraught with difficulty too. Often a young child only needs a very simple answer, like "Babies grow in the mummy's tummy". Children from three upwards are usually able to handle information about where babies come from, though it is not until they are about six or seven that they are able to understand the mechanics of sex. It is important to remember that sex is to do with feelings, too. So always talk about sex in terms of loving and caring, as well as the physical side, and be as honest as you can. This will make it easier to build a trusting relationship and for your child to share his feelings with you later on.

Sexual Stereotyping

Our society lays enormous emphasis on sex differences, and people even seem to need the reassurance of knowing a baby's sex before they know how to react to it. As a result, a whole range of outward symbols or codes are used to help tell baby boys and girls apart, although the old rules of pink for a girl and blue for a boy are largely outdated. For some people, knowing a baby's sex at a glance is something of a relief, because "appropriate" responses can be made: "Isn't she dainty?" or "Isn't he strong!"

Many parents, too, quickly begin reinforcing the baby's gender by dressing their girls in pretty dresses and boys in denims. But stereotypes already exist in people's minds: the baby with lots of blonde curls is invariably taken to be a girl; a baby with short, straight hair is assumed to be a boy. This stereotyping may seem unimportant but it can really influence the way in which people treat boys and girls, and the way boys and girls behave as a result.

In one recent study, a group of six-month-old babies were dressed in clothes typical of the opposite sex. Mothers invited to play with them were found to respond to the "girls" and "boys" very differently. When a baby "boy" cried, mothers tended to respond with lots of physical action such as lifting, swinging and tickling. With the "girls", mothers used soothing words and calming actions.

Boys are expected to (and do) enjoy outdoor physical activity, and can be dirty and messy with impunity; girls are usually expected to have more docile pursuits and are more likely to get told off for dirtying their clothes.

Some parents continue to apply different standards to boys and girls throughout the growing-up period. Girls are seen as needing greater protection and tend to be given more restrictions than their brothers, who may be given the freedom to roam beyond the home from a much earlier age.

Over the past 20 years, however, there has been a tremendous growth in awareness and questioning of traditional male and female roles and attitudes to these. It's important to realize the need for balance – on the one hand, to create a strong sense of sexual identity in your child, while on the other to try to free him or her from the clichés and assumptions that make it seem as if girls and boys are on opposite sides of a fence and will never be able to understand each other. From the very beginning your own attitude plays an influential part in how quickly and easily your child learns. From babyhood your child can distinguish a positive, and therefore approving reaction, from a negative one. If you approve of what he is doing, he will gain confidence and develop further. If you disapprove, he may lose interest.

Once your child is toddling, the range of toys available suddenly opens up. Rattles and activity boards are things of the past and the toys become more recognizably imitations of "real" things. But the emphasis should be on the stage of development and its accompanying skills rather than on the toy's suitability for a boy or girl.

For instance, all toddlers rapidly expand their construction skills and develop from being able to put one wooden block on top of another to fixing plastic building bricks into definite shapes and structures. This is a vital part of your child's exploration of the three-dimensional world. However, because in the adult world these are skills associated with building and engineering work, traditionally the domain of men, you may think of construction games as boys' rather than girls' toys.

But toys should not be regarded in the light of what your child is going to be when he or she grows up. Both boys and girls will develop the spatial aptitude and hand-eye co-ordination that these toys encourage. And they need to feel your approval to develop the confidence to experiment further and acquire more skills. They also need your approval if they are to enjoy fully what they learn.

Both boys and girls will have a favourite doll or cuddly animal which they feel attached to. It gives them security and is an object for their personal affections, outside the family. They will enjoy pushing their toy around in a baby walker or in a toy pram or pushchair. Once again, you shouldn't regard this as specifically a "girlish" activity. Your young toddler is enjoying the action rather than engaging in pretend play by adopting the role of mother.

Toddlers get the same fun out of riding a toy tractor or pushing around a toy bus. They are making things move, learning to pilot the objects over different surfaces and negotiate obstacles. They can see that a toy car or train is part of a mini-world but until they are around two and a half, toddlers' imaginations have not developed to the extent that they copy adult activity in organized play. At this early stage it is the activity itself that appeals, not the significance of that activity.

However, by about three years old, your child begins to adopt adult characters in pretend play. He will identify with the grown-ups close to him, or with those whose jobs have a clear function – like postmen, firemen or shopkeepers.

At this stage it is easy for girls to adopt their mother's role – they begin to play organized games with their dolls, acting as "Mummy". If they have a new baby brother or sister they will copy you by cradling a baby doll, bathing it and taking it out in a pram or pushchair. They will give "older" dolls a tea party or even organize them into an imaginary playgroup.

Boys can be encouraged to join in with – or initiate – this kind of play, learning important caring skills through it. But in mixed groups they usually feel that it is Daddy's role they should adopt. However, it is not always clear exactly what Daddy does. In many families Daddy leaves the house early and returns late from an invisible job. So boys may adopt as role models fantasy heroes like Superman or Batman who are also characters who come and go.

Dressing up is a good way for boys and girls to experiment with different roles for themselves. With a few simple props such as hats, bags and teatowels they can become characters from a favourite story or they can re-enact a visit to the doctor or dentist. Or your child can create these scenes by using puppets.

While girls play "house" they put a lot of energy into talking to the dolls – explaining and scolding much as you do with your child. This allows them to develop communication skills and girls are often found to be more articulate than boys. This may be because boys' "quiet" time is spent with more mechanical toys, such as building bricks or cars. They may talk about what they are building, or imitate the sound of cars on the road, but they don't have the same opportunity of reconstructing the emotions that are expressed when playing with dolls. Try to balance this by suggesting that your son include toy people in his building or car games. Once again, puppets are useful in encouraging communication.

For all forms of learning, confidence plays the greatest part in developing children's aptitude. So, in learning through play, boys need to develop a recognition of their caring and creative abilities. And this can best be achieved if both parents play an active part in playtime – each filling any gaps the other may leave.

It's important to remember that avoiding sexual stereotyping in your child's play is not simply a question of including boys in girls' games and vice versa, but depends on a degree of adjustment of your own attitudes. You may find that you have to make a few leaps of imagination in steering your child away from stereotyped perceptions. For example, when you play with toy cars or trains together don't always refer to the drivers as "he". Let your daughter have some toy cars and allow your young son to show an interest in toy pots and pans or toy brushes and hoovers. Remember that it is the play value of the toy that appeals to your child – feeling the movement of a toy bus or finding out how to brush up dust. It is important for young children to learn about all aspects of life and not to develop early inhibitions about "appropriate" behaviour.

It's also useful to know which areas of your child's personality can be developed or enhanced by particular toys or activities:

● Dolls and cuddly toys allow both boys and girls to display and articulate emotion. Your child develops responsibility in caring for a special toy.

● Cars and trains: both boys and girls enjoy the sensation of moving toy vehicles over different surfaces and the absorbing nature of this play expands a child's self-reliance.

● Domestic play: your child wants to copy you and develop the same abilities as you have. You can provide either sex with a duster or a toy broom to keep them happy.

● Building bricks develop your child's manipulative ability as well as an understanding of the three-dimensional construction skills that both sexes need to acquire.

● Dressing up allows children to feel what it's like to be "in someone else's shoes". It is a form of self-expression which also strengthens confidence and is an outlet for humour. It should be no stranger for a boy to dress up as a queen than for a girl to dress up as Daddy.

Sharing

A toddler's world is completely self-centred, and everything in it is "his". The key to understanding and dealing with your child's possessive behaviour is to accept it as a natural – if temporary – part of his development.

Experts on child development have established that a typical two-and-a-half-year-old wants complete possession of any object he is playing with, has played with, or might play with and is quite likely to go into a rage if he is denied his wish. While a tantrum is at its height, there is probably very little you can do about it; in fact insistent demands for sharing can make matters worse and your child more possessive.

A lot of children show more readiness to share around the age of three, although personality as well as age has some bearing on when this happens. And the structure of your family may also influence his willingness to share. An only child will grasp the concept of sharing a little later as the demand to share arises later and less often. Whereas if your child has elder brothers or sisters he will soon get used to the idea that toys are to be shared between everybody.

Generally speaking, the more secure and loved a child feels the easier he finds it to share. It is wise to remember that some quarrels, particularly between brothers and sisters, may not be about sharing toys but a way to demand attention and the lion's share of parental affection.

Instead of punishing your child for snatching his baby brother's toys and making him cry, try to make him feel special. Spend as much time alone with him as you can and talk to him about what pests babies can be but how they need bigger people to look after them. When he plays with his brother nicely, praise and reward him.

If your child shows a natural aversion to sharing you may be tempted to keep him in "solitary confinement" until he's learnt to share. But keeping a small child isolated is not the answer. Only by mixing with other children will he learn to cope with the grab and snatch of group play. If he starts hoarding all the play dough or instigates as tug-of-war, rather than feel embarrassed, do step in to distract and divert his attention. This is the best way to handle the situation at this stage. In your home environment, try and treat your two-year-old's belongings with respect. Before a playmate comes to visit, find out which of his favourite toys he wants you to put away for safekeeping and which he wouldn't mind sharing with his friend.

It is no use providing enough equipment for one child and expecting two to share it. Even if they are involved in the same activity give them their own equipment and space. Providing them with a pot of glue and a paint brush each and sitting them at opposite ends of the table will minimize conflicts. If they still arise, offer an alternative plaything to the one who grabs.

Duplicating big toys like tricycles and trucks will be well worth the expense so that the children can play side by side without competition. Some playthings, like a large sand-pit with plenty of tools, also work well for two. By trial and error, you'll soon find out which toys cause the least fights between two children – bricks, construction toys, puzzles, play people, for example, as long as there are enough pieces to keep them both happy.

Games that involve taking turns and role-playing are good for getting your child used to the idea of give and take and sharing. Some good ones are:
● Rocking boat – that takes two to play
● Trampolining – turns are the rule
● Wagon – pushing and being pushed
● Tea party – hosts and guests
● Shop – shopkeeper and customer
● Ball games – throwing or rolling
● Making a "team collage" – sharing glue, scissors, paint and magazines to cut out to make one giant picture together (any number of children).

It is no coincidence that most children start playgroup at around the age of three. This is the age when they begin to find playing together rather than merely alongside each other much more fun. This is also the age when your child's language develops rapidly and he'll be more responsive to verbal reasoning. He will listen to you explaining why he can't have all the colouring pens – that his playmates want to draw as well and that they will get bored and upset if he refuses to share.

It helps if a child feels that he gains rather than loses by sharing. With amusement you'll notice that little deals are going on between your child and his friends. He has learnt that to persuade his friend to lend him a desirable toy he has to offer an equally popular one in return.

Parting with sweets and chocolate is hard for any child. But try and encourage sharing treats especially when other children are around. If your child is given a bag of sweets by a visiting aunt or grandparent, persuade him to keep just a few for his best friend to share. On the other hand, you'll be surprised how commonly sharing and swapping lunchbox treats is practised in playgroups and nursery schools.

On a higher – and less materialistic – level your child will soon show signs that he has learnt to share other people's feelings. Seeing his best friend hurt by another child will make him want to comfort him. Or he may feel sympathetic towards a new child at playgroup who desperately wants to be included in the game.

Shock

Shock has nothing to do with being startled. It is a potentially fatal condition that occurs when a person's blood pressure becomes too low for the blood to flow normally through the tissues of the body and back to the heart. It can happen when a person loses a lot of blood or when the heart stops working properly. Although most of the body's vital organs can function for a limited time without enough blood, the brain and the heart cannot and death is caused if prompt action is not taken.

Shock may be caused by heavy bleeding (both internal and external; electric shock, which affects the heart; severe burns, which cause great fluid loss from the damaged skin; severe infection; dehydration after severe vomiting or diarrhoea; an abnormal reaction to medicines, bites or stings (like an allergic reaction, known as anaphylactic shock).

A person suffering from shock may have one or several of the following symptoms: pale bluish or greyish skin (especially under the fingernails and inside the lips); shallow, fast breathing; cold, clammy skin; a rapid, weak pulse; dizziness; blurred vision; sweating; thirst; restlessness. He may also become unconscious. Delayed shock can occur some time after an accident or injury so if your child is badly hurt see your doctor immediately even if he shows none of the symptoms of shock.

Always get medical treatment for shock. Meanwhile move your child as little as possible as this can make an injury worse, especially if you suspect he may have a broken bone or an internal haemorrhage after an injury or accident. If you are sure there are no broken bones, lay him on a blanket or coat and raise his legs so that they are higher than his chest, supporting them on cushions or pillows. Loosen any tight clothing, particularly around the neck, chest and waist. Turn his head to one side. Cover him with a blanket to keep him warm but do not let him get too hot. Never use a hot water bottle or electric blanket as these bring blood to the surface of the skin, allowing even less to get to the vital organs. If your child is unconscious, check that his airway is free and give resuscitation if necessary. Put him in the recovery position. Call for an ambulance or if no broken bones are suspected take him to your doctor or the nearest hospital accident and emergency department immediately. If he has lost a lot of blood a blood transfusion will be necessary.

◆ See also, **Artificial Respiration**, **First Aid**

Shyness

Some child development experts call shyness in babies "eight-month anxiety", because it's often at this age that babies first show their awareness that one or two people in their lives are extra-special and no one else will do. In fact, though eight months might be the "peak" age for this sort of behaviour, lots of babies between about four months and a year or older start to show the same nervousness. An unfamiliar face – or even a familiar one – doesn't produce a happy, sociable smile; instead, your baby turns his face away and may even start to cry. People who wear glasses sometimes have this effect on a baby if the baby's parents don't wear them, or a man with a beard if the baby's father is clean-shaven.

The best way to cope with this is not to force the pace. The majority of babies going through this stage come through it within a few months. Some do go on to be shy and clingy toddlers – but shyness can develop in toddlers without any previous signs. Treat it as a normal phase in your baby's development; don't insist on him sitting on Granny's lap if he's screaming with misery. Explain to people who might feel offended at the apparent rejection that you're quite sure it's nothing to do with them personally and that your baby reacts in the same way with other people as well.

Parents often describe their toddlers as "clingy". This is the sort of behaviour that means you can't leave your child alone even to go to the loo, and where your child insists on being cuddled on your lap right the way through a visit to a toddler group or to someone else's house.

This sort of toddler is very shy with other people, and seems to regard everyone bar Mum, Dad or other close family with deep suspicion. A usually talkative toddler might not say a word outside his own home, for example, and the idea of being able to leave him with a babysitter while you go out for the evening could seem unthinkable, in case he wakes up and howls in despair because you're not there.

While this stage lasts, it helps to leave your child only with someone he knows. If you are getting a babysitter, introduce the two of them to each other during the daytime on a few occasions before you leave the babysitter in sole charge. Also mention the person in conversation to your child to make her or him seem more familiar. Remember, though, that time away from your child is important and that it is definitely worth the risk of your child waking and being distressed. After all, he will get over it, and there could be every chance he might be perfectly happy even without you there.

If your child is still very shy by the age of three or so, when you'd perhaps expect him to enjoy nursery or playgroup, accept that you'll have to take things very gradually until he settles in. If he sticks to your side like glue, refuses to look the playleader in the eye and shows no inclination to make anything at all from the play dough unless you're by his side, don't give up hope. The best approach is to stay with him for a few sessions and then occasionally leave him for very short periods – perhaps 10 to 15 minutes at a time.

If this seems to be working, build on it. You might collect him early a few times rather than leaving him for the full session. Or invite a more confident member of the playgroup home to tea so that he can have a special friend there. It can take very shy children a term or more to begin to feel happy without you. A few children aren't really ready for separation until four or older, and continue to need a lot of support through the early months of school.

These days, it seems the more confident and extrovert you are, the more likely you are to succeed in life. We associate shyness with a lack of self-worth, and it is sometimes viewed as a real social handicap. It is normal for parents to worry that their child will grow into a shy adult, never "shining" in public or fully realizing his potential. But shyness is not necessarily a negative trait. It can signal greater sensitivity, an appealing modesty and a quiet intelligence that's just as valuable as louder, more obvious self-confidence. If it takes friends a little time to get to know him, that's not necessarily a bad thing.

Of course, at the same time as trying to draw your child out of his shyness, and give him confidence in other people, you must make it known that he should never get into a car or wander away from home with anyone at all – not even with friends – without asking you. Don't go into any gory details at this stage. It's enough to explain that you get very worried if you don't know exactly where he is at any time.

While for many children, shyness is just a response to an overwhelmingly busy world, for some children it can be the result of something that's happened to them or within the family. A shock like an unexpected stay in hospital – yours or his – for instance, can shatter your child's confidence. If your child has to be separated from you, try to minimize the effect. If he's in hospital, stay with him as much as you can. If you have to go into hospital, phone him and arrange for him to visit you as often as possible.

The death of a loved one, the birth of a new baby, a move of house – any of these life-changing events can make your child seek refuge in shyness. Some children show their confusion by being aggressive; others become more withdrawn. Let your child know that you understand how he feels and that it is a difficult time. Don't put pressure on him to pull himself together and behave "normally" if he's not ready for it. Very young children are best helped simply by being with you – even 15 minutes quiet cuddling time in the evening will help your child to regain his confidence.

Sibling Rivalry

One of the most obvious ways in which rivalry shows is when parents get on fine with each of their children individually, but as soon as they try to involve two children in the same activity, whether it's a bedtime story or a visit to the supermarket, things start to go wrong. From the children's point of view, it's as if each loses that sense of being the only person that matters to you. Your attention is, as far as they're concerned, divided and weakened and they can no longer feel so sure of your love.

As long as it seems that you're concentrating on your child, there's peace; but as soon as your attention shifts, then the noise and bad behaviour starts. A toddler, for example, might be playing happily while you're preparing a meal. The telephone rings and quite suddenly your child is whining for something to eat, clattering his toys, or even climbing on a chair to try to pull the telephone away from you. This is jealousy and the root cause is the same as that behind all sibling rivalry – children want the exclusive love of their parents. Everything that threatens, or seems to threaten, calls up jealous, attention-seeking behaviour.

While phone calls and visitors are temporary, brothers and sisters don't go away and, for a few unlucky children, seem to represent a permanent threat to the love they get from their parents. In rare cases childhood jealousy can last well into adult life. When this happens grown men and women bear grudges, get very sensitive or act in childishly competitive ways with their brothers or sisters unless they can unravel the problems from the past.

Why are these childhood feelings so deep? Why do the effects of jealousy between brothers and sisters do such damage to what is often an otherwise happy family life? The answer seems to be that the need to be loved by your parents is a very strong instinct present in the newborn baby, for whom a mother's love is literally a matter of life or death. This intense attachment plus the feeling of being central in the parents' world are powerful shaping forces for all children, but for firstborn and only children these feelings are likely to be longer lasting.

Although the amount of rivalry that exists between children within a family is a very individual thing, certain age gaps do seem to be more likely than others to cause resentment. Often it's most noticeable when there's a gap of between two and four years between children, as there are more potential comparisons that can be made between them, and more sharing – of similar toys and interests – to be faced. If you have children close together, say with only 16 or 18 months between them, there's generally less jealousy, perhaps because the elder is still too young to be aware of any threat from the new arrival.

If your first child is already four and a half or five, then again you're likely to find jealousy less of a problem. A child of this age has often built up quite a world of his or her own; nursery school and playmates provide a security in addition to the parents' love. Also, older children are better able to understand why babies might need more attention than themselves.

Usually children are most jealous of the child born immediately after them, whatever the difference in ages between them. So a firstborn may resent a second child but get on perfectly well with a third. But there are really no hard and fast rules about the order of birth or the gaps between children.

As well as the ages of your children contributing to rivalry, gender differences play their part as well. It's generally thought that jealousy is less common among children of the same sex, so that if you have two boys close in age, there's less chance of squabbling and jealousy than if a boy follows a girl or vice versa. But again, this is a general rule and many parents will have experiences to contradict it.

When a new child comes into the family you can do a lot to reduce feelings of resentment. Give other children plenty of warning before the baby arrives, to reduce the amount of change the other children have to cope with immediately around the time of the birth.

When talking about the new arrival to your three-, four- or five-year-old, try not to paint too rosy a picture. The three-year-old who is expecting a new playmate is bound to be disappointed when in reality he's faced with a crying infant who spends most of his time in his mother's arms. "The new baby will need your help as well as mine," is a better approach, as it offers potential for transforming your child's jealousy into a desire to be co-operative.

Later on, once problems begin to arise you'll probably tend to meet each situation as it comes. It's all too easy to be carried along from one household chore to another reacting to each child as he makes demands on you, especially if you've got two or three children under five to cope with. But as a rule it's better to meet the situation positively; try to anticipate and be prepared to take a definite line on what is happening. Even more important, try to arrange to spend some time every day with each child.

Classic inter-sibling jealousy is at work if:

● Your older child becomes babyish and demanding once there's a younger baby in the family.

● One child becomes destructive and difficult as soon as your attention is on the other child.

● There is pinching, pushing and kicking of a younger child by the elder once your back is turned.

● One child constantly tells tales to you about the other.

● The older child snatches toys or breaks up the games of the younger.

● There are quarrels over fairness in terms of watching television, food, treats and so on.

Asserting yourself, compromising and defending your possessions – or your ideas – are all things you do at some time in your life, and for most people the first testing ground for these qualities and skills is against the background of a loving family.

Many situations can trigger underlying feelings of jealousy but you'll probably find the biggest area of bickering among your children is over fairness. The question of whether or not you are being fair can crop up in a million and one situations daily in a household where there are two or more children vying for your attention.

Treating children fairly doesn't mean treating them equally. Each child is a unique individual and the way you respond to them should reflect this. It's appropriate for your eldest child to get more pocket money, stay up a little later or stay with Granny overnight. It's appropriate for you to devote more time in helping your toddler to get dressed, play with his toys, splash in the bath. The secret is to be very honest about why you are devoting extra time and energy to a particular child and to point out that there will be occasions when you'll treat the other child as special, too.

There will always be times when children fight or are resentful over something they think is unfair. In the end, it is best not to worry too much about it yourself. If you become involved in every squabble, then your children will see that it's a very good way of grabbing your attention. So keep cool and try to view the situation from the children's point of view.

When a four-year-old knocks down his toddler sister's brick tower or snatches a rattle from his baby brother, it is not because he wants to see a mess on the floor or he wants to play with the rattle, it's simply an opportunity to display anger. That feeling is real and unless you acknowledge it you're unlikely to make much progress with the situation.

If you immediately leap to the attack of the child who is worse behaved or who is moaning loudest about unfairness, that will only serve to confirm his feelings that you don't love him as much. Feeling rejected, he'll be more justified in striking out the next time a similar situation arises. Instead, attend to the "victim", and make it clear if you can that you're sure the other brother or sister is capable of acting better.

When you speak to the "guilty" party, let them know you understand their feelings. If your child is old enough he can be encouraged to talk about any feelings of unfairness. Make it clear that you appreciate how annoying the other child can be at times. Try to separate in your mind the child whom you love from the behaviour which you can't tolerate. Labelling a child as "selfish" or "unkind" can do a lot of damage to their self-esteem. Always make it clear that you love the child although you dislike their behaviour.

However much the jealousy and rivalry between your children gets you down, remember that most go through phases of a few months or at most a few years when this is a problem. Develop a strategy and stick to it – in this way you'll appear cool, assured and you may even be able to bring a little humour into the situation. Remember also that along with feelings of jealousy, there's usually a lot of affection and loyalty between your children. Build on the occasions when one child leaps to the defence of the other – even though they may have been fighting only a moment earlier. Praise the loyalty and ignore the petty jealousy and you'll bring out the best in your children. If you can approach rivalry in an equally positive way, then you have a good chance of guiding your children on to strong, happy relationships.

Sibling Status

It takes hard work and sensitivity on the part of parents to ensure harmony between brothers and sisters. Close-knit families are those where each child is treated as an important individual and the problems and talents of each child are given understanding and recognition.

Your first child will, for a while, have your undivided attention. He will have much love lavished on him from all quarters, especially if he is also the first grandchild. In the general enthusiasm there will probably be a baby book about him and mementos such as his first lock of hair will be cherished. Gifts from friends and family will pour in to welcome his arrival and then again for his first birthday. He will receive all the perks of being an only child and he will love it.

Of course, being the first child is not all wine and roses. There is a great deal of anxiety and tension around as people adjust to the idea of being a parent for the first time. The first child is often called the "experimental child" by experts, and a lot of the strain you feel when trying to cope with everything will be sensed by him.

Then, having got used to being the centre of the universe, your firstborn has to adjust to a rival when your second child is born. Coping with a new baby and having to deal with a jealous and demanding toddler can wear your patience a little thin at times. You have less time and energy to devote to your older child and he will resent this bitterly.

Your firstborn may well express some pretty horrid feelings towards your second child which might shock you. It is important to acknowledge these feelings and to talk them through gently and calmly, however appalled you are. Telling him that he is wrong to feel like that will only make him suffer in guilty silence and reinforce his fear that he has lost your love to the unwelcome newcomer. (See Sibling Rivalry.)

It can be difficult to be understanding towards your older child when he is in the middle of a full-blown tantrum and you have a new baby to look after. It is important, however, to try. It is vital to keep special, "quality" time for your older child.

As your first two children get a little older, subtle changes will take place. Your second child will move out of babyhood and will want to play with his sibling's more grown-up toys. Your older child will have to get used to sharing not only you but his possessions as well.

Fights over toys are a common feature around this time. Most parents tend to try to protect their younger, weaker offspring, and expect their older child to set a good example and be more responsible, when often this is not at all realistic. This can feel very much like taking sides to an older child.

Your firstborn could feel quite bewildered: he may be older, but his little brother or sister appears to have more power when the toy in question is snatched from his grasp and handed over to his crying sibling. It is very hard to know how to deal with these power struggles fairly.

Suggesting a different activity altogether is one option, but when passions are running high, distraction tactics do not always work. Under these circumstances removing the offending toy may be the only answer. Sometimes you will have to act as judge but only if both little warriors are in the frame of mind to be reasonable and this is rare. The more you encourage the fair discussion approach by setting a good example yourself, however, the more likely your children are to develop this strategy among themselves.

The arrival of a third child brings about changes for both children, but the youngest is likely to be more affected by them. He has to let go his role as the baby of the family and this can be tough. Suddenly, he becomes a middle child with no real status. If he is close in age to his older sibling and is of the same sex, he is also less likely to have things that are exclusively his.

Sharing his older brother's bedroom will tend to deny him his own space unless clear boundaries are set. Older children usually get the top, most desirable bunk so, if space allows, it is best to provide separate beds and chests of drawers. Hand-me-down clothes and toys make economic sense when young children are so expensive to run, but they do not help this middle child to gain any real sense of importance. So it is vital to make sure that he does have some toys and clothes that are his alone.

Teachers of children with special needs recognize that middle children are more likely to need extra help at school; they are also more liable to suffer from fairly frequent bouts of minor illness. This is due to the middle child's lack of status within the family. Being "piggy-in-the-middle" results in him needing to attract more attention by illness or learning problems.

Usually, a little special attention from a caring teacher helps this child catch up very quickly. These problems are less likely if there are two middle children who are close in age. They tend to develop a special bond and therefore feel less isolated.

You are likely to expect more from your eldest child at this time. Coping with a new baby is not easy, especially there are two older, more active and often quarrelsome youngsters around.

It is natural to expect your eldest child to be more responsible, to be less free with the thumps and to be generally better behaved. He will often be called upon to be tidier, not only to look after his own things but to clear up after his sibling as well. Older children can often be pushed harder to fulfil parental ambitions. This can be particularly true of a boy, while there can be more pressure on girls to "mother" younger siblings.

Childhood seems to last longer for the youngest child. He is likely to be less independent than the others, because the older children have been too willing to fetch, carry and do his fighting for him. Sometimes this last child is a late talker because the older members of his family will anticipate his needs so he has no need to speak. On the other hand he may be the loudest, if only to get a word in edgeways.

Older children are more likely to accuse your youngest of being spoilt or of being the favourite. This is because experience has led you as a parent to be less anxious about this child. Discipline is more likely to be softer and your general attitude more relaxed.

Perhaps one of the hardest lessons for young children to learn is that life simply is not fair. One of the ways you can help your children understand this is by being honest about it.

Too much responsibility heaped on to your eldest child is not fair but often it can't be helped. Your middle child may feel left out. Your youngest may always feel "too young" to join in. These "unfairnesses" are often easier to bear if the situation is acknowledged and calmly discussed.

One very important thing is that each child should have his own friends. It is tempting to expect your eldest child to allow his younger siblings to tag along with him and his friends. This is all right some of the time, but it can be infuriating for older children to have a brother or sister cluttering up games and activities that are not necessarily suitable for them.

The company of children their own age is a vital part of any child's development. Every child should be allowed time with his friends without having to combine it with child-care duties.

Your middle child especially needs friends of his own to give him a sense of importance. If he always has to tag along with big sister or brother he will always feel over-shadowed.

There are other ways of giving each child a sense of their own importance and place in the family:

● If you keep a baby book for your first child make sure you do the same for all your children.

● Bedtime should be graded according to age, youngest first, middle next and eldest last. Although this is harder on you than bundling them all off to bed together, it places a value on the status of each child.

● Pocket money should also be graded according to status. It is important that your eldest and middle children should have privileges as well as responsibilities.

It is impossible to make sure that each of your children is treated fairly at all times. The best you can ever hope to do is to treat each one as a valuable and much loved individual. Each one needs good quality time devoted to them alone. Each one also has special talents which need to be recognized and made the most of. They do not need to be compared with their siblings and found wanting. Each of your children needs to know that you love them for being exactly who they are.

◆ See also, **Favouritism**

Single Parents

Singe-parent families are no longer a rarity and are becoming more and more common. While the increasing divorce rate is one reason for this, changing attitudes have made being an unmarried mum more acceptable and some babies of single mums are conceived quite deliberately.

Whatever the reasons, having a baby without a partner to share the care is not an easy option. Bringing up children is hard work when there's two of you; it's even more so when there's just one.

The main problems you're likely to face are tiredness, stress and having less money than you'd like, and sometimes less than you need. Of course, having a partner doesn't automatically mean having help with child-care and no money problems, but figures do show that single parents are more likely than others to depend on state financial aid. They are also more likely to see medical help for anxiety and depression.

So much for the black side of life on your own. For many mums, the negatives are cancelled out by the sheer joy, sense of achievement and day-to-day pleasure of raising their child. Though some may wish for a partner, others are more than content to stay single.

In the early days and weeks of single motherhood, you're likely to find tiredness your major problem. If you're living alone, or are without support, the sheer weight of responsibility is likely to add to your feeling drained and exhausted.

Single mums need a strategy to cope. Can you arrange for occasional but regular help? Friends, relatives and neighbours often make the offer, so why not admit to difficulties, and pin someone down? Whether they clean and tidy up for you, wheel the baby out while you relax at home, or babysit, the break will do you wonders.

Also, without a partner's routine to consider you can at least live as you want to, go to bed in the evening if you need to, lie in if you can or go back to bed when your baby sleeps in the morning.

Later on, as your baby develops and becomes mobile, you may still feel tired much of the time, especially when your baby drops his daytime nap. On the positive side, your baby is likely to be in more of a feeding and sleeping routine, so arranging a regular favour can actually be easier.

Being a single parent can be traumatic. If you weren't expecting to be on your own, the sadness, the shock and the resentment can add to the loneliness. Even if you've gone into the situation by choice, reality may not square with the way you imagined motherhood to be.

Though you may feel proud and happy to have a baby, you can't escape the fact that society's norm is still seen to be the two-parent family. It's easy to start believing that it's your job to do the work of two parents, and to feel guilty and defeated when it's just not possible.

For some single mums, lack of money and lack of opportunity to socialize or to work outside the home mean isolation. You have few friends to confide in, and little to look forward to. This is bad enough for yourself, but you then begin to wonder if your child is being affected by the isolation as well – and so those feelings of guilt surface again.

To avoid falling victim to this isolation, try getting into the habit of phoning a friend perhaps once a day for a chat. Fix up a regular meeting with a group of new mums, taking it in turns to host it. You could put a note in your clinic asking for other single mums to get in touch, and find out about the local mothers and babies group.

Making decisions on your own, even everyday ones, is hard as well. Should you leave your baby to cry? What should you do if he seems off-colour? Is he ill enough to call the doctor? Should you start potty-training now? How do you explain what he is and isn't allowed to do? What do you do when he's climbed on a chair and on to the table for the fourth time that day – is he being intentionally naughty or is it normal?

Resenting your baby for presenting you with these worries and dilemmas, for restricting your options and for not always being the sunny, placid companion you'd like is understandable. You can feel this way and still love your baby dearly, though sometimes, when things are very bad, that love can lie deeply buried under other feelings. For a few mums, emotional and physical pressures can occasionally make them feel violent towards their babies.

If you realize a crisis is on the way, or you're already facing one, don't try to soldier on. You owe it to yourself just as much to your baby to seek help.

Sometimes, simple measures are the answer, like consciously relaxing when the tension builds up, making room in the day to be yourself, and making determined efforts to break out of your isolation. But taking control in this way may be impossible if you feel depressed, undervalued or if you are not valuing yourself.

In these circumstances, go to your doctor. A health visitor, midwife, or a counsellor experienced in the sorts of problems facing one-parent families may be other sources of support and may help you find some positive solutions.

Though cash may be short, it doesn't mean you can't look after yourself as well as the baby. If you can't afford the clothes or the hairdressing appointments you're used to, treat yourself to small luxuries like a favourite bath oil or shampoo. In the morning spend a few extra minutes on yourself – it's good for your morale.

When you're shopping for food, aim to eat healthily and don't always go for the cheapest. You can indulge yourself once in a while without spending a lot of money.

Getting out with or without your baby is a top priority, especially if you're living alone. While your baby is small, you'll be surprised at how easy it is to take him with you to all sorts of places. Tiny babies sleep anywhere that's warm and clean, while slightly older ones are comfortable in a carrycot or pram top. Noise almost never wakes them.

Small babies can be taken in a sling or baby carrier on public transport. If you're using a car, a removable safety seat doubles as a baby chair. And breastfeeding mothers are the most mobile: there's no need to make up feeds to take with you.

When your baby's older, he's less likely to sleep anywhere, and may have developed an evening routine you don't want to disrupt. In any case, you will want time to yourself, so think about arranging babysitters. Grand-parents often love to be asked and from time to time may be happy to have your baby overnight or for a whole weekend. Don't be shy about asking.

For many single mums, the major worry is money. You may want to work, but can't afford or arrange the necessary child-care. This lack of cash may mean you're living in poor-quality housing or accommodation that is too small for you and your baby.

The Child Support Agency help you get the maintenance due from your baby's father (if this is what you want). You may also qualify for state financial help. Self-help organizations and government offices will tell you how to apply and what you can claim.

Your national group for one-parent families may be useful, and local branches of the group can be helpful for social contact and for worthwhile information and support. Often they arrange holidays for single parents and their children. Ask other single parents what they've found are problems, and how they got round them. Discussions like these are a great way to make new friends, too.

If work is an option, a job with a workplace nursery, or flexible hours will be a bonus. A jobshare or part-time work can often fit in well with a child.

Another possibility is to study part-time while the child is small. Not everyone wants to work at this stage. Taking a course will give you an outside interest, contact with other people and the opportunity to improve your qualifications. This may give you better job prospects when you eventually return to work.

Though conventional views hold that children are deprived if they grow up with only one parent, more and more people are realizing that families come in all shapes and sizes. One-parent families need acceptance, support and hope for the future, not condemnation or even sympathy.

You'll discover that single-parent families are as different from each other, and as individual, as two-parent families. All families have practical and emotional problems but for most, love and mutual closeness help them through. You and your child will find there are positive sides to being on your own.

If you did not get on with your child's father and the choice was either to remain in a difficult, unhappy situation because it seemed somehow safer or easier at the time, or to try to make a go of it on your own with your baby, you may become increasingly glad of your decision. It was not an easy choice but you made it, you survived it, and you will undoubtedly in time feel stronger and more confident because of it.

Try to encourage a good relationship between your child and his grandparents. Days spent with Granddad have countless benefits – your child will enjoy a special growing closeness, and being the apple of your father's eye; your father will have a willing and eager companion for all his solitary pursuits and you will have some well deserved time off.

Children from one-parent families can develop a particularly close and special bond with the parent who cares for them, and a sense of their own worth and importance. The mothers, as they watch their babies grow into childhood, can feel strong and proud that they are coping alone, especially when they look back on problems they never thought they'd overcome.

Sinusitis

This is an infection of the sinuses (the air-filled spaces inside the bones around the eyes and nose which make the skull bones light and give the voice its resonance). The sinuses are narrow passages lined with the same mucus membrane as the nose. They drain into the nose, whose mucous membrane is connected to the upper part of the throat and, so an infection of the nose or throat can easily spread to them. Their lining then becomes inflamed and clogged with mucus. Sinusitis tends not to affect babies as their sinuses are not fully developed but is fairly common in children over three.

Sinusitis usually follows a cold, cough or sore throat. If the central cartilage of the child's nose is at all misshapen, this may predispose him to sinusitis as his sinuses will not be able to drain freely.

The main symptom of sinusitis is usually an ache or pain over the infected sinus, either in one or both cheeks or in the forehead. The affected area will feel tender when touched and the pain usually feels worse when the child bends forward or lies down. He may also have a fever, a greenish or yellowish discharge from his nose, and watering eyes.

Mild sinusitis will clear up on its own in two or three days. Severe attacks are rare in children but if your child should suffer one, consult your doctor who may prescribe antibiotics or decongestants. Steam inhalation can loosen the mucus and helps the sinuses to drain, but must be done very carefully in order not to burn your child with the scalding water. Many children also dislike the sensation of inhaling water vapour. If sinusitis recurs frequently, your doctor may advise a minor operation to wash out your child's sinuses.

◆ See also, **Catarrh**

Skin

The skin is the body's largest organ. It is made up of two layers: the epidermis (surface layer); and the dermis (lower layer). On most of the body the average thickness of the skin is 2 mm, but on the palms of the hands and the soles of the feet the epidermis in particular is much thicker than elsewhere. There is a layer of fat under the skin which helps to insulate the body.

The epidermis forms a tough protective layer on the outside of the body. It contains no blood vessels and the top layer that you can see and touch is made up of dead cells which are continually rubbed off and replaced by new cells. This happens because the cells in the lowest part of the epidermis are continually dividing and working their way to the surface. As they work their way upwards they fill up with a hard substance, keratin (a type of protein), and then die. Nails and hair are also derived from the epidermis.

The dermis contains a fibrous elastic tissue which gives the skin its strength and elasticity. It also contains blood and lymph vessels, nerve endings, muscles, hair follicles, sweat glands and sebaceous glands.

One in every ten cells in the lower part of the epidermis is a melanocyte or pigment-producing cell. These melanocytes produce melanin, the pigment that gives skin its colour. Everyone has approximately the same number of melanocytes, but in darker skinned people the melanocytes produce more melanin.

The skin's function is to protect the underlying tissues from heat, cold, sun, wind, chemicals and injury. As it is waterproof, it also keeps body fluids in and other liquids out and being supple it allows the body to move freely. The skin also plays an important part in keeping the body's temperature regular. If you get too hot, perhaps with a fever, sweat then evaporates and helps to cool the skin. The layer of subcutaneous fat just under the skin helps to keep heat in and the sensitive nerve endings in the dermis recognize touch, pressure, pain, cold and heat and transmit these messages to the brain. Traces of urea and other waste substances are excreted in sweat through the skin, and vitamin D is synthesized when the skin is exposed to light.

The condition of the skin often mirrors a person's health as both physical and mental upsets are reflected in it. If your child's skin is flushed, pale, excessively dry or sweaty, or if rashes or spots break out, it is always worth looking for an underlying cause and consulting your doctor if you are at all worried.

◆ See also, **Allergies**, **Athlete's Foot**, **Boils**, **Burns**, **Eczema**, **Hives**, **Impetigo**, **Rashes**, **Ringworm**, **Sunburn**, and **Warts**

Sleep Patterns

A newborn baby sleeps between 14 and 18 hours a day. Unfortunately for the parent, the baby doesn't do all his sleeping at once or at night when everyone else wants to sleep. Getting used to your newborn baby's sleep patterns is demanding, often frustrating and always exhausting.

If you are the frazzled parent of a newborn baby, do not despair, as over the next few months your baby will learn to sleep more during the night and less during the day, although the total amount of time he will spend sleeping will gradually lessen.

A baby will sleep almost anywhere if he is happy; there isn't any "specialist" equipment you need. Most babies up to 6 months old will sleep in a Moses basket, crib or carry-cot, which can be transported around with you almost anywhere. When he has outgrown these, the best thing to put him in is a cot. Ideally, this should have a side that can be lowered, so that you can get to him easily.

To get him used to his new bed, try placing the Moses basket or carry-cot inside the larger cot for the first week or so.

Start as early as possible to make your baby aware of the difference between night and day by putting him to bed in a cot or pram as soon as he shows signs of being sleepy so that he comes to associate these places with sleeping and by getting him up and bringing him into the living area when he is awake during the day. Make the difference between day and night clear by changing and feeding him quietly with no stimulation at night and encouraging him to go back to sleep immediately after a feed or a nappy change.

When a baby is very tiny, up to four months old, a good feed will usually send him off into a fairly deep sleep. As they get older babies tend to be more easily disturbed, as they start reacting to sounds around them. They also need less sleep. You could think about putting him in another room if he is sharing your room.

It is quite normal for a sleeping baby to make small movements: twitching fingers, toes and face – even a small smile! He may also make soft sighing, huffing and grumping noises, especially as he moves around.

A tiny baby may wake up hungry several times during the night. In order not to wake the baby any more than necessary for night feeds, have everything you need all prepared before bedtime. A very low light left on all the time will not disturb the baby and will give you enough light to see what you're doing without switching on the main light. After the age of three months most babies won't need night feeding.

If night feeding is left to one partner, he or she can feel decidedly fractious very quickly, due to lack of sleep. One way to work this out is to take it in turns, say every other night, to be on night duty. If the mother is breastfeeding she may be able to express her milk beforehand for her partner to give to the baby. For a bottle-fed baby, of course, either parent can feed him, so you can easily take turns.

An alternative for breastfeeding mothers is to stay in bed while your partner brings the baby to you and puts him back to bed when he has finished feeding. New parents feeling weary from lack of sleep can also try to go to bed early, regularly, and have naps during the day, if possible.

It is easy to feel concerned if your baby wakes during the night but this is usually due to a simple cause, such as a wet nappy. Or he may just need a cuddle. Gentle rocking movements and soft singing or humming to him will often help lull him back to sleep and be invaluable in the natural bonding process. Alternatively, you could get a musical box or a cassette tape, which many babies find very soothing.

The last thing you should do is lie awake in bed anxiously listening for the first sign of the baby waking up, then leaping out of bed to check that everything is all right. Often, after moving about in the cot for a moment or two, the baby will go back to sleep.

Repeatedly lifting him out of the cot at the first murmur can disturb his rhythm of sleep and can be the start of bad sleeping habits.

Obviously, a sensible balance should be made between getting out of bed like a jack-in-the-box every time the baby breathes, and ignoring him completely. If your baby sounds fretful or is crying, however, no delay should be made in checking to see if all is well.

All babies have their own personalities, and each will develop its own natural rhythm of sleep. The natural bonding process of parent and child tends to help build up an instinctive knowledge of sleep patterns which builds up confidence very quickly for first-time parents.

You can help to minimize sleep problems as the baby develops by establishing a clear bedtime routine so that your child gets used to the idea of there being a set time to go to sleep. This will probably consist of a bath, followed by a feed, a story or nursery rhymes then a kiss good night to everyone in the family before going off to his cot with his toys or comforter. If he cries go back and reassure him, but do not lift him out of the cot and he will soon associate being put in his cot with going to sleep.

A soft toy or a piece of blanket can help your child doze off so it is worth popping the same object into his cot with him every night. A dummy may also help, but never dip it in anything sweet. And do not let your baby doze off with a bottle as this can rot his teeth even before they come through.

If your baby wakes early and stays awake, it is because he has had enough sleep. You will have to decide whether you want quiet evenings or quiet mornings and adjust his schedule accordingly.

Similarly if your child wakes and cries in the night after giving up night feeds but is not ill or teething, leave him in his cot. Reassure him, change his nappy in his cot if necessary, but don't take him out.

Everyone will offer advice on your baby, and no less so on the subject of sleep. This can be reassuring, particularly when you hear tales of broken nights' sleep from other people. And don't forget that your GP, midwife and health visitor are all there to offer help and reassurance, whatever your problem.

◆ See also, **Sleep Problems**

Sleep Problems

Many sleep problems in babies and young children actually belong more to the parents than to the child. Babies naturally fall asleep when they need to and sleep for as long as they need. It is the way in which they take their sleep that can cause their parents problems. Human beings are diurnal (they sleep at night and are awake during the day) but babies and young children have to learn this pattern and they vary enormously in the length of time this takes.

After about six weeks (although the time this takes varies enormously) your child's sleep pattern will become more regular. He will still sleep for as long as he needs and is certainly not able to keep himself awake on purpose but he should be more aware of the difference between night and day.

You may be waking your baby if he still sleeps in your room, as no matter how quiet you try to be you will still make some noise when you come to bed and your movements in your sleep may disturb him during the night. If he has his own room you may wake him by going in to check on him while he is sleeping. Your baby is also now more aware of loud noises; perhaps traffic outside is disturbing him. Being too hot, too cold or hungry will wake him, as will nappy rash. He may also kick his covers off as he sleeps.

By the age of nine months, your baby will be able to keep himself awake. Sleep problems from this age onwards may come from being overtired and too tense to go to sleep at bedtime. Concentrate on a relaxing bedtime routine with no rough or boisterous games.

A change in routine of any kind can easily disrupt your child's sleeping patterns for some time afterwards. This is especially likely if he has to spend some time in hospital or goes to stay with relatives without you. Even going on holiday or moving to a new and unfamiliar room can disrupt his routine and you will need to spend time reassuring him and re-establishing the routine.

All adults go through periods of light and heavier sleep and also occasionally wake without even realizing it and babies and children do the same. Some frequently wake completely. If you just leave the child to cry when this happens he will become more and more distressed and difficult to settle, so go to him immediately and reassure him but again without lifting him out of his cot. He should soon learn to go back to sleep on his own. A comforter or soft toy may also help to reassure him.

Many children walk in their sleep and it can be very alarming for parents to find their child wandering about in a daze with open, expressionless eyes. Sleepwalkers often do not recognize or even see other people. If your child sleepwalks simply lead or carry him back to bed; do not try to wake him. Try not to mention these night wanderings to him during the day as he will not like to learn that he is doing things he can't remember and it will make him more anxious and less likely to go to sleep calmly. Most children soon grow out of this phase. Always fit a safety gate at the top of the stairs in case your child begins to sleepwalk.

Many children (and adults) are afraid of the dark and this naturally prevents them falling asleep peacefully. Accept this as something the child will grow out of and leave a night light on in his room or keep the hall light on. If he is afraid of monsters or other scary creatures in his room, you may

find it best to "chase" them away. But most children are quite able to be rational, and can be shown confidently that there really is nothing there.

Some children have their sleep disturbed because they wet the bed at night, although others sleep calmly through it. Most children can go through the night by the time they are two or three, but about one in ten children cannot, and some children have still not learned by the age of five or six.

If your child is not continent during the night he can be put in nappies to keep his pyjamas and bed clothes dry and stop him waking. Taking him to the bathroom before you go to bed may keep him dry for the rest of the night.

Never scold your child for wetting the bed at night. If a child reverts to bedwetting after having been dry this could be a sign of anxiety or illness, but otherwise it is quite normal for some children to take longer than others to learn to be dry all night.

◆ See also, **Insomnia**, **Night Frights**, **Potty Training**, **Sleep Patterns**

Slow Learners/Learning Disabilities

It is inevitable that some babies or toddlers will develop faster than others and this is true not only of the speed at which their bodies grow, but also of the rate at which their speech, movement and co-ordination progress. Some will be quick to speak and understand, to walk, dress or undress themselves, while for others all or some of these will take longer. The speed at which a baby or toddler develops is not necessarily an indication of how intelligent they will be, but if he is particularly slow there may be something wrong with the way in which his brain is working, which can lead to learning difficulties later on.

While this may not be the case with all slow early learners, a high proportion of those who are not speaking in two- or three-word sentences by the age of three will probably have learning difficulties in school, and some may have severe learning problems or even be mentally handicapped.

About three in every thousand children have severe learning difficulties or mental handicaps. In most cases there is a fault in the way the brain has developed, and the most common cause is Down's syndrome. Other less common genetic causes account for a fair proportion, and in other cases damage is caused either at birth, or after birth as a result of injury.

Often a baby will appear "normal" at birth and it may take two or even three years for it to become clear that the child is developing very slowly. Your health visitor or doctor will be able to help you decide whether your child is just a little slow to develop or whether there is real cause for concern. They, together with you, will monitor your baby's progress, and will refer you, if necessary, to a paediatrician. He or she will repeat the process, then carry out blood, urine tests and possibly X-rays in order to establish a cause for the slowness. The cause, if found, may not always be treatable, but since there may be genetic implications, it is important to know what it is.

A child with severe learning difficulties or mental handicap can learn, but will take a lot longer, and will need far more help than one who develops normally. As he reaches school age a "statement" of his educational needs will be made with local professionals and the local education authority. This will almost certainly involve the need for a good deal of individual attention and for teachers experienced in dealing with children with communication and other difficulties.

Autism is another problem that may only become obvious after the first two or three years of seemingly normal development. An autistic child may simply be rather unresponsive in the first few months of life, but towards the end of his first year you may start to find that he babbles very little (or maybe not at all) and that he does not like to be held or cuddled. He may avoid your gaze and spend a lot of time looking at his hands. He will probably be very slow to speak and understand and have difficulty relating to people, but may have walked fairly early and be good at sorting shapes or doing puzzles. Parents of autistic children will benefit from the sort of educational help provided for the mentally handicapped, but will also need extra help with behavioural problems.

Hyperactivity can also cause learning difficulties and sufferers often have to invest twice the amount of effort to achieve half the success of their classmates because of their poor concentration and specific related learning problems. Often they are poor listeners, forget instructions, lists or messages, are easily distracted, visually inattentive and "spaced out". They also find it difficult to sit still, socialize, and control their emotional impulses. It is important that parents and teachers recognize all this, and try to focus on successes rather than failures in activities both in and outside of school.

If you are concerned about your child and the rate at which he is developing it is always best to follow your instincts and discuss your worries with your doctor or a health visitor. At the same time you must always remember that each child is an individual and it is both unfair and unrealistic to expect your child to be doing the same or more than his peers.

◆ See also, **Hyperactivity**

Smacking

There are many debates about the benefits of smacking, and there are fashions too. One generation thinks it is the only way to teach small children, but the next is horrified at the idea. From a legal point of view, in Britain parents are currently allowed to smack their children, as are grandparents or other relatives in charge, but teachers in schools are forbidden to use corporal punishment.

Many child experts believe that smacking young children is wrong because, they say, it doesn't help your child to behave better and may actually make him more disobedient and aggressive.

Psychologists feel that the use of an adult's strength against a small child is unjust, and that smacking gives the message that "might is right" – a message the parents are probably trying to counter in other ways. Smacking may also make a child angry and resentful, and less respectful of his parents. As your child grows older and stronger he will try to get his own back and punish you, his parents, by acting in ways that distress you.

Another reason why psychologists are against physical punishment is that it tends to escalate. They argue that if you smack your child for doing something wrong, you will have to smack him harder when he does it again or when he does something worse. He will gradually become immune to mild slaps, so you smack him harder.

Your child may react angrily to physical punishment and begin to think that he is in the right and that you are in the wrong. He may also become afraid of you and learn to cover up his "crimes". Any relationship of trust between you and your child will be ruined as a result.

But there is an alternative view. Other experts believe that the occasional smack can't do much harm and many parents agree. They say a smack given while the child is actually being naughty is better than a punishment that comes into effect later.

For instance, as a punishment you can forbid your child his TV time, cancel an outing to the park or withhold his teatime treat, but there is a problem with this way of dealing with misbehaviour. By the time the punishment comes into effect, your child has probably forgotten all about the original offence, and you yourself may have calmed down and no longer feel that it matters. Your child will see this as inconsistent behaviour and he will not take your threats seriously.

Neither is it fair to threaten that you will "tell Daddy when he comes home". By that time your child again will have forgotten his naughtiness, and besides it will give him the idea that his father is a threatening person.

Those parents and experts who believe in smacking argue that a small child understands instantly why he has been punished. If he does something he has been told not to do, for example dropping toys down the toilet, and you smack him as soon as he does it, he learns cause and effect.

Those who are against smacking point out that there are better ways to teach children good behaviour. They suggest that you should talk to your child and explain what is wrong and why you are angry or hurt. It is much better to tell your child that you know he did not mean to be naughty and that you realize that he did not know that what he was doing was bad. Reassure him – tell him you're sure that he will not do it again.

There is a view that children want to be good because they want to be loved and to win your approval. If you withdraw your approval, or send your child out of the room, this can be a more effective way of changing his behaviour than smacking him. Children too young to follow your reasoning, that is most children under three, are best removed from the situation.

If your toddler keeps switching the TV on and off, just move him and keep doing so, over and over again, until he decides that it is no use trying any more. If your small child hits a playmate with a toy hammer, you must remember that he doesn't know what a hammer is or that it may hurt. Don't smack him but gently remove the toy and explain why he shouldn't do that again. Distract him with a story or another toy.

Many small children go through an aggressive phase – hitting, biting, spitting and pulling hair. To add to the embarrassment of onlooking parents, they often choose a child that is smaller than they are for their attacks. Your child is experimenting as he grows; he does not understand the pain he is causing. Try to explain gently as you lead him away. It would not be logical to smack him while telling him not to hit other children.

If you feel your child is very aggressive when he is with playmates, you may be expecting him to play with other children before he is ready to do so. Toddlers are not good at "playing" with other children until they are about three years old. If your child is older than this, but still showing signs of aggression, do not add to the violence by smacking him. Promise to stop his game and send away his friends if he does not improve his behaviour – and keep your promise if he doesn't listen.

There are also good arguments against the kind of parenting which explains everything to a child however. If a child is to learn that hitting causes pain, some psychologists say that the very best lesson you can give him is a smack. He understands then the kind of hurt he has caused his little playmates and, these experts argue, knowing what it feels like he will not do it again.

However, you should seek help if you find you're hitting your child very frequently, or if your punishments are getting harsher (such as giving hard smacks on exposed parts of the body). Also, ask for advice if your child is resorting to behaviour such as lying, stealing, hiding from you on a regular basis, and you find every day is filled with rows, and angry outbursts. Your doctor or health visitor should be able to advise you how best to deal with the situation.

Your toddler will test your patience until you are really irritated and an unpleasant scene occurs. But, if you smack him as he starts to misbehave, and then turn his attention elsewhere, you will keep calm and he will have something new to keep him occupied.

The worst thing you can do, according to all child experts, is to smack your child when you're tired and irritable. Smacking, if you believe in it, should be a form of discipline not a thoughtless slap. Yet this sort of physical reaction may be deliberately provoked by your child, for studies have shown that children who get very little attention will prefer to be smacked than to get no attention at all.

Your child may quickly realize that you notice him most when he is being naughty. When he is playing happily, you may leave him while you make a phone call, or just unwittingly ignore him as you get on with the housework.

So, if your child is frequently very naughty, try giving him lots of attention when he is good. Play with him and join in with him. Keep him near you, but walk out of the room when the bad behaviour starts. When dealing with under-twos, problems can often be avoided by thinking ahead about situations that are bound to cause conflict. For example, you needn't dread the weekly supermarket shopping trip. If you plan for lots of time and do your shopping slowly, you won't feel under stress and the expedition can be fun for you and your toddler. Tell your child in advance that he can have a treat at the end of it all, but not before. Give him something to keep him occupied while you shop – perhaps a small favourite toy or an apple. Let him take a book to look at or his teddy to play with as he sits in the supermarket trolley. Alternatively, get him to help you load things on to the trolley.

In your home you can reduce areas of conflict too: make your house 'child-proof' by packing away precious china ornaments, or dangerous bottles of bleach or your sewing box, where your child cannot reach them. That way, you will not feel anxious and you will not need to nag your child.

When he gets older, and can understand that china breaks and scissors are dangerous, you can bring out these more troublesome items again.

Consistency is probably the most important thing in helping your child learn the rights and wrongs of behaviour. It is crucial that both parents agree on methods of discipline, and on what constitutes good and bad behaviour.

Many behavioural problems come about because the parents are simply neither consistent nor clear in the rules they lay down for their children. If you let your child do something one day but the next day he is punished for the same action, he will become confused.

Decide in advance about a daily routine and don't vary it except for special occasions. If your children learn that they can watch TV at four o'clock for one hour and not at any other time during the day, you will avoid rows about switching the TV on and off at other times.

Bedtime is often another point of stress and family rows, but if you insist on a regular routine of bath, story and bed you'll find that your child will accept it and rarely argue with you. Once your children are in bed, be firm about not letting them get out of their bedroom again.

If you and your partner set a consistent routine in the home, you will help your children understand how you live and this should reduce the frequency of their unco-operative behaviour.

All experts agree that the best way to encourage your child to be calm and happy is through praise and encouragement. Always reward your child when he's done well or has been cheerfully playing. Give him big hugs or read his favourite story whenever he's been helpful.

Above all, it is important to realize that your child's greatest wish is to please you. If he is constantly nagged, shouted at or smacked he will feel that you do not love him and that he is not worth loving. Give him praise and affection, and be patient with him. You will have a happier and better balanced child, and you will be happier parents yourselves as a result.

Snake Bites

In Britain and parts of Europe the only venomous snake is the adder, or viper as it is also known. The other continents all have their share of deadly snakes, especially in tropical regions, but very few snakes bite unless provoked and it is very unlikely that you are running the risk of your child getting bitten when on holiday, in any part of the world. However, you should be on the alert for adders when walking in the countryside, even in Britain, as they are sluggish creatures that do not get out of the way, and there is a small risk of stepping on one by accident.

Poisonous snakes have fangs in their mouths, through which they can release venom (poison), which is injected into the victim when the snake bites. Most snake venom works by affecting the central nervous system and causes paralysis, or by interfering with the clotting of the blood. The puncture marks left on the skin by a snake bite are the fang marks through which the venom has been released. In most cases, shock is as great a danger as the poison itself.

A child who is bitten by a snake will first of all be extremely frightened and may be pale, sweating and shaking. The area around the bite will begin to swell and will be painful and the site of the bite itself will show the puncture, or usually a pair of puncture marks, in the skin. As the poison begins to spread, so will the pain of the bite, and this may be followed by a feeling of numbness.

If your child is bitten by a snake you must get him to the nearest place where medical treatment is available as soon as possible. In Europe, local pharmacies stock serum against adders and it is usually best to take the child straight to the nearest pharmacy. In the tropics, where snakebites can be more serious, take the child straight to the nearest hospital, where the appropriate serum will be given. Most hospitals stock all-purpose serum in areas where there is danger from a variety of snakes. But it will also be useful if you can describe the snake to help to identify it.

Before getting medical treatment, if possible you should wash or wipe clean the wound and cover it with a clean dressing. Reassure your child and keep him warm to help prevent shock. If he complains of pain it is safe to give him the appropriate dose of paracetamol for his age.

You should not apply a tourniquet, which can do more harm than good, or should you try to suck out the poison. Try to immobilize the limb with an improvised splint, if possible, to slow down the rate at which the poison can spread. Whether or not you are able to improvise a splint, keep the child lying down, and transport him in this position.

In order to prevent the possibility of snakebite when you are away on holiday, ask local people for advice before walking in the countryside. In most parts of Europe local pharmacists are well informed about the likely dangers of snakebites. If you are told that snakes are to be found in that area, make sure that you and your child are wearing trousers tucked in thick socks or long boots when walking. Carry a stick, and make sure that the grass is clear before sitting down. Remember that in the tropics there are many poisonous snakes and the risk of meeting one should be taken seriously.

Social Skills

It's important for your child to meet other children in order to develop his social skills. He needs to learn to share, to co-operate, to think about others, and he deserves the pleasure of companionship.

To begin with he won't seem to pay too much attention to his peers, but that is not to say that he is unaware of them. He will play happily, but independently alongside another baby. Although some babies are more sociable than others, most take pleasure in the company of those whom they can recognize as being "one of them". Once at playgroup or nursery, however, he will soon develop affiliations (and antagonisms). You can nurture these budding friendships (or even take the sting out of an antagonism) by inviting the other child to tea. But you do need to know what to expect.

The main lesson to be learned, and of course the main difficulty, in having another friend to visit, concerns sharing. Do be aware that it is perfectly natural for your child to be possessive. (Indeed, a child who does not have an appropriate sense of ownership may have more problems to deal with later in life.) Be prepared for the fact that both children will automatically want the same toy even if it has lain unregarded for months previously. Steel yourself for constant repetitions of "We must share, mustn't we", and "When we go to Alice's house she lets you play with her cars/dolls" and so on.

Decide in advance whether you are going to allow toys to be borrowed for a day or two. It's probably best not to if your child finds sharing difficult. Then at least he can get used to the idea that sharing does not include the trauma of having to be physically parted from something precious.

When your child is the host, he can be encouraged to feel very important, and also responsible. This is his house, his toys, his mummy, but it is also his responsibility to think about his guest's happiness. If you manage to balance these two factors, and your child is responsive to the idea, you will be able to watch him virtually swell with pride in his sense of importance and pleasurable responsibility.

How much you leave the two children alone depends very much on the ages and personalities of the children concerned, but there is a great deal to be said for staying on the sidelines as much as possible. This gives the children the best opportunity to think and to try to resolve their differences by themselves. If you are always there ready to jump in at the first sign of a squall they will never get used to working things out for themselves. On the other hand, you must not get so engrossed in other things that you miss your cue when they really do need you.

Soon your child will be invited to the other child's house. Here more lessons can be learned and advantages enjoyed.

Your child will need some preparation to be able to deal with being in a house where nothing is his, and where the habits and rituals may be just a little bit different. For his first invitations, it's easier on you both if he can go somewhere he has already visited with you.

Don't let him know if you have any anxieties about the visit. Send him off safe in the belief that you think he is capable of this activity and he will grow in self-confidence and rise to the occasion.

Small separations like this are very good preparation for more major events such as starting playschool or nursery. And it might come as quite a surprise to you to see how grown up your child seems when you go to pick him up after only a couple of hours away from you. He will have broadened his horizons, and will have coped with a situation over which, for once, you have little control. That is not to say, however, that he will necessarily be willing to tell you about it. Be prepared to listen if he wants to talk, but also allow him his privacy and his secrets.

See also, **Friendships for Children**, **Manners**, **Sharing**

Sore Throat

A sore throat is a common complaint that can occur on its own or as one of several symptoms. Even though it is so common, a sore throat has to be taken seriously in children as there is always the danger of infection spreading to the middle ear.

Sore throats are usually caused by an infection. They may be one of the symptoms of colds and flu or the child may also have tonsillitis or laryngitis. The swelling of the glands in mumps can also make the throat feel sore and a sore throat can be a symptom of scarlet fever.

Young children are often not able to recognize a sore throat and may complain of their mouth hurting or may simply have difficulty in swallowing and perhaps be a little off their food and generally unwell.

If you look inside the child's mouth you may see that the area round the back of the tongue is inflamed and if you feel the child's neck from ear to chin you may be able to detect hard little swollen lymph nodes, or you may find that the whole area feels swollen and tender. In babies the signs will be difficulty in feeding and general unhappiness and irritability.

Depending on the type of sore throat, the child may also have a high temperature.

More often than not the infection responsible for the sore throat is a viral rather than a bacterial one and antibiotics will make no difference. In the main the infection will clear itself within two or three days.

Make sure that a child with a sore throat has plenty of rest and keeps warm. Plenty of warm drinks such as lemon and honey or hot blackcurrant juice will help to soothe the throat as well as providing vitamin C and keeping the child's fluid level up.

If the child is not sleeping properly because of the soreness, or if his temperature is raised, he may be given the correct dose of paracetamol for his age to ease the pain or reduce the temperature.

For a straightforward case there is no need to call the doctor, but if the child is feverish, if there is a rash, if the sore throat lasts for more than three days or so, or if the child has earache or any other symptoms that worry you call your family doctor. The doctor will use a light to examine the child's throat and check that the tonsils and adenoids are not affected. The child's ears may also be examined to make sure that the infection has not spread. Antibiotics may be prescribed if the signs are that the child has a bacterial infection and the doctor may prescribe lozenges to soothe the throat, and give advice on how the child should be cared for. You may be asked to bring the child back for a check-up if the throat is not better by a set time.

If the sore throat is a symptom of another illness the doctor will prescribe the necessary treatment for that illness.

Speech

Before the age of two, several important things happen in your child's speech development. He cries, smiles, coos and babbles his way through the first few months of his life while you, in turn, smile, coo and babble back to him. By answering him in this way you teach him a valuable lesson – that communication works. Chattering comes next, and sounds for all the world like real conversation because, though he does not use "real" words, he includes the rises and falls in his voice that he picks up from you as you talk to him. Very shortly after this phase he starts to utter his first words.

To start with, pronunciation is often very odd, and this may continue even when your child has been talking for some time. Some sounds seem to be very difficult for young children. Most infants do not like the "s" and "f" sounds, and will often put other, easier letters in their place. Other tough ones for youngsters are the "g" and "k" sounds; your child may say "don" for gone and "tee" for key. On the other hand, children seem to love both "w" and "j" and will often substitute them for the much more difficult "l" and "r" sounds – saying "mewy-go-wound", for example.

Word endings can present a few problems too. Your child may not bother with them at all for a while. He may say "ha" for hat and "do" for dog. Clusters of letters like "spr" or "tr" can be very stricky for a young tongue to get around.

The quiet syllables like the "ba" in banana or the "gi" in giraffe cause most children trouble, which is why these words are almost invariably shortened to "nana" and, perhaps, "draff". And if a word defeats them completely, they may just make up a completely new word, which sounds nothing like the original.

Although your child may mispronounce words himself, he won't like you to do it. He hears a word correctly, but doesn't yet have enough control over his mouth and tongue to copy it accurately. It is always the best policy to teach by example and offer your child a good model of speech. It may sound "cute" to mimic his mistakes, but it will not teach him how to speak properly.

Your child will most likely stay in the one-word phase for up to a year and may become obsessed with naming things. Although this can be very irritating, it will help your child a great deal if you take notice of what he says. A simple response such as "Yes, that's your cup", or "I can see the dog", will be enough to satisfy him.

Children often use one word to describe all manner of things. "Nana" can mean all fruit; "Daddy" can mean all men. Experience will teach them that each type of fruit has a name of its own and so have people.

The next phase is the two-word phrase or sentence. Some children reach this stage before they are two, while most will not get to it until after their second birthday. Your child will understand far more than he will be able to say, because understanding must come before speech.

Once he masters the skill, your child will make more and more two-word sentences and will progress at the most astonishing rate. Some estimates put it at as many as four new combinations an hour, at its peak.

By the time your child is three he will be using longer and longer sentences. Sometimes he will stammer and stutter in his rush to tell you everything he has discovered. Try not to worry too much about this. It is simply that he is thinking far quicker than he is able to speak at this stage and in his enthusiasm he may get carried away.

A particular stumbling block at this time is words that keep changing their meaning according to circumstances. For example, the word "me". If Mummy says it, "me" means Mummy; if Daddy says it, "me" means Daddy; and from your child's point of view "me" means me. "You", "I" and "they" can be just as shifty, as can "it". "Here" and "there" are very tricky too.

No one gives grammar lessons to three- or four-year-olds so the best way to handle such shifty words is to give people and places their proper names. Instead of referring to "them" say "Granny and Grandad", for example. In place of "Put it there", try saying "Put it on the table".

Be tolerant of mistakes. If your child says "Me got red shoes", say "Yes you have, aren't they pretty? I have white shoes." He will eventually sort out the difference between "me" and "I" from the example you set with your corrective answers.

Of course, it is important to continue to encourage your child's efforts at talking. There are many ways to do this. As adults we like to be listened to when we are speaking; your child feels the same way.

Good conversations rely on there being interesting things to talk about. Children, like adults, can run dry if not stimulated, so you will need to take your child out and about. Playgroup or nursery school will give you both plenty of scope, as will trips to the shops or the park, or to see friends. More adventurous journeys to the seaside or a city farm will help to broaden your child's experience and his topics of conversation.

Books and television play an important role in increasing your child's store of language. Television is no use at all, however, if it is left on all the time as background noise. It is far better to choose special programmes and to enjoy them together. Your child will only learn from television, at this early stage, if he has someone with whom to discuss the programme he has watched, either during it or afterwards.

Books can be very helpful when trying to introduce the idea of opposites – big and small, long and short and so on. You could try making your own books as well as buying them or borrowing from the library. Encourage your child to draw a big ball and then a small one, stick the pictures into the book and label each picture.

You can have a big and small table and find things to put on it. Discuss the things you put in your collection and add a few things every day for a week. The following week it could be a long and short collection.

Your child will grasp the idea of singular and plural pretty quickly, and will soon learn to add an "s" to the end of a word. The exceptions to the rule will cause problems for a while, one sheep and lots of sheep being just one obvious example. By listening to you he will learn about these exceptions – there is no need to correct early mistakes.

The "ing" at the ends of words will also come fairly readily. "Run" and "running" will be easy, though "I runned" will be a common mistake. It is hardly surprising that children make these errors because they use logic. If one says "I laugh" and "I laughed", why shouldn't one say "I runned"?

For most children, the rules of everyday grammar are fairly well established by the time they are five or six. By then, your child will be telling you long and complicated stories with very few grammatical mistakes. He will not be able to tell you what an adjective is, or whether it should come before or after a noun. He will, however, be using lots of descriptive words and, what is more, he will get them in the right place.

If you and your partner speak different languages it can be difficult to decide whether to teach your child both at the same time, or whether to teach one first then introduce the other.

Some children have no trouble at all in coping with two languages, but others may be slow to pick up both. There is no way of telling in advance which sort your child will be. The answer is to take your cue from your child. If there are problems, then concentrate on one language at a time. It is, perhaps, best to choose the one his friends speak, otherwise there is a risk that he will become isolated.

Children whose parents have emigrated learn to speak the language of the new country more quickly if they are already fluent in their parents' mother tongue.

If you feel that your child's speech is not progressing as you would expect, it may be worth having his hearing checked, as good hearing is essential to normal speech and language development. Profound deafness is usually noticed early but the temporary, partial deafness caused by the common childhood complaint of "glue ear" (see separate entry) is harder to pick up. Here are some signs for you to look out for:

● Does your child suffer from lots of coughs and colds?
● Does your child seem to be in a world of his own a lot of the time?
● Does your child sometimes misunderstand what you say?
● Does he seem not to hear you if he can't also see you?
● Do other people have a lot of difficulty in understanding your child?

◆ See also, **Baby Talk**, **Hearing**

Spoilt Children

Everyone has their own views on what is and isn't a spoilt child and you must form your own. However, as a guide, new babies who cry and receive immediate attention cannot be said to be spoilt. Babies have very limited means of communication so it is unfair to ignore their cries. And children who charm their way into your favours are not spoilt either. Charm, and the ability to use it, can be great assets in life. Similarly, children who get what they want after asking for it reasonably and who would not be unduly upset if their request is turned down, are not spoilt.

Spoiling is something we are all probably guilty of to a greater or lesser extent. And it seems to be something that happens inevitably in spite of our best efforts to avoid it.

As children grow, so does their sense of self and with it their struggle for independence, first by learning to crawl and later by walking. All this is rightly welcomed by parents. One day, however, there usually comes a clash of wills. You want to do one thing and your little one wants to do another. It can be in the resolution of this clash that the seeds of a spoilt child are sown. You may, for example, want to take your child away from the playground so that you can do some shopping. To quieten the screams that follow your suggestion that it's time to go, you hand out some sweets and all is well. When you are busy, it's almost impossible to live life at your child's slow pace and it is only natural that you should want to avoid as many embarrassing "scenes" as possible.

But if giving out sweets to avoid a scene, or maybe even to save giving explanations of their actions, becomes routine, parents can soon find that the sweets are expected as a matter of routine. Children may even start to use them as a form of emotional blackmail to get their own way. In other words, "Give me some sweets or I'll make a scene and then you'll be sorry!"

If your child begis to get out of hand with his demands, try some of the following tactics:

● Ignore half-hearted demands; they may cease when your child realizes they are not getting a response.

● Explain firmly and clearly your views on the matter, and keep to them.

● Explain that you like and may reward good behaviour only.

● If you can bear to, ignore any tantrums.

● If necessary, give in – but only to the absolute minimum. So, for example, give just one or two sweets and not the whole packet.

Some parents find themselves at a loss to understand how things get so far out of control. But it is not difficult to see how it can happen. What began as a little reward or "bribe" on the parents' part, is seen by the child as a "payment". And it does not take long for a child to realize that he can ask or payment in advance.

However, this is not to say that "bribes" should never be used. But they should be used as infrequently as possible and preferably with a full

explanation as to why they are being offered. If, for example, you are all having a good time on the beach but you suddenly remember there is something you need to do elsewhere, it makes sense to reward your child for coming with you if it is not possible to leave him behind. But you must explain that the reward is only to compensate him for leaving the beach. This way, he will see the reward more as a one-off gift than something to be expected regularly.

Such bribes or rewards can also be a good way of seeing a child through an unpleasant, but unavoidable, experience, such as going to the dentist. A promise of some special treat afterwards can do a lot to lift a little one's spirits.

It follows from this that spoiling is not really about what is given to a child, but the way it is given. If a parent hands out treats and presents as a substitute for spending time with their child, there is no doubt that he will recognize this and become mercenary in the relationship, and when the treats that he has started to take for granted stop, the result can be a tantrum.

Whatever you do yourself, you are not the only person in your child's life. Aunts, uncles and grandparents, whatever they may say about you spoiling your child, are often the worst offenders.

It pays to keep a balanced attitude here. If you feel that any one person is going to spoil your child, politely but firmly outline your own views on the giving of sweets and presents and ask for those views to be respected. Try not to be too strict, though. Giving pleasure to children is one of the greatest "perks" of adult life and most of us fondly remember the person who came closest to spoiling us and breaking the rules in the eyes of our parents. Of course, whatever rules you make, you should always be prepared to break them on occasions. That is part of life and providing you explain your actions clearly, most children will appreciate that. And don't expect to eliminate all signs of being spoilt from your child. After all, if you love him you're bound to spoil him a little – and that includes kisses and cuddles.

◆ See also, **Temper Tantrums**

Sprains

There is some confusion about the difference between sprains and strains. Both can occur together, but strains are more common on their own. The symptoms are much the same and both injuries can result from the same kind of accident. In fact a sprain involves a tear in a ligament (the tough, fibrous and inelastic tissue between the two bones of a joint), while damage to the elastic muscle is known as a strain. Treatment is the same for both, but ligaments can be slow to heal, while muscles respond quickly.

Strains often occur as the result of falls and tumbles when children are playing and the muscles get overstretched as the child falls or lands. Sprains result from a joint being forced to bend beyond its normal capacity, damaging the ligaments which have very little "stretch". They become more likely as the child begins to take part in organized sport and they affect the knees and ankles as a result of football, dance, high jump and long jump, or the wrists and elbows from playing tennis and netball. Like strains, they can also be the consequence of a bad fall.

The symptoms of sprains and strains are swelling, pain, causing stiffness and preventing normal movement, and tenderness at the site of the injury.

Especially in the case of sprains there is often also bruising, and the pain can be severe.

Sprains frequently occur in the ankles (known as "twisted" ankle) and wrists, fingers, and knees. Muscular strains can occur anywhere in the body, but in children they are mostly in the same areas as sprains.

Children's sprains and strains usually respond quickly to home treatment. The swelling can be reduced by holding a cold compress (a pad of cloth soaked in cold water and wrung out) or a pack of frozen peas over the swollen area. This also soothes the pain for up to half an hour at a time.

When the initial swelling has gone down, support the injured muscle or joint with a crêpe bandage. This should be slightly stretched while you are applying it, but not applied so tightly that it affects the circulation.

The child should be discouraged from using the affected muscle or joint for a day or two. After this the swelling should have completely subsided and there should be little or no pain. If any bruising remains it can be made to disappear more quickly by applying a warm hot water bottle. It is now important for the child to exercise the injured area frequently but gently to restore full use. To encourage healing the child should still rest it when not doing the exercises.

In the vast majority of cses, the injury will soon heal, and the child will not need medical attention, but if the pain is severe, or if the swelling and pain continue for more than a day or two, you should take the child to the family doctor. He or she will examine the injury and decide whether further treatment is necessary. Painkillers may be prescribed to subdue the pain, and if an arm is affected the child may have to have it put in a sling. The doctor may also refer the child for physiotherapy.

In some cases a very bad sprain can be as troublesome as a fracture, and in others what appears to be a sprain can actually be a small fracture. The doctor may decide that the joint needs to be supported by a plaster for healing to take place properly, and may first send the child for X-rays to establish whether there is a fracture. More intensive physiotherapy may be necessary when this type of injury is healing, to make sure that the joint returns to normal strength and to prevent it from being susceptible to more injury in future.

Stammering

Speech involves the use of dozens of muscles in the lungs, throat and mouth, controlled and co-ordinated by the brain. It is little wonder that, especially between the ages of two and five when they are learning to speak, many children have minor speech impediments – even when there is nothing physically wrong.

A child who stammers gets stuck on the first parts of words, so that they get pronounced several times, interfering with the fluency of the child's speech. This can vary in severity from the occasional stutter when the child is excited to continual stammering which makes it very difficult to understand the child's speech. Generally, children who stammer can recite poetry or sing perfectly fluently.

All children benefit from being patiently helped and encouraged to speak. A mild stammer is nothing to be concerned about. But if your child stammers so badly that he has difficulty in making himself understood it could be that treatment could help him. Your doctor may refer him to a therapist who will assess his problem is and whether treatment is necessary.

Stammering or stuttering, especially when severe, or when combined with other problems such as facial tics, can be a sign of emotional disturbance. Try to assess whether for any reason your child is feeling insecure, tense or anxious, and see if there is anything you can do to help solve the problem. Do not be afraid to ask your doctor for advice.

Meanwhile, try not to fuss about the stammer. Help your child with words if he really wants you to, but otherwise patiently wait for him to get them out, and never hurry him or tease him about his stammer.

Most cases of stammering in children clear up spontaneously and completely; some persist into adult life; a few continue to worsen.

Stealing

◆ See **Lying**

Stepfathers

Whether it's after divorce, bereavement or some time spent as a single parent, welcoming a new partner into the family has today become quite commonplace. With one in three marriages ending in separation or divorce, stepfamilies are on the increase.

All too often, however, the alteration in the family make-up takes place without much conscious planning and preparation. Only afterwards do the pitfalls and mistakes become obvious, yet there are many areas that could be sorted out in advance.

Surveys have shown that in first marriages, problems with children come bottom of the list as causes of marital conflict. In second marriages, managing the children is the greatest source of strain and occupies a huge amount of the parents' energies. It's worth laying the foundations of your new relationship firmly and securely before plunging your children – and your new partner – into a potentially stressful situation.

Perhaps the most common mistake is to underestimate just how conservative small children are: they like to know exactly what to expect and what is going to happen in their lives. This doesn't mean that they are unadaptable, but rather that they need to be eased gently into changes.

A child's consciousness and awareness are quite different from an adult's. If you introduce a new "father" into the household quite suddenly, your child is very likely to think his world has been turned upside down. Insecurity can breed anxiety, with fears that other safe and known factors may just as easily change or disappear.

A child may begin to question a host of things that he previously took for granted. Displays of fear if you go out, clinginess and your child's sudden concern for the smooth running of everyday routines may be irritating for you, but they indicate his deep underlying need for your reassurance and attention.

Preparing your children gently doesn't mean you shouldn't give them clear explanations – you should. Children are perceptive and will pick up the truth for themselves so they'll respect you for being open with them from the start.

A four-year-old boy, for example, who is quite aware of changes behind the domestic scenes, will find it hard to experience separation from his real father and the later introduction of a stepfather if he hasn't been prepared for it in advance. To avoid upsetting him you may want to spare him the details about why his dad has moved away or for how long, and then when and how your new partner will fit into your lives. As a result, your little boy may feel confused – partly to blame for his father going away and partly angry with the stepfather. Although he may still be outgoing with his friends, he might become hostile and uncommunicative with adults.

It seems from all the research that children's major grievance when they are faced with their mother's remarriage is that they weren't consulted enough. This doesn't mean that you should make or break decisions according to what your child thinks, but that you should make every attempt to include your child in any decisions you make, talk about them and encourage him to say what's on his mind. Even a negative reaction is better than bottled up emotions. It helps, too, if you are calm and firm when you talk of your intentions.

Be prepared to be around more for your child. This may be difficult, especially if you are deeply involved in the new relationship, and even more if you work as well, but it will pay dividends. Children need to know they won't be pushed into the background and, added to that, they need extra love and security to help them over the transition.

One of the problems is the tendency to blame the situation for any small alteration in your child's behaviour. This may make you more anxious than you otherwise might be, to the extent that you interpret normal phases as evidence of the disturbing effect of the new situation.

It's important that you don't take on a lot of guilt. If you have done what you can to prepare the child, the guilt is unnecessary. Some questioning of yourself and your plans is only natural but don't let it undermine your belief in the rightness of your decisions.

Introducing your child to his prospective stepfather is best done in as non-threatening a way as possible. This means giving him – and your partner – a chance to meet as friends and build a real relationship. You could start with an afternoon out, with a shared meal at the end, then perhaps a whole day's outing. But don't only share treats. It's much fairer for your partner to see your child in normal circumstances too, such as bath and bed times.

One common hurdle is how to introduce the idea of your partner sleeping in your bed. For children this can come as quite a shock, especially if they are used to invading your bedroom each morning for their special time with you. Your children should be very familiar with your new boyfriend well before he stays overnight.

If you have only one child, then you might experience greater problems of acceptance of your new relationship as your child grieves for the closeness that existed between you both, especially if you have been alone together for some time, or all of your child's life.

If you have two or more children, you may find yourself coping with a variety of reactions. Your four-year-old may be over the moon, whereas your toddler may become clingy and demanding of your attention, even outwardly aggressive to your new partner. Again you need tact and lots of patience.

There are bound to be days when you fear that your child's resentment and hostility towards your partner will drive him away or make him have second thoughts about wanting to be with you. Your partner may quite rightly feel that it's not him you want as much as a helping hand with the children. You also run the risk of alienating your partner if you tend to side with your children too readily – and alienating them if you constantly defend him. This in turn may make you angry with your child. If you are aware of this "chain reaction", you're in a much better position to view each situation objectively and thus react less emotively.

Because you are having to cope with your child's reactions and your partner's, you can easily overlook your own needs in the situation. Balance is the key word here: balance between the different needs of which you are aware. You may find yourself giving in constantly to your child's whims and demands, however unreasonable, because you feel guilty about the break-up of your previous relationship. Although integrating your man into your family will take up a lot of energy, be kind to yourself too. You are also on the brink of a big change: you are deciding to spend your life with someone new. That relationship must be given a chance and you should be firm about ensuring "private" time with your prospective partner.

Try to be sensitive to your partner's reactions to your child. There will be times when he needs your support, just as you will need his on occasions. He'll be most likely to experience feelings of rejection – but you can help by pointing out the value in slowly forging relationships with your child and not expecting too much too soon. Being rebuffed by a child can be very painful – especially when there's a great desire to make the relationship work.

On the other hand, try to see things from your child's point of view: if you were previously single, then your child may be experiencing intense jealousy. If your new man is "replacing" an estranged father with whom he still has strong ties, then there's bound to be some resentment and lots of unfavourable comparisons, and your partner may feel an unwelcome outsider.

The mistake often lies in striving too hard for a fatherly closeness overnight: if you aim for a more casual bond – rather like friendship – then you will not be testing your child's loyalties so severely. If he tolerates and trusts him, this is a basis you can build on; do not enforce any kind of intimacy too soon.

On a practical level, you should make every attempt to include your partner in the everyday affairs of your household, once you have decided you want to share your life together. The worst thing for your partner to feel is that he's some kind of "spare part", hanging around on the outside of your family circle. In this respect, it's easier for him to find a valuable niche in terms of practical help – such as taking the kids to the park while you get housework out of the way, or taking them to the dentist or to school – than in terms of interfering with discipline or behaviour.

For many reasons, disciplining children is often the most problematic area in this delicate relationship. Stepfathers run the risk of going to opposite extremes in their reaction to their stepchildren. Either they are over-strict, or come to the new marriage with different standards from those the children are used to, or they hesitate to give their stepchildren any defined guidelines for fear of alienating them. Your partner may hold back from punishing your child – or even from giving him boundaries – because of the shakiness of his own relationship with them. But this can actually have the opposite effect of causing your child to lose respect for him.

You, as the mother, need to be very tactful on the subject of discipline – unless you decide to be in sole charge in this area. Before your new partner moves in, it's a good idea to make sure your views on how to treat children coincide – at least over major domestic issues. It's very confusing for a child to hear different messages about how he ought to behave. He is more likely to respect a united front. Don't just hope for the best; be prepared to discuss with your partner potential areas of conflict, such as table manners, watching TV, bedtimes, clearing up and how to deal with naughty behaviour. The best possible solution is to discuss your attitudes well before having to put them into practice.

However long the period of easing your partner into your life lasts, there will come a time when you decide to make the link permanent. Whether or not this entails marriage, you must let your child know exactly what is happening.

Meeting the demands of your child and your partner in a situation as delicate as this inevitably makes you feel as if you're engaged in some prolonged juggling act. In a sense, you always will be. But once the initial period of getting to know each other has passed and there's more familiarity and give and take, there's no need for your "new" family to be any more disadvantaged or less happy than a "normal" one.

Stings

Most insect stings and bites are completely harmless, merely causing temporary irritation. Bee and wasp stings can be painful, and can have severe effects in a few susceptible children; the stings of jellyfish can sometimes be troublesome, as can multiple stings, and bites from mosquitoes, ants and even gnats. In a few, rare cases children can have severe allergic reaction to stings, but normally they are a very minor problem.

When a child has been stung, his skin becomes red and swollen in the area around the sting. The skin may feel hot, and will be itchy or throbbing.

In a very few cases children have abnormal reactions to stings, with exaggerated swelling and soreness, and very occasionally being stung by a wasp or bee can produce symptoms of shock, with pallor, dilated pupils, shallow, fast breathing, cold, clammy skin, and possibly unconsciousness. This is known as "anaphylactic shock" and is treated as a medical emergency.

Normally, however, the only treatment needed is to cool the area by bathing it in cold water or rubbing it with an ice cube. When the skin is dry, calamine lotion can be applied to soothe it, and this treatment can be repeated frequently until the irritation has subsided. Even the more irritating jellyfish stings can be treated in this way, but first any traces of jellyfish should be wiped off the child's skin, and if possible the area should be washed with soap and water.

When stings cause severe irritation, this can be numbed by using one of the many preparations that are available in cream or aerosol spray form.

These are particularly useful at night, when the warmth of the bed can make the irritation worse and the child's sleep can be disturbed. Do not use them for more than a day or so, and if the problem persists see your family doctor.

If a child has an adverse reaction to a sting or is stung in several places, take him to the doctor. The doctor may prescribe antihistamine tablets or may give a steroid injection where there is a violent reaction. If a child shows signs of shock, call an ambulance or get him to hospital yourself as soon as possible as emergency treatment will be necessary.

◆ See also, **Bee Stings**, **Shock**, **Wasp stings**

Story-Telling

Children love the double thrill of hearing an exciting story while snuggling securely by the mother or father's side. Even babies will take comfort in the sound of your voice and the intimacy of a shared story, even if they don't actually understand it.

This early story-telling is a good way of helping you bond with each other, the process by which new parents and their child form a shared emotional commitment that will last a lifetime. As your child grows, you'll see the result of good early bonding when he climbs on to your lap to have a story read to him, for example, or when he seeks you out in particular from among a group of familiar adults, as his special friend.

Reading stories is a good way of developing your child's other skills, too. Let him reach for, and turn the pages as soon as he is able and he'll rapidly turn his unco-ordinated little fingers into nimble ones able to select an individual page or point out his favourite character.

If you adjust the pitch of your voice to suit the mood of the book it will not be long before you'll see a little head turning from book to you, and back to book again, desperately trying to make sense of what is happening. In time, he'll join in, exclaiming with delight at the more charming passages and shrieking with mock horror at the scary bits.

Participation like this is invaluable in helping your child develop his communication skills and he will soon apply these sounds to his own situations.

But it's not just the vocal ways of communcating that count. Studies of adults have revealed that nearly half of the impact of what we say is made by the way we use our bodies when we speak.

It follows from this that reading or telling stories with expression and animation is vital to your child's enjoyment of them. Some parents find this a bit of a stumbling block at first, having become unused to reading aloud. A good tip to get back into practice is to watch actors reading children's stories on TV. See how they look into your eyes from time to time as though really sharing the fun with you and listen to how they change their voice to match whichever new character is speaking. Remember, they rehearse their readings and it can pay dividends if you have a quick skim through a book before reading it to your child for the first time just to make sure you know what is happening and when.

You are bound to be appointed your child's number one story-teller in the family, but encourage others to take part too. Each of us brings a different perspective, however minor, to telling a story and children love to point out when someone has got something "wrong" compared to the way someone else tells the same tale. Your partner, grandparents, other relatives and friends all have a part to play – and will usually be delighted to be asked.

To the different versions of one story that a child hears, they will often add their own. And what a fascinating adaptation it can be with characters from their everyday real life skilfully inserted into both "good" and "bad" roles in the story. You can learn a lot from turning the tables and becoming the listening half of the story-telling session for a change: just as we sometimes discover daytime concerns surfacing in our dreams, so children use made-up stories to express their thoughts on life and secret fears.

Try not to worry if your best friend's child becomes "bad" in the story when you thought he should be "good". Children alter their opinions in an instant and everyone's roles are just as likely to have changed completely by the time you next listen to your little one.

Story-telling need not be restricted to bedtime; try to make any time story time. Simple stories can be made up for any situation – in the back of the car going to the shops or waiting for the bus.

Stories on tape are an absolute boon to the busy parent or the one who is simply worn out from reading. If your child has his own cassette recorder it will boost his sense of independence as he can select, insert and play his favourite stories all on his own. All the traditional stories and nursery rhymes are now available, plus many new ones too. They usually come with a book so children can follow the words and pictures as they listen. And the stories are read by professional actors so that the exciting bits really do sound exciting. Don't, however, allow tapes to replace your special time with your child.

Many of the fairy stories we tell our children actually have quite a scary plot. This seems to do little to put children off the stories however. In fact, the scarier they are, the more in demand they can become. Psychologists think that one of the possible reasons for this is that scary stories help children live out some of their own subconscious fears while in a safe environment. And providing that there is a happy ending, which there usually is, a scary story can actually help a child to come to terms with his fears. Remember though to stick to traditional stories rather than making up too scary a story of your own, and soften your voice for the scary bits if your child seems ill at ease; and give up the story altogether if it's too scary.

As soon as your child is old enough, take him along to your local library where the children's section will open up still more doors for him.

After watching you reading stories to him, your child will soon want to read stories to you too. Parents glow with pride at each new word their child learns – and rightly so, for the ability to read is one of the major gateways to children understanding the world around them.

Enjoy this stage of your child's development for what it is – the first faltering steps into the universe of books – and don't worry too much about mistakes. What he needs is constant encouragement and praise for trying and the more of this he receives, the quicker he is likely to progress. There are no rules as to when a child should learn to read. But what you can be sure of is that by reading and telling stories to him yourself, you are laying the foundations for his teachers in future years.

Strangulation

We use the term "strangulation" to mean compression of the neck, which reduces the supply of blood to the head, although medically strangulation is the cutting off of the blood supply to any part of the body, caused by local compression. However, here "strangulation" will be used in its everyday sense.

Strangulation causes irreversible brain damage and death unless the constriction is quickly removed and the child resuscitated, so rapid action is required. The risks should be avoided as much as possible. Anything tight round the neck causes compression of the jugular veins on either side of the neck. These are the veins through which blood from the head is returned to the heart to be supplied with fresh oxygen. When they are compressed the blood circulation is interfered with, and the brain is deprived of oxygen as blood is trapped in the head and its supply of oxygen is used up.

A child who is being strangled begins to struggle for breath and his face turns a livid purple or blue as the level of oxygen in the blood falls. Some of the blood vessels in the skin burst, causing a rash of tiny, bleeding points. Within two or three minutes the child loses consciousness, and within another three or four minutes he will die if he is not resuscitated.

If you have to treat a child who is suffering from strangulation try, if possible, to get someone else to get medical help while you give first aid.

First, remove whatever it is that is constricting the throat as quickly and calmly as you can (cutting it through if possible). Next, if the child is not breathing or if breathing is faint give mouth-to-mouth resuscitation (*see* Artificial Respiration) after clearing the child's mouth with your finger to make sure that there is nothing blocking the airways. If you are sure that there is no pulse give heart massage (*see* Cardiac Massage), stopping to give two breaths after every 5 presses on the heart.

When the child begins to breathe spontaneously again, place him in the recovery positon (*see* First Aid). Keep him warm and reassure him until medical help arrives, or call help if this has not already been done.

Babies and young children are most at risk from accidental strangulation as they do not understand the dangers of forcing their heads into restricted spaces or playing with loops of cord, and they are likely to panic and be unable to extract themselves if they do find themselves entangled.

Sources of danger are long cords attached to clothing or toys, fold-down washing lines with their loops of cord, and restraining apparatus from which babies and small children may be able to wriggle only to be strangled as they then fall out of bed or try to crawl away. You should also check for widely spaced slats or rails in cots. The ties on your child's cot bumpers should be kept short and should be regularly checked.

Parents can considerably reduce the risk of accidents by being aware of potential dangers when choosing and using restraining apparatus, toys and clothing.

As children grow up they should be taught about the dangers of having anything tight round the neck. They should not wear trailing scarves when on bicycles or tricycles because of the danger of the scarf being caught in the wheels, and they must be aware of danger when playing with ropes in "cowboys and Indians" or when swinging by ropes from trees or playing on swings.

Styes

A stye is a small boil on the edge of the eyelid, at the root of the lashes, and is usually caused by bacterial infection.

Bathing the affected area in an eye lotion or applying warm, moist compresses may be helpful. If the stye does not clear up within a day or two, however, take your child to your doctor who will prescribe an ointment or an alternative eye lotion.

Your child should not rub or touch the affected eyelid as this may spread the infection.

Suffocation

Suffocating or near-suffocating (known in non-medical terms as smothering) happens when the nose and mouth are blocked, preventing the child from breathing. This causes asphyxiation (lack of oxygen in the blood).

Asphyxiation is usually caused either by bedding, pillows or clothing covering the child's face and obstructing the airways when the child is asleep or by the child's face being covered by a plastic bag. It is tempting to a child to put things on his head and a plastic bag looks like an ideal dressing-up accessory. The bag clings to the child's face and makes him unable to breathe properly. The child panics, and is unable to remove it. Eventually he passes out through lack of oxygen.

The first sign of asphyxiation is difficulty in breathing. The child's breathing may become noisy and unless something is done may stop completely. This will cause the child to turn blue, then grey, and to become unconscious. It can also cause convulsions.

Immediate, cool-headed action is vital if you find a child being asphyxiated. If possible get someone else to call an ambulance while you attend to the child, but if there is no one else there, deal with the child first, losing no time.

First remove the obstruction by ripping off the polythene bag or pulling away bed clothing and make sure that there is good ventilation.

Check that there is no other reason for the child's airways being blocked (vomit or some object in his mouth, for example). Run your finger round the inside of the mouth to make sure that it is clear.

Put your cheek to the child's nose to feel for breathing and check whether the chest is rising and falling. Feel the pulse to check that the heart is beating.

If the child is still breathing and his heart is beating (even if he is unconscious) all you need to do is keep him lying down, in the recovery position (*see* First Aid), call an ambulance and watch over him while you wait for the ambulance to arrive.

If he appears not to be breathing you must administer artificial respiration at once, and if his heart is definitely not beating cardiac massage should be given. (Ideally these techniques should be learned in first aid classes, but in an emergency they should be tried regardless.)

Smothering can be fatal or it can cause irreversible brain damage if treatment is not given within a few minutes. To prevent accidents, make sure that children are told how dangerous it is to play with plastic bags. Keep in a safe place any plastic bags that are being saved for re-use and put them away immediately as shopping is unpacked.

Children should have firm pillows and babies should not have them at all. Choose night-clothes that will not ride up when the child is asleep and make sure the bed covers are well tucked in at the bottom to prevent them from being pulled up over the child's face.

◆ See also, **Artificial Respiration**, **Cardiac Massage**, **First Aid**

Sunburn

Most babies and young children have skins that are very sensitive to the sun, particularly if they are fair-haired and fair-skinned. However, it is always possible to prevent sunburn by controlling the amount of exposure to the sun a child has, and parents should always do this, as sunburn can ruin the holidays.

Sunburnt skin is red and sore, and feels hot and burning. In severe cases of sunburn the skin may blister, and there may also be intense itching. After several days the skin calms down, and then peels before returning to normal.

Resistance comes through the development of a tan, and this is best acquired through gradual exposure to the sun. The ultraviolet rays of the sun stimulate cells known as melanocytes to produce more of the skin pigment melanin, which darkens the skin and protects it from sunburn. The more gradual the exposure, the better the protection.

If your child does get sunburn, the best treatment is to dab on calamine lotion with cotton wool, and keep him indoors with the burnt parts exposed to the air. When he goes out, dress him in something loose and made of cotton, such as a soft old shirt or T-shirt, and at night make sure that the sheets on his bed are not rumpled, as the creases will make the sunburn more painful.

If the sunburnt skin causes pain this can be relieved with paracetamol in the dose recommended for the child's age, and it is safe to use lotions containing calamine or aloe vera or perhaps menthol or camphor. These can be obtained from a chemist without a doctor's prescription, and if in doubt about whether a cream is suitable for your child you can ask the pharmacist's advice. If the sunburn is severe, and if the skin is blistered, you should take the child to a doctor.

To prevent your child from getting sunburn, do not let him spend time in the sun when it is at its most intense (from 11 am to 2 pm) at the beginning of the holidays unless he has already built up a tan by playing outdoors during the spring and early summer. And bear in mind also that the sun can burn without seeming hot, especially if there is a cooling breeze, and when light is reflected by sea and snow. Burning can even take place on days of thin cloud, and the burning rays of the sun can also pass through very light clothing such as fine cotton lawn. For the first few days especially, make sure that while the child is outside, his back and head are protected by a shirt and hat.

Especially if his skin is fair, the child should not be exposed for more than about half an hour on the first day. This can be increased by about quarter of an hour a day over the first four or five days. If you apply a high-protection sun cream the time can be extended, but you must make sure that the cream is applied to all the exposed skin and is frequently re-applied, particularly after swimming.

Sunburn significantly increases the risk of later development of malignant melanoma (skin cancer).

Children with darker skins are lucky and their parents do not need to be so cautious. But even these children can get burnt if they spend hours in the strong sun when they are not used to it.

Sunstroke

When children have been exposed to too much sun they may suffer from heat stroke as well as getting sunburn. Mild cases of heat stroke caused by being in the sun are often referred to as "sunstroke". *See* the entry on Heat Stroke for symptoms and treatment.

Swallowed Objects

Babies and young children are always putting things in their mouths and these can sometimes get swallowed. If this happens to your child it is important for you not to panic. Many objects that were not intended to be swallowed will do no harm, but if the child swallows anything sharp, or small batteries like those used in calculators and musical birthdays cards, or if he is choking and unable to breathe, swift action is needed.

Especially when they are at the stage where they will put anything in their mouths (the worst time is usually between the ages of 3 and 18 months) children may swallow beads, pins, hairgrips, buttons, dried beans, washers, toy blocks, plastic bottle tops, metal can rings and all sorts of other objects.

You may actually see the child swallowing the object, but if not, the first sign may be coughing or choking as the object gets stuck at the entrance to the airway. Sometimes there will be no sign that anything is amiss until the object gets further down into the child's digestive tract and causes a blockage with pains and bloating in the tummy.

If the object was small and not sharp and if there is no adverse reaction, there is no need to do anything but wait for the object to pass out at the other end. This does not apply to batteries which, however small, can be dangerous, as some contain mercury which can leak. If your child swallows a battery take him straight to the nearest accident and emergency ward. In the case of any other small object, keep a check on the child's faeces (stools) to check that it has passed out (it is likely to take 24–48 hours). If the object does not appear in the stools or if the child has pain or swelling, seek medical help, either by making an appointment with your family doctor or by taking the child straight to the accident and emergency department of the nearest hospital if the symptoms are severe. An operation may be needed to remove the object.

If the child is coughing, encourage him to continue as this should dislodge the object, but if he is choking, he will be unable to breathe and urgent action is called for.

Some parents find that their children swallow things so frequently that they soon learn how to scoop them calmly out of the child's throat with a finger. Quickly look into the child's throat to see if there is something you could easily remove. If so, do this deftly, making quite sure that you do not push whatever it is further down the child's throat.

If you cannot easily remove the object, you must hold the child upside down and hope that the force of gravity will do the job. For a baby hold him firmly along one arm, with his head pointing downwards and supporting his jaw with your hand while you tap him firmly on the back between the shoulder blades with the other hand until the obstruction is clear. For a small child, sit down and hold him across your knees with his chest and head hanging down the side of your legs, and again tap him several times between the shoulder blades. (The strength of the tap should depend on the size of the child.) If you have nowhere to sit you can hold a baby or small child upside down by his feet and if possible get someone else to tap his back.

For an older, larger child who is too big to be placed across your knee the "abdominal thrust" method may be used: stand behind the victim and place both your arms just above his waist. Feel for the bottom of the ribs, where they join the breastbone, and then, with his head, arms and chest hanging forward, grab the fist of one of your hands with the other hand so that your arms are braced and press inward and upward quickly into the child's abdomen. Repeat several times if necessary.

A child who has swallowed batteries, eyebrow tweezers or any other sharp object, needs immediate medical attention. Call an ambulance, or if you can get him to hospital quickly by taking him yourself, do so, if possible getting someone to telephone to say that you are on your way.

In hospital the child will be examined manually and by X-ray. Once it has been confirmed that an object has been swallowed, and where it is, the object will then probably be removed surgically, although in some cases it may be thought preferable to leave it if it seems to be passing safely through the child's body.

As is so often the case accidents such as those involving swallowed objects may be prevented:

● Keep all small objects – from beads and buttons to building blocks as well as pills and tablets – out of your baby's reach.

● Check all rooms that your child has access to for small objects, when visiting other people as well as at home.

If your child persists in swallowing objects when he is past the baby and toddler stage, discuss this with your doctor. There may be some emotional problem at the root of this behaviour.

Swimming

There are many reasons why a child should learn to swim. The main purpose is, of course, to prevent a tragic drowning accident, and so it really is advisable to teach children to swim from a very early age. But it is also fun and a great way for your child to practise all kinds of skills. Regular trips to the swimming pool will help your child to develop his physical co-ordination, his self-confidence, and his ability to play, co-operate with and show concern for others – as well as his ability to look after himself. And don't forget, swimming can be very relaxing.

Once he feels secure in the water, your child may enjoy simply floating on the surface, as well as taking part in more boisterous play. So don't worry, you need not be an expert swimmer yourself to encourage his early water confidence, and introduce him to some of the fun of the swimming pool.

As long as your baby is well and free from any kind of infection, you can start taking him to an indoor pool once he's about 12 weeks old. This is very young, and not all parents will feel happy about putting such a small baby in the water, but you can check with your doctor if you are concerned. Make sure, though, that the water temperature is at least 28°C (82°F). Most shallow baby or learner pools are kept at 30°–32°C (86°–90°F), but larger, public pools are likely to be much cooler. It is also important that the air temperature is slightly warmer than the water, to stop your baby from getting cold.

If you decide not to take your baby swimming when he is very young, don't worry. You can wait until he's two or three. But the sooner you take him to a pool, the easier it will be for him to develop some of the simple reflexes which help to make water play fun. For example, once he develops the "diving reflex" he will instinctively stop water going up his nose when he goes under water. Young children can develop this reflex very easily.

Before you take your child to the pool, it is important to help him to feel happy and at home in water. Bath time gives you an ideal opportunity to do this. You can use a sponge to squeeze and trickle water over his body and face, so that he gets used to splashes, and to the feeling of water running over his head, face, ears and eyes. Make it fun and don't rush things. Teaching your child not to be afraid of water is very important. Give him toys to play with in the bath so that he associates water with pleasure. You can even introduce buoyancy aids such as inflatable arm bands into your play. This way they will already be familiar to him when it's time for your early trips to the swimming pool.

Once your baby or toddler is confident in the bath, and enjoys water play, he is ready for his first visit to the swimming pool. But try not to expect too much at first. He will need to get used to a strange, large, new place, full of unfamiliar sounds, sights and smells. It's a good idea to contact the pool authorities beforehand to find out when it is likely to be fairly quiet, and to check whether they have special times for parents with small children.

Your local pool may well offer a range of classes, including:
● a parent and baby class for parents with children between the ages of 3 and 18 months
● a parent and toddler class for parents with children aged from 18 months to 3 years old
● an infant class for slightly older children, to encourage confidence in the water without parents
● swimming classes for children from 4–5 years old upwards, including beginners, intermediate and advanced classes.

If you want to build up your own water confidence, there's usually a wide range of adult classes and women-only classes, too.

Treat your first visit to the pool as an extension of your play at home. Take a sponge so that you can continue to play trickling and splashing games and take some favourite bath toys. Keep the visit short, making sure that your child stays warm. You can build up to longer visits as he gets more active and confident.

Getting into the water is easier than you may think. If there are shallow steps into the pool, you can walk in slowly carrying your child, and then gradually sink down into the water until the shoulders of both of you are covered. Hold him gently but firmly, making sure that you keep eye contact with him all the time, and talk to him quietly as you gently bounce him up and down in the water. If at any time he seems distressed, stop what you are doing and try something else. Never force a nervous child into the water.

If you can't walk into the water but have to use a wall ladder, ask someone else to hand him down to you once you have got into the pool yourself. Don't be tempted to leave your toddler on the side while you climb in, just in case he wanders off.

Once you're in the water, you can continue building up your child's confidence through play. Once he has stopped clinging to you, you can have fun with floating and simple movement games. Most small babies can float quite easily on their backs, though remember that your baby's head is heavier than the rest of his body and he will need some support.

Make sure you are standing firmly on the bottom as you support your baby, and make sure he never drifts out of your reach. You can also support him firmly on his front, and move him gently backwards and forwards so that he gets used to the feeling of moving through the water. Put his favourite floating toys in the water, just out of reach. This will encourage him to try to "swim" as he reaches out for them. Once he's happy in the pool, you can start to introduce buoyancy aids such as arm bands. When they're fitted properly, he will be able to move about in the water on his own, while you stay close beside him for reassurance. There are a number of aids on the market – water wings, tubes and even swimming costumes with built-in buoyancy. Check these carefully for proper design before you buy them.

Don't worry if your child's first swimming movements are rather jerky. Just let him discover the fun and freedom of moving around independently in the water. And once he's really at ease, you can try a few games without the buoyancy aids. If you're with your partner or a friend, try supporting your child with one hand under his tummy and one under his chin, and launch him through the water to where your partner is waiting to catch him. And don't forget, always give him lots of praise and smiles as you play.

Your child learns naturally from copying others, and you can use this to help him. Show your toddler how you blow the water away from your mouth when it touches it. He'll love to see the bubbles you make, and you can encourage him to dip his mouth under the water to try to blow some of his own.

Hold on to the side of the pool and show him how you can kick your legs up and down to make big splashing movements. He may like to hold your hands rather than the side of the pool for his first attempts. Once he's got the idea, show him how to do the same thing holding on to a float. He'll begin to feel the thrill of moving through the water under his own steam. He won't be ready to learn proper strokes until he's three at the very least, and probably not until much later, but he'll have fun moving through the water on his own long before perfecting a technique.

If your child seems a bit uncertain about the water, try not to force him. After all, the unknown can be very frightening. Try to understand his fears, instead of insisting that he overcomes them. Visit the pool often and stay with him at the poolside, making sure he is warm and comfortable. And with any luck he'll want to join in himself after a few visits.

If you feel uncertain about the water yourself, visit the pool on your own before deciding whether or not you want to take your child. Ask if you can watch a mother and child session, or find out how crowded the pool is at the time you and your child are most likely to want to go.

If you do decide to take your child, try to organize a family outing with your partner, at least on the first trips. Having him there to support you may help your own confidence. But if you and your partner decide that you are both too nervous to take your child, try to make other arrangements rather than risk passing on your fears or deprive him of the pool pleasure altogether.

The most important lesson you can give your child is that swimming and water play are fun. Once he's hooked on the water – and old enough to want to develop his technique, you may want him to join a formal swimming class. Of course, if you're lucky he may get swimming lessons at school anyway, but if you feel he is ready for some instruction before that, make arrangements at your local pool.

Once your child starts lessons on his own, it doesn't mean that you can't continue to have fun together in the pool. In fact, his growing skills will open up lots of new activities and games. You can use the imitation skills he already has to play a game where everyone (perhaps a group of your child's friends) has to do what the leader does – crouch down under water, swim three strokes on their front, and so on. Take it in turns to play the leader.

You can also adapt lots of other playground games for the water. "Ring-a-ring-a-roses" is a good game to help your child get used to going under the surface, as you "all fall down". And different versions of tag will encourage him to learn how to change direction quickly and swim faster.

As soon as your child is old enough you should teach him the following "code" of behaviour at the pool:

● Walk, don't run, along the pool edge and in the changing areas.
● Understand that pushing other people into the water could hurt them.
● Look before jumping into the water.
● Avoid dangerous areas of the pool – deep areas, or areas under slides and diving boards.
● Stay near a parent or another adult in the swimming pool.
● Tell an adult immediately if someone is in any kind of trouble.
● Listen to any instructions from the lifeguards.
● Wear a bathing cap, especially for long hair.

More and more pools now have adventure slides and chutes. Small slides can be great fun for your child once he's happy about going under the water and being splashed, but most of the adventure chutes are not suitable – or open to – children under a certain size. Avoid disappointment by checking whether your child will be able to use a particular pool's facilities before setting out.

Some pools have wave machines which can send waves across the pool just like at the seaside. Lots of children find this very exciting. Wave machines are usually only turned on at intervals, and a horn or buzzer may sound to warn you. It is a good idea to warn your child about the buzzer, and let him watch what happens when the machine is turned on before deciding whether he wants to play in the waves. He must be able to swim, or you must hold him if he is to use the pool when the wave machine is working.

Remember that any public place can expose your child to the risk of common infections, and a swimming pool is no exception.

● Make sure that your child has been properly immunized. Ask your doctor if you are not sure what is necessary.

● Don't take your child swimming if he is unwell, especially if he has a chest infection, ear infection or sniffly nose.

● Make sure he has a wash or shower before and after going into the pool.

● Keep any cuts or grazes covered with waterproof plasters.

● Check regularly to see that he has not developed athlete's foot, verrucas or other skin problems. Ask your doctor of chemist's advice if you are concerned.

You might also find the following tips useful when planning a swimming outing:

● Do not take your child swimming immediately after a meal. Allow about two hours for food to be digested.

● Try to wear the same costume each time you go, so that your child can identify you easily at the pool.

● Take some snacks and drinks with you for afterwards. Swimming is likely to give your child an appetite.

● If your child uses arm bands, inflate them before you set out. They may be slightly bulky to carry, but it's easier than struggling with them at the poolside.

● Put everything you need in one large, preferably waterproof bag which you can leave at the side of the pool if you don't want to use a locker.

● Don't forget the basics – costumes, towels, soap, shampoo and a comb.

● Dress your child in the minimum of clothes needed to keep him warm. If possible, avoid socks and long trousers. Changing room floors are always wet, and shorts and skirts are less likely to trail in the puddles.

● If you intend to use a pool locker or hairdryer, remember to take some small change.

Finally, if your child is happy in the water, and has learnt some basic safety rules, both you and he can feel confident that he will be safe because he knows how to swim and look after himself.

Teeth and Dental Care

By the time your child is about two years old, his first set of teeth should be complete. These 20 primary teeth are commonly called the baby or milk teeth. Regular cleaning is vital for keeping the teeth and gums healthy and for fresh-smelling breath. Although a secondary set will start to replace the primary teeth from the age of about six, it is important to teach your child how to clean his first teeth properly as soon as possible. If he has not got into the habit of keeping them clean by the time his second set come through, he is likely to neglect these too and suffer pain and other problems later.

If the teeth are not cleaned regularly and thoroughly, unpleasant substances develop in the mouth and may cause tooth decay.

The most dangerous substance that damages teeth is plaque. This is an almost invisible layer of sticky, yellowish-white material, composed of dried saliva, microscopic particles of food and millions of bacteria. Plaque clings to the teeth and changes sugar in the mouth into acid, which attacks the enamel surface of the teeth. This is the start of tooth decay and, once it is established, it slowly moves deeper into the tooth, resulting in holes in the enamel which are known as cavities.

Gum disease is caused by plaque accumulating around, and just under the edge of the gums. If only the gum tissue is affected, the condition is called gingivitis.

Bad breath, soreness and inflammation of the gums, toothache and visible damage to the teeth are common symptoms of inadequate dental care. Even if they are brushed hard, your gums should not bleed if they are strong and healthy.

577

If allowed to worsen, gum disease, technically known as periodontal disease, can make the gums recede and may eventually affect deeper tissues, including the jaw bone. In some cases, the teeth become permanently loose.

Sometimes a child may complain of earache when a tooth is giving trouble. This is because the nerves in the side of the face are very close together and the pain caused by an inflammation of the ear may be easily confused with a toothache.

Because plaque is such a sticky substance, a child's teeth must be brushed thoroughly at least once a day to remove it. Being thorough is more important than cleaning the teeth frequently. On average, it takes about three minutes to remove all the plaque if you brush the teeth properly. Brushing your child's teeth quickly several times each day is not as effective as a really good clean after breakfast and before putting the child to bed. When your child is old enough to clean his own teeth, he will tend to copy what you have done, so always take time when cleaning his teeth. When brushing, work steadily around the outside of the teeth, and then clean the inside surfaces. Moving the brush around in small circles is the safest and most effective method, as it cleans the teeth without damaging the gums. Also, massage the gums by brushing them gently. Afterwards, make your child rinse out his mouth with water. When cleaning your child's teeth, the quality of the brush is considerably more important than using lots of toothpaste. A blob of paste about the size of a pea will be sufficient. But teeth cannot be cleaned properly with a frayed toothbrush, so check its condition and replace it when necessary – perhaps every three months or so.

Most dentists recommend a flat-headed nylon toothbrush with a short, straight handle as being the best for reaching the awkward corners of the mouth. Use a fairly soft brush to avoid damaging your child's delicate gums. He can progress to a slightly harder brush when he's older.

To discover whether all the plaque has been removed from your child's teeth, you can use disclosing tablets obtainable from a dentist or chemist. Your child should chew one of these tablets every so often and any remaining plaque will be dyed either bright red or blue. If you find it impossible to remove the plaque from your child's teeth, get this done by the dentist.

Better still, arrange for the dentist to check your child's teeth and gums regularly, even when they appear to be healthy. Any problems will be spotted before they become serious, and will be easier to treat.

Another way of cleaning the teeth is with a tooth-cloth. This ancient technique has been gaining popularity since it has been proved to prevent tooth decay. Any small piece of clean cloth may be used. Dampen the cloth, apply a little toothpaste to it, then hold the cloth over a finger and rub the paste on to the teeth and between them. The toothcloth may be used in addition to brushing, but should not be regarded as an alternative.

Although dental floss is not recommended for children, it is still a good idea for you to floss your teeth as children learn by copying adults, and they will need to know how to floss when they are older.

Dental floss is useful for cleaning the spaces between the teeth, where food particles can be trapped. Floss is a thin, silky yarn which is sometimes waxed to make it feel smoother. The waxed and unwaxed types are equally effective. A length of floss is drawn back and forth between the teeth to remove the plaque. Your dentist will be glad to demonstrate the most effective way of using it.

Some dentists believe that the best way to prevent tooth decay, especially in children, is to brush the teeth with fluoride toothpaste, and to use fluoride in other forms as well. In some regions, natural fluoride is inadquate in the water supply; in these areas, fluoride may be deliberately added to drinking water because of its effectiveness in protecting the teeth. Your local water authority will tell you whether your supply contains enough fluoride. If it does not, go to a chemist and purchase some fluoride drops or tablets to add to your drinking water. Alternatively your child could use a fluoride mouthwash.

If using fluoride drops, tablets or mouthwash, be sure to follow the directions as exceeding the dose does not offer extra protection and could, in extreme cases, cause mottling of the teeth.

Use the following guidelines to help you and your child fight the battle against tooth decay:

● Try to reduce the amount of unnecessary sugary food that your child eats as this is one of the main causes of tooth decay. Within minutes of eating anything containing sugar, bacteria on the teeth form acid. This helps to rot the teeth. Any type of sugar can contribute to decay.

● Do not prevent a child from eating honey and fruit as they are highly nutritious. However, as they contain sugar, make sure that his teeth are cleaned afterwards.

● Eating small amounts of sugar at intervals throughout the day is much worse than eating the same total amount all at once. If you must offer them at all, save sugary treats for mealtimes.

● If your child becomes hungry between meals, offer him a savoury snack, rather than cakes, biscuits, chocolate, sweets or ice cream.

Teething

Babies usually begin teething at around six months, and the process is not complete until the first back teeth or premolars appear when they are up to two or three years old. The baby teeth or milk teeth, properly known as primary teeth, begin to be replaced by permanent teeth from the time the child is about six years old, although the first permanent teeth to appear are usually the molars or back teeth, for which there are no equivalent primary teeth.

After the appearance of the molars the child's baby teeth gradually loosen and fall out and the permanent teeth take their place. It is not until the child is much older (usually 17 or 18) that the wisdom teeth grow and all 32 teeth are present.

The expression "teething" is usually used to refer to the process of the primary teeth appearing, which takes place over a period of a year or so.

When a baby is teething, his gums will be red and swollen at the site of the tooth that is about to emerge. This may make him fretful and disrupt his sleep as the swollen gum throbs painfully. Teething usually makes a baby dribble more than usual and he may put his fists into his mouth and bite on them for comfort. Symptoms will not be continuous, but can be observed each time a new tooth is about to appear.

Other symptoms are sometimes wrongly connected with teething. Teething does not cause unrelated symptoms, such as vomiting, lack of appetite or diarrhoea, although it can sometimes cause the child to have difficulty with feeding.

The premolars (the larger teeth at the sides of the mouth), which are cut when the child is between one and three years old, can cause much more pain and soreness than the teeth at the front, which come through first.

If your child is irritable or clinging look inside his mouth for any sign of sore and swollen gums, and feel the gum with your fingers. You will be able to feel the tooth under the gum if it is about to break through.

Give your child the cuddling he seems to be demanding as teething can be painful and he may feel very miserable. It is not a good idea to give pain relief medicines as the process will go on for such a long time as tooth after tooth breaks through.

Instead give the child a safety tested teething ring to bite on, or a rusk to chew. The child may also find it soothing if you cool your fingers in cold water and rub them over the sore gum. You can also buy cooling gels in your pharmacy to apply to the gums.

You can still breastfeed your child perfectly comfortably as his teeth appear, and he may actually need more nursing, partly just for the comfort and partly because when his gums are sore he may not feed as well as usual.

If the teething is going normally it is not necessary to see your doctor. However you should never put other symptoms down to teething and if your child has any other symptoms of illness while he is teething you should not hesitate to make a doctor's appointment.

If the gum is unusually swollen, if the baby is clearly in pain and not feeding properly, or if you are worried because a tooth seems to be taking a long time to come through, then you should also see your doctor about that. He or she may prescribe a mild analgesic to help the child over the difficulty, and in rare cases you may be advised to see a dentist if the gums are badly swollen.

Television and Videos

You may make a conscious decision not to have a television in your home, but there are still plenty of opportunities for your children to watch television and videos at other people's homes. So whether you approve or not, you have to accept the fact that your children are growing up with television, rather than without it. What you can do, however, is exercise some influence over how much and what your child watches when he is very young, and establish what you consider to be good viewing habits right from the start.

One reason why television has become such a prominent feature in home life is that it gives instant gratification. TV-watching is a passive activity that requires little or no effort from the viewer. One educationalist has described the appeal as being part of the "pleasure principle". Television can help the viewer travel to distant locations, experience many emotions such as joy and sadness, tension and relief, and learn about new subjects, without them even getting up out of a chair or opening a book. It is this passivity that worries many parents. Perhaps you also feel there is something slightly alarming about seeing your child sitting quite still, transfixed in front of the television and would rather see him trying to work out a puzzle, or playing a make-believe game with his toys.

The other alarming feature of television that causes great concern is violence. Banning specific programmes to eliminate violence, however, may not be as effective as you might think at first. Nightly newscasts, for example, are filled with graphic details of grisly murders and horrid accidents.

While younger children are not as captivated by the sophisticated violence and action of cops and robbers shows, their favourite cartoon may not be as gentle as it appears. If you watch closely, you'll see that most of the characters punch and hit each other with great regularity inflicting terrible wounds. Even the cuddliest-looking character can be quite violent.

Education is one of the areas where television straddles the line between being considered good or bad. It is bad when it distracts older children from doing their homework or reading, and good when it can be used as an educational tool.

Many of the programmes made specifically for pre-schoolers are designed to educate as well as entertain. If your child watches these programmes, make the most of the educational factor by trying to follow up on the lessons when the programme is over. Depending on how much time you have, read your child a story about a related subject, help him make a model of something featured in the programme, encourage him to draw a picture of what he remembers or sing the songs featured in the programme.

Whatever the programme content, be selective. Avoid letting your child "blanket watch". It can be very tempting when you're busy to let the television lull your child into a passive, quiet state so that you can get on with chores. This only starts bad viewing habits. Instead, put your child in a safe place and give him lots of toys to keep him occupied. It might not last as long, but the benefits will be greater.

Rather than just making an overall condemnation of television, think carefully about what it is exactly that you are particularly worried or concerned about:

● Are you concerned about the levels of bad language, violence and sex in the programmes your children watch?

● Is it difficult to get your children to turn off the TV long enough to eat a meal?

● Are you concerned about their eyesight and hearing because they want to sit too close or turn the volume up too high?

● Does it seem as if they aren't getting enough exercise and fresh air?

● Are their reading skills deteriorating because they never open a book?

The list could go on endlessly, with each parent having different concerns. Once you know what annoys you most, you'll be in a position to establish some ground rules that work in your household. As with all discipline problems, make sure you and your partner agree to enforce the same rules.

The viewing habits of young children and toddlers are, of course, easier to influence than those of school-aged children and teenagers. With younger children, you can simply put the television out of reach. This way you control when it is on or off. Sitting with your child while he's watching the TV is helpful, then you can point things out to him, helping him join in any activities suggested during the programme. And drawing up a schedule of TV-viewing that you are happy with will rule out the possibility of indiscriminate viewing. What isn't recommended, however, is totally banning all television, so that they will "blanket-watch" when they are not at home, whenever the opportunity presents itself.

Just like adults, children want to be like everyone else. So if all their friends have a favourite show, they don't want to be the odd one out, although this is something they feel more strongly as they get older. If you feel adamant that they shouldn't watch something, you just have to put your foot down and be firm. Say "No", advises one educationalist. If your child is old enough, you can try explaining exactly what you find objectionable about the banned programme.

Videos can be both a nightmare and a blessing for parents. On one hand, it's all too easy for older children to get hold of video "nasties" or to tape programmes you don't approve of and watch them when you aren't around.

On the other hand, videos can be an ideal means of settling many family disputes. If mealtimes clash with a favourite programme, for example, it can be taped for later viewing. Videos also take the tension out of situations when several people each want to watch different programmes.

Pre-recorded videos are also good as you can vet them for suitability before allowing your child to watch them. Then you can choose either to watch with your child as part of your "quiet time" together, or you can leave him to watch on his own, secure in the knowledge that what he is watching is not inappropriate in any way.

Many parents make the mistake of giving television too much importance in their children's lives by using it as a bribe. By all means tell your child that if he gets dressed quickly instead of dawdling, he can watch the television for an extra quarter of an hour that evening, but try not to use it as a reward/punishment tool all the time otherwise you risk crediting it with more importance than it really has.

In the end, you and your partner have to make up your own minds on how to settle the great television debate. Child-care experts and academic researchers are not in agreement on the effects of watching television. For every study clearly linking television violence with violent behaviour in children, there is another study concluding the two factors are unrelated. The one thing you can be certain of, however, is that your child will follow your lead if you and your partner spend every free minute in front of the TV, you cannot expect your children to behave differently.

The best way to see television and treat it, it would seem, is as a normal part of daily life.

Note: For safety's sake, always turn the television off at the mains before you go to bed, in case of lightning.

Temper Tantrums

Many children go through a phase of having temper tantrums, and although this is not a medical problem, it is a source of worry and alarm for parents when it happens.

These displays develop as the child begins to assert himself as an independent human being, particularly between the ages of two and three.

He has a strong will but his skills – both purely physical and in terms of understanding and self-expression – lag far behind. There are often provoking circumstances such as hunger, tiredness, momentary jealousy of a brother or sister or even over-excitement, but the tantrums may also come completely out of the blue. Very occasionally, if there are other symptoms, or if the tantrums go on well after the child is five years old, tantrums can be a sign of a deeper problem, but they are mostly just a normal part of the child's development.

Temper tantrums seem to turn your sweet little toddler into a demanding monster with whom you cannot reason or communicate at all. In a tantrum the child wants (or doesn't want) something and screams and screams, demanding (or refusing) it. Often the child screams until he loses his breath, or he may hold his breath until he is blue in the face. Once the tantrum is over he is his sweet, sunny self again.

Most experts in child behaviour advise that it is best to ignore tantrums as far as possible, while making sure that the child does not hurt himself – as he may act quite violently. The child is incapable of understanding reason while having a tantrum; if he is demanding something and you give in this will encourage him to have more tantrums in future; if he holds his breath and goes blue, he will begin to breathe again quite automatically, and the tantrum will soon blow itself out.

You will find your own way of dealing with the situation, and you may find it is not always the same.

Sometimes the best thing to do is to let the child get on with it, making sure from a distance that he does not hurt himself as he rolls on the floor or kicks about. Sometimes, however, you may sense that the child needs comfort and reassurance, and it will be best to hold him firmly on your knee while he storms. You may even decide occasionally that it is all right to give in, when you know that the child is tired and overwrought. Sometimes, also, it is possible to distract the child from his tantrum, with a joke (never at his expense) or by drawing his attention to something else.

Whatever happens, when your child has tantrums you must be calm yourself, and never show anxiety or anger by, for example, slapping the child to "bring him back to his senses".

You do not need to consult your doctor about temper tantrums unless these worry you unduly. But if they go on for too long or if they are accompanied by other symptoms which worry you, you may find it helpful to discuss this with your doctor. Make an appointment to go without your child if possible so that he does not realize you are worried. You will probably be reassured that everything is normal, but occasionally it may seem that the child is hyperactive or has some other problem, and further investigation may be needed to work out how the child can be helped.

◆ See also, **Spoilt Children**, **"Terrible Twos"**

Temperature for Babies

Knowing when your baby is at the correct temperature is an acquired skill. He is usually happy if he is neither too hot nor too cold, and the skin at the back of his head will feel about the same temperature as a warm adult hand. If the baby is too hot, the back of his head will feel moist and he will be a bit sweaty and uncomfortable. If the back of his head feels cool, then he probably needs more warmth, so keep a spare blanket handy.

Babies do not yet have the physical skills, such as shivering, to generate body heat, so the room where your baby is sleeping should be kept at about 24°C (75°F). This may feel too warm for the rest of the household, so heat the baby's room using a small heater with a safe thermostat.

Cover him with several layers of light-weight blankets and quilts, rather than one heavy blanket, and watch out for his hands and feet, which will quickly become cold if you're not careful. Socks and mittens might be needed.

Whilst warm, the room your baby sleeps in should be airy. Do ensure that you air the room regularly. Do this when you are bathing him or taking him for a walk. And even when the room is all cosy for him, it should not be stuffy. Leaving the top part of a window slightly open will provide enough fresh air.

"Terrible Twos"

Between the ages of two and three you may notice your child changing from an angelic baby into an individual whose behaviour angers and frustrates you. This alteration in personality is not unusual. It occurs because your toddler is growing up. He is beginning to form his own likes and dislikes and may no longer do what you want unquestioningly. He may refuse to eat or go to sleep at night, or he may appear to be stubborn with toilet training. Your attempts to overcome these difficulties may result in temper tantrums as he becomes frustrated by the demands made on him.

Do remember this is a time of great development for your child. At this age, his vocabulary increases rapidly and he is also acquiring new skills. It is not surprising, therefore, that he finds life trying and a bit confusing.

Despite his attempts at independence, however, he still relies on you for most of his needs, and this is a time when support from family and friends will be especially valuable, for both you and your child.

Sleep

Many two-year-old children wake regularly at night and demand attention. Additionally you may experience difficulty in settling him at bedtime, which can be very trying for you. Disturbed sleep night after night makes it hard for you to cope with normal activities the following day. It is important that you get rest and you may need help from family or babysitters to manage this.

What can you do? First, check with your doctor that there is no medical cause, such as an ear infection, for his night waking. Then look at his bedroom. Is it cold or is there a draught coming from a window? Is it too dark? If so, consider installing a night light to reassure him if he stirs.

His problem could stem from another cause. Think about his routine. Is he sleeping too much during the day? As your child grows up, he will need less sleep during the day. If he is in the habit of having a nap in the afternoon this could be the reason for his not sleeping through the night. Stop his naps, but change your routine if you can so that he doesn't notice the time when he would normally have one.

Anxiety may be a cause of disturbed nights, resulting in nightmares. Although it is difficult, try to find out if he is worrying about anything. Talk to him and reassure him when you put him to bed. Read him a short story at bedtime to take his mind off his fears. Cuddling a favourite soft toy may comfort him as he falls asleep.

A change in family life can also affect young children. Following the birth of a new baby there is a period of emotional upheaval as your attention switches to the new arrival. Your first child may feel resentful that he is no longer the baby of the house and may be making sleep or bedtime an issue as a result. His behaviour may disappoint you but don't worry and don't let him know. Give him extra attention during the day and involve him in the routine chores with the new baby. Asking him to fetch a nappy will give him a sense of achievement and may actually help you too.

There may be no obvious reason for your child's wakefulness. Children differ in temperament and some do simply seem to need less sleep than others. An early evening visit to a swimming pool may tire him too.

It is a good idea to establish a routine so that your child recognizes a set pattern building up to bedtime. If he is familiar with a routine, he will know what is expected of him and will probably go to bed without troublesome tantrums.

You may find it helpful to start with bathtime, as most children enjoy water play. Make his bath fun. Enjoy it with him and give him plenty of time to play.

Settle him into bed by reading a short story. He may well choose the same story each night as he will feel secure with the familiar words. Let him choose his favourite cuddly toy too.

If he wakes, deal with any obvious problem first. He may have a wet nappy, or he could be cold, or thirsty. Settle him back into bed, talk to him and, if necessary, repeat part of your bedtime routine by reading to him again. Do not rush.

On a cold night, when you are sleepy, you may be tempted simply to take him into your own bed. Try to avoid this, or be prepared to do it every time he wakes up. Once this habit develops, it can be very difficult to break.

If broken nights persist, take comfort. This is only a phase and fewer children aged three to four continue to wake in the night. The disturbed sleep pattern may even improve suddenly.

Eating

Whereas a few months ago your baby would eat contentedly, mealtimes may now resemble a battlefield. He may refuse to eat, throw food on the floor or scream if you challenge him.

This behaviour can be disheartening, especially if you have other children to feed at the same time. Stay calm. Your getting cross and angry will only make him more determined to have his own way. He may enjoy this attention and the effect it has on you. Don't worry, however, since few children develop nutritional problems as a result of this behaviour.

Establish regular mealtimes and maintain a good balanced diet. Avoid snacks between meals, if possible.

Toilet training

While some children may be dry at two, there are many who still wear nappies, refuse to use a potty and wet the bed. This is all quite normal behaviour. Don't be concerned if your friend's toddler is out of nappies and yours isn't; all children develop and reach this stage in their own time, and boys often seem to do so later than girls.

Encourage your child to use a potty. Praise him if he succeeds but be prepared for accidents. If he does wet himself, still put him on the potty so that he will begin to understand what is expected of him. Don't be surprised if this takes a long time and don't force him, as this will only result in frustration for you and distress for him.

Tantrums

Although tantrums may distress you, they are a normal phase at this stage of your child's development. It would be rare to find a toddler who has never thrown a temper tantrum. It is all part of the growing-up process and his need to express his independence.

It is important to let him explore the world around him but necessary to place restrictions on him for his own safety. This, in turn, can lead to temper tantrums. He is naturally curious to explore everything and becomes angry and frustrated with restrictions he cannot understand.

Also, he is at the age when he is easily frustrated when attempting to achieve tasks that are still beyond him. He is more likely, too, to have a tantrum if he is tired or hungry. Work out what leads to your child's tantrums and then try to avoid these situations.

When your child has a tantrum, it may be better to remove him from the situation, for example, if he is playing with other children or is in a shop, so you can be on your own with him. Try to distract him with a game or a toy; if this fails, stay calm and wait until the tantrum subsides. Reassurance and a cuddle will help.

Shyness

At about the age of two, your child may suddenly become quite shy, not wishing to leave your side. Whereas a few months earlier he may have been happy to be left playing at a friend's house, he will suddenly want you to stay in the room with him. This is a common occurrence at this age and nothing to worry about. It simply means that, although he is developing his skills and gaining independence, he still needs your reassurance and support during this important stage of his development.

This phase may not last long, so don't force him to stay somewhere without you as your support will help him gain confidence. If you feel the need for a break, perhaps he could stay with another member of the family whom he knows well, a grandparent or aunt for instance.

If you are concerned that your child is being difficult for reasons other than the usual "terrible two" scenarios, discuss your worries with your doctor in case there is an underlying medical cause.

Otherwise, be as patient and as supportive as you can, reminding yourself as often as necessary that this is just a phase.

◆ See also, **Potty-Training**, **Separation Anxiety**, **Shyness**, **Temper Tantrums**

Throwing and Catching

One of the most basic – but most versatile – toys you can give your child is a ball. He'll be absorbed for ages, watching it roll and spin, learning how to pick it up, drop it, throw, hit, kick and catch it – and once he has learnt these skills, there's a whole world of organized games just waiting for him to take part in.

You've only got to walk through your local park to realize how much fun adults and children alike get from a whole host of ball games, from simple "catch" to more complicated games, such as rounders, tennis, cricket, golf and, of course, football.

Playing with balls will help your child to develop a whole range of skills. Some of these are obvious, like learning to catch, or to hit a ball with a bat, but others you may not have thought about so much, like learning to follow rules, or to take turns.

None of these skills come naturally to your toddler or pre-school child. He will have to learn them, and learning takes practice. Some skills can be grasped when he is still very young, but others are more complex. So it helps to know which skills come first, or are easiest to learn, so you can help your child to practise them.

Learning to throw properly – like any other physical skill – involves not only using the abilities your child already has (like grasping and releasing objects, and moving his arms back and forth), but also learning to combine and control those actions. He'll need lots of practice before he can aim and throw a ball accurately.

As soon as he can sit steadily, without falling over as he leans forward to reach things, your baby will be able to roll a ball across the floor or table to you. Once he can stand and walk confidently, he'll learn to throw a ball overarm without losing his balance. And your two-year-old will be able to throw you a ball fairly accurately from several feet away. By the time he's four, and with a bit of practice, he should be capable of throwing a ball both under- and overarm fairly well.

Catching is a much more difficult skill for children to learn, and again needs lots of practice. It's easier to catch with both hands than with one, and your child will probably be able to do this with a largish ball when he's about three. But don't expect him to be catching confidently before he's at least five. Only then will he be able to go on to learn how to bounce a ball and catch it or throw it high up into the air by himself and catch it on the way down.

Again, your child may have been kicking vigorously from an early age. But learning to control those movements takes a lot of practice, especially if you've got to do it standing up. It's easier to kick something when you're standing still than when you're running, and also much easier to kick something that isn't moving itself.

Once your two-year-old can run, he should be able to kick a ball without overbalancing. He'll probably run or walk up to it, but he'll then stop before he kicks it. Once he can do that, he'll soon be able to kick a ball that is rolled to him. But it will be some time – probably not until he's about four – before he can run and kick a small ball without stopping first.

There are two very simple ways that you can help your child learn to kick, throw and catch. One is by playing with him yourself, using a variety of different objects and activities. And the other is by providing him with a number of balls of different sizes and material and other objects so that he can experiment and practise his developing skills by himself.

Learning should be fun, and your child will love it if you join in with his ball games. One way you can encourage him to aim and throw properly is by giving him a target to focus on. Try holding a box, or other container, for him to throw into. This not only gives him, quite literally, a "goal", but, by cheating slightly at first and moving the box, you can make sure that the ball goes in and that he scores.

Success is important in the early stages of learning, so remember to give him lots of praise. As he improves, you'll find you have to move the box less and less for him to score, and you can stand further and further away to make the game more difficult for him.

Another type of target worth trying is skittles. Children love knocking things over, and again, you can ensure that he's successful by putting them fairly close to him to begin with. Of course, you don't have to use proper skittles. Anything that he can knock over fairly easily will do. If he has difficulty with throwing, try standing behind him and holding the ball with him so that he gets the feel of the right movements.

Once your child is four or five years old he will be ready to play ball games with another child (and later with other children). Initially, your guidance and suggestions will be most welcome. At first, join in yourself or act as referee. Try and play the game with your child first on his own. Make sure he and his friend have the skills needed for the game you choose (they may get disheartened if they can't do what's expected). Don't use games with lots of rules as they won't be able to remember or stick to them all. Simplify games to one or two rules. For example, in simple cricket, tell him to run if he hits the ball and he's out if the ball hits the wicket.

Ball games like these with other children will help your child to develop basic social skills, such as taking turns and co-operation.

Tidying Up

Some children seem to be born tidy while others are oblivious to the mayhem they create. Even with the tidiest of children, however, clearing-up time can be an area for conflict, particularly when there are other children/siblings involved.

Perhaps the first step in confronting the issue is to have sensible expectations. While it is possible for a child under three to be tidy, it is not very likely, and he should not be made to feel bad about this.

Always restrict the number of toys in use at any one time. Then encourage your child to put these away before taking out others. This way he will not be overwhelmed by the amount of "mess" around him, and tidying up the toys is likely to be less of an issue.

Avoid toys or games with many tiny pieces until your child is old enough to understand that the game will be spoilt unless all the pieces are looked after and put away. He will more readily take on the responsibility for such games if he can appreciate that fact.

Your child will be reluctant to put away a puzzle he has completed or an elaborate construction he has been working on. Try to understand this, and wherever possible keep a corner available for his "works-in-progress".

It is often helpful to try and make clearing up a fun task, perhaps by racing to see who can clear up the most, or the quickest. Help your child to tidy up but don't do it for him otherwise he will come to expect this of you. Give him lots of praise for his efforts, and then move on to a rewarding activity. Avoid confrontations between siblings by making it a "group" activity.

Encouraging children to take a pride in their possessions is often the key to the problem. If they value their toys or books, and know that they will not necessarily be instantly replaced if lost or broken, children are bound to be more conscious of looking after them. From here it is a natural progression to tidying up each time they finish playing with something.

Finally, "a place for everything and everything in its place" is a valuable maxim: make it easy for your child by having fixed places for things, labelled or boxed wherever possible.

Time

A very young child experiences the world as here and now – if he wants something he wants it now. A child is not born with a sense of passing time; it is developed through experience.

Because the passage of time cannot be experienced directly – we cannot see it, hear it, touch it or taste it – it can be a difficult idea to teach. The notion of time is often the first abstract idea that children have to learn. Teaching it properly should be a slow, patient and careful process.

You can – and do, indirectly – talk about time from birth. Familiarize your child with the language of time by talking to him as you do things. Words such as "today" and "tomorrow" will not mean much to him for some time yet; what is important is that he is hearing them over and over again.

Greeting your child with a cheery "good morning" and flinging open the curtains with a comment on what kind of morning it is, will add "morning" to his bank of words.

At about 12–18 months of age, you can begin to enlist the help of your child's favourite toys to increase his knowledge and understanding of key words and phrases. Teddy can join in with the daily routine by having breakfast, lunch and tea with your child at the appropriate times. Last thing at night a review of Teddy's day can be made into a short bedtime chat.

Stories can add to your child's vocabulary of time. Again, favourite toys can play some of the leading characters in these adventures. Pepper these tales with "time" words – today, tomorrow, yesterday, morning, afternoon, evening and night. Phrases – "after a while", "a little later on" and "much later" – can be introduced with age and the stories can become more complicated.

Making a scrap book called "My Day" is a useful addition to your child's bookshelf and an enjoyable project for you to share. Begin by writing "In the morning..." with a large felt-tip pen on the first page, then illustrate it with pictures of various stages of your child's morning routine. A selection of photographs and drawings of getting up, getting dressed, eating breakfast and so on can be stuck in and labelled in the order in which these things happen.

The next section can begin with a picture of your child having lunch, followed by afternoon activities and bedtime.

At the age of two, your child will still be living mainly in the present. He will, however, begin to grasp the idea of "after". He will understand that he may have a biscuit "after" he has washed his hands, for example. To help him with this difficult idea, you could add pages to your scrapbook, with entries such as "After breakfast I clean my teeth", or "Before lunch I wash my hands". Add pictures and simple explanations as useful reminders.

Hospital games are a fun way to reinforce the notion of parts of the day and daily routines. As your child gets older this game can become more elaborate, but it is best to begin simply when he is about three.

Use cardboard boxes and teatowels to make beds and bedding for soft toys, who can become "patients". Your child can be the doctor or nurse. Improvise with a white shirt for a doctor's white coat, and use a strip of white cloth or card for a nurse's cap, and an apron.

Encourage your child to run through the sequence of a day. He can begin his patients' daily routine by waking them up and giving them a wash. Then comes breakfast and the doctor's round. Jigsaws and stories can amuse the patients until it is time for lunch. After lunch the patients can have their "treatments", like medicine or physiotherapy or fresh bandages. After treatment perhaps some songs and games will relieve the boredom until supper. After supper it is time for sleep.

The idea of yesterday, today and tomorrow is a very difficult one for your children to grasp. After all, these words change their meaning every day. You can help your child get a better understanding of these words and learn the days of the week in several ways:

● In the evening talk about the activities of the day with your child and, between you, produce a drawing and a written description for that day.

● As your child gets used to the idea, try making pictures in a different way to illustrate each day, such as a collage using fabrics, coloured paper or photographs.

● Talk about regular activities in the week, such as playgroup on Tuesdays and Thursdays.

● Ask your child questions such as "What did we do yesterday?" Prompt him gently, if necessary, to remind him of an event, then let him carry on. You can introduce the idea of minutes and hours to your child when he is between three and four years old. Kitchen timers and egg timers can be useful here – or even a stopwatch for an older child. Make a game out of timing various activities such as getting dressed.

This is especially useful if your child is infuriatingly slow to get dressed in the mornings, as it can help to speed him up. Set a kitchen timer for, say, five minutes, then ask your child to get as many clothes on as he can in the time. It is important to tell him how much time he has. Always allow plenty of time to begin with or else he will not want to play.

Ring the changes by seeing how many toys can be put away in the toy box in one, two or three minutes. There are many things you can time in this way to give your child the idea of how long a minute actually is. Join in by setting yourself a task to carry out in the same time.

Cooking is a practical way to illustrate time passing in minutes; you can also introduce hours depending on what you cook. An egg timer can be used for boiling an egg, or you can bake some potatoes for lunch or cakes for tea and set the timer for an hour or more. Fit out a pretend kitchen with a cooker, a tea set, pots and pans, so he can practise himself.

As your child's fourth birthday approaches you can introduce the clock face and talk about big hands and little hands. Bring in the idea of halves and quarters by cutting up cakes to share. A tea party with friends or for your child's toys is an excellent opportunity for this.

Growing things is a good way to learn about longer periods of time. Start with something that gives quick results, such as mustard and cress seeds: paint a face on an empty yoghurt pot and fill it with a little damp soil, then sprinkle the seeds on top of it. As long as you keep the soil moist, green "hair" should sprout within a few days.

Make a wall chart of what happens: "Monday... planted seeds, Tuesday... watered seeds, Wednesday... shoots beginning to show, Thursday... a full head of hair." The chart will not only help to plot the progress of both time and the seeds but will also help your child learn the days of the week in the right order.

As your child gets older he will be able to cope with the more delayed results of planting bulbs and perhaps managing his own patch of garden or a window box. Keeping a progress chart for these will help him learn about weeks and months.

When your child is about four, help him to grasp the idea of the passing year by making a birthday chart for his wall. Using a different coloured felt-tip pen for each month, write the names of the months in order on a large sheet of paper (the wrong side of a length of wallpaper is ideal), leaving a gap between each one.

Next, with your child's help, select photographs of family members and friends. Where there are no photographs encourage your child to draw or paint a small portrait. Sort the pictures into piles according to the month of the person's birthday. Take those in January and stick them to the chart in order. Write the name of the person and their birth-date next to the picture.

When the chart is completed, you and your child will be able to keep a check on the birthdays coming up each month. This will give you the opportunity to introduce all kinds of time words and phrases such as "next week", "in a fortnight" and "on the 11th" into your child's vocabulary.

Toys

First toys

Toys for babies can mean anything from the very latest expensive and imaginative invention to a classic rag doll or even a simple wooden spoon. Important factors are colours, shapes, and sounds, for these are the elements that please a baby too small to actually "play" with anything.

Things to hold that are easy to grip, will give your baby a lot of pleasure once he is able to hold objects. Try different spoons, or a ring shape. Bunches of objects, such as rings, beads and small plastic kitchen utensils strung on ribbons will also give your baby something to grip, as well as rattle, suck and chew. But make sure there are no detachable pieces.

Small cuddly toys like teddies or soft cubes or balls that your baby can hold and feel will become a favourite in the first few months, as your baby will respond to something squashy and lightweight, with a recognizable "face" and a pleasing texture. Other different textures can be explored in many ways – from a home-made beanbag to a seashell or a brightly coloured fabric picture book.

Baby rattles come in all shapes and colours and will fascinate your baby long before he is able to hold them himself. You'll have to shake and rattle them for him until he's about two months old.

A string of toys stretched across his pram or cot will help your baby learn how he can affect his world by his actions. At first he'll knock the toy accidentally and then notice how it moves or makes a sound. Eventually he will try to knock it deliberately, and will be delighted with the results.

Invest in a baby "gym". Your baby can lie underneath it watching characters dangling above him or playing with balls or mirrors on either side of him. Babies love to be surrounded by toys in this way and the "gym" is a great way to encourage hand-eye co-ordination too.

When you are giving your baby toys to play with always check that fixed-in parts (like teddies' eyes) are safe and firm, and that there are no points or sharp edges. Babies put everything in their mouths, so make sure the paint on toys is lead-free, and finally, never let your baby play unsupervised with anything that has a loop, ribbon or thin string.

Puppets

Puppets make excellent entertainment for all children, from young babies upwards. A small baby will watch while you dance two wooden spoon puppets in front of him, and young toddlers will giggle at finger puppets and silly voices for as long as you want to hold their attention.

After the age of three, your child will be able to help you make the puppets and contribute his own ideas for stories and characterization. He will also be able to work the puppets himself.

Wheeled toys

A mobile child is a happy child and yours will soon discover that riding anything with wheels is more than just great fun – it enables him to do things that he could not do before. The benefits of transport are quickly learnt.

You can safely introduce your baby to wheeled toys once he starts to totter by himself – there is little to be gained by pushing him before this. But once he has learned to control his leg muscles, and is toddling, he will be able to straddle toy trucks and, before you know it, he will be demanding a trike or a pair of roller skates.

A baby walker (a frame on wheels) is useful for short periods. A good one will be well padded and have at least six wheels, but you should always keep an eye on your baby when he is in it.

As soon as he is able to totter a few steps, he will be able to push a toddle truck. Choose one that is made for this purpose; toy prams and buggies may look suitable but they don't offer the same support.

Toddlers of both sexes love to push themselves along while straddling toy trucks, cars and small tricycles. This should be encouraged as it is excellent exercise for the legs. If your child has a toy that can be steered with a wheel or handlebar, so much the better, as he will learn to co-ordinate eye, leg and arm movements. Initially, he will not have much control over the steering and will probably zip round in circles and do uncontrolled zigzags. He will soon get this under control, however, and be able to determine exactly where he wants to go.

Many sit-and-ride toys have additional attractions built-in, like a secret boot or a hooter. These are fun playthings on their own but they also make the whole toy more appealing and will entice him into using it more often.

When the time arrives for your child to take on a pedal car, trike or bike – which will not be until he is about three – choose wisely. Pick something that is not only sturdy enough to last a few years but can also be adapted to suit your child as he grows. If you go for a bicycle, buy one that has stabilizing wheels at the back. These can be detached when your child wants to take off on just two wheels. The other essential thing to look out for is the chain, which must be completely enclosed.

Two-wheeled scooters, skateboards and roller skates demand both confidence and considerable balance from a child if he is not to end up with grazes and bruises. You can get padded, four-wheeled scooters – which are infinitely more stable than their two-wheeled counterparts – but even these are hard for a child to control. It is only really worthwhile thinking about getting a scooter for your child when he is at least four years old.

The fashion for skateboarding comes and goes, but it would be foolhardy to let a five-year-old loose on one. A better option is a steerable skateboard – a cross between a skateboard and a bicycle. One of these will enable your child to grasp hold of a pair of handlebars whilst riding the board. Even so, manufacturers do not recommend them for children under the age of four.

Roller skates are a different proposition altogether. Although they are great fun, they can also be extremely dangerous. If your child is between three and six, choose a type of skate where the wheels can be locked, either for walking or so that only forward movement is possible. Roller skating is great for developing a sense of balance but skates are very difficult for a small child to master, so provide plenty of support and padding.

Building and fitting toys

Construction kits, bricks, and puzzles all serve a purpose in improving hand control and visual co-ordination. The dexterity they encourage will be useful to your child later on when he is learning to write. Of course construction toys in particular will also provide opportunities for creative and imaginative play.

Cars and trains

Cars, trucks and trains have always been favourites with small children. There is an exhaustive range available and children never seem to tire of them. Again, these toys can send children on great flights of imagination, and also involve them in role-playing activities.

Dolls and soft toys

These may be used as special "friends" or comforters, or may become guests at imaginary tea parties or passengers on chair-trains. Children will also use them to play out events relating to family life – both real and fantasy. Dolls can help to bring out the more sensitive nurturing areas of your child's personality, although they may also be the victims of the bites and pinches he is trying not to inflict on real people.

Games

Games with rules and turns can help to develop a sense of good sportsmanship, co-operation and self-discipline. They also require a degree of manual dexterity when it comes to dice-throwing and moving small pieces around a board.

Don't forget that with very small children, anything can be a toy – a few saucepans are no less effective than a toy drum kit; a few cardboard boxes can be a construction kit; a sock can be a puppet, and so on. It may not be as expensive as you think to equip your child with a selection of fun, yet enduring and useful toys.

Guns and weapons

However much energy you put into promoting non-violence in play, there is always scope for turning bricks into guns, sticks into swords and so on. However, real "replica" weapons have been found to stimulate a more aggressive form of play, and may be best avoided.

Electronic toys

There is a wide range of pre-computer toys available which can be fun and educational at the same time, such as spelling and counting games where the machine will congratulate the child when he types in a right answer and beep when he chooses incorrectly.

These programmes are also useful in terms of familiarizing children with the concept of computers, which are an important part of our lives today.

For slightly older children (starting from around three to five years) there are many computer games, CD Roms and educational software all of which are invaluable both as learning aids and in helping them feel at ease with a keyboard.

If you store any of your own work or documents on the computer, make absolutely sure it's backed up, in case of disasters.

◆ See also, **Play**, **Safety**, **Sexual Stereotyping**, **Throwing and Catching**

Thumb-Sucking

◆ See **Comfort Habits**

Toadstool Poisoning

People tend to speak as though all mushrooms were edible and all "toadstools" poisonous. However, one of the most poisonous of all plants is a mushroom and the distinction between mushrooms and toadstools is a difficult one to make for someone who is not a botanist. It therefore makes better sense to speak of "fungi" poisoning, as all mushrooms and toadstools are different kinds of fungi.

Many fungi are poisonous to different degrees. Some of them merely give tummy ache, while others cause prolonged diarrhoea and sickness. The most dangerous fungi can cause damage to the heart, liver and kidneys, and to the blood cells and nervous system. In the case of a few species this can even cause death.

Although many poisonous fungi are unpleasant tasting, this is not always the case. And although some are very distinctive, this is not always so either. A toadstool which can cause death is Amanita muscari, and this is like the toadstools in children's fairy stories, with a bright red cap sprinkled with white spots; but Amanita phalloides, the death cap mushroom, looks quite similar to edible field mushrooms, yet is frequently fatal.

There are several toxins that may be present in fungi, but the two most dangerous of these are known as muscarine and phallin. Muscarine affects the activity of the nerve cells, and phallin behaves like snake poison, affecting the nerves to cause paralysis and acting destructively on the body's cells. The death cap (which contains phallin) eventually kills by destroying the liver and causing general weakening of the whole body, and young children are particularly susceptible to these effects.

It takes a varying amount of time for symptoms to appear. With the fungus Amanita muscari symptoms appear within one and a half to two hours, but with other fungi it usually takes longer. In some cases symptoms can disappear, only to return. A child who has eaten poisonous fungi may complain of tummy ache. He may be pale, cold and sweating, and may have diarrhoea and vomiting. In the worst cases these symptoms are followed by collapse.

If you know or suspect that your child has fungus poisoning, get him to hospital without delay. If you know what he has been eating, take a sample for identification, and keep a sample of his faeces and vomit, which may also help medical staff identify the poison.

Hospital treatment will depend on the poison and the severity of the symptoms. In some cases an antidote can be given and sometimes a gastric lavage will be given to remove the contents of the stomach. In some cases the child may merely be kept under observation, but in severe cases the child may have to be put on a life support machine and given intensive medical care.

The only course for prevention is to make it a strict rule never to allow children to eat wild fungi of any kind when out in the country, and not to pick mushrooms yourself unless you really know what you are doing. There are only a very few that are good to eat, compared with the huge numbers that are tasteless, inedible or poisonous, and even these can be dangerous if rotting.

In Britain there is not a strong tradition of fungus eating, but in most other parts of Europe many local people can readily identify those fungi that are worth eating. Local pharmacists often provide an excellent identification service and will give advice. In Britain, field rangers and other people working on national parks and nature reserves can often identify fungi. But you should never take advice from anyone unless you are quite sure they know what they are talking about.

Tonsillitis

Tonsillitis is an inflammation and swelling of the tonsils. It is not usually serious, but it can lead to complications, especially if it occurs frequently. It generally makes the child feel ill enough to spend time in bed.

Tonsillitis is caused by an infection. This may be viral or bacterial and can be very contagious, so that a child with tonsillitis should be kept away from other children to avoid spreading the infection.

The main symptom of tonsillitis is a very sore throat, sudden in onset, which can cause the child to have fits of coughing or to vomit. Within a few hours the child is very listless and has usually developed a fever. There may also be difficulty in swallowing food if the child still feels like eating.

If you feel the child's neck you will probably find that the lymph nodes are swollen at the sides of the neck and around the chin. You may be able to feel hard little nodules and the whole area around the ears and jaw-line may feel tender to the touch.

Inside the throat the child's tonsils will be enlarged and inflamed, and may be covered in yellow spots. These are formed by pus exuding from the crypts of the tonsils. The adenoids, although they are less easily visible, will also be inflamed. (You will be able to see the throat more clearly if you get the child to say "ah" while you hold his tongue down with the handle of a small spoon and shine a torch into the throat.)

Call your doctor if your child shows symptoms of tonsillitis with high fever, and in the meantime give him plenty of fluids to drink and keep his temperature down by sponging him with tepid water if he is very feverish. He will probably feel like going to bed, but if he does not he should be kept warm and should stay indoors.

The doctor will examine your child's throat and check to make sure that the infection has not spread to the ears. He or she may also take a swab from the child's throat to be sent for analysis to find out exactly what the infection is.

You will probably be advised to give the child paracetamol in the appropriate form and dose for his age to keep the fever under control, and the doctor may prescribe antibiotics for the infection if it is caused by bacteria. If the child has no appetite there is no need to worry about him not eating so long as he drinks plenty of fluids, but he may find that yoghurt and ice cream are soothing to his throat. As his appetite returns he will find it easier to swallow puréed foods at first.

If your child is beset with attacks of tonsillitis over a couple of years your doctor may advise you that he should have his tonsils removed (tonsillectomy). This involves a stay of two or three days in hospital and a recovery period of about two weeks. The operation is quite straightforward, although the child's throat will be raw for a while afterwards. Even though this operation is now performed much less commonly than it once was, it is still considered the best solution to repeated attacks of tonsillitis. The body functions perfectly well without tonsils.

Transport and Travel

The number of different types of transport used in the modern world can seem almost endless and discovering what different vehicles look like and what they are used for can form a valuable part of your child's education.

During a walk or drive, apart from familiar sights such as cars and buses, you may come across a fire engine with its siren wailing, an ambulance with its blue light flashing or, if you pass a building site, giant earthmovers and bulldozers busy at work.

Making your child aware of vehicles on the roads also allows you to introduce him to basic road safety. You can show him how to stop at the kerb and look both ways and tell him never to cross the road unless he is holding your hand. And you can point out the different types of pedestrian crossings and show him what to look for to let him know that it is safe to cross.

In the car, you can explain why he has to wear a seat belt and why children sit in the back of the car with the doors locked while Mummy or Daddy is driving.

When you go for a walk, you can use the cars and buses you see as a fun way to encourage your child's early skills in naming colours, counting and reading.

You can point out different cars and help him describe what colour they are, show him the numbers on the front of buses and number plates or count all the bicycles you see. And you can show him the writing which tells you which vehicle is a police car or ambulance or help him to recognize the sign for a bus stop.

Travelling on a bus or train will help your child to understand what transport is for and how we use it. He will experience differences in speed and in the time needed to get from place to place.

Travelling on public transport will give you the chance to talk to him about the different jobs involved – drivers, conductors, railway porters and ticket collectors. You can also introduce him to the idea of fares, to counting simple money and to looking at the numbers on his bus or train ticket. He will probably want to hold his own ticket and may want to keep it to make a collection.

Train stations, bus stations and airports are places full of activity, with plenty of things to see and talk about. But remember, these places can be frightening to a child who is not used to a lot of noise or to people rushing around, so prepare the way by talking about where you are going and what it is going to be like. And keep your visits short, so your child will not become bored or tired.

In stations and airports you can count trains, coaches and planes, spot numbers and destinations, and see the porters drive their luggage trolleys piled high with suitcases and bags.

You can find the departures and arrivals boards and have fun guessing where people are going or where they have come from. You may find it easier to choose a quiet vantage point where you can watch all the comings and goings from a safe distance – a window table at a station café is often a good corner to use, and most airports have special viewing areas where you can see the planes take off.

Museums may be less noisy and frightening than stations and airports, and are another useful way of learning about travel. There are a number of specialist transport museums, some focusing on only one form of transport – for example, vintage cars or aeroplanes. But you will find that many general museums or small local museums will have some exhibits and displays on travel as well.

You may be able to bring transport history alive for your child by taking him to a special show or event. Agricultural and farm shows may have pony and trap races or competitions; fairs may have miniature train rides; air shows may provide the chance to see old aeroplanes actually flying, and some steam trains have been restored or maintained for public use and can be the highlight of a fun day out.

One way that your child makes sense of his world is through play, and there are lots of toys, games, books and activities that you can give him which will enrich his understanding of transport and travel.

Some of the most popular children's toys are small cars, train sets and aeroplanes. Be careful to buy toys that are safe – beware of sharp edges, toxic parts or small pieces that are liable to be swallowed.

Playing with toy cars can help your child to understand how they work. He can see how the wheels go round, how the doors open and close and where the engine is kept under the bonnet. He can play out scenes such as going to the garage, and pretend to put petrol in the car just as he has seen you do.

Toy vehicles come in all shapes and sizes and include models such as tractors, cranes and petrol tankers as well as cars. Once he knows the purpose of each vehicle he can have endless fun pretending to be a crane operator or a tanker driver.

Rolling vehicles on different surfaces – over carpets or down slopes – or having races with friends, will allow your child to build up simple ideas of speed and resistance. And playing with vehicles that propel themselves, such as battery-operated cars and electric trains, will show him the function of engines and motors.

Encouraging your child to build his own vehicles is a useful way of absorbing what he has noticed and learnt on your trips and visits.

Keep a store of useful boxes and containers that he can glue together – cereal and tissues boxes can be ideal as car bodies and toilet roll centres can be cut up to make wheels. As he grows older, you will find that he gradually includes more detail such as door handles, headlights and number plates.

Building simple model planes at home can also be fun and a direct way of learning about flight. Paper darts are easy to fold and throw and have the added benefit of creating little damage.

There are also a number of general construction kits on the market which include wheels and other car and plane parts. Start him off with kits which have large pieces that he can manipulate and assemble easily.

Another way to help your child understand transport and travel is through painting. Painting pictures about journeys and talking about them will help him to make better sense of how travelling relates to time and space.

For example, he can talk about where the people in the pictures are going, how long they will take to get there and when they are coming back.

Painting can also be a good way of helping him to express any fears he may have about travelling. It can also be fun to make a scrapbook record of any special trips that you make. This can include tickets, programmes, postcards or any photographs you have taken.

Once your child has developed an understanding about transport and travelling you may be amazed at how creative his imaginary play will be. A simple box or chair can be converted into a car or bus with a paper plate becoming the steering wheel. And he may act out complicated games such as travelling to far off places, and picking up and setting down passengers.

Your child will soon be eager to extend his indoor imaginary play into more adventurous outdoor play with child-sized vehicles. At first he will need to be pushed by somebody as he sits in a toy car or on a bike, but gradually he will learn to propel himself, first by using his feet and later by using the pedals.

This is all part of learning about different ways of getting around and understanding how vehicles are propelled.

There are lots of simple picture books to help your very young child begin to identify trains, cars and buses. And there are also books for older pre-school children with illustrations covering a wider variety of vehicles. And story books are a wonderful source of travel tales for you and your child to enjoy together. You can choose between real or imaginary stories, between tales of trips to far-off lands or to familiar places or to visit people. You can select books about journeys by train, about space travel or even about travel under the sea. And you can remind him as you read, of any experiences he has had which are similar to those in the story.

Travel Sickness

Many people – adults and children alike – will be sick on a rough sea crossing, but it is common for young children to be so badly affected by travel sickness that any journey, whether by bus, boat, train, car or coach, becomes an almost intolerable trial for the whole family.

Doctors do not know exactly why travel sickness happens, but it is thought to be a consequence of upsetting the delicate balance mechanism in the inner ear. This balance may be more sensitive in young children, and certainly most do grow out of travel sickness as they get older. Travel sickness may start when your child is very young, possibly before the age of six months, or it may not become apparent until he is older, perhaps nearer two years old. However, once your child starts to feel, or be, sick on most journeys, the problem will probably continue until he reaches puberty and then will usually start to decrease.

The type of motion can have an effect on the severity of the sickness. Rough choppy movements often make a child more sick than smooth rolling ones, which is why more people are sick on boats than trains.

You can buy various over-the-counter medicines to take to prevent travel sickness, but it is advisable to consult your doctor first as some may have unpleasant side-effects such as a very dry mouth and overwhelming drowsiness. Promethazine (Avomine) may be recommended for children over 5 years, and dimenhydrinate (Dramamine) for those over 1 year. If you do give your child medicines, always follow the instructions carefully and make sure you give them at the recommended time in advance of the journey.

If you know that one form of travel, for example a boat journey, is more likely to make your child sick, try to choose an alternative, perhaps a combination of train and air. If you are driving, your child may be less sick if you can avoid routes and times when there will be a lot of stopping and starting. Driving at night on motorways may be best.

Eating a large greasy meal before a journey increases the likelihood of travel sickness, as does travelling on an empty stomach, so aim to have a light non-greasy meal beforehand and take a plentiful supply of plain water, plain biscuits and glucose sweets for the journey. Avoid fizzy drinks as these can make sickness worse.

Try to keep your child as still as possible as his own motion may make his sickness worse. Make sure a younger child is always securely fastened in his own car seat and an older one firmly strapped in with his seat belt so that he does not roll with the movement of the car on corners. Leaning his head against a cushion may also help as it has been found that travelling with the head tilted back, as if in a dentist's chair, disturbs the balance of the ears least. Try to keep his mind off being sick as dwelling on it is more likely to make him sick and don't keep asking him if he feels all right. Open the window slightly to let in fresh air.

Reading in cars can make even the best traveller feel sick, so provide your child with alternative entertainment, for example story cassettes and games the whole family can play. Similarly squabbling and fighting among children in the back seat can make sufferers feel worse, as can active play, so it is worth making an effort to keep children quietly occupied on all journeys.

Although travel sickness is not all in the mind, it can be made worse by the emotions. Once your child has started to feel sick it will be almost impossible to take his mind off it, but you may be able to prevent an attack by distracting him with games, a walk on deck if you are on a ship or simply by maintaining an interesting conversation.

Tummy-Ache

◆ See **Abdominal Pain**

Twins

Whether you were thrilled or dismayed when you discovered twins were on the way, remember that the unknown is usually more worrying than the real thing. You may wonder how you will cope with two tiny infants, particularly if they are your first. In practice, nature allows you time to learn the ropes, because newborn babies do very little except sleep, eat and sleep again. This may sound rather idealistic – but it really isn't far from the truth.

Starting at the beginning: where will they sleep? If you are unprepared, you can start them off in one cot or even a well-padded drawer. But however tiny they look, babies grow at an alarming rate, as well as kicking and throwing their arms around, so it's best to put them in separate cots fairly early on. Despite any fears you have about your twins disturbing each other if put in the same room, they won't wake each other up with crying, and some twins, particularly identical ones, need to be able to see each other before they will settle down.

Fresh air acts as a great lullaby and if a back garden or a balcony is available, putting the twins out in open air for a little while usually sends them to sleep. If possible, get a second pram so that they don't kick each other awake. Failing easy access to open spaces, dressing the babies in their

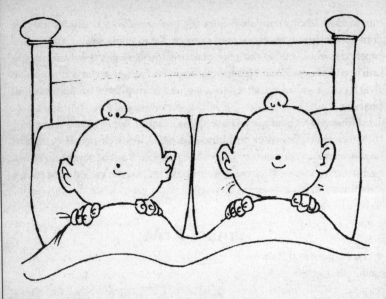

outdoor clothes and pushing their cots under an open window is a good substitute for a push in the park and is far less troublesome for you.

Feeds occupy a major part of the day but provided you play your cards right, they won't take up much more time than with one baby. Whether you breastfeed or bottle-feed, it is possible to feed both babies together, as long as you get everything together before you start.

Bottle feeding has the advantage over breastfeeding when it comes to sharing the job with your partner or a friend, and is a sensible alternative to breastfeeding if you are feeling exhausted. Keeping your energy levels up is vital.

To bottle feed the babies on your own, cradle one baby in the crook of your arm, with a bottle held in that hand, and have the other baby lying down by your side propped up with a pillow, sucking from a bottle held in your other hand.

For middle of the night demands, it's worth trying bottles of water. It's often enough to send them back to sleep, and not delicious enough to form a habit. But best of all, your partner can take turns getting up at night, leaving you to get a few hours of uninterrupted sleep.

When only one cries, and if it is not hunger, pick him up and comfort him and let the other one sleep. If he is hungry, feed both or you will be at it non-stop. If you do feed only one, make a mark on a blackboard or piece of paper to remind you who's the guzzler, because, however hard you try, you won't be able to remember which one had the last feed.

The same goes for vaccinations and medicines. Write down who had what and when. It may seem indelibly imprinted at the time, but the details fade fast, and it's important to be accurate.

When they start eating solids, the golden rule is one spoon, one dish, two (hopefully) open mouths, making you feel a bit like a mother bird feeding her chicks. As for the food itself, ready-prepared foods are convenient, but it does not take long for canned and bottled baby foods to become uneconomical with twins. A little of what the rest of the household is going to eat, puréed in a blender or a food processor, can be a good alternative.

Bathtime is fun. Babies love water from the earliest age and it should be a moment in the day when you too can be relaxed and enjoy it. Bath is best before a feed, so that the twins can go straight into their cots for a sound sleep afterwards. Some mothers find the morning ideal, others wait for the evening when proud fathers can take over or share the experience with them.

If you can't manage a double bathtime, no harm will come to them if you bath just one each day, with all the usual topping and tailing in between.

If you bought a layette, you may wonder why you bothered, because you will probably be inundated with presents of double everything. Friends and relatives tend to be over-generous when it comes to twins, so it is wise to make the most of this while it lasts and keep your clothes money for later – when the excitement of the birth has faded.

For the first few weeks, there is no need to dress the twins differently for day or night unless it's a special occasion. Don't worry if they spend all day in their babygrows – visitors will think them just as delightful and charming!

Undoubtedly, most of the clothes you are given will be two of a kind and maybe that's what you have bought too. While the babies are small it does not matter what they wear – they will certainly look cute dressed in identical outfits.

As they grow up and develop personalities, however, it is worth remembering that each twin is an individual, not half of a pair and needs to be seen as such by the outside world. So, allowing them to be different will make life a lot easier for them.

Obviously boy/girl twins won't have this problem, but single sex pairs, even when they are not identical, can cause confusion, and different clothes help friends, relatives and, later, teachers to tell them apart. Different hairstyles can help too.

That does not mean that your twins can't wear all the lovely things they have been given by well-meaning people who just can't help indulging their urge to dress twins identically.

Shopping for anything, whether it's food or clothes, can be a headache with twins. The easiest way of all, if possible, is to leave them at home – get someone to sit with them while you buy what you need calmly on your own.

If you are fortunate enough to have or be given hand-me-downs, it will save on the clothes bill. Since twins don't always grow at the same rate, particularly if they are non-identical, one may even pass clothes on to the other. If you have joined one of the many twins clubs, regular bring-and-buy mornings can offer lots of bargains.

Whatever clothes you buy, make sure that they are machine washable and easy care and declare a ban on fiddly buttons and bows. Easy on and easy off are the magic words, which will also let the twins start helping themselves when they get to that stage.

In fact, anything which makes life easier and streamlines your day is worth thinking about. So, if you live in a house with an upstairs and a downstairs, keeping a basket or bag of essentials – nappies, wipes, baby lotion, nappy bags, and perhaps a changing mat on both floors will save a lot of tearing up and down the stairs. And try to take an opportunity to rest whenever you can.

Watching twins grow up can be fascinating. Non-identical twins will be as like or as different as any other two children in the same family – except that they are born on the same day. They may be similar to or very different from one another. They might both be girls or both be boys or one of each. They will have developed from two separate eggs, fertilized by two separate sperm and been nourished in the womb by separate placentas.

Identical twins, on the other hand, result when a single egg is fertilized and later divides, so they will always be the same sex and always look alike. When in the womb, identical twins share the same placenta.

Twins often develop their own "secret" language which they understand clearly but sounds like nonsense to everyone else. The reason for this is nothing alarming or mystic. It is more due to the fact that they learn to speak by imitating what they hear and as they spend most of their time with each other they imitate and learn to understand what they are saying. So it is not really secret, just that other people might have difficulty in understanding it.

It is better to use normal language when you speak to them rather than imitate their funny words, but all toddlers take time learning to speak, so there's no need to worry about how their words come out.

Twins are almost inevitably compared to one another which is not necessarily fair to them. Of course it is difficult not to expect the same from each, but life is easier for them and you if they are not in competition with each other. Each twin will find his own level at his own speed and the best line you can take is to be encouraging and supportive to both children, whatever their respective achievements.

And when they are naughty, it is sometimes very difficult to know who is to blame, since they may protect each other. A good solution can be to aim for rewards for good behaviour instead of punishment for bad.

Most twins hate being lumped together after the first few years. And they like to have their own belongings and a corner of their room which is just theirs. They will obviously share big games and toys but they will be thrilled if you actually give each item to one of them. However difficult life with twins may be at times, it is also a fulfilling and rewarding experience.

Unconsciousness

Unconsciousness ranges in severity from a fleeting faint to a life-threatening coma. A child who is unconscious shows no awareness of his surroundings and cannot be roused. The condition arises because of changes in the brain caused by any of a variety of reasons.

The brain's activity can be measured as electrical impulses on a machine called an electroencephalograph (EEG). The impulses are presented as wave patterns, which vary considerably according to the degree of consciousness or unconsciousness. When someone is unconscious there are about three large waves a second, and as consciousness returns the waves increase in frequency until the pattern is a rapidly changing ten waves per second for a fully conscious person.

There are many possible causes of unconsciousness. It can be caused by a head injury or by shock due to blood loss as the result of an injury or to loss of body fluids during an illness or in extreme heat. Pressure on the brain caused by infections, bleeding or an abscess or tumour can cause unconsciousness, as can poisoning or lack of sugar in the blood.

Children who are hypoglycaemic (suffer from low blood sugar level) may fall into a coma. This will occur in children suffering from diabetes if given too much insulin. Children who have epileptic convulsions often have a brief period of unconsciousness after an attack and, strictly speaking, they are unconscious while having convulsions, even though they are moving.

Fainting is a very light form of unconsciousness brought on by reduction in the blood supply to the brain (see Fainting).

A child who is unconscious may simply be in a light faint from which he quickly recovers. If more deeply unconscious, he cannot be roused, and when he eventually does come round he may be confused and dazed, with no memory of where he is or what has happened. The state is medically known as a coma and in a deep coma all the normal reflexes are suppressed, so that, for example, the child would not automatically cough to clear his throat to stop him from swallowing blood or vomit after an accident.

We have all heard of cases where a child has been in a coma for days or weeks or longer after a bad accident. In most cases the child will recover within minutes. But unconsciousness is always serious and should be reported to the family doctor.

All cases of unconsciousness, apart from passing faints, need medical attention. If you find a child in a state of unconsciousness, the first thing to do is to remove any danger, and check for breathing and heartbeat.

If the child has been poisoned by gas, remove him to the fresh air if possible, or at least turn off the gas and open doors and windows. If he has been strangled, remove whatever is round his neck, if possible by cutting it away. If he is suffocating with his head inside a plastic bag, of course remove the bag (this is best done by tearing or cutting open the bag), and if he is having an electric shock, separate him from, or turn off, the appliance.

Next, clear the child's airway of any blockage, such as food or vomit, by drawing your finger quickly round the inside of the mouth, and staunch any bleeding. Check for breathing by putting your face to the child's mouth to listen and feel for breathing and by watching to see if his chest is rising and falling. If he is not breathing, check the pulse.

If the child is not breathing, give mouth-to-mouth resuscitation (*see* Artificial Respiration), and if in addition his heart is not beating, give heart massage (*see* Cardiac Massage).

If he does not need this treatment, put the child in the recovery position (*see* First Aid). Meanwhile, if possible get someone to call an ambulance while you take care of the child. If there is no one else there, wait until the heartbeat and breathing are restored before putting the child in the recovery position and calling help. Keep the child warm and be ready to reassure him if he comes round before professional help arrives.

If your child suffers from epilepsy you will get to know what the normal pattern of attacks is, and if it is usual for the child to remain unconscious for a while after an attack there is no need to call your doctor when this happens. However medical attention is needed if the child begins to have further convulsions without regaining consciousness. Place the child in the recovery position during an attack so that his tongue will not roll back and block the airway.

◆ See also, **Fainting**, **Febrile Convulsions**

Upset Stomach

Although parents should always be guided by their knowledge of their own child, the following are indications that medical help is needed when the child has tummy ache:

● acute abdominal pain which persists or becomes worse during a period of two to three hours

● abdominal pain with vomiting, diarrhoea or fever

● blood in the stools or in the urine

● weight loss with recurrent pains, rashes, fever, stiff neck or inability to stand bright lights accompanied by abdominal pain

● dry cough or breathing problems accompanied by abdominal pain

● pain accompanying any problems with passing water.

◆ See **Abdominal Pain**, **Constipation**, **Diarrhoea**, **Food Allergy**, **Food Poisoning**, **Gastroenteritis**, **Poisoning**, **Travel Sickness**, **Vomiting**

Urinary Tract Infections

The urinary tract consists of the kidneys, which filter waste products out of the blood to form urine; the ureters, through which urine is passed to the bladder; the bladder, where the urine is stored; and the urethra, through which urine is passed out of the body.

In children, infections of the urinary tract usually affect the bladder and/or urethra. Girls are more prone to infections of the urinary tract than are boys, since a girl's urethra is very much shorter than a boy's, and its outlet is situated much closer to the anus, so that there can be cross infection from the bowels.

Even though these infections are usually a minor nuisance rather than a serious illness, they have to be treated promptly as there is a danger of them passing up the urinary tract and affecting the kidneys. If a child suffers repeatedly from infections of the urinary tract this could mean that there is some abnormality which predisposes him to infection and the cause needs to be investigated. The most common childhood urinary tract infection is cystitis, which affects the bladder.

Infections of the urinary tract are usually caused by bacteria which are perfectly harmless in the bowels, but which cause irritation in the urethra and bladder. These bacteria can easily be transferred to the urethra. In girls this can happen when she wipes her bottom, especially if she wipes from back to front, and in boys it can happen when he handles his penis without washing his hands after wiping his bottom.

Symptoms of infection may show up in the urine itself, which may be cloudy or have an unpleasant "fishy" smell. The child may complain that it hurts to pass water, may want to pass water frequently, or may feel that he needs to empty his bladder and then find it difficult to do so. He may complain of pain in his tummy or low in the back, and in some cases he may even have a slight fever, feel nauseous or be sick. If a child who has previously been dry suddenly starts to wet the bed, this too could be a sign that there is something wrong. Most commonly the infection will just cause a stinging pain on passing water and the need to do so frequently, but often without producing very much urine.

If your child shows any of the symptoms of possible urinary tract infection he should see the family doctor immediately, as prompt treatment will ensure that the infection does not spread and become more serious. The doctor will probably ask you to collect a sample of the child's urine, which should be taken in the morning when it is at its most concentrated.

Laboratory tests will show whether there is infection present, and if this is so the doctor will probably prescribe antibiotics to cure it. He or she will also advise you to make sure that the child drinks plenty of fluids to dilute the urine and cause the child to pass water more frequently. This washes out bacteria and helps to cure the infection quickly.

If a child frequently has problems with urinary infections, the doctor may refer him to hospital to make sure that there is nothing else wrong.

Infections of the urinary tract may be prevented by:

- teaching girls to wipe their bottoms from front to back, and children of both sexes to wash their hands after defaecating
- making sure that children do not become constipated as this can interfere with the emptying of the bladder. Give them plenty of fresh fruits and vegetables and other forms of dietary fibre.
- encouraging your child to drink plenty of fluids – particularly plain water, so that the bladder is flushed out regularly and the urine does not become concentrated.

Vaccinations

The human body develops immunity to many viral and bacterial infections simply through exposure to them. This acquired immunity explains why the vast majority of people will generally get only one attack of an illness such as measles or chickenpox during their life. Humans as a species are also automatically immune to some diseases that affect animals.

In addition to these two types of natural immunity, there is a third type that can be conferred by means of vaccination or immunization. Because of this there are some diseases which formerly caused serious illness and even death which have now been brought under control or even eradicated worldwide.

The body deals with infection by manufacturing antibodies, special proteins which are specific to each particular infection. It stores information on the exact nature of these antibodies in the lymphocytes, and if the same infection attacks a second time, identical antibodies are then manufactured to fight it.

Immunization by vaccination is a way of provoking the body into producing antibodies to an infection without being submitted to the full-blown infection itself. If the immunized person later comes into contact with the agent of that infection the lymphocytes will get to work to produce antibodies and the infection will not be able to take hold.

The usual form of immunization is active immunization. This involves injecting small amounts of the virus or bacteria, either in inactivated (dead) or in live but much weakened form. The body is encouraged to produce antibodies, without actually making the child ill and the usual result is that lifelong immunity develops. This kind of immunization is given to babies and young children, to protect against diphtheria, polio, whooping cough, measles, mumps and rubella.

Passive immunization is used to treat people who have already caught the disease in question, or who are at risk of having caught it. It involves injecting immunoglobulin, which is rich in antibodies to that particular disease. Immunoglobulin is extracted from blood plasma provided by donors who have had the disease.

This form of immunization gives immediate protection, and is the type used, for example, if a child has had the sort of injury that might lead to tetanus or if a child has been in contact with someone who has hepatitis B. The effect of these injections wears off over time.

Since an immunization campaign was put in hand in Britain in 1942 smallpox has ceased to exist, whereas in the 1930s there were about 3,000 deaths a year from it in children under 15 in Britain alone.

Other diseases have now been banished. For example, poliomyelitis was also responsible for many deaths and many more cases of paralysis, and thanks to vaccination programmes put into effect in the United Kingdom since 1957 it has practically been wiped out.

A wide vaccination programme is now available to all children in developed countries, and most parents automatically take advantage of it. Some parents, however, do worry about the risks.

Only the whooping cough (pertussis) vaccination has proved controversial, since it was reported in 1974 that a very few children had to be admitted to hospital after the injection suffering from severe neurological illness. It could not be proved that the vaccination was responsible, but even so, as a result of this report many parents decided not to have their children immunized against whooping cough, and in the late 1970s and early 1980s there were new epidemics of the disease.

In extremely rare cases it is true that the vaccination has led to a child suffering from an illness related to the disease against which he has been vaccinated. But the risks of this happening are minute. For example, it is now estimated that the risk of side effects, including temporary ones, is something like 1 in 100,000 in the case of whooping cough vaccination, infinitely smaller than the risk of the child's having neurological complications as a result of actually catching a bad attack of the disease.

So the risk is negligible and is completely outweighed by the advantages. Parents who are worried, however, can seek reassurance from their family doctor.

Vomiting

Being sick seems to be a necessary part of childhood from babyhood onwards and although it is often unpleasant and upsetting for the child it is rarely due to anything seriously wrong. However, depending on the way in which the child is vomiting and whether there are other symptoms, vomiting can also be a sign of serious illness.

Parents learn to distinguish when their child needs to see the doctor and when the proper care at home is all that's needed. But it is always important to remember that the younger the child, the greater the danger from symptoms such as vomiting, diarrhoea and fever unless they clear up straight away.

The most usual cause of vomiting is irritation of the lining of the stomach, but this can be brought on by a number of different conditions, ranging from gastroenteritis and viral infections to serious conditions such as appendicitis. Overeating and eating contaminated food can also cause stomach irritation and vomiting. But many children also suffer from motion (travel) sickness, with acute vomiting, thought to be caused by confusing messages reaching the brain from the eyes and the centres of balance in the ears. A blow to the head can also cause vomiting, and this is a danger sign that the brain has been injured in some way. Migraines can stimulate vomiting by causing changes in the brain.

Babies often dribble back a little milk during and after feeds and this is not true vomiting, but is known as "possetting". In true vomiting the contents of the stomach are regurgitated quite forcefully. The child may be unusually pale and quiet for a while beforehand, but often in children, vomiting occurs with very little warning.

If possible, provide a bucket or bowl for the child to be sick into. If your child is being sick he will find it soothing and reassuring if you hold his forehead as he vomits, and afterwards he needs to be freshened up by having his face wiped with a cool flannel. If he is well enough he should clean his teeth to take away the unpleasant taste, and if he is in bed you can give him a glass of water to rinse his mouth out. Children are often sick quite suddenly, and the child's clothes and bedclothes may need to be changed. Make sure you keep the child well wrapped so that he does not get cold while he is out of bed if this happens. Put a child to bed when he has been sick and leave a bowl by his bed in case it happens again.

The most important thing, when a child is sick, is to make sure that his fluid intake is high to make up for the fluids lost in vomiting. Give him plenty of water and diluted fruit juice or squash, and if he has been very sick or sick several times add a pinch of salt and a teaspoonful of glucose to plain water and get him to sip this, to make up for the loss of salts and sugars this has caused.

Do not try to make the child eat, but gradually offer him easily digested foods such as thin soups with bits of plain bread floating in them, puréed fruit or vegetables, and yoghurt until his appetite gradually returns. Reintroduce fats, red meats, and strongly flavoured foods cautiously as the child gradually gets back to normal again.

Sickness from minor causes usually passes within about six hours. If the child is sick for longer than this, and the sickness is not coming under control, you should call your family doctor. With babies it is wise to seek advice sooner, because of the greater danger of dehydration.

Call your doctor immediately if the vomiting is accompanied by any of the following symptoms:

Children
● Severe pain, starting round the tummy button and travelling down to the lower right side (could be appendicitis).
● Pain in the neck and inability to look at bright light (could be meningitis).

Babies
● Red mucus in the stools and the baby obviously in pain (could be intussusception – bowel blockage).
● Diarrhoea, and baby seems unwell (could be gastroenteritis which is potentially dangerous in babies).
● Hernia (bulge in the tummy) and pain (could be umbilical hernia).

● In babies younger than 10 weeks, forceful vomiting during and after feeding (could be pyloric stenosis).

Babies and children
● Fever which you are unable to reduce by tepid sponging.
● Symptoms lasting more than six hours.
● Child not able to drink or retain fluids.

The doctor will need to know how long the vomiting has been going on, whether there has been diarrhoea, fever or any other symptoms and what the child has eaten. He or she will check to see whether the child has a fever and will advise you on how to care for the child at home. Oral rehydration powders may be prescribed – a properly balanced mixture of salts and sugars, which are added to water to provide a drink that makes sure that the body's lost salts, sugars and fluids are replaced.

If the doctor suspects that the cause of the vomiting is something other than a gastric infection the child may be taken to hospital for tests and possibly treatment.

◆ See also, **Gastroenteritis**, **Travel Sickness**

Walking

As early as four months, some babies enjoy being held upright on their parent's lap so that they can take some weight on their legs. By six months, they may enjoy "standing", while you support their weight, and flexing their knees; they may even learn to do a kind of "dance" with alternate feet. By approximately nine months, most babies can support their entire weight but they are still unable to balance on their own.

By 10 or 11 months, your baby may start to pull himself up by hanging on to convenient pieces of furniture, your legs, or the bars of his cot or playpen. At first, this is quite a nuisance because he doesn't know how to get down again. Often, he will fall at first, banging his head on the floor or furniture. Before long, he learns to plop himself down on his padded bottom or to let himself slide back to the ground, and he won't need to call for your help any more.

At first, being upright is its own reward. Soon, however, he wants to be moving. He rapidly learns to "cruise" around furniture, his playpen, or round your body as you sit on the floor. At first, he will move very tentatively, making sure he has a firm grip with one hand before releasing the other. Within a matter of weeks he can move quite quickly and confidently, often crossing from one piece of furniture to another despite quite a wide gap.

At some point, your baby will probably stand alone for the first time. He will let go of his support and stand with arms stretched out, not sure quite what to do next. He will start to wobble and immediately grab what he has been holding on to, otherwise he will fall. From this moment he will quickly progress to taking a step, then two, then three, in between one piece of furniture and another, and eventually he will launch out on his own.

When your baby first starts to stand upright he will look very odd to you. His arms and body seem too long for his short legs, his tummy sticks out, his legs are often bandy (nappies don't help here) and he has to hold his arms up at shoulder level in order to balance. As he grows in his second year, his body shape will become more appropriate for walking. Often his first attempts at walking are very comical – he seems unable to control his speed or direction and often ends up sitting down very suddenly.

Most parents are delighted and cannot help feeling proud when their child starts to take his first steps, and they see walking early as a sign that their child is a fast developer. However, the age at which a child walks is not necessarily linked to other skills. Sometimes, babies who are "sitters" develop better hand-eye co-ordination because they practise these skills more than a child who is busy toddling around. Sometimes, early crawlers become so fast and proficient at getting around on all fours that they have little incentive to try taking a slower and – from their point of view – more difficult way of getting around.

Walking early has advantages, but it has disadvantages too. While it's certainly easier to fold pushchairs at bus stops once your child can stand unsupported, for example, early walkers tend to be much more unstable and to have many more falls than those who learn later.

Early walkers probably take longer to progress to confident walking, running and climbing stairs than those who start two or three months later. Once late walkers start walking, they usually progress very quickly through these stages and it is soon impossible to tell which baby was walking at 9 months and which one was still a happy crawler at 18 months.

You may wonder if there is anything you can do to encourage your child to walk early. In fact, there is probably little that you can do to help, because studies have tended to show that the age at which a child walks is largely genetically determined; late or early walking tends to run in families.

There is also no evidence that baby walkers, baby bouncers, or holding your baby's arms while you walk him up and down will do anything to speed up the time when he'll launch out on his own. Indeed, it could be harmful to encourage your baby to walk before he is ready, because he is likely to fall and could damage himself, as well as newly gained confidence.

627

There has been a lot of concern about the safety of baby walkers and speculation about whether they actually help your baby to walk. The general consensus is that they do not, and some experts are even concerned that long periods spent in a baby walker can put a strain on the baby's muscles by keeping him in an artificial position. Furthermore, you must not leave your baby unattended in a baby walker, even for short periods. Active babies can turn the device over and become trapped. The baby can reach things that would normally be out of reach and if he falls down a step or bangs into something which overturns, he is likely to hurt himself more seriously than if he were not confined in a walker. It's important never to use as baby walker near steps, fires, ironing boards or other dangerous household equipment.

Push-along trolleys, cars or animals are very useful for your baby when he is at the stage between standing alone and learning to walk. It's important to select one which will not overbalance when your child pulls on the handle to lever himself up to a standing position. It also needs to be heavy enough to provide some resistance so that it doesn't run away from him when he pushes. You will need to be on hand to help him out, especially at the beginning, and also because it takes him a long time to learn how to turn it round when he reaches the end of the room.

Walking your baby along holding his hands is a game that many parents play, and some regret ever starting it because their baby requests it over and over again. But you should be aware that there is a danger of dislocating your child's arm if you pull it too hard in an awkward position, and especially if you tug on one arm. Again, helping your child along in this way won't speed up your baby's independent walking and may even slow it, as he starts to rely on you.

More fun for you and a better way of improving your child's confidence is sitting on the floor with arms stretched out and encouraging your child to take a step or two towards you. You are there to grab him should he fall, and to reward him with hugs, kisses and tickles should he succeed. Often late walkers are simply hesitant to take that first unsupported step; once they realize they can do it, there is no looking back.

Walking up and down stairs is a much more difficult skill to master for your young child and demands a lot more muscle control than walking in a – relatively – straight line. When he's about two-and-a-half years old, he will be able to walk up stairs alternating feet from step to step, while on his way down, he will still place both feet on the steps. Stairs are a tricky business – encourage him to hold on to the bannister and try not to rush him if he is taking his time.

Once your child is walking, a whole new world opens up for him, and for you too. Now you can go to parks and playgrounds and let him toddle around and explore without having to keep him confined to his push-chair. You can try out "baby bounce" sessions in local authority sports and leisure

centres where he can run around and climb on large mats, through tunnels, and play with outsize plastic-covered foam bricks. If you haven't done this before, this is the time to join mother-and-toddler groups and the "one o'clock clubs". Your child will enjoy playing with play houses, toddler trucks and pull-along toys and may even be adventurous enough to enjoy going on small slides or climbing frames.

Remember that although your child can walk or even run, it will be a long time before he can walk a long distance or follow you along the pavement. Although he may run with glee in the wrong direction and seem full of bounce, he will quickly tire of having to walk along by your side. At this age, he wants to stop and look at every object, walk up every garden path, open every gate and stop to examine every puddle. You will need to take a pushchair with you wherever you go for your own sanity as well as his safety, especially when walking along busy roads.

Your child will also quickly panic if you walk away from him to make him follow. He feels incapable of catching you up and will take such a move as a sign of desertion; he is more likely to sit on the pavement and howl than to run after you. Also, he will not hesitate to run out of your sight down the next aisle in the supermarket, but will howl with fear as soon as he realizes he can no longer see you. It's often kinder to sit him in the trolley with a fruit drink or healthy snack than let him run around and get lost.

Taking a newly walking child out on public transport can be a bit of a nightmare. He may be so keen to practise his new skills that he refuses to sit still. He may jump up and down on buses, run along station platforms, charge up and down the aisle in trains and want to look over the edge of the platform. A harness with reins can be a help in restraining him, but sometimes using these will only lead to a full-blown tantrum. Try to make sure he gets plenty of opportunity to run around at other times and take some books with you to look at when you know you will need to make him keep still.

Now he is upright, you may find you need to dress your child a little differently. Jogging suits and dungarees are still very practical, but stretch suits which cover the feet are now out. Dresses, which are impractical for a crawling baby, can now be worn by little girls. All-in-one snow suits may be too bulky and cumbersome for a toddler to walk in easily – a warm jacket may be better and allow more mobility.

It's best not to have anything on your baby's feet when you're indoors and he's learning to crawl, stand and walk. Even tight socks can constrict feet and prevent them growing properly, and they can prove slippery once your baby is crawling, standing and cruising.

Good shoes are essential once your child is walking properly and you go out of doors. It's important to go and have them properly fitted and to buy something which is comfortable and gives the foot proper support. Remember that first shoes get very badly scuffed at the front as your child is bound to do some crawling in them and a lot of falling over too. Have your baby's feet checked for size every two or three months as his feet can grow very quickly and often change shape too once he starts to walk.

Once your baby is walking he suddenly seems to leave babyhood behind and become a person in his own right. Many parents have noticed that their relationship changes at around this time, and older brothers and sisters, who were constantly asking for the baby to be taken away, as he is "spoiling my game", will suddenly start to involve him in it, treating him with new respect. Once your baby walks, he becomes a toddler and, inevitably, begins to assert his own personality. You need to be prepared for quite important changes in your relationship as you watch his first steps with such pride.

◆ See also, **Crawling**, **Feet**

Warts

Warts are very common, and usually quite harmless growths that are particularly likely to affect pre-teenage children.

The most common kind of wart is a small, round growth on the skin surface, which has a rough, pitted surface. The medical term for a wart is a verruca. When it grows on the sole of the foot it is usually a hard little knot more or less flush with the surface of the skin. The same is true of warts growing on the palms of the hands.

So-called plane warts, which are less common, but which usually occur only in children, are brown in colour and do not have a rough texture like the more common types of wart. Children are also prone to attacks of little white lumps known as molluscum contagiosum. These have nothing to do with warts.

Warts are the result of a viral infection which is spread by contact. The virus causes the skin cells to multiply in a disordered fashion so that a wart is effectively a benign tumour. It is thought that a break in the skin makes it easier for the infection causing warts to enter the skin.

The child eventually develops immunity to the virus causing the wart, and the wart disappears. This can happen within a few weeks or months, but it may take a matter of years. On the whole, once immunity has been developed the child stops getting warts, and people rarely get warts when they are older simply because they developed immunity as children. However, there are many varieties of the virus causing warts, so the child may have various types of wart before eventually becoming immune to all types.

Many magical cures have been suggested for warts over the centuries but there is no evidence that any of them works. Since all warts do eventually drop off as immunity develops, many apparent cures are simply the result of the infection having run its course.

There is no effective antibiotic against the virus causing warts, but various kinds of treatment are available. Although it is possible to get, without a prescription, paints and gels that are applied to warts, it is advisable to take your child to the family doctor if he develops warts. And never try to treat a wart on a child's face or genitals with gel or paint from the chemist's, as this can damage the surrounding, sensitive skin and cause scarring.

Unless the warts are causing the child distress the doctor will probably suggest that you wait for a time as they may disappear spontaneously quite quickly. Otherwise, he or she will prescribe the most suitable preparation for your child's skin and advise you how to apply it. The treatment has to be applied carefully, only to the wart and not to the surrounding skin, and between applications the hard skin is rubbed off with an emery board or pumice stone as it loosens.

Occasionally the doctor may decide that the wart should be removed by burning, scraping or freezing if it resists other treatments.

Wasp Stings

Only female wasps sting, but most wasps are females. Although wasp stings usually do little harm they are certainly alarming and unpleasant and wasps can make quite a nuisance of themselves in late summer. Very occasionally a child may be extra-sensitive to wasp stings, and may develop an allergic reaction with the signs of shock, which needs medical treatment; and stings in the mouth are also potentially dangerous.

Wasps generally do not leave their sting behind them, but if you look carefully you will see a small puncture mark on the child's skin where the wasp struck. The area round the mark will be red and sore and slightly swollen.

Many people believe that vinegar should be applied to wasps' stings, but this is just an old wives' tale, and the only effect the vinegar has is to cool the skin. This can be done better with an ice cube or a cold compress held over the sting.

A little cooling spray will soothe the sting and prevent it from flaring up. If the sting is obviously painful it is safe to give the appropriate dose of paracetamol.

If your child is one of the very few who develop a serious allergic reaction to wasp stings or if he has been stung by many wasps there may be severe swelling. The child may become pale and clammy, with rapid, shallow breathing. He will probably feel dizzy and may swoon or lapse completely into unconsciousness. These are signs that immediate medical help is needed.

If the child shows signs of shock, call an ambulance. If the child is conscious keep him warm, with his legs raised and supported so that they are above the level of his heart. If he is unconscious, put him in the recovery position (*see* First Aid), keep him warm, and be prepared to give artificial respiration (*see* Artificial Respiration) if he stops breathing while you are waiting for medical help to arrive.

If the sting is in the mouth, severe swelling may occur and this can affect breathing. Give the child ice cubes to suck, but if there is any sign of swelling or other worrying effects call your doctor or seek emergency help immediately.

If you are going to be outside when there are a lot of wasps or other biting insects about it may be a good idea to protect your child with an insect repellant as a preventive measure. These are available as creams, lotions and sprays from any chemist's shop. Try the repellant on a small area of skin first, in case the child's skin is oversensitive to it.

Perhaps more importantly, teach your child not to panic and flap his arms about at the sight of a wasp. Wasps are much less likely to sting if not provoked. Try to make sure also that the child pays attention when eating outside, to avoid the dangers of being stung in the mouth.

Weaning

The correct time to finish breastfeeding your baby is when it feels right for you and for him. This may sound vague and unhelpful if, at the moment, you're in the every early stages of feeding and getting to know your little one. Probably you are confused anyway by the conflicting advice and comments you are being given on the subject of your baby's nutrition. Try not to feel anxious because, as the weeks progress and you become attuned

24-HOUR GUIDE TO WEANING (Day divided into 5 meal times)

Baby is 4–5 months

Early morning breast feed	Breakfast & breast feed	Breast feed	Breast feed	Breast feed

Baby is 4½–5½ months

Early morning breast feed	Breakfast & breast feed	Lunch & breast feed	Breast feed	Breast feed

Baby is 5–6 months

Early morning breast feed	Breakfast & breast feed	Lunch	Supper	Breast feed

Baby is 6–7 months

Early morning breast feed	Breakfast	Lunch	Supper	Breast feed

Baby is 7–8 months

Drink of water or diluted juice	Breakfast	Lunch	Supper	Drink of water or diluted juice

to your baby's needs and gain more confidence in your own instincts, you will know when it is right for both of you to finish breastfeeding.

As with so many other areas of child-care, there really is no absolute right or wrong because every baby and every mother is entirely different, and it is very important to use the information given here simply as a rough guide.

There are a few women and babies who suddenly go from breastfeeding several times a day to not feeding at all but this is usually for special reasons. The usual sequence of events is more gradual as you and your baby mutually "lose interest" in breastfeeding because solid food is playing an increasing role in your baby's diet. Breastfeeding will become less frequent (see chart), until it only occurs last thing at night and/or first thing in the morning for reasons of comfort and security rather than for nutritional needs because, actually, your baby is getting his food from other sources.

Some women do get totally "addicted" to breastfeeding and this means that their babies become hooked in the same way. When this happens, breastfeeding may continue into toddlerhood and sometimes even until the child starts full-time school, although usually he will call a halt himself at this stage.

There is, of course, no rush to stop if you and your child are both happy to go on. You should, however, be aware of your child's development and make sure that he's growing naturally towards independence, and that it is not feelings of insecurity or other fears and anxieties which are making him cling to breastfeeding. Also, if you're planning another baby at this stage, your first child could take it very badly indeed if you suddenly stop breastfeeding him because you are feeling the fatigue of early pregnancy.

Most mothers of twins tend to give up breastfeeding earlier than women with just one baby, because it is very tiring to feed two babies and is definitely more time-consuming. It is also difficult to feed twins in public if, as is quite normal, they are both hungry at the same time. Sometimes one twin loses interest in the breast earlier than the other and this can make their mother feel that she is giving more attention to the one who wants to continue feeding. However, usually they stop at around the same age.

If you feel you have had enough of breastfeeding after five or six months – or even less – you can begin to gently wean him from the breast. The first feeds to do away with are the daytime ones. Make sure that solids are always given first and the breast feed last, so that you know he is filling up with food and not with your milk. Many babies, surprisingly, don't even seem to notice when you omit to finish off their mealtime with a breast feed, probably because they're so interested in the new adventure of solids. However, if your baby does become very distressed, continue to breastfeed him, and wait until the next day and a different mealtime to try again.

It can be very helpful when weaning from the breast if your partner or another helper can take care of your baby's mealtime for you, and thereby break your baby's connection between food, you and the breast.

The practice of getting your baby off to sleep in the evening by nursing him at the breast, although essential in the very early days, can cause problems as your baby matures. Babies become attached to a routine, and will not change habits easily.

You nurse him off to sleep, tiptoe with him to his cot, put him down, but a few hours later he's awake again, and you give him the breast to comfort him back to sleep Try to break this routine as soon as you can. Ask your partner to soothe the baby to sleep at night, perhaps with a little water from a baby cup to quench his thirst. An even better idea is to try to get your baby into the routine of lying down in his cot at bedtime before he is actually asleep, so that it is time and place he connects with sleep, and not the breast habit.

As weaning progresses it is important to remember to supplement your baby's fluid intake but this shouldn't be with calorie-laden or sweetened drinks. Remember, your baby will not be taking much nutritionally from breastfeeding at this stage. He is using the breast for occasional comforting feeds. It's also a good idea to avoid introducing the bottle as a breast substitute, as you risk starting up a whole new habit which could go on and on. Choose sensible baby beakers instead and try to promote the idea of drinking water at least some of the time as well as unsweetened diluted fruit juice and baby milk.

You may decide to stop breastfeeding because you find it too exhausting or it limits your mobility. Breastfeeding does sap your energy, and it is important to remember that when you first give up completely it is unwise to plunge into strenuous activities. Give your body a little time to get back to normal. If you haven't exercised or worked at all while breastfeeding, ease yourself into these things very gently. Also, while you may feel some sense of release when you give up, and are enjoying more mobility don't forget your baby's feelings. Remember that breastfeeding was for your baby a comforting close experience, and while you may be keen to resume lots of activities, do make time to compensate your child with extra cuddles and affection.

If you wean very gradually you shouldn't experience much discomfort when you stop breastfeeding, although some women do complain of soreness and tingling pains but these usually disappear within a couple of days. If your discomfort is great, and lasts more than a week, visit your doctor. With gradual weaning your breasts will return more or less to their pre-pregnancy size and shape. If you haven't already bought new bras, and been properly measured by a trained corsetry assistant then now is definitely the time to do so. You may feel that your breasts are smaller and less attractive than before, but probably, you have got used to their increased size during pregnancy and feeding, and have forgotten how they were before.

Quite a few mothers report a sense of loss when weaning from the breast is finally completed, especially if they are not going to have any more children. If this is the case with you, it means that you have made the most of this stage in your baby's growth and naturally you will regret the end of this special intimacy with your baby. Don't worry – there are many, many more stages in his development to look forward to and enjoy. If you experience serious feelings of depression for more than a fortnight, however, there might be other causes, and you should talk to your doctor.

◆ See also, **Breastfeeding**, **First Foods**

Whooping Cough

This disease, medically known as pertussis, is still fairly common in childhood, although it is easily prevented by immunization. In very young babies it can, very rarely, be fatal, and it is frightening and unpleasant for children of any age, even though full recovery is the norm.

Whooping cough is caused by bacteria, which are passed from child to child during coughing fits. Because the early symptoms are so similar to those of the common cold, parents may not realize that a child is infectious until it is too late and other children have been infected. If your child seems to have a cold and has in the previous ten days or so been in contact with someone who has whooping cough, it is best to assume that he has contracted the disease and keep him away from other children. He will be infectious for at least three weeks after the first attack.

The cause of the "whoop" lies in the fact that, because the coughing fits attack so suddenly, the child has no chance to draw breath, because the glottis at the opening of the windpipe closes spontaneously, and at the end of a bout of coughing the child is almost suffocating. He quickly learns to breathe in against the resistance of the glottis, and this makes the characteristic noise.

Small babies sometimes fail to acquire this knack, which is partly why the disease is more dangerous for them, and it is also possible for a child with whooping cough not to make the "whooping" noise.

You are unlikely to suspect that the illness is whooping cough in the early stages unless the child has been in contact with someone known to have the disease.

The full symptoms will not begin to develop until a week or more after the common cold symptoms, when the cough gets worse and the "whoop" develops. The whooping cough attacks in violent prolonged bouts which leave the child almost suffocating. The cough produces phlegm at the end of an attack, when the child gasps for breath in a characteristic "whooping" way, and then will often retch or vomit. In many cases the child feels quite well once he has recovered from the coughing attack, until the next attack comes on.

As with many illnesses, the symptoms are not equally violent in all children. Some children have mild attacks of whooping cough which can be mistaken for a cold at every stage, but, unlike those of a cold, the symptoms last and last. In many cases, it is 10 or 12 weeks before the child recovers from a bad case of whooping cough, and even mild cases take several weeks.

A serious case of whooping cough is in any case alarming and debilitating for a child. But in some unusual cases, especially in babies, or if the child has a weakness, complications may develop.

The chief complication is that of secondary chest infection, which may lead to pneumonia and cause permanent lung damage; but whooping cough can, in up to 2 per cent of cases, also cause encephalitis (inflammation of the brain), and the coughing fits can cause a burst blood vessel in the brain and, in susceptible children, epileptic fits. These complications are less likely to result if the child receives good medical care, and it is important to call your doctor as soon as you suspect that your child has whooping cough.

Although whooping cough is caused by bacteria, it is not simple and straightforward and there is no real cure for it. The doctor may decide to take a throat swab to establish whether the illness really is whooping cough. Antibiotics will probably be prescribed to prevent secondary infections and limit the period during which the child is infectious. In the case of a baby, the doctor may decide that he should be taken to hospital to make sure that he does not suffer from any complications, and otherwise he or she will advise on the care of the child. You will be able to help the child during coughing fits by supporting him in a sitting position, and reassuring him to keep him calm.

You may find that a moist atmosphere, provided by bowls of steaming hot water, helps during an attack, and you should not expose the child to cigarette smoke. You will need to make sure that bowls are available for the child to vomit into. Giving him frequent small meals may help him to keep food down, and, as always when a child is ill, he should be given plenty of fluids to help prevent dehydration.

If the child feels quite well between attacks, he need not spend the time in bed, but he must be kept away from school and should not be allowed to do anything strenuous until he is better. Especially at night he will probably feel very ill and frightened during coughing fits, and will need a great deal of comforting. If possible, he should not be left alone, so try to ensure that someone is there to reassure him when he has night-time attacks.

There is a vaccine for whooping cough, and although this is not absolutely effective in preventing the disease, any child who has had the vaccine will suffer from only a mild form if he subsequently contracts it.

However, there are some problems connected with the vaccine. The first is that it cannot be given to babies before they are three months old, so that very small babies most at risk cannot be protected. The second problem is that there has been some controversy connected with the vaccine itself, with some reports having linked the vaccine with brain damage in young children. How definite, and, if so, how serious these risks are has still not been fully established. For certain children (for example those who come from families with a history of epilepsy) the vaccine may not be advisable; but the overwhelming evidence is that there would be epidemics of whooping cough if a widespread vaccination programme was not carried out, and that most children are much more at risk from the illness and its complications than from the vaccine.

◆ See also, **Vaccinations**

Work (Going Back To)

If you decide, for whatever reason, to go back to work while your child is at home, take comfort from the thought that there is no proof that it is harmful for children to have a working mum.

When you find yourself feeling anxious and guilty, concentrate, instead, on the positive aspects of the situation. Spending time with someone other than just you gives your child the benefit of affection from another source. He will learn to be sociable, if he goes to a childminder. If you enjoy your job, chances are you will be happier and more relaxed during the time you actually spend with your child. You will often hear this referred to as "quality time". Use this time to play with your child, and let him know how much you love him. This way he won't feel neglected when you are at work.

Also, it is wrong to think that you are letting your child down or that it is your fault if he becomes ill or hurts himself while you're away. These things could just as easily happen if you were at home all day and you should not feel guilty.

You may find you are one of the many mothers who choose to go back to work even if they do not need the money. No matter how much they love their child, many mothers do not enjoy spending the entire day at home with a small child.

Depression is just one of the problems that can hit mothers when they find themselves at home with no one to talk to. The chores mount up, loneliness sets in and it can seem pointless, if not futile, to put on nice clothes in the morning when they are just going to be drooled on or food-encrusted by lunch time. If this is how you feel, you are probably not doing anyone any favours by staying at home.

Although it is often difficult to detach yourself from a baby, the younger he is the easier it will be for him. A toddler who has been used to spending the day with you will find it more difficult if you are suddenly, regularly away from home.

Tearful scenes and tantrums can be difficult and emotionally draining for you. To make the situation less traumatic, take your child to visit the childminder a few times before you start leaving him on his own. If your child is to be looked after by a friend or relative, leave him with them for just a couple of hours every day for a week or two so he gets used to the idea of your going out and coming back. It will be much less draining for you, and you will be able to concentrate on your work if you can go off with a kiss and a hug, rather than tears.

By the time your child reaches about three years, it is important he starts learning how to interact with other people, even if you have been at home until then. By this age, you should be able to explain in simple terms that you are going to work and will be back later in the day, and that you aren't abandoning him.

If you are planning to return to work after your baby is born, it's never too soon to think about how you will arrange childcare and organize your daily life. Even if you are newly pregnant, it isn't too soon to consider the alternatives. Think about the costs involved and how much help and support your partner will give.

Going off to work won't be as simple as when you just had yourself to get ready. You will need time to get your child ready and to pack his bag. Also you will have even less time to do the increased amount of housework and washing.

Your partner will have a vital role to play in any plans you make. Make sure you both understand exactly how much you expect him to help and what you expect him to do. If one of you takes your child to the minder, perhaps the other one can pick him up. If your baby still isn't sleeping through the night, your partner will have to take turns getting up to care for him.

If you plan to rely on neighbours, friends or other family members on a regular basis, find out exactly how much time they are willing to give. Even the most understanding employer will soon lose patience if you constantly let her down because of unreliable child-care. Also, unless you are satisfied your child is being well cared for, it will be difficult to concentrate on your work.

Several factors should be considered before you decide what job to take. Your old job may not be as suitable as it was before the baby was born. If, for

example, it involves long-distance travelling or frequent or unpredictable overtime, you may want to consider a new job. Also, most childcare is expensive, so you might want to think about a job closer to home to save on travelling costs and, as a bonus, on time.

Before deciding on a job, have a chat with your employer to find out what the attitude is towards your having to stay at home occasionally. No matter how well you plan, there are bound to be times when your child-care arrangements break down – perhaps your childminder is ill, or one of her children needs to be taken to hospital, or your own child is unwell and needs you to look after him. It happens to every working mum sooner or later.

Finances are often the determining factor in the type of child-care parents select. Three popular forms are a childminder, a mother's help or a nanny.

Childminders are the least expensive and, consequently, the most frequently used. They generally have children of their own and so are happy to be able to earn some extra money from home.

They tend to look after several children at the same time in their own home. Often they will have been "vetted" and will have fulfilled basic requirements in terms of safety, hygiene, cooking skills, knowledge of children and so on. Your local council may have a list of people with vacancies in your area. Some childminders will look after babies as little as eight weeks old.

Before committing yourself, be sure to visit the childminder's home when other children are there so you can see what they are like, what they are doing and what type of food they are given. Some points to consider are:

● What does the fee cover? Are meals and snacks included? Do you have to provide nappies? Is there an extra charge if you are late picking up your child after work?

● What alternatives are available if the childminder is ill?

● How much discipline is there? Is the childminder too strict, or are the children allowed to run wild all day?

● How good are the play facilities? Are there any educational toys or games available?

A mother's help is an untrained person who comes to your home; she is likely to be under 20. Some will generally do some housework as well as providing child-care.

Nannies are the most expensive form of child-care because they are often trained. They may be day nannies or live-in, in which case they may expect "perks" like their own TV or the use of a car. If you have nearby friends with young children, it is often economical to consider sharing a day nanny or mother's help.

Two other forms of child-care are local council or church-administered nurseries and day-care centres. Unfortunately, these are not available everywhere. Your local council or other mothers should be able to advise you on what is available in your area. Most nurseries and day-care centres have waiting lists, so if you find one you like, put your name down as soon as possible, even if your child isn't born yet.

Some employers either operate crèches at the workplace or contribute towards the cost of a local nursery. It is also worth checking if your partner's employer offers such a benefit.

◆ See also, **Nannies, Nurseries and Playgroups**

Working From Home

If you want to work from home, you first need to ask yourself some basic questions. How much time have you got? Do you want to work while your child is around, or in the evenings or full-time? Do you have space to work in? Are you aiming for pocket money or a substantial income? Do you want to be an occasional earner, a self-employed freelance, or to build a business? (Bear in mind that building a business takes a lot of time and hard work.)

Having established these basics you must then assess your skills. Can you build on past work experience, such as teaching, typing or hairdressing; a hobby, such as pottery or gardening; or skills such as sewing or cooking? Or is there a course in something new and different that interests you at a local college which could help you earn at home?

You could also look for gaps in local services. Study noticeboards and small ads in papers. Think about what's missing in your area and what might be needed. Then, sound out ideas on people you know.

Marketing yourself is necessary whatever you do. Cards in local shops or libraries are cheapest and an ad in the local paper is often highly effective. But word of mouth works wonders – so spread the word among friends, neighbours and acquaintances. And ask your partner and friends to tell people too.

Image is important and using headed notepaper and business cards definitely looks professional, but always remember that image needs to be backed up by a genuinely good product or service.

One job that many mothers with small children opt for is childminding. It's hard work, you must really like children, and it won't make you rich, but you should never be short of work.

If you want to childmind you must register with your local Social Services Department who will visit to check your home. Once registered you'll be put on a list and can advertise yourself directly.

Another popular home-based job is selling. There's a huge market for second-hand clothes and equipment – and you need nothing but garment rails and space. You could build up a stock of baby clothes and equipment and keep a proportion of the selling price. Contact sellers and buyers through surgeries, clinics and playgroups. Or, if baby clothes don't hold much appeal, you could do a similar thing with upmarket second-hand clothes for adults. You will probably find many customers among your friends.

You can also sell things you've made – crafts, pottery, hand-knitted jumpers – inviting round friends and friends of friends to see the range and take orders.

Party-planning involves organizing get-togethers to sell products for outside companies and getting paid on commission. For this you need a wide circle of contacts. Avoid companies that expect you to buy products before selling them.

Home-based catering may be a good choice if you enjoy cooking. It can mean anything from cooking dishes for friends' freezers to preparing novelty cakes or buffet lunches.

You could approach local offices and businesses with the offer of fresh, tasty sandwiches. Or, if you feel more ambitious, advertise yourself as providing buffet lunches for special occasions. Or you could develop a speciality, such as party food, or selling home-made cakes to your local health-food or delicatessen store.

Whichever route you prefer, you must record expenses meticulously and at least double the cost of ingredients when charging. Find out about catering legislation from your local Environmental Health Office.

Typing can easily be done from home and some companies pay well if you're reliable and efficient. Look through the telephone book and write to local colleges or firms you'd like to work for; put up ads, and/or try contacting companies you've worked for in the past.

Book-keeping can also be done at home, though you'll need to do a course if you are not experienced. Writing, researching, translating or editing are also options – though highly competitive ones.

As well as making all these jobs much easier, new technology is also opening up fresh possibilities for working from home. Computers can be used for anything from word processing to data analysis, so it's well worth developing computer skills. Some companies employ large numbers of home-based computer workers.

Sewing and knitting can be good money-spinners as long as you don't under-charge. (Make a contract with yourself that you're not going to work for less than a certain amount per hour.) Curtains, blinds and loose covers are often profitable, though they take confidence and experience. Or you may like to specialize – say in children's clothes, wedding dresses, or cushion covers – or just do simple clothes alterations.

You can also do sewing as an outworker for big companies, but out-working (which also includes work such as stuffing envelopes and sorting buttons) is generally badly paid and boring. Knitting machinists, however, can earn reasonably well working for local designers. So though the machine costs a lot this can be recouped by knitting jumpers for firms, designers and your own contacts. Upholstery is a less common choice but there's quite a market for it in some areas. You'll probably have to do a course first and you'll need nifty fingers, space and kind neighbours (it's noisy).

Making jewellery, candles, soft toys or lavender bags is fun but it's hard to make a serious income after deducting the cost of materials and your time. Nevertheless, some people have done well at these or more practical crafts such as furniture painting, lampshade making or picture framing.

Selling is usually the hardest part. You can sell through friends, acquaintances, a market stall (ask your local council what's available), car boot sales or shops (these take a hefty cut).

There are countless other jobs you can do from home, including tutoring, reflexology, flower arranging, massage, or taking in lodgers or paying guests. You can get lodgers through universities and local colleges but make sure you always establish terms first.

Although working from home may sound like the perfect option for mothers of small children, there are several factors that need serious consideration:

Child-care

You might be able to work at home while your tiny baby sleeps – but a toddler is different. If you are working in the day you may have to organize child-care for at least some of the time. You will have to learn to shut yourself away.

For very small children out of sight is often out of mind. If someone else is looking after your child, let her get on with it. Don't rush out each time you hear a whimper or scream – it could be interpreted as criticism. Child-care isn't cheap so take this into account when assessing costs and benefits of working from home.

Overheads

As well as child-care you need to take into account the costs of lighting, heating, stationery and so on. Keep all receipts and bills so that expenses can be claimed against tax.

You will, of course, have to deal with your own tax and national insurance which can be difficult on top of all your other responsibilities.

Loneliness

You may find yourself feeling very isolated, missing the stimulation of adult company yet still having to deal with all the pressures of work.

If you do choose to work at home you will have to accept that you'll be more tired – running a home with small children is a full-time job in itself. If you work evenings and nights while your child sleeps, keep some evenings free each week – or you'll quickly get worn out. Combining work and family life is hard because you can't really leave either behind. Inevitably housework will suffer so learn to shut the door sometimes on unmade beds and unwashed clothes. Get all the help and labour-saving gadgets you can and be disciplined about setting aside work time and ruthless about casual visitors and social telephone calls.

Worms

There are several kinds of worms that can live in the human intestines – usually doing little harm. Children seem particularly vulnerable to threadworms, which are extremely infectious and can affect everyone in the family. In some parts of the world, particularly where the weather is hot and sanitation is poor, worms can be a great problem, causing debilitating diseases. The technical term for worms that are parasites of human beings is "helminths". These are divided into three main types: roundworms or nematodes; tapeworms or cestodes; and flatworms or trematodes.

Threadworms can be passed from person to person as eggs can get on to the child's hands when he scratches. If the child puts his fingers into his mouth this causes reinfection, and when he touches other people he can transfer the eggs to them. Eggs also drop off into the general household dust and linger in bedding and on towels. The eggs can also contaminate food.

The eggs that enter the digestive tract hatch out in the intestines, and when the female is fully developed she makes her way out of the child's body via the anus and lays more eggs there.

Threadworms are the most common worm and cause anal itching. As the worms are active at night this causes the child's sleep to be disturbed. Although they usually affect the child's anus (back passage) they can also sometimes get into a girl's urethra (front passage) and vagina. This can cause pain on passing water, and there may also be a vaginal discharge. Some of the worms are passed out of the body in the faeces (stools), and are visible as tiny white threads.

Most roundworms are only found in conjunction with tropical climates and poor sanitation, where their eggs can contaminate food. Some types of roundworm are normally parasites of dogs and cats from an infected animal. Again they hatch out in the intestines, where they then lay their eggs. Eggs may be excreted before they hatch and are passed on through poor hygiene.

Roundworms usually cause no symptoms, but are visible as white worms of the size of an earthworm when they are passed out of the body in the faeces. A child who is badly affected may look thin and feel slightly unwell.

647

The eggs of tapeworms can infect both pork and beef. They are killed by thorough cooking, but can enter the digestive system if meat that has not been thoroughly cooked is eaten. In most countries meat is checked by inspectors before it is allowed to be put on sale and is very rarely contaminated by tapeworms.

Tapeworms have been linked to various kinds of digestive upset, but again there are no specific symptoms until the worm is expelled from the body. A "tapeworm" is actually a colony of separate cestodes, each segment (proglottis) being a separate parasite. These worms, as their name implies, are like a length of tape or ribbon and can be alarmingly long.

Fortunately, once they have been identified, worms are easily treated, and although the very thought of them makes people feel squeamish there is no reason to feel embarrassed if you suspect that your child has worms. Take him straight to the doctor, who will prescribe a drug known as piperazine (Pripsen) for threadworms or roundworms, or niclosamide (Yomesan) for tapeworms. Make sure that you follow the instructions carefully when giving the drug, so that the right amount is taken at the right time.

Since threadworms' eggs can so easily be passed from person to person, the doctor may well advise you to treat everyone in the family (including yourself) as well as the child, and this is a sensible precaution. It is also important to observe the strictest standards of hygiene, washing your hands and scrubbing under the nails after going to the lavatory, before eating, and when about to handle food. Don't let children share towels and sheets if anyone in the family has worms, keep the infected child's finger-nails short so that they cannot harbour eggs, and make sure that boys and girls alike wear pyjamas in bed so that their fingers are less likely to come into contact with the eggs.

Useful Addresses

Action Against Allergies
7 Strawberry Hill Road
Twickenham
Middlesex
Tel. 0181-892 2711

Active Birth Centre
25 Bickerton Road
London N19 5JT
Tel. 0171-561 9006

Association for Post-natal Illness
25 Jerdan Place
London SW6 1BE
Tel. 0171-778 0868

Association of Breastfeeding Mothers
26 Fermshaw Close
London SE26 4TH
Tel. 0181-778 4769

British Standards Institute
Sales and Enquiries
Linford Wood
Milton Keynes MK14 6LE
Tel. 01908-220022

The Children's Society
(*advice for families involved in divorce*)
Edward Rudolph House
Margery Street
London WC1X OJL
Tel. 0171-837 4299

Contact A Family
70 Tottenham Court Road
London W1P OHA
Tel. 0171-383 3555

CRY-SIS
(*support for parents of crying babies*)
B.M. Families
London WC1N 3XX
Tel. 0171-404 5011

Family Planning Association
27–35 Mortimer Street
London W1N 7RG
Tel. 0171-636 7866

Gingerbread
(*support for one-parent families*)
16–17 Clerkenwell Close
London EC1R OAA
Tel. 0171-336 8183

Handicapped Adventure Playground Association
Pryors Bank, Bishops Park
London SW6
Tel. 0171-736 4443

Health Education Authority
30 Great Peter Street
London SW1
Tel. 0171-222 5300

Hyperactive Children's Support Group
71 Whyke Lane
Chichester
West Sussex PO19 2LD
Tel. 01903-725 182

Kidscape
(*support for victims of bullying*)
152 Buckingham Palace Road
London SW1W 9TR
Tel. 0171-730 3300

La Leche League of Great Britain
Box 3424
London WC1N 3XX
Tel. 0171-242 1278

Left Handed Shop
57 Brewer Street
London W1R 3FB
Tel. 0171-437 3910

Meet-a-Mum Association
14 Willis Road
Croydon
Surrey CRO 2XX
Tel. 0181-665 0357

MENCAP
123 Golden Lane
London EC1Y 0RT
Tel. 0171-454 0454

Miscarriage Association
Clayton Hospital
Northgate
Wakefield WF1 3JS
Tel. 01924-200799

**National Association for
Gifted Children**
540 Eldergate
Milton Keynes
Buckinghamshire
Tel. 01908-673677

**National Association for the
Welfare of Children in Hospital
(NAWCH)**
Argyle House
Euston Road

London NW1 2SD
Tel. 0171-833 2041

National Asthma Campaign
Providence House
Providence Place
London N1 ONT
Tel. 0171-226 2260

National Childbirth Trust
Alexandra House
Oldham Terrace
London W3 6NH
Tel. 0181-992 8637

**National Childminding
Association**
8 Masons Hill
Bromley
Kent BR2 9EY
Tel. 0181-464 6164

**National Council for
One-parent Families**
255 Kentish Town Road
London NW5 2LX
O171-267 1361

**National Deaf Children's
Society**
15 Dufferin Street
London EC1
Tel. 0171-250 0123
(Helpline: 0800 252380)

National Eczema Society
4 Tavistock Place
London WC1H 9RA
Tel. 0171-388 4097

National Marriage Guidance Council
Herbert Grey College
Little Church Street
Rugby
Works CV21 3AP
Tel. 01788 73241

National Stepfamily Association
Hatton Place
London EC1
Tel. 0171-209 2460

Parentline & the National Helpline for Parents
Tel. 01702-559900

Patients' Association
8 Guilford Street
London WC1N 1DT
Tel. 0171-242 3460

Pre-school Playgroups Association
61–63 Kings Cross Road
London WC1X 9LL
Tel. 0171-923 3534

Relate
Little Church Street
Rugby
Tel. 01788 573241

Royal National Institute for the Blind (RNIB)
224 Great Portland Street
London W1N 6AA
Tel. 0171-388 1266

Royal Society for the Prevention of Accidents (ROSPA)
Helpline: 0121- 248 2244

St John's Ambulance
(*for advice or information / courses on first aid*)
National Headquarters
Edwina Mountbatten House
63 York Street
London W1H 1PS
Tel. 0171-258 3456

Twins and Multiple Births Association (TAMBA)
PO Box 30
Little Sutton
South Wirral L66 1TH
Tel. 0151-348 0020

Working Mothers Association
77 Holloway Road
London N7 8JZ
Tel. 0171-700 5771

Further Reading

Babies, Dr Christopher Green, Vermillion, London

Babywatching, Desmond Morris, Jonathan Cape, London

Solve Your Child's Sleep Problems, Dr Richard Ferber, SK, London

Toddler Taming, Dr Christopher Green, Vermillion, London

Understanding Your 1 Year Old [and 2 through to 8], The Tavistock Institute, London

101 Essential Tips on Baby Care, Dorling Kindersley, London

The Royal Society of Medicine: Family Health Encyclopaedia, Bloomsbury, London

Baby and Child, Penelope Leach, Penguin, London

BMA Family Health Encyclopaedia, Dorling Kindersley, London

The Practical Guide to Pregnancy and Childcare, Karen Sullivan, Parragon, Bristol

New Parents, ed. Dr David Harvey, Mandarin, London

Dr Spock's Baby and Child Care for the Nineties, Dr Benjamin Spock and Dr Michael B. Rothenberg, Simon & Schuster, London

Great Ormond Street Book of Baby and Child Care, Bodley Head, London

The Family Encyclopedia of Medicine & Health, Robinson, London